Lecture Notes in Artificial Intelligence   1828

Subseries of Lecture Notes in Computer Science
Edited by J. G. Carbonell and J. Siekmann

Lecture Notes in Computer Science

Edited by G. Goos, J. Hartmanis and J. van Leeuwen

Springer
Berlin
Heidelberg
New York
Barcelona
Hong Kong
London
Milan
Paris
Singapore
Tokyo

Ron Sun   C. Lee Giles (Eds.)

Sequence Learning

Paradigms, Algorithms, and Applications

Springer

Series Editors

Jaime G. Carbonell,Carnegie Mellon University, Pittsburgh, PA, USA
Jörg Siekmann, University of Saarland, Saarbrücken, Germany

Volume Editors

Ron Sun
University of Missouri-Columbia
CECS Department
201 Engineering Building West, Columbia, MO 65211-2060, USA
E-mail: rsun@cecs.missouri.edu

C. Lee Giles
NEC Research Institute
4 Independence Way, Princeton, NJ 08540, USA
E-mail: giles@research.nj.nec.com

Cataloging-in-Publication Data applied for

Die Deutsche Bibliothek - CIP-Einheitsaufnahme

Sequence learning : paradigms, algorithms, and applications / Ron Sun ;
C. Lee Giles (ed.). - Berlin ; Heidelberg ; New York ; Barcelona ;
Budapest ; Hong Kong ; London ; Milan ; Paris ; Singapore ; Tokyo :
Springer, 2001
    (Lecture notes in computer science ; Vol. 1828 : Lecture notes in
    artificial intelligence)
    ISBN 3-540-41597-1

CR Subject Classification (1998): I.2, F.1, F.2

ISBN 3-540-41597-1 Springer-Verlag Berlin Heidelberg New York

Springer-Verlag Berlin Heidelberg New York
a member of BertelsmannSpringer Science+Business Media GmbH
© Springer-Verlag Berlin Heidelberg 2001
Printed in Germany

Typesetting: Camera-ready by author, data conversion by PTP Berlin, Stefan Sossna
Printed on acid-free paper   SPIN 10721179   06/3142   5 4 3 2 1 0

Preface

This book is intended for use by scientists, engineers, and students interested in sequence learning in artificial intelligence, neural networks, and cognitive science. The book will introduce essential algorithms and models of sequence learning and develop them in various ways. With the help of these concepts, a variety of applications will be examined. This book will allow the reader to acquire an appreciation of the breadth and variety within the field of sequence learning and its potential as an interesting area of research and application. The reader is presumed to have basic knowledge of neural networks and AI concepts.

Sequential behavior is essential to intelligence and a fundamental part of human activities ranging from reasoning to language, and from everyday skills to complex problem solving. Sequence learning is an important component of learning in many task domains — planning, reasoning, robotics, natural language processing, speech recognition, adaptive control, time series prediction, and so on. Naturally, there are many different approaches towards sequence learning. These approaches deal with different aspects of sequence learning. This book provides an overall framework for this field.

November 2000   Ron Sun
                                                                    C. Lee Giles

Contributors

Frédéric Alexandre
CORTEX, LORIA
B.P. 239
54506 Vandœuvre-lès-Nancy, France
Frederic.Alexandre@loria.fr
www.loria.fr/equipes/cortex

Pierre Baldi
Information and Computer Science
University of California at Irvine
Irvine, CA 92697, USA
pfbaldi@ics.uci.edu
www.ics.uci.edu/~pfbaldi

Raju S. Bapi
Computer & Information Sciences
University of Hyderabad
Hyderabad 500 046, India
rajubapi@erato.atr.co.jp
www.erato.atr.co.jp/~rajubapi

Søren Brunak
Center for Bio. Sequence Analysis
Technical University of Denmark
DK-2800 Lyngby, Denmark
brunak@cbs.dtu.dk
www.cbs.dtu.dk/staff/brunak.html

Jean-Cédric Chappelier
DI–LIA, EPFL
INR (Ecublens)
CH-1015 Lausanne, Switzerland
jean-cedric.chappelier@epfl.ch
liawww.epfl.ch/~chaps

Samuel Ping-Man Choi
Computer Science Department
Hong Kong University
of Science and Technology
Clear Water Bay, Kowloon
Hong Kong, China
pmchoi@cs.ust.hk
www.cs.ust.hk/~pmchoi

Paul Cohen
Department of Computer Science
University of Massachusetts
Amherst, MA 01003, USA
cohen@cs.umass.edu
www-eksl.cs.umass.edu/~cohen

Kenji Doya
Information Sciences Division
ATR International
2-2 Hikaridai, Seika
Soraku, Kyoto, 619-0288, Japan
doya@isd.atr.co.jp
www.erato.atr.co.jp/~doya

Laura Firoiu
Computer Science Department
University of Massachusetts
Amherst, MA 01003-4610, USA
lfiroiu@cs.umass.edu
www-eksl.cs.umass.edu

Paolo Frasconi
Systems and Computer Science
University of Florence
Via di Santa Marta 3
50139 Firenze, Italy
paolo@dsi.unifi.it
www.dsi.unifi.it/~paolo

Hervé Frezza-Buet
ERSIDP, Supélec
2 rue Edouard Belin
F-57070 Metz, France
Herve.Frezza-Buet@supelec.fr
www.ese-metz.fr/metz/personnel/frezza

C. Lee Giles
NEC Research Institute
4 Independence Way
Princeton, NJ 08540, USA
giles@research.nj.nec.com
external.nj.nec.com/homepages/giles

Marco Gori
Ingegneria dell'Informazione
Università di Siena
Via Roma, 56
I-53100 Siena, Italy
marco@ing.unisi.it
www-dii.ing.unisi.it/~marco

Stephen Grossberg
Center for Adaptive Systems
Boston University
677 Beacon Street
Boston, MA 02215, USA
steve@cns.bu.edu
www.cns.bu.edu/Profiles/Grossberg

Alain Grumbach
Département Informatique et Réseaux
ENST
46 rue Barrault
F-75634 Paris Cedex 13, France
grumbach@enst.fr
www.infres.enst.fr/~grumbach

Christian Lebiere
Human Computer Interaction Institute
Carnegie Mellon University
5000 Forbes Avenue
Pittsburgh, PA 15213, USA
cl+@cmu.edu
act.psy.cmu.edu

Tim Oates
Computer Science Department
University of Massachusetts
Amherst, MA 01003-4610, USA
oates@cs.umass.edu
www-eksl.cs.umass.edu

Rainer W. Paine
Center for Adaptive Systems
Boston University
677 Beacon Street
Boston, MA 02215, USA
rpaine@bu.edu
www.cns.bu.edu/pub/rpaine

Gianluca Pollastri
Information and Computer Science
University of California at Irvine
Irvine, CA 92697, USA
gpollast@ics.uci.edu
www.ics.uci.edu/~gpollast

Marco Ramoni
Knowledge Media Institute
The Open University
Milton Keynes MK7 6AA, UK
m.ramoni@open.ac.uk
www.kmi.open.ac.uk

Nicolas Rougier
CORTEX, LORIA
B.P. 239
54506 Vandœuvre-lès-Nancy, France
Nicolas.Rougier@loria.fr
www.loria.fr/equipes/cortex

Juergen Schmidhuber
IDSIA
Galleria 2, 6928 Manno
Lugano, Switzerland
juergen@idsia.ch
www.idsia.ch/~juergen

Paola Sebastiani
Mathematics and Statistics
University of Massachusetts
Amherst, MA 01003, USA
sebas@math.umass.edu
www.math.umass.edu

Giovanni Soda
Systems and Computer Science
University of Florence
Via di Santa Marta 3
50139 Firenze, Italy
giovanni@dsi.unifi.it
www.dsi.unifi.it

Diego Sona
Dipartimento di Informatica
Università di Pisa
Corso Italia, 40
Pisa, Italy
sona@di.unipi.it
www.di.unipi.it/~sona

Alessandro Sperduti
Dipartimento di Informatica
Università di Pisa
Corso Italia 40
Pisa, Italy
perso@di.unipi.it
www.di.unipi.it/~perso

Ron Sun
CECS Deptartment
University of Missouri
Columbia, MO 65211, USA
rsun@cecs.missouri.edu
www.cecs.missouri.edu/~rsun

Gerald Tesauro
IBM T. J. Watson Research Center
30 Saw Mill River Road
Hawthorne, NY 10532 USA
tesauro@watson.ibm.com
www.research.ibm.com/infoecon

Dieter Wallach
Institut fur Psychologie
Universitaet Basel
Bernoullistr. 16
CH-4056 Basel, Switzerland
wallachd@ubaclu.unibas.ch
www.unibasel.ch/psycho/wallach.html

DeLiang Wang
Center for Cognitive Science
Ohio State University
2015 Neil Ave.
Columbus, OH 43210, USA
dwang@cis.ohio-state.edu
www.cis.ohio-state.edu/~dwang

Dit-Yan Yeung
Computer Science Department
Hong Kong University
of Science and Technology
Clear Water Bay, Kowloon
Hong Kong, China
dyyeung@cs.ust.hk
www.cs.ust.hk/~dyyeung

Mohammed J. Zaki
Computer Science Department
Rensselaer Polytechnic Institute
110 8th Street
Troy, NY 12180, USA
zaki@cs.rpi.edu
www.cs.rpi.edu/~zaki

Nevin L. Zhang
Computer Science Department
Hong Kong University
of Science and Technology
Clear Water Bay, Kowloon
Hong Kong, China
lzhang@cs.ust.hk
www.cs.ust.hk/~lzhang

Table of Contents

Biologically Inspired Sequence Learning Models

Introduction to Sequence Learning

Ron Sun

CECS Department, University of Missouri
Columbia, MO 65211, USA

1 Introduction

Sequential behavior is essential to intelligence, and it is a fundamental part of human activities ranging from reasoning to language, and from everyday skills to complex problem solving. In particular, sequence learning is an important component of learning in many task domains — planning, reasoning, robotics, natural language processing, speech recognition, adaptive control, time series prediction, financial engineering, DNA sequencing, and so on.

Naturally, there are many different approaches towards sequence learning, resulting from different perspectives taken in different task domains. These approaches deal with somewhat differently formulated sequential learning problems (for example, some with actions and some without), and/or different aspects of sequence learning (for example, sequence prediction vs. sequence recognition).

Sequence learning is clearly a difficult task. More powerful algorithms for sequence learning are needed in all of these afore-mentioned domains. It is our view that the right approach to develop better techniques, algorithms, models, and theories is to first better understand the state of the art in different disciplines related to this topic. There seems to be a need to compare, contrast, and combine different existing techniques, approaches, and paradigms, in order to develop better and more powerful algorithms. Currently, existing techniques and algorithms include recurrent neural networks, hidden Markov models, dynamic programming, reinforcement learning, graph theoretical models, search based models, evolutionary computational models, symbolic planning models, production rule based models, and so on.

Especially important to this topic area is the fact that work on sequence learning has been going on in several different disciplines such as artificial intelligence, neural networks, cognitive science (human sequence learning, e.g., in skill acquisition), and engineering. We need to examine the field in a cross-disciplinary way and take into consideration all of these different perspectives on sequence learning. Thus, we need interdisciplinary gatherings that include researchers from all of these orientations and disciplines, beyond narrowly focused meetings on specialized topics such as reinforcement learning or recurrent neural networks.

A workshop on neural, symbolic, and reinforcement methods for sequence learning (co-chaired by Ron Sun and Lee Giles) was held on August 1st, 1999, preceding IJCAI'99, in Stockholm, Sweden. The following issues concerning sequence learning were raised and addressed:

R. Sun and C.L. Giles (Eds.): Sequence Learning, LNAI 1828, pp. 1–10, 2000.
© Springer-Verlag Berlin Heidelberg 2000

(1) Underlying similarities and differences among different models, including (1.1) problem formulation (ontological issues), (1.2) mathematical comparisons, (1.3) task appropriateness, and (1.4) performance analysis and bounds.

(2) New and old models, and their capabilities and limitations, including (2.1) theory, (2.2) implementation, (2.3) performance, and (2.4) empirical comparisons in various domains.

(3) Hybrid models, including (3.1) foundations for synthesis or hybridization, and (3.2) advantages, problems, and issues of hybrid models.

(4) Successful sequence learning applications and future extensions, including (4.1) examples of successful applications, (4.2) generalization and transfer of successful applications, and (4.3) what is needed for further enhancing the performance of these successful applications.

In this book, we will be mostly concerned with items 1, 2 and 4, focusing on exploring similarities, differences, capabilities, and limitations of existing and new models, in relation to various task domains and various sequence learning problems.

2   Problem Formulations and Their Relationships

One aim of the present volume is to better understand different formulations of sequence learning problems.

With some necessary simplification, we can categorize various sequence learning problems that have been tackled into the following categories: (1) sequence prediction, in which we want to predict elements of a sequence based on the preceding element(s); (2) sequence generation, in which we want to generate elements of a sequence one by one in their natural order; and (3) sequence recognition, in which we want to determine if a sequence is a legitimate one according to some criteria; in addition, (4) sequential decision making involves selecting a sequence of actions, to accomplish a goal, to follow a trajectory, or to maximize (or minimize) a reinforcement (or cost) function that is normally the (discounted) sum of reinforcements (costs) that are received along the way (see Bellman 1957, Bertsekas and Tsitsiklis 1995).

These different sequence learning problems can be more precisely formulated as follows (assume a deterministic world for now):

- *Sequence prediction*: $s_i, s_{i+1}, ..., s_j \longrightarrow s_{j+1}$, where $1 \leq i \leq j < \infty$; that is, given $s_i, s_{i+1}, ..., s_j$, we want to predict s_{j+1}. When $i = 1$, we make predictions based on all of the previously seen elements of the sequence. When $i = j$, we make predictions based only on the immediately preceding element.
- *Sequence generation*: $s_i, s_{i+1}, ..., s_j \longrightarrow s_{j+1}$, where $1 \leq i \leq j < \infty$; that is, given $s_i, s_{i+1}, ..., s_j$, we want to *generate* s_{j+1}. (Put in this way, it is clear that sequence prediction and generation are essentially the same task.)
- *Sequence recognition*: $s_i, s_{i+1}, ..., s_j \longrightarrow$ *yes or no*, where $1 \leq i \leq j < \infty$; that is, given $s_i, s_{i+1}, ..., s_j$, we want to determine if this subsequence is

legitimate or not. (There are alternative ways of formulating the sequence recognition problem, for example, as an one-shot recognition process, as opposed to an incremental step-by-step recognition process as formulated here.)

With this formulation, sequence recognition can be turned into sequence generation/prediction, by basing recognition on prediction (see the chapter by D. Wang in this volume); that is, $s_i, s_{i+1}, ..., s_j \longrightarrow yes$ (a recognition problem), if and only if $s_i, s_{i+1}, ..., s_{j-1} \longrightarrow s_j^p$ (a prediction problem) and $s_j^p = s_j^a$, where s_j^p is the prediction and s_j^a is the actual element.

Sequence learning (either generation, prediction, or recognition) is usually based on models of legitimate sequences, which can be developed through training with exemplars. Models may be in the form of Markov chains, hidden Markov models, recurrent neural networks, and a variety of other forms. Expectation-maximization, gradient descent, or clustering may be used in training (see e.g. the chapters by Oates and Cohen and by Sebastiani et al in this volume). Such training may extract "central tendencies" from a set of exemplars.

– *Sequential decision making* (that is, sequence generation through action-s): there are several possible variations. In the goal oriented case, we have $s_i, s_{i+1}, ..., s_j; s_G \longrightarrow a_j$, where $1 \leq i \leq j < \infty$; that is, given $s_i, s_{i+1}, ..., s_j$ and the goal state s_G, we want to choose an action a_j at time step j that will likely lead to s_G in the future. In the trajectory oriented case, we have $s_i, s_{i+1}, ..., s_j; s_{j+1} \longrightarrow a_j$, where $1 \leq i \leq j < \infty$; that is, given $s_i, s_{i+1}, ..., s_j$ and the desired next state s_{j+1}, we want to choose an action a_j at time step j that will likely lead to s_{j+1} in the next step. In the reinforcement maximizing case, we have $s_i, s_{i+1}, ..., s_j \longrightarrow a_j$, where $1 \leq i \leq j < \infty$; that is, given $s_i, s_{i+1}, ..., s_j$ we want to choose an action a_j at time step j that will likely lead to receiving maximum total reinforcement in the future. The calculation of total reinforcement can be in terms of discounted or undiscounted cumulative reinforcement, in terms of average reinforcement, or in terms of some other functions of reinforcement (Bertsekas and Tsitsiklis 1996, Kaelbling et al 1996, Sutton and Barto 1997).

The action selection can be based on the immediately preceding element (i.e., $i = j$), in which case a Markovian action policy is in force; otherwise, a non-Markovian action policy is involved (McCallum 1996, Sun and Sessions 2000). Yet another possibility is that the action decisions are not based on preceding elements at all (i.e., $s_i, s_{i+1}, ..., s_j$ are irrelevant), in which case an open-loop policy is used (Sun and Sessions 1998) while in the previous two cases, closed-loop policies are involved, as will be discussed later.

Note that, on this view, sequence generation/prediction can be viewed as a special case of sequential decision making.

The above exposition reveals the relationship among different categories of sequence learning, under the assumption of a deterministic world. Another assumption in the above discussion is that we considered only closed-loop situations: that is, we deal only with one step beyond what is known or done. For open-loop prediction, generation, or action, we can have the following formalizations:

- *Sequence prediction:* $s_i, s_{i+1}, ..., s_j \longrightarrow s_{j+1}, ..., s_{j+k}$, where $1 \leq i \leq j < \infty$ and $k > 1$; that is, given $s_i, s_{i+1}, ..., s_j$, we want to be able to predict $s_{j+1}, ..., s_{j+k}$.
- *Sequence generation:* $s_i, s_{i+1}, ..., s_j \longrightarrow s_{j+1}, ..., s_{j+k}$, where $1 \leq i \leq j < \infty$ and $k > 1$.
- *Sequential decision making:* $s_i, s_{i+1}, ..., s_j; G \longrightarrow a_j, ..., a_{j+k}$, where $1 \leq i \leq j < \infty$ and $k > 1$; that is, given $s_i, s_{i+1}, ..., s_j$ and a goal state, a goal trajectory, or a reinforcement maximizing goal, we want to choose actions a_j through a_{j+k} that may lead to that goal.

The formulation of sequence recognition (either incremental or one-shot) is not changed, as sequence recognition has nothing to do with being either closed-loop or open-loop.

To extend our discussion from a deterministic world to a stochastic world, we may specify a probability distribution in place of a deterministic prediction/generation as adopted above. Predictions and generations can then be probabilistic: a distribution is calculated concerning an element in a sequence: $p(s_{j+1}|s_i.....s_j)$. Recognition may also be probabilistic: a probability $p(s_{j+1})$ may be calculated so as to determine how likely a sequence is a legitimate one. In cases where action is involved, the transition to a new element (i.e., a new state) after an action is performed can be stochastic (determined by a probability distribution): $p_{a_j}(s_j, s_{j+1})$, where action a_j is performed in state s_j at step j, and s_{j+1} is a new state resulting from the action. The action selection in such cases can also be probabilistic, whereby an action is selected from an action probability distribution $p(s_j, a_j)$, where s_j is a state and a_j is an action, In such cases, we may find the best stochastic action policy, i.e., the optimal action probability distribution in each state.

In addition to addressing these types of tasks, there are also other models that address additional issues arising out of, or along with, these above categories of sequence learning tasks. For example, we may want to segment a sequence (i.e., perform *sequential segmentation*) for the sake of compressing the description of sequences (Nevill-Manning and Witten 1997), or for the sake of better dealing with temporal dependencies (Sun and Sessions 2000, McCallum 1996). We may even form hierarchies of sequential segmentation (see the chapter by Sun and Sessions in this volume). We may also create modular structures during sequence learning (i.e, perform *modularization*) to facilitate learning processes, such as in Singh (1994), Tham (1995), Thrun and Schwartz (1995), and Sun and Peterson (1999). In addition, sequence filtering is also a common task.

3   Characterizing Sequence Learning Models

There are many existing models for different types of sequence learning discussed above. They vary greatly in terms of applicable domain, emphasis, or learning algorithm. We can characterize them along several major dimensions as follows:

- learning paradigm (whether supervised, unsupervised, reinforcement based, or knowledge based learning is used)
- implementation paradigm (whether neural networks, symbolic rules, or lookup tables are used for implementation)
- whether the world is probabilistic or deterministic (in terms of the determination of next elements)
- whether the world is Markovian or non-Markovian
- whether the task is closed-loop or open-loop
- whether action is involved or not
- whether an action policy is deterministic or stochastic (when action is selected)
- applicable domains — e.g., market agents (see the chapter by Tesauro), speech and language processing (e.g., Wermter et al 1996), navigation learning (e.g., Sun and Peterson 1998, 1999), or motor sequence learning (see the chapters by Bapi and Doya and by Grossberg and Paine).

Let us briefly review and compare several major approaches to sequence learning, such as recurrent neural networks, symbolic planning, dynamic programming (value iteration or policy iteration), and reinforcement learning (such as Q-learning), while keeping in mind these afore-mentioned dimensions.

First of all, there are a number of neural network models for dealing with sequences, such as recurrent backpropagation networks (see the review chapters by Sona and Sperduti and by Chappelier et al). Such networks typically use hidden nodes as memory, which represents a condensed record of the previously encountered subsequence. The hidden nodes are connected back to the input nodes and are used in subsequent time steps, so that the previous states are taken into account. Recurrent backpropagation networks are widely used for sequence prediction and generation (Frasconi et al 1995, Giles et al 1995). A potential shortcoming of such networks is that they require supervised learning and therefore may not be suitable for typical sequential decision making learning scenarios (whereby there is no teacher input, beside sparse reinforcement signals). There have also been associative networks proposed for sequence learning (see, e.g., Guyon et al 1988, Kleinfeld and Sompolinsky 1988). In this volume, Baldi et al, Sona and Sperduti, and Chappelier et al discussed various forms of recurrent backpropagation networks. Wang discussed more structured networks of his own design for sequence learning.

A good solution for learning sequential decision making, as well as sequence prediction/generation, is the temporal difference method, as described by e.g. Sutton and Barto (1997) and Watkins (1989). In general, there is an evaluation function and/or an action policy. The evaluation function generates a value,

$e(x)$, for a current state (input) x, which measures the goodness of x. An action a is chosen according to a certain action policy, based on the evaluation function $e(x)$. An action performed leads to a new state y and a reinforcement signal r. We then modify (the parameters of) the evaluation function so that $e(x)$ is closer to $r + \gamma e(y)$, where $0 < \gamma < 1$ is a discount factor. At the same time, the action policy may also be updated, to strengthen or weaken the tendency to perform the chosen action a, according to the error in evaluating the state: $r + \gamma e(y) - e(x)$. That is, if the situation is getting better because of the action, increase the tendency to perform that action; otherwise, reduce the tendency. The learning process is dependent upon the temporal difference in evaluating each state. *Q-learning* (Watkins 1989) is a variation of this method, in which the policy and the evaluation function are merged into one function $Q(x, a)$, where x is the current state and a is an action. Much existing work shows that Q-learning is as good as any other reinforcement learning algorithms (Lin 1992, Tesauro 1992). However, reinforcement learning is problematic when the input state space is continuous or otherwise large in which case reinforcement learning using table lookup is no longer applicable, and connectionist implementations are not guaranteed successful learning (Lin 1992, Tesauro 1992). In this volume, the chapters by Schmidhuber, by Sun and Sessions, by Choi et al, and by Tesauro are concerned with various extensions of reinforcement learning, for dealing with non-Markovian dependencies, co-learning in multi-agent systems, and so on.

Another approach for sequential decision making is explicit symbolic planning as developed in artificial intelligence. From an overall goal, a number of subgoals are generated that are to be accomplished in a certain order; then, from each of these subgoals, a number of subsubgoals are generated, and so on, until each of these goals can be accomplished in one step. Subgoals are generated based on domain knowledge. Alternatively, partial ordering of primitive actions can be incrementally established from known domain knowledge, and then a total ordering of actions is produced based on partial ordering, which constitutes a plan for action sequencing. The shortcomings of the planning approach are the following: (1) a substantial amount of prior knowledge is required in this approach, which is not always readily available; (2) a high computational complexity is inherent in this approach; (3) symbolic planning may be unnatural for describing some simple reactive sequential behavior, as pointed out by advocates of situated action (e.g., Agre and Chapman 1990). Recently, Inductive Logic Programming techniques (Lavrac and Dzeroski 1994) have been developed, which can be used to learn symbolic knowledge from exemplars and thus partially remedies one problem of symbolic planning.

Hidden Markov models (HMM) can be used for sequence learning (including generation and recognition; Baum 1972). This type of model learns underlying state transition probability distributions from which overt observation data are generated. Sequence generation can evidently be handled by this type of model. Sequence recognition can also be accomplished based on hidden Markov models by computing probabilities of generating sequences from underlying models. In this volume, a number of chapters deal with extending and enhancing known

HMM algorithms, by considering, e.g., clustering of HMMs (as in Oates and Cohen), multiple HMMs with transitions among them (as in Choi et al), or incorporating input/output relations and bidirectional (forward and backward) predictions (as in Baldi et al).

Another approach suitable for a variety of types of sequence learning is evolutionary computation (EC). EC is a "weak" method for knowledge-lean heuristic search. It updates its knowledge based (mostly) on the acquired experience of an entire generation (each member of which goes through many training trials) at the end of all their trials. It can be used to tackle all types of sequence learning because of the generality of this learning method (see, e.g., Grefenstette 1992, Meeden 1995, as well as the chapter by Schmidhuber in this volume).

There are also other ways in which sequence learning can be performed, extensions and variations of existing methods can be explored, and advances beyond existing work can be made (see, e.g., Wang and Alkon 1993, Giles and Gori 1998).

Given the variety of different approaches for sequence learning, we may compare, and combine, some of these approaches. In this volume, the chapter by Sona and Sperduti and, to a lesser extent, the chapter by Chappelier et al compare (informally) a variety of different models for sequence learning, and illustrate their respective strengths and weaknesses. Clearly, these different techniques are suitable for somewhat different learning situations, and a clear and formal understanding of this aspect is yet to be achieved. In terms of combining different techniques to form some sorts of hybrid models, there are clearly many possibilities, for example, combining symbolic rules and neural networks for implementing reinforcement learning (Sun and Peterson 1998), or combining symbolic planning and reinforcement learning to produce action sequences (Dearden and Boutilier 1997, Sun and Sessions 1998). There are also proposals for combining EC and recurrent neural networks for sequence learning. Hybridization is definitely an issue worthy of further consideration.

4   Applications

A number of applications of sequence learning are reported in this volume. For example, Baldi et al discussed protein secondary structure prediction. Sabastiani et al focused on robot sensory processing. Bapi and Doya analyzed motor sequence learning. Tesauro explored automatic pricing in e-commerce. Zaki dealt with data mining in large databases of sequential data.

There are, of course, many other areas of applications for sequence learning that are not covered by the present volume due to space limitation. In fact, sequence learning is arguably the most prevalent form of human and animal learning. In classical studies of instrumental conditioning, sequencing is central (Anderson 1995). In human skill learning, sequentiality is often the most important aspect (Willingham et al 1989, Sun et al 2000; see also the chapter by Lebiere and Wallach in this volume). In human high-level problem solving and reasoning, sequences are also essential (Anderson 1995). Therefore, when building intelligent systems to emulate human intelligence and cognition, we must pay serious attention to sequences, including sequence learning.

5   Further Issues

One difficult issue in sequence learning is temporal (non-Markovian) dependencies, especially long-range dependencies. A current situation may be dependent on what happened before, and sometimes on what happened a long time ago. Many existing models have difficulties dealing with such temporal dependencies. For example, it is well known that many recurrent neural networks models cannot deal well with long-range dependencies (see the chapter by Chappelier et al). Dealing with long-range dependencies is even harder for reinforcement learning. Many heuristic methods (e.g., McCallum 1996, Sun and Sessions 2000) may help to facilitate learning of temporal dependencies to some extent, but they break down in cases of long-range dependencies. The methods described in the chapters by Zaki and by Schmidhuber may have some potential in dealing with this issue.

Another issue in sequence learning is hierarchical structuring of sequences. Many real-world problems give rise to sequences that have clear hierarchical structures: a sequence is made up of subsequences and they in turn are made up of subsubsequences, and so on. The difficulty lies in how we automatically identify these subsequences and deal with them accordingly. This issue is somewhat related to the issue of temporal dependencies, as hierarchical structures are often determined based on temporal dependencies. Learning hierarchical structures may help to reduce or even eliminate temporal dependencies. It may also help to compress the description of sequences. For learning hierarchical sequences with no action involved, there are some existing methods for segmentation (e.g., Nevill-Manning and Witten 1997). For learning hierarchical action sequences, the reinforcement learning methods developed in the chapter by Sun and Sessions showed some potential.

Yet another issue concerns complex or chaotic sequences often encountered in real-world applications such as time series prediction or neurobiological modeling (Wang and Alkon 1993). There has been a substantial amount of work in this area. However, not enough understanding has been achieved. Much more work is needed and further progress is expected in this area. The same can be said about hybridization of existing sequence learning techniques as mentioned earlier.

6   Concluding Remarks

The importance of sequential behavior and sequence learning in intelligence and cognition cannot be over-estimated. The mistake of earlier AI and Machine Learning has been downplaying the role of sequential behavior and sequence learning (which has been corrected to some large extent recently). We hope that this book serves to emphasize, and bring to the attention of the scientific and engineering communities, the importance of this problem. In this introduction,

I tried to present a unified view of a variety of sequence learning formulations, paradigms, and approaches, to give some coherence to this topic. This book, I hope, is the first step toward establishing a more unified, more coherent conceptual framework for the study of sequence learning of various types.

References

P. Agre and D. Chapman, (1990). What are plans for? In: P. Maes, ed. *Designing Autonomous Agents*. Elsevier, New York.

J. Anderson, (1995). *Learning and Memory*. John Wiley and Sons, New York.

L. E. Baum, (1972). An inequality and associated maximization technique in statistical estimation for probabilistic functions of a Markov process. *Inequalities*, 3, 1-8.

R. Bellman, (1957). *Dynamic Programming*. Princeton University Press, Princeton, NJ.

D. Bertsekas and J. Tsitsiklis, (1996). *Neuro-Dynamic Programming*. Athena Scientific, Belmont, MA.

R. Dearden and Boutilier, (1997). Abstraction and approximate decision theoretic planning. *Artificial Intelligence*. 89, 219-283.

P. Frasconi, M. Gori, and G. Soda, (1995). Recurrent neural networks and prior knowledge for sequence processing. *Knowledge Based Systems*. 8, 6, 313-332.

C.L. Giles and M. Gori, (eds.) (1998). *Adaptive Processing of Sequences and Data Structures*. Springer, Heidelberg, Germany.

C.L. Giles, B.G. Horne, and T. Lin, (1995). Learning a class of large finite state machines with a recurrent neural network. *Neural Networks*, 8 (9), 1359-1365.

J. Grefenstette, The evolution of strategies for multiagent environments. *Adaptive Behavior*. 1(1). 65-90.

I. Guyon et al, (1988). Storage and retrieval of complex sequences in neural networks. *Physical Review A*, 38, 6365-6372.

L. Kaelbling, M. Littman, and A. Moore, (1996). Reinforcement learning: a survey. *Journal of Artificial Intelligence Research*, 4, 237-285.

D. Kleinfeld and H. Sompolinsky, (1988). Associative neural network models for the generation of temporal patterns. *Biophysics Journal*, 54, 1039-1051.

N. Lavrac and S. Dzeroski, (1994). *Inductive Logic Programming*. Ellis Horword, New York.

L. Lin, (1992). Self-improving reactive agents based on reinforcement learning, planning, and teaching. *Machine Learning*. 8, pp.293-321.

A. McCallum, (1996). Learning to use selective attention and short-term memory in sequential tasks. *Proc. Conference on Simulation of Adaptive Behavior*. 315-324. MIT Press, Cambridge, MA.

L. Meeden, (1995). An incremental approach to developing intelligent neural network controllers for robots. *Adaptive Behavior*.

C. Nevill-Manning and I. Witten, (1997). Identifying hierarchical structure in sequences: a linear-time algorithm. *Journal of Artificial Intelligence Research*, 7, 67-82.

S. Singh, (1994). *Learning to Solve Markovian Decision Processes*. Ph.D Thesis, University of Massachusetts, Amherst, MA.

R. Sun, E. Merrill, and T. Peterson, (2000). From implicit skills to explicit knowledge: a bottom-up model of skill learning. *Cognitive Science*, in press.

R. Sun and T. Peterson, (1998). Autonomous learning of sequential tasks: experiments and analyses. *IEEE Transactions on Neural Networks*, 9, 6, pp.1217-1234.

R. Sun and T. Peterson, (1999). Multi-agent reinforcement learning: weighting and partitioning. *Neural Networks*, 12, 4-5. pp.127-153.

R. Sun and C. Sessions, (1998). Learning plans without a priori knowledge. *Proceedings of WCCI-IJCNN'98*, vol.1, 1-6. IEEE Press, Piscataway, NJ. A longer version to appear in: *Adaptive Behavior*.

R. Sun and C. Sessions, (2000). Self-segmentation of sequences: automatic formation of hierarchies of sequential behaviors. *IEEE Transactions on Systems, Man, and Cybernetics: Part B Cybernetics*, Vol.30, No.3, 403-418.

R. Sutton and A. Barto, (1997). *Reinforcement Learning*. MIT Press, Cambridge, MA.

T. Tesauro, (1992). Practical issues in temporal difference learning. *Machine Learning*. 8, 257-277.

C. Tham, (1995). Reinforcement learning of multiple tasks using a hierarchical CMAC architecture. *Robotics and Autonomous Systems*. 15, 247-274.

S. Thrun and A. Schwartz, (1995). Finding structure in reinforcement learning. *Neural Information Processing Systems 7*, MIT Press, Cambridge, MA.

L. Wang and D. Alkon, (eds.) (1993). *Artificial Neural Networks: Oscillations, Chaos, and Sequence Processing*. IEEE Computer Society Press, Los Alamitos, CA.

C. Watkins, (1989). *Learning with Delayed Rewards*. Ph.D Thesis, Cambridge University, Cambridge, UK.

S. Wermter et al, (ed.) (1996). *Connectionist and Statistical Approaches to Natural Language Processing*. Springer, Heidelberg, Germany.

D. Willingham, M. Nissen, and P. Bullemer, (1989). On the development of procedural knowledge. *Journal of Experimental Psychology: Learning, Memory, and Cognition*. 15, 1047-1060.

Sequence Learning via Bayesian Clustering by Dynamics

Paola Sebastiani[1], Marco Ramoni[2], and Paul Cohen[3]

[1] Department of Mathematics and Statistics, University of Massachusetts, Amherst
[2] Knowledge Media Institute, The Open University
[3] Department of Computer Science, University of Massachusetts, Amherst

1 Introduction

Suppose one has a set of univariate time series generated by one or more unknown processes. The problem we wish to solve is to discover the most probable set of processes generating the data by clustering time series into groups so that the elements of each group have similar dynamics. For example, if a batch of time series represents sensory experiences of a mobile robot, clustering by dynamics might find clusters corresponding to abstractions of sensory inputs (Ramoni, Sebastiani, Cohen, Warwick, & Davis, 1999).

The method presented in this chapter transforms each time series into a Markov Chain (MC) and then clusters time series generated by the same MCs. A MC represents a dynamic process as a transition probability matrix. If we regard each time series as being generated by a stochastic variable, we can construct a transition probability matrix for each observed time series. Each row and column in the matrix represents a state of the stochastic variable, and the cell values are the probabilities of transition from one state to each other state of this variable in the next time step. A transition probability matrix is learned for each time series in a training batch of time series. Next, a Bayesian clustering algorithm groups time series that produce similar transition probability matrices. The task of the clustering algorithm is two-fold: to find the set of clusters that gives the best partition of time series according to some measure, and to assign each time series to one cluster.

Clustering can be simply a matter of grouping objects together so that the average similarity of a pair of objects is higher when they are in the same group and low when they are in different groups. Numerous clustering algorithms have been developed along this principle (Fisher, 2000). Our algorithm, called Bayesian Clustering by Dynamics (BCD), does not use a measure of similarity between MCs to decide if two time series need to belong to the same cluster but it uses a different principle: Both the decision of whether to group time series and the stopping criterion are based on the posterior probability of the clustering, that is, the probability of the clustering conditional on the data observed. In other words, two time series are assigned to the same cluster if this operation increases the posterior probability of the clustering, and the algorithm stops when the posterior probability of the clustering is maximum. Said in yet another way,

R. Sun and C.L. Giles (Eds.): Sequence Learning, LNAI 1828, pp. 11–34, 2000.

BCD solves a Bayesian model selection problem, where the model it seeks is the most probable partition of time series given the data. To increase efficiency, the algorithm uses an entropy-based heuristic and performs a hill-climbing search through the space of possible partitions, so it yields a local-maximum posterior probability clustering.

The algorithm produces a set of clusters, where each cluster is identified by a MC estimated from the time series grouped in the cluster. Given the model-based probabilistic nature of the algorithm, clusters induced from the batch of time series have a probability distribution which can be used for reasoning and prediction so that, for example, one can detect cluster membership of a new time series or forecast future values. Although a MC is a very simple description of a dynamic process, BCD has been applied successfully to cluster robot experiences based on sensory inputs (Ramoni et al., 1999), simulated war games (Sebastiani, Ramoni, Cohen, Warwick, & Davis, 1999), as well as the behavior of stocks in market and automated learning and generation of Bach's counterpoint. A conjecture of the success of the algorithm is that describing a dynamic process as a MC can be enough to capture the common dynamics of different time series without resorting to complex models as, for example, Hidden Markov Models (Rabiner, 1989).

The reminder of this chapter is organized as follows. We describe BCD in Section 2. Section 3 shows how to make classification and prediction with clusters of dynamics. An application of the algorithm to cluster robot sensory inputs is in Section 4. Section 5 describes related and future work and conclusions are in the last section of this chapter.

2   Bayesian Clustering by Dynamics

Suppose we are given a batch of m time series that record the values $1, 2, ..., s$ of a variable X. Consider, for example, the plot of three time series in Figure 1. Each time series records the values of a variable with five states — labeled 1 to 5 — in 50 time steps. It is not obvious that the three time series are observations of the same process. However, when we explore the underlying dynamics of the three series more closely, we find, for example, that state 2 is frequently followed by state 1, and state 3 is followed disproportionately often by state 1. We are interested in extracting these types of similarities among time series to identify time series that exhibit similar dynamics. To cluster time series by their dynamics, we model time series as MCs. For each time series, we estimate a transition matrix from data and then we cluster similar transition matrices.

2.1   Learning Markov Chains

Suppose we observe a time series $S = (x_0, x_1, x_2, ..., x_{t-1}, x_t, ..)$, where each x_t is one of the states $1, ..., s$ of a variable X. The process generating the sequence S is a first order MC if the conditional probability that the variable X visits state j

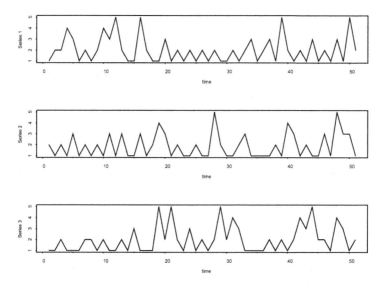

Fig. 1. Plot of three time series

at time t, given the sequence $(x_0, x_1, x_2, ..., x_{t-1})$, is only a function of the state visited at time $t-1$ (Ross, 1996). Hence, we write

$$p(X_t = j | (x_0, x_1, x_2, ..., x_{t-1})) = p(X_t = j | x_{t-1}),$$

with X_t denoting the variable X at time t. In other words, the probability distribution of the variable X at time t is *conditionally independent* of the values $(x_0, x_1, x_2, ..., x_{t-2})$, once we know x_{t-1}. This conditional independence assumption allows us to represent a MC as a vector of probabilities $p_0 = (p_{01}, p_{02}, ..., p_{0s})$, denoting the distribution of X_0 (the initial state of the chain) and a matrix P of transition probabilities, where $p_{ij} = p(X_t = j | X_{t-1} = i)$, so that

$$
P = (p_{ij}) = \begin{array}{c|cccc} & \multicolumn{4}{c}{X_t} \\ X_{t-1} & 1 & 2 & \cdots & s \\ \hline 1 & p_{11} & p_{12} & \cdots & p_{1s} \\ 2 & p_{21} & p_{22} & \cdots & p_{2s} \\ \vdots & & \cdots & & \\ s & p_{s1} & p_{s2} & \cdots & p_{ss} \end{array}
$$

Given a time series generated by a MC, we wish to estimate the probabilities p_{ij} of state transitions $(i \to j) \equiv (X_{t-1} = i \to X_t = j)$ from the data. This is a well known statistical estimation problem whose solution is to estimate p_{ij} as n_{ij}/n_i, where $n_i = \sum_j n_{ij}$ and n_{ij} is the frequency of the transitions $(i \to j)$ observed in the time series (Bishop, Fienberg, & Holland, 1975). Briefly, the estimate is found in this way:

1. First, we need to identify the *sampling model*, that is, the probability distribution from which the observed data were generated. Typically, the sampling model is known up to a vector of unknown parameters θ, which we wish to estimate from the data. In our problem, the sampling model is the transition probability matrix P, which is a set of independent discrete distributions, one for each row of P. The vector of parameter θ is given by the set of conditional probabilities (p_{ij}).

2. The sample data S and the sampling model allow us to write down the *likelihood function* $p(S|\theta)$: The probability of the data given the sampling model and θ. Since data are observed, $p(S|\theta)$ is only a function of θ and we estimate θ by finding the value which maximizes the likelihood function. This procedure returns the *Maximum Likelihood estimate* of θ and, hence, the parameter value that makes the observed data most likely.

The assumption that the generating process is a MC implies that transitions from state i of the variable X are independent of transitions from any of the other states of the variables. Therefore, rows of the transition probability matrix P are independent distributions. Data relevant to the ith row distribution are the n_i transitions $(i \rightarrow j)$, for any j, observed in the time series and the probability of observing the transitions $(i \rightarrow 1), \cdots, (i \rightarrow s)$ with frequencies $n_{i1}, \cdots, n_{is}$ is $\prod_j p_{ij}^{n_{ij}}$. A discrete random variable with probability mass function proportional to $\prod_j p_{ij}^{n_{ij}}$ has a multinomial distribution (Bishop et al., 1975). By independence, the likelihood function is the product:

$$p(S|\theta) = \prod_{i=1}^{s} \prod_{j=1}^{s} p_{ij}^{n_{ij}} \tag{1}$$

and depends on the data only via n_{ij}. Maximization of $p(S|\theta)$, with the constraint that $\sum_j p_{ij} = 1$, for all i, returns the estimate $\hat{p}_{ij} = n_{ij}/n_i$.

This estimate uses only the observed data while one may have some prior information about a MC to take into account during the estimation of θ. A Bayesian approach provides a formal way to use both prior information and data to estimate θ. This is achieved by regarding θ as a random variable, whose density $p(\theta)$ encodes prior knowledge. Data are used to update the prior density of θ into the posterior density $p(\theta|S)$ by Bayes' Theorem:

$$p(\theta|S) = \frac{p(S|\theta)p(\theta)}{p(S)}$$

and the estimate of θ is the posterior expectation of θ (Ramoni & Sebastiani, 1999).

To choose the prior, we suppose we have some background knowledge that can be represented in terms of a hypothetical time series of length $\alpha - s^2 + 1$ in which the $\alpha - s^2$ transitions are divided into $\alpha_{ij} - 1$ transitions of type $(i \rightarrow j)$. This background knowledge gives rise to a $s \times s$ contingency table, homologous to the frequency table, containing these hypothetical transitions

$\alpha_{ij} - 1$ that are used to formulate a conjugate prior[1] with density function $p(\theta) \propto \prod_{i=1}^{s} \prod_{j=1}^{s} p_{ij}^{\alpha_{ij}-1}$. This is the density function of s independent *Dirichlet* distributions, with hyper-parameters α_{ij}. Each Dirichlet distribution is a prior to the parameters $p_{i1}, \cdots, p_{is}$ associated with the ith row conditional distribution of the matrix P. Standard notation denotes one Dirichlet distribution associated with the conditional probabilities $(p_{i1}, ..., p_{is})$ by $D(\alpha_{i1}, ..., \alpha_{is})$. The distribution given by independent Dirichlet is called a Hyper-Dirichlet distributions (Dawid & Lauritzen, 1993) and it is commonly used to model prior knowledge in Bayesian networks (Ramoni & Sebastiani, 1999). We will denote such a Hyper-Dirichlet distribution by $HD(\alpha_{ij})_s$, where the index s denotes the number of independent Dirichlet distributions defining the Hyper-Dirichlet.

By letting α_i denote $\sum_j \alpha_{ij}$, this prior distribution assigns probability α_{ij}/α_i to the transition $(i \rightarrow j)$, with variance $(\alpha_{ij}/\alpha_i)(1 - \alpha_{ij}/\alpha_i)/(\alpha_i + 1)$. For fixed α_{ij}/α_i, the variance is a decreasing function of α_i and, since small variance implies a large precision about the estimate, α_i is called the *local precision* about the conditional distribution $(p_{i1}, \cdots, p_{is})$ and indicates the level of confidence about the prior specification. The quantity $\alpha = \sum_i \alpha_i$ is the *global* precision, as it accounts for the level of precision of all the s conditional distributions defining the sampling model. We note that, when α_{ij} is constant, $\alpha_{ij}/\alpha_i = 1/s$ so that all transitions are supposed to be equally likely. Priors with this hyper-parameter specification are known as symmetric priors (Good, 1968).

A Bayesian estimation of the probabilities p_{ij} is the posterior expectation of p_{ij}. By conjugate analysis (Ramoni & Sebastiani, 1999), the posterior distribution of θ is still Hyper-Dirichlet with updated hyper-parameters $\alpha_{ij} + n_{ij}$ and the posterior expectation of p_{ij} is

$$\hat{p}_{ij} = \frac{\alpha_{ij} + n_{ij}}{\alpha_i + n_i}. \tag{2}$$

Equation 2 can be rewritten as

$$\hat{p}_{ij} = \frac{\alpha_{ij}}{\alpha_i} \frac{\alpha_i}{\alpha_i + n_i} + \frac{n_{ij}}{n_i} \frac{n_i}{\alpha_i + n_i} \tag{3}$$

which shows that $\hat{p}_{ij}$ is an average of the estimate n_{ij}/n_i and of the quantity α_{ij}/α_i, with weights depending on α_i and n_i. When $n_i \gg \alpha_i$, the estimate of p_{ij} is approximately n_{ij}/n_i, and the effect of the prior is overcome by data. However, when $n_i \ll \alpha_i$, the prior plays a role. In particular, the Bayesian estimate 2 is never 0 when $n_{ij} = 0$.

Example 1. Table 1 reports the frequencies of transition n_{ij} $i, j = 1, ..., 5$ observed in the first time series in Figure 1 and the learned transition matrix when the prior global precision is $\alpha = 5$ and $\alpha_{ij} = 1/5$. The matrix $\hat{P}$ describes a dynamic process characterized by frequent transitions between states 1, 2 and 3 while states 4 and 5 are visited rarely. Note that although the observed frequency table is sparse, as 14 transitions are never observed, null frequencies of

---

[1] A prior distribution is said to be conjugate when it has the same functional form as the likelihood function

Table 1. Frequency and transition matrices for the first time series in Figure 1.

	1	2	3	4	5			1	2	3	4	5
1	3	12	3	0	3		1	0.15	0.55	0.15	0.01	0.15
2	11	1	2	2	0		2	0.66	0.07	0.13	0.13	0.01
3	6	0	0	0	1		3	0.78	0.03	0.03	0.03	0.15
4	0	0	2	0	0		4	0.07	0.07	0.73	0.07	0.07
5	0	4	0	0	0		5	0.04	0.84	0.04	0.04	0.04

$$N= \qquad \Rightarrow \qquad \hat{P}=$$

some transitions do not induce null probabilities. The small number of transitions observed from state 3 ($n_3 = 7$), state 4 ($n_4 = 2$) and state 5 ($n_5 = 4$) do not rule out, for instance, the possibility of transitions from 3 to either 2, 3 or 4. A summary of the essential dynamics is in Figure 2 in which double headed paths represent mutual transitions. Transitions with probability smaller than 0.05 are not represented.

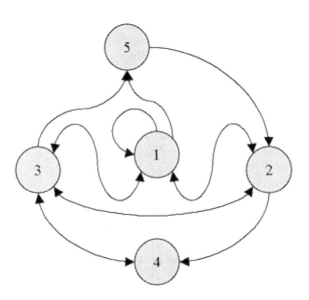

Fig. 2. Markov Chain induced from data.

2.2 Clustering

The second step of the learning process is an unsupervised agglomerative clustering of time series on the basis of their dynamics. The available data is a set

$S = \{S_i\}$ of m time series and the task of the clustering algorithm is two-fold: finding the set of clusters that gives the best partition of the data and assigning each time series S_i to one cluster, without fixing the number of clusters in advance.

Formally, clustering is done by regarding a partition as a discrete variable C with states $C_1, \ldots, C_c$ that are not observed. Each state C_k of the variable C labels, in the same way, time series generated by the same MC with transition probability matrix P_k and, hence, it represents a cluster of time series. The number c of states of the variable C is unknown but it is bounded above by the total number of time series in the data set S: The maximum number of clusters is obtained when each time series is generated by a different MC. Thus, initially, each time series has its own label. The clustering algorithm then tries to relabel those time series that are likely to have been generated by the same MC and thus merges the initial states $C_1, \ldots, C_m$ into a subset $C_1, \ldots, C_c$, with $c \leq m$. Figure 3 provides an example of three different relabelings of a data set S of four time series. Each relabeling determines a model so that, for example, model M_1 is characterized by the variable C having three states C_1, C_2 and C_3 with C_1 labeling time series S_1 and S_2, C_2 labeling S_3 and C_3 labeling S_4. In models M_2 and M_3, the variable C has only two states but they correspond to different labeling of the time series and hence different clusters.

The specification of the number c of states of the variable C and the assignment of one of its states to each time series S_i define a statistical model M_c. Thus, we can regard the clustering task as a Bayesian model selection problem, in which the model we are looking for is the most probable way of re-labeling time series, given the data. We denote by $p(M_c)$ the prior probability of each model M_c and then we use Bayes' Theorem to compute its posterior probability, and we select the model with maximum posterior probability. The posterior probability of M_c, given the sample S, is $p(M_c|S) \propto p(M_c)p(S|M_c)$ where $p(S|M_c)$ is the *marginal likelihood*. This marginal likelihood differs from the likelihood function because it is only a function of the model M_c, while the likelihood function depends on parameters θ quantifying the model M_c. Therefore, the marginal likelihood is computed by averaging out the parameters from the likelihood function. We show next that, under reasonable assumptions on the sample space, the adoption of a particular parameterization for the model M_c and the specification of a conjugate prior lead to a simple, closed-form expression for the marginal likelihood $p(S|M_c)$.

Given a model M_c, that is, a specification of the number of states of the variable C and of the labeling of the original time series (or, equivalently, conditional on the specification of c clusters of time series), we suppose that the marginal distribution of the variable C is multinomial, with cell probabilities $p_k = p(C = C_k|\theta)$. We also suppose that the MCs generating the time series assigned to different clusters C_k are independent, given C, and that time series generated by the same MC are independent. We denote by $P_k = (p_{kij})$ the transition probability matrix of the MC generating time series in cluster C_k and

Original Data		Partitions	

Cluster Time Series

$$M_1 = \begin{array}{cc} C_1 & S_1 \\ C_1 & S_2 \\ C_2 & S_3 \\ C_3 & S_4 \end{array}$$

Cluster Time Series			Cluster Time Series	
C_1	S_1	$\longrightarrow M_2 =$	C_1	S_1
C_2	S_2		C_2	S_2
C_3	S_3		C_2	S_3
C_4	S_4		C_1	S_4

Cluster Time Series

$$M_3 = \begin{array}{cc} C_1 & S_1 \\ C_1 & S_2 \\ C_1 & S_3 \\ C_2 & S_4 \end{array}$$

Fig. 3. Three models corresponding to different re-labeling of four time series.

denote the cell probabilities by $p_{kij} = p(X_t|X_{t-1} = i, C_k, \theta)$. Therefore, the overall likelihood function is

$$p(S|\theta) = \prod_{k=1}^{c} p_k^{m_k} \prod_{ij=1}^{s} p_{kij}^{n_{kij}}$$

where n_{kij} denotes the observed frequency of transitions $(i \to j)$ observed in all time series assigned to cluster C_k, and m_k is the number of time series that are assigned to cluster C_k. Compared to Equation 1, the likelihood is a product of terms corresponding to each cluster and each factor is weighted by the cluster probability $p_k^{m_k}$. We now define a prior density for θ as a product of $c \times s + 1$ Dirichlet densities. A Dirichlet is the prior distribution assigned to (p_k), say $D(\beta_1, ..., \beta_c)$. The other $c \times s$ densities correspond to c independent Hyper-Dirichlet distribution $HD(\alpha_{kij})_s$, each distribution $HD(\alpha_{kij})_s$ being assigned to the parameters p_{kij} of the MC generating the time series in cluster C_k. The marginal likelihood is then given by

$$p(S|M_c) = \int p(S|\theta)p(\theta)d\theta$$

and it is easy to show (by using the same integration techniques in (Cooper & Herskovitz, 1992)) that

$$p(S|M_c) = \frac{\Gamma(\beta)}{\Gamma(\beta+m)} \prod_{k=1}^{c} \frac{\Gamma(\beta_k + m_k)}{\Gamma(\beta_k)} \prod_{i=1}^{s} \frac{\Gamma(\alpha_{ki})}{\Gamma(\alpha_{ki} + n_{ki})} \prod_{j=1}^{s} \frac{\Gamma(\alpha_{kij} + n_{kij})}{\Gamma(\alpha_{kij})}$$

where $\Gamma(\cdot)$ denotes the Gamma function, $n_{ki} = \sum_j n_{kij}$ is the number of transitions from state i observed in cluster C_k, $\sum_k m_k = m$ and $\beta = \sum_k \beta_k$.

Once the *a posteriori* most likely partition has been selected, the transition probability matrix P_k associated with the cluster C_k can be estimated as

$$\hat{p}_{kij} = \frac{\alpha_{kij} + n_{kij}}{\alpha_{ki} + n_{ki}}$$

and the probability of $C = C_k$ can be estimated as

$$\hat{p}_k = \frac{\beta_k + m_k}{\beta + m}.$$

We conclude this section by suggesting a choice of the hyper-parameters α_{kij} and β_k. We use symmetric prior distributions for all the transition probabilities considered at the beginning of the search process. The initial $m \times s \times s$ hyper-parameters α_{kij} are set equal to $\alpha/(ms^2)$ and, when two time series are assigned to the same cluster and the corresponding observed frequencies of transitions are summed up, their hyper-parameters are summed up. Thus, the hyper-parameters of a cluster corresponding to the merging of m_k time series will be $m_k\alpha/(ms^2)$. An alternative solution is to distribute the initial precision α uniformly, across clusters, so that the hyper-parameters of a model with c clusters are $\alpha/(cs^2)$. In both ways, the specification of the prior hyper-parameters requires only the prior global precision α, which measures the confidence in the prior model, and the marginal likelihood of different model is a function of the same α. An analogous procedure can be applied to the hyper-parameters β_k associated with the prior estimates of p_k. Empirical evaluations have shown that the magnitude of the α value has the effect of zooming out differences between dynamics of different time series, so that, increasing the value of α produces an increasing number of clusters.

2.3   A Heuristic Search

To implement the clustering method described in the previous section, we should search all possible partitions and return the one with maximum posterior probability. Unfortunately, the number of possible partitions grows exponentially with the number of time series and a heuristic method is required to make the search feasible.

A good heuristic search could be to merge, or agglomerate, first pairs of time series producing similar transition probability tables. What makes two tables similar? Recall that each row of a transition probability table corresponds to a probability distribution over states at time t given a state at time $t-1$. Let P_1 and P_2 be tables of transition probabilities of two MCs. Because each table is a collection of s row conditional probability distributions, rows with the same index are probability distributions conditional on the same event. The measure of similarity that BCD uses is therefore an average of the Kulback-Liebler distances between row conditional distributions. Let p_{1ij} and p_{2ij} be the probabilities of the transition $X_t = j|X_{t-1} = i$ in P_1 and P_2. The Kulback-Liebler distance of the two probability distributions in row i is $D(p_{1i}, p_{2i}) = \sum_{j=1}^s p_{1ij} \log(p_{1ij}/p_{2ij})$. The average distance between P_1 and P_2 is then $D(P_1, P_2) = \sum_i D(p_{1i}, p_{2i})/s$.

Iteratively, BCD computes the set of pairwise distances between the transition probability tables, sorts the generated distances, merges the two time series with closest transition probability tables and evaluates the result. The evaluation asks whether the resulting model M_c, in which two time series are assigned to the same cluster is more probable than the model M_s in which these time series are generated by different MCs, given the data S. If the probability $p(M_c|S)$ is higher than $p(M_s|S)$, BCD updates the set of transition probability tables by replacing them with the table resulting from their merging. Then, BCD updates the set of ordered distances by removing all the ordered pairs involving the merged MCs, and by adding the distances between the new MC and the remaining MCs in the set. The procedure repeats on the new set of MCs. If the probability $p(M_c|S)$ is not higher than $p(M_s|S)$, BCD tries to merge the second best, the third best, and so on, until the set of pairs is empty and, in this case, returns the most probable partition found so far. The rationale of this search is that merging similar MCs first should result in better models and increase the posterior probability sooner thus improving the performance of the hill-climbing algorithm. Empirical evaluations in controlled experiments appear to support this intuition (Ramoni et al., 1999). Note that the similarity measure is just used as a heuristic guide for the search process rather than a grouping criterion.

3   Reasoning and Prediction with Clusters of Dynamics

The BCD algorithm partitions a batch S of m time series into c clusters. Each cluster C_k groups time series generated by the MC with transition probability P_k, which is estimated as $(\hat{p}_{kij}) = (\alpha_{kij} + n_{kij})/(\alpha_{ki} + n_{ki})$. The grouping of time series into clusters provides estimates of the marginal probability that a future time series is generated from the MC with transition probability P_k. This probability is the quantity $\hat{p}_k = (\beta_k + m_k)/(\beta + m)$. The probabilities $\hat{p}_k$ and $\hat{p}_{kij}$ can be used to recognize the cluster from which a new time series is generated by using Bayesian predictive-sequential inference (Cowell, Dawid, Lauritzen, & Spiegelhalter, 1999).

Suppose we observe a transition (x_0, x_1), with x_0 chosen, and we know that this transition can be generated only from one of the c MCs estimated from the c clusters, and we wish to decide which of the c MCs is more likely to be the generating model. Conditional on the transition (x_0, x_1), we can compute the probability that each of the c MCs is the generating process by using Bayes' Theorem:

$$p(C_k|x_0, x_1) = \frac{p(x_0, x_1|C_k)p(C_k)}{p(x_0, x_1)}.$$

The quantity $p(C_k|x_0, x_1)$ is the probability that the generating process is the MC in cluster C_k, given the transition (x_0, x_1), while $p(x_0, x_1|C_k)$ is the probability of observing the transition (x_0, x_1), given that the generating process is the MC in cluster C_k. Bayes' Theorem lets us update the prior probability $p(C_k)$ into the posterior probability $p(C_k|x_0, x_1)$ via the updating ratio $p(x_0, x_1|C_k)/p(x_0, x_1)$, and the posterior probability distribution over the clusters can be used to choose the MC which, most likely, generated the transition (x_0, x_1).

We only need to compute the updating ratio and, hence, the conditional probability $p(x_0, x_1|C_k)$, for any C_k, and the marginal probability $p(x_0, x_1)$. This marginal probability is computed as

$$p(x_0, x_1) = \sum_k p(x_0, x_1|C_k)p(C_k)$$

so that the crucial quantity to compute remains the conditional probability $p(x_0, x_1|C_k)$. If the value x_0 is chosen deterministically, the probability $p(x_0, x_1|C_k)$ is simply the transition probability $p(x_1|C_k, x_0)$, which, if $x_0 = i$ and $x_1 = j$, is $\hat{p}_{kij}$, and the posterior probability of cluster C_k is

$$p(C_k|x_0, x_1) = \frac{p(x_1|C_k, x_0)p(C_k)}{\sum_k p(x_1|C_k, x_0)p(C_k)} . \tag{4}$$

The updating becomes slightly more complex when more than one transition is observed. Suppose, for example, we observe the sequence $\tilde{S} = (x_0, x_1, x_2)$ and, hence, the pair of transitions (x_0, x_1) and (x_1, x_2). The posterior distribution over the clusters, conditional on $\tilde{S}$, is

$$p(C_k|x_0, x_1, x_2) = \frac{p(x_0, x_1, x_2|C_k)p(C_k)}{p(x_0, x_1, x_2)}$$

and the updating ratio is now $p(x_0, x_1, x_2|C_k)/p(x_0, x_1, x_2)$. As before, the marginal probability $p(x_0, x_1, x_2)$ is $\sum_k p(x_0, x_1, x_2|C_k)p(C_k)$ and the quantity to compute is $p(x_0, x_1, x_2|C_k)$. This probability can be factorized as

$$p(x_0, x_1, x_2|C_k) = p(x_0, x_1|C_k)p(x_2|C_k, x_0, x_1) = p(x_1|C_k, x_0)p(x_2|C_k, x_1). \tag{5}$$

The first simplification $p(x_0, x_1|C_k) = p(x_1|C_k, x_0)$ is the same used above. The second simplification $p(x_2|C_k, x_0, x_1) = p(x_2|C_k, x_1)$ is a consequence of the Markov assumption. Both probabilities are then given by the estimates $\hat{p}_{kij}$ and $\hat{p}_{kjl}$ if $x_0 = i$, $x_1 = j$, and $x_2 = l$.

Simplification of Equation 5 determines this expression for the marginal probability $p(x_0, x_1, x_2)$:

$$p(x_0, x_1, x_2) = \sum_k p(x_0, x_1, x_2|C_k)p(C_k) = \sum_k [p(x_1|C_k, x_0)p(C_k)]p(x_2|C_k, x_1)$$

so that the posterior probability $p(C_k|x_0, x_1, x_2)$ is given by

$$p(C_k|x_0, x_1, x_2) = \frac{[p(x_1|C_k, x_0)p(C_k)]p(x_2|C_k, x_1)}{\sum_k [p(x_1|C_k, x_0)p(C_k)]p(x_2|C_k, x_1)}.$$

Now, from Equation 4, we have that $p(x_1|C_k, x_0)p(C_k)$ is proportional to $p(C_k|x_0, x_1)$, with a proportionality constant independent of k. Therefore, we can rewrite $p(C_k|x_0, x_1, x_2)$ above as

$$p(C_k|x_0, x_1, x_2) = \frac{p(x_2|C_k, x_1)p(C_k|x_0, x_1)}{\sum_k p(x_2|C_k, x_1)p(C_k|x_0, x_1)}$$

which is identical to formula 4 with $p(C_k|x_0, x_1)$ playing the role of $p(C_k)$. This property is the core of the predictive-sequential approach: For any sequence $\tilde{S} = (x_0, x_1, x_2, \cdots)$, the posterior distribution over the clusters can be computed sequentially, by using each transition (x_{t-1}, x_t) in turn to update the current prior distribution into a posterior distribution using formula (4). The posterior distribution will become the prior for the next updating. This result is used in the next section.

4   Bayesian Clustering of Sensory Inputs

This section begins with a description of the robot used in the experiments. It then proceeds by analyzing the application of BCD to the unsupervised generation of a representation of the robot's experiences, and finally shows how to use this abstract representation to enable the robot to classify its current situation and predict its evolution.

Fig. 4. The Pioneer 1 robot.

4.1   The Robot and Its Sensors

Our robot is the Pioneer 1 depicted in Figure 4. It is a small platform with two drive wheels and a trailing caster, and a two degree of freedom paddle gripper (the two metal arms coming out of the platform). For sensors, the Pioneer 1 has shaft encoders, stall sensors, five forward pointing and two side pointing sonars, bump sensors, and a pair of infra-red sensors at the front and back of its gripper. The bump sensors signal when the robot has touched an object so, for example, they go on when the robot pushes or bumps into something. The infra-red sensors at the front and back of the gripper signal when an object is within the grippers. The robot has also a simple vision system that reports the location and size of colored objects. Our configuration of the Pioneer 1 has roughly forty streams of sensor data, though the values returned by some are derived from others.

Table 2. Robot's sensors and their range of values.

Sensor name	Interpretation	Range of values
r.vel	velocity of right wheel	-600–600
l.vel	velocity of left wheel	-600–600
grip.f	infra-red sensor at the front of the gripper	0=off; 1=on
grip.r	infra-red sensor at the rear of the gripper	0=off; 1=on
grip.b	bumper sensor	0=off; 1=on
vis.a	number of pixels of object in the visual field	0–40,000
vis.x	horizontal location of object in the visual field	-140 = nearest 140= furthest
vis.y	position of object in the visual field	0 = most left, 256= most right

We will focus attention on 8 sensors, described in Table 2. Figure 5 shows an example of sensor values recorded during 30 seconds of activity of the robot. The velocity-related sensors r.vel, l.vel, as well as the sensors of the vision system vis.a, vis.x and vis.y take continuous values and were discretized into 5 bins of equal length, labeled between .2 and 1. The vis.a sensor has a highly skewed distribution so that the square root of the original values were discretized. Hence, the category .2 for both sensors r.vel l.vel represents values between -600 and -340, while .4 represents values between -360 and -120, .6 represents values between -120 and 120 and so on. Negative values of the velocities of both wheels represent the robot moving backward, while positive velocities of both wheels represent forward movements. Both negative and positive velocities of the wheels result in the robot turning. The first two plots show sensory values of the left and right wheel velocity from which we can deduce that the robot is probably not moving during the first 5 seconds (steps 1 to 50) or moving slowly (the bin labeled 0.6 represents range of velocity between -120 and 120). After the 5th second, the robot turns (the values of the velocity of the two wheels are discordant) stops and then moves forward, first at low velocity then at increasing velocity until stops, begins moving backward (as the velocity of both wheels is negative) and then forward again. Note that the sensors grip.f and grip.b go on and stay on in the same time interval. Furthermore, the dynamic of the sensor vis.a shows the presence of an object of increasing and decreasing size in the visual field, with maximum size corresponding to the time in which the sensors of the wheel velocity record a change of trend. The trend of the other two sensors of the vision system, vis.x and vis.y, both support the idea that the robot is moving toward an object, bumps into it, and then moves away.

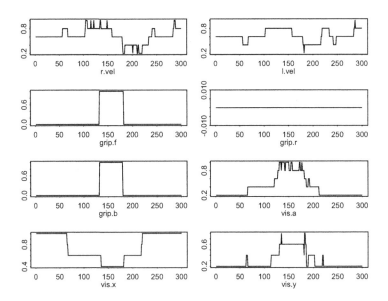

Fig. 5. Sensory inputs recorded by the robot during 30 seconds. The x-axes report the time, measured every 1/10 of a second.

The robot is programmed to engage in several different activities, moving toward an object, loosing sight of an object, bumping into something, and all these activities will have different sensory signatures. If we regard the sequence of sensory inputs of the robot as a time series, different sensory signatures can be identified with different dynamic processes generating the series. It is important to the goals of our project that the robot's learning should be *unsupervised*, which means we do not tell the robot when it has switched from one activity to another. Instead, we define a simple *event marker* — a simultaneous change of at least three sensors — and we define an *episode* as the time series between two consecutive event markers. The available data is then a set of episodes for each sensor and the statistical problem is to cluster episodes having the same dynamics. The next section will apply the BCD algorithm to solve this problem.

4.2   Clustering the Robot Sensory Inputs

In this section we describe the results obtained with the BCD algorithm on a data set of 11,118 values recorded, for each of the 8 sensors in Table 2, during an experimental trial that lasted about 30 minutes. The event marker led us to split the original time series into 36 episodes, of average length 316 time steps. The shortest episode was 6 time steps long and the longest episode was 2917 time steps.

Table 3. Size of clusters found by the BCD algorithm for the sensor vis.a. Brackets before a pair of numbers indicate that the clusters were produced by splitting the episodes belonging to one cluster only for a smaller value of α.

				α	
Sensor	1	5	10	20	40
					11
				18	7
vis.a	34	34	$\begin{cases} 18 \\ 16 \end{cases}$	$\begin{cases} 13 \\ 3 \end{cases}$	$\begin{cases} 10 \\ 3 \end{cases}$
					3
	2	2	2	2	2

We ran our implementation of the BCD algorithm on the set of 36 episodes for each sensor, using different values for the precision α, while β was set equal to 1. Table 3 shows the number of clusters created by the BCD algorithm for the sensor vis.a, for some of the values of α used in this experiment. A small value of the precision α leads BCD to identify two clusters, one merging 34 episodes, the other merging two episodes. Increasing values of α make the BCD algorithm create an increasing number of clusters by monotonically splitting a single cluster of 34 episodes. For example, this cluster is split into two clusters of 18 and 16 episodes, when $\alpha = 10$. The cluster collecting 16 episodes is then split into two of 13 and 3 episodes, for $\alpha = 20$, and then, when $\alpha = 40$, the cluster of 18 episodes is split into two clusters of 11 and 7 episodes, while the cluster of 13 episodes is split into two clusters of 10 and 3 episodes. Larger values of α make BCD create an even larger number of clusters, some of which represent MC learned from very sparse frequency matrices, so we decide to stop the algorithm for $\alpha = 40$, in order to avoid overfitting.

The pictures in Table 4 represent the *essential* dynamics of the MCs induced from the BCD algorithm with the 36 episodes of the sensor vis.a. Thus, neither transitions with probability inferior to 0.01 are represented in the chains nor are the uniform transition probabilities of visiting all states. We stress here that the interpretation of the dynamics represented by the MCs is our own one — we looked at the transition probability matrices and labeled the dynamics according to our knowledge of the robot's perception system — and it is by no means

Table 4. MCs learned with the BCD algorithm from the 36 episodes of the sensor vis.a.

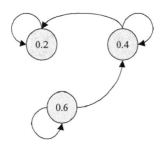

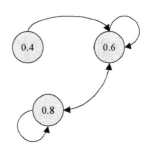

Cluster 1: *Object disappearing.*   Cluster 2: *Object approaching.*

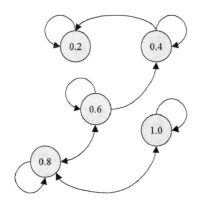

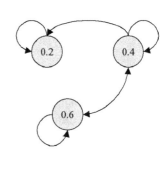

Cluster 3: *Object moving back and forth.*   Cluster 4: *Object appearing.*

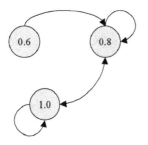

Cluster 5: *Object approaching.*   Cluster 6: *No object in sight.*

knowledge acquired by the robot. So, for example, the first chain represents a dynamic process concentrated on the first three states of the sensor vis.a. State 0.2 represents the presence, in the robot's visual field, of an object of size varying between 0 and 1600 pixels, state 0.4 represents the presence of an object of size between 1600 and 6400 pixels, while state 0.6 represents the presence of an object of size between 6400 and 14,400 pixels. The maximum size is given by 40,000 pixels so that values between 0 and 14,400 represent an object that, at most, takes 1/4 of the visual field. Now the dynamics between these three states can be that either the sensor value is constant or decreases because it visits a state preceding itself, so that the overall dynamics is that of an object of decreasing size in the visual field that eventually disappears. The interpretation of the other dynamics was deduced in a similar way. Interestingly, the last chain represents essentially a deterministic process, in which the sensor value is constant in state 0.2 showing that there is no object in the robot's visual field.

Similar results were found for the other sensors related to the robot's vision system. For example, the values of the sensors vis.x and vis.y produce two clusters for $\alpha = 1$ and eight clusters for $\alpha = 40$. The values of the other sensors tend to produce a smaller number of clusters and to need a much higher prior precision to induce clusters: the minimum value of the precision to obtain at least 2 clusters was 20 for the sensor l.vel; 40 for the sensors r.vel, grip.f and grip.r; and it was 45 for the sensor grip.b. We used the same approach described above to choose a value of α: we run the BCD algorithm for increasing values of α and stopped the algorithm when it began producing MCs with very sparse frequency tables.

We found three clusters of MCs for both the sensors l.vel and r.vel ($\alpha = 45$ and 50), representing dynamics concentrated on null or negative values of the velocity, null or positive values of the velocity and a mixture of those. We found two clusters for the dynamics of sensor grip.f ($\alpha = 40$), the first one representing a process in which the gripper front beam stays off with high probability and with small probability goes on and stays on, while, in the second one, there is a larger probability of changing from the off to the on state. Hence, the second cluster represents more frequent encounters with an object. The episodes for the sensor grip.r were partitioned in three clusters ($\alpha = 40$), one representing rapid changes from the on to the off state, followed by a large probability of staying off; one representing rare changes from the off to the on state, or the other way round, followed by a large probability of staying in that state; the last one representing the sensor in the on state. The episodes for the sensor grip.b were partitioned in two clusters, one representing rare changes from the off to the on state, or the other way round, followed by a large probability of staying in that state; the last one representing the sensor in the on state. So, for example, the first cluster represents the sensor dynamics when the robot is not near an object but, when it is, it pushes it for some time. The second cluster is the sensor dynamics when the robot is pushing an object. Finally, the three clusters found for the sensor vis.x ($\alpha = 5$) discriminate the sensor dynamics when an object is far from the robot, or near the robot or a mixture of the two. The four clusters of dynamics for the sensor vis.y ($\alpha = 1$) distinguish among an object moving from the left of the robot's visual field to the center, from the left to the right, from the right to the left, or in front of the robot.

The interpretation of the dynamic processes, represented by the clusters that the BCD algorithms found for each sensor, is our own and not the robot's one. An interesting and still open question is what the robot learned from these clusters. The clusters found by the BCD algorithm assign a label to each episode so that, after this initial cluster analysis, the robot can replace each episode with a label representing a combination of 8 sensor clusters. Now, episodes labeled with the same combination of sensor clusters represent the same "activity" characterized by the same sensor dynamic signature. For example, one such activity is characterized by the combination cluster 1 for r.vel, cluster 3 for l.vel, cluster 1 for grip.f, grip.r and grip.b, cluster 2 for vis.a and vis.x and cluster 1 for vis.y. This activity is repeated in 7 of the 36 episodes. Using our interpretation of the dynamics represented by the clusters, we can deduce that this activity represents the robot that rotates and moves far from an object (the velocity of the wheels are discordant, and the size of the object in the visual field decreases and becomes null) and hence we have a confirmation that this activity is meaningful. However, as far as the robot's world in concerned, this activity is nothing more than a combination of sensory dynamics.

This process of labeling the episodes in activities by replacing each sensor episode by the cluster membership reduces the initial 36 episodes into 22 different activities, some of which are experienced more than once. Thus, the robot learned 22 different activities characterized by different dynamic signatures.

4.3   Reasoning with Clusters of Dynamics

Results of Section 3 can be used to provide the robot with tools to recognize the cluster it is in, given sensor data. We consider here the six clusters of dynamics learned for the vis.a sensor. From the data in Table 3, one can see that the probability distribution over the 6 clusters in Figure 4 is

C_k	C_1	C_2	C_3	C_4	C_5	C_6
$\hat{p}_k$	0.19	0.30	0.06	0.09	0.09	0.27

This probability distribution is estimated using $\hat{p}_k = (\beta_k + m_k)/(\beta + m)$ with $\beta = 1$ and $\beta_k = 1/6$. Each cluster, in turns, represent a MC with transition probability learned from the time series merged in the cluster. For example, the transition probability of the MC in cluster C_1 is the table

$$\hat{P}_1 = \begin{array}{c|ccccc} & 0.2 & 0.4 & 0.6 & 0.8 & 1 \\ \hline 0.2 & 1.00 & 0.00 & 0.00 & 0.00 & 0.00 \\ 0.4 & 0.52 & 0.12 & 0.12 & 0.12 & 0.12 \\ 0.6 & 0.02 & 0.10 & 0.82 & 0.02 & 0.02 \\ 0.8 & 0.20 & 0.20 & 0.20 & 0.20 & 0.20 \\ 1 & 0.20 & 0.20 & 0.20 & 0.20 & 0.20 \end{array}$$

Suppose now we observe the sequence $S = (0.2, 0.2, 0.4, 0.6)$. The posterior distribution over the clusters C_k, conditional on the first transition $(0.2, 0.2)$ is computed using formula 4. Since $\hat{p}_{k11}$ is 1.00 for $k = 1, 2, 6$, 0.20 for $k = 3$, and 0.43 for $k = 4, 5$, there follows that $p(0.2, 0.2) = 0.83$ and $p(0.2, 0.2|C_1)p(C_1) = 0.194$; $p(0.2, 0.2|C_2)p(C_2) = 0.301$; $p(0.2, 0.2|C_3)p(C_3) = 0.012$; $p(0.2, 0.2|C_4)p(C_4) = 0.036$; $p(0.2, 0.2|C_5)p(C_5) = 0.017$; and $p(0.2, 0.2|C_6)p(C_6) = 0.271$. Formula 4 gives the posterior distribution over the clusters

C_k	C_1	C_2	C_3	C_4	C_5	C_6
$p(C_k|0.2, 0.2)$	0.24	0.36	0.01	0.04	0.02	0.33

This distribution, compared to those learned from the data, assigns more weight to clusters C_1, C_2 and C_6 and the most likely cluster generating transition $(0.2, 0.2)$ appears to be C_2. When we use this updated distribution over the clusters as prior for the next updating, conditional on transition $(0.2, 0.4)$, the distribution turns out to be

C_k	C_1	C_2	C_3	C_4	C_5	C_6
$p(C_k|0.2, 0.2, 0.4)$	0.00	0.04	0.10	0.67	0.15	0.04

and the most likely cluster is C_4. Indeed, from Figure 4, we see that cluster C_4 assigns high probability to the transition $(0.2, 0.4)$. The next updating produces

C_k	C_1	C_2	C_3	C_4	C_5	C_6
$p(C_k|0.2, 0.2, 0.4, 0.6)$	0.00	0.00	0.61	0.08	0.24	0.06

so that likely generating clusters are C_3 and C_5. Note that cluster C_3 is the most likely and indeed it is the only cluster that gives high probability to the sequence $(0.2, 0.2, 0.4, 0.6)$.

This procedure can be used to reason with longer sequences so that the robot can recognize the cluster it is in and use this to make decisions.

5   Future and Related Work

Although the description of BCD in this paper assumes a batch of *univariate* time series for reasons of simplicity, we have extended it to the *multivariate* case. Suppose one has a multivariate time series of k variable each of which takes, say, v values. A first solution is trivial and consists of recoding these series into a single one, as it was generated by a variable taking v^k values, one for each combination of values of the original variables. The difficulty here is computational: the transition probability table for the encoding variable will have $(v^k)^2$ probabilities to estimate. A more sophisticated approach relies on some assumptions of conditional independence among the variable dynamics so that each cluster becomes a set of MCs with independent transition probability tables (Ramoni, Sebastiani, & Cohen, 2000).

BCD models time series as first order MCs. More complex models involve the use of k-order Markov chains (Saul & Jordan, 1999), in which the memory of the

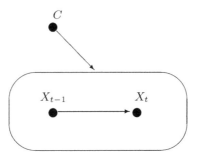

Fig. 6. Graphical representation of the model used by BCD.

time series is extended to a window of k time steps, or Hidden Markov Models (MacDonald & Zucchini, 1997), in which hidden variables H are introduced to decompose the complex auto-regressive structure of the time series into smaller pieces. Hidden Markov Models were originally introduced in speech recognition (Rabiner, 1989) and are nowadays applied in many fields ranging from DNA and protein sequencing (Lio & Goldman, 1998) to robotics (Firoiu & Cohen, 1999). Despite their popularity, Hidden Markov Models make assumptions that are questionable on the basis of recent results about the identifiability of hidden variables (Settimi & Smith, 1998) because identifiability of the hidden variables may impose strong constraints on the auto-regressive structure of the series. At first glance it may appear that BCD and Hidden Markov Models are similar technologies, and indeed we have used Hidden Markov Models for some robot learning tasks (Firoiu, Oates, & Cohen, 1998), but they are quite different. BCD approximates the process generating time series with MCs and clusters similar MCs by creating a variable C which represents cluster membership. Conditional on each state of the variable C, the model for the time series is a MC with transition probability $p(X_t = j|X_{t-1} = i, C_k)$. Graphically, this assumption is represented by the model in Figure 6. The oval represents a MC and C separates different ovals, so that, conditional on $C = C_k$ we have $p(X_t = j|X_{t-1} = i, C_k)$ and this is independent of other MCs.

In a Hidden Markov Model, the hidden variable H (or variables) allows one to compute the transition probabilities among states as $p(x_t|x_{t-1}, H_k) = p(x_t|H_k)$, so that conditioning on the state of the hidden variable makes the dependence of x_t on x_{t-1} vanish. Figure 7 represents graphically this assumption. A detailed explanation of the difference between a Hidden Markov Model and the model used by BCD can be found in (Smyth, 1997) and the description of an algorithm to cluster Hidden Markov Model is reported by Smyth (Smyth, 1999).

The Bayesian modeling-based approach used in BCD is similar in nature to the Bayesian clustering methods developed by Raftery (Banfield & Raftery, 1993; Fraley & Raftery, 1998) and Cheeseman (Cheeseman & Stutz, 1996) for static

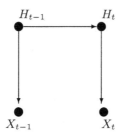

Fig. 7. Graphical representation of a Hidden Markov Model.

data. Recent work (Ridgeway, 1998; Smyth, 1999) attempted to extend the idea to dynamic processes without, however, succeeding in finding a closed form solution, as the one we have identified. Ridgway (Ridgeway, 1998) proposed to approximate the marginal likelihood using Markov Chain Monte Carlo methods. Smyth (Smyth, 1999) represents a clustering of time series as a mixture of a known number of components and estimates the parameters of the mixture via the EM algorithm. Thus, in his approach, clustering reduces to an estimation problem, while BCD seeks the best clustering as solution of a model selection problem. Furthermore, all these methods assume the number of clusters to be known, while BCD searches for the number of clusters with the highest posterior probability, and relies on an heuristic method to efficiently explore the space of possible partitions.

Methodology aside, BCD is similar in some respects to some other algorithms for clustering time series. To assess the dissimilarity of a pair of multivariate, real-valued time series, Oates (Oates et al., 1999) applies dynamic time warping to force a series to fit the other as well as possible; the residual lack of fit is a measure of dissimilarity, which is then used to cluster episodes. Rosenstein (Rosenstein & Cohen, 1998) solves the problem by first detecting events in time series, then measuring the root mean squared difference between values in two series in a window around an event. In Rosenstein's method, two time series are compared moment by moment for a fixed interval. In Oates's approach, a series is stretched and compressed within intervals to make it fit the other as well as possible. The former method keeps time rigid, the latter makes time elastic. If the duration of a sequence within a series is important to the identity of the series — if clustering should respect durations — the former method is probably preferable to the latter. BCD is even more extreme because it transforms a time series, in which durations might be important, into a table of state transitions, which is inherently atemporal. For instance, one cannot tell by looking at a transition table whether a transition $X_t = j | X_{t-1} = i$ occurred before or after a transition $X_{t'} = j | X_{t'-1} = i$.

The problem of finding dependencies between states in time series has been studied by several authors (Howe, 1992; Oates & Cohen, 1996; Friedman, Murphy, & Russell, 1998). The current work is unique in its approach to *clustering* time series by the dependency structure that holds among states, and in particular, its ability to differentiate time series that have different dependency structures.

6 Conclusions

This chapter presented BCD a model-based Bayesian algorithm to cluster time series generated by the same process. Although in this chapter we applied BCD to cluster time series of robot's sensory values, the algorithm has been applied successfully to identify prototypical dynamics in simulated war games, music composition and tracking of financial indexes. Our conjecture for this success is that, in those applications, approximating the true generating process by a first order MC was enough to capture the essential dynamics thus providing the algorithm with the information needed to partition the original set of time series into groups. However, approximating a dynamic process by a MC has limitations: for example the order with which transitions are observed in a time series is lost and this may be a serious loss of information. The results given in Section 3 can be used to assess the adequacy of the Markov assumption, by using clusters found by the algorithm to solve some classification or prediction task.

Acknowledgments

This research is supported by DARPA/AFOSR under contract(s) No(s) F49620-97-1-0485. The U.S. Government is authorized to reproduce and distribute reprints for governmental purposes notwithstanding any copyright notation hereon. The views and conclusions contained herein are those of the authors and should not be interpreted as necessarily representing the official policies or endorsements either expressed or implied, of DARPA/AFOSR or the U.S. Government.

References

Banfield, J. D., & Raftery, A. E. (1993). Model-based gaussian and non-gaussian clustering. *Biometrics*, *49*, 803–821.

Bishop, Y. M. M., Fienberg, S. E., & Holland, P. W. (1975). *Discrete Multivariate Analysis: Theory and Practice*. MIT Press, Cambridge, MA.

Cheeseman, P., & Stutz, J. (1996). Bayesian classification (AutoClass): Theory and results. In *Advances in Knowledge Discovery and Data Mining*, pp. 153–180. MIT Press, Cambridge, MA.

Cooper, G. F., & Herskovitz, E. (1992). A Bayesian method for the induction of probabilistic networks from data. *Machine Learning*, *9*, 309–347.

Cowell, R. G., Dawid, A. P., Lauritzen, S. L., & Spiegelhalter, D. J. (1999). *Probabilistic Networks and Expert Systems*. Springer, New York, NY.

Dawid, A. P., & Lauritzen, S. L. (1993). Hyper Markov laws in the statistical analysis of decomposable graphical models. *Annals of Statistics, 21*, 1272–1317. Correction ibidem, (1995), *23*, 1864.

Firoiu, L., & Cohen, P. (1999). Abstracting from robot sensor data using hidden Markov models. In *Proceedings of the Sixteenth International Conference on Machine Learning (ICML-99)*, pp. 106–114. Morgan Kaufmann, San Mateo, CA.

Firoiu, L., Oates, T., & Cohen, P. (1998). Learning regular languages from positive evidence. In *Proceedings of the Twentieth Annual Meeting of the Cognitive Science Society*, pp. 350–355. Lawrence Erlbaum, Mahwah, NJ.

Fisher, D. (2000). Conceptual clustering. In Klosgen, W., & Zytkow, J. (Eds.), *Handbook of Data Mining and Knowledge Discovery*. Oxford University Press, Oxford.

Fraley, C., & Raftery, A. E. (1998). How many clusters? Which clustering methods? Answers via model-based cluster analysis. Tech. rep. 329, Department of Statistics, University of Washington.

Friedman, N., Murphy, K., & Russell, S. (1998). Learning the structure of dynamic probabilistic networks. In *Proceedings of the Fourteenth Annual Conference on Uncertainty in Artificial Intelligence (UAI–98)*, pp. 139–147. Morgan Kaufmann, San Mateo, CA.

Good, I. J. (1968). *The Estimation of Probability: An Essay on Modern Bayesian Methods*. MIT Press, Cambridge, MA.

Howe, A. E. (1992). Analyzing failure recovery to improve planner design. In *Proceedings of the Tenth National Conference on Artificial Intelligence (AAAI-92)*, pp. 387–392. Morgan Kaufmann.

Lio, P., & Goldman, N. (1998). Models of molecular evolution and phylogeny. *Genome Research, 8*, 1233–1244.

MacDonald, I. L., & Zucchini, W. (1997). *Hidden Markov and other Models for discrete-values Time Series*. Chapman and Hall, London.

Oates, T., & Cohen, P. (1996). Searching for structure in multiple streams of data. In *Proceedings of the Thirteenth International Conference on Machine Learning*, pp. 346–354. Morgan Kaufmann, San Mateo, CA.

Oates, T., Schmill, M., & Cohen, P. (1999). Identifying qualitatively different experiences: Experiments with a mobile robot. In *Proceedings of the Sixteenth International Joint Conference on Artificial Intelligence (IJCAI-99)*. Morgan Kaufmann, San Mateo, CA.

Rabiner, L. (1989). A tutorial on Hidden Markov Models and selected applications in speech recognition. *Proceedings of the IEEE, 77*(2), 257–285.

Ramoni, M., & Sebastiani, P. (1999). Bayesian methods. In Berthold, M., & Hand, D. J. (Eds.), *Intelligent Data Analysis. An Introduction*, pp. 129–166. Springer, New York, NY.

Ramoni, M., Sebastiani, P., & Cohen, P. (2000). Multivariate clustering by dynamics. In *Proceedings of the Seventeenth National Conference on Artificial Intelligence (AAAI-2000)*. Morgan Kaufmann, San Mateo, CA.

Ramoni, M., Sebastiani, P., Cohen, P., Warwick, J., & Davis, J. (1999). Bayesian clustering by dynamics. Tech. rep. KMi-TR-78, Knowledge Media Institute, The Open University, Milton Keynes, United Kingdom.

Ridgeway, G. (1998). Finite discrete markov process clustering. Tech. rep. MSR-TR-97-24, Microsoft Research, Redmond, WA.

Rosenstein, M., & Cohen, P. (1998). Concepts from time series. In *Proceedings of the Fifteenth National Conference on Artificial Intelligence (AAAI-98)*, pp. 739–745. Morgan Kaufmann, San Mateo, CA.

Ross, S. M. (1996). *Stochastic Processes*. Wiley, New York, NY.

Saul, L. K., & Jordan, M. I. (1999). Mixed memory Markov models: Decomposing complex stochastic processes as mixture of simpler ones. *Machine Learning, 37*, 75–87.

Sebastiani, P., Ramoni, M., Cohen, P., Warwick, J., & Davis, J. (1999). Discovering dynamics using Bayesian clustering. In *Proceedings of the Third International Symposium on Intelligent Data Analysis (IDA-99)*, pp. 199–209. Springer, New York, NY.

Settimi, R., & Smith, J. Q. (1998). On the geometry of Bayesian graphical models with hidden variables. In *Proceedings of the Fourteenth Annual Conference on Uncertainty in Artificial Intelligence (UAI–98)*, pp. 472–479. Morgan Kaufmann, San Mateo, CA.

Smyth, P. (1997). Clustering sequences with hidden Markov models. In Mozer, M., Jordan, M., & Petsche, T. (Eds.), *Advances in Neural Information Precessing*, pp. 72–93. MIT Press, Cambridge, MA.

Smyth, P. (1999). Probabilistic model-based clustering of multivariate and sequential data. In *Proceedings of the Seventh International Workshop on Artificial Intelligence and Statistics (Uncertainty 99)*, pp. 299–304. Morgan Kaufmann, San Mateo, CA.

Using Dynamic Time Warping to Bootstrap HMM-Based Clustering of Time Series

Tim Oates, Laura Firoiu, and Paul R. Cohen

Computer Science Department
University of Massachusetts

1 Introduction

Given a source of time series data, such as the stock market or the monitors in an intensive care unit, there is often utility in determining whether there are qualitatively different regimes in the data and in characterizing those regimes. For example, one might like to know whether the various indicators of a patient's health measured over time are being produced by a patient who is likely to live or one that is likely to die. In this case, there is a priori knowledge of the number of regimes that exist in the data (two), and the regime to which any given time series belongs can be determined post hoc (by simply noting whether the patient lived or died). However, these two pieces of information are not always present.

Consider a system that produces multivariate, real-valued time series by selecting one of K hidden Markov models (HMMs), generating data according to that model, and periodically transitioning to a different HMM. Only the time series produced by the system are observable. In particular, K and the identity of the HMM generating any given time series are not observable. Given a set of time series produced by such a system, this paper presents a method for automatically determining K, the number of generating HMMs, and for learning the parameters of those HMMs.

HMMs are an attractive framework for modeling time series for two reasons. First, there are simple and efficient algorithms for inducing HMMs from time series data. Second, they have been demonstrated empirically to be capable of modeling the structure of the generative processes underlying a wide variety of real-world time series. HMMs have met with success in domains such as speech recognition (Jelinek 1997), computational molecular biology (Baldi *et al.* 1994), and gesture recognition (Bregler 1997).

Given a set of time series, it is possible to induce an HMM that models these data. However, algorithms for inducing HMMs do not directly address the problem of identifying qualitatively different regimes in the data; they simply attempt to fit a single model that accounts for all of the data as well as possible, regardless of whether the data were generated by a single underlying process or multiple processes.

Our approach to addressing the above limitation of HMMs involves obtaining an initial estimate of K (the number of regimes in the time series) by unsupervised clustering of the time series using dynamic time warping (DTW)

R. Sun and C.L. Giles (Eds.): Sequence Learning, LNAI 1828, pp. 35–52, 2000.
© Springer-Verlag Berlin Heidelberg 2000

as a similarity metric. In addition to producing an estimate of K, this process yields an initial partitioning of the data. As later sections will explain, DTW is related to HMM training algorithms but is weaker in several respects. Therefore, the clusters based on DTW are likely to contain mistakes. These initial clusters serve as input to a process that trains one HMM on each cluster and iteratively moves time series between clusters based on their likelihoods given the various HMMs. Ultimately the process converges to a final clustering of the data and a generative model (the HMMs) for each of the clusters.

The remainder of the paper is organized as follows. Section 2 reviews HMMs and the algorithms used to induce HMMs from data. One such algorithm, the Viterbi algorithm, is explored in some detail. Section 3 describes dynamic time warping and its use as a distance measure between multivariate time series for the purpose of unsupervised clustering. Section 4 shows that despite surface dissimilarities between DTW and the Viterbi algorithm, under certain restricted conditions both algorithms optimize the same criterion. Section 5 describes an algorithm that takes advantage of the tight relationship between DTW and the Viterbi algorithm by using DTW to bootstrap the process of fitting HMMs to data containing multiple regimes. Section 6 presents the results of experiments with this approach using artificial data, and section 7 concludes and points to future work.

2   Hidden Markov Models

Sources of time series data abound. For example, the world's financial markets produce volumes of such data on a daily, hourly, minute-by-minute and even second-by-second basis. Investors attempt to understand the processes underlying these markets and to make predictions about the directions in which they will move by analyzing time series of the prices of individual stocks, market averages, interest rates, exchange rates, etc.

Of fundamental importance to the endeavor of time series analysis – regardless of whether the series are generated by financial markets, monitors in a nuclear power plant, or the activities of customers at a web site – is the construction of models from data. In this context, a model is a concise representation of the data in a time series that ideally lays bare the structure in the data and, therefore, provides information about the real-world process underlying its generation.

One type of model that has proven to be useful when working with time series data from many different kinds sources is the hidden Markov model (HMM). It is possible to model time series containing either discrete values or real values within the HMM framework. In the former case a discrete HMM is used, and in the latter case a continuous HMM is used.

We begin our discussion of HMMs with a formal specification of the elements of discrete HMMs, following the presentation in (Rabiner 1989) (an excellent tutorial to which the interested reader is referred), and then generalize to the continuous case. This will include a brief discussion of various algorithms for, among other things, inducing HMMs from data. Following this background material, one of these algorithms (the Viterbi algorithm) will be explored in more detail in preparation for a comparison with DTW in section 4.

2.1 HMM Fundamentals

The following items comprise a discrete HMM:

- a set of N states, $\{1,\ldots,N\}$
- an alphabet of M output symbols, $\Sigma = \{\sigma_1,\ldots,\sigma_M\}$
- a set of output probabilities, $B = \{b_{i,j}|1 \leq i \leq N, 1 \leq j \leq M\}$
- a set of state transition probabilities, $A\{a_{i,j}|1 \leq i \leq N, 1 \leq j \leq N\}$
- an initial state probability distribution, $\pi = \{p_1,\ldots,p_N\}$

A time series of values is generated by a discrete HMM as follows. At every time step the HMM is in one of its N states. The state in which the HMM begins at the first time step is chosen according to the initial state distribution π. An element of Σ is then selected according to the output distribution of the current state and that symbol is emitted. Next, the HMM transitions to a new state based on the transition distribution of the current state. Finally, this process of selecting an output symbol and transitioning to a new state repeats.

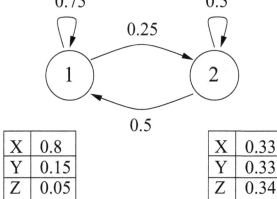

Fig. 1. An example of a discrete Hidden Markov model.

To make these ideas and the related notation clear, consider the discrete HMM shown in figure 1. This HMM has $N = 2$ states. The initial state distribution, $\pi = \{0.9, 0.1\}$, indicates that the HMM will begin in state 1 with probability 0.9 and in state 2 with probability 0.1. Note that $\sum_{i=1}^{N} \pi_i = 1$.

At each time step, one of the $M = 3$ symbols in $\Sigma = \{X, Y, Z\}$ will be chosen and emitted. The probability with which a given element of Σ will be chosen depends on the set of output probabilities:

$$B = \{b_{i,j} | 1 \leq i \leq N, 1 \leq j \leq M\}$$

The value of $b_{i,j}$ is the probability that the jth symbol in Σ (i.e. σ_j) will be emitted in state i. Note that the output probabilities for each state must sum to one, i.e. $\sum_{j=1}^{M} b_{i,j} = 1$. For the HMM in the figure, $b_{1,1}$ is the probability that σ_1, which is X, will be emitted in state 1. This probability is 0.8. Likewise, the probability of emitting $\sigma_2 = Y$ in state 1 is $b_{1,2} = 0.15$, and the probability of emitting $\sigma_3 = Z$ in state 2 is $b_{2,3} = 0.34$. Clearly, time series generated by the HMM in figure 1 will be elements of Σ^*, i.e. the Kleene closure over Σ.

Once an output symbol is chosen and emitted, the HMM makes a transition to a new state selected according to the set of state transition probabilities:

$$A = \{a_{i,j} | 1 \leq i \leq N, 1 \leq j \leq N\}$$

The value of $a_{i,j}$ is the probability of transitioning to state j given that the current state is i. Note that the sum of the transition probabilities for each state must sum to 1, i.e. $\sum_{j=1}^{N} a_{i,j} = 1$. For example, the probability of transitioning from state 1 to state 2 is $a_{1,2} = 0.25$, whereas the probability of transitioning from state 2 to itself is $a_{2,2} = 0.5$.

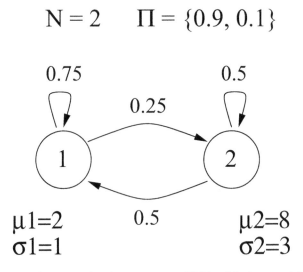

Fig. 2. An example of a continuous Hidden Markov model.

A continuous HMM differs from a discrete one in that the output symbols are emitted from a probability density instead of a distribution. The most commonly used density is the normal density with mean μ and standard deviation σ. Consider the continuous HMM shown in figure 2. It is essentially the HMM shown in figure 1, except there is no discrete alphabet Σ, and the set of output probabilities, B, has been replaced with two normal densities, one for each state. When the HMM is in state 1, a real value chosen from the normal density with mean $\mu_1 = 2$ and standard deviation $\sigma_1 = 1$ will be emitted. When the HMM is in state 2, a real value chosen from the normal density with mean $\mu_2 = 8$ and standard deviation $\sigma_1 = 3$ will be emitted. A time series containing 100 time steps generated by this HMM is shown in figure 3.

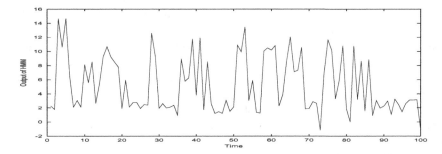

Fig. 3. A time series generated by the HMM in figure 2.

Given a time series generated by an HMM, the activity of the HMM is observed indirectly through the sequence of outputs. Therefore, the states are said to be hidden. Hidden Markov models are an extension of standard Markov models in which the output at each state is simply the index of the state, so an output sequence identifies the state sequence that produced it. It is both possible and common to extend the definition of HMMs to allow for the emission of a vector of discrete or real values at each time step rather than just a single value as described above.

Let λ be an HMM (either discrete or continuous), and let $O = \{o_1, \ldots, o_L\}$ be a sequence of observations (i.e. a time series) gathered over L time steps. There exist dynamic programming algorithms to solve the following problems:

1. determine the probability of observing O given that it was generated by λ, i.e. $p(O|\lambda)$
2. find the sequence of states through λ that maximizes the probability of O (the Viterbi algorithm)
3. determine the parameters of λ (e.g. the state transition and emission probabilities) that maximize the probability of O (the Baum-Welch algorithm)

The solution to the first problem allows us to evaluate how well a given model matches a given observation sequence, and therefore to choose among multiple competing models the one that best "fits" the data. The solution to the second problem makes it possible to uncover that which is hidden, the sequence of states that is most likely given the data. If it is assumed that the data were generated by an HMM, the solution to problem 3 makes it possible to find the parameters of the HMM that maximizes the probability of the data. An important caveat is that this maximization is not done globally with respect to all possible parameter values. Rather, it occurs over a local neighborhood of initial parameters values generated by the Baum-Welch algorithm.

2.2   The Viterbi Algorithm

Let $O = \{o_1, \ldots, o_L\}$ be an observation sequence containing L values, and let $S = \{s_1, \ldots, s_L\}$ be a sequence of L states through HMM λ. Let $p(O|S, \lambda)$ be the probability of observing O given state sequence S. The Viterbi algorithm uses dynamic programming to find a state sequence out of the N^L possible state sequences of length L that maximizes $p(O|S)$. (We will drop the λ when its identity is either clear from the context or unimportant.) Note that there may be more than one state sequence that maximizes the probability of the observation sequence.

Given a state sequence and an observation sequence, how does one compute $p(O|S)$? This is best explained via an example. Let λ be the discrete HMM shown in figure 1. Let $O = \{X, X, Z\}$ and let $S = \{1, 2, 1\}$. For O to occur given S, the HMM must begin in state 1, which occurs with probability $\pi(1) = 0.9$, and emit an X, which occurs with probability $b_{1,1} = 0.8$. The HMM must then transition to state 2 (with probability $a_{1,2} = 0.25$) and emit an X (with probability $b_{2,1} = 0.33$). Finally, the HMM must transition back from state 2 to state 1 (with probability $a_{2,1} = 0.5$) and emit a Z (with probability $b_{1,3} = 0.05$). Because all of these various events are independent, the final probability is the product of the individual probabilities:

$$
\begin{aligned}
p(\{X, X, Z\}|\{1, 2, 1\}) &= p(\{o_1, o_2, o_3\}|\{s_1, s_2, s_3\}) \\
&= \pi_{s_1} b_{o_1, s_1} a_{s_1, s_2} b_{o_2, s_2} a_{s_2, s_3} b_{o_3, s_3} \\
&= \pi_{s_1} b_{o_1, s_1} \Pi_{t=2}^{3} a_{s_{t-1}, s_t} b_{o_t, s_t}
\end{aligned}
\tag{1}
$$

For arbitrary observation and state sequences of length L, equation 1 generalizes as follows:

$$
p(O|S) = \pi_{s_1} b_{o_1, s_1} \Pi_{t=2}^{L} a_{s_{t-1}, s_t} b_{o_t, s_t}
\tag{2}
$$

We can simplify the notation of equation 2 by defining a special state 0 such that the probability of transition from state 0 to state i is π_i and the probability of transitioning into state 0 is 0 (i.e. $a_{0,i} = \pi_i$ and $a_{i,0} = 0$). If the HMM starts in state 0 with probability 1, then state 0 serves the function of the initial state probability distribution. We have not changed the output behavior of the HMM, but equation 2 can now be rewritten as follows:

$$
\begin{aligned}
p(O|S) &= \Pi_{t=1}^{L} a_{s_{t-1}, s_t} b_{s_t} \\
&= \Pi_{t=1}^{L} p(s_t|s_{t-1}) p(o_t|s_t)
\end{aligned}
\tag{3}
$$

For the sake of clarity in the remaining discussion, $a_{s_t,s_{t-1}}$ has been replaced with $p(s_t|s_{t-1})$ and b_{o_t,s_t} has been replaced with $p(o_t|s_t)$. The Viterbi algorithm returns a state sequence S that maximizes equation 3.

It will prove to be useful later to note that any state sequence that maximizes 3 also maximizes $\ln(p(O|S))$:

$$\ln(p(O|\lambda)) = \ln(\Pi_{t=1}^{L} p(s_t|s_{t-1})p(o_t|s_t))$$

$$= \sum_{t=1}^{L} \ln(p(s_t|s_{t-1})p(o_t|s_t))$$

$$= \sum_{t=1}^{L} \ln(p(s_t|s_{t-1})) + \sum_{t=1}^{L} \ln(p(o_t|s_t)) \tag{4}$$

For continuous HMMs in which the output in state i is drawn from a normal distribution with mean μ_i and standard deviation σ_i, equation 4 simplifies as follows:

$$\ln(p(O|\lambda)) = \sum_{t=1}^{L} \ln(p(s_t|s_{t-1})) + \sum_{t=1}^{L} \ln(p(o_t|s_t))$$

$$= \sum_{t=1}^{L} \ln(p(s_t|s_{t-1})) + \sum_{t=1}^{L} \ln\left(\frac{1}{\sqrt{2\pi}\sigma_i} e^{-\frac{(o_t-\mu_i)^2}{2\sigma_i^2}}\right)$$

$$= \sum_{t=1}^{L} \ln(p(s_t|s_{t-1})) + \sum_{t=1}^{L} \left(\ln(1) - \ln(\sqrt{2\pi}\sigma_i) + \ln\left(e^{-\frac{(o_t-\mu_i)^2}{2\sigma_i^2}}\right)\right)$$

$$= \sum_{t=1}^{L} \ln(p(s_t|s_{t-1})) - \sqrt{2\pi} \sum_{t=1}^{L} \ln(\sigma_i) - \sum_{t=1}^{L} \frac{(o_t-\mu_i)^2}{2\sigma_i^2} \tag{5}$$

We will return to equation 5 in section 4 where we formally specify the relationship between the Viterbi algorithm and DTW.

3   Dynamic Time Warping

This section describes dynamic time warping and its use as a measure of similarity for unsupervised clustering of time series. Recall that our ultimate goal is to discover qualitatively different regimes in time series data and to identify the individual HMMs that underly them. Given a suitable measure of similarity, we can discover qualitatively different regimes by clustering the time series. Each cluster should then correspond to a regime. DTW is such a measure of similarity. We begin with an explanation that appeals to intuition of DTW and how it is used in unsupervised clustering of time series, and then describe the algorithm more formally in preparation for a comparison of DTW and the Viterbi algorithm in section 4.

3.1   The Intuition Behind DTW and Clustering

Using the notation of section 2, let O denote a multivariate time series spanning L time steps such that $O = \{o_1, \ldots, o_L\}$. The o_i are vectors of values containing one element for the value of each of the component univariate time series at time i. Given a set of m multivariate time series, we want to obtain, in an unsupervised manner, a partition of these time series into subsets such that each subset corresponds to a qualitatively different regime.

If an appropriate measure of the similarity of two time series is available, clustering followed by prototype extraction is a suitable unsupervised learning method for this problem. Finding such a measure of similarity is difficult because time series that are qualitatively the same may be quantitatively different in at least two ways. First, they may be of different lengths, making it difficult or impossible to embed the time series in a metric space and use, for example, Euclidean distance to determine similarity. Second, within a single time series, the rate at which progress is made can vary non-linearly. The same pattern may evolve slowly at first and then speed up, or it may begin quickly and then slow down. Such differences in rate make similarity measures such as cross-correlation unusable.

DTW is a generalization of classical algorithms for comparing discrete sequences (e.g. minimum string edit distance (Corman, Leiserson, & Rivest 1990)) to sequences of continuous values (Sankoff & Kruskall 1983). It was used extensively in speech recognition, a domain in which the time series are notoriously complex and noisy, until the advent of Hidden Markov Models which offered a unified probabilistic framework for the entire recognition process (Jelinek 1997).

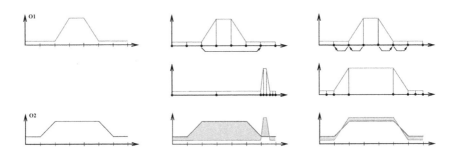

Fig. 4. Two time series, O_1 and O_2, (the leftmost column) and two possible warpings of O_1 into O_2 (the middle and rightmost columns).

Given two time series, O_1 and O_2, DTW finds the warping of the time dimension in O_1 that minimizes the difference between the two series. Consider the two univariate time series shown in Figure 4. Imagine that the time axis of O_1 is an elastic string, and that you can grab that string at any point corresponding to a time at which a value was recorded for the time series. Warping of the time dimension consists of grabbing one of those points and moving it to a new location. As the point moves, the elastic string (the time dimension) compresses in the direction of motion and expands in the other direction. Consider the middle column in Figure 4. Moving the point at the third time step from its original location to the seventh time step causes all of the points to its right to compress into the remaining available space, and all of the points to its left to fill the newly created space. Of course, much more complicated warpings of the time dimension are possible, as with the third column in Figure 4 in which four points are moved.

Given a warping of the time dimension in O_1, yielding a time series that we will denote O_1', one can compare the similarity of O_1' and O_2 by determining, for example, the area between the two curves. That area is shown in gray in the bottom row of Figure 4. Note that the first warping of O_1 in which a single point was moved results in a poor match, one with a large area between the curves. However, the fit given by the second, more complex warping is quite good. In general, there are exponentially many ways to warp the time dimension of O_1. DTW uses dynamic programming to find the warping that minimizes the area between the curve in time that is a low order polynomial of the lengths of O_1 and O_2, i.e. $O(|O_1||O_2|)$.

DTW returns the optimal warping of O_1, the one that minimizes the area between O_1' and O_2, and the area associated with that warping. The area is used as a measure of similarity between the two time series. Note that this measure of similarity handles nonlinearities in the rates at which time series progress and is not affected by differences in the lengths of the time series. In general, the area between O_1' and O_2 may not be the same as the area between O_2' into O_1. However, a symmetrized version of DTW exists that essentially computes the average of those two areas based on a single warping (Kruskall & Liberman 1983). Although a straightforward implementation of DTW is more expensive than computing Euclidean distance or cross-correlation, there are numerous speedups that both improve the properties of DTW as a distance metric and make its computation nearly linear in the length of the time series with a small constant.

Given m time series, we can construct a complete pairwise distance matrix by invoking DTW $O(m^2)$ times. We then apply a standard hierarchical, agglomerative clustering algorithm that starts with one cluster for each time series and merges the pair of clusters with the minimum average intercluster distance (Everitt 1993). Without a stopping criterion, merging will continue until there is a single cluster containing all m time series. To avoid that situation, we do not merge clusters for which the mean intercluster distance is significantly different from the mean intracluster distance as measured by a t-test. The number of clusters remaining when this process terminates is K, the number of regimes in the time series.

Finally, for each cluster we select a prototype. Two methods commonly used are to choose the cluster member that minimizes the distance to all other members of the cluster, and to simply average the members of the cluster. The advantage of the latter method is that it smooths out noise that may be present in any individual data item. Unfortunately, it is only workable when the cluster

elements are embedded in a metric space (e.g. Cartesian space). Although we
cannot embed time series in a metric space, DTW allows us to use a combination
of the two methods as follows. First, we select the time series that minimizes distance to all other time series in a given cluster. Then we warp all other patterns
into that centroid, resulting in a set of patterns that are all on the same time
scale. It is then a simple matter to take the average value at each time point
over all of the series and use the result as the cluster prototype.

3.2   A More Rigorous Discussion of DTW

This section describes DTW more formally than the previous one. There are
two reasons for this. The primary motivation is the development of ideas and
notation that will make it possible in section 4 to explicitly state the similarities
between the Viterbi algorithm and DTW. A secondary motivation is simply to
present a more conventional account of DTW. The use of areas between warped
time series as the measure to be minimized is somewhat non-standard, whereas
the use of the sum of Euclidean distances between points (after warping) is rather
common. The discussion in this section will focus on the latter measure.

Let W and Y be multivariate, real-valued time series of length L_W and L_Y,
respectively, such that:

$$W = w_1 w_2 \ldots w_{L_W}$$
$$Y = y_1 y_2 \ldots y_{L_Y}$$

Given $t_y \in \{1, 2, \ldots, L_Y\}$ and $t_w \in \{1, 2, \ldots, L_W\}$, let ϕ be a warping function
that maps elements of W onto elements of Y as follows:

$$\phi(t_w) = t_y$$

That is, for any given element in W whose index is t_w, ϕ returns the index in Y
to which that element is mapped, i.e. t_y.

Let d be a distance measure, such as Euclidean distance. Then DTW uses
dynamic programming to determine ϕ such that the following sum is minimized:

$$D_\phi = \sum_{t_w=1}^{L_W} d(w_{t_w}, y_{\phi(t_w)}) \tag{6}$$

It is common for d to compute the squared difference. When W and Y are
univariate, this yields:

$$D_\phi = \sum_{t_w=1}^{L_W} (w_{t_w} - y_{\phi(t_w)})^2 \tag{7}$$

Note that this is rather different from using the area between Y and the warped
version of W as the measure that is to be minimized. For example, it is possible
that ϕ maps all points in W to a single point in Y, in which case that warped
version of W spans 0 time steps and D_ϕ is simply the sum of the distances

between all of the points in W and the single point in Y to which they are mapped.

In practice, certain constraints are typically placed on ϕ to avoid such situations. Those commonly reported in the DTW literature are:

- **Boundary Conditions:** This constraint forces the first element of W to map to the first element of Y (i.e. $\phi(1) = 1$) and the last element of W to the last element of Y (i.e. $\phi(L_W) = L_Y$).
- **Monotonicity:** This constraint ensures that the warping maintains the temporal ordering of points in W (though clearly not the temporal interval between them), i.e. $\phi(t_i) \geq \phi(t_j)$ for $t_i \geq t_j$.
- **Continuity:** Under this rubric falls a large number of constraints that limit, for example, the degree to which the time dimension can be warped.

4 A Unified View of HMMs and DTW

Given two time series W and Y, dynamic time warping finds a mapping of points in W to points in Y such that the difference between the warped version of W and Y is minimized. In contrast, given a time series W and an HMM λ, the Viterbi algorithm finds the state sequence S through λ for which $p(O|S)$ is maximized. On the face of it, these two algorithms are quite different. DTW operates on two time series and the Viterbi algorithm operates on a time series and an HMM. DTW minimizes a measure of dissimilarity and the Viterbi algorithm maximizes a probability.

Despite the apparent differences between DTW and the Viterbi algorithm, this section will show that under certain circumstances these two algorithms are in fact optimizing the same criterion. Given two time series W and Y, it is possible to construct an HMM based on Y such that the state sequence returned by the Viterbi algorithm (the one that maximizes $p(O|S)$) and the mapping returned by DTW (the one that minimizes the dissimilarity of the time series) are equivalent.

Using the notation of section 3.2, let W and Y be univariate, real-valued time series of length L_W and L_Y, respectively, such that:

$$W = w_1 w_2 \ldots w_{L_W}$$
$$Y = y_1 y_2 \ldots y_{L_Y}$$

(The results below generalize trivially to the multivariate case.) Let λ_Y be the continuous HMM constructed from Y as follows:

1 Create one state in λ_Y for each element of Y.
2 Let the output density of state i be the normal density with mean $\mu_i = y_i$ and standard deviation $\sigma_i = \sigma$. Note that the mean of the normal density in any given state depends on a value in Y, but the standard deviation is a constant which is independent of the state and Y.
3 Set all transition probabilities to $\alpha = 1/N$. That is, all states are equally likely as next states regardless of the current state.

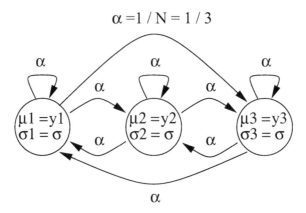

Fig. 5. An HMM constructed from the time series $Y = \{y_1, y_2, y_3\}$. For each element of Y there is a state with a normal output density with mean $\mu_i = y_i$ and standard deviation $\sigma_i = \sigma$. All transition probabilities are the same, i.e. $\alpha = 1/N = 1/3$.

An example of a continuous HMM constructed in this manner for $Y = \{y_1, y_2, y_3\}$ is shown in figure 5.

Given W and λ_Y, the Viterbi algorithm finds a state sequence that maximizes $p(W|S, \lambda_Y)$ or, equivalently, $\ln(p(W|S, \lambda_Y))$ as given by equation 5. Because all state transitions in λ_Y have the value α and all standard deviations have the value σ, we can simplify equation 5 as follows:

$$
\begin{aligned}
\ln(p(W|S, \lambda_Y)) &= \sum_{t=1}^{L_W} \ln(p(s_t|s_{t-1})) - \sqrt{2\pi} \sum_{t=1}^{L_W} \ln(\sigma_i) - \sum_{t=1}^{L} \frac{(w_t - \mu_i)^2}{2\sigma_i^2} \\
&= \sum_{t=1}^{L_W} \ln(\alpha) - \sqrt{2\pi} \sum_{t=1}^{L_W} \ln(\sigma) - \sum_{t=1}^{L_W} \frac{(w_t - y_{s_t})^2}{2\sigma^2} \\
&= L_W \ln(\alpha) - L_W \sqrt{2\pi} \ln(\sigma) - \frac{1}{2\sigma^2} \sum_{t=1}^{L_W} (w_t - y_{s_t})^2 \qquad (8)
\end{aligned}
$$

That is, given an HMM λ_Y constructed from time series Y as described above, finding a state sequence S that maximizes $p(Y|S, \lambda_Y)$ is equivalent to finding a state sequence that maximizes equation 8.

The first two terms in equation 8 are constant, and thus can be ignored for the purpose of maximization. Therefore, $\ln(p(W|S, \lambda_Y)$ is maximized when the third term in that equation is maximized. Because σ is a positive constant and $(w_t - y_{s_t})^2$ is positive, we have:

$$
-\frac{1}{2\sigma^2} \sum_{t=1}^{L_W} (w_t - y_{s_t})^2 \leq 0
$$

Therefore, by finding a state sequence that minimizes the following expression, the Viterbi algorithm maximizes equation 8:

$$\sum_{t=1}^{L_W}(w_t - y_{s_t})^2$$

Because states in λ_Y are in a one-to-one correspondence with elements of Y, the state sequence returned by the Viterbi algorithm is also a mapping of elements in W to elements of Y. That is, the state sequence specifies for each w_i which state produced that value. Furthermore, as we have just demonstrated, this sequence is one that minimizes the sum of squared differences between the elements of W and the elements of Y onto which they are mapped. By equation 7, this is exactly what DTW does: it finds a mapping of points in W to points in Y that minimizes the sum of squared differences.

5 Clustering with DTW and HMMs

This section presents an algorithm for clustering time series using only HMMs, and then shows how the utility of that algorithm is greatly enhanced by the information obtained by first clustering the time series with DTW.

5.1 Clustering with HMMs

Definition of "acceptance" of an output sequence by an HMM The assumption underlying our method of clustering with HMMs is that all of the sequences that belong in a cluster were generated by the same HMM and, as such, have high probabilities under this HMM. If a sequence has a high probability under a model, we consider it to be generated, or "accepted", by the model. If it has a low probability we consider it to be "rejected". We apply a simple statistical test to check whether an observed sequence O is generated by a given model λ. We generate a large sample of sequences from the model λ. From this sample we calculate the empirical probability distribution (see "Computer Intensive Methods" in (Cohen 1995)) of $\log(P(o|\lambda))$[1], the log-likelihood of the sequences generated by the model. Let L be the log-likelihood of O under the model, i.e. $L = log(P(O|\lambda))$. We then test the hypothesis that L is drawn from the probability distribution of the log-likelihood of the sequences generated by the model λ. Specifically, we test that:

$$P_\lambda(log\text{-}likelihood \leq L) > threshold$$

and reject the null hypothesis if the probability is below the threshold. If the hypothesis is rejected and L is considered not to be drawn from the probability distribution of the log-likelihood of the sequences generated by λ, then we infer that the sequence O is not accepted by the model λ.

---

[1] In order to eliminate the influence of the sequence length we actually take the average log-likelihood, $\frac{\log(P(o|\lambda))}{sequence\ length}$

HMM-based clustering of output sequences Due to the above assumption, the task of clustering the sequences is equivalent with the task of finding a set of hidden Markov models that accept disjoint subsets of the original set of sequences. A set of sequences can be clustered by fitting an HMM to all the sequences in the set and then applying a fixed point operation that refines the HMM and "shrinks" the initial set to the subset of sequences accepted by the resulting HMM. Given a set S of sequences and a model HMM, the fixed-point operation is:

- $S_0, S_0' \longleftarrow S$
- repeat
    - $S_0 \longleftarrow S_0'$
    - re-train the HMM with S_0
    - $S_0' \longleftarrow$ the sequences in S_0 accepted by the HMM
- until $S_0 = S_0'$

Clustering of the set S proceeds then by repeating the fixed point operation for the set $(S \setminus S_0)$ of remaining sequences and so forth, until no sequence remains unassigned.

The fixed-point operation converges because at each iteration, S can either shrink or stay the same. In the extreme case, S is reduced to one sequence only and not to the empty set, because it is unlikely that an HMM trained exactly with one sequence will not accept it.

5.2   Clustering with DTW + HMMs

When fitting an HMM to a set of sequences, the induction algorithm will try to fit all the sequences in the set equally well. Because the number of states is set in advance and not learned from the data, it is not clear how the states are "allocated" to the different sequences. It is likely that the states' observation probability distributions will cover the regions in the observation space most often visited by the given sequences and that the state probability transitions will be changed accordingly. This means that if the set contains sequences generated by distinct models, it is likely that the induced HMM will be a "compromise" between the original models (the most frequent states of either generating model will appear in the learned model). It is not clear what this compromise model is. Because the training algorithm converges to a local maximum, the resulting HMM is highly dependent on the initial model from which the training algorithm starts.

Therefore, if we assume that the sequences in a training set were generated by some hidden Markov models and our task is to identify these models, then it is advantageous to start the HMM clustering algorithm with even an appro-ximate initial clustering. If the majority of sequences in the initial cluster come from the same model, then it is likely that the learned compromise HMM will be closer to this one (the learned states do not have to cover the regions in the observation space frequently visited by the other HMM). Since the DTW clustering technique can provide a good initial partition, the HMM clustering algorithm is initialized with it. For each cluster in the DTW partitioning, an HMM is created by applying the fixed-point operation described in the previous section to the sequences of the cluster. The remaining sequences from each DTW cluster are then checked against the HMMs of the other DTW clusters. Finally, if any sequences are still unassigned to an HMM, they are placed in a set that is clustered solely by HMM clustering.

6   Experiments

We tested our algorithm on an artificial dataset generated as in (Smyth 1997), from two hidden Markov models. The two hidden Markov models that generated the artificial dataset each have two states, one that emits one symbol from the normal density with mean 0 and variance 1, $\mathcal{N}(0, 1)$, and one that emits one symbol from $\mathcal{N}(3, 1)$. The two models differ in their transition probability matrices. These matrices are:

$$A_{HMM_1} = \begin{pmatrix} .6 & .4 \\ .4 & .6 \end{pmatrix}$$

$$A_{HMM_2} = \begin{pmatrix} .4 & .6 \\ .6 & .4 \end{pmatrix}$$

As explained in (Smyth 1997) this is only apparently an easy problem.

Because the output of the states is continuous and we implemented our clustering algorithm with discrete HMMs, we discretized the output values with a Kohonen network with 20 units (so the output alphabet has 20 symbols in our experiments). Again as in (Smyth 1997), the training set consists of 40 sequences. The first 20 are generated by HMM_1 and the last 20 by HMM_2. Each sequence has length 200.

The clusters resulting from DTW alone are shown below. For each cluster the indices of the time series belonging to that cluster are shown. Ideally, cluster 1 would contain indices 0 through 19 and cluster 2 would contain indices 20 through 39.

- cluster 1: 1 2 3 4 5 6 9 10 11 12 13 15 17 18 19 23 24 33 35 37
- cluster 2: 0 7 8 14 16 20 21 22 25 26 27 28 29 30 31 32 34 36 38 39

The resulting DTW+HMM clustering is:

- cluster 1: 1 2 3 4 5 6 9 10 11 13 14 15 16 18
- cluster 2: 20 21 22 24 26 27 29 30 31 34 36 37 38 39
- cluster 3: 0 8 12 17 19 23 25 28 33
- cluster 4: 7 32 35

The transition matrices of the four HMMs are:

$$A_{HMM_1} = \begin{pmatrix} .69 & .30 \\ .38 & .61 \end{pmatrix}$$

$$A_{HMM_2} = \begin{pmatrix} .29 & .70 \\ .64 & .35 \end{pmatrix}$$

$$A_{HMM_3} = \begin{pmatrix} .55 & .44 \\ .53 & .46 \end{pmatrix}$$

$$A_{HMM_4} = \begin{pmatrix} .49 & .50 \\ .46 & .53 \end{pmatrix}$$

It can be noticed that the HMM clustering "cleans" the clusters obtained by DTW. For example, the sequences 33, 35, 37, that appear in the first cluster in the DTW partitioning, are removed by the HMM clustering, and the resulting DTW+HMM cluster has only sequences generated by the first model. The second cluster has only sequences generated by the second model, too. It can also be noticed that when HMM clustering alone is applied for the sequences removed from the DTW clusters, the resulting clusters, 3 and 4, have mixed sequences. Thus, HMM clustering alone does not work well: when trained with mixed sequences a compromise HMM is learned, rather than an HMM close to one of the true models. The transition matrices for the first two models are very different: each HMM fits the idiosyncrasies of the sequences emitted by the true models. As for the last two models, each of them is a compromise between the two original HMMs. The above results indicate that further improvement might be obtained by alternating DTW and HMM clustering in repeated iterations.

We ran experiments where we applied the inverse fixed-point operation; that is, the set of sequences assigned to one HMM was "grown" starting from the prototype returned by DTW clustering:

- the initial HMM is created from the prototype sequence
- iterate until the set of accepted sequences does not change:
  - test all the sequences in the DTW cluster for membership to the current HMM
  - retrain the HMM with the set of accepted sequences

Because it is not guaranteed that at each iteration the set of accepted sequences grows - a previously accepted sequence may no longer be accepted after retraining - the process does not always converge. Another problem with starting the fixed-point operation from the prototype is that the initial HMM might overfit the prototype and accept no other sequence. Despite these problems, we intend to pursue this method of clustering because it holds promise for better clustering than by HMM alone. HMM clustering is hindered by the unknown number of states: with enough states the HMM has enough branches to accommodate different output sequences; with few states it may over generalize and again accept different sequences. Provided that the adequate number of states is found, creating the HMM from the prototype may lead to a model with one "main" (very likely) state path. Such a model corresponds to our intuitive notion of similarity of time series: the observed output sequences are generated by random walks along similar state sequences.

We also applied the technique to clustering time series of robot sensor values. The time series were collected during several simple experiences: the robot was approaching, pushing or passing an object. While we do not know the true clusters in the robot data, we considered a good clustering one which reflects the kinds of experiences enumerated above. We observed the same effect of "cleaning" the DTW clusters by the HMM, but the set of sequences removed by the HMM fixed-point operation was large and poorly clustered by the HMM clustering method. Also, the initial DTW clustering of robot data is not as good as the one for artificial data. As such, the HMM clustering algorithm does not benefit from the initial DTW partition. In this case, both DTW clustering and HMM clustering alone are better than the DTW + HMM combination. These are the results obtained by HMM clustering alone for the robot data. For each time series we marked the events that we considered important, for example "push red object" or "pass red object on left". These results illustrate the problem of "branchy" HMMs, that accept distinct sequences on different state paths.

- **cluster 1, prototype 91**
    - 4 8 20 31 63 **91** 112 134: push red object
    - 16 36 54 138: pass red object on right
    - 107 123 127 129: pass red object on left
    - 96: approach right red object
- **cluster 2, prototype 94**
    - 1 6 41 58 61 77: crash into red object
    - **94** 98: approach left red object
- **cluster 3, prototype 125**
    - 59 73 **125**: push red object
    - 18: crash into red object
- **cluster 4, prototype 116**
    - 45 75 **116**: pass red object on right
    - 32: crash into red object
    - 158: push red object
- **cluster 5, prototype 146**
    - 80 **146**: crash into red object

We think that the problem of the unknown number of HMM states must be solved before trying to cluster and represent real data with HMMs. We plan to apply the minimum description length principle for tackling this difficult problem.

7   Conclusion

We presented a hybrid time series clustering algorithm that uses dynamic time warping and hidden Markov model induction. The algorithm worked well in experiments with artificial data. The two methods complement each other: DTW produces a rough initial clustering and the HMM removes from these clusters the sequences that do not belong to them. The downside is that the HMM removes some good sequences along with the bad ones. We suggested possible ways of improving the method and are currently working on validating them.

References

[Baldi *et al.* 1994] Baldi, P.; Chauvin, Y.; Hunkapiller, T.; and McClure, M. 1994. Hidden Markov models of biological primary sequence information. *Proceedings of the National Academy of Sciences* 91(3):1059–1063.

[Bregler 1997] Bregler, C. 1997. Learning and recognizing human dynamics in video sequences. In *Proceedings of the IEEE Conference on Computer Vision and Pattern Recognition*, 568–574.

[Cohen 1995] Cohen, P. R. 1995. *Empirical Methods for Artificial Intelligence.* Cambridge: The MIT Press.

[Corman, Leiserson, & Rivest 1990] Corman, T. H.; Leiserson, C. E.; and Rivest, R. L. 1990. *Introduction to Algorithms.* MIT Press.

[Everitt 1993] Everitt, B. 1993. *Cluster Analysis.* John Wiley & Sons, Inc.

[Jelinek 1997] Jelinek, F. 1997. *Statistical Methods for Speech Recognition.* MIT Press.

[Kruskall & Liberman 1983] Kruskall, J. B., and Liberman, M. 1983. The symmetric time warping problem: From continuous to discrete. In *Time Warps, String Edits and Macromolecules: The Theory and Practice of Sequence Comparison.* Addison-Wesley.

[Rabiner 1989] Rabiner, L. 1989. A tutorial on hidden markov models and selected applications in speech recognition. *Proceedings of the IEEE* 77(2):257–285.

[Sankoff & Kruskall 1983] Sankoff, D., and Kruskall, J. B. 1983. *Time Warps, String Edits and Macromolecules: The Theory and Practice of Sequence Comparison.* Addison-Wesley.

[Smyth 1997] Smyth, P. 1997. Clustering sequences with hidden markov models. In *Advances in Neural Information Processing 9.*

Anticipation Model for Sequential Learning of Complex Sequences*

DeLiang Wang

Department of Computer and Information Science
and Center for Cognitive Science
The Ohio State University

1 Introduction

One of the fundamental aspects of human intelligence is the ability to process temporal information (Lashley, 1951). Learning and reproducing temporal sequences are closely associated with our ability to perceive and generate body movements, speech and language, music, etc. A considerable body of neural network literature is devoted to temporal pattern generation (see Wang, 2001, for a recent review). These models generally treat a temporal pattern as a sequence of discrete patterns, called a temporal sequence. Most of the models are based on either multilayer perceptrons with backpropagation training or the Hopfield model of associative recall. The basic idea for the former class of models is to view a temporal sequence as a set of associations between consecutive components, and learn these associations as input-output transformations (Jordan, 1986; Elman, 1990; Mozer, 1993). To deal with temporal dependencies beyond consecutive components, part of the input layer is used to keep a trace of history, behaving as short-term memory (STM). Similarly, for temporal recall based on the Hopfield associative memory, a temporal sequence is viewed as associations between consecutive components. These associations are stored in extended versions of the Hopfield model that includes some time delays (Sompolinsky & Kanter, 1986; Buhmann & Schulten, 1987; Heskes & Gielen, 1992). To deal with longer temporal dependencies, high-order networks have been proposed (Guyon et al., 1988).

1.1 Learning Complex Sequences

One of the main problems with the above two classes of models lies in the difficulty in retrieving complex temporal sequences, where the same part may occur many times in the sequence. Though proposed remedies can alleviate the problem to some degree, the problem is not completely resolved. In multilayer perceptrons, a blended form of STM becomes increasingly ambiguous when temporal dependencies increase (Bengio et al., 1994). The use of high-order units

---

* Thanks to X. Liu for his help in typesetting. The preparation of this chapter was supported in part by an ONR YIP award and a grant from NUWC.

in the Hopfield model requires a huge number of connections to deal with long range temporal dependencies, or the model yields ambiguities.

More recently, Bradski et al. (1994) proposed an STM model, which exhibits both recency and primacy, where the former means that more recent items in a sequence are better retained and the latter means that the beginning items are less prone to forgetting. Both recency and primacy are characteristics of human STM. In addition, their model creates new representations for repeated occurrences of the same symbol, thus capable of encoding complex sequences to a certain extent. Granger et al. (1994) proposed a biologically motivated model for encoding temporal sequences. Their model uses a competitive learning rule that eventually develops sequence detectors at the end of sequence presentation. Each detector encodes a sequence whereby the beginning component has the highest weight, and the subsequent components have successively lower weights. They claim that the network has an unusually high capacity. However, it is unclear how their network reads out the encoded sequences. Baram (1994) presented a model for memorizing vector sequences using the Kanerva memory model (Kanerva, 1988). The basic idea is similar to those models that are based on the Hopfield model. Baram's model uses second-order synapses to store the temporal associations between consecutive vectors in a sequence, but the model deals only with sequences that contain no repeating vectors. Rinkus (1995) proposed a model of temporal associative memory, based on associations among random sequences. The associations are encoded using a method similar to the associative memory of Willshaw et al. (1969). However, the model needs an additional operation that maps a sequence component in a semi-random vector and remembers the mapping for later decoding.

Based on the idea of using STM for resolving ambiguities, Wang and Arbib (1990) proposed a model for learning to recognize and generate complex sequences . With an STM model, a complex sequence is acquired by a learning rule that associates the activity distribution in STM with a context detector (for a rigorous definition see Section 2). For sequence generation, each component of a sequence is associated with a context detector that learns to associate with the component. After successful training, a beginning part of the sequence forms an adequate context for activating the next component, and the newly activated component joins STM to form a context for activating the following component. This process continues until the entire sequence is generated. A later version (Wang & Arbib, 1993) deals with the issues of time warping and chunking of subsequences. In particular, sequences in this version can be recognized in a hierarchical way and without being affected by presentation speed. Hierarchical recognition enables the system to recognize sequences whose temporal dependencies are much longer than the STM capacity. In sequence generation, the system is capable of maintaining relative timing among the components while the overall rate can change.

Recently, L. Wang (1999) proposed to use multi-associative neural networks for learning and retrieving spatiotemporal patterns. STM is coded by systematic delay lines. The basic idea is that, when dealing with complex sequences , one pattern is allowed to be associated with a set of subsequent patterns, and disambiguation can be eliminated by intersecting multiple sets associated by the previous pattern, the pattern prior to the previous pattern, and so on. It is easy to see that a complex sequence can be unambiguously generated with a sufficient number of systematic delay lines. Associations between spatial patterns are established through single units in a competitive layer. A major drawback of the multi-associative network model is that much of system architecture and many network operations are algorithmically described, rather than arising from an autonomous neural network (e.g., no discussion on how set intersection is neurally implemented).

1.2   Sequential Learning Problem

A comprehensive model of temporal sequence learning must address the issue of sequentially learning multiple sequences; that is, how are new sequences learned after some sequences have been acquired? One way of learning multiple sequences is to use simultanous training, where many sequences are learned at once. A model that can learn one sequence can generally be extended to learn multiple sequences with simultaneous training. A straightforward way is to concatenate multiple sequences into a single long sequence. Given that each sequence has a unique identifier, a model can learn all of the sequences if it can learn the concatenated sequence. However, sequential learning of multiple sequences is an entirely different matter. It is a more desirable form of training because it allows the model to acquire new sequences without bringing back all the previously used sequences - a form of *incremental learning* . Incremental learning not only conforms well with human learning, but also is important for many applications that do not keep all the training data and where learning is a long-term on-going process.

It turns out that incremental learning is a particularly challenging problem for neural networks. In multilayer perceptrons, it is well recognized that the network exhibits so called catastrophic interference, whereby later training disrupts the traces of previous training. It was pointed out by Grossberg (1987), and systematically revealed by McCloskey and Cohen (1989) and Ratcliff (1990). Many subsequent studies attempt to address the problem, and most of proposed remedies amount to reducing overlapping in hidden layer representations by some form of orthogonalization, a technique used long ago for reducing cross-talks in associative memories (see Kruschke, 1992, Sloman & Rumelhart, 1992, and French, 1994). Most of these proposals are verified only by small scale simulations, which, together with the lack of rigorous analysis, make it difficult to judge to what extent the proposed methods work. It remains to be seen whether a general remedy can be found for multilayer perceptions. Associative memories are less susceptible to the problem, and appear to be able to incorporate more patterns easily so long as the overall number of patterns does not exceed the memory capacity. However, the Hopfield model has a major difficulty in dealing with correlated patterns with overlapping components (Hertz et al., 1991). The Hopfield model has been extended to deal with correlated patterns (Kantor &

Sompolinsky, 1987), and Diederich and Opper (1987) proposed a local learning rule to acquire the necessary weights iteratively. The local learning rule used by them is very similar to the perceptron learning rule. Thus, it appears that such a scheme for dealing with correlated patterns would suffer from catastrophic interference.

The major cause of catastrophic interference is the *distributedness* of representations; the learning of new patterns needs to use and alter those weights that participate in representing previously learned patterns. There is a tradeoff between distributedness and interference. Models that use non-overlapping representations, or local representations, do not exhibit the problem. For example, the ART model (Carpenter & Grossberg, 1987) does not have the problem because each stored pattern uses a different weight vector and no overlapping is allowed between any two weight vectors.

During sequential learning , humans show some degree of interference. Retroactive interference has been well documented in psychology (Crooks & Stein, 1991), which occurs when learning a later event interferes with the recall of earlier information. In general, the similarity between the current event and memorized ones is largely responsible for retroactive interference (Barnes & Underwood, 1959; Chandler, 1993; Bower et al., 1994). Animals also exhibit retroactive interference (Rodriguez et al., 1993). The existence of retroactive interference suggests that events are not independently stored in the brain, and related events are somehow intertwined in the memory. Although recall performance of the interfered items decreases, it still is better than the chance level, and it is easier to relearn these items than to learn them for the first time. This analysis suggests that a memory model that stores every item independently cannot adequately model human/animal memory. From the computational perspective, the models that store different events in a shared way have a better storage efficiency than those that do not. In summary, a desired memory model should exhibit some degree of retroactive interference when learning similar events, but not catastrophic interference.

In this chapter, we describe the *anticipation model* for temporal sequence learning (Wang & Yuwono, 1995; Wang & Yuwono, 1996). Similar to Wang and Arbib (1990), an STM model is used for maintaining a temporal context. In learning a temporal sequence, the model actively anticipates the next component based on STM. When the anticipation is correct, the model does nothing and continues to learn the rest of the sequence. When the anticipation is incorrect, namely a mismatch occurs, the model automatically expands the context for the component. A one-shot (single step) normalized Hebbian learning rule is used to learn contexts, and it exhibits the mechanism of temporal masking, where a sequence masks its subsequences in winner-take-all competition. The anticipation model can learn to generate an arbitrary sequence by self-organization, thus avoiding supervised teaching signals as required in Wang and Arbib. Furthermore, the model is examined in terms of its performance on sequential training tasks. We show that the anticipation model is capable of incremental learning , and exhibits retroactive interference but not catastrophic interference. Extensive simulations reveal that the amount of retraining is relatively independent of the number of sequences stored in the model. Furthermore, a mechanism of chunking is described that creates chunks for recurring subsequences. This chunking mechanism significantly improves training and retraining performance.

The remaining part of the chapter is organized as follows. In Section 2, the anticipation model is fully defined. Section 3 introduces several rigorous results of the anticipation model. In Section 4, we provide simulation results of the model, in particular for learning many sequences incrementally. The simulation results suggest that incremental learning in the anticipation model is capacity-independent, or unaffected by the number of stored sequences. Section 5 describes the chunking mechanism and shows how chunking improves the learning performance. Section 6 provides some general discussions about the anticipation model. Finally, Section 7 concludes the chapter.

2 Anticipation Model

We follow the terminology introduced by Wang and Arbib (1990). Sequences are defined over a symbol set Γ, which consists of all possible symbols, or spatial (static) patterns. Sequence S of length N over Γ is defined as p_1-p_2-...-p_N, where $p_i (1 \leq i \leq N) \in \Gamma$ is called a component of S. The sequence p_j-p_{j+1}-...-p_k, where $1 \leq j \leq k \leq N$, is a *subsequence* of S, and the sequence p_j-p_{j+1}-...-p_N where $1 \leq j \leq N$, is a *right subsequence* of S. In general, in order to produce a component by its predecessors in a sequence, a prior subsequence is needed. For example, to produce the first "P" in the sequence M-I-S-S-I-S-S-I-P-P-I requires the prior subsequence S-I-S-S-I. This is because I-S-S-I is a recurring subsequence. Hence, the *context* of p_i is defined as the shortest prior subsequence of p_i that uniquely determines p_i in S. The *degree* of p_i is the length of its context. The degree of S is the maximum degree of all of the components of S. Therefore, a *simple sequence*, where each component is unique, is a degree 1 sequence and a *complex sequence*, which contains recurring subsequences, is a sequence whose degree is greater than 1.

2.1 Basic Network Description

We now describe the basic components of the anticipation model. Fig. 1 shows the architecture of the network. The network consists of a layer of n input terminals, each associated with a shift-register (SR) assembly, and a layer of m context detectors, each associated with a modulator. Each SR assembly contains r units, arranged so that the input signal stimulating an input terminal shifts to the next unit every time step. SR assemblies serve as STM for input signals. Each detector receives input from all SR units, and there are lateral connections, including self-excitation, within the detector layer that form winner-take-all architecture. These connections and competitive dynamics lead to the detector that receives the greatest ascending input from SR units to be the sole winner of the entire detector layer. In addition to the ascending and lateral connections, each detector also connects mutually with its corresponding modulator, which in turn connects directly with input terminals.

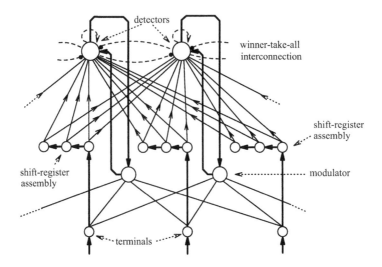

Fig. 1. Architecture of the anticipation model. Thin solid lines denote modifiable connections, and thick or dash lines denote fixed connections. The connections between terminals and modulators are bidirectional.

The model internally anticipates the next component and compares it with the external input through the modulator layer. Each modulator unit receives upward connections from every individual terminal. In addition, it receives a downward connection from its respective detector. An active detector enables its corresponding modulator in the next time step (assuming some delay). Once enabled, the modulator performs one-shot learning that updates its connection weights from the terminals. Since only one terminal corresponding to an input component can be active at any time step, one-shot learning leads to one-to-one connection from an active terminal to an enabled modulator. Basically, this one-shot learning establishes the association between a context detector and the next input component. If the active terminal and the enabled modulator do not match next time when the detector is activated, the anticipated activation of the modulator will be absent. This mismatch will be detected by the modulator, which in turn will send a signal to its respective detector to expand the context that the detector is supposed to recognize.

2.2   Model Description

The activity of detector i at time t, $E_i(t)$, is defined as:

$$E_i(t) = g(\sum_{j,k} W_{i,jk} g(V_{jk}(t), A_i), \theta_i) \tag{1}$$

$$g(x, y) = \begin{cases} x & \text{if } x \geq y \\ 0 & \text{otherwise} \end{cases} \tag{2}$$

where $W_{i,jk}$ is the connection weight from the kth SR unit of assembly j to detector i. $V_{jk}(t)$ is the activity of this SR unit at time t. θ_i is an adjustable threshold for the detector, which is initialized to 0. θ_i may be increased when detector i wins winner-take-all competition in the detector layer, to be discussed later. A_i is defined later in (5). The activity $V_{jk}(t)$ is given as follows,

$$V_{jk}(t) = \begin{cases} I_j(t) & \text{if } k = 1 \text{ (head unit)} \\ \max(0, V_{j,k-1}(t-1) - \delta) & \text{otherwise} \end{cases} \tag{3}$$

where $I_j(t)$ is the binary activity of terminal j, that is, $I_j(t) = 1$ if the corresponding symbol of terminal j is being presented to the network at time t, and $I_j(t) = 0$ otherwise. Due to the nature of sequential input, at most one terminal has its I equal to 1 at t. δ is a decay parameter. Eq. 3 provides an implementation of the STM model described earlier, i.e., an input activity is held for a short time but decays gradually in a shift-register assembly. If assembly j is stimulated by an input at time t, namely $I_j(t) = 1$, according to (3) the end unit of the assembly gets activated at time $t + r - 1$, and its activity $V_{jr}(t+r-1) = max(0, 1 - \delta(r-1))$. Apparently, the input cannot be held longer than r steps, the limit of STM capacity. Given r, in order for the input to be held for r steps, the parameter must be chosen so that $1 - \delta(r - 1) > 0$. That is, $\delta < 1/(r - 1)$.

As mentioned earlier, all the detector units in the detector layer form a winner-take-all network. The detailed dynamics of winner-take-all can be found in Grossberg (1976). In such a competitive network, the activity of each detector evolves until the network reaches equilibrium, at which point the detector with the highest initial activity becomes the only active unit. The network takes a short time to reach equilibrium. This time period should be much shorter than the duration of one sequence component. Therefore, we assume that each discrete time step is longer than the time needed for the winner-take-all mechanism to settle at an equilibrium.

The learning rule for each detector i is a Hebbian rule (Hebb, 1949) plus normalization to keep the overall weight a constant (von der Malsburg, 1973; Wang & Arbib, 1990), and it is denoted as a *normalized Hebbian rule*,

$$\hat{W}_{i,jk}(t + 1) = W_{i,jk}(t) + \alpha O_i(t) g(V_{jk}(t), A_i) \tag{4a}$$

$$W_{i,jk}(t + 1) = \frac{\hat{W}_{i,jk}(t + 1)}{\alpha C + \sum_{jk} \hat{W}_{i,jk}(t + 1)} \tag{4b}$$

where α is a gain parameter or learning rate. A large α makes training fast. It is easy to see that very large α leads to approximate one-shot learning. As mentioned earlier, winner-take-all competition in the detector layer will activate a single unit from the layer. To indicate the outcome while omitting the details of competitive dynamics, let $O_i(t)$ equal 1 if detector i is the winner of the competition, or 0 otherwise. Function g, as defined in (2), serves as a gate to let in the influences of only those SR units whose activities are greater than or equal to A_i. A_i is the sensitivity parameter of unit i. The lower the sensitivity parameter the more SR units can be sensed by a winning detector, and thus more connections of the detector can be modified according to (4a). Furthermore, the sensitivity parameter A_i is adaptive by itself:

$$A_i = \begin{cases} 1 & \text{if } d_i = 0 \\ \max(0, 1 - \delta(d_i - 1)) & \text{if } d_i > 0 \end{cases} \tag{5}$$

where d_i, indicating the degree of detector i, is a non-negative integer, initialized to 0. δ is the decay parameter introduced in (3). According to (5), A_i is equal to 1 when $d_i = 0$ or 1, and decreases until 0 as d_i increases. Since value 1 is the activity level of the corresponding head unit when some assembly is stimulated, detector i will only sense one SR unit - a head unit - when $d_i = 0$ or 1. When d_i increases, more SR units are sensed. Except when $d_i = 0$, d_i is equal to the number of units that detector i can sense when it becomes a winner. The constant C in (4b) is positive, and its role will be described in Sect. 3. The connection weight $W_{i,jk}$ is initialized to $1/[r(1+C)+\epsilon]$, where ϵ is a small random number introduced to break symmety between the inputs of the detectors, which may cause problems for competitive dynamics.

Let unit z be the winner of the competition in the detector layer. As a result of the updated connection weights, the activity of unit z will change when the same input is presented in the future. More specifically, E_z is monotonically non-decreasing as learning takes place. This observation will be further discussed in the next section. The resulting, increased, activity in (1) is then used to update the threshold of unit z. This is generally described as:

$$\theta_i(t+1) = \theta_i(t) + O_i(E_i^*(t+1) - \theta_i(t)) \tag{6}$$

where $E_i^*(t+1)$ is the activity of i based on the new weights, i.e. $E_i^*(t+1) = \sum_{jk} W_{i,jk}(t+1)g(V_{jk}(t), A_i)$. Thus, θ_i is adjusted to if unit i is the winner. Otherwise, θ_i remains the same. Due to this adjustment, unit z increases its threshold so that it will be triggered only by the same subsequence whose components have been sensed during weight updates by (4a). The above threshold can be relaxed (lowered) a little when handling sequences with certain distortions. This way, subsequences very close to the training one can also activate the detector.

A modulator receives both a top-down connection from its corresponding detector and bottom-up connections from input terminals (Fig. 1). We assume that the top down connection modulates the bottom-up connections by a multiplicative operation. Thus, the activity of modulator i is defined as,

$$M_i(t) = O_i(t-1) \sum_{j=1}^{n} R_{ij} I_j(t) \tag{7}$$

where R_{ij} is a binary weight of the connection from terminal j to modulator i. All R_{ij}'s are initialized to 0. We assume that the top-down signal takes one step to reach its modulator. Because at most one terminal is active ($I(t) = 1$) at any time, $M_i(t)$ is also a binary value. If $O_i(t-1) = 1$ and $M_i(t) = 0$ then the modulator sends a feedback signal to its corresponding detector. Upon receiving this feedback signal, the detector increases its degree, thus lowering its sensitivity parameter A_i (see Eq. 5). Quantitatively, d_i is adjusted as follows:

$$d_i = \begin{cases} d_i + O_i(t-1) & \text{if } M_i(t) = 0 \\ d_i & \text{otherwise} \end{cases} \tag{8}$$

The situation where $O_i(t-1) = 1$ and $M_i(t) = 0$ is referred to as a *mismatch*. A mismatch occurs when an anticipated component in the sequence does not appear, to be explained shortly. Thus the degree of a context detector increases when a mismatch occurs.

Finally, one-shot learning is performed on the bottom-up connection weights of the modulator of the winning detector z,

$$R_{zj} = I_j(t) \tag{9}$$

This one-shot learning sets the connection weights of modulator z to the current activities of the input terminals. Since there is only one active terminal at time t, i.e., the one representing the current input symbol, only one bottom-up weight of the modulator is equal to one, and all the others are zero. This training results in a one-to-one association between a modulator and a terminal.

We now explain under what condition a mismatch occurs, which leads to an increment of the degree of the winning detector. According to (7), a mismatch occurs when $O_i(t-1) = 1$ and $\sum_{j=1}^{n} R_{ij} I_j(t) = 0$. Since at any time, only one bottom-up weight of modulator i equals 1 and only one input terminal (I_j) is active, mismatch occurs when the non zero weight and the terminal with non zero input do not coincide. But one-shot learning of Eq. 9 establishes a non zero link only between a modulator and the next input terminal. Therefore, a mismatch occurs if the link between detector i and an input terminal established last time when detector i was activated does not coincide with the active input terminal this time (at time t). The bottom-up links of a modulator established between the modulator (or the corresponding detector) and the next input component are used for the modulator to anticipate the next component in sequence generation. Thus a mismatch corresponds to where the anticipated input symbol does not match with the actual input during sequence training. Since R_{ij}'s are all initialized to 0, following (7) a mismatch is bound to occur the first time a pair of consecutive components is presented, which then increases the degree of the detector for the first component from 0 to 1. If the sequence to be learned is a simple sequence, like A-B-C-D-E, it suffices to increase the degrees of all involved detectors to 1. For complex sequences , though, the degree of the relevant detectors need further increase until no mismatch occurs.

The training is repeated each time step. After all sequence components have been presented, the entire cycle of training, referred to as a *training sweep*, is repeated. The training phase is completed when there is no mismatch during the last training sweep. In this case the network correctly anticipates the next component for the entire sequence. The completion of the learning phase can be detected in various ways. For example, a global unit can be introduced to sum up all feedback from modulators to their respective context detectors during a training sweep. In this case, an inactive global unit by the end of a sweep signals the end of the training phase.

3   Analytical Results

In this section, we summarize several analytical results on the anticipation model. These results are listed in the form of propositions without proofs, and the interested reader is referred to Wang and Yuwono (1995; 1996) for detailed proofs of these results.

*Proposition*1. The normalized Hebbian rule of (4) with the following choice of parameter C

$$C > \frac{\delta r(r-1)}{6}[1 + \frac{\delta+2}{1-\delta(r-1)}] \tag{10}$$

leads to a property called *temporal masking*: the detector of sequence S is preferred to the detectors of the right subsequences of S. In other words, when sequence S occurs, the detector that recognizes S masks those detectors that recognize the right subsequences of S. This property is called temporal masking, following the term *masking fields* introduced by Cohen and Grossberg (Cohen & Grossberg, 1987), which state that larger spatial patterns are preferred to smaller ones when activating their corresponding detectors.

Inequality (10) tells us how to choose C based on the value of δ in order to ensure that the detector of a sequence masks the detectors of its left subsequences. The smaller is δ, the smaller is the right-hand-side of (10), and thus the smaller C can be chosen to satisfy the inequality. As a degenerate case, if $\delta = 0$, (10) becomes $C > 0$, and this corresponds to exactly the condition of forming masking fields in static pattern recognition (Cohen & Grossberg, 1987). Therefore, (10) includes masking fields as a special case. In temporal processing, δ reflects forgetting in STM, and thus cannot be 0. On the other hand, δ should be smaller than $1/(r-1)$ in order to fully utilize SR units for STM (see the discussion in Sect. 2.2), thus the degree of the learnable sequences (see Eq. 3).

*Proposition*2. The following two conclusions result from the learning algorithm: (a) At any time, a detector can be triggered by only a single sequence; (b)

Except for initial training, once a unit is activated by sequence S, it can only be activated by S or a sequence that has S as a right subsequence. Because of (a), one can say that a detector is *tuned* to the unique sequence which can trigger a detector.

*Proposition*3. An anticipation model with m detectors, and r SR units for each of n SR assemblies can learn to generate an arbitrary sequence S of length $\leq m$ and degree $\leq r$, where S is composed of symbols from Γ with $|\Gamma| \leq n$.

Once training is completed, the network can be used to generate the sequence it has been trained on. During sequence generation, the learned connections from input terminals to modulators are used reversely for producing input components. Sequence generation is triggered by the presentation of the first component, or a sequence identifier. This presentation will be able to trigger an appropriate detector which then, through its modulator, leads to the activation of the second component. In turn, the newly activated terminal adds to STM, which then forms an appropriate context to generate another component in the sequence. This process continues until the entire sequence is generated.

Aside from Proposition 3, learning is efficient - it generally takes just a few training sweeps to acquire a sequence. This is because the anticipation model employs the strategy of least commitment. The model views, as a default, the sequence to be learned as a simple one, and expands the contexts of sequence components only when necessary. Another feature of the model is that, depending on the nature of the sequence, the system can yield significant sharing among context detectors: the same detector may be used for anticipating the same symbol that occurs many times in a sequence. As a result, the system needs fewer detectors to learn complex sequences than the model of Wang and Arbib (1990; 1993).

The above results are about learning a single sequence, whereby a sequence is presented to the network one component at a time during training. When dealing with multiple sequences, each sequence is assumed to be unique, because learning a sequence that has been acquired corresponds to recalling the sequence. We assume that the first component of a sequence represents the unique identifier of the sequence. To facilitate the following exposition, we define a *sequential learning procedure* as the following. The training process proceeds in rounds. In the first round, the first sequence is presented to the network in repeated sweeps until the network has learned the sequence. The second round starts with the presentation of the second sequence. Once the second sequence is acquired by the network, the network is checked to see if it can generate the first sequence correctly when presented with the identifier of the sequence. If the network can generate the first sequence, the second round ends. Otherwise, the first sequence is brought back for retraining. In this case, the first sequence is said to be *interfered* by the acquisition of the second sequence. If the first sequence needs to be retrained, the second sequence needs to be checked again after the retraining of the first sequence is completed, since the latter lead to the interference of the second sequence. The second round completes when both sequences can be produced by the network. In the third round, the third sequence is presented to the network repeatedly until it has been learned. The network is then checked to see if it can generate the first two sequences; if yes, the third round is completed; if not, retraining is conducted. In the latter case, retraining is always conducted on the sequences that are interfered. The system sequentially checks and retrains each sequence until every one of the three sequences can be generated by the network - that ends the third round. Later sequences are sequentially trained in the same manner. It is possible that a sequence that is not interfered when acquiring the latest sequence gets interfered as a result of the retraining of some other interfered sequences. Because of this, retraining is conducted in a systematic fashion as the following. All of the previous sequences plus the current one are checked sequentially and retrained if interfered. This retraining process is conducted repeatedly until no more interference occurs for every sequence learned so far. Each such process is called a *retraining cycle*. Thus a round in general consists of repeated retraining cycles.

If a system exhibits catastrophic interference, it cannot successfully complete a sequential learning procedure with multiple sequences. The system instead will show endless *oscillations* between learning and relearning different sequences. In the case of two sequences, for example, the system can only acquire one sequence - the latest one used in a sequential training procedure. Thus, the system will be stuck in the second round.

*Proposition*4. Given sufficient numbers of detectors and SR units for each shift-register assembly, the anticipation model can learn to produce a finite number of sequences sequentially.

In Proposition 4, the number of units in each SR assembly, or the STM capacity, must be sufficient to handle long temporal dependencies in the context of multiple sequences. It should be clear that the complexity of a sequence may increase when it is trained with other sequences. For example, X-A-B-C and Y-A-B-D are both simple sequences when taken separately. But when the system needs to memorize both sequences, A-B becomes a repeating sequence, and as a result both become complex sequences . We define the *degree of a set of sequences* as the maximum length of all the shortest prior sequences that uniquely determine all the components of all the sequences in the set. Because the first component of each sequence is its unique identifier, the definition of the set degree does not depend on how this set of sequences is ordered. Moreover, the degree of a set of sequences must be smaller than the length of the longest sequence in the set. With this definition, it is sufficient to satisfy the condition of Proposition 3 if the number of SR units in each assembly is greater than or equal to the set degree.

The sequential learning procedure is not necessary for the validity of Proposition 4. A more natural procedure of sequential training is postpone retraining until interfered sequences need to be recalled in a specific application. This procedure is more consistent with the process of human learning. One often does not notice memory interference until being tested in a psychological experiment or daily life. This learning procedure blurs the difference between learning a new sequence for the first time and relearning an interfered sequence. Proposition 4 essentially implies that more and more sequences will be acquired by the system as the learning experience of the model extends. This is an important point. As a result, the anticipation model can be viewed as an open learning system. No rigid procedure for sequential training is needed for the system to increase its long-term memory capacity. The model automatically increases the capacity by just focusing on learning the current sequence. Also, the number of detectors needed to satisfy Proposition 4 can be significantly smaller than the upper limit of $\sum_{i=1}^{k}(|S_i| - 1)$ for k sequences. This is because detectors can be shared within the same sequence as well as across different sequences. This will be further discussed in the next section.

4   Simulation Results

To illustrate the model's capability in learning an arbitrarily complex sequence, we show the following computer simulation for learning input sequence $<TO$ - BE - OR - NOT - TO - $BE>$. The simulated network has 24 detector units, 24 terminals, and 6 SR units for each shift-register assembly (144 SR units in total). Figure 2 shows the activity trace of the network from a simulation run. We use symbol '#' as the end marker, and symbol '-' as a distinct symbol separating meaningful words. The network learned the sequence in 5 training sweeps. In the last training sweep, the system correctly anticipates every component of the sequence, as shown in the last column of the figure. After this training, the entire sequence can be correctly generated by the presentation of its first component, T in this case, and the activity trace will be the same as the last sweep of training. The degree of the sequence is 6, used to set r.

Once one sequence is learned, a right subsequence of the sequence can be generated from a middle point of the sequence. In the above example, with symbol R as the initial input the network will correctly generate the remaining part of the sequence $<-NOT$ - TO - $BE>$. Component R was chosen because it forms the degree 1 context for its successor '-'. In general, it requires a subsequence as an input to generate the remaining part of the sequence. A subsequence can activate an detector which then produces a certain component. The component can then join the subsequence to activate another detector, and so on, until the remaining part is fully generated. This feature of the model conforms with the experience that one can often continue a familiar song or a piece of music being exposed to a part of it.

Proposition 4 guarantees that the anticipation model does not suffer from catastrophic interference. Interference exists nonetheless in sequential training, because committed detectors may be seized by later training or retraining to make different anticipation. For example, assume that the system is sequentially trained with two simple sequences, S_a: C-A-T and S_b: E-A-R. After S_a is learned, the training with S_b will lead to the following situation. The previously established link from A to T will be replaced by a link from E-A to R. Thus, S_a

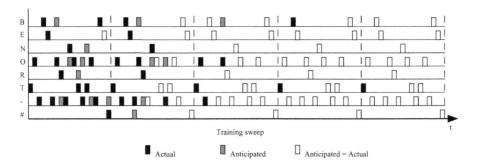

Fig. 2. Training and generation of the sequence $<TO\text{-}BE\text{-}OR\text{-}NOT\text{-}TO\text{-}BE>$. The activity traces of the input terminals are shown, where a black box represents an actual terminal activity, a gray box represents an anticipated activity that does not match the actual input, and a white box represents a match between an anticipated and an actual input activity. The training phase takes 5 training sweeps. The generation process is initiated by presenting the first component of the sequence, T. The parameter values used are: $\alpha = 0.2$, $\delta = 0.1$, and $C = 3.0$.

is interfered and cannot be generated after S_b is acquired. The critical question is what kind of interference is exhibited by the model, and how severely does it affect learning performance? The extent of interference depends on the amount of overlap between the sequence to be learned and the sequences already stored in the memory. Clearly, if a new sequence has no component in common with the stored sequences, the sequence can be trained as if nothing had been learned by the model. In this sense, interference is caused by the similarity between the sequence and the memory. This is consistent with psychological studies on retroactive interference (see Sect. 1.2).

Knowing that the amount of interference, and thus retraining, depends on the overlap of the sequences to be learned, we wanted to evaluate the system by arbitrarily selecting a domain that contains a lot of overlaps among the sequences. The database of the sequences used consists of the titles of all sessions that were held during the 1994 *IEEE International Conference on Neural Networks* (ICNN-94). This database has 97 sequences, as listed in Table 1. These titles are listed without any change and in exactly the same order as they appear in the final conference program, even retaining the obvious mistakes printed on the program. Evident from the table, there are many overlapping subsequences within the database. Thus, these sequences provide a good testbed for evaluating sequential training and retroactive interference.

For training with this database, the chosen network has 131 input terminals - 34 for the symbol set (26 English letters plus "#", " " (space), ".", "&", "?", "-", ":", and "/") and 97 for the identifiers of the 97 sequences. Each SR assembly contains 40 units. Also, the network needs at least 1,088 detectors and 1,088 modulators. Hence, the network has a total of 7,567 units. The parameters of the network are: $\alpha = 0.2$, $\delta = 1/40$ and $C = 535$. To measure the extent of interference, we record the number of retraining sweeps required to eliminate

Table 1. Sequence Base for Sequential Training

no.	Sequence	no.	Sequence
1	Social & philosophical implications of computational intelligence	50	Image recognition
2	Neurocontrol research: real-world perspectives	51	Medical applications
3	Fuzzy neural systems	52	Parallel architectures
4	Advanced analog neural networks and applications	53	Associative memory I
5	Neural networks for control	54	Pattern recognition IV
6	Neural networks implementations	55	Supervised learning III
7	Hybrid systems I.D.	56	Learning and memory IV
8	Artificial life	57	Intelligent control IV
9	Learning and recognition for intelligent control	58	Economic/Finance/Business applications
10	Artificially intelligent neural networks	59	Machine vision I
11	Hybrid systems II	60	Machine vision
12	Supervised learning X	61	Architecture I
13	Intelligent neural controllers: algorithms and applications	62	Supervised learning V
14	Who makes the rules?	63	Speech I
15	Pulsed neural networks	64	Robotics
16	Fuzzy neural systems II	65	Associative memory II
17	Neural networks applications to estimation and identification	66	Medical applications II
18	Adaptive resonance theory neural networks	67	Modular/Digital implementations
19	Analog neural chips and machines	68	Pattern recognition VI
20	Learning and memory I	69	Robotics II
21	Pattern recognition I	70	Unsupervised learning I
22	Supervised learning I	71	Optimization I
23	Intelligent control I	72	Applications in image recognition
24	Neurobiology	73	Architecture III
25	Cognitive science	74	Optimization II
26	Image processing III	75	Supervised learning VII
27	Neural network implementation II	76	Associative memory IV
28	Applications of neural networks to power systems	77	Robotics III
29	Neural system hardware I	78	Speech III
30	Time series prediction and analysis	79	Unsupervised learning II
31	Probabilistic neural networks and radial basis function networks	80	Neurodynamics I
32	Pattern recognition II	81	Applications I
33	Supervised learning II	82	Applied industrial manufacturing
34	Image processing I	83	Applications II
35	Learning and memory II	84	Architecture IV
36	Hybrid systems III	85	Optimization III
37	Artificially intelligent networks II	86	Applications in image recognition II
38	Fast learning for neural networks	87	Unsupervised learning III
39	Industry application of neural networks	88	Supervised learning VIII
40	Neural systems hardware II	89	Neurodynamics II
41	Image processing II	90	Computational intelligence
42	Nonlinear PCA neural networks	91	Optimization using Hopfield networks
43	Intelligent control III	92	Supervised learning IX
44	Pattern recognition III	93	Applications to communications
45	Supervised learning III	94	Applications III
46	Applications in power	95	Unsupervised learning IV
47	Time series prediction and analysis II	96	Optimization IV
48	Learning and memory III	97	Applications
49	Intelligent robotics		

all interference for every round of sequential training. This number is a good indicator of how much retraining is needed to store all of the sequences that have been sequentially presented to the system. Also, we record the number of intact uninterfered (intact) sequences right after the acquisition of the latest sequence. Figure 3 shows the number of intact sequences and the number of retraining sweeps plotted against training rounds.

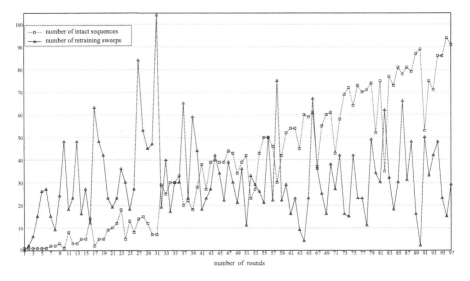

Fig. 3. The number of intact sequences and the number of retraining sweeps with respect to training rounds during training with the Table 1 database.

Several conclusions can be drawn from this simulation result. The first and the most important conclusion is that the number of retraining sweeps seems independent of the size of the previous memory. The overall curve for retraining sweeps remains flat, even though there is large variation across different training rounds. We view this result as particularly significant because it suggests that, in the anticipation model, the amount of interference caused by learning a new sequence does not increase with the number of previously memorized sequences. This conclusion not only conforms intuitively with human performance of long-term learning, but also makes the model feasible to provide a reliable sequential memory that can be incrementally updated later on. Hence, new items can be incorporated into the memory without being limited by those items already in the memory. We refer to this property of sequential learning/memory as *capacity-independent incremental learning/memory*. The anticipation model exhibits this property because a learned sequence leaves its traces across the network, involving a set of distributed associations between subsequences and context detectors (see Fig. 1). On the other hand, each context detector stores its context locally. When a new sequence is learned, it employs a group of context detectors, some of which may have been committed, thus causing interference. But as the sequential memor y becomes large, so is the number of context detectors. Out of these detectors, only a certain number of them will be interfered as a result of learning a new sequence. The number of interfered detectors tends to relate to the new sequence itself, not the size of the sequential memory . Contrasting capacity-independent incremental learning , catastrophic interference would require simultaneous retraining of the entire memory when a new item is to be learned. The cost of retraining when catastrophic interference occurs can be prohibitive if the size of memory is not so small. Ruiz de Angulo and Torras (1995) presented a study on sequential learning of multilayer perceptrons, and reported that their model can learn sequentially several most recent patterns. Although it is a better result than original multilayer perceptrons, their model appears unable to support a sizable memory. The high variations in the number of retraining sweeps are caused by the overlaps between the stored sequences. For long overlapping subsequences, many sweeps may be needed to resolve the interference caused by overlaps.

The second conclusion is that the number of intact sequences increases with rounds of sequential training approximately linearly. This is to be expected given the result on the amount of retraining. Again, there are considerable variations from one round to another. Since interference is caused by the overlap between a new sequence and the stored sequences, another way of looking at this result is the following. As the memory expands, relatively the fewer items in the memory will overlap with the new sequence.

Figure 4 illustrates the detailed retraining process during round 96. Right after the model has learned S_{96} of Table 1, the only interfered sequence is S_{14}. After S_{14} is retrained, S_{96} is interfered and has to be retrained. This finishes the first retraining cycle for round 96. During the second cycle, S_{71} is found to be interfered. After S_{71} is retrained, S_{96} is interfered again and has to be retrained. The retraining with S_{71} alternates with that of S_{96} for three more cycles. Notice the large overlap between S_{71}: "*OPTIMIZATION* I" and S_{96}: "*OPTIMIZATION* IV". In cycle 6, several more sequences are interfered. After retraining them sequentially, all of the first 96 sequences have been learned successfully.

To examine the amount of detector sharing, we compare the detector use in the anticipation model with one in which no detector is shared by different components (see for example Wang & Arbib, 1993). Without detector sharing, the number of detectors needed to acquire all of the 97 sequences is $\sum_{i=1}^{97}(|S_i| - 1)$, which equals 2520. As stated earlier, the anticipation model needs 1,088 detectors to learn all of the sequences. Thus, the detector sharing in the anticipation model cuts required context detectors by nearly a factor of 2.5.

5   Context Learning by Chunking

Even though the amount of retraining does not depend on the number of stored sequences in the memory, retraining can still be expensive. As shown in Fig. 3, it usually takes dozens of retraining sweeps to fully incorporate a new sequence.

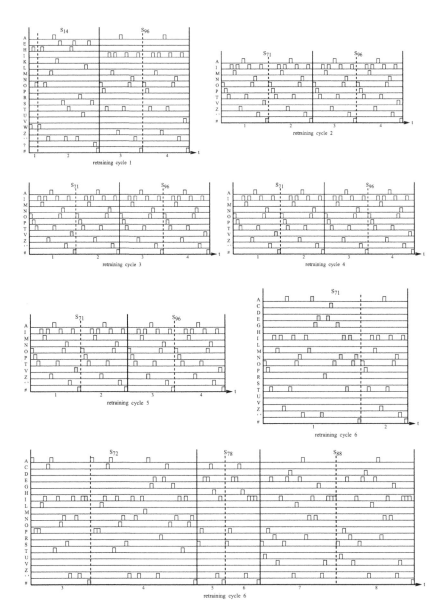

Fig. 4. Retraining process during round 96 of Fig. 3. Each row represents the activity trace of an input terminal indicated by the corresponding input symbol. White boxes represent correctly anticipated terminal activities in sequence generation, whereas gray boxes represent terminal activities which do not match anticipated ones. Solid vertical lines separate training sweeps of different sequences, and dash vertical lines separate training sweeps of the same sequence. Cycle numbers are indicated under each panel. Time runs from left to right.

Our analysis of the model indicates that repeated sweeps are usually caused by the need to commit a new detector and gradually expand the context of that detector in order to resolve ambiguities caused by long recurring subsequences. For example, consider the situation that the system has stored the following two sequences

S_c: "JOE LIKES 0"

S_d: "JAN LIKES 1",

and the network is to learn the sequence

S_e: "DEB LIKES 2".

There is an overlapping subsequence between S_c and S_d: "LIKES". A common situation before S_e is learned is that there are two detectors, say u_1 and u_2, tuned to the contexts of "E LIKES" and "N LIKES", respectively. While S_e is being trained, neither u_1 nor u_2 can be activated and a new detector, say u_3, must be committed to anticipate "2" (u_3 needs to recognize only "S" since "S" cannot activate either u_1 or u_2). Suppose now the network is to learn yet another sequence,

S_f: "DIK LIKES 3".

S_e and S_f will take turns to capture u_3 and gradually increase its degree until u_3 can detect either "B LIKES" or "K LIKES". Eventually, another detector, say u_4, will be committed for the other sequence. This gradual process of degree increment is the major factor causing numerous retraining sweeps.

The above observation has led to the following extended model for cutting the amount of retraining. The basic idea is to incorporate a chunking mechanism so that newly committed detectors may expand their contexts from chunks formed previously, instead of from the scratch.

The extended model consists of a dual architecture, shown in Figure 5. The dual architecture contains a *generation network* (on the left of Fig. 5), which is almost the same as the original architecture (see Fig. 1), and another similar network, called the chunking network (on the right of Fig. 5). The two networks are mutually connected at the top. The *chucking network* does not produce anticipation, and thus does not need a layer of modulators. Because of this, the detectors in this network do not increase their degrees by a mismatch. Besides, the chunking network mirrors every process occurring in the generation network.

At any time step during training, there is a pair of winning detectors in the dual architecture, each corresponding to one network. The algorithm is designed so that the winning detector of the chunking network has a degree less by 1 than the degree of the winning detector of the generation network. In addition, a newly committed detector of the generation network may take a degree which is 1 plus the degree of the activated chunk detector. We refer to the detectors of the chunking network as *chunk detectors*. The interaction between the two networks takes place via the two-way connections between the two networks

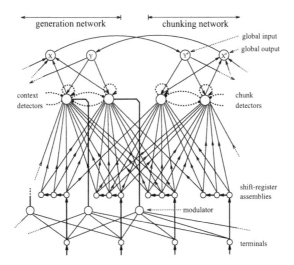

Fig. 5. Dual architecture of the extended anticipation model for chunking. The architecture consists of two mutually connected networks: the generation network and the chunking network. The connections to and from global input and output units have fixed weights. See the caption of Fig. 1 for other notations.

(Fig. 5). The introduction of the chunk detectors can speed up learning when a subsequence (a chunk) occurs multiple times in the input flow. More specifically, assume that a context detector u_i of degree d has learned to recognize a context, and a corresponding chunk detector $u_{i'}$ of degree $d-1$ has learned a chunk which is a right subsequence of the context learned by u_i. If the chunk occurs at least twice, then there will be a time when $u_{i'}$ is activated but u_i is not. Through the learning process an uncommitted context detector, say u_j, is activated (thus committed). Instead of starting from degree 1, u_j starts its degree at the value of d, leading to a significant reduction of training/retraining sweeps. The speedup in sequential training comes with a cost. Obviously, the addition of another network - the chunking network - adds both to the size of the overall network and to additional computing time. The formal description of the chunking network is given in Wang and Yuwono (1996).

Before presenting simulation results with chunking, we explain using the earlier example how the dual architecture helps speed up training. After training with S_c and S_d, there will be a context detector tuned to either "*E LIKES*" or "*N LIKES*". This, in turn, will lead to the formation of the chunk "*LIKES*"; that is, a chunk detector will be tuned to "*LIKES*" since the detector has a degree that is one less than that of the corresponding context detector. After the chunk is formed, Se can be acquired easily - the detector that is trained to associate with "2" can obtain its appropriate degree in just one sweep, thanks to the formation of the chunk "*LIKES*". Similarly, S_f can be acquired quickly.

To show the effectiveness of the chunking network, we present simulations using the same sequences (Table 1) and the same procedure as in the previous section. To complete the training, the dual architecture requires 1,234 context detectors as compared to 1,088 without chunking, and 436 chunk detectors. Other parts of the network are the same as used in the previous section. Figure 6 gives the result. A comparison between Fig. 6 and in Fig. 3 shows that the former ends up with only a few more intact sequences. This indicates that, in the dual architecture, later training causes almost the same amount of interference. On the other hand, when the chunking is incorporated, the number of retraining sweeps on the whole is cut dramatically. The total number of retraining sweeps during the entire training is 1,104 when the chunking network is included. This is compared to 3,029 without the chunking network, hence a reduction of the overall amount of sequential training almost by three-fold.

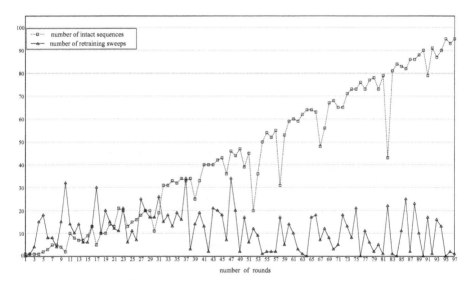

number of rounds

Fig. 6. The number of intact sequences and the number of retraining sweeps with respect to training rounds during training with the Table 1 database with the dual architecture.

For a comparison with Fig. 4 which illustrates the retraining process of round 96, Figure 7 shows the detailed retraining process during round 96 using the dual architecture. Right after S_{96} is learned, three sequences are interfered: S_{59}, S_{60} and S_{86}. After S_{59}: "*MACHINE VISION* I" is retrained, S_{60}: "*MACHINE VISION* II" can be correctly generated without further retraining. This interesting situation arises because the two sequences have a large overlap and it is the overlapping part that is interfered during training S_{96}. Thus, when the overlapping part is regained during retraining with S_{59}, both S_{59} and S_{60} can be recalled correctly. The system needs another sweep to regain S_{86}. After the first retraining cycle, all of the first 96 sequences have been acquired.

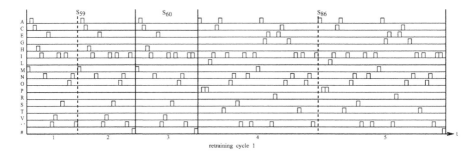

Fig. 7. Retraining process during round 96 of Fig. 6. The interference with S_{60} is eliminated as a result of retraining S_{59}. See the caption of Fig. 4 for notations.

6   Further Discussion

The idea of anticipation-based learning seems to be consistent with psychological evidence on human learning of sequential behaviors. Meyer (1956) noted that expectation is key to music cognition. When a temporal sequence is repeatedly presented to subjects, according to Nissen and Bullemer (1987), the reaction to a particular component in the sequence becomes faster and faster, and the reaction time to a component in a repeated sequence is much shorter than when it occurs in random sequences. The latter finding rules out the possibility that the reduction in reaction time is due to the familiarity with a component. These findings have been confirmed by later experiments (Willingham et al., 1989; Cohen et al., 1990). The results suggest that the subjects have developed with practice some form of anticipation before a particular component actually occurs in the sequence. It is observed that in learning temporal sequences human subjects can even be explicitly aware of the temporal structure of a sequence, and predict what comes next in the sequence (Nissen & Bullemer, 1987; Willingham et al., 1989; Curran & Keele, 1993).

As analyzed earlier, the anticipation model does not suffer from catastrophic interference. When multiple sequences are presented to the model sequentially, some degree of interference occurs. But this kind of interference can be overcome by retraining the interfered sequences. Extensive computer simulations indicate that the amount of retraining does not increase as the number of sequences stored in the model increases. The anticipation model is characteristic of capacity-independent incremental learning during sequential training. These results, plus the fact that interference is caused by the overlap between a new sequence and stored sequences, suggest that the behavior of the model in sequential learning resembles aspects of retroactive interference.

After a sequence S is learned, it can be generated by its beginning component - the sequence identifier. Partial sequence generation can also be elicited by a subsequence of S. If a sufficient subsequence is presented, the rest of S can be generated entirely. Partial generation may stop before the rest of the sequence is completed. For example, after the sequence: X-A-B-C-D-E-A-B-C-D-F is learned, the presentation of A activates the subsequence B-C-D, but not the rest. The anticipation model exhibits partial generation because a sequence is stored as a chain of associations, each of which is triggered by a context, or a subsequence. This property of the model is consistent with our experience that we are able to pick up a familiar song, a melody, or an action sequence (like *Tai Chi*) from the middle.

As shown in Sect. 5, the model's capability of chunking repeated subsequences within a sequence and between sequences substantially reduces the amount of retraining and improves the overall efficiency of learning. Without chunking, recurring subsequences must be learned from the scratch. The basic idea behind current chunking is to learn a recurring subsequence just once and store it as a chunk, so that the next time the subsequence occurs the model can simply use the chunk as a basic component. Chunking is a fundamental characteristic of human information processing (Miller, 1956; Simon, 1974). We note that, though the present model has addressed some aspects of chunking, the general issue of automatic chunking is very challenging and remains an open problem. What constitutes a chunk? A chunk is often taken to be a meaningful subsequence (such as a word), but it may also be just a convenient way of breaking a long sequence into shorter subsequences for facilitating further processing. In the anticipation model, a chunk corresponds to a repeated subsequence. This is a reasonable definition in the present context. The model, through its mechanism of context learning , provides a neural network basis for forming such chunks. On the other hand, this definition of a chunk does not capture the richness of general chunking. Chunking depends critically on the STM capacity (Miller, 1956). Furthermore, different people, may have different ways of chunking the same sequence in order to overcome STM limitations and memorize the sequence. Chunking also depends on general knowledge and custom. For example, we tend to chunk a 10-digit telephone number in the U.S. into three chunks: the first three digits corresponding to an area code, then the next three digits to a district code, and the last four digits. However, the same 10-digit number may well be chunked differently in another country.

Proposition 4 and the property of capacity-independent incremental learning together enable the anticipation model to perform long-term automatic learning of temporal sequences. The system is both adaptive and stable, and its long-term memory capacity increases gradually as learning proceeds. Thus, the anticipation model provides a *sequential memory* , which can store and recall a large number of complex sequences .

7 Summary

In this chapter, we have presented the anticipation model - a neural network model - that learns and generate complex temporal sequences. In the anticipation model, sequences are acquired by one-shot learning that obeys a normalized Hebbian learning rule, in combination with a competitive mechanism realized by a winner-take-all network. During learning and generation, the network actively anticipates the next component on the basis of a previously anticipated context. A mismatch between the anticipation and the actual input triggers self-organization of context expansion. Analytical results on the anticipation model, presented in Sect. 3, ensure that the model can learn to generate any complex sequences . Multiple sequences are acquired by the model in an incremental fashion, and large-scale simulation results strongly suggest that the model exhibits capacity-independent incremental learning . As a result, the anticipation model provides an effective sequential memory . In addition, by incorporating a form of chunking we have demonstrated significant performance improvement in learning many sequences that have significant overlaps.

Finally, the anticipation model argues (see also Wang & Arbib, 1993) from a computational perspective for the chaining theory of temporal behavior, which was rejected by Lashley (1951) but supported by recent psychological studies of serial order organization (Murdock, 1987; Lewandowsky & Murdock Jr., 1989). Simple associative chaining between adjacent sequence components is too limited to be true. However, if chaining between remote components and chunking of subsequences into high-order components are allowed, the basic idea of associative chaining can give rise to much more complex temporal behaviors, going much beyond what was realized by Lashley (1951). The anticipation model shows how learning and generation of complex temporal sequences can be achieved by self-organizing in a neural network.

References

Baram, Y. (1994). Memorizing binary vector sequences by a sparsely encoded network. *IEEE Transactions on Neural Networks*, **5**(6), 974-981.

Barnes, J. M., & Underwood, B. J. (1959). 'Fate' of first-list associations in transfer theory. *Journal of Experimental Psychology*, **58**, 97-105.

Bengio, Y., Simard, P., & Frasconi, P. (1994). Learning long-term dependencies with gradient descent is difficult. *IEEE Transactions on Neural Networks*, **5**(2), 157-166.

Bower, G. H., Thompson-Schill, S., & Tulving, E. (1994). Reducing retroactive interference: An interference analysis. *Journal of Experimental Psychology: Learning, Memory, and Cognition*, **20**, 51-66.

Bradski, G., Carpenter, G. A., & Grossberg, S. (1994). STORE working memory networks for storage and recall of arbitrary temporal sequences. *Biological Cybernetics*, **71**, 469-480.

Buhmann, J., & Schulten, K. (1987). Noise-driven temporal association in neural networks. *Europhysics Letters*, **4**, 1205-1209.

Carpenter, G. A., & Grossberg, S. (1987). A massively parallel architecture for a self-organizing neural pattern recognition machine. *Computer Vision, Graphs, and Imaging Processing*, **37**, 54-115.

Chandler, C. C. (1993). Accessing related events increases retroactive interference in a matching test. *Journal of Experimental Psychology: Learning, Memory, and Cognition*, **19**, 967-974.

Cohen, A., Ivry, R. I., & Keele, S. W. (1990). Attention and structure in sequence learning. *Journal of Experimenal Psychology*, **16**, 17-30.

Cohen, M. A., & Grossberg, S. (1987). Masking fields: A massively parallel neural architecture for learning, recognizing, and predicting multiple groupings of patterned data. *Applied Optics*, **26**, 1866-1891.

Crooks, R. L., & Stein, J. (1991). *Psychology: Science, behavior, and life*. Fort Worth, TX: Holt, Rinehart and Winston.

Curran, T., & Keele, S. W. (1993). Attentional and nonattentional forms of sequence learning. *Journal of Experimental Psychology: Learning, Memory, and Cognition*, **19**, 189-202.

Diederich, S., & Opper, M. (1987). Learning of correlated patterns in spin-like glass networks by local learning rules. *Physical Review Letters*, **58**, 949-952.

Elman, J. L. (1990). Finding structure in time. *Cognitive Science*, **14**, 179-211.

French, R. M. (1994). Dynamically constraining connectionist networks to produce distributed, orthogonal representations to reduce catastrophic interference. In *Proceedings of the Sixteenth Annual Conference of the Cognitive Science Society*, (pp. 335-340). Hillsdale, NJ: Erlbaum.

Granger, R., Whitson, J., Larson, J., & Lynch, G. (1994). Non-Hebbian properties of long-term potentiation enable high-capacity encoding of temporal sequences. *Proceedings of the National Academy of Sciences of USA*, **91**, 10104-10108.

Grossberg, S. (1976). Adaptive pattern classification and universal recoding: I. Parallel development and coding of neural feature detectors. *Biological Cybernetics*, **23**, 121-134.

Grossberg, S. (1987). Competitive learning: From interactive activation to adaptive resonance. *Cognitive Science*, **11**, 23-63.

Guyon, I., Personnaz, L., Nadal, J. P., & Dreyfus, G. (1988). Storage and retrieval of complex sequences in neural networks. *Physics Review A*, **38**, 6365-6372.

Hebb, D. O. (1949). *The Organization of behavior*. New York: Wiley & Sons.

Hertz, H., Krogh, A., & Palmer, R. G. (1991). *Introduction to the theory of neural computation*. Redwood City, CA: Addison-Wesley.

Heskes, T. M., & Gielen, S. (1992). Retrieval of pattern sequences at variable speeds in a neural network with delays. *Neural Networks*, bf 5, 145-152.

Jordan, M. I. (1986). Attractor dynamics and parallelism in a connectionist sequential machine. In *Proceedings of the Eighth Annual Conference of the Cognitive Science Society*, (pp. 531-546). Hillsdale, NJ: Erlbaum.

Kanerva, P. (1988). *Sparse distributed memory.* Cambridge, MA: MIT Press.

Kantor, I., & Sompolinsky, H. (1987). Associative recall of memory without errors. *Physics Review A*, bf 35, 380-392.

Kruschke, J. K. (1992). ALCOVE: An exemplar-based model of category learning. *Psychological Review*, **99**, 22-44.

Lashley, K. S. (1951). The problem of serial order in behavior. In L. A. Jeffress (Ed.), *Cerebral mechanisms in behavior* (pp. 112-146). New York: Wiley & Sons.

Lewandowsky, S., & Murdock Jr., B. B. (1989). Memory for serial order. *Psychological Review*, **96**, 25-57.

McCloskey, M., & Cohen, N. J. (1989). Catastrophic interference in connectionist networks: The sequential learning problem. *Psychology of Learning and Motivation*, **24**, 109-165.

Meyer, L. B. (1956). *Emotion and meaning in music.* Chicago, IL: University of Chicago Press.

Miller, G. A. (1956). The magical number seven, plus or minus two: Some limits on our capacity for processing information. *Psychological Review*, **63**, 81-97.

Mozer, M. C. (1993). Neural net architectures for temporal sequence processing. In A. Weigend & N. Gershenfeld (Ed.), *Predicting the future and understanding the past* (pp. 243-264). Redwood City, CA: Addison-Wesley.

Murdock, B. B. J. (1987). Serial-order effects in a distributed-memory model. In D. S. Gorfein & R. R. Hoffman (Ed.), *Memory and learning: The Ebbinghaus centennial conference* (pp. 227-310). Hillsdale, NJ: Erlbaum.

Nissen, M. J., & Bullemer, P. (1987). Attentional requirements of learning: Evidence from performance measures. *Cognitive Psychology*, **19**, 1-32.

Ratcliff, R. (1990). Connectionist models of recognition memory: Constraints imposed by learning and forgetting function. *Psychological Review*, **97**, 285-308.

Rinkus, G. J. (1995). TEMECOR: an associative, spatio-temporal pattern memory for complex state sequences. In *Proceedings of World Congress on Neural Networks*, (pp. I.442-I.448). Washington DC:

Rodriguez, W. A., Borbely, L. S., & Garcia, R. S. (1993). Attenuation by contextual cues of retroactive interference of a conditional discrimination in rats. *Animal Learning & Behavior*, **21**, 101-105.

Ruiz de Angulo, V., & Torras, C. (1995). On-line learning with minimal degradation in feedforward networks. *IEEE Transactions on Neural Networks*, **6**, 657-668.

Simon, H. A. (1974). How big is a chunk? *Science*, **183**, 482-488.

Sloman, S. A., & Rumelhart, D. E. (1992). Reducing interference in distributed memories through episodic gating. In A. F. Healy, S. M. Kosslyn, & R. M. Shiffrin (Ed.), *From learning theory to connectionist theory: Essays in honor of William K. Estes* (pp. 227-248). Hillsdale, NJ: Erlbaum.

Sompolinsky, H., & Kanter, I. (1986). Temporal association in asymmetric neural networks. *Physics Review Letters*, **57**, 2861-2864.

von der Malsburg, C. (1973). Self-organization of orientation sensitive cells in the striate cortex. *Kybernetik*, **14**, 85-100.

Wang, D. L. (2001). Temporal pattern processing. In M. A. Arbib (Ed.), *Handbook of brain theory and neural networks*, Second Edition (to appear). Cambridge MA: MIT Press.

Wang, D. L., & Arbib, M. A. (1990). Complex temporal sequence learning based on short-term memory. *Proceedings of the IEEE*, **78**, 1536-1543.

Wang, D. L., & Arbib, M. A. (1993). Timing and chunking in processing temporal order. *IEEE Transactions on Systems, Man, and Cybernetics*, **23**, 993-1009.

Wang, D. L., & Yuwono, B. (1995). Anticipation-based temporal pattern generation. *IEEE Transactions on Systems, Man, and Cybernetics*, **25**, 615-628.

Wang, D. L., & Yuwono, B. (1996). Incremental learning of complex temporal patterns. *IEEE Transactions on Neural Networks*, **7**, 1465-1481.

Wang, L. (1999). Multi-associative neural networks and their applications to learning and retrieving complex spatio-temporal sequences. *IEEE Transactions on Systems, Man, and Cybernetics - Part B: Cybernetics*, **29**, 73-82.

Willingham, D. B., Nissen, M. J., & Bullemer, P. (1989). On the development of procedural knowledge. *Journal of Experimental Psychology: Learning, Memory, and Cognition*, **15**, 1047-1060.

Willshaw, D. J., Buneman, O. P., & Longuet-Higgins, H. C. (1969). Nonholographic associative memory. *Nature*, **222**, 960-962.

Bidirectional Dynamics for Protein Secondary Structure Prediction

Pierre Baldi[1], Søren Brunak[2], Paolo Frasconi[3], Gianluca Pollastri[1], and Giovanni Soda[3]

[1] University of California at Irvine
[2] The Technical University of Denmark
[3] University of Florence

1 Introduction

Connectionist models for learning in sequential domains are typically dynamical systems that use hidden states to store contextual information. In principle, these models can adapt to variable time lags and perform complex sequential mappings. In spite of several successful applications (mostly based on hidden Markov models), the general class of sequence learning problems is still far from being satisfactorily solved. In particular, learning sequential translations is generally a hard task and current models seem to exhibit a number of limitations. One of these limitations, at least for some application domains, is the causality assumption. A dynamical system is said to be *causal* if the output at (discrete) time t does not depend on future inputs. Causality is easy to justify in dynamics that attempt to model the behavior of many physical systems. Clearly, in these cases the response at time t cannot depend on stimulae that the system has not yet received as input. As it turns out, non-causal dynamics over infinite time horizons cannot be realized by any physical or computational device. For certain categories of *finite* sequences, however, information from both the past and the future can be very useful for analysis and predictions at time t. This is the case, for example, of DNA and protein sequences where the structure and function of a region in the sequence may strongly depend on events located both upstream and downstream of the region, sometimes at considerable distances. Another good example is provided by the off-line translation of a language into another one. Even in the so-called "simultaneous" translation, it is well known that interpreters are constantly forced to introduce small delays in order to acquire "future" information within a sentence to resolve semantic ambiguities and preserve syntactic correctness.

Non-causal dynamics are sometimes used in other disciplines (for example, Kalman smoothing in optimal control or non-causal digital filters in signal processing). However, as far as connectionist models are concerned, the causality assumption is shared among all the types of models which are capable of mapping input sequences to output sequences, including recurrent neural networks and input-output HMMs (IOHMMs) (Bengio & Frasconi, 1996). In this paper, we develop a new family of non-causal adaptive architectures where the underlying dynamics are factored using a pair of chained hidden state variables. The two

R. Sun and C.L. Giles (Eds.): Sequence Learning, LNAI 1828, pp. 80–104, 2000.
© Springer-Verlag Berlin Heidelberg 2000

chains store contextual information contained in the upstream and downstream portions of the sequence, respectively. The output at time t is then obtained by combining the two hidden representations. Interestingly, the same general methodology can be applied to many different classes of graphical models for time series, such as recurrent neural networks, IOHMMs, tree structured HMMs, and switching state space models (Ghahramani & Jordan, 1997). For concreteness, however, in the rest of this paper we focus exclusively on IOHMMs and recurrent neural networks.

The main motivation of this work is an application to the problem of protein secondary structure (SS) in molecular biology. The task can be formulated as the translation of amino acid input strings into corresponding output strings that describe an approximation of the proteins' 3D folding. This is a classic problem in bioinformatics which has been investigated for several years under the machine learning perspective, and for which significant performance improvements are still expected. Protein SS prediction can be formulated as the problem of learning a synchronous sequential translation, from strings in the amino acid alphabet to strings in the SS alphabet. The task is thus a special form of grammatical inference (Angluin & Smith, 1983). Nonetheless, to the best of our knowledge no successful applications of grammatical inference algorithms (neither symbolic, neither based on connectionist architecture) have been reported. Instead, the current best predictors are based on feedforward neural networks fed by a fixed-width window of amino acids, which by construction cannot capture relevant information contained in distant regions of the protein. Our proposal is motivated by the assumption that both adaptive dynamics and non-causal processing are needed to overcome the drawbacks of local fixed-window approaches. While our current system achieves an overall performance exceeding 75% correct prediction (at least comparable to the best existing systems) the main emphasis here is on the development of new algorithmic ideas.

The chapter is organized as follows. In Section 2, we shortly review the literature on protein SS prediction. In Sections 3 and 4, we introduce the two novel non-causal architectures: bidirectional IOHMMs (BIOHMMs) and bidirectional RNNs (BRNNs). In Section 5, we describe the protein datasets used in the experimental evaluation of the proposed system. Finally, in Section 6 we report preliminary prediction results on the SS prediction task using our best system which is based on ensembles of BRNNs.

2   Prediction of Protein Secondary Structure

Proteins are polypeptides chains carrying out most of the basic functions of life at the molecular level. The chains can be viewed as linear sequences over the 20-letter amino acid alphabets that fold into complex 3D structures essential to their function. One step towards predicting how a protein folds is the prediction of its secondary structure. The secondary structure consists of local folding regularities often maintained by hydrogen bonds, and traditionally subdivided into three classes: alpha helices, beta sheets, and coils, representing all the rest. The sequence preferences and correlations involved in these structures have made secondary structure prediction one of the classical problems in computational molecular biology. Moreover, this is one application where machine learning methods, particularly neural networks, have had considerable impact yielding the best performing algorithms to date (Rost & Sander, 1994).

The basic architecture used in the early work of Qian and Sejnowski (1988) is a fully connected MLP with a single hidden layer that takes as input a *local* fixed-size window of amino acids (the typical width is 13), centered around the residue for which the secondary structure is being predicted. A significant improvement was obtained by cascading the previous architecture with a second network to clean up the output of the lower network. The cascaded architecture reached a performance of $Q_3 = 64.3\%$, with the correlations $C_\alpha = 0.41$, $C_\beta = 0.31$, and $C_\gamma = 0.41$ — see (Baldi et al., 1999) for a review of the standard performance measures used in this chapter. Although this approach has proven to be quite successful, using a local fixed width window has well known drawbacks. First, the size of the input window must be chosen a priori and a fair choice may be difficult. Second, the number of parameters grows with the window size. This means that permitting certain far away inputs to exert an effect on the current prediction is paid in terms of parametric complexity. Hence, one of the main dangers of the Qian and Sejnowski's architectures is the overfitting problem.

Most of the subsequent work on predicting protein secondary structure using NNs has been based on architectures with a local window, although a lot of effort has been put on devising several improvements. Rost and Sander (1993b, 1993a) started with Qian and Sejnowski's architecture, but used two methods to address the overfitting problem. First, they used early stopping. Second, they used ensemble averages (Hansen & Salamon, 1990; Krogh & Vedelsby, 1995) by training different networks independently, using different input information and learning procedures. But the most significant new aspect of their work is the use of multiple alignments, in the sense that profiles (i.e. position-dependent frequency vectors derived from multiple alignments), rather than raw amino acid sequences, are used in the network input. The reasoning behind this is that multiple alignments contain more information about secondary structure than do single sequences, the secondary structure being considerably more conserved than the primary sequence. Although tests made on different data sets can be hard to compare, the method of Rost and Sander, which resulted in the PHD prediction server (Rost & Sander, 1993b, 1993a, 1994), still reaches the top levels of prediction accuracy ($Q_3 = 72\%$, measured using 7-fold cross validation). In the 1996 Asilomar competition CASP2, the PHD method reached $Q_3 = 74\%$ accuracy, thus performing much better than virtually all other methods used for making predictions of secondary structure.

Another interesting recent NN approach is the work of Riis and Krogh (1996), who address the overfitting problem by careful design of the NN architecture. Their approach has four main components. First, they reduce the number of free parameters by using an adaptive encoding of amino acids, that is, by letting the NN find an optimal and compressed representation of the input letters. Second, the authors design a different network for each of the three classes, using biological prior knowledge. For example, in the case of alpha-helices, they exploit the helix periodicity by building a three-residue periodicity between the first and second hidden layers. Third, Riis and Krogh use ensembles of networks and filtering to improve the prediction. The networks in each ensemble differ, for instance, in the number of hidden units used. Finally, the authors use multiple alignments together with a weighting scheme. Instead of profiles, for which the correlations between amino acids in the window are lost, predictions are made first from single sequences and then combined using multiple alignments. Most important, perhaps, the basic accuracy achieved is $Q_3 = 66.3\%$ when using seven-fold cross-validation on the same database of 126 non-homologous proteins used by Rost and Sander. In combination with multiple alignments, the method reaches an overall accuracy of $Q_3 = 71.3\%$, and correlation coefficients correlations $C_\alpha = 0.59$, $C_\beta = 0.50$, and $C_\gamma = 0.41$. Thus, in spite of a considerable amount of architectural design, the final performance is practically identical to (Rost & Sander, 1994). More recently, Cuff and Barton (1999) have compared and combined the main existing predictors. On the particular data sets used in their study, the best isolated predictor is still PHD with $Q_3 = 71.9\%$.

A more detailed review of the secondary structure prediction problem and corresponding results can be found in (Baldi & Brunak, 1998). The important information however is that there is an emerging consensus of an accuracy upper bound, slightly above 70-75%, to any prediction method based on *local* information only. By leveraging evolutionary information in the form of multiple sequence alignments, performance seems to top at the 72-74% level, in spite of several attempts with sophisticated architectures. Thus it appears today that to further improve prediction results one must use distant information, in sequences and alignments, which is not contained in *local* input windows. This is particularly clear in the case of beta sheets where stabilizing bonds can be formed between amino acids far apart. Using long-ranged information, however, poses two formidable related challenges: (1) avoiding overfitting related to large-input-window MLPs (2) being able to detect the *sparse* and weak long-ranged signal and combine it with the significant local information, while ignoring the bulk of less relevant distant information.

The limitations associated with the fixed-size window approach can be mitigated using other connectionist models for learning sequential translators, such as recurrent neural networks (RNNs) or input-output hidden Markov models (IOHMMs). Unlike feedforward nets, these models employ state dynamics to store contextual information and they can adapt to variable width temporal dependencies. Unfortunately there are theoretical reasons suggesting that, despite an adequate representational power, RNNs cannot possibly learn to capture long-ranged information because of the vanishing gradient problem (Bengio et al., 1994). However, it is reasonable to believe that RNNs fed by a *small* window of amino acids can capture some distant information using less adjustable weights than MLPs. The usual definition of RNNs only allows "past" context to be used but, as it turns out, useful information for prediction is located both downstream and upstream of a given residue. The architectures described in the next sections remove these limitations.

3   IOHMMs and Bidirectional IOHMMS

3.1   Markovian Models for Sequence Processing

Hidden Markov models (HMMs) have been introduced several years ago as a tool for probabilistic sequence modeling. The interest in this area developed particularly in the Seventies, within the speech recognition research community, concerned at that time with the limitations of template-based approaches such as dynamic time-warping. The basic model was very simple, yet so flexible and effective that it rapidly became extremely popular. During the last years a large number of variants and improvements over the standard HMM have been proposed and applied. Undoubtedly, Markovian models are now regarded as one of the most significant state-of-the-art approaches for sequence learning. Besides speech recognition (see e.g. (Jelinek, 1997) for more recent advances), important application of HMMs include sequence analysis in molecular biology (Baldi et al., 1994; Krogh et al., 1994; Baldi & Chauvin, 1996; Baldi & Brunak, 1998), time series prediction (Andrew & Dimitriadis, 1994), numerous pattern recognition problems such as handwriting recognition (Bengio et al., 1995; Bunke et al., 1995), and, more recently, information extraction (Freitag & McCallum, 2000). HMMs are also very closely related to stochastic regular languages, making them interesting in statistical natural language processing (Charniak, 1993). The recent view of the HMM as a particular case of Bayesian networks (Bengio & Frasconi, 1995; Lucke, 1995; Smyth et al., 1997) has helped the theoretical understanding and the ability to conceive extensions to the standard model in a sound and formally elegant framework.

The basic data object being considered by the standard model is limited to a *single sequence* of observations (which may be discrete or numerical, and possibly multivariate). Internally, standard HMMs contain a *single* hidden state variable X_t which is repeated in time to form a Markov chain (see Figure 1). The Markov property states that X_{t+1} is conditionally independent of $X_1, \ldots, X_{t-1}$ given X_t. Similarly, each emission variable Y_t is independent of the rest given X_t. These conditional independence assumptions are graphically depicted using the Bayesian network of Figure 1. More details about the basic model can be found in (Rabiner, 1989).

Some variants of standard HMMs are conceived as extensions of the internal structure of the model. For example, factorial HMMs (Ghahramani & Jordan, 1997) contain more than just one hidden state variable (see for example the middle of Figure 1) and can also introduce complex probabilistic relationships amongst state variables. However, the data interface towards the external world essentially remain the same and the basic data objects being processed are still single sequences.

Another direction that can be explored to extend the data types that can be dealt with Markovian models is the direction of modeling. A standard HMM

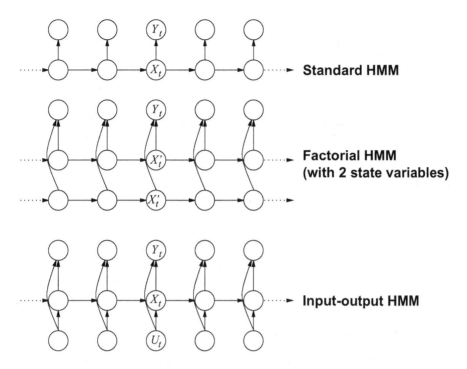

Fig. 1. Bayesian networks for standard, factorial, and input-output HMMs.

is a generative model. When used in classification tasks (as in isolated word recognition), one model per class is introduced and each model is typically trained on positive examples only. This means that no competition among classes is introduced when estimating the parameters and there is no associative probabilistic mapping from a sequence to a class variable. Learning is thus unsupervised because the model is trained to estimate an *unconditional* probability density (in a sense, we might say that a weak form of supervision occurs because class membership of training examples is only used to select the model to which the sequence is presented but each model is not aware of other classes). A fully supervised method for training HMMs has been early proposed by Brown (1987). The method modifies the function to be optimized and, instead of using maximum likelihood estimation, it relies on maximum mutual information (MMI) between the model and the class variable. In this way, the set of models employed in a classification task allows to estimate the *conditional* probability of the class *given* the input sequence, thus effectively introducing supervision in the learning process, as noted by Bridle (1989) and Bengio & Frasconi (1994). However, the MMI approach only allows to associate a single output variable to the input sequence. A more general supervised learning problem for sequences consists of associating a whole output sequence to the input sequence. This is the common sequence learning setting when using other machine learning approaches, such as recurrent neural networks. This extension cannot be achieved by a modification of the optimization procedure but requires a different architecture, called input-output HMM (IOHMM).

As shown at the bottom of Figure 1, three classes of variables are considered. The emission Y_t is called in this case `output` variable. Hidden states in IOHMMs are conditionally dependent on the *input* variable U_t. In this way, state transition probabilities, although stationary, are non-homogeneous because the probability of transition is controlled by the current input. The resulting model is thus similar to a stochastic *translating* automaton (i.e. it can be used to estimate the conditional probability of the output sequence given the input sequence), but IOHMMs can also deal with *continuous* input and output variables. This can be easily achieved by employing feedforward neural networks as models of the conditional probabilities $P(Y_t|X_t, U_t)$ and $P(X_t|X_{t-1}, U_t)$ that define the parameterization of the model. This technique is described in detail in (Baldi & Chauvin, 1996) and in (Bengio & Frasconi, 1996), along with details about inference and learning algorithms. These topics are summarized later on in Sections 3.3 and 3.4 for the more general case of the bidirectional architecture presented in this paper.

3.2   The Bidirectional Architecture

A bidirectional IOHMM is a non-causal model of a stochastic translation defined on a space of finite sequences. Like IOHMMs, the model describes the conditional probability distribution $P(\boldsymbol{Y}|\boldsymbol{U})$, where $\boldsymbol{U} = U_1, U_2, \cdots, U_T$ is a generic input sequence and $\boldsymbol{Y} = Y_1, Y_2, \cdots, Y_T$ the corresponding output sequence. Although in the protein application described below both $\boldsymbol{U}$ and $\boldsymbol{Y}$ are symbolic sequences, the theory holds for sequences of continuous (possibly multivariate) sequences as well. The model is based on two Markov sequences of hidden state variables, denoted by $\boldsymbol{F}$ and $\boldsymbol{B}$, respectively. For each time step, F_t and B_t are discrete variables with realizations (states) in $\{f^1, \cdots, f^n\}$ and $\{b^1, \cdots, b^m\}$, respectively. As in HMMs, F_t is assumed to have a causal impact on the next state F_{t+1}. Hence, F_t stores contextual information contained on the left of t (propagated in the *forward* direction). Symmetrically, B_t is assumed to have a causal impact on the state B_{t-1}, thus summarizing information contained on the right of t (propagated in the *backward* direction).

As in other Markov models for sequences, several conditional independence assumptions are made, and can be described by a Bayesian network as shown in Fig. 2. In particular, the following factorization of the joint distribution holds:

$$P(\boldsymbol{Y}, \boldsymbol{U}, \boldsymbol{F}, \boldsymbol{B}) = \prod_{t=1}^{T} P(Y_t|F_t, B_t, U_t)P(F_t|F_{t-1}, U_t)P(B_t|B_{t+1}, U_t)P(U_t) \quad (1)$$

Two boundary variables, B_{T+1} and F_0 are needed to complete the definition of the model. For simplicity we assume these variables are given, i.e. $P(B_{T+1} = b^1) = P(F_0 = f^1) = 1$, although generic (trainable) distributions could be

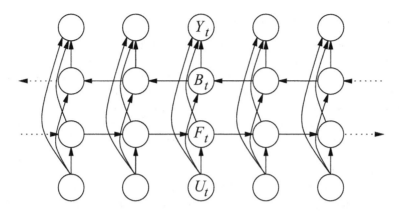

Fig. 2. Bayesian networks for the bidirectional IOHMM.

specified. The suggested architectures can be viewed as a special form of factorial IOHMMs (with obvious relationships to factorial HMMs and hidden Markov decision trees (Ghahramani & Jordan, 1997)) where the state space is factorized into the state variables F_t and B_t.

3.3 Parameterization

The parameters of a Bayesian network specify the local conditional distribution of each variable given its parents. In the case of BIOHMMs, the local conditional distributions are $P(Y_t|F_t, B_t, U_t)$, $P(F_t|F_{t-1}, U_t)$, and $P(B_t|B_{t+1}, U_t)$. Unconditional distributions for root nodes (i,e, $P(U_t)$) do not need to be modeled if we assume that there are no missing data in the input sequences. A quite common simplification is to assume that the model is *stationary*, i.e. the above conditional distributions do not vary over time. Stationarity can be seen as a particular form of parameter sharing that significantly reduces the degrees of freedom of the model. In the discrete case, parameters can be explicitly represented using conditional probability tables. Unfortunately the tables can become very large when nodes have many parents, or variables have large state spaces. Hence, a more constrained reparameterization is often desirable and can be achieved using the neural network techniques. In (Baldi & Chauvin, 1996), the general approach is demonstrated in the context of HMMs for protein families using, for the emission probabilities, a single hidden layer shared across all HMM states. In the case of BIOHMMs, the approach can be extended by introducing three separate feedforward neural networks for modeling the local conditional probabilities $P(B_t|B_{t+1}, U_t), P(F_t|F_{t-1}, U_t), P(Y_t|F_t, B_t, U_t)$. Alternatively, a modular approach using a different MLP for each state can be pursued (Baldi et al., 1994; Bengio & Frasconi, 1996). The modular approach is also be possible with BIOHMMs, although in this case the number of subnetworks would become $n+m+nm$ (one subnetwork for each state b^i, f^j, and one for each pair (b^i, f^j)).

3.4   Inference and Learning

The basic theory for inference and learning in graphical models is well established, and can readily be applied to the present architecture. For conciseness,
we focus on the main aspects only. A major difference between BIOHMMs
and IOHMMs or HMMs is that the Bayesian network for BIOHMMs is not
singly connected. Hence direct propagation algorithms such as Pearl's algorithm
(1988) cannot be used for solving the inference problem. Rather, we adopt the
general junction tree algorithm (Jensen et al., 1990). Given the regular structure of the network, the junction tree can be constructed by hand. Cliques are
$\{U_t, F_t, B_t, Y_t\}$, $\{U_t, F_t, B_t, F_{t-1}\}$, and $\{U_t, F_t, B_t, B_{t+1}\}$. Assuming B_t and F_t
have the same number of states (i.e., $n = m$) space and time complexities are
$O(KTn^3)$, where K is the number of input symbols ($K = 20$ in the case of proteins). However, it should be noted that often in a sequence translation problem
input variables are all observed (this is the case, at least, in the protein problem)
and thus we know a priori that the nodes U_t always receive evidence, both in the
learning and recall phases. Therefore, we can reduce the complexity by a factor
K since only those entries which are known to be non-zero need to be stored and
used in the absorption computations. In the case of proteins, this simple trick
yields a speed up factor of about 20, the size of the input amino acid alphabet.
The advantage is even more pronounced if, instead of a single amino acid, the
input U_t is obtained by taking a window of amino acids, as explained later on.

Learning is formulated in the framework of maximum likelihood and is solved
by the expectation maximization (EM) algorithm. EM is a family of algorithms
for maximum likelihood estimation in the presence of missing (or hidden) variables (in our case, forward and backward states F_t and B_t are the hidden
variables). Let $\mathcal{D}_c$ denote the complete data (input and output sequences U and
Y, plus the hidden state sequences F and B) and let $\mathcal{D}$ denote the incomplete
data (only the input and output sequences). Furthermore, let L_c denote the
complete data likelihood, i.e.

$$L_c(\boldsymbol{\theta}; \mathcal{D}_c) = \prod_{\text{training sequences}} P(\boldsymbol{Y}, \boldsymbol{F}, \boldsymbol{B} | \boldsymbol{U}, \boldsymbol{\theta}).$$

Since forward and backward states are not observed, $\log L_c(\boldsymbol{\theta}; \mathcal{D}_c)$ is a random
variable that cannot be optimized directly. However, given an initial hypothesis
$\hat{\boldsymbol{\theta}}$ on the parameters and observed variables $\boldsymbol{U}$ and $\boldsymbol{Y}$, it is possible to compute
the expected value of $\log L_c(\boldsymbol{\theta}; \mathcal{D}_c)$. Thus, an EM algorithms iteratively fills in
missing variables according to the following procedure:

E-step Compute the auxiliary function

$$Q(\boldsymbol{\theta}, \hat{\boldsymbol{\theta}}) \doteq E[\log L_c(\hat{\boldsymbol{\theta}}; \mathcal{D}_c) | \boldsymbol{\theta}, \mathcal{D}]$$

M-step Update the parameters by maximizing $Q(\boldsymbol{\theta}, \hat{\boldsymbol{\theta}})$ with respect to $\boldsymbol{\theta}$, i.e.

$$\hat{\boldsymbol{\theta}} \leftarrow \arg\max_{\boldsymbol{\theta}} Q(\boldsymbol{\theta}, \hat{\boldsymbol{\theta}})$$

and repeat until convergence.

A well known result is that the above procedure will converge to a local maximum of the likelihood function (Dempster et al., 1977). A variant of the above procedure, called *generalized* EM (GEM) consists of computing a new parameter vector $\hat{\theta}$ such that $Q(\hat{\theta}, \hat{\theta}) > Q(\theta, \hat{\theta})$ (instead of performing full optimization). GEM will also converge to a local maximum, although convergence rate may be slower.

In the case of belief networks, the E-step essentially consists of computing the expected sufficient statistics for the parameters. In our case these statistics are the following expected counts:

- $N^f_{j,l,u}$: expected number of (forward) transitions from f^l to f^j when the input is u $(j, l = 1, \ldots, n; u = 1, \ldots, K)$;
- $N^b_{k,\ell,u}$: expected number of (backward) transitions from b^ℓ to b^k when the input is u $(k, \ell = 1, \ldots, m; u = 1, \ldots, K)$;
- $N^y_{i,j,k,u}$: expected number of times output symbol i is emitted at a given position t when the forward state at t is f^j, backward state at t is b^k, and the input at t is u.

Basically, expected sufficient statistics are computed by inference using the junction tree algorithm as a subroutine. If local conditional probabilities were modeled by multinomial tables, then the M-step would be straightforward: each entry in the table would be replaced by the corresponding normalized expected count (Heckerman, 1997). However, in our case the M-step deserves more attention because of the neural network reparameterization of the local conditional probabilities. In fact, maximizing the function $Q(\theta, \hat{\theta})$, requires the neural network weights θ to be adapted to perfectly fit the normalized expected sufficient statistics. Even in the absence of local minima, a complete maximization would require an expensive inner gradient descent loop, inside the outer EM loop. Hence, we resorted to a generalized EM algorithm, where a single gradient descent step is performed inside the main loop. The expected sufficient statistics are used as "soft" targets for training the neural networks. In particular, for each output unit, the backpropagation delta-error term is obtained as the difference between the unit activation (before the softmax) and the corresponding expected sufficient statistic. For example, consider the network for estimating the conditional probability of the output Y_t, given the forward state F_t, the backward state B_t, and the input symbol U_t. For each sequence and for each time step t, let $a_{i,t}$ be the activation of the i-th output unit of this network when fed by $F_t = f^j$, $B_t = b^k$ and $U_t = u_t$ (where u_t is fixed according to the input training sequence). Let $z_{i,j,k,t} = \exp(a_{i,t})/(\sum_\ell \exp(a_{\ell,t})$. We have $z_{i,j,k,t} = P(Y_t = y^i | F_t = f^j, B_t = b^k, U_t = u_t, \theta)$. Moreover, let $\hat{z}_{i,j,k,t} = P(Y_t = y^i, F_t = f^j, B_t = b^k, U_t = u_t, \text{training data}, \hat{\theta})$ denote the contribution in this sequence at position t to the expected sufficient statistics (obviously, $\hat{z}_{i,j,k,t} = 0$ if the observed output at position t, $\overline{y}_t \neq y^i$). Then, the error function for training this network is given by

$$C = \sum_{\text{training sequences}} \sum_t \sum_{i,j,k} \hat{z}_{i,j,k,t} \log z_{i,j,k,t}. \tag{2}$$

Similar equations hold for the other two networks modeling $P(F_t|F_{t-1}, U_t)$, and $P(B_t|B_{t+1}, U_t)$.

4   Bidirectional Recurrent Neural Nets

4.1   The Architecture

The basic idea underlying the architecture of BIOHMMs can be adapted to recurrent neural networks. Suppose in this case F_t and B_t are two vectors in $I\!R^n$ and $I\!R^m$, respectively. Then consider the following (deterministic) dynamics, in vector notation:

$$F_t = \phi(F_{t-1}, U_t) \tag{3}$$
$$B_t = \beta(B_{t+1}, U_t) \tag{4}$$

where $\phi()$ and $\beta()$ are adaptive nonlinear transition functions. The vector $U_t \in I\!R^K$ encodes the input at time t (for example, using one-hot encoding in the case of amino acids). Equations 3 and 4 are completed by the two boundary conditions $F_0 = B_{T+1} = 0$. Transition functions $\phi()$ and $\beta()$ are realized by two MLPs $\mathcal{N}_\phi$ and $\mathcal{N}_\beta$, respectively. In particular, for MLP $\mathcal{N}_\beta$ we have:

$$b_{i,t} = \sigma\left(\sum_{j=1}^{N_\beta} w_{ij} h_{j,t}\right) \quad i = 1, \ldots n \tag{5}$$

where σ is the logistic function, N_β is the number of hidden units in MLP $\mathcal{N}_\beta$, $b_{i,t}$ is the i-th component of B_t and

$$h_{j,t} = \sigma\left(\sum_{\ell=1}^{N_\beta} w_{j,\ell} b_{\ell,t+1} + \sum_{\ell=1}^{k} v_{j,\ell} u_{\ell,t}\right) \quad j = 1, \ldots, N_\beta \tag{6}$$

is the output of j-th hidden unit. In the above equations, $w_{ij}, w_{j,\ell}$ and $v_{j,\ell}$ are adaptive weights. Network $\mathcal{N}_\phi$ is described by similar equations except that the forward state F_t is used instead of the backward state B_t.

Also, consider the mapping

$$Y_t = \eta(F_t, B_t, U_t) \tag{7}$$

where $Y_t \in I\!R^s$ is the output prediction and $\eta()$ is realized by a third MLP $\mathcal{N}_\eta$. In the case of classification, s is the number of classes and $\mathcal{N}_\eta$ has a softmax output layer so that outputs can be interpreted as conditional class probabilities. The neural network architecture resulting from eqs. 3,4, and 7 is shown in Fig. 3, where for simplicity all the MLPs have a single hidden layer (several variants are conceivable by varying the number and the location of the hidden layers). Like in Elman's simple recurrent networks, the hidden state F_t is copied back

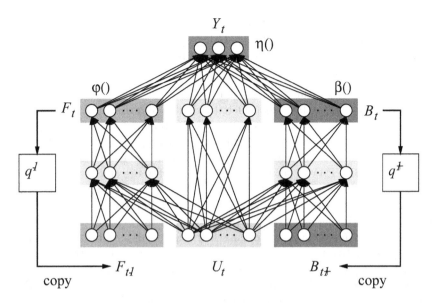

Fig. 3. A bidirectional RNN.

to the input. This is graphically represented in Fig. 3 using the causal *shift operator* q^{-1} that operates on a generic temporal variable X_t and is symbolically defined as $X_{t-1} = q^{-1}X_t$. The shift operator with the composition operation forms a multiplicative group. In particular, q, the inverse (or non-causal) shift operator is defined $X_{t+1} = qX_t$ and $q^{-1}q = 1$. As shown in Fig. 3, a non-causal copy is performed on the hidden state B_t. Clearly, if we remove the backward chain $\{B_t\}$ we obtain a standard first-order RNN. A BRNN is stationary if the connection weights in networks $\mathcal{N}_\beta$, $\mathcal{N}_\phi$ and $\mathcal{N}_\eta$ do not change over time. Stationarity will be assumed throughout the paper. It is worth noting that using MLPs for implementing $\beta()$ and $\phi()$ is just one of the available options as a result of their well known universal approximation properties. Similar generalizations of second-order RNN (Giles et al., 1992) or recurrent radial basis functions (Frasconi et al., 1996) are easily conceivable following the approach here described.

4.2   Inference and Learning

As for standard RNNs, it is convenient to describe inference and learning in BRNNs by unrolling the network on the input sequence. The resulting graphical model has exactly the same form as the BIOHMM network shown in Fig. 2. Actually, the BRNN can be interpreted as a Bayesian network, except for some differences as explained below. First, causal relationships among nodes linked by a directed edge should be regarded as deterministic rather than probabilistic. In particular, $P(Y_t|F_t, B_t, U_t)$ should be regarded as a delta-Dirac distribution centered on a value corresponding to $Y_t = \eta(F_t, B_t, U_t)$. Similarly,

$P(F_t|F_{t-1}, U_t)$ and $P(B_t|B_{t+1}, U_t)$ are replaced by Dirac distributions centered at $F_t = \phi(F_{t-1}, U_t)$ and $B_t = \beta(B_{t+1}, U_t)$, respectively. The second difference is that state variables in this case are vectors of real variables rather than symbols in a finite alphabet.

The inference algorithm in BRNNs is straightforward. Starting from $F_0 = 0$, all the states F_t are updated from left to right, following eq. 3. Similarly, states B_t are updated from right to left using the boundary condition $B_{T+1} = 0$ and following eq. 4. After forward and backward propagation have taken place, predictions Y_t can be computed using eq. 7. The main advantage with BRNNs (compared to BIOHMMs) is that inference is much more efficient. The intuitive reason is that in the case of BRNNs, the hidden states F_t and B_t evolve independently (without affecting each other). However, in the case of BIOHMMs, F_t and B_t, although conditionally independent given U_t, become dependent when Y_t is also given (as it happens during learning). This is reflected by the fact that cliques relative to B_t and F_t in the junction tree contain triplets of state variables, thus yielding a time complexity proportional to n^3 for each time step (if both variable have the same number of states n). In the case of BRNNs, assuming that MLPs $\mathcal{N}_\beta$ and $\mathcal{N}_\phi$ have $O(n)$ hidden units, time complexity is only proportional to n^2 for each time step and this can be further reduced by limiting the number of hidden units.

The learning algorithm is based on maximum-likelihood. For simplicity we limit our discussion to classification. In this case, the cost function (or negative log likelihood) has the form of a cross-entropy:

$$C(\mathcal{D}; \boldsymbol{\theta}) = \sum_{\text{training sequences}} \sum_{i=1}^{s} \overline{y}_{i,t} \log y_{i,t}$$

where $\overline{y}_{i,t}$ is the target output (equal to 1 if the class at position t is i, and equal to 0 otherwise) and $y_{i,t}$ is the i-th output of $\mathcal{N}_\eta$ at position t. Optimization is based on gradient descent, where gradients are computed by a noncausal version of backpropagation through time. The intuitive idea behind backpropagation through time is to flatten-out cycles in the recurrent network by unrolling the recursive computation of state variables over time. This essentially consists of replicating the transition network for each time step, so that a feedforward network with shared weights is obtained. The same unrolling procedure can be applied in more general cases than just sequences. For example it can be applied to trees and graphs, provided that the resulting unrolled network is acyclic (Goller & Kuechler, 1996; Frasconi et al., 1998). In the case of BRNNs, it is immediate to recognize that the unrolling procedure yields an acyclic graph (if we only look at the main variables Y_y, B_t, F_t, and U_t, the unrolled network has the same topology as the Bayesian network shown in Figure 2). The unrolled network can be divided into slices associated with different position indices t, and for each slice there is exactly one replica of each network $\mathcal{N}_\phi$, $\mathcal{N}_\beta$, and $\mathcal{N}_\eta$.

The error signal is first computed for the leaf nodes (corresponding to the output variables Y_t):

$$\delta_{i,t} \doteq \frac{\partial C}{\partial a_{i,t}} = \overline{y}_{i,t} - y_{i,t} \quad i = 1, \ldots, s; \ t = 1, \ldots, T$$

where $a_{i,t}$ denotes the activation of the i-th output unit of $\mathcal{N}_\eta$ (before the soft-max). Then error is then propagated over time (in both directions) by following any reverse topological sort of the unrolled net. For example, the delta-errors of $\mathcal{N}_\phi$ at position t are computed from the delta-errors at the input of $\mathcal{N}_\eta$ at t, and from the delta-errors at the first n inputs of $\mathcal{N}_\phi$ at position $t + 1$. Similarly, the delta-errors of $\mathcal{N}_\beta$ at position t are computed from the delta-errors at the input of $\mathcal{N}_\eta$ at t, and from the delta-errors at the last m inputs of $\mathcal{N}_\beta$ at position $t - 1$. Obviously, the computation of delta-errors also involves backpropagation through the hidden layers of the MLPs. Since the model is stationary, weights are shared among the different replicas of the MLPs at different time steps. Hence, the total gradients are obtained by summing all the contributions associated to different time steps. There are three possibilities: First, if i and j are any pair of connected neurons within the same position slice t, $\delta_{i,t}$ denotes the delta-error of unit i at t, and $x_{j,t}$ denotes the output of neuron j at t, then

$$\frac{\partial C}{\partial w_{ij}} = \sum_{t=1}^{T} \delta_{i,t} x_{j,t}.$$

Second, if i is in the hidden layer of $\mathcal{N}_\beta$ at slice t and j is in the output layer of $\mathcal{N}_\beta$ at slice $t + 1$, then

$$\frac{\partial C}{\partial w_{ij}} = \sum_{t=1}^{T} \delta_{i,t} b_{j,t+1}.$$

Finally, if i is in the hidden layer of $\mathcal{N}_\phi$ at slice t and j is in the output layer of $\mathcal{N}_\phi$ at slice $t - 1$, then

$$\frac{\partial C}{\partial w_{ij}} = \sum_{t=1}^{T} \delta_{i,t} f_{j,t-1}.$$

4.3   Embedded Memories and Other Architectural Variants

One of the principal difficulties when training standard RNNs is the problem of vanishing gradients. In (Bengio et al., 1994), it is shown that one of the following two undesirable situations necessarily arise: either the system is unable to ro-bustly store past information about its inputs, or gradients vanish exponentially. Intuitively, in order to contribute to the output at time t, the input signal at time $t - \tau$ must be propagated in the forward chain through τ replicas of the NN that implements the state transition function. However, during gradient compu-tation, error signals must be propagated backward along the same path. Each propagation step involves a multiplication between the error vector and the Ja-cobian matrix associated with the transition function. Unfortunately, when the

dynamics develop attractors that allow the system to reliably store past information, the norm of the Jacobian is < 1. Hence, when τ is large, gradients of the
error at time t with respect to inputs at time $t - \tau$ tend to vanish exponentially.
Similarly, in the case of BRNNs, error propagation in both the forward and the
backward chains is subject to exponential decay. Thus, although the model has
in principle the capability of storing remote information, such information cannot be learnt effectively. Clearly, this is a theoretical argument and its practical
impact needs to be evaluated on a per case basis.

In practice, in the case of proteins, the BRNN can reliably utilize input information located within about ± 15 amino acids (i.e., the total effective window
size is about 31). This was empirically evaluated by feeding the model with
increasingly long protein fragments. We observed that the average predictions
at the central residues did not significantly change if fragments were extended
beyond 41 amino acids. This is an improvement over standard NNs with input
window sizes ranging from 11 to 17 amino acids (Rost & Sander, 1994; Riis &
Krogh, 1996). Yet, there is presumably relevant information located at longer
distances that our model have not been able to discover so far.

To limit this problem, we propose a remedy motivated by recent studies of
NARX networks (Lin et al., 1996). In these networks, the vanishing gradients
problem is mitigated by the use of an explicit delay line applied to the output,
which provides shorter paths for the effective propagation of error signals. The
very same idea cannot be applied directly to BRNNs since output feedback,
combined with bidirectional propagation, would generate cycles in the unrolled
network. However, as suggested in (Lin et al., 1998), a similar mechanism can be
implemented by inserting multiple delays in the connections among hidden state
units rather than output units. The modified dynamics in the case of BRNNs
are defined as follows:

$$
\begin{aligned}
F_t &= \phi(F_{t-1}, F_{t-2}, \ldots, F_{t-s}, I_t) \\
B_t &= \beta(B_{t+1}, B_{t+2}, \ldots, B_{t+s}, I_t).
\end{aligned}
\tag{8}
$$

The explicit dependence on forward or backward states introduces *shortcut*
connections in the graphical model, forming shorter paths along which gradients
can be propagated. This is akin to introducing higher order Markov chains in
the probabilistic version. However, unlike Markov chains where the number of
parameters would grow exponentially with s, in the present case the number
of parameters grows only linearly with s. To reduce the number of parameters,
a simplified version of Eq. 8 limits the dependencies to state vectors located s
residues apart from t:

$$
\begin{aligned}
F_t &= \phi(F_{t-1}, F_{t-s}, I_t) \\
B_t &= \beta(B_{t+1}, t + s, I_t).
\end{aligned}
\tag{9}
$$

Another variant of the basic architecture which also allows to increase the effective window size consists in feeding the output networks with a window in the
forward and backward state chains. In this case, the prediction is computed as

$$
O_t = \eta(F_{t-k}, \ldots, F_{t+k}, B_{t-k}, \ldots, B_{t+k}, I_t).
\tag{10}
$$

5   Datasets

The assignment of the SS categories to the experimentally determined 3D structure is nontrivial and is usually performed by the widely used DSSP program (Kabsch & Sander, 1983). DSSP works by assigning potential backbone hydrogen bonds (based on the 3D coordinates of the backbone atoms) and subsequently by identifying repetitive bonding patterns. Two alternatives to this assignment scheme are the programs STRIDE and DEFINE. In addition to hydrogen bonds, STRIDE uses also dihedral angles (Frishman & Argos, 1995). DEFINE uses difference distance matrices for evaluating the match of interatomic distances in the protein to those from idealized SS (Richards & Kundrot, 1988). While assignment methods impact prediction performance to some extent (Cuff & Barton, 1999), here we concentrate exclusively on the DSSP assignments. A number of data sets were used to develop and test our algorithms. We will refer to each set using the number of sequences contained in it. The first high quality data used in this study was extracted from the Brookhaven Protein Data Bank (PDB) (Bernstein & et al., 1977) release 77 and subsequently updated. We excluded entries if:

- They were not determined by X-ray diffraction, since no commonly used measure of quality is available for NMR or theoretical model structures.
- The program DSSP could not produce an output, since we wanted to use the DSSP assignment of protein secondary structure (Kabsch & Sander, 1983).
- The protein had physical chain breaks (defined as neighboring amino acids in the sequence having C^α-distances exceeding 4.0Å).
- They had a resolution worse than 1.9Å, since resolutions better than this enables the crystallographer to remove most errors from their models.
- Chains with a length of less than 30 amino acids were also discarded.
- From the remaining chains, a representative subset with low pairwise sequence similarities was selected by running the algorithm #1 of Hobohm et al. (1992), using the local alignment procedure search (rigorous Smith-Waterman algorithm) (Myers & Miller, 1988; Pearson, 1990) using the pam120 matrix, with gap penalties -12, -4.

Thus we obtained a data set consisting of 464 distinct protein chains, corresponding to 123,752 amino acids, roughly 10 times more than what was available in (Qian & Sejnowski, 1988). Another set we used is the EMBL non-redundant PDB subsets that can be accessed by ftp at the site ftp.embl-heidelberg.de. Data details are in the file /pub/databases/pdb_select/README. The extraction is based on the file /pub/databases/pdb_select/1998_june.25.gz containing a set of non-redundant (25%) PDB chains. After removing 74 chains on which the DSSP program crashes, we obtained another set of 824 sequences, overlapping in part with the former ones. In addition, we also used the original set of 126 sequences of Rost and Sander (corresponding to 23,348 amino acid positions) as well as the complementary set of 396 non-homologue sequences (62,189 amino acids) prepared by Cuff and Barton (1999). Both sets can be downloaded at

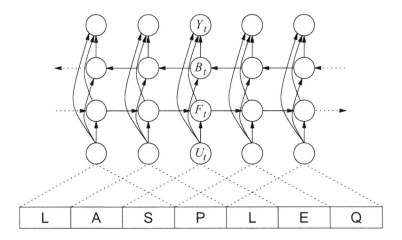

Fig. 4. Unfolded bidirectional model for protein SS prediction. The model receives as input an explicit window of amino acids of size w ($w = 3$ in the figure).

http://circinus.ebi.ac.uk:8081/pred_res/. Finally, we also constructed two more data sets, containing all proteins in PDB which are at least 30 amino acids long, produce DSSP output without chain breaks, and have a resolution of at least 2.5 Å. Furthermore the proteins in both sets have less than 25% identity to any of the 126 sequences of Rost and Sander. In both sets, internal homology is reduced again by Hobohm's #1 algorithm, keeping the PDB sequences with the best resolution. For one set, we use the standard 25% threshold curve for homology reduction. For the other set, however, we raise, the threshold curve by 25%. The set with 25% homology threshold contains 826 sequences, corresponding to a total of 193,249 amino acid positions, while the set with 50% homology threshold contains 1180 sequences (282,303 amino acids). Thus, to the best of our knowledge, our experiments are based on the currently largest available corpora of non-redundant data. In all but one experiment (see below), profiles were obtained from the HSSP database (Schneider et al., 1997) available at http://www.sander.embl-heidelberg.de/hssp/.

6   Architecture Details and Experimental Results

We carried out several preliminary experiments to tune up and evaluate the prediction system. DSSP classes were assigned to three secondary structure classes α, β, and γ as follows: α is formed by DSSP class H, β by E, and γ by everything else (including DSSP classes F, S, T, B, and I). This assignment is slightly different from other assignments reported in the literature. For example, in (Riis & Krogh, 1996), a contains DSSP classes H, G, and I. In the CASP competition (Moult & et al., 1997; CASP3, 1998), α contains H, and G, while β contains E, and B. In a first set of experiments, we used the 824 sequences dataset and reserved 2/3 of the available data for training, and 1/3 for testing. We trained several BRNNs of different sizes and different architectural details. In all experiments, we set $n = m$ and we tried different values for n and k (see Eq. 10). The number of free parameters varied from about 1400 to 2600. Qualitatively we observed that using $k > 0$ can improve accuracy, but increasing n beyond 12 does not help because of overfitting. Results for this method, without using profiles, are summarized in the first rows of Table 1. By comparison, we also trained several feedforward NNs on the same data. The best feedforward NN achieved $Q_3 = 67.2\%$ accuracy using a window of 13 amino acids. By enriching the feedforward architecture with adaptive input encoding and output filtering, as in (Riis & Krogh, 1996), 68.5% accuracy was achieved (output filtering actually increases the length of the input window). Hence, the best BRNN outperforms our best feedforward network, even when additional architectural design is included. Subsequent experiments included the use of profiles. Table 1 reports the best results obtained by using multiple alignments, both at the input and output levels. Profiles at the input level consistently yielded better results. The best feedforward networks trained in the same conditions achieve $Q_3 = 73.0\%$ and 72.3%, respectively.

Table 1. Experimental results using a single BRNN and 1/3 of the data as test set. h_ϕ, h_β and h_η are the number of hidden units for the transition networks $\mathcal{N}_\phi$, $\mathcal{N}_\beta$ and the output network $\mathcal{N}_\eta$ respectively. We always set $h_\phi = h_\beta$.

Profiles	n	k	h_ϕ	h_η	W	Accuracy
No	7	2	8	11	1611	$Q_3 = 68.7\%$
No	9	2	8	11	1899	$Q_3 = 68.8\%$
No	7	3	8	11	1919	$Q_3 = 68.6\%$
No	8	3	9	11	2181	$Q_3 = 68.8\%$
No	20	0	17	11	2601	$Q_3 = 67.6\%$
Output	9	2	8	11	1899	$Q_3 = 72.6\%$
Output	8	3	9	11	2181	$Q_3 = 72.7\%$
Input	9	2	8	11	1899	$Q_3 = 73.3\%$
Input	8	3	9	11	2181	$Q_3 = 73.4\%$
Input	12	3	9	11	2565	$Q_3 = 73.6\%$

In a second set of experiments (also based on the 824 sequences), we combined several BRNNs to form an ensemble, as in (Krogh & Vedelsby, 1995), using a simple averaging scheme. Different networks were obtained by varying architectural details such as n, k, and the number of hidden units. Combining 6 networks using profiles at the input level we obtained the best accuracy $Q_3 = 75.1\%$, measured in this case using 7-fold cross validation. We also tried to include in the ensemble a set of 4 BRNNs using profiles at the output level but performance in this way slightly decreased to 75.0%. A study for assessing the capabilities of the model in capturing long ranged information was also performed. Results indicate that the model is sensitive to information located within about ±15 amino acids. Although this value is not very high, it should be remarked that typical feedforward nets reported in the literature do not exploit information beyond $\tau = 8$. To further explore the long-range information problem we conducted another set of experiments using BRNNs with simplified embedded memories (see Eq. 9). In this case, as for the results reported in Table 1, we used a single model (rather than a mixture) and the test set method (1/3 of the available data) for measuring accuracy. We tried all values of s from 1 to 10, but in no case we could observe a significant performance improvement on the test set. Interestingly, our experiments showed that using shortcuts reduces the convergence difficulties associated with vanishing gradients: accuracy on the training set increased from 75.7% using no shortcuts to 76.9% with $s = 3$. On the other hand, the gap between training set and test set performance also increased. Thus overfitting offset the convergence improvement, probably because long-range information is too sparse and noisy.

Another experiment was conducted by training on all the 824 sequences and using the official test sequences used at the 1998 CASP3 competition. In this case, we adopted a slightly different class assignment for training (DSSP classes H, G, and I were merged together). The CASP3 competition was won by one of the two programs entered by D. Jones, which selected 23 out of 35 proteins obtaining a performance of $Q_3 = 77.6\%$ per protein, or $Q_3 = 75.5\%$ per residue (Jones, 1999). We evaluated that system on the whole set of 35 proteins by using Jones' prediction server at http://137.205.156.147/psiform.html. It achieved $Q_3 = 74.3\%$ per residue and 76.2% per protein. On the same 35 sequences our system achieved $Q_3 = 73.0\%$ per residue and $Q_3 = 74.6\%$ per protein. A test set of 35 proteins is relatively small for drawing general conclusions. Still, we believe that this result confirms the effectiveness of the proposed model, especially in consideration of the fact that Jones' system builds upon more recent profiles from TrEMBL database (Bairoch & Apweiler, 1999). These profiles contain many more sequences than our profiles, which are based on the older HSSP database, leaving room for further improvements of our system.

Table 2. First confusion matrix derived with an ensemble of 6 BRNNs with 2/3-1/3 data splitting. First row provides percentages of predicted helices, sheets, and coils within (DSSP-assigned) helices.

	pred α	pred β	pred γ
α	78.61%	3.13%	18.26%
β	5.00%	61.49%	33.51%
γ	10.64%	9.37%	79.99%

To further compare our system with other predictors, as in (Cuff & Barton, 1999), we also trained an ensemble of BRNNs using the 126 sequences in the Rost and Sander data set. The performance on the 396 test sequences prepared by Cuff

Table 3. Same as above. First row provides percentages of (DSSP-assigned) helices, sheets, and coils within the predicted helices.

	α	β	γ
pred α	80.77%	3.74%	15.49%
pred β	5.11%	73.17%	21.72%
pred γ	11.71%	15.63%	72.66%

and Barton is $Q_3 = 72.0\%$. This is slightly better than the 71.9% score for the single best predictor (PHD) amongst (DSC, PHD, NNSSP, and PREDATOR) reported in (Cuff & Barton, 1999). This result is also achieved with the CASP class assignment. Finally, we also trained an ensemble of 6 BRNNs using the set containing 826 sequences with less than 25% identity to the 126 sequences of Rost and Sander. When tested on the 126 sequences, the system achieves $Q_3 = 74.7\%$ per residue, with correlation coefficients $C_\alpha = 0.692$, $C_\beta = 0.571$, and $C_\gamma = 0.544$. This is again achieved with the harder CASP assignment. In contrast, the $Q_3 = 75.1\%$ described above was obtained by 7 fold cross-validation on 824 sequences and with the easier class assignment ($H \rightarrow \alpha$, $E \rightarrow \beta$, the rest $\rightarrow \gamma$). The same experiment was performed using the larger training set of 1,180 sequences having also less than 25% identity with the 126 sequences of Rost and Sander, but with a less stringent redundancy reduction requirement. In this case, and with the same hard assignment, the results are $Q_3 = 75.3\%$ with correlation coefficients $C_\alpha = 0.704$, $C_\beta = 0.583$, and $C_\gamma = 0.550$. The corresponding confusion matrices are given in Tables 2 and 3. Table 4 provides a summary of the main results with different datasets.

Table 4. Summary of main performance results.

Training sequences	Test sequences	Class assignment	Performance
824 (2/3)	824 (1/3)	Default	$Q_3 = 75.1\%$
824	35	CASP	$Q_3 = 73.0\%$
126	396	CASP	$Q_3 = 72.0\%$
826	126	CASP	$Q_3 = 74.7\%$
1180	126	CASP	$Q_3 = 75.3\%$

Although in principle bidirectional models can memorize all the past and future information using the state variables F_t and B_t, we also tried to employ a window of amino acids as input at time t. In so doing, the input U_t for the model is a window of w amino acids centered around the t-th residue in the sequence (see Fig. 4). As explained in the previous sections, both with BIOHMMs and BRNNs the prediction Y_t is produced by an MLP fed by U_t (a window of amino acids) and the state variables F_t and B_t. Hence, compared to the basic architecture of Qian and Sejnowski, our architecture is enriched with more contextual information provided by the state variables. The main advantage of the present proposal is that w can be kept quite small (even reduced to a single amino acid), and yet relatively distant information propagated through the state variables. Because of stationarity (weight sharing) this approach allows a better control over the number of free parameters, thus reducing the risk of data overfitting.

In a set of preliminary experiments, we have tried different architectures and model sizes. In the case of BIOHMMs, the best result was obtained using $w = 11$, $n = m = 10$, 20 hidden units for the output network and 6 hidden units for the forward and backward state transition networks. The resulting model has about 10^5 parameters in total. The correct residue prediction rate is 68%, measured by reserving $1/3$ of the available sequences as a test set. This result was obtained without using output filtering or multiple alignments. Unfortunately, $n = 10$ seems too small a number for storing enough contextual information. On the other hand, higher values of n are currently prohibitive for today's computational resources since complexity scales up with n^3.

In the case of BRNNs, we were able to obtain slightly better performances, with significant computational savings. A set of initial experiments indicated that redefining the output function as $Y_t = \eta(F_{t-k}, \ldots, F_{t+k}, B_{t-k}, B_{t+k}, U_t)$ and using $w = 1$ yields the best results. In subsequent experiments, we have trained 4 different BRNNs with $n = m$ varying from 7 to 9, and k varying from 2 to 4. The number of free parameters varies from about 1400 to 2100. An RNN can develop quite complex nonlinear dynamics and, as a result, n BRNN state units are able to store more context than n BIOHMM discrete states. The performances of the 4 networks are basically identical, achieving about 68.8% accuracy measured on the test set. While these results do not lead to an immediate improvement, it is interesting to remark that using a static MLP we obtained roughly the same accuracy only after the insertion of additional architectural design as in (Riis & Krogh, 1996): adaptive input encoding and output filtering. More precisely, the MLP has $w = 13$, with 5 units for adaptive encoding (a total of about 1800 weights) and achieves 68.9%. Interestingly, although the 4 BRNNs and the static MLP achieve roughly the same overall accuracy, distributions of errors on the three classes are quite different. This suggests that combining predictions from filtered MLP and BRNNs could improve performance. Indeed, by constructing an ensemble with the five networks, accuracy increased to 69.5%. Finally we enriched the system using an output filtering network on the top of the ensemble and adding multiple alignment profiles as provided by the HSSP database (Schneider et al., 1997). In this preliminary version of the system, we have not included commonly used features like entropy and number of insertions and deletions. The performance of the overall system is 73.3%.

In a second set of experiments, we measured accuracy using 7-fold cross validation. The usage of more training data in each experiments seems to have a positive effect. The performance of the five networks ensemble is 69.6% without alignments and 73.7% using alignments. We must remark that these results are not directly comparable with those reported by Rost and Sander (1994) because our dataset contains more proteins and the assignment of residues to

SS categories is slightly different (in our case the class *coil* includes everything except DSSP classes 'H' and 'E').

The last experiment is based on a set of 35 proteins from the 1998 edition of "Critical Assessment of Protein Structure Prediction" (Moult & et al., 1997; CASP3, 1998). This unique experiment attempts to gauge the current state of the art in protein structure prediction by means of blind prediction. Sequences of a number of target proteins, which are in the process of being solved, are made available to predictors before the experimental structures are available. Although we tried our system only after the competition was closed, we believe that result obtained on this dataset are still interesting. Our system achieved 71.78% correct residue prediction on the 35 sequences. A direct comparison with other systems is difficult. The best system (labeled JONES-2 in the CASP3 web site) achieves 75.5% correct residue prediction on a subset of 23 proteins (performance of JONES-2 on the remaining 12 proteins is not available). It should be also remarked that, in the CASP evaluation system, DSSP class 'G' (3-10 helix) is assigned to 'H' and DSSP class 'B' (beta bridge) is assigned to 'E'. Moreover, accuracy is measured by averaging the correct prediction fraction over single proteins, thus biasing sensitivity towards shorter sequences. Using this convention, our accuracy is 74.1% on 35 proteins while JONES-2 achieves 77.6% on 23 proteins. If we focus only on the 24 proteins for which our network has the highest prediction confidence (the criterion is based on the entropy at the softmax output layer of the network), then the performance of our system is 77.5%, although it is likely that in so doing we are including sequences which are easy to predict. More importantly, JONES-2 results have been obtained using profiles from TrEMBL database (Bairoch & Apweiler, 1999). These profiles contain many more sequences than our profiles which are based on the older HSSP database. We believe that this leaves room for further improvements.

7   Conclusion

In this paper, we have proposed two novel architectures for dealing with sequence learning problems in which data is not obtained from physical measurements over time. The new architectures remove the causality assumption that characterize current connectionist approaches to learning sequential translations. Using BRNNs on the protein secondary structure prediction task appears to be very promising. Our performance is very close to the best existing systems although our usage of profiles is not as sophisticated. One improvement of our prediction system could be obtained by using profiles from the TrEMBL database.

Acknowledgements. The work of PB is in part supported by an NIH SBIR grant to Net-ID, Inc. The work of SB is supported by a grant from the Danish National Research Foundation. The work of PF and GS is partially supported by a "40%" grant from MURST, Italy.

References

Andrew, F., & Dimitriadis, M. (1994). Forecasting probability densities by using hidden markov models with mixed states. In Weigend, A. S., & Gershenfeld, N. (Eds.), *Time Series Prediction: Forecasting the Future and Understanding the Past*. Addison-Wesley.

Angluin, D., & Smith, C. H. (1983). A survey of inductive inference: Theory and methods. *ACM Comput. Surv.*, *15*(3), 237–269.

Bairoch, A., & Apweiler, R. (1999). The SWISS-PROT protein sequence data bank and its supplement TrEMBL in 1999. *Nucleic Acids Res*, pp. 49–54.

Baldi, P., & Brunak, S. (1998). *Bioinformatics: The Machine Learning Approach*. MIT Press, Cambridge, MA.

Baldi, P., Brunak, S., Chauvin, Y., & Nielsen, H. (1999). Assessing the accuracy of prediction algorithms for classification: an overview. Submitted for publication.

Baldi, P., & Chauvin, Y. (1996). Hybrid modeling, HMM/NN architectures, and protein applications. *Neural Computation*, *8*(7), 1541–1565.

Baldi, P., Chauvin, Y., Hunkapillar, T., & McClure, M. (1994). Hidden Markov models of biological primary sequence information. *Proc. Natl. Acad. Sci. USA*, *91*, 1059–1063.

Bengio, Y., & Frasconi, P. (1995). An input output HMM architecture. In Tesauro, G., Touretzky, D., & Leen, T. (Eds.), *Advances in Neural Information Processing Systems 7*, pp. 427–434. The MIT Press.

Bengio, Y., & Frasconi, P. (1996). Input-output HMM's for sequence processing. *IEEE Trans. on Neural Networks*, *7*(5), 1231–1249.

Bengio, Y., Simard, P., & Frasconi, P. (1994). Learning long-term dependencies with gradient descent is difficult. *IEEE Trans. on Neural Networks*, *5*(2), 157–166.

Bengio, Y., & Frasconi, P. (1994). Credit assignment through time: Alternatives to backpropagation. In Cowan, J. D., Tesauro, G., & Alspector, J. (Eds.), *Advances in Neural Information Processing Systems*, Vol. 6, pp. 75–82. Morgan Kaufmann Publishers, Inc.

Bengio, Y., LeCun, Y., Nohl, C., & Burges, C. (1995). LeRec: A NN/HMM hybrid for on-line handwriting recognition. *Neural Computation*, *7*(6), 1289–1303.

Bernstein, F. C., & et al. (1977). The protein data bank: A computer based archival file for macromolecular structures. *J. Mol. Biol.*, *112*, 535–542.

Bridle, J. S. (1989). Training stochastic model recognition algorithms as networks can lead to maximum mutual information estimation of parameters. In D.S.Touretzky (Ed.), *Advances in Neural Information Processing Systems*, Vol. 2, pp. 211–217. Morgan Kaufmann.

Brown, P. (1987). *The Acoustic-Modeling problem in Automatic Speech Recognition*. Ph.D. thesis, Dept. of Computer Science, Carnegie-Mellon University.

Bunke, H., Roth, M., & Schukat-Talamazzini, E. (1995). Off-line Cursive Handwriting Recognition Using Hidden Markov Models. *Pattern Recognition*, *28*(9), 1399–1413.

CASP3 (1998). Third community wide experiment on the critical assessment of techniques for protein structure prediction. Unpublished results available in `http://predictioncenter.llnl.gov/casp3`.

Charniak, E. (1993). *Statistical Language Learning*. MIT Press.

Cuff, J. A., & Barton, G. J. (1999). Evaluation and improvement of multiple sequence methods for protein secondary structure prediction. *Proteins, 34*, 508–519.

Dempster, A. P., Laird, N. M., & Rubin, D. B. (1977). Maximum-likelihood from incomplete data via the EM algorithm. *Journal of Royal Statistical Society B, 39*, 1–38.

Frasconi, P., Gori, M., Maggini, M., & Soda, G. (1996). Representation of finite state automata in recurrent radial basis function networks. *Machine Learning, 23*, 5–32.

Frasconi, P., Gori, M., & Sperduti, A. (1998). A general framework for adaptive processing of data structures. *IEEE Trans. on Neural Networks, 9*(5), 768–786.

Freitag, D., & McCallum, A. (2000). Information extraction with hmm structures learned by stochastic optimization. In *Proc. AAAI*.

Frishman, D., & Argos, P. (1995). Knowledge-based secondary structure assignment. *Proteins, 23*, 566–579.

Ghahramani, Z., & Jordan, M. I. (1997). Factorial hidden Markov models. *Machine Learning, 29*, 245–274.

Giles, C. L., Miller, C. B., Chen, D., Chen, H. H., Sun, G. Z., & Lee, Y. C. (1992). Learning and extracting finite state automata with second-order recurrent neural networks. *Neural Computation, 4*(3), 393–405.

Goller, C., & Kuechler, A. (1996). Learning task-dependent distributed structure-representations by backpropagation through structure. In *IEEE International Conference on Neural Networks*, pp. 347–352.

Hansen, L. K., & Salamon, P. (1990). Neural network ensembles. *IEEE Trans. on Pattern Analysis and Machine Intelligence, 12*, 993–1001.

Heckerman, D. (1997). Bayesian networks for data mining. *Data Mining and Knowledge Discovery, 1*(1), 79–119.

Hobohm, U., Scharf, M., Schneider, R., & Sander, C. (1992). Selection of representative data sets. *Prot. Sci., 1*, 409–417.

Jelinek, F. (1997). *Statistical Methods for Speech Recognition*. MIT Press.

Jensen, F. V., Lauritzen, S. L., & Olosen, K. G. (1990). Bayesian updating in recursive graphical models by local computations. *Comput. Stat. Quarterly, 4*, 269–282.

Jones, D. (1999). Protein secondary structure prediction based on position-specific scoring matrices. *Journal of Molecular Biology*, pp. 195–202.

Kabsch, W., & Sander, C. (1983). Dictionary of protein secondary structure: pattern recognition of hydrogen-bonded and geometrical features. *Biopolymers, 22*, 2577–2637.

Krogh, A., Brown, M., Mian, I. S., Sjolander, K., & Haussler, D. (1994). Hidden Markov models in computational biology: Applications to protein modeling. *J. Mol. Biol.*, pp. 1501–1531.

Krogh, A., & Vedelsby, J. (1995). Neural network ensembles, cross validation, and active learning. In Tesauro, G., Touretzky, D., & Leen, T. (Eds.), *Advances in Neural Information Processing Systems 7*, pp. 231–238. The MIT Press.

Lin, T., Horne, B. G., & Giles, C. L. (1998). How embedded memory in recurrent neural network architectures helps learning long-term temporal dependencies. *Neural Networks, 11*(5), 861–868.

Lin, T., Horne, B. G., Tino, P., & Giles, C. L. (1996). Learning long-term dependencies in NARX recurrent neural networks. *IEEE Transactions on Neural Networks, 7*(6), 1329–1338.

Lucke, H. (1995). Bayesian belief networks as a tool for stochastic parsing. *Speech Communication, 16*, 89–118.

Moult, J., & et al. (1997). Critical assessment of methods of protein structure prediction (CASP): Round II. *Proteins, 29*(S1), 2–6. Supplement 1.

Myers, E. W., & Miller, W. (1988). Optimal alignments in linear space. *Comput. Appl. Biosci., 4*, 11–7.

Pearl, J. (1988). *Probabilistic Reasoning in Intelligent Systems : Networks of Plausible Inference.* Morgan Kaufmann.

Pearson, W. R. (1990). Rapid and sensitive sequence comparison with FASTP and FASTA. *Meth. Enzymol.*, pp. 63–98.

Qian, N., & Sejnowski, T. J. (1988). Predicting the secondary structure of glubular proteins using neural network models. *J. Mol. Biol., 202*, 865–884.

Rabiner, L. R. (1989). A tutorial on hidden Markov models and selected applications in speech recognition. *Proceedings of the IEEE, 77*(2), 257–286.

Richards, F. M., & Kundrot, C. E. (1988). Identification of structural motifs from protein coordinate data: secondary structure and first-level supersecondary structure. *Proteins, 3*, 71–84.

Riis, S. K., & Krogh, A. (1996). Improving prediction of protein secondary structure using structured neural networks and multiple sequence alignments. *J. Comput. Biol., 3*, 163–183.

Rost, B., & Sander, C. (1993a). Improved prediction of protein secondary structure by use of sequence profiles and neural networks. *Proc. Natl. Acad. Sci. USA, 90*(16), 7558–7562.

Rost, B., & Sander, C. (1993b). Prediction of protein secondary structure at better than 70 % accuracy. *J. Mol. Biol., 232*(2), 584–599.

Rost, B., & Sander, C. (1994). Combining evolutionary information and neural networks to predict protein secondary structure. *Proteins*, pp. 55–72.

Schneider, R., de Daruvar, A., & Sander, C. (1997). The hssp database of protein structure-sequence alignments. *Nucleic Acids Research, 25*, 226–230.

Smyth, P., Heckerman, D., & Jordan, M. I. (1997). Probabilistic independence networks for hidden markov probability models. *Neural Computation, 9*(2), 227–269.

Time in Connectionist Models

Jean-Cédric Chappelier[1], Marco Gori[2], and Alain Grumbach[3]

[1] DI–LIA, EPFL, Lausanne (Switzerland)
[2] Dipartimento di Ingegneria dell'Informazione, Universitá di Siena, Siena (Italy)
[3] Département Informatique, ENST, Paris (France)

1 Introduction

The prototypical use of "classical" connectionist models (including the multi-layer perceptron (MLP), the Hopfield network and the Kohonen self-organizing map) concerns *static* data processing. These classical models are not well suited to working with data varying over time. In response to this, temporal connectionist models have appeared and constitute a continuously growing research field. The purpose of this chapter is to present the main aspects of this research area and to review the key connectionist architectures that have been designed for solving temporal problems.

The following section presents the fundamentals of temporal processing with neural networks. Several temporal connectionist models are then detailed in section 3. As a matter of illustration, important applications are reviewed in the third section. The chapter concludes with the presentation of a promising future issue: the extension of temporal processing to even more complex structured data.

2 Fundamentals

Before actually getting into the fundamentals of temporal connectionist models, we have to clarify some possible confusion between different kinds of time representation.

The issue we are concerned with is the study of models which are able to take the *"natural"* time of a problem into account. Some ambiguity may arise from the fact that some models also have an *internal* use of time. This internal time does not however correspond to any temporal dimension of the problem dealt with; the problem considered by such a model could even be static (e.g. image recognition). Internal use of time is only necessary for the model's own dynamics (e.g. for relaxation of inner states to some equilibrium as in the Hopfield's network).

To make the difference clear, we shall speak of *external* time for the time of the problem which is considered. Some sort of mixed computation could of course happen where the use of internal time is also extended to the processing of the input sequence. To the best of the authors' knowledge however, no such link between internal and external time has ever been investigated in the literature.

The chapter focuses only on neural network architectures that handle the temporal problem, i.e. that deal with external time.

R. Sun and C.L. Giles (Eds.): Sequence Learning, LNAI 1828, pp. 105–134, 2000.

Several aspects of time may be involved in temporal problems. These aspects correspond to different properties of time such as:

- time as a simple *order relation* (where time only consists of an index used to order events, e.g. the time embedded in the reading of a sentence);
- time as *metrics* (e.g. the time involved in speech, where duration is meaningful);
- *discrete* time versus *continuous* time;
- time over a *finite* versus *infinite* interval (never ending problems).

2.1   A Short Historical Overview

The chronological ordering of temporal connectionist models is characterized by the increase of the integration of time in the architecture.

A first phase in the development of temporal neural networks is characterized by architectures based on classical models, but *locally* modified so as to take the time dimension into account. For instance, recurrent networks based on the MLP were introduced. They include backward links with a one time step delay that represents the ordering relation between two successive inputs. This kind of approach typically focuses on *temporal sequence learning*.

For example, (Jordan, 1986) designed such an architecture in which the output vector at time $t-1$ is concatenated to the input vector at time t.[1] This architecture was used for modelling the sequence of movements of a robot arm.

(Elman, 1990) also designed a similar architecture, in which the hidden vector rather than the output vector is concatenated to the input vector. This architecture was successfully used for sentence processing.

These modifications of the architecture also affect the learning process: the backward links have to be taken into account. The learning algorithm used in this case, called "back-propagation through time", is a generalisation of the standard back-propagation learning algorithm (see for instance the paper of (Williams & Peng, 1990)).

A second phase in the development of temporal neural networks still considered classical architectures but focused on configuring their parameters more *globally* so as to be able to accommodate enough temporal informations for solving the problem. A first important parameter which can take into account the time dimension is the input vector: this could be a temporal window over the input signal for example. This choice triggers other choices such as the dimension of the hidden layers which needs to be proportional to the dimension of the input temporal window. A good prototype from this second phase is the TDNN (Lang et al., 1990)[2]. This kind of architecture typically focuses on *temporal pattern recognition* of the kind needed in speech processing.

After the use of adapted classical architectures, a third phase appeared in the development: architectures specially designed for time processing appeared. Most

---

[1] see section 3.2 for further details on this architecture.
[2] This model is described in section 3.1.

of them are inspired by our knowledge of information processing in "natural" neural networks. These try to mimic one or several of their characteristics such as:

1. propagation delays on connections;
2. neurons sending discrete pulses rather than continuous activity (i.e. "spiking neurons");
3. neuron activity being also a function of time; for instance introducing some refractory period;
4. synchronization between neuron populations.

For instance, RST (Chappelier & Grumbach, 1998) which has been applied to finding the moving part of an image, uses properties 2 and 3 above[3].

Considering architectures using spiking neurons, (Maass, 1997b) studied their computational power and showed that they have at least the same computational power as a classical MLP, but need fewer neurons.

Although several other architectures have also been designed with this kind of approach, we are still only at the beginning of this third phase.

2.2   Time Integration in Connectionist Models

Let us now detail the different approaches of time integration in connectionist models such as sketched out in the previous section. The hierarchy of models detailed hereafter is summarized in figure 1 (see also the paper of (Chappelier & Grumbach, 1994)).

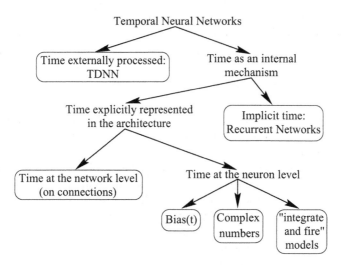

Fig. 1. A classification of connectionist models with respect to time integration.

---

[3] A description of this architecture is given in section 3.4.

External Representation of Time. The first approach in the integration of time into connectionist models consists in not introducing it *directly* in the architecture, rather leaving the time representation outside the neural network. The idea is to preprocess the data so that classical static connectionist models can proceed with the temporal task. Time is preprocessed through a time to space transformation; the network accessing then only spatial information, a dimension of which has semantics related to time[4].

Researchers who have taken this approach include (Simpson & Deich, 1988), (Gorman & Sejnowski, 1988), (Bengio et al., 1989) and (Goldberg & Pearlmutter, 1989). One typical model of this category is the well known TDNN (Lang et al., 1990), which is described in section 3.1.

(Elman, 1990) points out that there are several disadvantages with this kind of approach. First, it requires some buffering: how long should the buffer be and how often does the network look at it? This approach imposes therefore a rigid limit on the duration of patterns, which is not necessarily appropriate to the real temporal input. Secondly, no difference is made between relative and absolute temporal positions. Most of these architectures do not even have any representation of absolute temporal position at all. Finally, these methods also suffer from inadequate/inflexible time windowing and from over-training caused by an excessive number of weights, even if some clever strategies are used to share weights over time (as in TDNN).

Time as an Internal Index. Time itself can be introduced into connectionist models at several levels. First of all, time can be used as an index in a sequence of network states. There is no actual representation of time in the network strictly speaking but rather a use of time as an internal variable controlling the inner mechanism. We may say in this case that time is *implicitly* present in the model. This kind of network is typically illustrated by *recurrent networks* (RNNs, described further in section 3.2). As explained later, these models are nevertheless very powerful for temporal processing of sequences.

Time at the Connection Level. A step further in the introduction of time in a neural model is to represent it explicitly at the level of the network either on connections or at the neuron level (or both).

In the case where time is represented at the level of connections, it is usually done by some delays of propagation on the connections ("temporal weights"), or more generally by some convolution of the neuron input by a given temporal kernel. The works of (Béroule, 1987), (Jacquemin, 1994) and (Amit, 1988) are, among others, three different but representative approaches of connections carrying temporal information.

Problems that are tackled with such architectures typically involve temporal matching between events.

---

[4] For instance, one effective way of constructing a spatial representation of temporally-occurring information (which is not only limited to neural computing) is to create the power spectrum of the incoming information and use it as a static input image.

Time at the Neuron Level. At the level of the neuron itself, there are several ways of introducing time, depending on how temporal information will be represented by the neural network activity. The two main approaches are:

- the information is contained in the time sequence of the neuron activities;
- the neuron activity consists of discrete events ("pulses" or "spikes"), the information being conveyed by the timings of these events.

These two points of view are summarized in figure 2.

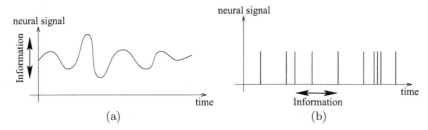

(a)   (b)

Fig. 2. An illustration of the two different points of view on temporal coding at the neuron level: a) variations (in time) of the amplitude of the neuron signal; b) different timings of neural events.

Static neural networks can clearly be emulated by the first type of temporal neural networks as they constitute a very special case (no time). It is furthermore interesting to notice that "static" neural networks can also be emulated with infinite precision in the second framework (Maass, 1997a, 1997b), the activity of a given static neural network being transcoded into a set of timings of a spiking neural network. Networks of spiking neurons therefore have at least the same computational power as classical neural networks.

The introduction of time at the neuron level can be done either by simulating biological properties or by building up neuron models from an engineering point of view, introducing time without specific biological inspiration.

The first approach usually leads to neuron models based on differential equations (Rinzel & Ermentrout, 1989; Abbott & Kepler, 1990). The model most often used in this context is the so-called "integrate and fire" model, or the "leaky-integrator". The principle underlying these models consists in summing the inputs of the neuron over a period of time. When this sum becomes greater than a given threshold (specific to each neuron), the neuron state changes. For a survey of this kind of model, we refer to the paper of (Gerstner, 1995).

On the other hand, the engineering approach is often purely algebraic:

- by changing the usual representation (scalar) to complex numbers (Vaucher, 1996),
- or by introducing an artificial time varying bias (Horn & Usher, 1991),

– or by considering that standard equation of neural networks $y_j = f\left(\sum w_{ij} x_i\right)$ concerns equilibrium and could be generalized to

$$\tau \frac{dy_j}{dt} = -y_j + f\left(\sum_i w_{ij} x_i\right)$$

which is finally equivalent to an "integrate and fire" model.

The introduction of time at the neuron level often leads to dynamical properties and complex behaviours implying oscillations (Horn & Usher, 1991) and synchronizations at the network level (Hirch, 1991; Ramacher, 1993; Lumer & Huberman, 1992).

2.3   Temporal Components of Connectionist Models

Having detailed the different approaches to the time integration in connectionist models, we are now able to detail the different temporal components used in these models.

Any connectionist architecture that processes temporal patterns contains two (at least conceptually) distinct components: a short-term **memory** and a **predictor**[5].

The short term memory has to retain those aspects of the input sequence that are relevant for the problem. The predictor, on the other hand, uses the content of the short term memory to predict/classify and produce some output.

These two modules can either be embedded in each other or be as explicitly distinct as, for instance, in the model of (Catfolis, 1994), which consists of a RNN followed by a MLP. When explicit, the predictor will most generally be a classical static connectionist architecture.

Concerning the short term memory, several types are considered which can be classified along three axes: memory *form*, memory *content* and memory *plasticity*. These concepts were introduced rather informally by (Mozer, 1994). In order to formalize them a little further, we define a memory as some function f of time and previous inputs: $f(t, x(t-1), ..., x(t-k))$.

Memory form

The memory form deals with the function f itself. It can be as simple as a buffer containing the k most recent inputs[6]. This kind of memory is used within the spatial approach to time representation.

But the memory form does not have to necessarily consist of the raw input sequence itself. It could include some transformation of the representation of the input. Such types of memory form include decaying neuronal activity or delayed connections performing some convolution of the neuron input signal[7].

---

[5] Several other authors make this distinction including (Mozer, 1994) and (de Vries & Principe, 1992).

[6] In this case the function f returns a vector of size k consisting of $x(t-1), ..., x(t-k)$.

[7] For instance $f = K(t) \otimes x(t)$ for some function K being the "kernel" of the memory.

Memory content

The memory content is related to the number of arguments f actually takes into account. This can be related to the Markovian/non-Markovian aspect of the problem. "Markovian" means that the output at any time step can be determined uniquely from the input and target values for a given number of time steps in the recent past[8]. It is the purpose of the memory to keep these past values, either directly or combined with previous memory/output states.

Notice that Markovian problems of order higher than 1 can always be transformed into a Markovian problem of order 1. In the context of neural networks, this transformation leads to some "delay lines" where the input at a given time step is augmented with copies of k past inputs. However, if k is large, the network is likely to be overwhelmed by large amounts of redundant and irrelevant information. A standard technique for reducing the number of weights is so-called "weight sharing" or "weight tying", constraining a given set a weights to have the same (unspecified) numerical value[9]. Sharing of weights is linked to some known symmetries of the problems. However it should be emphasised that using RNNs rather than delay lines keeps down the number of parameters to be learned.

Non-Markovian problems, in which outputs are dependent on inputs that are an unbounded distance in the past, require the memory content to depend on some internal states[10].

Memory plasticity

Memory plasticity focuses on how the memory evolves through time[11], which can formally be defined as $\frac{\partial f}{\partial t}$.

The memory can either be *static*, when all its parameters are fixed in advance, or *adaptive*. Adaptive memory consisting in learning either delays (Bodenhausen & Waibel, 1991; Unnikrishnan et al., 1991), decay rates (Mozer, 1989; Frasconi et al., 1992) or some other parameters characterizing the memory (de Vries & Principe, 1992).

Static memories are mentioned here since they still can be of some interest when there is adequate domain knowledge to constrain the type of information that should be represented in the memory. For instance, the memory may have a high resolution for recent events and decreasing resolution for more distant ones as illustrated by the work of (Tank & Hopfield, 1987).

2.4   The Computational Power of Temporal Connectionist Models

On the basis of the classification made in the previous sections, this section addresses the question of the kind of temporal problems connectionist models can actually handle.

---

[8] i.e. depends only on a *temporal neighbourhood* of the input.

[9] For a illustration of that point, see TDNN explained in the next section.

[10] which are not explicited in the chosen presentation of the memory form f but rather "hidden" in the t (first argument) dependency of f.

[11] i.e. "adapting" or "learning".

Standard (Static) Networks. It is widely known that classical neural networks[12], even with one single hidden layer, are universal function approximators (Hornik et al., 1989; Hornik, 1991). This means that any continuous function with compact domain and compact range can be approximated with an arbitrarily degree of precision with regard to the norm of uniform convergence by a network of this type (provided that it has enough hidden neurons). This universality theorem provides a theoretical framework for the application of MLPs to various problem domains and explains their success.

Such feedforward networks, inherently static, can nevertheless have some applications in temporal domain, as already explained in the last two sections. The most simple temporal problems could be handled using feedforward networks. Indeed, MLPs are enough to learn such mapping where the input data at each time step contains enough information to determine the output at that time, (i.e. where $o(t) = F(i(t))$, with i is the input and o the output of the network).

It can furthermore be proved that such static models implement some nonlinear generalization of usual statistical AR-predictors; i.e. $o(t) = F(i(t), ..., i(t - k))$ (Lapedes & Farber, 1987).

Recurrent Networks. Similarly to the universality of static neural-networks in function approximation, recurrent neural networks (RNNs) are universal approximators of dynamical systems (Funahashi & Nakamura, 1993). It is also easy to show that RNNs can simulate any arbitrary finite state machine (FSA) (Cleeremans et al., 1989). (Siegelmann & Sontag, 1995) have even shown that a RNN can simulate any Turing Machine.

In the case where the previous output is needed as well as the current input to determine the output, i.e. if $o(t) = F(i(t), o(t - 1))$, simple RNNs with feedback weighted connections from the ordinary target nodes (such as Jordan networks) or even feedforward networks with 'teacher forcing' techniques could be employed (Rohwer, 1994).

In the most general case however, the approximation theorem mentioned before constitutes only a theoretical result as they do not say anything on how a given machine should be approximated. These theorems do unfortunately not imply that RNNs could easily be trained from examples to do complex temporal tasks.

This is the reason why relatively few cases have been reported showing the successful learning of *complex* dynamics by fully connected RNNs. One of the reasons lies in the cost of the computing of the error gradient for large scale RNNs. High-order Markovian problems present severe difficulties to temporal neural networks. Although some preliminary solutions have been proposed (Bengio et al., 1993; Hochreiter & Schmidhuber, 1997b), the computation of long time dependencies still remains a major problem for RNNs. For a good overview and critique on this point, we refer to the contribution of (Hochreiter & Schmidhuber, 1997a).

---

[12] more precisely MLP.

Spiking Neural Networks. It can be demonstrated (Maass, 1994, 1996) that a "spiking neural network"[13] is at least as powerful as a Turing machine. This means that such an architecture is, with a finite number of neurons and with a boolean input, able to simulate in real-time any Turing machine with a finite number of tapes.

Furthermore, spiking neural networks are strictly more powerful than Turing machine. Indeed they can also simulate some machine that a Turing machine can not, since spiking neural networks are able to handle computation with real numbers (differences of temporal events).

It is then easy to claim that spiking neural networks are unlimited with respect to temporal computing. However, the problem remains that, as with RNNs, such a powerful theorem does unfortunately not tell us *how* a given function can be learned by such networks. Still, the implementation of several fundamental functions (such as multiplication, addition, comparison) has been detailed by (Maass, 1996).

Summary. As far as estimation is concerned, a parallel could be made between usual statistical estimators, that are inherently linear, and non-linear estimators resulting from temporal neural networks. The non-linear equivalent of autoregressive (AR) estimator is the "standard" MLP, whereas non-linear equivalent of autoregressive with moving average (ARMA) estimators are represented by RNNs (Connor et al., 1992; Connor & Martin, 1994). Temporal connectionist models therefore appear to be a richer and more powerful family of estimators than the usual linear ones.

A summary of all the temporal potentialities of connectionist models is given in table 1.

Table 1. A summary of theoretical properties of temporal connectionist models.

connectionist model	able to emulate	non-linear generalization of estimator
standard static networks	continuous mapping	AR
RNNs	dynamical system/Turing Machine	ARMA
spiking neural networks	Turing machine	any?

3   Most Relevant Temporal Connectionist Models

The aim of this section is to present in detail some temporal connectionist models in order to more concretely illustrate the theoretical issues presented up to here.

---

[13] i.e. a connectionist architecture built on spiking neurons and having some propagation delay on the connections;

3.1   TDNN

The "Time-Delay Neural Network" (TDNN) model is a modification of the MLP architecture, the input of which consists of a "delay line", i.e. a whole set of "time-slices" as illustrated in figure 3. This set of time slices is shifted from left to right at each time step. The hidden layer is also divided into sub-slices (which are not shifted but computed from the previous layer). In order to keep the time consistency, the weights are set to be equal among time slices. In that sense, times slices "share" a unique weight set (one for each layer). For instance the weight of the connection from the first neuron of a time slice of the input layer to the first corresponding neuron of the hidden layer is always the same among all time slices of the input layer (see figure 3).

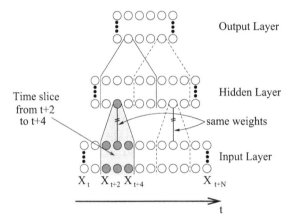

Fig. 3. TDNN architecture: a MLP architecture modified so that units take their inputs from only a part of the previous layer corresponding to a time slice. Different time slices are represented with different line styles. All time slices of a given layer share the same weights.

This model has been introduced by (Lang et al., 1990) in a speech recognition context. The problem considered there was to recognize four kinds of phoneme. The input of the TDNN consisted in a sequence of spectrogram "slices".

3.2   Recurrent Networks

Recurrent neural networks (RNNs) constitute the major family of temporal connectionist models. A RNN can be defined in the most general way as a neural network containing at least one neuron the state of which depends either directly or indirectly on at least one of its anterior states. Formally, a RNN can be described by an equation like:

$$\mathbf{X}_t = f\left(\mathbf{X}_{t-1}, \mathbf{U}_t, t, \Theta_t^f\right)$$
$$\mathbf{Y}_t = g\left(\mathbf{X}_t, t, \Theta_t^g\right)$$

$$(1)$$

where $\mathbf{U}$ stands for the input signal sequence, $\mathbf{Y}$ for the output sequence and Θs for the parameters of the network (typically the weights). $\mathbf{X}$ represents the set of recurrent variables.

There are a huge number of RNNs which have been proposed by various groups (Jordan, 1986; Williams & Zipser, 1989; Narendra & Parthasarathy, 1990; Elman, 1990; Back & Tsoi, 1991; de Vries & Principe, 1992). Some of these architectures do not bear much resemblance (at least superficially) to one another. There were therefore many attempts to find unifying themes in this variety of architectures (Narendra & Parthasarathy, 1990; Nerrand et al., 1993; Tsoi & Back, 1997; Tsoi, 1998).

As a matter of illustration, we now detail three examples of RNNs.

Jordan and Elman Networks. The (Jordan, 1986) and (Elman, 1990) architectures are RNNs both based on the MLP architecture. They consist of adding recurrent links from one part of the network to the input layer, either from the output layer ((Jordan, 1986), figure 4a) or from the hidden layer ((Elman, 1990), figure 4b). At time $t - 1$, the recurrent part is copied into the input layer as a complement to the actual input vector at time t (i.e. the signal to be processed). When computing a new output, the information goes downstream as in a classical MLP, from the input to the output layer. The complementary input vector, that is copied after each computation step, thus represents context information about the past computation.

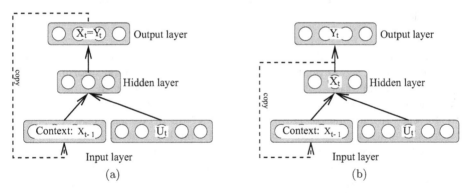

Fig. 4. Two typical recurrent neural networks: (a) Jordan's and (b) Elman's architectures.

Mathematically speaking, the Elman's network is described by the following simplification[14] of equation 1:

$$\begin{aligned} \mathbf{X}_t &= f\left(\mathbf{X}_{t-1}, \mathbf{U}_t, \Theta^f\right) \\ \mathbf{Y}_t &= g\left(\mathbf{X}_t, \Theta^g\right) \end{aligned} \tag{2}$$

---

[14] $\mathbf{X}_t$ and $\mathbf{Y}_t$ do not depend directly on t, and Θs do not depend on t at all.

where $\mathbf{U}$ is the actual input vector sequence, $\mathbf{X}$ is the vector sequence of neuron states from the hidden layer and $\mathbf{Y}$ is the vector sequence of states from the output layer (see figure 4b). Θ^f represents the set of weights from the input layer to the hidden layer, Θ^g the set of weights from the hidden layer to the output layer and the f and g functions represent a vectorial form of the usual sigmoidal function. Notice that the input layer of the network is made up of the concatenation of $\mathbf{U}_t$ and $\mathbf{X}_{t-1}$.

Similarly, Jordan's architecture can also be expressed in terms of another simplification of equation 1 as:

$$\begin{aligned} \mathbf{X}_t &= f\left(\mathbf{X}_{t-1}, \mathbf{U}_t, \Theta^f\right) \\ \mathbf{Y}_t &= \mathbf{X}_t \end{aligned} \tag{3}$$

where $\mathbf{X}$ is the vector sequence of states from the output layer (as well as $\mathbf{Y}$ for notation compatibility purposes). The function f needs however to be developed further. It results from the combination of the hidden and the output layer computations:

$$f\left(\mathbf{X}_{t-1}, \mathbf{U}_t, \Theta^f\right) = f_2\left(f_1\left(\mathbf{X}_{t-1}, \mathbf{U}_t, \Theta^{(1)}\right), \Theta^{(2)}\right)$$

with f_1 representing the computation of hidden layer states from input layer states, f_2 the computation of output layer states from hidden layer states and $\Theta^f = (\Theta^{(1)}, \Theta^{(2)})$.

Jordan and Elman networks are typically used for memorizing (and recalling) sequences such as poems (sequences of words), robot arm movements (sequences of positions), etc...

δ-NARMA. The δ-NARMA neural network model (Bonnet et al., 1997c, 1997b) was designed for signal prediction. Let us consider a temporal information sequence, for instance the daily number of railroad travellers from Paris to Lyon. Assume we know this number from three years ago up until yesterday. How can we forecast the number of travellers of today? Such problems can be tackled with usual statistical methods, such as ARMA models. But these methods have at least two important drawbacks: they cannot take into account non-stationary information and they are unable to deal with non-linear temporal relationships. These limitations are the major reasons why the neural network approach has been investigated. The problem is now: how to design a connectionist architecture which is devoted to temporal forecasting?

D. Bonnet answered this question by the design of the δ-NARMA neural network. This network takes as inputs the values of the variable from date $t - p$ to date $t - 1$ $(p \geq 2)$. The output is the predicted value of the variable for date t. The architecture has two levels: the ε-NARMA neuron and the δ-NARMA network.

An ε-NARMA neuron is a recurrent neuron. But, instead of feeding the output value back into the input vector, it feeds the error from $t - q$ to $t - 1$ (i.e. the difference between the predicted output value and the real output value) back into the input vector (see figure 5). In all other ways, it acts like a standard neuron.

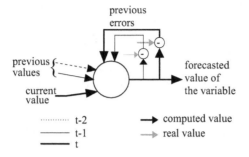

Fig. 5. An ε-NARMA neuron.

There are two main differences with the neuron model of (Frasconi et al., 1992): **the recurring information**, which is the neuron output *error* in the ε-NARMA architecture whereas it is the neuron output itself in Frasconi's model, and *the number of values which are fed back*: only the last one in Frasconi's architecture and the last q values in an ε-NARMA neuron.

A δ-NARMA network consists of an MLP network with ε-NARMA neurons.

The learning algorithm is an adaptation of the classical stochastic back-propagation.

In such a forecasting problem, the time dimension is twofold: an order relation, and a phenomenon which is captured at periodical time points (day or month). These characteristics are grounded in the architecture through two features: the input vector which takes into account the previous values of the forecasted variable, and recurrent connections which mean that the forecasted value depends on the previous errors.

This architecture has been successfully applied to railroad traffic prediction where it gave better results than usual statistical methods (Bonnet et al., 1997a).

3.3   Temporal Extensions of Kohonen Maps

There have been several attempts at integrating temporal information into Self-Organizing Feature Maps[15].

As for other classical connectionist models, a first technique consists of adding temporal information externally, on the input of the map. For example, exponential averaging of inputs and delay lines were considered (Kangas, 1990; Kohonen, 1991).

Another common method is to use layered maps so that the second map tries to capture the spatial dynamics of the input moving on the first map (Kangas, 1990; Morasso, 1991).

---

[15] also called "Kohonen Maps".

A third approach that has been investigated, consists of integrating memory into the map, typically with some exponential decay of activities (e.g. by using leaky-integrator neurons) (Privitera & Morasso, 1993; Chappell & Taylor, 1993).

Another example of this kind of approach is given by the work of (Euliano & Principe, 1996). They add a spatio-temporal coupling to Kohonen maps so as to create temporally and spatially localized neighbourhoods. The spatio-temporal coupling is based on travelling waves of activity which attenuate over time. When these travelling waves reinforce one another, temporal activity wavefronts are created which are then used to enhance the possibility of a given neuron being active[16] in the next cycle.

Finally, more mathematically grounded approaches were developed by (Kopecz, 1995), (Mozayyani et al., 1995) or (Chappelier & Grumbach, 1996).

(Kopecz, 1995) creates a Kohonen map with a lateral coupling structure which has symmetric and antisymmetric coupling (for temporal ordering). Once trained, the antisymmetric weights allow active regions of the map to trigger other regions in the map, thus reproducing the trained temporal pattern.

(Mozayyani et al., 1995) use a coding with complex numbers where the time dimension is embedded into the phase of the complex representation.

(Chappelier & Grumbach, 1996) embed the map into a high dimensional space, classifying temporal inputs as functions of time (i.e. map inputs are no longer 2 or 3-D vectors but higher dimension vectors, each vector representing a function of time).

3.4   Networks of Spiking Neurons

Synfire Chains. Synfire chains were proposed by (Abeles, 1982) as a model of cortical function. A synfire chain consists of small layers of neurons connected together in a feedforward chain so that a wave of activity propagates from layer to layer in the chain. Interest in them has grown because they provide a possible explanation for otherwise mysterious measurements of precise neural activity (so-called "spike") timings. Many spatio-temporal patterns can be stored in a network where each neuron participates in several chains (chains are different but have non-empty intersections) although this introduces crosstalk noise which ultimately limits the network capacity. This capacity is however non zero allowing the effective use of such a model. It should furthermore be noted that since only a small fraction of neurons are active at a given time, many synfire chains can be simultaneously active, providing a possible mechanism for a higher level of organization.

RST. The approach of (Chappelier & Grumbach, 1998) consists of embedding spatial dimensions into the network and integrating time at both neuron and

---

[16] technically: "to win".

connection levels. The aim is to take both spatial relationships (e.g. as between neighbouring pixels in an image) and temporal relationships (e.g. as between consecutive images in a video sequence) into account at the architecture level.

Concerning the spatial aspect, the network is embedded into the actual space (2 or 3-D), the metrics of which directly influence its structure through a connection distribution function. A given number of neurons is randomly distributed in a portion of the space delimited by two planes, the input and output layers. Links are then created between the neurons according to their neighbourhood in the embedding space.

For the temporal aspect, they used a leaky-integrator neuron model with a refractory period and post-synaptic potentials[17]. The implemented model is mainly described by two variables: a membrane potential V and a threshold θ. V is the sum of a specific potential U and an external potential I which stands for the input of the neuron. Most of the time V is less than θ. Whenever V reaches θ, the neuron "fires". It sends a spike to the downstream neurons and changes its state as follows: θ is increased by some amount called adaptation or fatigue and the specific potential U is lowered down to a post-spike value. When the neuron does not fire, the variables U and θ decay exponentially to their resting values.

The input of a given neuron is the sum over space (all the input neurons of the considered neuron) and time (all the firing instants of its input neurons). In order to provide temporal robustness, the spikes sent by inputs are received as post-synaptic potentials described by a function of the kind $t \mapsto t \cdot \exp(1 - t/\tau)$.

The propagation of neuron spikes in the network as spatiotemporal synchronized waves enables RST to perform time and space correlation detection, e.g. motion detection in a video sequence (see figure 6). Spike synchronization plays the main role in RST for filtering static input patterns from moving ones.

4   Applications

A major reason of interest in connectionist models of intelligent processes is that they have been successfully applied to an impressive number of different application domains (e.g. see the book of (Fogelman-Soulié & Gallinari, 1998)). In many applications these models are required to deal with time and exhibit different dynamic behaviour.

4.1   Speech Processing

Most problems from automatic speech recognition are very difficult to address using traditional pattern recognition approaches designed for static data types. Speech has an inherent dynamic nature and, therefore, an effective model needs to be able to capture important temporal dependencies. The use of temporal

---

[17] for more details on "integrate and fire" neurons, we refer to the paper of (Gerstner, 1995) or the book of (MacGregor & Lewis, 1977).

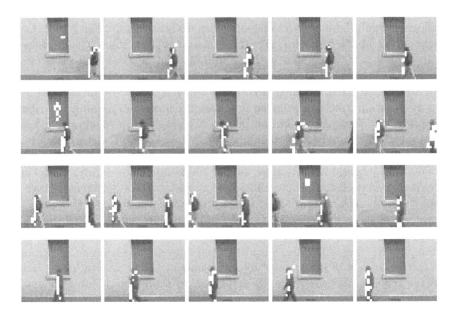

Fig. 6. Application of RST network to motion detection in video sequences. The response of the network (i.e. spiking neurons) is superimposed as white squares on the original input images.

connectionist models for speech processing is motivated by a number of different reasons:

- Speech recognition and speech understanding, due to the huge amount of variability in the signal, require high learning capabilities;
- large-scale speech processing projects (e.g. ARPA) have demonstrated the importance of high performance at the phonetic level;
- the statistical hypotheses of the best current models (hidden Markov models) are quite restrictive;
- learning and prior knowledge can be framed homogeneously in connectionist models;
- connectionist models are an intrinsically parallel computational scheme which turns out to be useful for very demanding applications.

Connectionist models have been proposed for both phoneme recognition or isolated word recognition with interesting results (e.g. see the book of (Gori, 1992)).

Phoneme Recognition. The first problem consists of coding a given speech utterance by means of the corresponding phonemes. The speech signal is typically pre-processed so as to produce a sequence of frames, each composed of a vector of discriminative features (e.g. spectral parameters). In practice, the frames are produced at a rate[18] which is related to the speed of the commands that the brain uses to control the articulatory system. A possible approach to predicting phonemes is to simply rely on a fixed speech window composed of a predefined number of frames. Unfortunately, the information required to predict different phonemes is spread over a significantly varying number of frames (Bourlard & Morgan, 1994, 1998). RNNS are much better suited for dealing with such a problem. The basic problem of choosing a suitable speech window is in fact overcome by the inherent dynamical nature of the model. The input can simply be taken at frame level and the network is expected to capture the temporal dependencies which turn out to be useful for an effective phoneme classification. A possible recurrent architecture for this problem can consist of a simple one-layer network which takes a single speech frame as input and in which only self-loop connections are adopted. The speech signal is processed frame by frame along time and for each speech frame the neural network outputs a prediction of the corresponding phoneme. It has been pointed out that this architecture turns out to be suitable to incorporate the *forgetting behaviour* that a phoneme classifier is expected to exhibit (Bengio et al., 1992). Basically, the phoneme classification is supposed to depend on the speech frame being processed and on the close frames, but it is supposed not to depend on remote information. Very successful results for the problem of phoneme recognition on the DARPA-TIMIT speech data base have been found by (Robinson, 1994), where, in addition to the adoption of recurrent architectures, proper integration schemes with hidden Markov models are proposed.

Isolated Word Recognition. In principle, RNNs can also be used for isolated word recognition. Isolated words are in fact sequences of speech frames that can properly be labelled at the end by a target for specifying the sequence membership. Unfortunately, in spite of the experimental efforts of many research groups, this direct approach has not produced very successful results yet. There are at least two major reasons for this experimental lack of result. First, isolated words are sequences composed of hundreds of frames and it is now well-known that long-term dependencies are difficult to capture by a gradient-based learning algorithm (Bengio et al., 1994). Hence, RNN-based classifiers develop the trend to perform the prediction on the basis of the last part of the word, which is in fact a strong limitation especially when dealing with large dictionaries. Second, regardless of the architecture and weights, RNNs are difficult to use when the number of classes becomes very large. Basically, RNNs inherit the property of MLPs in exhibiting very strong discrimination capabilities but also the poor scaling with respect to the number of classes.

4.2   Language Processing

Theoretical foundations of natural language have been swinging, pendulum-like, between fully symbolic-based models, to approaches more or less based on stati-

---

[18] in the order of magnitude of 10 ms.

stics. Since the renewal of interest in neural networks, the connectionist approach has been immediately recognized as a neat way of dealing with the inherent uncertainty of natural languages. Languages, however, have also an inherently sequential nature and, therefore, only connectionist models that incorporate time[19] are good candidates for language processing. Typical tasks in language processing propose time as an external variable acting at different levels. For instance, lexical analyses require processing letters of a given alphabet in a sequential way, whereas in syntactical analyses, time is used to scan different words composing a sentence. In the last few years, RNNs appeared to be very well-suited for performing interesting language processing tasks.

Prediction of Linguistic Elements. Let us consider the problem of predicting linguistic elements. A preliminary investigation was carried out by (Servan-Schreiber et al., 1991) concerning the prediction of terminal items for Reber's grammar (Reber, 1976) (see figure 7).

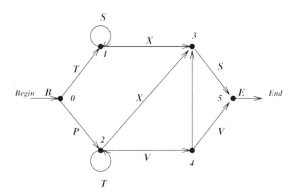

Fig. 7. An automaton representation of Reber's finite-state grammar.

Elman's recurrent network was used for the experiments. The network had an input aimed at coding the symbols and some context units representing the state. The output layer had the same number of units as the input layer and one-hot coding[20] was adopted for the symbols of both layers. For each time step, a symbol from the alphabet of a Reber string was provided at the input and the recurrent network was asked to predict the next one. The training was carried out with a sample of Reber strings and the network subsequently exhibited very good generalization capabilities. Interestingly enough, the network developed automata-like internal representations and was even capable of performing correctly on arbitrarily long sequences.

---

[19] at least as an order relation.

[20] an exclusive coding in which one and only one output neuron is high.

Early experiments shown in the article of (Elman, 1990) were aimed at predicting the next word of a given part of a small sentence. The lexical items (inputs and outputs) were presented in a localist form using basis vectors. Hence, lexical items were orthogonal to one another and there was no encoding of the item's category membership.

Other interesting language processing tasks were presented by (Elman, 1991). His simple RNN was trained to learn the correctness of a given sentence on the basis of the presentation of positive and negative examples. For instance, Elman studied the problem of detecting the *agreement* of nouns with their verbs. Thus, for example, `John feeds dogs` and `Girls sees Mary` are grammatical and un-grammatical, respectively. No information concerning the grammatical role (subject/object, etc.) is provided to the network. The grammar of the language used in the experiment is given in Table 2

S → NP VP `` . ''
NP → PropN | N | N RC
VP → V (NP)
RC → who NP VP | who VP (NP)
N → boy | girl | cat | dog | boys | girls | cats | dogs
PropN → John | Mary
V → chase | feed | see | hear | walk | live | chases | feeds | sees | hears | walks | lives

Additional restrictions:

- number agreement between N and V within clause, and (where appropriate) between head N and subordinate V.
- verb arguments:
  chase, feed: require a direct object
  see, hear: optionally allow a direct object
  walk, live: preclude a direct object
  (observed also for head/verb relations in relative clauses)

Table 2. The grammar used by (Elman, 1990) for different language tasks, like noun-verb agreement, verb argument structure, and interactions with relative clauses.

The network is expected to learn that there are items which function as what we would call nouns, verbs, etc. and then must learn which items are examples of singular or plural, and which nouns are subjects and objects. Related successful experiments have been carried out concerning the verb argument structure, and the interactions with relative clauses.

Grammatical Inference. The theoretical result stating that a RNN can behave as an automaton is fully illustrated by some applications of RNNs to natural language processing. Unlike automata, however, the neural activations are continuous-valued variables and, therefore, an understanding of the network's internal representation developed during the training, is non trivial. RNNs are basically adaptive parsers the behaviour of which depends upon the parameters developed during the training. Formally, an *adaptive neural parser* can be regarded as a 4-tuple $\{U, X, \Phi, Z\}$, where $U \in R^M$ is the *alphabet of symbols*, $X \in R^N$ is the *state*, $\Phi(W) : R^N \times R^M \to R^N$ is the *state transition function* which depends on a vector of parameters $W \in R^P$, and $Z : R^N \to \{0, 1\}$ is the *decision function* that decides whether a given state is accepted or not. Given a set of labelled examples, one could try to relate the learning of the network and the developed internal representation with the grammar which generates the language. In the literature, the grammatical inference of the hidden rule is stated as the search for a parser capable of classifying the strings. The inference process adapts the neural parser to the given learning set by means of a search in the parameter space that defines the state transition function $\Phi(W)$.

In order to process symbolic strings by neural networks, each symbol of the input alphabet Σ has to be encoded. Basically, Σ is mapped to a set of vectors $\mathcal{U} = \{U_1, \ldots, U_S\}$ ($U_k \in \mathcal{R}^M$) and each string of Σ^* corresponds to a sequence of vectors that is used as input to the RNN[21]. The classification of each string is decided looking at the output of neuron N at the end of the input sequence.

The training set is composed of a set of L pairs (s, d), where $s \in \mathcal{U}^*$ and $d \in \{d^+, d^-\}$, being $d^+, d^- \in \mathcal{R}$. The learning algorithm adapts the neural network parameters by using a back-propagation through time (e.g. see the paper of (Williams & Peng, 1990)).

When processing symbolic strings by RNNs, the state vector X describes complex trajectories. As proposed by (Kolen, 1994), these trajectories can be studied in the framework of Iterated Function Systems (IFSs).

Basically, the symbolic interpretation emerges from partitioning the state space into a set of regions that are associated to the states of a finite machine. The volume of these regions defines the *resolution* of the extraction process.

The number of such regions provides interesting information concerning the rule extraction process. The more regions approximate the network trajectories, the more detailed description and, consequently, the more likely is the extracted machine to have a larger number of states (see figure 8). Equivalent states can of course be removed by using a state minimization algorithm for finite state machines. There is experimental evidence that beyond a certain number of clusters, the extraction of the finite machine with the corresponding state minimization does not produce an increasing number of states but, instead, a maximum value is reached.

These basic steps for performing grammatical inference in the case of finite state machines are summarized in figure 9.

Most problems of language processing have been tackled by using Elman's recurrent network. However, second-order RNNs are more suitable for extracting

---

[21] The notation Σ^* denotes the set of all the possible sequences created using the vectors contained in Σ.

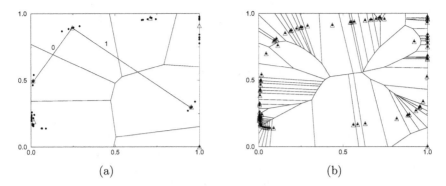

Fig. 8. Finite State Automaton (FSA) extraction algorithm using a neural parser with a two-dimensional state space. (a) The number of regions is 7. The extracted FSA approximates exactly the network behaviour on all the strings with length up to 6. The transition rules from state 1 are shown. (b) The number of regions is 77. This number of clusters is necessary in order to have the same behaviour of the network on all the strings with length up to 11. The corresponding minimization yields an equivalent 31 states machine.

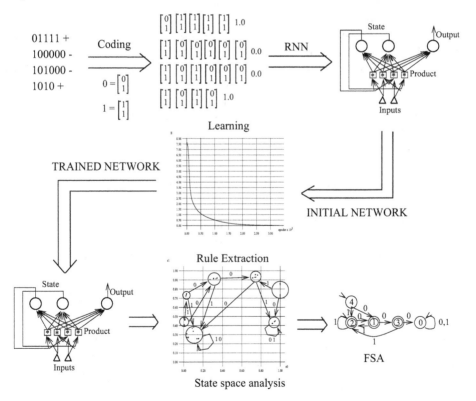

Fig. 9. Grammatical inference using neural networks: The learned configuration is subsequently used for the extraction of symbolic rules.

the internal representation and, consequently for grammatical inference (e.g. see the paper of (Miller. & Giles, 1993) or the one of (Omlin & Giles, 1996)).

Parsing with Simple-Synchrony Networks. Simple Synchrony Networks (SSNs) (Lane & Henderson, 1998, 2000) are an extension of RNNs, adding another usage of internal time in order to represent structural constituents[22]. This extension does however not change the way external time[23] is dealt with.

More precisely, SSNs can be seen as RNNs of pulsing units, which enables them to represent structures and to generalize across structural constituents. The SSN approach consists in representing structural constituents directly, rather than using usual RNN indirect encoding. The structural relationships are represented by synchrony of neuron activation pulses, leading to an incremental representation of the structure over the constituents. Indeed, SNNs extend the incremental outputs of RNNs with as many output neurons as required by Temporal Synchrony Variable Binding (Shastri & Ajjanagadde, 1993). The central idea is to divide each time period into several phases, each phase being associated with a unique constituent. For an input sentence of n words, the representation of the syntactic structure in the output is achieved by the unfolding of that structure in a temporal sequence of n phases in which unit synchrony represents some relationship between constituents in the structure (for instance the father-son relationship).

SSNs have been successfully applied on standard Natural Language parsing problems: taking English sentences drawn from a corpus of naturally occurring text, the model incrementally outputs a hierarchical structure representing how the words fit together to form constituents (i.e. a parse tree of the input sentence).

5   Extension: From Temporal to Structured Data Types

The learning of sequential information is the first step toward the adaptive computation of dynamic data types. RNNs, as presented in section 3.2, were conceived so as to exhibit a dynamic behaviour for incorporating time, i.e. dealing with temporal sequences.

From the structure point of view, any discrete sequence of real-valued variables defined over a time interval can be regarded as a list, which is in fact the simplest conceivable dynamic data type. RNNs can therefore be seen as good candidates for list processing and even more structured data types.

Early research in this direction was carried out by (Pollack, 1990) who introduced the RAAM model, which is capable of dealing with trees with labels in the leaves.

---

[22] non-terminals in the case of Natural Language parsing
[23] word sequence in the case of Natural Language sentences.

Processing Lists. If we represent an input signal sequence **U** of a RNN by a list in which each node, indexed by v, contains a real-valued vector $\mathbf{U}_v$, the general computational scheme described by equations 1 (page 114), and aimed at producing the output list **Y**, can be written:

$$\begin{aligned} \mathbf{X}_v &= f\left(q^{-1}\mathbf{X}_v, \mathbf{U}_v, v, \Theta_v^f\right) \\ \mathbf{Y}_v &= g\left(\mathbf{X}_v, v, \Theta_v^g\right), \end{aligned} \tag{4}$$

where q^{-1} is the operator that, when applied to state $\mathbf{X}_a$, returns the state $\mathbf{X}_b$ of the next node of a.[24]

The model defined by equation 4 can itself be structured in the sense that the generic variable $X_{i,v}$ might be independent of $q^{-1}X_{j,v}$. Likewise other statements of independence might involve input-state variables and/or state-output variables. An explicit statement of independence is a sort of prior knowledge on the mapping that the machine is expected to learn. In general these statements can also be different for different nodes and can be conveniently expressed by a graphical structure that is referred to as a *recursive network*.

Lists can in fact be processed by means of an *encoding network* which is constructed by unfolding the input through the list. The corresponding network is created by associating each node of the list with input, state, and output variables, respectively. The state variables are connected graphically following the reverse direction of the list traversal, and the input and the output variables are connected with the associated state variables.

Generalization to Directed Ordered Acyclic Graphs. A nice extension of time sequences can be gained in the framework of dynamic data structures. Basically, giving a list corresponds with assigning a set of tokens where an order relation is defined. When paying attention to "temporal relations", a directed graph seems to be the most natural extension of list, in the sense that any directed graph is a way of defining a partial order over a set of homogeneous tokens. In particular, let us consider a directed ordered acyclic graph (DOAG) so that for any node v one can identify a set, potentially empty, of ordered children $ch[v]$. For each node, one can extend the next-state equation (4) as follows

$$\begin{aligned} \mathbf{X}_v &= f\left(\mathbf{X}_{ch[v]}, \mathbf{U}_v, v, \Theta_v^f\right) \\ \mathbf{Y}_v &= g\left(\mathbf{X}_v, v, \Theta_v^g\right). \end{aligned} \tag{5}$$

In the case of binary trees, the state associated with each node is calculated as a function of the attached label and of the states associated with the left and right children, respectively. The operators q_L^{-1} and q_R^{-1} make it possible to address the information associated with the left and right children of a given node and, therefore, straightforwardly generalize the temporal delay operator q^{-1}. Of course, for any node, the children must be ordered so as to be able to

---

[24] The operator q^{-1} is introduced here in order to make the extension to more complex data structures easier. In the context of lists representing temporal sequences, it corresponds to the former time step, that is $q^{-1}\mathbf{X}_t \doteq \mathbf{X}_{t-1}$.

produce different outputs for binary trees $\{r, L, R\}$ and $\{r, R, L\}$. A list is just a special case of a binary tree in which one of the children is null.

The construction holds for any DOAG provided that a special node s of the graph, referred to as the *supersource*, is given together with the graph.

The computation of $\mathbf{Y}_v$ in the case of graphs is also more involved than the one associated with the simple recursive model of equations (4). The DOAG somehow represents the state update scheme, i.e. a graphical representation of the computation taking place in the recursive neural network (see figure 10). This graph plays its own role in the computation process either because of the information attached to its nodes or for its topology. This state update graphical representation emphasizes the structure of independence of some variables in the state-based model of equation 5. For instance, a classic structure of independence arises when the connections of any two state variables $\mathbf{X}_v$ and $\mathbf{X}_w$ only take place between components $X_{i,v}$ and $X_{i,w}$ with the same index i. In the case of lists, this assumption means that only *local-feedback* connections are permitted for the state variables. Basically, the knowledge of a recursive network yields topological constraints which often make it possible to cut the number of learning parameters significantly.

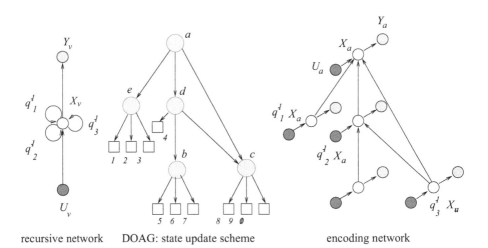

recursive network   DOAG: state update scheme   encoding network

Fig. 10. Construction of the encoding network corresponding to a recursive network and a directed ordered acyclic graph. Proper frontier (initial) states are represented by squares. The encoding network inherits the structure of the input graph. When making the functional dependence explicit, the encoding network becomes a neural network, which is used to calculate the corresponding output.

Furthermore, the information attached to the recursive network needs to be integrated with a specific choice of functions f and g which must be suitable for learning the parameters. A connectionist assumption for functions f and g turns out to be adequate especially to fulfil computational complexity requirements. The first-order recursive neural network is one of the simplest architectural choices. In this case, equation 5 becomes:

$$\mathbf{X}_v = \sigma \left(\mathbf{A}_v \cdot q^{-1}\mathbf{X}_v + \mathbf{B}_v \cdot \mathbf{U}_v\right)$$
$$\mathbf{Y}_v = \sigma \left(\mathbf{C}_v \cdot \mathbf{X}_v\right).$$

$$(6)$$

Matrix $\mathbf{A}_v \in \mathcal{R}^{n,n}$ contains the weights associated with the feedback connections, whereas matrix $\mathbf{B}_v \in \mathcal{R}^{n,m}$ contains the weights associated with the input-neuron connections. Finally, $\mathbf{C}_v \in \mathcal{R}^{p,n}$ is the parameter for the definition of the state-output map. These equations produce the next-state and the output values by relying on a first-order equation, in which the outputs are bounded by using a squashing function[25]. An in-depth analysis of this models can be found in (Frasconi, Gori, & Sperduti, 1998; Frasconi, 1998).

Concerning the learning, since the structure of the encoding neural network is inherited by both the DOAG and the recursive network, the encoding neural network is essentially a feedforward network. Hence the back-propagation algorithm for feedforward neural networks can be conveniently extended to data structures. The learning algorithm is in this case referred to as *back-propagation through structure* (Sperduti, 1998).

6   Conclusion

We gave in this chapter an overview of what is presently going on in the field of temporal connectionist models. The aim was not to be as exhaustive as possible but to exhibit the main concepts, ideas and applications in this area.

Temporal connectionist models already have the power to do arbitrary computations with time-varying data with the advantage of learning from examples. Fundamental theorems about their potential capabilities already exist. They however still need to find efficient ways to be used in practice: existing training methods still suffer from their inability to deal with very long time dependencies. Although the success so far of capturing and classifying temporal information with neural networks is still limited, the approach looks very promising and benefits from a rapid growth.

Acknowledgements. The authors would like to thank James B. Henderson, the reviewers and editors for their helpful comments on this chapter, and Peter Weyer-Brown for his careful proofreading of the manuscript.

---

[25] In equation 6, $\sigma(\cdot)$ denotes a vector of squashing functions operating on n of neurons.

References

Abbott, L. F., & Kepler, T. B. (1990). Model neurons : from Hodgkin-Huxley to Hopfield. In Garrido, L. (Ed.), *Statistical Mechanics of Neural Networks*, pp. 5–18. Springer.

Abeles, M. (1982). *Local cortical circuits: an electrophysiological study (Studies of brain functions, Vol. 6)*. Springer Verlag.

Amit, D. J. (1988). Neural network counting chimes. *Proc. Nat. Acad. Sci. USA, 85*, 2141–2145.

Back, A., & Tsoi, A. (1991). FIR and IIR Synapses: A New Neural Network Architecture for Time Series Modeling. *Neural Computation, 3*(3), 375–385.

Bengio, Y., Cardin, R., de Mori, R., & Merlo, E. (1989). Programmable Execution of Multi-Layered Networks for Automatic Speech Recognition. *Communications of the ACM, 32*, 195–199.

Bengio, Y., Frasconi, P., & Simard, P. (1993). The problem of learning long-term dependencies in recurrent networks. In *IEEE Transactions on Neural Networks*, pp. 1183–1195 San Francisco. IEEE Press. (invited paper).

Bengio, Y., Mori, R. D., & Gori, M. (1992). Learning the Dynamic Nature of Speech with Back-propagation for Sequences. *Pattern Recognition Letters, 13*(5), 375–386.

Bengio, Y., Simard, P., & Frasconi, P. (1994). Learning long-term dependencies is difficult. *IEEE Trans. on Neural Networks, 5*(2), 157–166.

Béroule, D. (1987). Guided propagation inside a topographic memory. In *1st int. conf. on neural networks*, pp. 469–476 San Diego. IEEE.

Bodenhausen, U., & Waibel, A. (1991). The Tempo2 algorithm: adjusting time delays by supervised learning. In Lippmann, R. P., Moody, J., & Touretzky, D. S. (Eds.), *Advances in Neural Information Processing Systems*, Vol. 3, pp. 155–161 San Mateo (CA). Morgan Kaufmann.

Bonnet, D., Perrault, V., & Grumbach, A. (1997a). Daily Passenger Traffic Forecasting using δ-NARMA Neural Networks. In *Proceedings of the World Congress on Railroad Research (WCRR'97)*, pp. CD–ROM.

Bonnet, D., Perrault, V., & Grumbach, A. (1997b). δ-NARMA neural network: a new approach to signal prediction. *IEEE Transaction on Signal Processing, 45*(11), 2799–2810.

Bonnet, D., Perrault, V., & Grumbach, A. (1997c). δ-NARMA neural networks: a connectionist extension of ARARMA models. In Verleysen, M. (Ed.), *Proceedings of the European Symposium on Artificial Neural Networks*, pp. 127–132 Brussels (Belgium). D Facto.

Bourlard, H., & Morgan, N. (1994). *Connectionist Speech Recognition – A Hybrid Approach*. Kluwer Academic Publishers.

Bourlard, H., & Morgan, N. (1998). Hybrid HMM/ANN Systems for Speech Recognition: Overview and New Research Directions. In Giles, C. L., & Gori, M. (Eds.), *Adaptive Processing of Sequences and Data Structures*, Vol. 1387 of *Lecture Notes in Artificial Intelligence*, pp. 389–417. Springer.

Catfolis, T. (1994). Mapping a complex temporal problem into a combination of static and dynamic neural networks. *Sigart Bulletin, 5*(3), 23–28.

Chappelier, J.-C., & Grumbach, A. (1994). Time in Neural Networks. *Sigart Bulletin, 5*(3), 3–10.

Chappelier, J.-C., & Grumbach, A. (1996). A Kohonen Map for Temporal Sequences. In *NEURAP'95* Marseille.

Chappelier, J.-C., & Grumbach, A. (1998). RST: a Connectionist Architecture to Deal with Spatiotemporal Relationships. *Neural Computation*, *10*(4), 883–902.

Chappell, G. J., & Taylor, J. G. (1993). The Temporal Kohonen Map. *NN*, *6*, 441–445.

Cleeremans, A., Servan-Schreiber, D., & McClelland, J. (1989). Finite State Automata and Simple Recurrent Networks. *Neural Computation*, *1*, 372–381.

Connor, J., Atlas, L. E., & Martin, D. R. (1992). Recurrent network and NARMA modelling. In Hanson, S. J., Lippmann, R. P., Moody, J. E., & Touretzky, D. S. (Eds.), *Advances in Neural Information Processing Systems*, Vol. 4, pp. 301–308. Morgan Kaufmann, San Mateo (CA).

Connor, J., & Martin, D. R. (1994). Recurrent neural networks and robust time series prediction. *IEEE Transactions on Neural Networks*, *5*(2), 240–253.

de Vries, B., & Principe, J. C. (1992). The Gamma model. A new neural model for temporal processing. *Neural Networks*, *5*, 565–576.

Elman, J. L. (1990). Finding structure in time. *Cognitive Science*, *14*(2), 179–211.

Elman, J. L. (1991). Distributed representations, simple recurrent networks, and grammatical structure. *Machine Learning*, *7*(2), 195–226.

Euliano, N. R., & Principe, J. C. (1996). Spatio-Temporal Self-Organizing Feature Maps. In *IJCNN'96*, Vol. 4, pp. 1900–1905.

Fogelman-Soulié, F., & Gallinari, P. (Eds.). (1998). *Industrial Applications of Neural Networks*. World Scientific Publishing Co.

Frasconi, P. (1998). An introduction to learning structured information. In Giles, C. L., & Gori, M. (Eds.), *Adaptive Processing of Sequences and Data Structures*, Vol. 1387 of *Lecture Notes in Artificial Intelligence*, pp. 99–120. Springer.

Frasconi, P., Gori, M., & Soda, G. (1992). Local Feedback Multi-Layered Networks. *Neural Computation*, *4*(2), 120–130.

Frasconi, P., Gori, M., & Sperduti, A. (1998). A general framework for adaptive processing of data structures. *IEEE Transactions on Neural Networks*, *9*, 768–786.

Funahashi, K., & Nakamura, Y. (1993). Approximations of dynamical systems by continuous time recurrent neural networks. *Neural Networks*, *6*(6), 801–806.

Gerstner, W. (1995). Time structure of the activity in neural network models. *Physical Review E*, *51*, 738–758.

Goldberg, K. Y., & Pearlmutter, B. A. (1989). Using Backpropagation with Temporal Windows to Learn the dynamics of the CMU Direct-Drive Arm II. In Touretzky, D. S. (Ed.), *Advances in Neural Information Processing Systems*, Vol. 1. Morgan-Kaufmann.

Gori, M. (Ed.). (1992). *Neural Networks for Speech Processing*. Lint.

Gorman, R. P., & Sejnowski, T. J. (1988). Analysis of hidden units in a layered network trained to classify sonar targets. *NN*, *1*, 75–89.

Hirch, M. W. (1991). Network dynamics : Principles and problems. In Paseman, F., & Doebner, H. (Eds.), *Neurodynamics, Series on neural networks*, pp. 3–29. World Scientific.

Hochreiter, S., & Schmidhuber, J. (1997a). Bridging Long Time Lags by Weight Guessing and "Lond Short Term Memory". In Silva, F. L., Principe, J. C., & Almeida, L. B. (Eds.), *Spatiotemporal Models in Biological and Artificial Systems*, pp. 65–72. IOS Press.

Hochreiter, S., & Schmidhuber, J. (1997b). Long Short-Term Memory. *NC*, *9*(8), 1735–1780.

Horn, D., & Usher, M. (1991). Parallel activation of memories in an oscillatory neural network. *Neural Computation*, *3*(1), 31–43.

Hornik, K. (1991). Approximation capabilities of multilayer feedforward networks. *NN*, *4*, 251–257.

Hornik, K., Stinchcombe, M., & White, H. (1989). Multilayer feedforward neural networks are universal approximators. *NN*, *2*(5), 359–366.

Jacquemin, C. (1994). A Temporal Connectionnist Approach to Natural Language. *Sigart Bulletin*, *5*(3), 12–22.

Jordan, M. I. (1986). Attractor dynamics and parallelism in a connectionist sequential machine. In *Proc. of the 8th annual conference on Cognitive Science*. Erlbaum.

Kangas, J. (1990). Time-Delayed Self-Organizing Maps. In *Proceedings of IJCNN'90*, Vol. II, pp. 331–336.

Kohonen, T. (1991). The HyperMap Architecture. In T. Kohonen, K. Makisara, O. S., & Kangas, J. (Eds.), *Artificial Neural Networks*, pp. 1357–1360. North-Holland.

Kolen, J. F. (1994). Recurrent Networks: State Machines or Iterated Function Systems?. In Mozer, M. C., Smolensky, P., Touretzky, D. S., Elman, J. L., & Weigend, A. S. (Eds.), *Proceedings of the 1993 Connectionist Models Summer School*, pp. 203–210 Hillsdale NJ. Erlbaum.

Kopecz, K. (1995). Unsupervised Learning of Sequences on Maos with Lateral Connectivity. In *Proceedings of ICANN'95*, Vol. 2, pp. 431–436.

Lane, P. C. R., & Henderson, J. B. (1998). Simple Synchrony Networks: Learning to parse natural language with Temporal Synchrony Variable Binding. In Noklasson, L., Boden, M., & Ziemke, T. (Eds.), *Proc. of 8th Int. Conf. on Artificial Neural Networks (ICANN'98)*, pp. 615–620 Skövde (Sweden).

Lane, P. C. R., & Henderson, J. B. (2000). Incremental Syntactic Parsing of Natural Language Corpora with Simple Synchrony Networks. *IEEE Transactions on Knowledge and Data Engineering, to appear*. Special Issue on Commenctionist Models for Learning in Structured Domains.

Lang, K. J., Waibel, A. H., & Hinton, G. E. (1990). A time-delay neural-network architecture for isolated word recognition. *Neural Networks*, *3*(1), 23–44.

Lapedes, A. S., & Farber, R. (1987). Nonlinear signal processing using neural networks: prediction and system modelling. Tech. rep. LA-UR-87-2662, Los Alamos National Laboratory, Los Alamos (CA).

Lumer, E. D., & Huberman, B. A. (1992). Binding hierarchies : a basis for dynamic perceptual grouping. *NC*, **4**, 341–355.

Maass, W. (1994). On the computationnal complexity of networks of spiking neurons. In *NIPS'94 Proc.*, Vol. 7. MIT-Press.

Maass, W. (1996). Lower bounds for the computational power of networks of spiking neurons. *Neural Computation*, *8*(1), 1–40.

Maass, W. (1997a). Analog Computing with Temporal Coding in Networks of Spiking Neurons. In Silva, F. L., Principe, J. C., & Almeida, L. B. (Eds.), *Spatiotemporal Models in Biological and Artificial Systems*, pp. 97–104. IOS Press.

Maass, W. (1997b). Networks of spiking neurons: the third generation of neural network models. *Neural Networks*, *10*(9), 1659–1671.

MacGregor, R. J., & Lewis, E. R. (1977). *Neural Modeling, Electric signal processing in the neurons systems*. Plenum Press.

Miller., C. B., & Giles, C. L. (1993). Experimental Comparison of the Effect of Order in Recurrent Neural Networks. *Int. Journal of Pattern Recognition and Artificial Intelligence*, *7*(4), 849–872.

Morasso, P. (1991). Self-Organizing Feature Maps for Cursive Script Recognition. In T. Kohonen, K. Makisara, O. S., & Kangas, J. (Eds.), *Artificial Neural Networks*, pp. 1323–1326. North-Holland.

Mozayyani, N., Alanou, V., Dreyfus, J., & Vaucher, G. (1995). A Spatio-Temporal Data-Coding Applied to Kohonen Maps. In *International Conference on Artificial Neural Networks*, Vol. 2, pp. 75–79.

Mozer, M. C. (1994). Neural Net Architectures for Temporal Sequence Processing. In Weigend, A., & Gershenfeld, N. (Eds.), *Time Series Prediction*, pp. 243–264. Addison–Wesley.

Mozer, M. (1989). A Focused Back-Propagation Algorithm for Temporal Pattern Recognition. *Complex Systems*, *3*, 349–381.

Narendra, K. P., & Parthasarathy, K. (1990). Identification and Control of Dynamical Systems using Neural Networks. *IEEE Transactions on Neural Networks*, *1*, 4–27.

Nerrand, O., Roussel-Ragot, P., Personnaz, L., Dreyfus, G., & Marcos, S. (1993). Neural networks and nonlinear adaptive filtering: unifiying concepts and new algorithms. *Neural Computation*, *5*, 165–197.

Omlin, C., & Giles, C. (1996). Constructing Deterministic Finite-State Automata in Recurrent Neural Networks. *Journal of the ACM*, *43*(6), 937–972.

Pollack, J. B. (1990). Recursive distributed representations. *Artificial Intelligence*, *46*(1–2), 77–106.

Privitera, C. M., & Morasso, P. (1993). A New Approach to Storing Temporal Sequences. In *Proc. IJCNN'93*, pp. 2745–2748.

Ramacher, U. (1993). Hamiltonian dynamics of neural networks. *Neural Networks*, *6*(4), 547–557.

Reber, A. S. (1976). Implicit learing of synthetic languages: The role of the instructional set. *Journal of Experimental Psycology: Human Learning and Memory*, *2*, 88–94.

Rinzel, J., & Ermentrout, G. B. (1989). Analysis of Neural Excitability and Oscillations. In Koch, C., & Segev, I. (Eds.), *Methods in Neural Modeling – From Synapses to Networks*, pp. 135–169. MIT Press.

Robinson, T. (1994). An application of recurrentn nets to phone probability estimation. *IEEE Trans. on Neural Networks*, *5*(2), 298–305.

Rohwer, R. (1994). The Time Dimension of Neural Network Models. *Sigart Bulletin*, *5*(3), 36–44.

Servan-Schreiber, Cleeremans, A., & McClelland, J. (1991). Graded state machines: The representation of temporal contingencies in simple recurrent networks. *Machine Learning*, *7*(2), 161–194.

Shastri, L., & Ajjanagadde, V. (1993). From simple associations to systematic reasoning: a connectionist representation of rules, variables and dynamic bindings using temporal synchrony. *Behavioral and Brain Sciences*, *16*, 417–494.

Siegelmann, H. T., & Sontag, E. D. (1995). On the Computational Power of Neural Nets. *Journal of Computers and System Sciences*, *50*, 132–150.

Simpson, P. K., & Deich, R. O. (1988). Neural networks, fuzzy logic and acoustic pattern generation. In *Proceedings of AAAIC'88*.

Sperduti, A. (1998). Neural Network for Processing Data Structures. In Giles, C. L., & Gori, M. (Eds.), *Adaptive Processing of Sequences and Data Structures*, Vol. 1387 of *Lecture Notes in Artificial Intelligence*, pp. 121–144. Springer.

Tank, D. W., & Hopfield, J. J. (1987). Neural computation by concentring information in time. *Proc. Nat. Acad. Sci. USA*, *84*, 1896–1900.

Tsoi, A. C. (1998). Recurent Neural Network Architectures: An Overview. In Giles, C. L., & Gori, M. (Eds.), *Adaptive Processing of Sequences and Data Structures*, Vol. 1387 of *Lecture Notes in Artificial Intelligence*, pp. 1–26. Springer.

Tsoi, A. C., & Back, A. (1997). Discrete time recurrent neural network architectures: A unifying review. *NeuroComputing*, *15*(3 & 4), 183–223.

Unnikrishnan, K. P., Hopfield, J. J., & Tank, D. W. (1991). Connected-digit speaker-dependent speech recognition using a neural network with time delay connections. *IEEE Transaction on Signal Processing*, *39*(3), 698–713.

Vaucher, G. (1996). Neuro-Biological Bases for Spario-Temporal Data Coding in Artificial Neural Networks. *Lecture Notes in Computer Science, 1112*, 703ff.

Williams, R. J., & Peng, J. (1990). An Efficient Gradient-Based Algorithm for On-Line Training of Recurrent Network Trajectories. *Neural Computation, 2*(4), 490–501.

Williams, R., & Zipser, D. (1989). A Learning Algorithm for Continually Running Fully Recurrent Neural Networks. *Neural Computation, 1*(3), 270–280.

On the Need for a Neural Abstract Machine

Diego Sona and Alessandro Sperduti

Dipartimento di Informatica
Università di Pisa

1 Introduction

The complexity of learning tasks and their variety, as well as the number of different neural networks models for sequence learning is quite high. Moreover, in addition to architectural details and training algorithms peculiarities, there are other relevant factors which add complexity to the management of a neural network for the adaptive processing of sequences. For example, training heuristics, such as adaptive learning rates, regularization, and pruning, are very important, as well as insertion of a priori domain knowledge. All these issues must be considered and matched with the complexity of the application domain at hand. This means that the successful application of a neural network to a real world domain has to answer to several questions on the type of architecture, training algorithms, training heuristics, and knowledge insertion, according to the problem complexity.

At present, these questions cannot be easily answered, due to the lack of a computational tool encompassing all the relevant issues. We observe that some authors [45] [67] [70] [12] [19] [36] [20] [24] tried to unify different architectures and learning algorithms. However, none of their proposals is complete. The same situation is encountered when considering software simulators and neural specification languages: all of them are restricted to specific models and do not allow the user to develop new models.

On the basis of these observations, we argue for the need for a Neural Abstract Machine, i.e., a formal, and precise definition of the basic (and relevant) objects as well as operations which are manipulated and performed, respectively, by neural computation.

To define the Neural Abstract Machine, we suggest to use Abstract State Machines (ASMs). ASMs have been extensively used for the formal design and analysis of various hardware systems, algorithms and programming languages semantics. They allow to specify formal systems in a very simple way, while preserving mathematical soundness and completeness.

In Section 2 we briefly review the different issues arising when considering learning sequences. On the basis of this review, in Section 3, we argue about the need for a Neural Abstract Machine. Abstract State Machines are briefly presented in Section 4 and a very simple example of how they can be applied to neural networks is discussed in Sections 5 and 6. Conclusions are drawn in Section 7.

R. Sun and C.L. Giles (Eds.): Sequence Learning, LNAI 1828, pp. 135–161, 2000.
© Springer-Verlag Berlin Heidelberg 2000

2   A Brief Overview on Sequence Learning by Neural Networks

In the following we will briefly outline the main issues in sequence learning by neural networks. The presence of a large number of different neural architectures and learning algorithms is pointed out. The main computational and complexity known results on architecture power and learning are discussed. The most important issues concerning training heuristics and knowledge insertion in recurrent networks are briefly reported. Moreover, we argue about the difficulties in developing successful neural solutions for application problems.

2.1   Domains, Tasks, and Approaches to Sequence Learning

Informally, a sequence is a serially ordered set of atomic entities. Sequences (the simplest kind of dynamic data structure) typically occur in learning domains with temporal structure, where each atom corresponds to a discrete *time* point. For example, variables in a financial forecasting problem are sampled at successive instants, yielding an instance space formed by discrete-time sequences of observations. Automatic speech recognition systems contain front-end acoustic modules that learn to translate sequences of acoustic attributes into sequences of phonetic symbols. Other examples of temporal data can be found in problems of automatic control or digital signal processing. In all these cases, data gathering involves a digital sampling process. Hence, serial order in sequences is immediately associated with the common physical meaning of time. There are however other kinds of data that can be conveniently represented as sequences. For example, consider a string of symbols obtained after preprocessing in syntactic approaches to pattern recognition. Also consider problems of molecular biology, in which DNA chains are represented as strings of symbols associated to protein components. Such strings can also be effectively represented as sequences, although *time* in these cases do not play any role in a strictly physical meaning. Time, in the domain of sequences, has therefore the more abstract meaning of *coordinate* used to address simple entities which are *serially ordered* to form a more complex structure. More complex situations arises when considering sequences combining both symbolic and numerical data, as may happen in medical applications.

There are different learning tasks involving sequences. Typical tasks are classification, time series prediction (with different order of prediction), sequential transduction, and control. Sometimes it is also useful to try to approximate probability distributions over sequence domains, as well as to discover meaningful clusters of sequences. This is particularly useful when performing Knowledge Discovery and Data Mining.

The complexity and variety of problems in sequence learning is so high that it would be naive to think that a single approach suffices to master the field. According to the nature of data and learning tasks, different approaches has been defined and explored, such as Recurrent Neural Networks, Hidden Markov

Models, Reinforcement Learning (dynamic programming), Evolutionary Computation, Rule-based Systems, Fuzzy Systems, and so on. Recently, the feeling that a combination of more approaches to face real-world problems is needed is emerging in the scientific community. Unfortunately, foundations on how to rigorously proceed with this combination have yet to emerge.

2.2 Representations and RNN Architectures

Neural networks architectures for sequence learning can be broadly classified into two classes, according to the way time is represented: *explicitly* or *implicitly*.

Explicit time representation is also referred to as algebraic representation of time, since input and output events at different time steps are explicitly represented as unrelated variables on which an algebraic model operates, i.e., the *whole* input subsequence from time 1 to time t is mapped into the output using a *static* relationship. From a practical point of view, this means that a buffer holding the external inputs to the system, as they are received, must be used. Basically, with an explicit representation of time, *temporal* processing problems are converted into *spatial* processing problems, thus allowing one to use simpler static models, such as feed-forward neural networks. Typical architectures belonging to this class of networks are feed-forward networks looking at the input sequences through a window of prefixed size and Time-Delay networks, which exploit this window approach also for hidden activations. The networks in this class have been related with FIR filters, since they can be considered as nonlinear versions of these filters. Moreover, from a computational point of view, this class of networks is strictly related to Definite-Memory Sequential Machines.

Implicit time representation assumes *causality*, i.e., the output at time t only depends on the present and past inputs. If causality holds, then the *memory* about the past can be stored into an *internal state*. From a practical point of view, internal representations can be obtained by *recurrent connections*. To this class of networks belong Fully Connected networks, NP networks, NARX networks, Recurrent Cascade Correlation networks, and so on. According to the type of topology involving the recurrent connections, different types of memory can be implemented (e.g., input (transformed) memory, hidden (transformed) memory, output (transformed) memory). Moreover, in discrete-time networks, different kinds of temporal dependencies can be expressed by resorting to different Discrete-Time Operators, such as the standard *shift operator*, the *delta operator*, the *gamma operator*, the *rho operator*, and so on. Because of the internal state, this class of networks is strictly related to IIR filters, and to several classes of sequential machines (such as Finite State Sequential Machines, Finite-Memory Sequential Machines, etc.). A good overview of all these different architectural aspects can be found in [67].

2.3 Training Algorithms

There is a huge variety of training algorithms for recurrent neural networks. Almost all training algorithms for recurrent neural networks are based on gradient descent. Among these the most popular algorithms are Back-propagation Through Time (BPTT) [44], Real Time Recurrent Learning (RTRL) [75] developed for on-line training, Kalman (Extended) Filter (EKF) [74] [49], and Temporal Difference [62] [63]. As for feed-forward networks [10], second order or quasi-second order methods can be defined for recurrent neural networks (see [66] for an overview).

Moreover, there is a class of constructive algorithms which exploit the gradient to build up the network architecture during training, according to the training data complexity. Within this class we can mention Recurrent Cascade-Correlation [18], a partition algorithm using Radial Basis Functions [68], and Recurrent Neural Trees [60].

There is also a class of stochastic learning algorithms for recurrent networks. For example, EM [17] (or GEM) can be used to train feed-forward [8] and recurrent networks [42]. Also Evolutionary Algorithms (Genetic Algorithms) can be used to train recurrent networks [52] [9]. Notice that Evolutionary Algorithms can be considered constructive algorithms, since with a suitable representation of the recurrent network, more and more complex networks can evolve within a population of networks.

2.4 Training Heuristics

The successful training of a neural network can not usually be obtained by just running the selected training algorithm on any configuration for the network architecture and learning parameters. There are several additional issues which must be considered. This is particularly true for recurrent networks.

For example, the size of the state variable is very relevant. Moreover, an important issue is which kind of delay lines should be used in the network, since a correct choice may help in capturing the right temporal dependencies, hidden into the training data. So usually it is useful to have multi-step delay lines within the recurrent network.

In addition, in order to facilitate training, it may be important to choose the right representation for the starting state or even to have the possibility to learn it [21]. Also connectivity can be very critical: fully connected networks allow for the discovery of high-order correlations, while a sparse connectivity can significantly speed up training and return very good solutions where high-order correlations are not relevant. Similarly, training times can be reduced by using a learning rule which exploits truncated gradients, or by using an adaptive learning rate.

Finally, in order to have some guarantee that the trained network will show some generalization capability, regularization [76] [66] and/or pruning (during and post training) [31] [48] [66] should be used.

These are just some of the issues which must be taken in consideration when training a recurrent neural network. Thus training a recurrent network is not just a problem of choosing a suitable architecture and learning algorithm: several different heuristics should be applied to fill in the missing information about the learning task.

2.5   Computational Power and Learning Facts

Training heuristics are useful, however it is important to discover computational and complexity limitations and strengths of network architectures and learning algorithms, since these may help us in avoiding to loose time and resources with computational devices which are not suited for the learning task at hand. Several results concerning computational power and learning complexity for recurrent neural networks have be obtained.

Concerning computational power, among positive results we can mention that recurrent networks can model any first order discrete-time, time invariant, non-linear system (see for example [54] [59]). In addition, it has been observed that recurrent neural networks with just 2 neurons can exhibit chaos [64] [15]. This last result is interesting since it testifies that even a trivial network can show a very complex behavior, thus implicitly demonstrating that, in principle, very complex computations could be performed by this network. Finally, some recurrent architectures, such as fully recurrent and NARX networks, are Turing equivalent [56] [57] [55].

On the other side, some recurrent architectures have limited computational power. For example, single layer recurrent networks cannot represent all Finite State Automata [32] (while Elman networks can because of the presence of the output layer [39]). Similarly, some constructive methods for RNN (i.e., Recurrent Cascade Correlation) generate networks which are computationally limited [27] [38].

Concerning learning, it has been proved that gradient descent based algorithms for RNNs converge for bounded sequences and constraints on learning rate [40]. Unfortunately, however, the loading problem [35] for RNNs (i.e., finding a set of weights consistent with the training data) is unsolvable [72]! Moreover, even if several recurrent architectures have the computational capability to represent arbitrary nonlinear dynamical systems, gradient-based training suffers long-term dependencies [11] [41], showing difficulties in learning even very simple dynamical behaviors. The problem of long-term dependencies can be understood as the inability of gradient descent algorithms (when used on several of the most common RNN architectures) to store error information concerning past inputs which are far in time from the present input. Some heuristics have been proposed to try to reduce the problem of vanishing gradient information [29] [53] [41] [34], however, none of them is able to completely remove it.

2.6   Knowledge Insertion and Refinement

From Section 2.5 it is clear that RNNs which are computationally very powerful are also very difficult to train. In fact, it would be wonderful to have a recurrent architecture which is computational complete, i.e., Turing equivalent, *and* also easy to train (see Figure 1).

Some authors have proposed to exploit a priori information on the application domain to master learning complexity. From the point of view of generalization, this idea is supported by theoretical results on the decomposition of the error of

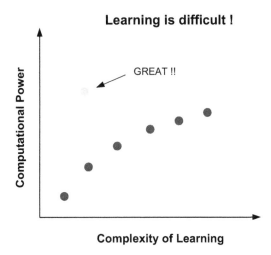

Fig. 1. Learning is difficult: as soon as the computational power of the RNN increases, the complexity of training the network increases exponentially. It would be great to have a powerful RNN which is easy to train.

a neural network into Bias and Variance [26]. These results suggest that in order for a neural network to properly learn the desired function, some significant prior structure should be given to the network.

There are different ways to implement the above idea. One possibility is to give some *hints* to the network on specific properties of the desired function (see for example [1] [6] [58] [3] [2] [5] [4]) or to *insert* prior knowledge in form of rules into the neural network and then to train it using a standard learning algorithm (for the case of dynamically-driven recurrent neural networks see [16] [22] [7] [23] [46]). A variant of this approach considers the possibility to *refine* rough knowledge (see for example [43] [30] [29]) by *extracting* knowledge coded into the neural networks through algorithms which take in input a neural network and return a set of rules or a FSM for sequence domains (see for example [47] [28] [65] [15]). These rules are then inserted back into the neural network and the cycle insertion/training/extraction is repeated several times.

It is usually believed that the above approach helps learning since it may reduce the number of functions that are candidate for the desired function. Moreover, due to the inserted knowledge, training times should be reduced. Unfortunately, while the above statements may be true for specific and (often) small domains, in general there are at least two reasons for the above approach to fail. First of all, the insertion of rules or FSM into neural networks implies that a good amount of the network structure is predetermined, as well as several of the values for the weights. This turns out to create some difficulties to the learning process (especially if the learning algorithm is based on gradient descent), which has to satisfy the additional constraints imposed by the knowledge insertion, i.e., very often the neural units are saturated and thus they are difficult to train by using a gradient descent approach. Moreover, rule (or DFA) extraction from neural networks is not so easy as it was expected. For example, some criticisms about the reliability of DFA extraction from recurrent neural networks have been raised in [37]. Although a partial solution to these criticisms has been given in [73], the problem of reliable extraction of knowledge from neural networks is still a research subject. For example, recently, an approach based on reinforcement learning for extracting complete action plans from sequences has been proposed [61]

2.7   Application Requirements

Application fields are many and diverse. This diversity implies the need for different approaches, ranging from symbolic to sub-symbolic techniques. Given a specific problem, several are the questions which need to be answered for a successful, flexible, and portable solution. When using RNNs, some typical questions are:

What is the appropriate RNN architecture(s) for the problem to be solved ?
What is the appropriate RNN training algorithm(s) ?
How can a priori knowledge be best used ?
What to do if no existing architecture/algorithm is suited for the problem to be solved (development of new architecture/algorithm ?)
How can a RNN be integrated with other approaches ?

The possibility to give correct answers to these questions in a short time is related to the availability of specification languages for prototyping and experimentation. Unfortunately, it must be stressed that even if many neural network simulators have been developed (e.g., Aspirin/Migraines, Rochester Connectionist Simulator, NNSYSID, Stuttgart Neural Network Simulator, Toolkit for Mathematica, just to mention a few), as well as specification languages for neural networks (e.g., EpsiloNN, Neural Simulation Language), they implement a restricted set of specific models for dealing mostly with static data. At our knowledge, there is no single specification language which may support the user in giving an answer to all the above questions, especially when considering the development of new architectures and/or algorithms. The situation is even worst when considering the integration of RNNs with symbolic approaches.

2.8   Unifying Theories

The lack of a "universal" neural specification language is mainly due to a lack of synthesis of the main concepts and results in the neural network field. Up to now, several different architectures and training algorithms have been devised. Many of the new improvements however are just small and insignificant changes to existing architectures and/or algorithms. Furthermore, since the research is not based on a general framework, it is difficult to focus on the study of background important properties. For this reason some researchers have felt the need to try to develop, especially for dynamical systems, a general framework able to describe the foundations of both architectures and learning algorithms.

Nerrand et al. [45] describe a general framework that encompasses algorithms for feed-forward and recurrent neural networks, and algorithms for parameter estimation of non-linear filters. Specifically, feed-forward networks are viewed as transversal filters, while recurrent networks as recursive filters. Their approach is based on the definition of a canonical form which can be used as a building block for the training algorithms based on gradient estimation. A similar approach is followed also by Santini et al. [51].

Tsoi and Back [69] and Tsoi [67] propose a unifying view of discrete time feed-forward and recurrent network architectures, basing their work on systems theory with linear dynamics. In this case canonical forms are used to group similar architectures and a unifying description is obtained by exploiting a notation based on matrices.

Wan and Beaufays [71] [70] suggest an approach, exploiting *flow graph theory*, to construct and manipulate block diagrams representing neural networks. Gradient algorithms for temporal neural networks are derived on the basis of a set of simple block diagram manipulation rules.

A computational approach is followed by Berthold et al. [12] [19] [36] [20]. In their works Graph Grammars (see [50]) are used to formally specify neural networks and their corresponding training algorithms. One of the benefits of using this formal framework is the support for proving properties of the training algorithms. Moreover, the proposed methodology can be used to design new network architectures along with the required training algorithms.

A proposal for the unification of deterministic and probabilistic learning in structured domains, thus including as special cases feed-forward and recurrent neural networks, has been proposed by Frasconi et al. [24], where graphical models are used to describe in a unified framework both neural and probabilistic (Bayesian Networks) transductions involving data structures. The basic idea is to represent functional dependencies within an adaptive device by graphical models. The graphical models are then "unfolded" over the data structure to make explicit all the functional dependencies into the data. This process generates an encoding network which can be implemented either by a neural or a Bayesian network.

3   Need for a Neural Abstract Machine

As argued in Section 2.8, current neural network simulators and specification languages have too many drawbacks in order to be a valid tool for the development of successful neural solutions to applications problems. First of all they are too specific, since they typically implement a restricted set of neural models. Then, it is usually not possible, or very difficult, to slightly modify the specification of a given standard model, to combine different models, to insert a priori knowledge, and to develop a new model. Only some of them can deal with sequences (or structures). Finally, as pointed out in [25], in several application domains, it is not possible to assume both *causality* and *stationarity*, and at our knowledge none of them is able to cope with these requirements.

What we really need is to further develop the unifying approaches described in the previous section so to reach the full specification of a Neural Abstract Machine, i.e., a "universal" theory of neural computation, where all the basic and relevant neural concepts, and only them, are formally defined and used. For example, we must have the possibility to give a specification of input data types (static vectors, sequences, structures) and how to represent them (e.g., one-hot encoding, distributed representation, etc.), i.e., the object to be manipulated by the neural network. Then we must have the possibility to specify the operation types and their representation, e.g., functional dependencies, deterministic o probabilistic functions, gradient propagation, growing operators, compositional rules, pruning, knowledge insertion, shift operators, weight sharing, and so on. Finally, we have to master basic computational concepts and their implementation, e.g., model of computation, unrolling in time, unfolding on the structure, (non-)causality, (non-)stationarity, and so on.

When all these entities are defined and ways of implementing them are specified, to face an application problem we just have to write a few lines of "neural code" based on the neural abstract machine!! What we suggest is to perform a computational synthesis of the relevant issues in neural computing, recognizing the basic atoms of neural computation and how these basic atoms can be combined in order both to reproduce known neural models and to develop new architectures and learning algorithms, without the need to recode everything in a standard programming language such as Java, or C++. By using an analogy with the history of computers, we have to move from combinatorial or sequential circuits (current neural networks) to a Von Neumann machine (the Neural Abstract Machine).

4 Abstract State Machines

In order to devise a formal description of the *Neural Abstract Machine*, we need to decide which type of specification method to use. It is difficult to take such a decision choosing among many formal methods, since a lot of available theories are not practical for the description of complex dynamic real-world systems [14]. We think that the *Evolving Algebras*, devised by Gurevich [33], present some useful features for the *Neural Abstract Machine* formal development. Furthermore, this formalism has been intensively used for the formal design and analysis of various hardware systems, algorithms and programming languages semantics, showing an astonishing simplicity while preserving mathematical soundness and completeness. The main reason for its simplicity is the imperative specification style that, in contrast to conventional algebraic specification methods, allows an easier understandability. This leads to an easy definition of formal and informal requirements, turning them into a satisfactory *ground model* [14], i.e. a formal model that satisfies all the system requirements. Moreover, as stated in Börger's work [13], the evolving algebras have many other features that can help when devising a system or defining a language semantics:

- The *freedom of abstraction*, that allows incremental development of systems by stepwise refinement through a vertical hierarchy of intermediate models;
- The *information hiding* and the *precise definition of interfaces*, that helps the horizontal structuration of modules. In practice, when using a function we do not care about its implementations, we are interested only in the interface;
- The *scalability* to complex real-world systems;
- The easy *learning* and *usability* of the model.

4.1 Domains and Dynamic Functions

When specifying a system or a language semantics some entities must be defined. In particular, the basic object classes and the set of elementary operations on objects, i.e. the basic *domains* and *functions*. Each domain represents a category of elements that contributes to the definition of the whole system. These domains are completely abstract, since they represent some sort of information that will be specified later. For example, a generic neural network is built up by a linked set of computational units. In order to formalize a neural network with an Evolving Algebra *(EA)*, we may define two basic domains: the *NEURONS* set and the *CHANNELS* set. Note that this is only one of all possible formalizations of the basic elements of a neural network. Even if usually within the EA framework the domains are static, it is also possible to have dynamic domains [33]. This is very useful for our project, since there are many neural architectures that grow or shrink (through pruning) during training. Furthermore, the time unfolding of recurrent networks and the graph unfolding of recursive networks is done at run-time, thus we can not assume to have static networks.

Once the system domains have been defined, the set of all properties and elementary operations must be specified by corresponding functions. A function is defined in a mathematical sense as:

A function is a set of $(n + 1)$-tuples, where the $(n + 1)$-th element is functionally dependent from the first n elements (its arguments) [14].

Typically, each system operation updates a value (e.g. a memory location in an hardware system) given a set of other values (e.g registers). In the ASM framework this corresponds to the *dynamic function update* or *destructive assignment* defined as:

$$f(t_1, \ldots, t_n) \leftarrow t$$

where f is an arbitrary n-ary function as defined above, $t_1, \ldots, t_n$ are the function parameters defined in some domains, and t is the value at which the function is set. The *EA*s are so general that each used term could be of any complexity or abstraction. Continuing with the previous neural example, we can define the function that given a channel returns its strength parameter as:

$$weight : CHANNELS \rightarrow \mathbb{R} \ .$$

Since during training the weights of the network are changed, the update of one channel weight can be formalized as:

$$weight(C_i) \leftarrow weight(C_i) + \ \delta_w(C_i) \ ,$$

where C_i is an object belonging to the domain $CHANNELS$, and δ_w is a function that returns the amount of weight update associated to the specified channel (a real number).

4.2   Abstract States and Transition Instructions

Thanks to the EA's freedom of abstraction and information hiding properties, it is possible to produce rigorous high level specifications without worrying about the future design. This is accomplished using the concepts of *abstract state* and *abstract transition function*. It is for this reason that Evolving Algebras are nowadays also termed *Abstract State Machines* (ASM). The ASM concept of abstract state should not be confused with the notion of state used in finite state automata:

> The ASM abstract state is a collection of domains and dynamic functions defined on the domains.

The abstract states are subject to integrity constraints that partially describe the machine behavior. More clearly, when a system is in a state, the set of all reachable states is limited by the machine specification. Even if the notation used for the constraints formulation is not limited by any programming language, in order to describe the ASM behavior a set of basic actions have been designed. These actions constitute the set of abstract transition functions also termed *machine abstract instructions*. The dynamic function updates are the basic operations by which the behavior of a system can be described. However, they are inadequate for a complete system description, so the model needs to be enriched with control operators, frequently termed *rules*. The most general of these operators is the *guarded assignment*:

> **if** *Cond* **then** *Updates*

where *Cond* is a condition (the constraint), and *Updates* consists of finitely many function updates, which are executed simultaneously. At this point we have all the ingredients for an ASM system behavior description [13,14]:

> **Definition of Abstract State Machines.** An ASM $\mathcal{M}$ is a finite set of guarded function updates, used for evolving step by step the machine. When $\mathcal{M}$ is in a state $\mathcal{S}$, all guard conditions are evaluated (with standard logic), and all instructions with the verified guard condition are

selected. Then, all the *update functions* of all selected instructions are simultaneously executed, transforming the state S into a new state S'. This procedure of the ASM M is iteratively applied as long as possible (i.e. until there are not verified rule conditions). The ASM *run* can be defined as the set of all transitions that bring the machine M from the initial state S to the final state S', where no more rules have the verified guard.

The above definition shows how simple is the ASMs concept, since it is the only notion one has to know about the ASM semantics in order to be able to use this formalism.

4.3   ASM Rules and Graphical Representation

As previously stated, all the needed ingredients for a system behavior description with ASMs have been introduced. Nevertheless, the model is so general that a free use of programming notation is permitted. Even if a general rule for ASMs is that, unless there is an important reason, it is better to avoid the use of complex non-standard concepts or notations, in order to simplify the designer work, some simple and generic rules have been introduced in the ASMs formalism:

- **skip;**
- $p(t_1, \ldots, t_m);$
- **forall** f **in** *Dom* **such that** *Cond(f)*
        Rule;
- **choose** f **in** *Dom* **such that** *Cond(f)*
        Rule;

where, f is a function signature, *Dom* is a domain to which the given signature must belong, and *Cond* is an arbitrary condition on the function. The first rule, obviously, does nothing. The second rule represents a collection of rules. The third and the fourth rules allow a selection of rules to be executed. Note that with the last rule a sort of explicit nondeterminism has been introduced. An alternative nondeterministic solution could be to modify the ASMs semantic definition by allowing the firing at each step of only one of all fireable updates.

    In order to further simplify the design phase of a system also a graphical representation for the previous rules has been introduced. The guarded update is an instruction that allows the ASM transition from a state S to a state S', thus the guarded update rule can be rewritten as:

   if ($currentstate = S$) & (*Cond*) **then**
        Updates
        $currentstate \leftarrow S'$

Which can be graphically represented by the following diagram:

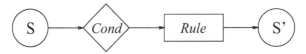

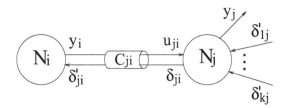

Fig. 2. A graphical representation of the required communication messages between channels and neurons. The signals u and y are the neuron input and output, δ is the gradient information computed by the neuron, and $\delta' = \delta w$ is the gradient information computed by the channel.

Note that the rectangular box may also contain a set of rules. This is very helpful when formalizing a problem with a top-down approach, because a complex concept can be expressed by a box, and left for future expansion.

5 A Sketch of Feed-Forward Network Specification

Our approach to the *Neural Abstract Machine* (NAM) is based on the idea of a kernel able to process feed-forward neural networks. In this section we provide a simplified high level formal description of such kernel, adopting a joined bottom-up and top-down approach, and showing some operational details with ASMs. Note that this is only a (not rigorous) exercise in order to give an idea about how ASMs technology can be applied. In particular we show the main features on which we are working for the NAM project.

5.1 Neurons and Channels Domains Specification

As stated in Section 4.1, in order to design an ASM, the set of basic domains must be defined. In our framework, since a net is viewed as a collection of neurons and connections (channels), we define the *NEURONS* and the *CHANNELS* domains, which represent the basic block categories compounding a neural network.

In view of the learning process, besides to neurons, we can assume that channels are "active" entities[1], i.e., able to update autonomously the associated weight, on the basis of the gradient information. In Figure 2 all the required communications between a channel and a neuron unit are shown.

Our basic assumption is that the kernel of the system is based on a *Neural Control Machine* (NCM), which dynamically generates the neural network connecting the basic blocks (channels and neurons), controls the flow of computation, furnishes the input data, and eventually the error information. The NCM

---

[1] The assumption that a channel is an active entity is not a requirement. According to the actual implementation, it may also be a passive entity accessed and modified by a *Neural Control Machine*.

should be able to manipulate also constructive algorithms, such as Cascade Correlation. In order to have this ability, the NCM should be able to communicate with each channel or neuron during the operative phase, sending signals such as *freeze* (or *de-freeze*). Moreover, the NCM needs to be able to dynamically create or destroy units during training, thus changing the neural architecture. The advantage of using the ASMs formal specification method is that such operations can be easily formalized with suitable function assignments.

5.2   Architecture Manipulation Functions

As previously stated, we have two basic block categories, represented by the *NEURONS* and *CHANNELS* domains.

In order to control the basic behavior of neurons and channels we need to define some functions over the domains *NEURONS* and *CHANNELS*. For instance, we need functions that, given a computational object, belonging to one of the two domains, return the "names" of all the other objects connected to it. Thus, for each domain, we need two functions, *source* and *dest*, which return the sources and the destinations for a given unit (N) or channel (C) during the forward phase:

$$source_C : CHANNELS \rightarrow NEURONS$$
$$dest_C : CHANNELS \rightarrow NEURONS$$

$$source_N : NEURONS \rightarrow \mathrm{P}(CHANNELS)$$
$$dest_N : NEURONS \rightarrow \mathrm{P}(CHANNELS)$$

where P denotes the power set. In our formalization while a neuron may have many source and destination channels, a channel has only one source and one destination neuron. Nevertheless, higher order connections, which have multiple sources and/or multiple destinations, can be easily modeled by the following new definition:

$$source_C : CHANNELS \rightarrow \mathrm{P}(NEURONS).$$

Since the Neural Control Machine needs to access all resources of the implemented neural network (neurons and channels), two functions are required:

$$all\_neurons : \mathrm{P}(NEURONS)$$
$$all\_channels : \mathrm{P}(CHANNELS)$$

which return the set of all neurons and the set of all channels used by the network. Furthermore, in order to know which are the input and the output units of the neural network the NCM requires the following two functions:

$$in\_layer \ : \mathrm{P}(NEURONS)$$
$$out\_layer : \mathrm{P}(NEURONS)$$

We assume that the NCM uses a data flow computational paradigm, i.e. the computation starts when the NCM transmits data to the *in_layer* units, and finishes when all units in the *out_layer* have computed the output, and no computation for other units needs to be performed. Moreover, it is responsibility of the NCM to implement the backward propagation of the gradient information across the network. Even in this case, a data flow computation is performed.

The previously defined functions allow the generation of a neural network. Actually, after the creation of a set of computational units $n_i \in NEURONS$ and $c_{ij} \in CHANNELS$, the network can be built up by a set of simple assignments like the followings:

$$source_C(c_{ij}) \leftarrow n_j$$
$$dest_C(c_{ij}) \leftarrow n_i$$

$$source_N(n_i) \leftarrow \{c_{ih}, \ldots, c_{ik}\}$$
$$dest_N(n_i) \leftarrow \{c_{mi}, \ldots, c_{ni}\}$$

5.3   Units Computation Functions

Each computational unit behavior may be described by three basic functions for each direction of the flow of computation (either forward or backward): the *input function*, the *state transition function* and the *output function*. In the following we show the functions characterizing the forward computation of the neural units.

The input function of the neural units during the forward phase could be described by the following interface:

$$in\_forw_N : NEURONS \rightarrow INPUT,$$

where *INPUT* is a new domain introduced for generalize the data description. With this approach the specifications can be left for future refinements, however, we can imagine that each channel transmits to a neuron a pair of data, formed by the signal conveyed by the channel and the weight associated to the channel. In this way, each neuron can use any internal computation function. For this reason we can assume $INPUT \equiv P((\mathbb{R}, \mathbb{R}))$. As a result of this choice, accessing the input of a neuron with the function in_forw, a list of couples is returned.

Obviously, data are returned only if previously sent to the neuron by all channels. For this reason when data are ready on the output interface of all channels they are copied in the input function with the following assignment:

$$in\_forw_N(n_i) \leftarrow \{out\_forw_C(c_{ih}), \ldots, out\_forw_C(c_{ik})\}$$

where $c_{ki}, \ldots, c_{hi}$ could be previously determined using the function $source_N(n_i)$, and out_forw_C is the channel output function. This way of processing emphasizes the data-flow paradigm implicitly assumed by our system. In fact, the internal computation can be done only when all data are ready in the input side of the neuron, i.e. when the neural unit possesses all the required inputs.

At this point the neurons can carry out the internal computations of the input data. In order to do this the following functions are required:

$$compute\_forw_N : INPUT \to STATE$$
$$output\_function_N : STATE \to OUTPUT$$

The function $compute\_forw_N$ computes the internal state of the neuron (e.g. the net value), and the function $output\_function_N$ computes the output value starting from the internal state. As previously stated for the $INPUT$ domain, also the $STATE$ and the $OUTPUT$ domains can be left unspecified for future refinements, however, for the sake of presentation, we assume $STATE \equiv OUTPUT \equiv \mathbb{R}$. Note that, the state is not strictly necessary in feed-forward networks, however it allows the storing of information needed by the backward phase.

Two other functions are needed for accessing the $STATE$ and $OUTPUT$ values of the neuron:

$$state\_forw_N : NEURONS \to STATE$$
$$out\_forw_N : NEURONS \to OUTPUT$$

They can be instantiated as follows:

$$state\_forw_N(n_i) \leftarrow compute\_forw_N(in\_forw_N(n_i))$$
$$out\_forw_N(n_i) \leftarrow output\_function_N(state\_forw_N(n_i))$$

Note that the function $compute\_forw_N$ does not take into account the previous state, so there is no memory of the past. If the memory is required, as in neural networks with short term memory, the function interface and the state transition may be changed in the following way:

$$compute\_forw_N : STATE \times INPUT \to STATE$$
$$state\_forw_N(n_i) \leftarrow compute\_forw_N(state\_forw_N(n_i), in\_forw_N(n_i))$$

Even if the proposed functions give just a partial definition for the feed-forward computation of a neural unit, they show how a neural model can be devised with ASMs. The backward propagation of the neuron unit is not much different from the forward propagation, and also the channel functions (either forward or backward) are similar to the neuron functions. It is theoretically interesting to note that, with such a block approach, neurons and channels are very similar. In an object oriented programming language the $NEURONS$ and $CHANNELS$ domains could be two classes inheriting from the same class.

5.4   The Neural Control Machine

Here, we are going to describe a possible formalization of the feed-forward part of the Neural Control Machine. In Figure 3 we show the part of the NCM, that

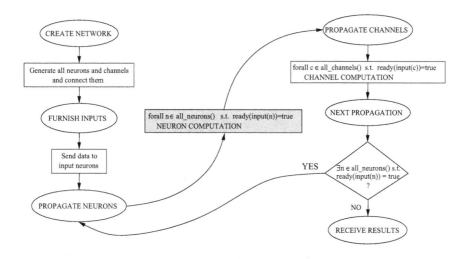

Fig. 3. This flowchart shows the part of NCM involved in the forward propagation of data in a feed-forward neural network. The NCM generates a neural network with a specified topology, then it furnishes an input to the network and propagates it through the network.

starting from a clear blackboard, creates a network and forward propagates a given input data till an output result is returned.

The first step of the NCM is the creation of the neural network. This can be accomplished creating all the neurons and all the required channels. Then, all the objects are linked. When the network is ready, the forward propagation of one input data can be accomplished. In order to do this, the data is sent to the input neurons of the network (known through the function *in_layer*). After that, the propagation of data starts. The machine iteratively propagates data through all neurons and channels. When the network output is ready, the NCM can collect it from the output units (known through the function *out_layer*).

In order to show how the freedom of abstraction property of the ASMs can help when incrementally developing by stepwise refinement, we have refined the neuron computation procedure left undefined in Figure 3. The specification of this computation is given in Figure 4.

When for a neuron the data is ready in input, it is copied into an internal working area for fast and easy access during the further computation. At this point the internal state is computed using the function $compute\_forw_N$ and the result is internally stored assigning it to the function $state\_forw_N$. Finally, the output result can be computed using the function $output\_function_N$ over the internal state and the result is stored by means of the function out_forw_N.

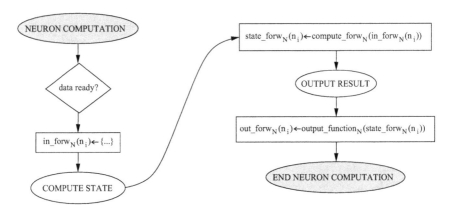

Fig. 4. This flowchart is an example of refinement of the NEURON COMPUTATION left unexplained in the flowchart of Figure 3. When a data is ready in input, it is assigned to the internal memory working area, then the internal state is computed, and finally the output result of the neuron is computed.

6   Some Details of the Neural Abstract Machine for Sequences

We have previously explained the basic behavior of the NAM kernel able to process feed-forward networks. In this section we provide a simple high level formal description of the part of Neural Abstract Machine devoted to the treatment of recurrent networks for structured data.

As previously stated (see Section 3), in order to define the NAM we need a general unifying theory of all different types of neural networks architectures and training algorithms. Even if some unification works have already appeared, we use here only a limited set of such ideas, since most of them are addressed to the internal organization of networks and their learning algorithms.

In particular, the work by Tsoi and Back [69] and Tsoi [67] showed that several recurrent networks can be reduced to a canonical recurrent form. Furthermore, if all cycles in the network are controlled by a delay operator, the forward and learning operations of a recurrent network can be easily reduced to the forward and learning operations of a feed-forward encoding network with identical behavior and weights[2]. For example, when considering a recurrent network where internal loops are controlled by a delay operator of one time step (i.e q^{-1}), the system transitions could be represented by the following Mealy model:

$$X_t = f_t(X_{t-1}, U_t) \quad \text{and} \quad Y_t = g_t(X_t, U_t), \tag{1}$$

---

[2] The weights of the recurrent network are shared among all layers of the transformed net.

where X_t is the internal state at time t, U_t is the input at time t, Y_t is the computed output at time t, f_t and g_t are the transition function and the output function at time t. Note that, even if the state transition is recursive, the functions f_t and g_t are intrinsically non-recursive, in fact the past information (i.e. the previous system computation) does not belong to the function f_t but is given to it as an external information. This show that the recursive system can be easily modeled by a suitable composition of non-recursive functions. Note also that the given specification assumes the possibility of a non stationary system, where functions f_t and g_t change over time.

It is clear at this point that given a data set and a (recurrent) network specification, the *Neural Abstract Machine* should be able to devise the parametric non-recursive functions f_t and g_t by which to define the feed-forward neural network that behaves as the recurrent network. In other words the NAM should be able to use the formal description[3] of a (recurrent) neural network in conjunction with the data set in order to find the optimal solution for the network parameters.

For a better understanding of the expected behavior of the NAM, let us reconsider Equations 1, which explain how the recurrent network can be dynamically unfolded over a sequence, generating a feed-forward network (also called *encoding network*). Informally, the encoding network is derived by dynamically unfolding the temporal operations of the recurrent network over each element of the observed sequence. Specifically, the recurrent network without the delayed links is replicated for each element of the sequence, and then each delayed link from neural unit i to unit j is mapped into a corresponding link from unit i to unit j of adjacent layers in the new feed-forward network (see Figure 5). In this way, for each input sequence a different feed-forward network is generated.

Since we can assume that all recurrent neural networks can be reduced to feed-forward networks, we now try to formalize a machine able to apply this transformation.

6.1   The Unfolding Machine

Let us study the high-level description of the unfolding process when the input data is constituted by sequences. The process to which we are interested in can be easily expressed by the (ASMs based) flowchart shown in Figure 6, where the first part of a sequence processing is shown.

Notice that the machine needs to access a database of sequences located somewhere. We are not interested in details such as how it is made and where it is stored. As first operation the machine "loads" a sequence from the database into the machine working area. This is then followed by the unfolding operation. The cycle that controls the unfolding is based on the idea that a sequence can be represented as a directed graph composed of nodes connected as shown in the following:

---

[3] In order to give a formal description of a neural network, also a *Neural Language* should be defined.

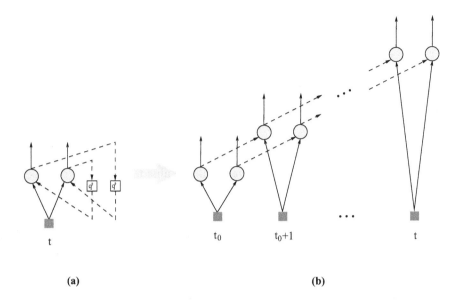

(a)   **(b)**

Fig. 5. Given an input sequence, a recurrent network (a) can be unfolded in time, originating an equivalent feed-forward network called encoding network (b).

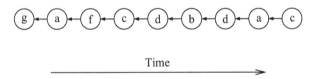

Time

Specifically, note that we assume the inverse orientation of the arcs with respect to the time of elaboration. The reason is that, using this approach, we can further extend the machine to the processing of structures, such as trees, forests and more in general DOAGs (Directed Ordered Acyclic Graphs). In fact, a recurrent network can be applied to structured data by unfolding it over the structure in a way which is very similar to the one used for sequences[4].

In the flowchart there are not operational details about the algorithm, there is only a (very) high level description of the unfolding operation. The first step only asserts that a sequence must be loaded for future processing. The second step is based on the assumption that all the elements (termed nodes from now on) of the loaded sequence can be marked as "visited" or "not visited". The second step is a loop over all not visited nodes, stating that at each iteration, for each element of the frontier, the encoding network must be extended unfolding the recurrent network.

---

[4] Note that sequences are a particular instance of DOAG.

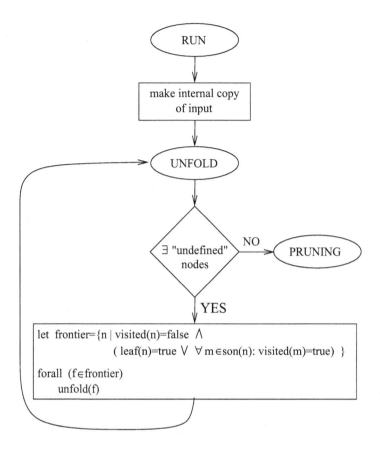

Fig. 6. Flowchart for the processing of sequences by a recurrent network. The feed-forward encoding network, for each sequence, is generated by unfolding the recurrent network on the input sequence. Notice that the machine is defined to work also for structured data, such as trees.

During the first iteration, the frontier is constituted by all leaves of the data structure (i.e. the first element of the sequence). From the second step on, the frontier is determined by all those nodes still not visited for which all sons have been visited. The loop stops when the roots are reached (i.e. the last element of the sequence). When there are no more undefined elements (i.e. all elements of the data have been used for the unfolding operation) the *Unfolding Machine* leaves the control to the *Pruning Machine*, which, in the case of complex data structure, removes portions of the encoding network, for which no gradient information must be computed. At the end of this process the encoding network is ready to be used.

The mathematical description of the frontier computation is based on some simple functions. The function *visited*(n) returns a boolean value indicating whether the node n has been visited during the unfolding loop, the function *leaf*(n) returns a boolean value that signal whether a node is a leaf of the structure, and finally, *son*(n) returns the set of all nodes m that have the node n as father.

The most important and complex part of the *Unfolding Machine* is the function *unfold*(n) that, for each node n of the structured data (e.g. an element of a sequence), must dynamically create the feed-forward encoding network.

7   Conclusions

Sequence Processing is a very complex task. According to the learning problem different approaches can be used. Neural networks for sequence are especially useful when data is numerical and noisy, or when uncertainty characterizes the learning task.

Training a recurrent neural network, however, is not a trivial task. Several choices about the network architecture, as well as the training algorithm must be taken. Moreover, heuristics must be used to set the learning rates, the regularization tools, the pruning procedure, and so on.

When present, a priori knowledge should be used to reduce the burden of training a network. In some cases, this may speed up learning and improve the generalization ability of the network. However, in general, learning remains difficult, also considering the long-term dependencies.

To successfully apply recurrent neural networks in real world domains, all the above choices must be taken in the shortest time and in the most reliable way. At present, no software tool is available to support all the aspects described above, including the rapid development of ad hoc new neural network models.

Recalling some recent attempts to find a unifying theory for (recurrent) neural networks, we suggested to push this challenge further, since this would create the theoretical basis on which to build a *Neural Abstract Machine*. This machine could be used to formally define a sort of neural programming language for fast prototyping and development of neural solutions to sequence (and structured) learning problems. As computational formalism we suggested to use the *Abstract State Machines* (ASM), which allow to describe the *Neural Abstract Machine* at different levels of abstraction and detail, while preserving simplicity of presentation and comprehension. A very brief and preliminary example of how to use ASM for neural networks was discussed.

Finally, we stress that the development of a *Neural Abstract Machine* would: *1)* help in understanding what is really needed and worth to be used in (recurrent) neural networks; *2)* create a universal computational language for neural computation; *3)* improve the possibility to integrate, at a computational level, neural networks with other approaches such as expert systems, Bayesian networks, fuzzy systems, and so on.

References

1. Abu-Mostafa, Y. S., 1990. Learning from Hints in Neural Networks. *Journal of Complexity* 6:192–198.
2. Abu-Mostafa, Y. S., 1993a. Hints and the VC Dimension. *Neural Computation* 5, no. 2:278–288.
3. Abu-Mostafa, Y. S., 1993b. A Method for Learning From Hints. In *Advances in Neural Information Processing Systems*, eds. S. J. Hanson, J. D. Cowan, and C. L. Giles, vol. 5, pp. 73–80. Morgan Kaufmann, San Mateo, CA.
4. Abu-Mostafa, Y. S., 1995a. Financial Applications of Learning from Hints. In *Advances in Neural Information Processing Systems*, eds. G. Tesauro, D. Touretzky, and T. Leen, vol. 7, pp. 411–418. The MIT Press.
5. Abu-Mostafa, Y. S., 1995b. Hints. *Neural Computation* 7, no. 4:639–671.
6. Al-Mashouq, K. A. and Reed, I. S., 1991. Including Hints in Training Neural Nets. *Neural Computation* 3, no. 3:418–427.
7. Alquézar, R. and Sanfeliu, A., 1995. An Algebraic Framework to Represent Finite State Machines in Single-Layer Recurrent Neural Networks. *Neural Computation* 7, no. 5:931–949.
8. Amari, S., 1995. Information Geometry of the EM and em Algorithms for Neural Networks. *Neural Networks* 8, no. 9:1379–1408.
9. Angeline, P. J., Saunders, G. M., and Pollack, J. P., 1994. An Evolutionary Algorithm That Constructs Recurrent Neural Networks. *IEEE Transactions on Neural Networks* 5, no. 1:54–65.
10. Battiti, T., 1992. First- and Second-Order Methods for Learning: Between Steepest Descent and Newton's Method. *Neural Computation* 4, no. 2:141–166.
11. Bengio, Y., Simard, P., and Frasconi, P., 1994. Learning Long-Term Dependencies with Gradient Descent is Difficult. *IEEE Transactions on Neural Networks* 5, no. 2:157–166.
12. Berthold, M. and Fischer, I., 1997. Formalizing Neural Networks Using Graph Transformations. In *Proceedings of the IEEE International Conference on Neural Networks*, vol. 1, pp. 275–280. IEEE.
13. Börger, E., 1995. Why Use Evolving Algebras for Hardware and Software Engineering? In *SOFSEM'95, 22nd Seminar on Current Trends in Theory and Practice of Informatics*, ed. J. W. Miroslav BARTOSEK, Jan STAUDEK, vol. 1012 of *Lecture Notes in Computer Science*, pp. 236–271. Berlin Heidelberg New York: Springer-Verlag.
14. Börger, E., 1999. High Level System Design and Analysis using Abstract State Machines. In *Current Trends in Applied Formal Methods (FM-Trends 98)*, eds. D. Hutter, W. Stephan, P. Traverso, and M. Ullmann, vol. 1641 of *Lecture Notes in Computer Science*, pp. 1–43. Berlin Heidelberg New York: Springer-Verlag.
15. Casey, M., 1996. The Dynamics of Discrete-Time Computation, with Application to Recurrent Neural Networks and Finite State Machine Extraction. *Neural Computation* 8, no. 6:1135–1178.
16. Das, S., Giles, C. L., and Sun, G. Z., 1992. Learning Context-free Grammars: Limitations of a Recurrent Neural Network with an External Stack Memory. In *Proceedings of The Fourteenth Annual Conference of the Cognitive Science Society*, pp. 791–795. San Mateo, CA: Morgan Kaufmann Publishers.
17. Dempster, A. P., Laird, N. M., and Rubin, D. B., 1977. Maximum likelihood from incomplete data via the EM algorithm (with discussion). *Journal of the Royal Statistical Society series B* 39:1–38.

18. Fahlman, S., 1991. The Recurrent Cascade-Correlation Architecture. In *Advances in Neural Information Processing Systems 3*, eds. R. Lippmann, J. Moody, and D. Touretzky, pp. 190–196. San Mateo, CA: Morgan Kaufmann Publishers.

19. Fischer, I., Koch, M., and Berthold, M. R., 1998a. Proving Properties of Neural Networks with Graph Transformations. In *Proceedings of the IEEE International Joint Conference on Neural Networks*, pp. 457–456. Anchorage, Alaska.

20. Fischer, I., Koch, M., and Berthold, M. R., 1998b. Showing the Equivalence of Two Training Algorithms - Part2. In *Proceedings of the IEEE International Joint Conference on Neural Networks*, pp. 441–446. Anchorage, Alaska.

21. Forcada, M. L. and Carrasco, R. C., 1995. Learning the Initial State of a Second-Order Recurrent Neural Network during Regular-Language Inference. *Neural Computation* 7, no. 5:923–930.

22. Frasconi, P., Gori, M., Maggini, M., and Soda, G., 1991. A Unified Approach for Integrating Explicit Knowledge and Learning by Example in Recurrent Networks. In *International Joint Confernece on Neural Networks*, pp. 811–816.

23. Frasconi, P., Gori, M., and Soda, G., 1995. Recurrent Neural Networks and Prior Knowledge for Sequence Processing: A Constrained Nondeterministic Approach. *Knowledge Based Systems* 8, no. 6:313–332.

24. Frasconi, P., Gori, M., and Sperduti, A., 1998. A General Framework for Adaptive Processing of Data Structures. *IEEE Transactions on Neural Networks* 9, no. 5:768–786.

25. Frasconi, P., Gori, M., and Sperduti, A., 2000. Integration of Graphical-Based Rules with Adaptive Learning of Structured Information. In *Hybrid Neural Symbolic Integration*, eds. S. Wermter and R. Sun. Springer-Verlag. To appear.

26. Geman, S., Bienenstock, E., and Doursat, R., 1992. Neural Networks and the Bias/Variance Dilemma. *Neural Computation* 4, no. 1:1–58.

27. Giles, C. L., Chen, D., Sun, G.-Z., Chen, H.-H., Lee, Y.-C., and Goudreau, M. W., 1995. Constructive Learning of Recurrent Neural Networks: Limitations of Recurrent Casade Correlation and a Simple Solution. *IEEE Transactions on Neural Networks* 6, no. 4:829–836.

28. Giles, C. L., Miller, C. B., Chen, D., Chen, H. H., Sun, G. Z., and Lee, Y. C., 1992. Learning and Extracted Finite State Automata with Second-Order Recurrent Neural Networks. *Neural Computation* 4, no. 3:393–405.

29. Giles, C. L. and Omlin, C. W., 1993a. Extraction, Insertion and Refinement of Symbolic Rules in Dynamically-Driven Recurrent Neural Networks. *Connection Science* 5, no. 3:307–337.

30. Giles, C. L. and Omlin, C. W., 1993b. Rule Refinement with Recurrent Neural Networks. In *1993 IEEE International Conference on Neural Networks (ICNN'93)*, vol. II, p. 810. Piscataway, NJ: IEEE Press.

31. Giles, C. L. and Omlin, C. W., 1994. Pruning Recurrent Neural Networks for Improved Generalization Performance. *IEEE Transactions on Neural Networks* 5, no. 5:848–851.

32. Goudreau, M. W., Giles, C. L., Chakradhar, S. T., and Chen, D., 1993. On Recurrent Neural Networks and Representing Finite State Recognizers. In *Third International Conference on Artificial Neural Networks*, pp. 51–55. The Institution of Electrical Engineers, London, UK.

33. Gurevich, Y., 1995. Evolvin Algebras 1993: Lipari Guide. In *Specification and Validation Methods*, ed. E. Börger, pp. 9–36. Oxford University Press.

34. Hochreiter, S. and Schmidhuber, J., 1997. Long Short Term Memory. *Neural Computation* 9, no. 8:123–141.

35. Judd, J. S., 1989. *Neural Network Design and the Complexity of Learning*. MIT press.

36. Koch, M., Fischer, I., and Berthold, M. R., 1998. Showing the Equivalence of Two Training Algorithms - Part1. In *Proceedings of the IEEE International Joint Conference on Neural Networks*, pp. 441–446. Anchorage, Alaska.

37. Kolen, J. F., 1994. Fool's Gold: Extracting Finite State Machines from Recurrent Network Dynamics. In *Advances in Neural Information Processing Systems*, eds. J. D. Cowan, G. Tesauro, and J. Alspector, vol. 6, pp. 501–508. Morgan Kaufmann Publishers, Inc.

38. Kremer, S., 1996. Finite State Automata that Recurrent Cascade-Correlation Cannot Represent. In *Advances in Neural Information Processing Systems 8*, eds. D. Touretzky, M. Mozer, and M. Hasselno. MIT Press. 612-618.

39. Kremer, S. C., 1995. On the Computational Power of Elman-Style Recurrent Networks. *IEEE Transactions on Neural Networks* 6, no. 4:1000–1004.

40. Kuan, C.-M., Hornik, K., and White, H., 1994. A Convergence Result for Learning in Recurrent Neural Networks. *Neural Computation* 6, no. 3:420–440.

41. Lin, T., Horne, B. G., Tiño, P., and Giles, C. L., 1996. Learning Long-Term Dependencies in NARX Recurrent Neural Networks. *IEEE Transactions on Neural Networks* 7, no. 6:1329–1338.

42. Ma, S. and Ji, C., 1998. Fast Training of Reccurent Networks Based on the EM Algorithm. *IEEE Transactions on Neural Networks* 9, no. 1:11–26.

43. Maclin, R. and Shavlik, J. W., 1992. Refining Algorithms with Knowledge-Based Neural Networks: Improving the Chou-Fasman Algorithm for Protein Folding. In *Computational Learning Theory and Natural Learning Systems*, eds. S. Hanson, G. Drastal, and R. Rivest. MIT Press.

44. McClelland, J. L. and Rumelhart, D. E., 1987. *PARALLEL DISTRIBUTED PROCESSING, Explorations in the Microstructure of Cognition. Volume 1: Foundations Volume 2: Psychological and Biological Models*. MIT Press. The PDP Research Group, MIT.

45. Nerrand, O., Roussel-Ragot, P., Personnaz, L., Dreyfus, G., and Marcos, S., 1993. Neural Networks and Nonlinear Adaptive Filtering: Unifying Concepts and New Algorithms. *Neural Computation* 5, no. 2:165–199.

46. Omlin, C. and Giles, C., 1996. Constructing Deterministic Finite-State Automata in Recurrent Neural Networks. *Journal of the ACM* 43, no. 6:937–972.

47. Omlin, C. W., Giles, C. L., and Miller, C. B., 1992. Heuristics for the Extraction of Rules from Discrete-Time Recurrent Neural Networks. In *Proceedings International Joint Conference on Neural Networks 1992*, vol. I, pp. 33–38.

48. Pedersen, M. W. and Hansen, L. K., 1995. Recurrent Networks: Second Order Properties and Pruning. In *Advances in Neural Information Processing Systems*, eds. G. Tesauro, D. Touretzky, and T. Leen, vol. 7, pp. 673–680. The MIT Press.

49. Puskorius, G. V. and Feldkamp, L. A., 1994. Neurocontrol of Nonlinear Dynamical Systems with Kalman Filter Trained Recurrent Networks. *IEEE Transactions on Neural Networks* 5, no. 2:279–297.

50. Rozemberg, G., Courcelle, B., Ehrig, H., Engels, G., Janssens, D., Kreowski, H., and Montanari, U., eds., 1997. *Handbook of Graph Grammars: Foundations*, vol. 1. Workd Scientific.

51. Santini, S., Bimbo, A. D., and Jain, R., 1995. Block structured recurrent neural netorks. *Neural Networks* 8:135–147.

52. Saunders, G. M., Angeline, P. J., and Pollack, J. B., 1994. Structural and Behavioral Evolution of Recurrent Networks. In *Advances in Neural Information*

Processing Systems, eds. J. D. Cowan, G. Tesauro, and J. Alspector, vol. 6, pp. 88–95. Morgan Kaufmann Publishers, Inc.

53. Schmidhuber, J., 1992. Learning Complex, Extended Sequences Using the Principle of History Compression. *Neural Computation* 4, no. 2:234–242.

54. Seidl, D. and Lorenz, D., 1991. A structure by which a recurrent neural network can approximate a nonlinear dynamic system. In *Proceedings of the International Joint Conference on Neural Networks*, vol. 2, pp. 709–714.

55. Siegelmann, H., Horne, B., and Giles, C., 1997. Computational capabilities of recurrent NARX neural networks. *IEEE Trans. on Systems, Man and Cybernetics* In press.

56. Siegelmann, H. T. and Sontag, E. D., 1991. Turing Computability with Neural Nets. *Applied Mathematics Letters* 4, no. 6:77–80.

57. Siegelmann, H. T. and Sontag, E. D., 1995. On the Computational Power of Neural Nets. *Journal of Computer and System Sciences* 50, no. 1:132–150.

58. Simard, P., Victorri, B., Le Cun, Y., and Denker, J., 1992. Tangent Prop—A Formalism for Specifying Selected Invariances in an Adaptive Network. In *Advances in Neural Information Processing Systems*, eds. J. E. Moody, S. J. Hanson, and R. P. Lippmann, vol. 4, pp. 895–903. Morgan Kaufmann Publishers, Inc.

59. Sontag, E., 1993. Neural Networks for control. In *Essays on Control: Perspectives in the Theory and its Applications*, eds. H. L. Trentelman and J. C. Willemsd, pp. 339–380. Boston, MA: Birkhauser.

60. Sperduti, A. and Starita, A., 1997. Supervised Neural Networks for the Classification of Structures. *IEEE Transactions on Neural Networks* 8, no. 3:714–735.

61. Sun, R. and Sessions, C., 1998. Extracting plans from reinforcement learners. *Proceedings of the 1998 International Symposium on Intelligent Data Engineering and Learning*, eds. L. Xu, L. Chan, I. King, and A. Fu, pp.243–248. Springer-Verlag.

62. Sutton, R. S., 1988. Learning to Predict by the Methods of Temporal Differences. *Machine Learning* 3:9–44.

63. Tesauro, G., 1992. Practical Issues in Temporal Difference Learning. *Machine Learning* 8:257–277.

64. Tino, P., Horne, B., and C.L.Giles, 1995. Fixed Points in Two–Neuron Discrete Time Recurrent Networks: Stability and Bifurcation Considerations. Tech. Rep. UMIACS-TR-95-51 and CS-TR-3461, Institute for Advance Computer Studies, University of Maryland, College Park, MD 20742.

65. Towell, G. G. and Shavlik, J. W., 1993. Extracting Refined Rules from Knowledge-Based Neural Networks. *Machine Learning* 13:71–101.

66. Tsoi, A., 1998a. Gradient Based Learning Methods. In *Adaptive Processing of Sequences and Data Structures: Lecture Notes in Artificial Intelligence*, eds. C. Giles and M. Gori, pp. 27–62. New York, NY: Springer Verlag.

67. Tsoi, A., 1998b. Recurren Neural Network Architectures: An Overview. In *Adaptive Processing of Sequences and Data Structures: Lecture Notes in Artificial Intelligence*, eds. C. Giles and M. Gori, pp. 1–26. New York, NY: Springer Verlag.

68. Tsoi, A. and Tan, S., 1997. Recurrent Neural Networks: A constructive algorithm and its properties. *Neurocomputing* 15, no. 3-4:309–326.

69. Tsoi, A. C. and Back, A., 1997. Discrete Time Recurrent Neural Network Architectures: A Unifying Review. *Neurocomputing* 15:183–223.

70. Wan, E. A. and Beaufay, F., 1998. Diagrammatic Methods for Deriving and Relating Temporal Neural Network Algorithms. In *Adaptive Processing of Sequences and Data Structures: Lecture Notes in Artificial Intelligence*, eds. C. Giles and M. Gori, pp. 63–98. New York, NY: Springer Verlag.

71. Wan, E. A. and Beaufays, F., 1996. Diagrammatic Derivation of Gradient Algorithms for Neural Networks. *Neural Computation* 8, no. 1:182–201.

72. Wiklicky, H., 1994. On the Non-Existence of a Universal Learning Algorithm for Recurrent Neural Networks. In *Advances in Neural Information Processing Systems*, eds. J. D. Cowan, G. Tesauro, and J. Alspector, vol. 6, pp. 431–436. Morgan Kaufmann Publishers, Inc.

73. Wiles, J. and Bollard, S., 1996. Beyond finite state machines: steps towards representing and extracting context-free languages from recurrent neural networks. In *NIPS'96 Rule Extraction from Trained Artificial Neural Networks Workshop*, eds. R. Andrews and J. Diederich.

74. Williams, R. J., 1992. Some Observations on the Use of the Extended Kalman Filter as a Recurrent Network Learning Algorithm. Tech. Rep. NU-CCS-92-1, Computer Science, Northeastern University, Boston, MA.

75. Williams, R. J. and Zipser, D., 1988. A Learning Algorithm for Continually Running Fully Recurrent Neural Networks. Tech. Rep. ICS Report 8805, Institute for Cognitive Science, University of California at San Diego, La Jolla, CA.

76. Wu, L. and Moody, J., 1996. A Smoothing Regularizer for Feedforward and Recurrent Neural Networks. *Neural Computation* 8, no. 3:461–489.

Sequence Mining in Categorical Domains:
Algorithms and Applications

Mohammed J. Zaki

Computer Science Department
Rensselaer Polytechnic Institute, Troy, NY

1 Introduction

This chapter focuses on sequence data in which each example is represented as a sequence of "events", where each event might be described by a set of predicates, i.e., we are dealing with categorical sequential domains. Examples of sequence data include text, DNA sequences, web usage data, multi-player games, plan execution traces, and so on.

The sequence mining task is to discover a set of attributes, shared across time among a large number of objects in a given database. For example, consider the sales database of a bookstore, where the objects represent customers and the attributes represent authors or books. Let's say that the database records the books bought by each customer over a period of time. The discovered patterns are the sequences of books most frequently bought by the customers. An example could be that, "70% of the people who buy Jane Austen's *Pride and Prejudice* also buy *Emma* within a month." Stores can use these patterns for promotions, shelf placement, etc. Consider another example of a web access database at a popular site, where an object is a web user and an attribute is a web page. The discovered patterns are the sequences of most frequently accessed pages at that site. This kind of information can be used to restructure the web-site, or to dynamically insert relevant links in web pages based on user access patterns. Other domains where sequence mining has been applied include identifying plan failures [15], selecting good features of classification [7], finding network alarm patterns [4], and so on.

The task of discovering all frequent sequences in large databases is quite challenging. The search space is extremely large. For example, with m attributes there are $O(m^k)$ potentially frequent sequences of length k. With millions of objects in the database the problem of I/O minimization becomes paramount. However, most current algorithms are iterative in nature, requiring as many full database scans as the longest frequent sequence; clearly a very expensive process.

In this chapter we present SPADE (Sequential PAttern Discovery using Equivalence classes), a new algorithm for discovering the set of all frequent sequences. The key features of our approach are as follows: 1) We use a *vertical id-list* database format, where we associate with each sequence a list of objects in which it occurs, along with the time-stamps. We show that all frequent sequences can be enumerated via simple temporal joins (or intersections) on id-lists. 2) We

R. Sun and C.L. Giles (Eds.): Sequence Learning, LNAI 1828, pp. 162–187, 2000.

use a lattice-theoretic approach to decompose the original search space (lattice) into smaller pieces (sub-lattices) which can be processed independently in main-memory. Our approach requires a few (usually three) database scans, or only a single scan with some pre-processed information, thus minimizing the I/O costs. 3) We decouple the problem decomposition from the pattern search. We propose two different search strategies for enumerating the frequent sequences within each sub-lattice: breadth-first and depth-first search.

SPADE not only minimizes I/O costs by reducing database scans, but also minimizes computational costs by using efficient search schemes. The vertical id-list based approach is also insensitive to data-skew. An extensive set of experiments shows that SPADE outperforms previous approaches by a factor of two, and by an order of magnitude if we have some additional off-line information. Furthermore, SPADE scales linearly in the database size, and a number of other database parameters.

We also discuss how sequence mining can be applied in practice. We show that in complicated real-world applications, like predicting plan failures, sequence mining can produce an overwhelming number of frequent patterns. We discuss how one can identify the most interesting patterns using pruning strategies in a post-processing step. Our experiments show that our approach improves the plan success rate from 82% to 98%, while less sophisticated methods for choosing which part of the plan to repair were only able to achieve a maximum of 85% success rate. We also showed that the mined patterns can be used to build execution monitors which predict failures in a plan before they occur. We were able to produce monitors with 100% precision, that signal 90% of all the failures that occur.

As another application, we describe how to use sequence mining for feature selection. The input is a set of labeled training sequences, and the output is a function which maps from a new sequence to a label. In other words we are interested in selecting (or constructing) features for sequence classification. In order to generate this function, our algorithm first uses sequence mining on a portion of the training data for discovering frequent and distinctive sequences and then uses these sequences as features to feed into a classification algorithm (Winnow or Naive Bayes) to generate a classifier from the remainder of the data. Experiments show that the new features improve classification accuracy by more then 20% on our test datasets.

The rest of the chapter is organized as follows: In Section 2 we describe the sequence discovery problem and look at related work in Section 3. In Section 4 we develop our lattice-based approach for problem decomposition, and for pattern search. Section 5 describes our new algorithm. An experimental study is presented in Section 6. Section 7 discusses how the sequence mining can be used in a real planning domain, while Section 8 describes its use in feature selection. Finally, we conclude in Section 9.

2   Problem Statement

The problem of mining sequential patterns can be stated as follows: Let $\mathcal{I} = \{i_1, i_2, \cdots, i_m\}$ be a set of m distinct *items* comprising the alphabet. An *event* is a non-empty unordered collection of items (without loss of generality, we assume that items of an event are sorted in lexicographic order). A *sequence* is an ordered list of events. An event is denoted as $(i_1 i_2 \cdots i_k)$, where i_j is an item. A sequence α is denoted as $(\alpha_1 \rightarrow \alpha_2 \rightarrow \cdots \rightarrow \alpha_q)$, where α_i is an event. A sequence with k items $(k = \sum_j |\alpha_j|)$ is called a *k-sequence*. For example, $(B \rightarrow AC)$ is a 3-sequence.

For a sequence α, if the event α_i occurs before α_j, we denote it as $\alpha_i < \alpha_j$. We say α is a *subsequence* of another sequence β, denoted as $\alpha \preceq \beta$, if there exists a one-to-one order-preserving function f that maps events in α to events in β, that is, 1) $\alpha_i \subseteq f(\alpha_i)$, and 2) if $\alpha_i < \alpha_j$ then $f(\alpha_i) < f(\alpha_j)$. For example the sequence $(B \rightarrow AC)$ is a subsequence of $(AB \rightarrow E \rightarrow ACD)$, since $B \subseteq AB$ and $AC \subseteq ACD$, and the order of events is preserved. On the other hand the sequence $(AB \rightarrow E)$ is not a subsequence of (ABE), and vice versa.

The database $\mathcal{D}$ for sequence mining consists of a collection of input-sequences. Each input-sequence in the database has an unique identifier called *sid*, and each event in a given input-sequence also has a unique identifier called *eid*. We assume that no sequence has more than one event with the same time-stamp, so that we can use the time-stamp as the event identifier.

An input-sequence $\mathcal{C}$ is said to *contain* another sequence α, if $\alpha \preceq \mathcal{C}$, i.e., if α is a subsequence of the input-sequence $\mathcal{C}$. The *support* or *frequency* of a sequence, denoted $\sigma(\alpha, \mathcal{D})$, is the the total number of input-sequences in the database $\mathcal{D}$ that contain α. Given a user-specified threshold called the *minimum support* (denoted *min_sup*), we say that a sequence is *frequent* if occurs more than *min_sup* times. The set of frequent k-sequences is denoted as $\mathcal{F}_k$. A frequent sequence is *maximal* if it is not a subsequence of any other frequent sequence.

Given a database $\mathcal{D}$ of input-sequences and *min_sup*, the problem of mining sequential patterns is to find all frequent sequences in the database. For example, consider the input database shown in Figure 1. The database has eight items (A to H), four input-sequences, and ten events in all. The figure also shows all the frequent sequences with a minimum support of 50% (i.e., a sequence must occur in at least 2 input-sequences). In this example we have a two maximal frequent sequences, ABF and $D \rightarrow BF \rightarrow A$.

Some comments are in order to see the generality of our problem formulation: 1) We discover sequences of *subsets* of items, and not just single item sequences. For example, the set BF in $(D \rightarrow BF \rightarrow A)$. 2) We discover sequences with arbitrary *gaps* among events, and not just the consecutive subsequences. For example, the sequence $(D \rightarrow BF \rightarrow A)$ is a subsequence of input-sequence 1, even though there is an intervening event between D and BF. The sequence symbol $\rightarrow$ simply denotes a *happens-after* relationship. 3) Our formulation is general enough to encompass almost any categorical sequential domain. For example, if the input-sequences are DNA strings, then an event consists of a single item (one of A, C, G, T). If input-sequences represent text documents, then each word

DATABASE		
SID	Time (EID)	Items
1	10	C D
1	15	A B C
1	20	A B F
1	25	A C D F
2	15	A B F
2	20	E
3	10	A B F
4	10	D G H
4	20	B F
4	25	A G H

FREQUENT SEQUENCES

Frequent 1-Sequences

A	4
B	4
D	2
F	4

Frequent 2-Sequences

AB	3
AF	3
B->A	2
BF	4
D->A	2
D->B	2
D->F	2
F->A	2

Frequent 3-Sequences

ABF	3
BF->A	2
D->BF	2
D->B->A	2
D->F->A	2

Frequent 4-Sequences

D->BF->A	2

Fig. 1. Original Input-Sequence Database

(along with any other attributes of that word, e.g., noun, position, etc.) would comprise an event. Even continuous domains can be represented after a suitable discretization step.

Once the frequent sequences are known, they can be used to obtain rules that describe the relationship between different sequence items. Let α and β be two sequences. The *confidence* of a sequence rule $\alpha \Rightarrow \beta$ is the conditional probability that sequence β occurs, given that α occurs in an input-sequence, given as

$$Conf(\alpha \Rightarrow \beta, \mathcal{D}) = \frac{\sigma(\alpha \to \beta, \mathcal{D})}{\sigma(\alpha, \mathcal{D})}.$$

Given a user-specified threshold called the *minimum confidence* (denoted *min_conf*), we say that a sequence rule is *confident* if $Conf(\alpha, \mathcal{D}) \geq min\_conf$. For example, the rule $(D \to BF) \Rightarrow (D \to BF \to A)$ has 100% confidence.

3   Related Work

The problem of mining sequential patterns was introduced in [2]. They also presented three algorithms for solving this problem. The *AprioriAll* algorithm was shown to perform better than the other two approaches. In subsequent work [12], the same authors proposed the GSP algorithm that outperformed *AprioriAll* by up to 20 times. They also introduced maximum gap, minimum gap, and sliding window constraints on the discovered sequences.

We use GSP as a base against which we compare SPADE, as it is one of the best previous algorithms. GSP makes multiple passes over the database.

In the first pass, all single items (1-sequences) are counted. From the frequent items a set of *candidate* 2-sequences are formed. Another pass is made to gather their support. The frequent 2-sequences are used to generate the candidate 3-sequences. A pruning phase eliminates any sequence at least one of whose subsequences is not frequent. For fast counting, the candidate sequences are stored in a *hash-tree*. This iterative process is repeated until no more frequent sequences are found. For more details on the specific mechanisms for constructing and searching hash-trees, please refer to [12].

Independently, [10] proposed mining for *frequent episodes*, which are essentially frequent sequences in a single long input-sequence (typically, with single items events, though they can handle set events). However our formulation is geared towards finding frequent sequences across many different input-sequences. They further extended their framework in [9] to discover *generalized episodes*, which allows one to express arbitrary unary conditions on individual sequence events, or binary conditions on event pairs. The MEDD and MSDD algorithms [11] discover patterns in multiple event sequences; they explore the rule space directly instead of the sequence space.

Sequence discovery bears similarity with association discovery [1,16,14]; it can be thought of as association mining over a temporal database. While association rules discover only intra-event patterns (called itemsets), we now also have to discover inter-event patterns (sequences). Further, the sequence search space is much more complex and challenging than the itemset space; the set of all frequent sequences is a superset of the set of frequent itemsets.

4   Sequence Enumeration: Lattice-Based Approach

Theorem 1. *Given a set $\mathcal{I}$ of items, the ordered set $\mathcal{S}$ of all possible sequences on the items, induced by the subsequence relation $\preceq$, defines a hyper-lattice with the following two operations: the* join, *denoted $\bigvee$, of a set of sequences $A_i \in \mathcal{S}$ is the set of minimal common supersequences, and the* meet, *denoted $\bigwedge$, of a set of sequences is the set of maximal common subsequences. More formally,*

Join: $\bigvee\{A_i\} = \{\alpha \mid A_i \preceq \alpha \text{ and } A_i \preceq \beta \text{ with } \beta \preceq \alpha \Rightarrow \beta = \alpha\}$

Meet: $\bigwedge\{A_i\} = \{\alpha \mid \alpha \preceq A_i \text{ and } \beta \preceq A_i \text{ with } \alpha \preceq \beta \Rightarrow \beta = \alpha\}$

Note that in a regular lattice the join and meet refers to the unique minimum upper bound and maximum lower bound. In a hyper-lattice the join and meet need not produce a unique element; instead the result can be a set of minimal upper bounds and maximal lower bounds. In the rest of this chapter we will usually refer to the sequence hyper-lattice as a lattice, since the sequence context is understood.

Figure 2 shows the sequence lattice induced by the maximal frequent sequences ABF and $D \to BF \to A$, for our example database. The *bottom* or least element, denoted $\perp$, of the lattice is $\perp = \{\}$, and the set of *atoms* (elements

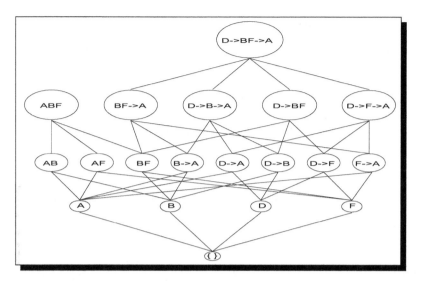

Fig. 2. Lattice Induced by Maximal Frequent Sequences ABF and $D \to BF \to A$

directly connected to the bottom element), denoted $\mathcal{A}$, is given by the frequent items $\mathcal{A} = \{A, B, D, F\}$. To see why the set of all sequences forms a hyper-lattice, consider the join of A and B; $A \vee B = \{(AB), (B \to A)\}$. As we can see the join produces two minimal upper bounds (i.e., minimal common super-sequences). Similarly, the meet of two (or more) sequences can produce a set of maximal lower bounds. For example, $(AB) \wedge (B \to A) = \{(A), (B)\}$, both of which are the maximal common sub-sequences.

In the abstract the sequence lattice can be potentially infinite, since we can have arbitrarily long sequences. Fortunately, in all practical cases not only is the lattice bounded (the longest sequence can have $C \cdot T$ items, where C is the maximum number of events per input-sequence and T is the maximum event size), but the set of frequent sequences is also very sparse (depending on the *min_sup* value). For our example, we have $C = 4$ and $T = 4$, thus the longest sequence can have at most 16 items.

The set of all frequent sequences is closed under the meet operation, i.e., if X and Y are frequent sequences, then the meet $X \wedge Y$ (maximal common subsequence) is also frequent. However, it is not closed under joins since X and Y being frequent, doesn't imply that $X \vee Y$ (minimal common supersequence) is frequent. The closure under meet leads to the well known observation on sequence frequency:

Lemma 1. *All subsequences of a frequent sequence are frequent.*

What the lemma says is that we need to focus only on those sequences whose subsequences are frequent. This leads to a very powerful pruning strategy, where we eliminate all sequences, at least one of whose subsequences is infrequent. This property has been leveraged in many sequence mining algorithms [12,10,11].

4.1   Support Counting

Let's associate with each atom X in the sequence lattice its *id-list*, denoted $\mathcal{L}(X)$, which is a list of all input-sequence (*sid*) and event identifier (*eid*) pairs containing the atom. Figure 3 shows the id-lists for the atoms in our example database. For example consider the atom D. In our original database in Figure 1, we see that D occurs in the following input-sequence and event identifier pairs $\{(1, 10), (1, 25), (4, 10)\}$. This forms the id-list for item D.

A		B		D		F	
SID	EID	SID	EID	SID	EID	SID	EID
1	15	1	15	1	10	1	20
1	20	1	20	1	25	1	25
1	25	2	15	4	10	2	15
2	15	3	10			3	10
3	10	4	20			4	20
4	25						

Fig. 3. Id-lists for the Atoms

D		D -> B			D -> B F				D -> B F -> A				
SID	EID(D)	SID	EID(D)	EID(B)	SID	EID(D)	EID(B)	EID(F)	SID	EID(D)	EID(B)	EID(F)	EID(A)
1	10	1	10	15	1	10	20	20	1	10	20	20	25
1	25	1	10	20	4	10	20	20	4	10	20	20	25
4	10	4	10	20									

Fig. 4. Naive Temporal Joins

Lemma 2. *For any $X \in \mathcal{S}$, let $J = \{Y \in \mathcal{A}(\mathcal{S}) | Y \preceq X\}$. Then $X = \bigvee_{Y \in J} Y$, and $\sigma(X) = |\bigcap_{Y \in J} \mathcal{L}(Y)|$, where $\bigcap$ denotes a temporal join of the id-lists, and $|\mathcal{L}(Z)|$, called the* cardinality *of $\mathcal{L}(Z)$, denotes the number of distinct sid values in the id-list for a sequence Z.*

The above lemma states that any sequence in $\mathcal{S}$ can be obtained as a temporal join of some atoms of the lattice, and the support of the sequence can be obtained by joining the id-list of the atoms. Let's say we wish to compute the support of sequence $(D \rightarrow BF \rightarrow A)$. Here the set $J = \{D, B, F, A\}$. We can perform temporal joins one atom at a time to obtain the final id-list, as shown in Figure 4. We start with the id-list for atom D and join it with that of B. Since the symbol $\rightarrow$ represents a temporal relationship, we find all occurrences of B after a D in an input-sequence, and store the corresponding time-stamps or eids, to obtain $\mathcal{L}(D \rightarrow B)$. We next join the id-list of $(D \rightarrow B)$ with that of atom F, but this time the relationship between B and F is a non-temporal one, which we call an *equality* join, since they must occur at the same time. We thus find all occurrences of B and F with the same eid and store them in the id-list for $(D \rightarrow BF)$. Finally, a temporal join with $\mathcal{L}(A)$ completes the process.

Space-Efficient Joins If we naively produce the id-lists (as shown in Figure 4) by storing the eids (or time-stamps) for all items in a sequence, we waste too much space. Using the lemma below, which states that we can always generate a sequence by joining its lexicographically first two $k - 1$ length subsequences, it is possible to reduce the space requirements, by storing only (sid,eid) pairs (i.e., only two columns) for any sequence, no matter how many items it has.

Lemma 3. *For any sequence $X \in \mathcal{S}$, let X_1 and X_2 denote the lexicographically first two $(k - 1)$-subsequences of X. Then $X = X_1 \vee X_2$ and $\sigma(X) = |\mathcal{L}(X_1) \cap \mathcal{L}(X_2)|$.*

The reason why this lemma allows space reduction is because the first two $k - 1$ length sequences, X_1 and X_2, of a sequence X, share a $k - 2$ length prefix. Since they share the same prefix, it follows that the eids for the items in the prefix must be the same, and the only difference between X_1 and X_2 is in the eids of their last items. Thus it suffices to discard all eids for the prefix, and to keep track of only the eids for the last item of a sequence.

Figure 5 illustrates how the idlist for $(D \rightarrow BF \rightarrow A)$ can be obtained using the space-efficient idlist joins. Let $X = (D \rightarrow BF \rightarrow A)$, then we must perform a temporal join on its first two subsequences $X_1 = (D \rightarrow BF)$ (obtained by dropping the last item from X), and $X_2 = D \rightarrow B \rightarrow A$ (obtained by dropping the second to last item from X). Then, recursively, to obtain the id-list for $(D \rightarrow BF)$ we must perform a equality join on the id-list of $(D \rightarrow B)$ and $(D \rightarrow F)$. For $(D \rightarrow B \rightarrow A)$ we must perform a temporal join on $\mathcal{L}(D \rightarrow B)$ and $\mathcal{L}(D \rightarrow A)$. Finally, the 2-sequences are obtained by joining the atoms directly. Figure 5 shows the complete process, starting with the initial vertical database of the id-list for each atom. As we can see, at each point only (sid,eid) pairs are stored in the id-lists (i.e., only the eid for the last item of a sequence are stored). The exact details of the temporal joins are provided in Section 5.3, when we discuss the implementation of SPADE.

Lemma 4. *Let X and Y be two sequences , with $X \preceq Y$. Then $|\mathcal{L}(X)| \geq |\mathcal{L}(Y)|$.*

This lemma says that if the sequence X is a subsequence of Y, then the cardinality of the id-list of Y (i.e., its support) must be equal to or less than the cardinality of the id-list of X. A practical and important consequence of this lemma is that the cardinalities of intermediate id-lists shrink as we move up the lattice. This results in very fast joins and support counting.

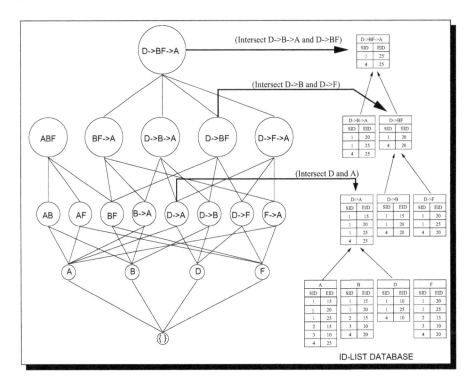

Fig. 5. Computing Support via Space-Efficient Temporal Id-list Joins

4.2   Lattice Decomposition: Prefix-Based Classes

If we had enough main-memory, we could enumerate all the frequent sequences by traversing the lattice, and performing temporal joins to obtain sequence supports. In practice, however, we only have a limited amount of main-memory, and all the intermediate id-lists will not fit in memory. This brings up a natural question: can we decompose the original lattice into smaller pieces such that each piece can be solved independently in main-memory. We address this question below.

Define a function $p : (\mathcal{S}, N) \rightarrow \mathcal{S}$ where $\mathcal{S}$ is the set of sequences, N is the set of non-negative integers, and $p(X, k) = X[1 : k]$. In other words, $p(X, k)$ returns the k length prefix of X. Define an equivalence relation θ_k on the lattice $\mathcal{S}$ as follows: $\forall X, Y \in \mathcal{S}$, we say that X is related to Y under θ_k, denoted as $X \equiv_{\theta_k} Y$ if and only if $p(X, k) = p(Y, k)$. That is, two sequences are in the same class if they share a common k length prefix.

Figure 6 shows the partition induced by the equivalence relation θ_1 on $\mathcal{S}$, where we collapse all sequences with a common item prefix into an equivalence class. The resulting set of equivalence classes is $\{[A], [B], [D], [F]\}$. We call these first level classes as the *parent* classes.

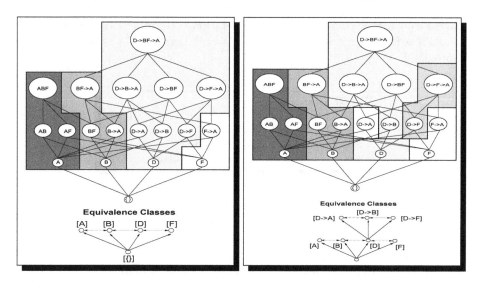

Fig. 6. a) Equivalence Classes of $\mathcal{S}$ Induced by θ_1, b) Classes of $[D]_{\theta_1}$ Induced by θ_2

Lemma 5. *Each equivalence class $[X]_{\theta_k}$ induced by the equivalence relation θ_k is a sub-(hyper)lattice of $\mathcal{S}$.*

Each $[X]_{\theta_1}$ is thus a hyper-lattice with its own set of atoms. For example, the atoms of $[D]_{\theta_1}$ are $\{D \to A, D \to B, D \to F\}$, and the bottom element is $\perp = D$. By the application of Corollary 3, we can generate the supports of all the sequences in each class (sub-lattice) using temporal joins. If there is enough main-memory to hold temporary id-lists for each class, then we can solve each $[X]_{\theta_1}$ independently.

In practice we have found that the one level decomposition induced by θ_1 is sufficient. However, in some cases, a class may still be too large to be solved in main-memory. In this scenario, we apply recursive class decomposition. Let's assume that $[D]$ is too large to fit in main-memory. Since $[D]$ is itself a lattice, it can be decomposed using the relation θ_2. Figure 6 shows the classes induced by applying θ_2 on $[D]$ (after applying θ_1 on $\mathcal{S}$). Each of the resulting six parent classes, $[A]$, $[B]$, $[D \to A]$, $[D \to B]$, $[D \to F]$, and $[F]$, can be processed independently to generate frequent sequences from each class. Thus depending on the amount of main-memory available, we can recursively partition large classes into smaller ones, until each class is small enough to be solved independently in main-memory.

5   SPADE: Implementation Issues

In this section we describe the implementation of SPADE. Figure 7 shows the high level structure of the algorithm. The main steps include the computation of the frequent 1-sequences and 2-sequences, the decomposition into prefix-based parent equivalence classes, and the enumeration of all other frequent sequences via BFS or DFS search within each class. We will now describe each step in some more detail.

SPADE $(min\_sup, \mathcal{D})$:
  $\mathcal{F}_1 = \{$ frequent items or 1-sequences $\}$;
  $\mathcal{F}_2 = \{$ frequent 2-sequences $\}$;
  $\mathcal{E} = \{$ equivalence classes $[X]_{\theta_1} \}$;
  for all $[X] \in \mathcal{E}$ **do** *Enumerate-Frequent-Seq*($[X]$);

Fig. 7. The SPADE Algorithm

5.1   Computing Frequent 1-Sequences and 2-Sequences

Most of the current sequence mining algorithms [2,12] assume a *horizontal* database layout such as the one shown in Figure 1. In the horizontal format the database consists of a set of input-sequences. Each input-sequence has a set of events, along with the items contained in the event. In contrast our algorithm uses a *vertical* database format, where we maintain a disk-based id-list for each item, as shown in Figure 3. Each entry of the id-list is a (sid, eid) pair where the item occurs. This enables us to check support via simple id-list joins.

Computing $\mathcal{F}_1$: Given the vertical id-list database, all frequent 1-sequences can be computed in a single database scan. For each database item, we read its id-list from the disk into memory. We then scan the id-list, incrementing the support for each new sid encountered.

sid	$(item, eid)$ pairs
1	(A 15) (A 20) (A 25) (B 15) (B 20) (C 10) (C 15) (C 25) (D 10) (D 25) (F 20) (F 25)
2	(A 15) (B 15) (E 20) (F 15)
3	(A 10) (B 10) (F 10)
4	(A 25) (B 20) (D 10) (F 20) (G 10) (G 25) (H 10) (H 25)

Fig. 8. Vertical-to-Horizontal Database Recovery

Computing $\mathcal{F}_2$: Let $N = |\mathcal{F}_1|$ be the number of frequent items, and A the average id-list size in bytes. A naive implementation for computing the frequent 2-sequences requires $\binom{N}{2}$ id-list joins for all pairs of items. The amount of data read is $A \cdot N \cdot (N - 1)/2$, which corresponds to around $N/2$ data scans. This is clearly inefficient. Instead of the naive method we propose two alternate solutions:

1. Use a preprocessing step to gather the counts of all 2-sequences above a user specified lower bound. Since this information is invariant, it has to be computed once, and the cost can be amortized over the number of times the data is mined.
2. Perform a vertical-to-horizontal transformation on-the-fly. This can be done quite easily, with very little overhead. For each item i, we scan its id-list into memory. For each (sid, eid) pair, say (s, e) in $\mathcal{L}(i)$, we insert (i, e) in the list for input-sequence s. For example, consider the id-list for item A, shown in Figure 3. We scan the first pair $(1, 15)$, and then insert $(A, 15)$ in the list for input-sequence 1. Figure 8 shows the complete horizontal database recovered from the vertical item id-lists. Computing $\mathcal{F}_2$ from the recovered horizontal database is straight-forward. We form a list of all 2-sequences in the list for each sid, and update counts in a 2-dimensional array indexed by the frequent items.

5.2   Enumerating Frequent Sequences of a Class

Figure 9 shows the pseudo-code for the breadth-first and depth-first search. The input to the procedure is a set of atoms of a sub-lattice S, along with their id-lists. Frequent sequences are generated by joining the id-lists of all pairs of atoms (including a self-join) and checking the cardinality of the resulting id-list against min_sup.

```
Enumerate-Frequent-Seq(S):
    for all atoms A_i ∈ S do
        T_i = ∅;
        for all atoms A_j ∈ S, with j ≥ i do
            R = A_i ∨ A_j;
            L(R) = L(A_i) ∩ L(A_j);
            if σ(R) ≥ min_sup then
                T_i = T_i ∪ {R}; F_|R| = F_|R| ∪ {R};
        end
        if (Depth-First-Search) then Enumerate-Frequent-Seq(T_i);
    end
    if (Breadth-First-Search) then
        for all T_i ≠ ∅ do Enumerate-Frequent-Seq(T_i);
```

Fig. 9. Pseudo-code for Breadth-First and Depth-First Search

SPADE supports both breadth-first (BFS) and depth-first (DFS) search. In BFS we process all the child classes at a level before moving on to the next level, while in DFS, we completely solve all child equivalence classes along one path before moving on to the next path. DFS also requires less main-memory than BFS. DFS needs only to keep the intermediate id-lists for two consecutive classes along a single path, while BFS must keep track of id-lists for all the classes in two consecutive levels. Consequently, when the number of frequent sequences is very large, for example in dense domains or in cases where the *min_sup* value is very low, DFS may be the only feasible approach, since BFS can run out of virtual memory.

The sequences found to be frequent at the current level form the atoms of classes for the next level. This recursive process is repeated until all frequent sequences have been enumerated. In terms of memory management it is easy to see that we need memory to store intermediate id-lists for at most two consecutive levels. The depth-first search requires memory for two classes on the two levels. The breadth-first search requires memory of all the classes on the two levels. Once all the frequent sequences for the next level have been generated, the sequences at the current level can be deleted.

5.3   Temporal Id-List Join

We now describe how we perform the id-list joins for two sequences. Consider an equivalence class $[B \rightarrow A]$ with the atom set $\{B \rightarrow AB, B \rightarrow AD, B \rightarrow A \rightarrow A, B \rightarrow A \rightarrow D, B \rightarrow A \rightarrow F\}$. If we let P stand for the prefix $B \rightarrow A$, then we can rewrite the class to get $[P] = \{PB, PD, P \rightarrow A, P \rightarrow D, P \rightarrow F\}$. One can observe the class has two kinds of atoms: the event atoms $\{PB, PD\}$, and the sequence atoms $\{P \rightarrow A, P \rightarrow D, P \rightarrow F\}$. We assume without loss of generality that the event atoms of a class always precede the sequence atoms. To extend the class it is sufficient to join the id-lists of all pairs of atoms. However, depending on the atom pairs being joined, there can be upto three possible resulting frequent sequences (these are the three possible minimal common super-sequences):

1. **Event Atom with Event Atom**: If we are joining PB with PD, then the only possible outcome is new event atom PBD.
2. **Event Atom with Sequence Atom**: If we are joining PB with $P \rightarrow A$, then the only possible outcome is new sequence atom $PB \rightarrow A$.
3. **Sequence Atom with Sequence Atom**: If we are joining $P \rightarrow A$ with $P \rightarrow F$, then there are three possible outcomes: a new event atom $P \rightarrow AF$, and two new sequence atoms $P \rightarrow A \rightarrow F$ and $P \rightarrow F \rightarrow A$. A special case arises when we join $P \rightarrow A$ with itself, which can produce only the new sequence atom $P \rightarrow A \rightarrow A$.

We now describe how the actual id-list join is performed. Consider Figure 10, which shows the hypothetical id-lists for the sequence atoms $P \rightarrow A$ and $P \rightarrow F$. To compute the new id-list for the resulting event atom $P \rightarrow AF$, we simply need to check for *equality* of (sid,eid) pairs. In our example, the only matching pairs are $\{(8, 30), (8, 50), (8, 80)\}$. This forms the id-list for $P \rightarrow AF$. To compute the id-list for the new sequence atom $P \rightarrow A \rightarrow F$, we need to check for a *temporal*

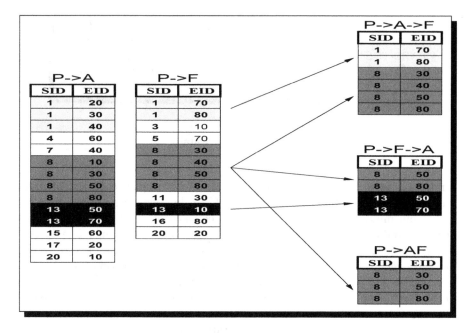

Fig. 10. Temporal Id-list Join

relationship, i.e., for a given pair (s, t_1) in $\mathcal{L}(P \rightarrow A)$, we check whether there exists a pair (s, t_2) in $\mathcal{L}(P \rightarrow F)$ with the same sid s, but with $t_2 > t_1$. If this is true, it means that the item F follows the item A for input-sequence s. In other words, the input-sequence s contains the pattern $P \rightarrow A \rightarrow F$, and the pair (s, t_2) is added to the pattern's id-list. Finally, the id-list for $P \rightarrow F \rightarrow A$ can be obtained in a similar manner by reversing the roles of $P \rightarrow A$ and $P \rightarrow F$. The final id-lists for the three new sequences are shown in Figure 10. Since we join only sequences within a class, which have the same prefix (whose items have the same eid or time-stamp), we need only to keep track of the last item's eid for determining the equality and temporal relationships. As a further optimization, we generate the id-lists of all the three possible new sequences in just one join.

6   Experimental Results

In this section we study the performance of SPADE by varying different database parameters and by comparing it with the GSP algorithm. GSP was implemented as described in [12]. For SPADE results are shown only for the BFS search. Experiments were performed on a 100MHz MIPS processor with 256MB main memory running IRIX 6.2. The data was stored on a non-local 2GB disk.

Synthetic Datasets The synthetic datasets are the same as those used in [12], albeit with twice as many input-sequences. We used the publicly available dataset generation code from the IBM Quest data mining project [5]. These datasets

Dataset	C	T	S	I	D	Size (MB)
C10-T2.5-S4-I1.25-D(100K-1000K)	10	2.5	4	1.25	100,000	18.4-184.0
C10-T5-S4-I2.5-D200K	10	5	4	2.5	200,000	54.3
C20-T2.5-S4-I2.5-D200K	20	2.5	4	2.5	200,000	66.5
C20-T2.5-S8-I1.25-D200K	20	2.5	8	1.25	200,000	76.4

Fig. 11. Synthetic Datasets

mimic real-world transactions, where people buy a sequence of sets of items. Some customers may buy only some items from the sequences, or they may buy items from multiple sequences. The input-sequence size and event size are clustered around a mean and a few of them may have many elements. The datasets are generated using the following process. First N_I maximal events of average size I are generated by choosing from N items. Then N_S maximal sequences of average size S are created by assigning events from N_I to each sequence. Next a customer (or input-sequence) of average C transactions (or events) is created, and sequences in N_S are assigned to different customer elements, respecting the average transaction size of T. The generation stops when D input-sequences have been generated. Like [12] we set $N_S = 5000$, $N_I = 25000$ and $N = 10000$. Figure 11 shows the datasets with their parameter settings. We refer the reader to [2] for additional details on the dataset generation.

PLAN DATABASE											
PlanId	Time	EventId	Action	Outcome	Route	From	To	AtLocation	Cargo	Vehicle	VehicleId	Weather
1	10	78	Move	Success	Delta-Exodus	Delta	Exodus			Helicopter	Heli1	Good
1	20	84	Load	Success				Exodus	People7		Heli1	
1	30	85	Move	Flat	Exodus-Barnacle-Abyss	Exodus	Barnacle			Helicopter	Heli1	Fair
1	40	101	Unload	Crash				Barnacle	People7	Helicopter	Heli1	Hazardous
2	10	7	Move	Flat	Delta-Calypso-Delta	Delta	Calypso			Truck	Truck1	Good
2	20	10	Move	Breakdown	Delta-Calypso-Delta	Calypso	Delta			Truck	Truck1	Good

Fig. 12. Example Plan Database

Plan Dataset This real dataset was obtained from a planning domain. The input consists of a database of plans for evacuating people from one city to another. Each plan has a unique identifier, and a sequence of actions or events. Each event is composed of several different attributes including the event time, the unique event identifier, the action name, the outcome of the event, and a set of additional parameters specifying the weather condition, vehicle type, origin and destination city, cargo type, etc. Some example plans are shown in Figure 12. Each plan represents an input-sequence (with sid = PlanId). Each distinct attribute and value pair is an item. For example, *Action=Move*, *Action=Load*, etc., are all distinct items. A set of items forms an event (with eid = Time). For example, the second row of the first plan corresponds to the event *(84, Load, Success, Exodus, People7, Heli1)*.

The data mining goal is to identify the causes of plan failures. Each plan is tagged *Failure* or *Success* depending on whether or not it achieved its goal. We mine only the dataset of bad plans, which has 77 items, 202071 plans (input-sequences), and 829236 events in all. The average plan length is 4.1, and the average event length is 7.6.

6.1   Comparison of SPADE with GSP

Figure 13 compares SPADE with GSP, on different synthetic and the plan datasets. Each graph shows the results as the minimum support is changed from 1% to 0.25%. Two sets of experiments are reported for each value of support. The bar labeled SPADE corresponds to the case where we computed $\mathcal{F}_2$ via the vertical-to-horizontal transformation method described in Section 5.1. The times for GSP and SPADE include the cost of computing $\mathcal{F}_2$. The bars labeled SPADE-F2 and GSP-F2 correspond to the case where $\mathcal{F}_2$ was computed in a pre-processing step, and the times shown don't include the pre-processing cost.

The figures clearly indicate that the performance gap between the two algorithms increases with decreasing minimum support. SPADE is about twice as fast as GSP at lower values of support. In addition we see that SPADE-F2 outperforms GSP-F2 by an order of magnitude in most cases. Another conclusion that can be drawn from the SPADE-F2 and GSP-F2 comparison is that nearly all the benefit of SPADE comes from the improvement in the running time after the $\mathcal{F}_2$ pass since both algorithms spend roughly the same time in computing $\mathcal{F}_2$. Between $\mathcal{F}_3$ and $\mathcal{F}_k$, SPADE outperforms GSP anywhere from a factor of three to an order of magnitude.

6.2   Scaleup

We study how SPADE performs with increasing number of input-sequences. Figure 14 shows how SPADE scales up as the number of input-sequences is increased ten-fold, from 0.1 million to 1 million (the number of events is increased from 1 million to 10 million, respectively). All the experiments were performed on the *C10-T2.5-S4-I1.25* dataset with different minimum support levels ranging from 0.5% to 0.1%. The execution times are normalized with respect to the time for the 0.1 million input-sequence dataset. It can be observed that SPADE scales almost linearly. SPADE also scales linearly in the number of events per

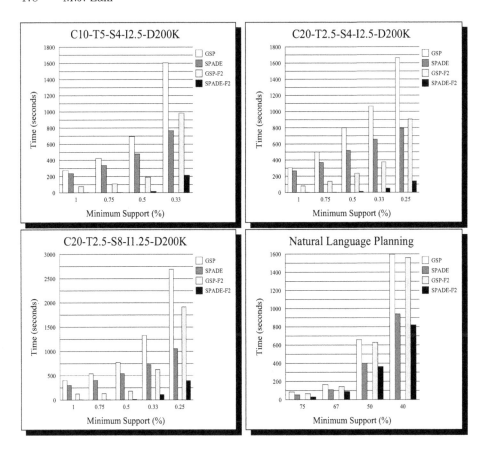

Fig. 13. Performance Comparison: Synthetic and Plan Datasets

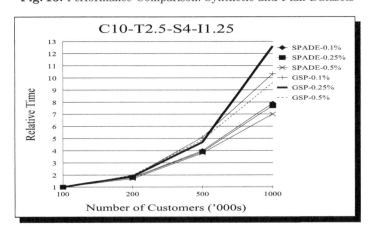

Fig. 14. Scale-up: Number of Input-Sequences

input-sequence, event size and the size of potential maximal frequent events and sequences [13].

7   Application I: Predicting Plan Failures

We saw in the last section that SPADE is an efficient and scalable method for mining frequent sequences. However, the mining process rarely ends at this stage. The more important aspect is how to take the results of mining and use them effectively within the target domain. In this section we briefly describe our experiences in applying sequence mining in a planning domain to predict failures before they happen, and to improve the plans.

Using SPADE to find the frequent sequences we developed a system called PLANMINE [15], which has been integrated into two applications in planning: the IMPROVE algorithm for improving large, probabilistic plans [6], and plan monitoring.

IMPROVE *automatically* modifies a given plan so that it has a higher probability of achieving its goal. IMPROVE runs PLANMINE on the execution traces of the given plan to pinpoint defects in the plan that most often lead to plan failure. It then applies qualitative reasoning and plan adaptation algorithms to modify the plan to correct the defects detected by PLANMINE.

We applied SPADE to the planning dataset to detect sequences leading to plan failures. We found that since this domain has a complicated structure with redundancy in the data, SPADE generates an enormous number of highly frequent, but unpredictive rules [15]. Figure 15 shows the number of mined frequent sequences of different lengths for various levels of minimum support when we ran SPADE on the bad plans. At 60% support level we found an overwhelming number of patterns (around 6.5 million). Even at 75% support, we have too many patterns (38386), most of which are quite useless for predicting failures when we compute their confidence relative to the entire database of plans. Clearly, all potentially useful patterns are present in the sequences mined from the bad plans; we must somehow extract the interesting ones from this set.

We developed a three-step pruning strategy for selecting only the most predictive sequences from the mined set:

1. *Pruning Normative Patterns*: We eliminate all *normative* rules that are consistent with background knowledge that corresponds to the normal operation of a (good) plan, i.e., we eliminate those patterns that not only occur in bad plans, but also occur in the good plans quite often, since these patterns are not likely to be predictive of bad events.
2. *Pruning Redundant Patterns*: We eliminate all *redundant* patterns that have the same frequency as at least one of their proper subsequences, i.e., we eliminate those patterns q that are obtained by augmenting an existing pattern p, while q has the same *frequency* as p. The intuition is that p is as predictive as q.
3. *Pruning Dominated Patterns*: We eliminate all *dominated* sequences that are less predictive than any of their proper subsequences, i.e., we eliminate those

patterns q that are obtained by augmenting an existing pattern p, where p is shorter or more general than q, and has a higher *confidence* of predicting failure than q.

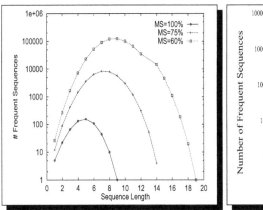 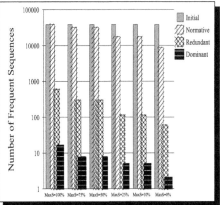

Fig. 15. a) Number of Frequent Sequences; b) Effect of Different Pruning Techniques

Figure 15 shows the reduction in the number of frequent sequences after applying each kind of pruning. After normative pruning (by removing patterns with more than 25% support in good plans), we get more than a factor of 2 reduction (from 38386 to 17492 sequences). Applying redundant pruning in addition to normative pruning reduces the pattern set from 17492 down to 113. Finally, dominant pruning, when applied along with normative and redundant pruning, reduces the rule set from 113 down to only 5 highly predictive patterns. The combined effect of the three pruning techniques is to retain only the patterns that have the highest confidence of predicting a failure, where confidence is given as:

$$Conf(\alpha) = \frac{\sigma(\alpha, \mathcal{D}_b)}{\sigma(\alpha, \mathcal{D}_b + \mathcal{D}_g)}$$

where $\mathcal{D}_b$ is the dataset of bad plans and $\mathcal{D}_g$ the dataset of good plans.

These three steps are carried out *automatically* by mining the good and bad plans separately and comparing the discovered rules from the unsuccessful plans against those from the successful plans. There are two main goals: 1) to improve an existing plan, and 2) to generate a plan monitor for raising alarms. In the first case the planner generates a plan and simulates it multiple times. It then produces a database of good and bad plans in simulation. This information is fed into the mining engine, which discovers high frequency patterns in the bad plans. We next apply our pruning techniques to generate a final set of rules that are highly predictive of plan failure. This mined information is used for fixing the plan to prevent failures, and the loop is executed multiple times till no further improvement is obtained. The planner then generates the final plan. For the second goal, the planner generates multiple plans, and creates a database of good and bad plans (there is no simulation step). The high confidence patterns are mined as before, and the information is used to generate a plan monitor that raises alarms prior to failures in new plans.

7.1   Experiments

Plan Improvement We first discuss the role of PLANMINE in IMPROVE, a fully automatic algorithm which modifies a given plan to increase its probability of goal satisfaction [6]. Table 1 shows the performance of the IMPROVE algorithm on a large evacuation domain that contains 35 cities, 45 roads, and 100 people. We use a domain-specific greedy scheduling algorithm to generate initial plans for this domain. The initial plans contain over 250 steps.

Table 1. Performance of IMPROVE (averaged over 70 trials).

	initial plan length	final plan length	initial success rate	final success rate	num. plans tested
IMPROVE	272.3	278.9	0.82	0.98	11.7
RANDOM	272.3	287.4	0.82	0.85	23.4
HIGH	272.6	287.0	0.82	0.83	23.0

We compared IMPROVE with two less sophisticated alternatives. The RANDOM approach modifies the plan randomly five times in each iteration, and chooses the modification that works best in simulation. The HIGH approach replaces the PLANMINE component of IMPROVE with a technique that simply tries to prevent the malfunctions that occur most often. As shown in Table 1, PLANMINE improves the plan success rate from 82% to 98%, while less sophisticated methods for choosing which part of the plan to repair were only able to achieve a maximum of 85% success rate.

Plan Monitoring Figure 16a shows the evaluation of the monitors produced with PLANMINE on a test set of 500 (novel) plans. The results are the averages over 105 trials, and thus each number reflects an average of approximately 50,000 separate tests. Note that *precision* is the ratio of correct failure signals to the total number of failure signals, while *recall* is the percentage of failures identified. The figure clearly shows that our mining and pruning techniques produce excellent monitors, which have 100% precision with recall greater than 90%. We can produce monitors with significantly higher recall, but only by reducing precision to around 50%. The desired tradeoff depends on the application. If plan failures are very costly then it might be worth sacrificing precision for recall. For comparison we also built monitors that signaled failure as soon as a fixed number of malfunctions of any kind occurred. Figure 16b shows that this approach produces poor monitors, since there was no correlation between the number of malfunctions and the chance of failure (precision).

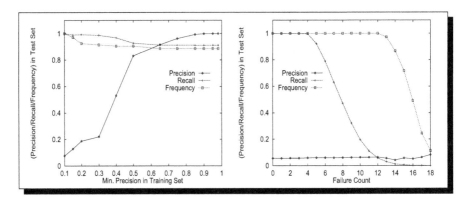

Fig. 16. a) Using PLANMINE for Prediction; b) Using Failure Count for Prediction

8   Application II: Feature Selection

Our next application of sequence mining is for feature selection. Many real world datasets contain irrelevant or redundant attributes. This may be because the data was collected without data mining in mind, or because the attribute dependences were not known a priori during data collection. It is well known that many data mining methods like classification, clustering, etc., degrade prediction accuracy when trained on datasets containing redundant or irrelevant attributes or features. Selecting the right feature set can not only improve accuracy, but can also reduce the running time of the predictive algorithms, and can lead to simpler, more understandable models. Good feature selection is thus one of the fundamental data preprocessing steps in data mining.

Most research on feature selection to-date has focused on non-sequential domains. Here the problem may be defined as that of selecting an optimal feature subset of size l from the full m-dimensional feature space, where ideally $l \ll m$. The selected subset should maximize some optimization criterion such as classification accuracy or it should faithfully capture the original data distribution.

Selecting the right features in sequential domains is even more challenging than in non-sequence data. The original feature set is itself undefined; there are potentially an infinite number of sequences of arbitrary length over d categorical attributes or dimensions. Even if we restrict ourselves to some maximum sequence length k, we have potentially $O(m^k)$ subsequences over m dimensions.

The goal of feature selection in sequential domains is to select the best subset of sequential features out of the m^k possible sequential features (i.e., subsequences). We now briefly describe FEATUREMINE [7], a scalable algorithm based on SPADE, that mines features to be used for sequence classification. The input database consists of a set of input-sequences with a class label. Let β be a sequence and c be a class label. The confidence of the rule $\beta \Rightarrow c$ is given as $\sigma(\beta, \mathcal{D}_c)/\sigma(\beta, \mathcal{D})$ where $\mathcal{D}_c$ is the subset of input-sequences in $\mathcal{D}$ with class label c. Our goal is to find all frequent sequences with high confidence. Figure 17a shows a database of customers with labels. There are 7 input-sequences, 4 belonging to class c_1, and 3 belonging to class c_2. In general there can be more than two classes. We are looking for different min_sup in each class. For example, while C is frequent for class c_2, it's not frequent for class c_1. The rule $C \Rightarrow c_2$ has confidence $3/4 = 0.75$, while the rule $C \Rightarrow c_1$ has confidence $1/4 = 0.25$.

EID	Time	Items	Class
1	10	A B	
	20	B	c1
	30	A B	
2	20	A C	
	30	A B C	c1
	50	B	
3	10	A	
	30	B	c1
	40	A	
4	30	A B	
	40	A	c1
	50	B	
5	10	A B	c2
	50	A C	
6	30	A	c2
	40	C	
7	20	C	c2

FREQUENT SEQUENCES

Class = c1
min_freq (c1) = 75%

A	100%
B	100%
A->A	100%
AB	75%
A->B	100%
B->A	75%
B->B	75%
AB->B	75%

Class = c2
min_freq (c2) = 67%

A	67%
C	100%
A->C	67%

New Boolean Features

EID	A	A->A	B->A	B	AB	A->B	B->B	AB->B	C	A->C	Class
1	1	1	1	1	1	1	1	1	0	0	c1
2	1	1	0	1	1	1	1	1	1	0	c1
3	1	0	1	1	0	1	0	0	0	0	c1
4	1	1	1	1	1	1	1	1	0	0	c1
5	1	1	1	1	1	0	0	0	1	1	c2
6	1	0	0	0	0	0	0	0	1	1	c2
7	0	0	0	0	0	0	0	0	1	0	c2

(Examples)

Fig. 17. a) Database with Class Labels, b) New Database with Boolean Features

We now describe how frequent sequences $\beta_1, ..., \beta_n$ can be used as features for classification. Recall that the input to most standard classifiers is an example represented as vector of feature-value pairs. We represent a example sequence α as a vector of feature-value pairs by treating each sequence β_i as a boolean feature that is true iff $\beta_i \preceq \alpha$. For example, suppose the features are $f_1 = A \rightarrow D$, $f_2 = A \rightarrow BC$, and $f_3 = CD$. The input sequence $AB \rightarrow BD \rightarrow BC$ would be represented as $\langle f_1, 0 \rangle, \langle f_2, 1 \rangle, \langle f_3, 0 \rangle$. Figure 17b shows the new dataset created from the frequent sequences of our example database of Figure 1a.

FEATUREMINE uses the following heuristics to determine the "good" features: 1) features should be frequent, 2) they should be distinctive of at least one class, and 3) feature sets should not contain redundant features. FEATUREMINE employs pruning functions, similar to the three outlined in the last section, to achieve these objectives. Further all pruning constraints are directly integrated into the mining algorithm itself, instead of applying pruning as a post-processing step. This allows FEATUREMINE to search very large spaces efficiently, which would have been infeasible otherwise.

8.1   Experiments

To evaluate the effectiveness of FEATUREMINE, we used the feature set it produces as input to two standard classification algorithms: Winnow [8] and Naive Bayes [3]. We ran experiments on three datasets described below. In each case, we experimented with various settings for min_sup, max_w (maximum event size), and max_l (maximum number of events) to generate reasonable results.

Random Parity We first describe a non-sequential problem on which standard classification algorithms perform very poorly. Each input example consists of N parity problems of size M with L distracting, or irrelevant, features. Thus are a total of $N \times M + L$ boolean-valued features. Each instance is assigned one of two class labels (ON or OFF) as follows. Out of the N parity problems (per instance), if the weighted sum of those with even parity exceeds a threshold, then the instance is assigned class label ON, otherwise it is assigned OFF. Note that if $M > 1$, then no feature by itself is at all indicative of the class label ON or OFF, which is why parity problems are so hard for most classifiers. The job of FEATUREMINE is essentially to figure out which features should be grouped together. We used a min_sup of .02 to .05, $max_l = 1$ and $max_w = M$.

FireWorld We obtained this dataset from simple forest-fire domain [7]. We use a grid representation of the terrain. Each grid cell can contain vegetation, water, or a base. We label each instance with SUCCESS if none of the locations with bases have been burned in the final state, or FAILURE otherwise. Thus, our job is to predict if the bulldozers will prevent the bases from burning, given a partial execution trace of the plan. For this data, there were 38 items to describe each input-sequence. In the experiments reported below, we used $min\_sup = 20\%$, $max_w = 3$, and $max_l = 3$, to make the problem tractable.

Spelling To create this dataset, we chose two commonly confused words, such as "there" and "their", "I" and "me", "than" and "then", and "your" and "you're", and searched for sentences in the 1-million-word Brown corpus containing either word [7]. We removed the target word and then represented each word by the word itself, the part-of-speech tag in the Brown corpus, and the position relative to the target word. For "there" vs. "their" dataset there were 2917 training examples, 755 test examples, and 5663 feature/value pairs or items. Other datasets had similar parameters. In the experiments reported below, we used a min_sup = 5%, $max_w = 3$, and $max_l = 2$.

For each test in the parity and fire domains, we generated 7,000 random training examples. We mined features from 1,000 examples, pruned features that did not pass a chi-squared significance test (for correlation to a class the feature was frequent in) in 2,000 examples, and trained the classifier on the remaining

Table 2. Classification Results (FM denotes features produced by FEATUREMINE)

Experiment	Winnow	WinnowFM	Bayes	BayesFM
parity, $N = 5, M = 3, L = 5$	.51 (.02)	.97 (.03)	.50 (.01)	.97 (.04)
parity, $N = 3, M = 4, L = 8$	.49 (.01)	.99 (.04)	.50 (.01)	1.0 (0)
parity, $N = 10, M = 4, L = 10$	.50 (.01)	.89 (.03)	.50 (.01)	.85 (.06)
fire, time $= 5$	.60 (.11)	.79 (.02)	.69 (.02)	.81 (.02)
fire, time $= 10$	.60 (.14)	.85 (.02)	.68 (.01)	.75 (.02)
fire, time $= 15$	.55 (.16)	.89 (.04)	.68 (.01)	.72 (.02)
spelling, their vs. there	.70	.94	.75	.78
spelling, I vs. me	.86	.94	.66	.90
spelling, than vs. then	.83	.92	.79	.81
spelling, you're vs. your	.77	.86	.77	.86

5,000 examples. We then tested on 1,000 additional examples. The results in Table 2 are averages from 25-50 such tests. For the spelling correction, we used all the examples in the Brown corpus, roughly 1000-4000 examples per word set, split 80-20 (by sentence) into training and test sets. We mined features from 500 sentences and trained the classifier on the entire training set.

Table 2, which shows the average classification accuracy using different feature sets, confirms that the features produced by FEATUREMINE improved classification performance. We compared using the feature set produced by FEATUREMINE with using only the primitive features themselves, i.e. features of length 1. The standard deviations are shown, in parentheses following each average, except for the spelling problems for which only one test and training set were used. Both Winnow and Naive Bayes performed much better with the features produced by FEATUREMINE. In the parity experiments, the mined features dramatically improved the performance of the classifiers and in the other experiments the mined features improved the accuracy of the classifiers by a significant amount, often more than 20%.

9   Conclusions

In this chapter we presented SPADE, a new algorithm for fast mining of sequential patterns in large databases. Unlike previous approaches which make multiple database scans and use complex hash-tree structures that tend to have sub-optimal locality, SPADE decomposes the original problem into smaller subproblems using equivalence classes on frequent sequences. Not only can each equivalence class be solved independently, but it is also very likely that it can be processed in main-memory. Thus SPADE usually makes only three database scans – one for frequent 1-sequences, another for frequent 2-sequences, and one more for generating all other frequent sequences. If the supports of 2-sequences is available then only one scan is required. SPADE uses only simple temporal join operations, and is thus ideally suited for direct integration with a DBMS.

An extensive set of experiments was conducted to show that SPADE outperforms the best previous algorithm, GSP, by a factor of two, and by an order of magnitude with precomputed support of 2-sequences. Further, it scales linearly in the number of input-sequences and other dataset parameters.

We discussed how the mined sequences can be used in a planning application. A simple mining of frequent sequences produces a large number of patterns, many of them trivial or useless. We proposed novel pruning strategies applied in a post-processing step to weed out the irrelevant patterns and to locate the most interesting sequences. We used these predictive sequences to improve probabilistic plans and for raising alarms before failures happen.

Finally, we showed how sequence mining can help select good features for sequence classification. These domains are challenging because of the exponential number of potential subsequence features that can be formed from the primitives for describing each item in the sequence data. The number of features, containing many irrelevant and redundant features, is too large to be practically handled by today's classification algorithms. Our experiments using several datasets show that the features produced by mining predictive sequences significantly improves classification accuracy.

References

1. Agrawal, R., Mannila, H., Srikant, R., Toivonen, H., and Verkamo, A. I. (1996). Fast discovery of association rules. In Fayyad, U. and et al, editors, *Advances in Knowledge Discovery and Data Mining*, pages 307–328. AAAI Press, Menlo Park, CA.
2. Agrawal, R. and Srikant, R. (1995). Mining sequential patterns. In *11th Intl. Conf. on Data Engg.*
3. Duda, R. O. and Hart, P. E. (1973). *Pattern Classification and Scene Analysis.* John Wiley and Sons.
4. Hatonen, K., Klemettinen, M., Mannila, H., Ronkainen, P., and Toivonen, H. (1996). Knowledge discovery from telecommunication network alarm databases. In *12th Intl. Conf. Data Engineering.*
5. IBM. *http://www.almaden.ibm.com/cs/quest/syndata.html.* Quest Data Mining Project, IBM Almaden Research Center, San Jose, CA 95120.
6. Lesh, N., Martin, N., and Allen, J. (1998). Improving big plans. In *15th Nat. Conf. AI.*
7. Lesh, N., Zaki, M. J., and Ogihara, M. (2000). Scalable feature mining for sequential data. *IEEE Intelligent Systems and their Applications*, 15(2):48-56. Special issue on Data Mining.
8. Littlestone, N. (1988). Learning quickly when irrelevant attributes abound: A new linear-threshold algorithm. *Machine Learning*, 2:285–318.
9. Mannila, H. and Toivonen, H. (1996). Discovering generalized episodes using minimal occurences. In *2nd Intl. Conf. Knowledge Discovery and Data Mining.*
10. Mannila, H., Toivonen, H., and Verkamo, I. (1995). Discovering frequent episodes in sequences. In *1st Intl. Conf. Knowledge Discovery and Data Mining.*
11. Oates, T., Schmill, M. D., Jensen, D., and Cohen, P. R. (1997). A family of algorithms for finding temporal structure in data. In *6th Intl. Workshop on AI and Statistics.*

12. Srikant, R. and Agrawal, R. (1996). Mining sequential patterns: Generalizations and performance improvements. In *5th Intl. Conf. Extending Database Technology*.

13. Zaki, M. J. (1998). Efficient enumeration of frequent sequences. In *7th Intl. Conf. on Information and Knowledge Management*.

14. Zaki, M. J. (1999). Parallel and distributed association mining: A survey. *IEEE Concurrency*, 7(4):14–25. Special issue on Parallel Data Mining.

15. Zaki, M. J., Lesh, N., and Ogihara, M. (1998). PLANMINE: Sequence mining for plan failures. In *4th Intl. Conf. Knowledge Discovery and Data Mining*.

16. Zaki, M. J., Parthasarathy, S., Ogihara, M., and Li, W. (1997). New algorithms for fast discovery of association rules. In *3rd Intl. Conf. on Knowledge Discovery and Data Mining*.

Sequence Learning in the ACT-R Cognitive Architecture: Empirical Analysis of a Hybrid Model

Christian Lebiere[1] and Dieter Wallach[2]

[1] Human Computer Interaction Institute, Carnegie Mellon University, USA
[2] Department of Psychology, University of Basel, Switzerland

1. Introduction

A hallmark of Cognitive Science is its interdisciplinary approach to the study of the structures and mechanisms of human and artificial cognitive systems. Over the past decade, sequential pattern acquisition has attracted the attention of researchers from Computer Science, Cognitive Psychology and the Neurosciences. Methodologies for the investigation of sequence learning processes range from the exploration of computational mechanisms to the conduct of experimental studies and the use of event-related brain potentials, functional magnetic resonance imaging and positron emission tomography (Clegg, DiGirolamo, & Keele 1998; Curran 1998). This interest in sequential pattern acquisition is also understandable from an evolutionary perspective: sequencing information and learning of event contingencies are fundamentally important processes without which adaptive behavior in dynamic environments would hardly be possible. From sequencing continuous speech to learning operating sequences of technical devices or acquiring the skill to play a musical instrument, learning of event sequences seems to be an essential capability of human (and artificial) cognition. It is therefore not surprising that we are witnessing a tremendous interest in sequence learning in the disciplines contributing to Cognitive Science. This chapter presents and analyses a model of sequence learning based on the ACT-R theory (Anderson 1993; Anderson & Lebiere 1998). The model is rooted in, and has been successfully applied to, empirical studies using the serial reaction task that was introduced by Nissen and Bullemer (1987).

A large variety of empirical studies using the serial reaction time paradigm have explored the conditions under which subjects display sensitivity to the sequential structure of events. In a typical sequence learning experiment subjects are exposed to visuospatial sequences in a speeded compatible response mapping serial reaction time task. Participants are asked to react as quickly and accurately as possible with a discriminative response to the location of a target stimulus that may appear at one of a limited number of positions. Usually these target stimuli consist of signals that are presented in one of several horizontally aligned positions on a computer screen. Responses most frequently require participants to press keys that spatially match these positions. Unbeknownst to the subjects, the presented sequence of visual signals follows a well-defined systematicity resulting in a continuous stream of structured events to which subjects have to respond. Depending on the respective experiment, the systematicity of signals follows one of three types of patterns: it executes a deterministically repeating sequence of fixed length (*Simple Repeating Paradigm;* e.g. Willingham, Nissen, & Bullemer 1989), it is constructed on the basis of the output of a probabilistic and noisy finite state-grammar (*Probabilistic Sequence Paradigm;* e.g. Jimenez, Mendez, & Cleeremans 1996), or it is generated by a complex set of rules (*Deter-*

R. Sun and C.L. Giles (Eds.): Sequence Learning, LNAI 1828, pp. 188-212, 2000.
© Springer-Verlag Berlin Heidelberg 2000

ministic Rule-based paradigm; e.g. Stadler 1989) that allows the construction of several alternative deterministic signal successions (Cleeremans & Jimenez 1998, p. 325). Sequence learning and thus sensitivity to the sequential constraints is said to have been expressed when (1) subjects exposed to systematic event sequences show faster response latencies than those responding to random event sequences, or (2) response times of subjects increase significantly when systematic sequences are temporarily switched to random sequences. The faster response times are interpreted as resulting from acquired knowledge about the event pattern that allows subjects to prepare their responses. Figure 1 illustrates a prototypical data pattern to be found when using the serial reaction task (Nissen & Bullemer 1987). As the graph shows, response latencies from subjects exposed to structured sequences in blocks 1-5 increase distinctly when the event succession is temporary switched to a random presentation in blocks 6 and 7 and decrease again when switched back to the systematic sequence in blocks 8 and 9. The amount of sequence learning can be assessed indirectly by contrasting response latencies to structured sequences with reaction times to randomly presented events.

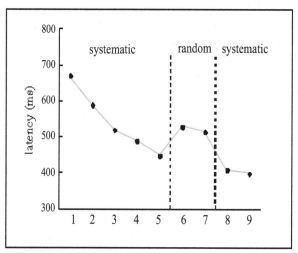

Figure 1. A prototypical data pattern in a study of sequence learning.

A broad range of experimental studies in sequence learning report to have demonstrated functional dissociations between performance in sequence learning (as revealed indirectly by contrasting latencies in systematic vs. random blocks) and conscious awareness of a sequence (as assessed by direct post-task measures). These dissociations have led researchers to speculate that the serial reaction task and post-task tests might tap two independent knowledge bases: *implicit* learning that can only be expressed in immediate task performance, and *explicit* learning[1] that can

---

[1] Frensch (1998) identifies no less than eleven different definitions of implicit learning in the field — "a diversity that is undoubtedly symptomatic of the conceptual and methodological difficulties facing the field" (Cleeremans, Destrebecqz, & Boyer, 1998, p. 407). Berry and Dienes (1993) provide a largely theory-neutral definition by referring to learning as *implicit* when subjects acquire

be verbalized or used to predict event sequences. Investigating the role of consciousness in learning has become a major focus in experimental studies of sequential pattern acquisition and the field has flourished along with research on artificial grammar learning (Reber 1993) and complex system control (Berry & Broadbent 1984) into one of the major paradigms for investigating implicit learning processes.

In contrast to the extraordinarily wide body of experimental data available on serial pattern acquisition, theory development to explain the empirically observed phenomena has been surprisingly scarce. Much of the experimental work has concentrated on investigating the conditions under which phenomena like unconscious learning is likely to occur or when attentional resources are required for learning, while the development of detailed computational models of empirical data has been largely neglected. An important exception is Cleeremans's model based on *simple recurrent networks* (1993; Cleeremans & McClelland 1991; Jimenez et al. 1996) which has been applied to a wide set of experimental data, including the classical study of Lewicki et al. (1988) and its conceptual replications by Perruchet, Gallego, & Savy (1990) and Ferrer-Gil (1994). A simple recurrent network (SRN; Elman 1990) uses a fully-connected, three-layer, back-propagation architecture that allows the network to predict the next element of a sequence based upon the current stimulus and the network's sensitivity to the temporal context in which consecutive stimuli occur. Sensitivity to the temporal context of a SRN is derived by utilizing fixed one-to-one recurrent connections between hidden units and context units that encode the activation vector of a previous time step's hidden units. Over time, these recurrent connections then enable contextual information to differentiate different parts of a sequence.

A SRN seems to provide a particular natural account for implicit learning phenomena since all the knowledge of the network is stored in its connections and may thus only be expressed through performance — a phenomenon which is a central component in definitions of implicit learning (Berry & Dienes 1993). However, a current major limitation of SRNs seems to be that they "do not account for explicit learning or the difference between it and implicit learning but could perhaps be expanded to do so" (Stadler & Roedinger 1998, p. 126). Cleeremans and Jimenez (1998, p. 350) note that modeling some effects would "probably require additional learning mechanisms (e.g., mechanisms based on explicit memory for salient aspects of the material) that are not all captured by the model". It remains to be seen how such mechanisms can be integrated into the architecture of a SRN.

Hybrid architectures provide a potentially fruitful way of integrating implicit and explicit knowledge. The CLARION architecture (Sun 1999) can be described as a two-level architecture where the *top-level* uses a *localist* representation (with each representational unit representing a distinct entity), while the *bottom level* is based on *distributed* representations (where an entity to be represented corresponds to a pattern of activation among a set representational units). Conscious knowledge is encoded in the representational nodes of CLARION's *top-level* and is assumed to be accessible and explicit. Implicit knowledge resides in the distributed representations of CLARION's *bottom level* and is inaccessible to conscious processing. Learning at the top-level is described as explicit one-shot hypothesis-testing, while the bottom-level provides gradual weight-tuning mechanisms. Based on the task, the outcomes of the two levels can be altered with the top level generally involving controlled processing and the bottom-level being governed by

---

information without intending to do so, and in such a way that the resulting knowledge is difficult to express using direct post-task tests.

automatic processing. The CLARION architecture has successfully been applied to modeling human data from a number of implicit learning paradigms, including sequence learning (Sun 1999). According to CLARION, implicit learning is triggered by a situation that is too complex to be handled by the explicit processes at the top level and is thus processed by the bottom level which can better cope with complex relations in the environment. As Sun (1999) shows, the interplay of CLARION's two levels provides a natural account for the relationship of explicit and implicit knowledge in contributing to human performance.

2.   An ACT-R theory of sequence learning

Recently, Lebiere and Wallach (1998; in prep.) have proposed a theory of sequence learning based on the ACT-R cognitive architecture (Anderson 1993; Anderson & Lebiere 1998). ACT-R is a hybrid production system that distinguishes between a permanent procedural memory and a permanent declarative memory. Procedural knowledge is encoded in ACT-R using modular condition-action-rules (*productions*) to represent potential actions to be taken when certain conditions are met. Declarative structures called *chunks* are used to store factual knowledge in declarative memory. Chunks encode knowledge as structured, schema-like configurations of labeled slots that can be organized hierarchically. A representation of goals in a goal stack is utilized to control information processing whereby exactly one chunk is designated to be the active goal of the system. Knowledge represented symbolically by chunks and productions is associated with *sub-symbolic* (i.e. real-valued) numerical quantities that control which productions are used and which chunks are retrieved from memory. These quantities reflect past statistics of use of the respective symbolic knowledge structures and are learned by Bayesian learning mechanisms derived from a *rational analysis* of cognition (Anderson 1990). Generally, subsymbolic learning allows ACT-R to adapt to the statistical structure of an environment.

A basic assumption of the ACT-R theory of sequence learning is that the mappings between stimulus locations and response keys in an experiment are encoded as chunks. Each chunk associates the respective stimulus location on the screen to the desired response key. These declarative representations essentially represent a straightforward explicit encoding of the experimental instructions informing the subjects of the stimulus-response mappings. When a stimulus is observed, the chunk representing the mapping between that stimulus location and the associated response key will be retrieved. Each retrieval results in the immediate reinforcement of that chunk through ACT-R's base-level learning mechanism that strengthens a chunk to reflect its frequency of use. Formally, activation reflects the log posterior odds that a chunk is relevant in a particular situation. The activation A_i of a chunk i is computed as the sum of its *base-level activation B_i* plus its *context activation*:

$$A_i = B_i + \sum_j W_j S_{ji} \qquad \textbf{Activation Equation}$$

In determining the context activation, W_j designates the attentional weight given the focus element j. An element j is in the focus, or in context, if it is part of the current goal chunk (i.e. the value of one of the goal chunk's slots). S_{ji} stands for the strength of association from element j to a chunk i. ACT-R assumes that there is a limited capacity of source activation and that each goal element emits an equal amount of activation. Source activation capacity is typically assumed to be *1*, i.e. if there are *n* source elements in the current focus each receives a source activation of *1/n* (Anderson & Lebiere 1998). The *associative strength* S_{ji} between an activation source *j* and a chunk *i* is a measure of how often *i* was needed (i.e. retrieved in a production) when chunk *j* was in the context. Associative strengths provide an estimate of the log likelihood ratio measure of how much the presence of a cue *j* in a goal slot increases the probability that a particular chunk *i* is needed for retrieval to instantiate a production.

The base level activation of a chunk is learned by an architectural mechanism to reflect the past history of use of a chunk *i*:

$$B_i = \ln \sum_{j=1}^{n} t_j^{-d} \approx \ln \frac{nL^{-d}}{1-d} \qquad \textbf{Base-Level Learning Equation}$$

In the above formula t_j stands for the time elapsed since the *jth* reference to chunk *i* while *d* is the memory decay rate and *L* denotes the life time of a chunk (i.e. the time since its creation). As Anderson and Schooler (1991) have shown, this equation produces the Power Law of Forgetting (Rubin & Wenzel 1996) as well as the Power Law of Learning (Newell & Rosenbloom 1981).

When retrieving a chunk to instantiate a production, ACT-R selects the chunk with the highest activation A_i. However, some stochasticity is introduced in the system by adding gaussian noise of mean 0 and standard deviation σ to the activation A_i of each chunk. In order to be retrieved, the activation of a chunk needs to reach a fixed retrieval threshold τ that limits the accessibility of declarative elements. If the gaussian noise is approximated with a sigmoid distribution, the probability *P* of chunk *i* to be retrieved by a production is:

$$P = \frac{1}{1+e^{-\frac{A_i-\tau}{s}}} \qquad \textbf{Retrieval Probability Equation}$$

where $s=\sqrt{3}\sigma/\pi$. The activation of a chunk *i* is directly related to the latency of its retrieval by a production *p*. Formally, retrieval time T_{ip} is an exponentially decreasing function of the chunk's activation A_i:

$$T_{ip} = Fe^{-fA_i} \qquad \textbf{Retrieval Time Equation}$$

where *F* is a time scaling factor. In addition to the latencies for chunk retrieval as given by the *Retrieval Time Equation*, the total time of selecting and applying a production is determined by executing the actions of a production's action part, whereby a value of 50 ms is typically assumed for elementary internal actions. External actions, such as pressing a key, usually have a longer latency determined by the ACT-R/PM perceptual-motor module (Byrne & Anderson 1998).

In summary, subsymbolic activation processes in ACT-R make a chunk active to the degree that past experience and the present context (as given by the current goal) indicates that it is useful at this particular moment. In the ACT-R sequence learning model, these reinforcements will lead to higher activation levels for the chunks that map stimulus positions to the keys to be pressed, which then results in faster response latencies. This speedup will occur independently of whether the stimulus sequence is systematic or random because it only depends upon the frequency of each retrieval.

The fundamental assumption of the ACT-R model of sequence learning is the *persistence of (working) memory*. ACT-R states that the components of the current goal are sources of activation. If the new goal is to respond to a particular stimulus with a certain response, we assume that the previous stimulus (i.e. the central element of the previous goal) remains in the encoding of the new goal. This assumption has two important implications. First, since every goal contains both the previous stimulus and the next one, when that goal is popped and becomes a chunk in declarative memory, it contains a record of a small fragment of the sequence. The set of these chunks constitutes the model's *explicit* knowledge of the sequence. The second implication is that when the chunk encoding the mapping between the current stimulus and the proper response key is retrieved, both the current stimulus and the previous one are components of the goal and thus sources of activation. This co-occurrence between previous stimulus (as a source of activation) and current stimulus (as a component of the mapping chunk being retrieved) is automatically learned by ACT-R in the association strengths between source stimulus and mapping chunk and thus facilitates further processing. The subsymbolic strengths of associations between consecutive sequence fragments constitute the model's *implicit* knowledge of the sequence. An additional assumption of the model controls the way chunks are built by determining the exact nature of the previous context that persists in the current goal. If no correct anticipation or guess was made as to the identity of the current stimulus, then that stimulus persists in the next goal, leading to the creation of the next pair of the sequence as described above. However, if the current stimulus could be correctly guessed by retrieving a chunk mapping the current context to that stimulus, i.e. if the current piece of sequence is already known, then the current goal, which is identical to the chunk retrieved, persists in the next goal as a more complex context, allowing the next piece of sequence to be encoded using the current one. Therefore, while all memory chunks only encode pairs, longer sequences can be represented because the first element of the pair can be a chunk as well as a basic stimulus.

Table 1 describes the procedural knowledge that uses the declarative encodings, both implicit and explicit, to perform the task. The basic goal, as expressed in the instructions to the sequence learning experiments, is to map the location of a screen stimulus to a key and press that key as a response. Production *Input* checks that no stimulus has been encoded yet and checks if one is present and if so encodes it and places its location in the current goal. Production *Map-Location* then retrieves the chunk from declarative memory that maps this location to the proper response key, and places the key in the goal. Production *Type-Key* then types the respective key and pops the goal. Before a stimulus has appeared, production *Guess* attempts to retrieve a chunk that holds a piece of the sequence starting with the current context, and if successful uses that chunk to anticipate which stimulus will appear and which key to press. Once the stimulus appears, if the anticipation was correct then the retrieved key can be typed directly without the need for mapping location to key. Otherwise, the production *Bad-Guess* withdraws the prepared response, which requires mapping the actual stimulus location to a different key. When a response has been given, if no correct guess was made then the production *Next-Pair* creates and focuses on a new goal with the current stimulus as the context, which will lead to the encoding of the next pair of stimuli. If a correct guess was made, however, then the production *Higher-Chunk* focuses on a new goal with the current goal as the next context, leading to the creation of a new chunk encoding the current piece of sequence together with the next stimulus.

Input	Guess
IF the goal is to respond to a stimulus and no stimulus has been encoded yet THEN check if a *stimulus* is present and encode it	IF the goal is to respond to a stimulus given a previous *context* and there is no stimulus present and no guess has been made and *context* was in the past most often followed by *stimulus* responded to by *key* THEN guess that the next stimulus will be *stimulus* and prepare to respond with *key*
Map-Location	
IF the goal is to respond to a stimulus and no key has been prepared to respond to *stimulus* and *key* is associated to *stimulus* THEN get ready to respond with *key*	
Type-Key	*Bad-Guess*
IF the goal is to respond to a stimulus and a response with *key* has been prepared THEN type *key*	IF the goal is to respond to a stimulus and a *guess* was made that is different from the encoded *stimulus* THEN withdraw the prepared response *key*
Next-pair	*Higher-Chunk*
IF the goal is to respond to a stimulus and a response was made without a correct guess THEN focus on a new goal with the stimulus as context	IF the goal is to respond to a stimulus and a response was made with correct guess THEN focus on a new goal with this goal as context

Table 1: Productions to perform the mapping of a stimulus to a response key

The Act-R theory of sequence learning precisely specifies mechanisms and memory structures on a level that is sufficient to implement a computational model which generates qualitative and quantitative predictions that can be compared to empirical data. To explore the scope of the theory, we have modeled three seminal studies in the field (Willingham, Nissen, & Bullemer 1989; Perruchet & Amorim 1992; Curran & Keele 1993). The experimental conditions in these studies vary widely with regard to the type of sequence used, the length of the sequence, the distribution of systematic vs. random blocks, the number and length of blocks, the Response-to-Stimulus Interval used and whether the serial reaction task was presented as a single task or in combination with a secondary task ("tone counting"). Our validation of the ACT-R model was not restricted to comparing model-generated and empirical data on a single dimension, but comprised a comparison of latencies, learning trajectories, errors, stimulus anticipations, individual differences as well as the structure of acquired chunks. In our view, the comparison of model predictions and empirical data presented in Lebiere and Wallach (1998; in prep.) provides clear evidence for the broad empirical scope and integrative character of the ACT-R approach to sequence learning, overcoming the lack of theoretical development in the field that was criticized in the introduction to this chapter. While the reader is referred to Lebiere and Wallach, (1998; in prep.) for an extensive discussion of the modeling results, the next section presents a fine-grained sensitivity analysis of the ACT-R model.

3. Empirical Analysis

The goal of this section is to report the results of a detailed sensitivity analysis of the model's performance as a function of a number of its parameters and of the experimental conditions to which it is applied. Conducting such a sensitivity analysis opens up the possibility of investigating the behavioral and computational effects of certain internal and external model manipulations and thus allows for a precise analysis of the implications of a model's underlying theoretical assumptions. Although Van Lehn, Brown and Greeno (1984) have forcefully argued in favor of detailed "model experiments" more than fifteen years ago, sensitivity analyses are still the exception in cognitive modeling: "Cognitive science has given psychology a new way of expressing models of cognition that is much more detailed and precise than its predecessors. But unfortunately, the increased detail and precision in *stating* models has not been accompanied by correspondingly detail and precise arguments *analyzing and supporting* them" (Van Lehn, Brown, & Greeno 1984, p. 237). This section presents a fine-grained analysis of variations of central model and experiment parameters including:

- sequence type, i.e. whether the stimuli composing the sequence appear only once (*unique* sequence), multiple times (*ambiguous* sequence) or both (*mixed* or *hybrid* sequence).
- rate of memory decay, which controls how fast a sequence can be learned (and forgotten).
- noise in chunk activation, which controls the stochasticity of the model.
- threshold τ on memory retrieval, which controls how much activation is needed for memory retrieval. It is expressed here, and varies inversely to, the Response-to-Stimulus Interval used in experimental studies.
- change in the sequence, i.e. how fast an old sequence can be unlearned and a new one learned.
- choice of knowledge representation, i.e. whether the sequence is encoded in hierarchical chunks or in fixed-length chunks, and in that case what the impact of the chunk length is.

The model analysis will be primarily empirical, with results being reported for the average of 1000 Monte Carlo runs of the model over 20 blocks of 12 stimuli, unless otherwise specified. Whenever tractable, the empirical results will be supplemented by a formal analysis of the model using the ACT-R equations introduced with the model. Due to the complexity of the model and the approximations inherent in some of the equations themselves, the results derived by the formal analysis are only approximate but are nonetheless useful in understanding the empirical results and the parameters that control them. The results and analyses are reported for three dependent measures of the performance of the model:

1. Response Time (RT) is the most widely used behavioral measure in cognitive psychology. In the ACT-R model, response time is a measure both of how likely each element of the sequence is to be correctly retrieved from memory as well as of the amount of practice and context of the chunk holding that element.
2. Odds of Guessing measure the likelihood of anticipating, correctly or incorrectly, each stimulus by attempting to retrieve the next element of the sequence from memory. It is

correlated but does not directly correspond to response time because of the possibility of incorrectly guessing the next stimulus and the context effects involved in mapping that stimulus.

3. Odds of Error is another standard behavioral measure in cognitive psychology. In this model, it measures the likelihood of incorrectly anticipating the next stimulus through memory retrieval and is at most equal to the odds of guessing. It reflects the general confusion of the model about the identity of the sequence.

While those quantitative measures are related, they express different characteristics of the model's behavior. The trade-offs involved in trying to optimize these measures are a fundamental part of human cognition. Studying how these measures vary as a function of the parameters described previously should yield important insights into the model's predictions about the powers and limits of human cognition.

3.1 Sequence Type

Intuitively, some sequences should be harder to learn than others. The difficulty in learning a sequence depends upon the bias of the model, but a good general measure of difficulty for sequences of discrete elements is the ambiguity in the succession of stimuli. In our empirical analysis of the model we will use three types of sequence, listed in increasing order of difficulty:

1. *Unique sequences* in which each stimulus only appears once in each repetition of the sequence, e.g. **a b c d**, if **a**, **b**, **c** and **d** denote the possible spatial positions of a stimulus. In unique sequences the next stimulus can always be unambiguously predicted from the previous one.
2. *Mixed* or *hybrid sequences* in which some stimuli are always followed by the same stimuli but some are not, e.g. **a b c b d c**, where **a** and **d** are unique stimuli but **b** and **c** are not.
3. *Ambiguous sequences* in which all stimuli appear multiple times in the sequence and no stimulus can be unambiguously predicted from the previous one, e.g. **a b c b a d c a c d b d**. That sequence is a particular type of ambiguous sequence called a de Bruijn sequence (de Bruijn 1946), because each stimulus in the sequence is followed once and only once by all other stimuli (e.g. **a** is followed once by **b**, **c** and **d**).[2]

Figure 2 reports the results of applying the model to each type of sequence in terms of reaction times (RT) and odds of guessing, averaged per training block of 12 stimuli over 1000 runs. Since there are four distinct stimulus positions, the unique sequence is repeated three times per block and the mixed sequence twice per block while the ambiguous sequence appears once per block. Reaction times and odds are plotted on a log-log scale as a function of training block. In human subjects unique sequences are the easiest to learn and can be learned unconsciously over time (Cohen, Ivry, & Keele 1990) while ambiguous sequences are the hardest to learn and are thought to require attentional effort to be acquired (Curran & Keele 1993; but see Stadler 1995 and Frensch, Lin, & Buchner 1998 for diverging evidence), with mixed sequences being a mid-

---

[2] In typical de Bruijn sequences each stimulus is also followed by itself once, but we adhered here to a convention of not repeating consecutive stimuli. Any such repeating sequences can be straightforwardly converted into a non-repeating sequence by simply deleting one of the repeating stimuli.

dle case. Not surprisingly, this is also the case for our model, both in terms of reaction times and odds of guessing, with learning in unique sequences being consistently faster than in ambiguous sequences. Learning in mixed sequences is between the two but closer to unique sequences than to ambiguous sequences. The reason for this latter effect is that mixed sequences are built in memory starting with their unique stimuli, because unlike for ambiguous stimuli the next stimulus position can be reliably predicted from the current stimulus alone, i.e. from retrieving the basic chunks encoding pairs of stimuli. Thus learning in mixed sequences will be primarily determined by its unique stimuli than by its ambiguous stimuli.

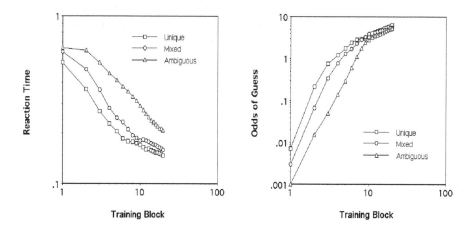

Figure 2. Reaction times and odds of guessing for the three types of sequences.

Performance, both in terms of reaction times and odds of guessing, improves roughly linearly on the log-log scale, meaning that it follows the power law of practice (Newell & Rosenbloom 1981) ubiquitous in human performance. This result is a direct consequence of how activation grows with practice and how performance is determined by activation. Assuming without loss of generality that activation reduces to its base-level component, the approximate form of ACT-R's Base-Level Learning Equation can be combined with the Retrieval Time Equation to yield a power function of response time as a function of the amount of practice n:

$$RT \cong Fe^{-f\left(\log n^{1-d}+C\right)} \cong Fn^{-f(1-d)}$$ **RT Practice Equation**

Note that given the default values used for the latency exponent parameter f and the base-level decay rate d of 1.0 and 0.5 respectively, this yields the power law slope of about 0.5 observed on the left of Figure 2. Similarly, the Base-Level Learning Equation can be combined with the Retrieval Probability Equation to yield a power function of the odds of retrieval (i.e. guessing the position of the next stimulus) as a function of the amount of practice:

$$Odds \cong e^{(\log n^{1-d}-C)} \Big/ s \cong Cn^{1-d} \Big/ s$$ **Odds Practice Equation**

While performance improvement is generally linear on the log-log scale, the curves are actually composed of two separate quasi-linear segments of different slopes. This is another consequence of the way the sequence is learned, i.e. by starting with a pair of stimuli and iteratively adding chunks on that root to cover the whole sequence. In the first phase of the learning, all pairs can be learned in parallel because retrieval is infrequent and the context usually defaults to the previous stimulus. However, when the pairs of stimuli can be retrieved and the model attempts to build longer sequences, learning becomes increasingly sequential with ultimately a single set of chunks spanning the whole sequence. Thus learning still follows a power law but becomes much slower as indicated by the much-reduced slope of the improvement. Note that the transition from the first to the second phase happens faster for the unique sequence than for the mixed and for the ambiguous sequences because each training block contains three repetitions of the unique sequence and two of the mixed sequence for only one of the ambiguous sequence.

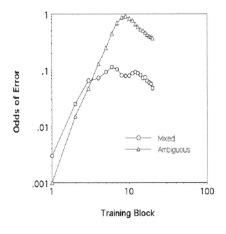

Figure 3. Odds of error for mixed and ambiguous sequences.

Finally, one can examine the performance of the model in terms of the odds of error of the process of guessing the next stimulus as plotted in Figure 3. Because each stimulus is unambiguously predicted by its predecessor in unique sequences, no errors occurred in that case and the odds of error are only plotted for mixed and ambiguous sequences[3]. Odds of error initially increase in the first learning phase as chunks encoding pairs of stimuli become more active and the odds of guessing increase[4], then decrease as the model enters the second learning phase and re-

---

[3] A mechanism called partial matching that adjusts chunk activations according to the degree of match could produce errors for unique sequences as well but was not activated in the model for simplicity reasons.

[4] Interestingly, for the first half-dozen training blocks odds of error for ambiguous sequences are almost equal to odds of guessing, meaning that almost all guesses are incorrect. This is an interesting property of the interaction between de Bruijn sequences and base-level decay, in which the most active chunks are those encoding the most recent appearances of the stimulus, which predict the other stimuli than the one about to occur.

trievals are based on unambiguous contexts rather than ambiguous stimuli. Odds of error are initially higher for mixed sequences than for ambiguous sequences because the odds of guessing are much higher, but odds of error at and after the maximum are about an order of magnitude lower for mixed sequences than for ambiguous sequences. In conclusion, by any of the three measures used to assess performance, the model exhibits the same qualitative sensitivity as human subjects to sequence difficulty reflecting stimuli ambiguity (Cohen et al. 1990).

3. 2Memory Decay Rate

Another characteristic of human sequence learning, indeed of any type of memory, is decay, i.e. the gradual forgetting of information (Rubin & Wenzel 1996). Forgetting is often described as an unnecessary shortcoming of human cognition. In a subsequent section, we will see that it is in fact an essential attribute in dealing with a changing world. But even when considering a single sequence as in this section, it can have desirable effects. Figure 4 plots the two measures of learning speed, reaction times and odds of guessing, as a function of practice for memory decay rates d of 0.25, 0.5 (the default) and 0.75[5]. As expected, a higher decay rate slows down learning both in terms of reaction time and odds of retrieval while a lower decay rate speeds it up. Since the analysis in the previous section showed that performance is a power of $1-d$, the difference between the low and the medium noise (as measured by the ratio $1-0.25/1-0.5=1.5$) is larger than the difference between medium and high noise ($1-0.5/1-0.75=2.0$). More generally, differences in performance tend to get amplified at the low end, as was the case in the previous section. The graph for odds of guessing confirms the analysis of the Odds Practice Equation with the slope of the curve reflecting the $1-d$ exponent while the impact on reaction time primarily reflects the influence of d on the constant factor F' rather than the slope.

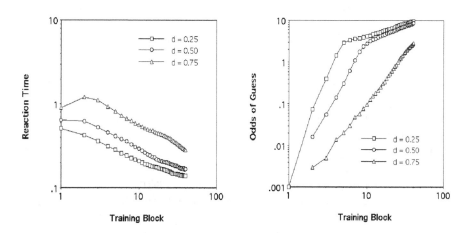

Figure 4. Reaction times and odds of guessing for three memory decay rates.

---

[5] The ambiguous sequence described in the previous section was used because it generated higher error rates but similar results could be obtained with the mixed (or any non-unique) sequence as well.

While lower decay rates uniformly increase learning speed, they have a less beneficial effect on the error rate. Figure 5 plots the odds of error as a function of practice and as a function of the odds of guessing for 40 training blocks. Odds of error are initially higher for lower decay rates, then reverse that trend after reaching their maximum. Part of the reason for the initially higher error rates for low decay rates is that their odds of guessing are higher as well, as Figure 4 established. But that is not the whole story, as the second part of Figure 5 demonstrates. The odds of error are initially the same for equivalent odds of guessing for all decay rates, but lower decay rates, which produce faster learning, also lead to significantly higher maximum error rates before decreasing in the second learning phase as longer, less ambiguous segments of the sequence are constructed. Conversely, the high decay rate that produced slow learning also helps in limiting the odds of error to a maximum that is less than half of the lowest decay rate.

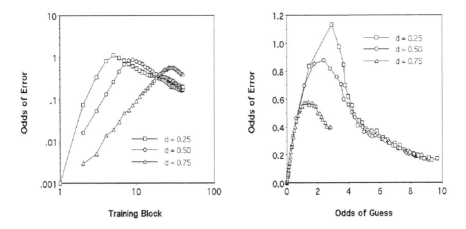

Figure 5. Odds of error as a function of practice and of odds of guessing for 3 memory decay rates.

In conclusion, forgetting in the form of memory decay, while making for slower learning also helps in limiting the number of errors. This suggests a tradeoff in which a decay rate is used that provides for reasonably fast learning while keeping errors down. Such a rate might well be the ACT-R default rate of 0.5, which provides a learning speed almost as fast as the lower decay rates (see Figure 4) but has a significantly lower error peak (see Figure 5). Very similar results can be obtained by analyzing the influence of the threshold in activation that a chunk must reach to be successfully retrieved (or equivalently the Response-to-Stimulus Interval of the experiment since retrieval time is determined by activation). A low retrieval threshold, like a low decay rate, will allow faster learning at the expense of higher error rates. A high retrieval threshold, while preventing retrieval in the early stages of learning, will also yield fewer errors. Thus a threshold on retrieval that requires a certain amount of practice to allow a memory to be recalled is not necessarily a cognitive limitation but instead might serve the role of preventing interference between memory items by delaying their recall until they are reliably established.

3.3 Activation Noise

Random noise in the activation quantities controlling the retrieval of memory chunks also appears, like memory decay, to be purely a limitation of human memory without any redeeming value. Indeed, it was introduced in ACT-R primarily to provide error profiles comparable to those of human subjects. However it turns out that stochasticity has advantageous consequences as well. Figure 6 plots the reaction times and odds of guessing as a function of three activation noise levels S of 0.1, 0.25 (our default used in many other simulations, e.g. Lebiere (1998, 1999) and Lebiere & West (1999)) and 0.5. The effect on speed of learning is mixed: while lower noise levels produce faster performance, they also lead to lower odds of guessing, at least initially. The reason for this divergence lies in the different ways in which activation affects those measures of performance. Noise is symmetrically distributed around a mean of 0. Since the retrieval time is a negative exponential function of activation, negative noise amounts will slow down retrieval more than positive amounts will speed it up. This will lead to slower retrievals in average for higher noise levels. As can be seen in the first part of Figure 6, the default noise level of 0.25 is only slightly slower than the low noise level of 0.1, but the higher noise level of 0.5 is markedly slower.

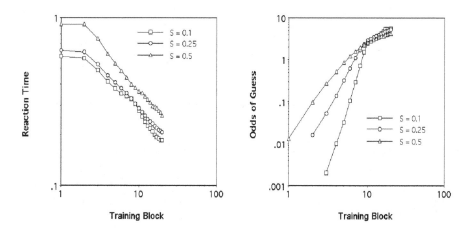

Figure 6. Reaction times and odds of guessing for three activation noise levels.

The impact of noise on odds of retrieval, i.e. guessing the next stimulus' position, will depend on whether chunk activation is higher or lower than the retrieval threshold. If it is lower, as it is early in the learning, activation noise can only help in reaching the threshold. Therefore, the larger the amount of noise, the better the odds that the chunk can be retrieved. However, consistently with the Odds Practice equation, the slope of the odds curve as a function of practice is inversely proportional to the noise level S, and, after the first learning phase, the relationship is inverted. The reason is that the average activation for the chunks encoding pairs of stimuli is now higher than the threshold and adding noise can only increase the risk of retrieval failures. But because it helps in retrieving the newer chunks that still have low activation, the total effect of noise in the second learning phase is weak and its main consequence is the beneficial effect of activation noise in speeding up the first learning phase.

With increased odds of guessing come increased odds of error, as demonstrated in the first part of Figure 7. Higher noise also means higher odds of error through almost all the training except the time of maximum error at about the 10th training block. However, as the second part of Figure 7 establishes, those increased odds of error mostly reflect the increased odds of guessing. Only in the second part of the learning does higher noise lead to slightly higher odds of error for equal odds of guessing.

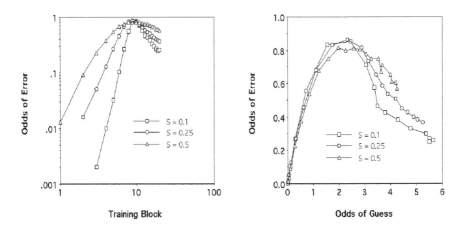

Figure 7. Odds of error as a function of practice and of odds of guessing for 3 activation noise levels.

Once again, a tradeoff emerges, this time between faster initial learning, but slightly higher error rates resulting from higher noise levels. The standard noise value of 0.25 seems like a good compromise, but the optimal value will depend on the relative importance of initial versus long-term performance.[6] This in turn will depend upon the rate at which the environment changes, which is the focus of the next section.

3.4 Sequence Change

The results presented in the previous sections referred to a model that learned a sequence given a clean, empty memory without any existing knowledge to interfere with the new sequence. Real life, of course, is not always so convenient. Sequences in the real world, be it weather, speech or stock market data, always change, frequently without warning. This section analyzes the performance of the ACT-R model that is trained on a sequence that is then changed to a different

---

[6] A way out of this tradeoff would be to have a variable noise level, initially high to provide fast learning then gradually decreasing to bring down the error rate. Lebiere (1998, 1999) observed that this gradual noise reduction with practice would also help account for long-term learning in domains such as cognitive arithmetic and is related to the technique of simulated annealing used in the Boltzmann Machine (Ackley, Hinton, & Sejnowsky, 1985).

one. Specifically, the model learns the standard unique sequence **a b c d** for 10 training blocks, then learns another unique but incompatible sequence, **d c b a**, for 20 training blocks. Only the performance in those latter 20 blocks is plotted in the following graphs. The results would have been qualitatively similar but quantitatively less distinguishable if other types of sequences were used because those sequences would have had small fragments in common that would have permitted some knowledge transfer from one sequence to the next. For example, two ambiguous de Bruijn sequences have in common all pairs of stimuli.

As one would expect phenomena such as forgetting and stochasticity to impact the model's ability to switch from one sequence to the next, the sensitivity analysis carried out in the two previous sections on memory decay rate and activation noise level is repeated here, with striking results as can be seen in Figure 8. While higher decay rates still make for slower performance in terms of reaction time, the difference tends to disappear over time. Moreover, while higher decay rates also yields lower odds of guessing, the shape of the curves is very different, with odds of guessing for lower decay rates starting very high and going even higher before gradually decreasing while odds of guessing for higher decay rates starting much lower and decreasing before gradually picking up. The reason for this behavior is that the model keeps retrieving the old sequence when the new one is introduced, a process that for low enough decay rates is self-sustaining and effectively blocks out the new sequence for many training blocks. For high decay rates such as 0.75, forgetting is strong enough to quickly wipe out the old sequence, decreasing the odds of guessing, before the new sequence is gradually learned.

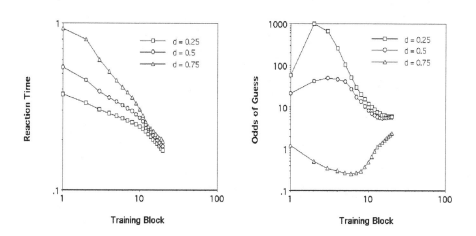

Figure 8. Reaction times and odds of guessing for three memory decay rates.

Figure 9, which plots the odds of error, makes clear the downside of low decay rates in the presence of a changing environment. The odds of error for low decay rates become very large because the model keeps anticipating the old sequence and only very gradually decline to about even at the end of the 20 training blocks. In contrast, for the high decay rate the odds of error start about even and are down to almost zero by the end of the 20 blocks. The second part of Figure 9 plots the odds of error as a function of guessing odds, displaying a very interesting trajectory in that state space. The vertical bifurcation in the graph suggests a phase transition for a given value of the decay parameter[7]. For lower decay rates, odds of guessing and error grow very large before slowly decreasing, while for higher decay rates the model adopts the sensible strategy of mostly stopping guessing until the new sequence can be acquired to minimize errors.

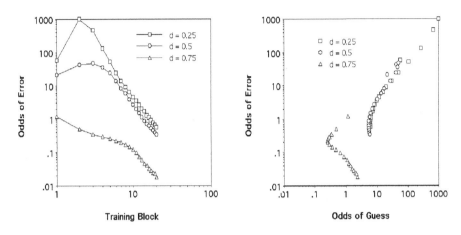

Figure 9. Odds of error as a function of practice and of odds of guessing for 3 memory decay rates.

A similar analysis for activation noise levels yields much the same results, reported in Figure 10 and 11.

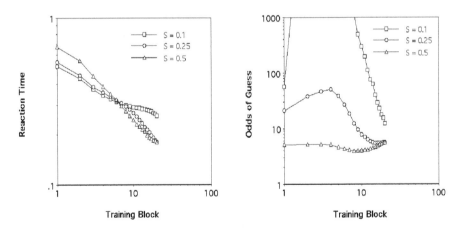

Figure 10. Reaction times and odds of guessing for three activation noise levels.

---

[7] Lebiere (1998, 1999) found a similar bifurcation for activation noise values, with values higher than a certain threshold leading in the limit to chaotic behavior while values lower than that threshold yielding convergence to a stable memory state.

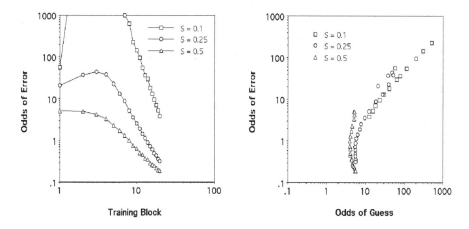

Figure 11. Odds of error as a function of practice and of odds of guessing for three noise levels.

If anything, low noise levels such as 0.1 yield even more undesirable extreme behavior than low decay rates, yielding very high error rates and slow performance because the lack of sufficient stochasticity prevents adapting to the new sequence. That is because memory reinforcement is a dynamic process with its own feedback loop. Retrieving an item from memory reinforces it, which in turns makes it more likely to be retrieved. Thus, if the system has sufficient stochasticity, the new sequence, while weaker at first than the first one, can be retrieved early by chance, which then lets it get established earlier. A very deterministic system, on the other hand, takes much longer to let purely external reinforcement gradually push the activation of the new sequence above that of the initial one, with the help of memory decay. One can observe that the middle activation noise value of 0.25 yields fairly good results, converging by the end of the 20 training blocks to the results for the best value of 0.5, while performance for the lower noise value of 0.1 remains quite poor.

In conclusion, this analysis confirms and greatly reinforces the conclusion that forgetting and stochasticity are not undesirable characteristics of a suboptimal cognitive system but are instead fundamental tools in adapting to a changing environment. Moreover, the default values of the parameters controlling those phenomena in ACT-R, namely memory decay rate and chunk activation noise, might well be close to the optimum for a wide range of conditions.

3.5 Knowledge Representation

A fundamental characteristic of our sequence learning model is the way it represents the sequence by building chunk pairs first from basic stimuli then from other chunks, gradually stretching to span the whole sequence. This representation is very flexible, allowing the storage of sequences of arbitrary length. But a disadvantage is that the representation of any given sequence is still of a finite length and when the model reaches the end it fails to anticipate the next stimulus and must start anew. An alternative representation would be to simply store the sequence in chunks of a given fixed length by storing all subsequences of that length, essentially achieving a tiling effect. For example, if all chunks are of length 2, i.e. pairs, one would represent the unique sequence **a b c d** by storing the 4 chunks **a-b, b-c, c-d** and **d-a**.[8] The model would operate essentially unchanged other than for the simplification of not needing to build chunks more complex than pairs of stimuli. Figure 12 plots the learning provided by that model for the three standard types of sequences. Generally, odds of guessing increase very quickly and indefinitely according to the power law of the Odds Practice Equation, while reaction times also decrease quickly to the minimum reflecting the fan (Anderson 1974) of each sequence element. Ambiguous sequences are still more difficult than unique sequences for the same reason as the original model, namely that the stimuli appear in multiple positions, and therefore in multiple chunks, thereby diluting the activation spreading from the context.

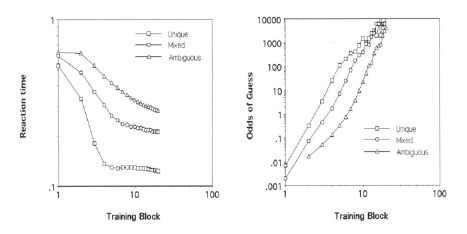

Figure 12. Reaction times and odds of guessing for the pair model on the 3 types of sequences.

However, while unique sequences are learned without errors, Figure 13 shows conclusively that the error rates for mixed and ambiguous sequences gradually increase until reaching a plateau determined by the inherent ambiguity of the sequence given this fixed representation. For example, since ambiguous sequences have no stimulus that by itself identifies its successor without ambiguity, it has the highest error rate.

---

[8] These two models essentially reflect the general choice between fixed and flexible windows which also arises in other frameworks such as neural networks. The original model that gradually build its context corresponds to Elman's (1990) recursive networks while the fixed-length model corresponds to networks with fixed-input fields such as *NetTalk* (Sejnowski & Rosenberg, 1987).

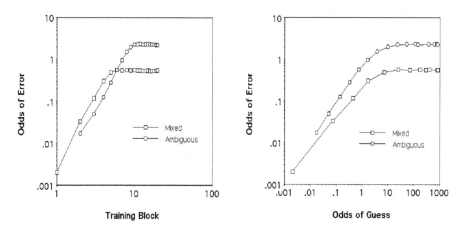

Figure 13. Odds of error as a function of practice and of odds of guessing for the pair model.

An obvious solution is to simply increase the length of the fixed chunks, say from pairs to triplets. This effectively allows the model to learn all types of sequences without any errors, but Figure 14 establishes that that perfection comes at a cost. While reaction times are still quite fast, odds of guessing still increase according to a power law but much more slowly. For example, at the end of the 20 training blocks, the odds of anticipating the next stimulus of an ambiguous sequence are still less than even. This is a direct consequence of the increased dilution of spreading activation resulting from the growth in the size of the chunks, leading each stimulus to appear in more chunks and making them less predictive.

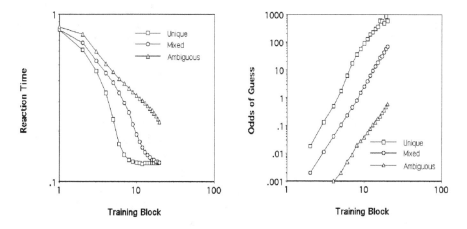

Figure 14. Reaction times and odds of guessing for the triplet model on the 3 types of sequences.

Thus, smaller chunks such as pairs cannot adequately represent ambiguous sequences while larger chunks such as triplets are much too slow in building chunks. This suggests that, perhaps like human cognition, the original model, despite its flaws such as its tendency to make errors, might still represent the optimal solution for representing and accessing sequences.

4. Discussion

While the elements of the sequences learned by this model are discrete, many sequences encountered in real life are composed of continuous quantities, for example the prices on the stock market. Fortunately, there is a straightforward way to extend the model to handle sequences of continuous quantities by using ACT-R's partial-matching mechanism. While the sequence is still represented by symbolic chunks, the retrieval of chunks is affected by the similarities between the values that they hold. Specifically, the chunk with the highest match score is retrieved, where match score is a function of the chunk activation and its degree of mismatch to the desired values:

$$M_{ip} = A_i - MP \sum_{v,d} (1 - Sim(v,d))$$ **Partial Match Equation**

where $Sim(v,d)$ is the similarity between the desired value v held in the goal and the actual value d held in the retrieved chunk, allowing the representation of continuous quantities. Thus even if no chunk in memory perfectly matches the current context, a likely occurrence with an infinite amount of continuous values, the chunk holding the closest value can be retrieved if its match score after subtracting the mismatch between values from its activation is still higher than the retrieval threshold. A shortcoming of partial matching is that there will always be a residual error for the imperfection of the match. Lebiere (1999) proposed a generalization of the retrieval mechanism called *blending* which allows the retrieval and averaging of values from multiple chunks rather than a single one, providing for sequences of continuous values a powerful kind of interpolation that has proved useful for a range of paradigms of implicit learning (Wallach & Lebiere 1999; Gonzalez, Lebiere & Lerch 1999). Specifically, the value retrieved is:

$$V = Min \sum_i P_i (1 - Sim(V, V_i))^2$$ **Blending Equation**

where P_i is the probability of retrieving chunk i and V_i is the value held by that chunk. Unfortunately, space limitations do not allow for a detailed analysis of the application of this model extension to continuous sequences.

The ACT-R model also has the capacity to learn the "noisy" finite-state grammars of Cleeremans and McClelland (1991). In that paradigm, continuous sequences are generated from a finite-state grammar looping onto itself, with a small probability (e.g. 15%) of substituting at each point in the sequence a random stimulus for the one prescribed by the grammar. Like the SRN networks used by Cleeremans and McClelland, the chunks built by the ACT-R model can span as large a segment of the sequence as necessary. Moreover, if several possible stimuli can follow the current sequence fragment, they will be anticipated with a probability equal to their conditional probability of occurrence in the sequence since the activations of a chunk represent the odds of that chunk occurring in the environment. This correspondence between ACT-R and SRN is to be expected since ACT-R uses Bayesian learning mechanisms and neural networks have been shown to converge to Bayesian optimum under certain conditions (Mitchell, 1997).

Perhaps the main advantage of a cognitive architecture such as ACT-R is its generality, specifically the ability to apply a model, if not literally then in the form of design patterns and parameter values, to a very different task than the one for which it was developed. For example, Lebiere and West (1999) applied this model of sequence learning with great success to the classic game of Paper Rock Scissors. Interestingly, for reasons of comparability with an existing neural network model, they chose the fixed-length chunk representation described in the previous section. They concluded that the default parameters used by the model presented here provided excellent performance that matched human behavior quite well, confirming the analysis presented here. Moreover the pair model provided the best fit to the initial performance of human subjects while the triplet model provided the best fit to their long-term performance, supporting the original variable-length representation which starts with pairs of stimuli and gradually builds longer sequences upon them. Another related model is the model of list learning of Anderson et al. (1997). Like the sequence learning model, it acquires a list of items by building chunks associating indices in the list to the items stored at that position. The indices have two components, one being the identity of the subgroup holding the item and the other is the position of the item in that subgroup. Clearly there is a parallel between those indices and the context elements of chunks in this model that should be pursued further. Finally, Lebiere (1998; 1999) performed a sensitivity analysis of a model of lifetime learning of cognitive arithmetic that yielded many of the same conclusions as this analysis, including the desirability of characteristics such as forgetting, stochasticity and retrieval failure to learning even in as precise an environment as formal mathematics. One can therefore conjecture that the lessons drawn from the analysis presented here are applicable not only to this particular domain but to many other cognitive tasks as well.

5. Conclusion

This chapter presents a model of sequence learning based on the ACT-R cognitive architecture. This model acquires sequences by gradually learning small pieces of the sequence in symbolic structures called chunks. The availability of those chunks is a function of their numerical parameters, which are estimated by the architecture's Bayesian learning mechanisms to reflect the structure of the environment. Therefore, the sequence is represented both explicitly in the symbolic chunks as well as implicitly in their real-valued parameters. In a recent review, Cleeremans et al. (1998, p. 414) identify the following properties for successful learning models in the field:

- Learning involves elementary association processes that are highly sensitive to the statistical features of the training set.
- Learning is incremental, continuous, and best characterized as a by-product of ongoing processing.
- Learning is based on the processing of exemplars and produces distributed knowledge.
- Learning is unsupervised and self-organizing.

The ACT-R approach to sequential pattern acquisition seems to be well characterized by the properties listed above: the model learns to encode chunks (i.e. *exemplars*) from basic stimuli that *gradually* stretch to span the whole sequence. Learning of elementary *associations* between subsequent objects is conceptualized by the model as a non-deliberate *by-product* of performance that is highly sensitive to the *statistical* features of the particular training sequence. Learning is *unsupervised* in the sense that the model essentially starts with the encoding of instructions on the respective stimulus-key mappings and *incrementally* builds up explicit and implicit knowledge (i.e. chunks and their subsymbolic association values) to prepare responses in the serial reaction task.

This chapter presented a detailed analysis of the model's sensitivity to its parameters and experimental conditions. The main conclusion is that two central characteristics of cognitive models, stochasticity and forgetting, are in fact essential in optimizing the performance of the model. We also studied alternative knowledge representations and found them to have advantages but also serious shortcomings relative to the standard model. This model is related to a number of other ACT-R models applied to a wide range of domains, and it is hoped that both the techniques used here and the conclusions drawn are applicable to a wide range of cognitive domains.

References

Ackley, D.H., Hinton, G.E., & Sejnowsky, T.J. (1985). A learning algorithm for Boltzmann machines. *Cognitive Science, 9,* 147-169.

Anderson, J.R. (1974). Retrieval of propositional information from long-term memory. *Cognitive Psychology, 5,* 451-474.

Anderson, J.R. (1990). *The adaptive character of thought.* Hillsdale: LEA.

Anderson, J.R. (1993). *Rules of the Mind.* Hillsdale: LEA.

Anderson, J. R., Bothell, D., Lebiere, C. & Matessa, M. (1998). An integrated theory of list memory. *Journal of Memory and Language*, 38, pp. 341-380.

Anderson, J.R. & Lebiere, C. (1998). *The atomic components of thought.* Mahwah: LEA.

Anderson, J.R. & Schooler, L.J. (1991). Reflections of the environment in memory. *Psychological Science, 2,* 396-408.

Berry, D.C. & Broadbent, D.E. (1984). On the relationship between task performance and verbalizable knowledge. *Quarterly Journal of Experimental Psychology, 36A,* 209-231.

Berry, D.C. & Dienes, Z. (1993). *Implicit learning: Theoretical and empirical issues.* Mahwah: LEA.

Byrne, M.D. & Anderson, J.R. (1998). Perception and action. In J.R. Anderson & C. Lebiere (Eds.). *The atomic components of thought* (pp. 167-200). Mahwah: LEA.

Cleeremans, A. (1993). *Mechanisms of implicit learning.* Cambridge, MA: MIT Press.

Cleeremans, A. & McClelland, J.L. (1991). Learning the structure of event sequences. *Journal of Experimental Psychology: General, 3,* 235-253.

Cleeremans, A., Destrebecqz, A., & Boyer, M. (1998). Implicit learning: news from the front. *Trends in Cognitive Science, 10,* 406-416.

Cleeremans, A. & Jimenez, L. (1998). Implicit sequence learning: The truth is in the details. In M.A. Stadler & P.A. Frensch (Eds.). *Handbook of implicit learning* (p. 323-364). Thousand Oaks, CA: Sage.

Clegg, B.A., DiGirolamo, G.J., & Keele, S.W. (1998). Sequence Learning. *Trends in Cognitive Science, 8,* 275-281.

Cohen, A., Ivry, R., & Keele, S.W. (1990). Attention and structure in sequence learning. *Journal of Experimental Psychology: Learning, Memory and Cognition, 16,* 17-30.

Curran, T. (1998). Implicit sequence learning from a cognitive neuroscience perspective. In M.A. Stadler & P.A. Frensch (Eds.). *Handbook of implicit learning* (p. 365-400). Thousand Oaks, CA: Sage.

Curran, T. & Keele, S.W. (1993). Attentional and nonattentional forms of sequence learning. *Journal of Experimental Psychology: Learning, Memory and Cognition, 19,* 189-202.

de Bruijn, N. G. (1946). A combinatorial problem. *Nederl. Akad. Wetensch. Proc.* 49, 758-764.

Elman, J.L. (1990). Finding structure in time. *Cognitive Science, 14,* 179-211.

Ferrer-Gil, E. (1994). La unidad de aprendizaje en procesamiento no consciente: Un análisis experimental [The unit of learning in unconscious processing: An experimental analysis]. *Psicologemas, 7,* 195-217.

Frensch, P.A. (1998). One concept, multiple meanings: On how to define the concept of implicit learning. In M.A. Stadler & P.A. Frensch (Eds.). *Handbook of implicit learning* (p. 47-104). Thousand Oaks, CA: Sage.

Frensch, P.A., Lin, J., & Buchner, A. (1998). Learning versus behavioral expression of the learned: The effects of a secondary tone-counting task on implicit learning in the serial reaction task. *Psychological Research, 61,* 83-98.

Gonzalez, C, Lebiere, C., & Lerch, F. J. (1999). ACT-R Learning in a Real-Time Dynamic Decision-Making Task. Presented at the *1999 ACT-R, Workshop*, George Mason University, Fairfax, Va.

Jimenez, L., Mendez, C., & Cleeremans, A. (1996). Comparing direct and indirect measures of implicit learning. *Journal of Experimental Psychology: Learning, Memory and Cognition, 22,* 948-969.

Lebiere, C. (1998). *The dynamics of cognition: an ACT-R model of cognitive arithmetic.* Ph.D. Dissertation. Technical Report CMU-CS-98-186. Also available on the web at http://reports-archive.adm.cs.cmu.edu/

Lebiere, C. (1999). The dynamics of cognition: an ACT-R model of cognitive arithmetic. *Kognitionswissenschaft, 8,* 5-19.

Lebiere, C., & Wallach, D. (1998). Eine deklarative Theorie des Sequenzlernens. Paper presented at the *Forty First Conference of the German Psychological Society*, Dresden, Germany.

Lebiere, C., & Wallach, D. (in prep.). Implicit does not imply procedural: A declarative theory of sequence learning. Manuscript in preparation.

Lebiere, C., & West, R. L. (1999). A dynamic ACT-R model of simple games. In *Proceedings of the Twenty-First Conference of the Cognitive Science Society*, pp. 296-301. Mahwah, NJ: Erlbaum.

Lewicki, P., Hill, T., & Bizot, E. (1988). Acquisition of procedural knowledge about a pattern of stimuli that cannot be articulated. *Cognitive Psychology, 20,* 24-37.

Mitchell, T. M. (1997). *Machine Learning.* McGraw-Hill.

Nattkemper, D. & Prinz, W. (1997). Stimulus and response anticipation in a serial reaction task. *Psychological Research, 60,* 98-112.

Newell, A. & Rosenbloom, P.S. (1981). Mechanisms of skill acquisition and the power law of practice. In J.R. Anderson (Ed.).*Cognitive skills and their acquisition* (pp. 1-56). Hillsdale, LEA.

Nissen, M.J. & Bullemer, P. (1987). Attentional requirements of learning: Evidence from performance measures.*Cognitive Psychology, 19,* 1-32.

Perruchet, P. & Amorim, M.-A. (1992). Conscious knowledge and changes in performance in sequence learning: Evidence against dissociation. *Journal of Experimental Psychology: Learning, Memory and Cognition, 18,* 785-800.

Perruchet, P., & Gallego, J. & Savy, I. (1990). A critical reappraisal of the evidence for unconscious abstraction of deterministic rules in complex experimental situations. *Cognitive Psychology, 22,* 493-516.

Reber, A. (1993). *Implicit learning and tacit knowledge.* New York: Oxford University Press.

Rubin, D.C. & Wenzel, A.E. (1990). One hundred years of forgetting: A quantitative description of retention. *Psychological Review, 103,* 734-760.

Sejnoski, T.J., Rosenberg, C. R. (1987). Parallel networks that learn to pronounce English text. *Complex Systems*, vol.1, no.1, 145-68.

Stadler, M.A. (1995). Role of attention in implicit learning. *Journal of Experimental Psychology: Learning, Memory and Cognition, 21,* 819-827.

Stadler, M.A. (1989). On learning complex procedural knowledge. *Journal of Experimental Psychology: Learning, Memory and Cognition, 15,* 1061-1069.

Stadler, M.A. & Roediger, H.L. (1998). The question of awareness in research on implicit learning. In M.A. Stadler & P.A. Frensch (Eds.). *Handbook of implicit learning* (p. 105-132). Thousand Oaks, CA: Sage.

Sun, R. (1999). Accounting for the computational basis of consciousness: A connectionist approach. *Consciousness and Cognition, 8,* 529-565.

VanLehn, K., Brown, J.S. & Greeno, J. (1984). Competitive argumentation in computational theories of cognition. In W. Kintsch, J.R. Miller & P.G. Polson (Eds.). *Methods and tactics in cognitive science (pp. 235-262).* Hillsdale, NJ: LEA.

Wallach, D., & Lebiere, C. (1999). Example-based models of control problems. Paper presented at the *1999 ACT-R Workshop*, George-Mason University, Fairfax, VA. See http://hfac.gmu.edu/actr99/.

Wallach, D. & Lebiere, C. (2000). Learning of event sequences: An architectural approach. In J. Aasman & N. Taatgen (Eds.). *Proceedings of the third international conference on cognitive modeling* (pp. 271-279). Groningen: Universal Press.

Willingham, D.B., Nissen, M.J., & Bullemer, P. (1989). On the development of procedural knowledge. *Journal of Experimental Psychology: Learning, Memory and Cognition, 15,* 1047-1060.

Sequential Decision Making Based on Direct Search

Jürgen Schmidhuber

IDSIA, Galleria 2, 6928 Manno (Lugano), Switzerland

1 Introduction

The most challenging open issues in sequential decision making include partial observability of the decision maker's environment, hierarchical and other types of abstract credit assignment, the learning of credit assignment algorithms, and exploration without *a priori* world models. I will summarize why direct search (DS) in policy space provides a more natural framework for addressing these issues than reinforcement learning (RL) based on value functions and dynamic programming. Then I will point out fundamental drawbacks of traditional DS methods in case of stochastic environments, stochastic policies, and unknown temporal delays between actions and observable effects. I will discuss a remedy called the success-story algorithm, show how it can outperform traditional DS, and mention a relationship to market models combining certain aspects of DS and traditional RL.

Policy learning. A learner's modifiable parameters that determine its behavior are called its policy. An algorithm that modifies the policy is called a learning algorithm. In the context of sequential decision making based on reinforcement learning (RL) there are two broad classes of learning algorithms: (1) methods based on dynamic programming (DP) (Bellman, 1961), and (2) direct search (DS) in policy space. DP-based RL (DPRL) learns a value function mapping input/action pairs to expected discounted future reward and uses online variants of DP for constructing rewarding policies (Samuel, 1959; Barto, Sutton, & Anderson, 1983; Sutton, 1988; Watkins, 1989; Watkins & Dayan, 1992; Moore & Atkeson, 1993; Bertsekas & Tsitsiklis, 1996). DS runs and evaluates policies directly, possibly building new policy candidates from those with the highest evaluations observed so far. DS methods include variants of stochastic hill-climbing (SHC), evolutionary strategies (Rechenberg, 1971; Schwefel, 1974), genetic algorithms (GAs) (Holland, 1975), genetic programming (GP) (Cramer, 1985; Banzhaf, Nordin, Keller, & Francone, 1998), Levin Search (Levin, 1973, 1984), and adaptive extensions of Levin Search (Solomonoff, 1986; Schmidhuber, Zhao, & Wiering, 1997b).

Outline. DS offers several advantages over DPRL, but also has some drawbacks. I will list advantages first (section 2), then describe an illustrative task unsolvable by DPRL but trivially solvable by DS (section 3), then mention a few theoretical results concerning DS in general search spaces (section 4), then point out a major problem of DS (section 5), and offer a remedy (section 6 and section 7).

R. Sun and C.L. Giles (Eds.): Sequence Learning, LNAI 1828, pp. 213–240, 2000.

2   Advantages of Direct Search

2.1   DS Advantage 1: No States

Finite time convergence proofs for DPRL (Kearns & Singh, 1999) require (among other things) that the environment can be quantized into a finite number of discrete states, and that the topology describing possible transitions from one state to the next, given a particular action, is known in advance. Even if the real world was quantizable into a discrete state space, however, for all practical purposes this space will be inaccessible and remain unknown. Current proofs do not cover apparently minor deviations from the basic principle, such as the world-class RL backgammon player (Tesauro, 1994), which uses a nonlinear function approximator to deal with a large but finite number of discrete states and, for the moment at least, seems a bit like a miracle without full theoretical foundation. Prior knowledge about the topology of a network connecting discrete states is also required by algorithms for partially observable Markov decisicion processes (POMDPs), although they are more powerful than standard DPRL, e.g., (Kaelbling, Littman, & Cassandra, 1995; Littman, Cassandra, & Kaelbling, 1995). In general, however, we do not know *a priori* how to quantize a given environment into meaningful states.

DS, however, completely avoids the issues of value functions and state identification — it just cares for testing policies and keeping those that work best.

2.2   DS Advantage 2: No Markovian Restrictions

Convergence proofs for DPRL also require that the learner's current input conveys all the information about the current state (or at least about the optimal next action). In the real world, however, the current sensory input typically tells next to nothing about the "current state of the world," if there is such a thing at all. Typically, memory of previous events is required to disambiguate inputs. For instance, as your eyes are sequentially scanning the visual scene dominated by this text you continually decide which parts (or possibly compressed descriptions thereof) deserve to be represented in short-term memory. And you have presumably *learned* to do this, apparently by some unknown, sophisticated RL method fundamentally different from DPRL.

Some DPRL variants such as $Q(\lambda)$ are limited to a very special kind of exponentially decaying short-term memory. Others simply ignore memory issues by focusing on suboptimal, memory-free solutions to problems whose optimal solutions do require some form of short-term memory (Jaakkola, Singh, & Jordan, 1995). Again others can in principle find optimal solutions even in partially observable environments (POEs) (Kaelbling et al., 1995; Littman et al., 1995), but they (a) are practically limited to very small problems (Littman, 1996), and (b) do require knowledge of a discrete state space model of the environment. To various degrees, problem (b) also holds for certain hierarchical RL approaches to memory-based input disambiguation (Ring, 1991, 1993, 1994; McCallum, 1996; Wiering & Schmidhuber, 1998). Although no discrete models are necessary for

DPRL systems with function approximators based on recurrent neural networks (Schmidhuber, 1991c; Lin, 1993), the latter do suffer from a lack of theoretical foundation, perhaps even more so than the backgammon player.

DS, however, does not care at all for Markovian conditions and full observability of the environment. While DPRL is essentially limited to learning reactive policies mapping current inputs to output actions, DS in principle can be applied to search spaces whose elements are general algorithms or programs with time-varying variables that can be used for memory purposes (Williams, 1992; Teller, 1994; Schmidhuber, 1995; Wiering & Schmidhuber, 1996; Sałustowicz & Schmidhuber, 1997).

2.3 DS Advantage 3: Straight-Forward Hierarchical Credit Assignment

There has been a lot of recent work on hierarchical DPRL. Some researchers address the case where an external teacher provides intermediate subgoals and/or prewired macro actions consisting of sequences of lower-level actions (Moore & Atkeson, 1993; Tham, 1995; Sutton, 1995; Singh, 1992; Humphrys, 1996; Digney, 1996; Sutton, Singh, Precup, & Ravindran, 1999). Others focus on the more ambitious goal of automatically learning useful subgoals and macros (Schmidhuber, 1991b; Eldracher & Baginski, 1993; Ring, 1991, 1994; Dayan & Hinton, 1993; Wiering & Schmidhuber, 1998; Sun & Sessions, 2000). Compare also work presented at the recent NIPS*98 workshop on hierarchical RL organized by Doina Precup and Ron Parr (McGovern, 1998; Andre, 1998; Moore, Baird, & Kaelbling, 1998; Bowling & Veloso, 1998; Harada & Russell, 1998; Wang & Mahadevan, 1998; Kirchner, 1998; Coelho & Grupen, 1998; Huber & Grupen, 1998).

Most current work in hierarchical DPRL aims at speeding up credit assignment in fully observable environments. Approaches like HQ-learning (Wiering & Schmidhuber, 1998), however, additionally achieve a qualitative (as opposed to just quantitative) decomposition by learning to decompose problems that cannot be solved at all by standard DPRL into several DPRL-solvable subproblems and the corresponding macro-actions.

Generally speaking, non-trivial forms of hierarchical RL almost automatically run into problems of partial observability, even those with origins in the MDP framework. Feudal RL (Dayan & Hinton, 1993), for instance, is subject to such problems (Ron Williams, personal communication). As Peter Dayan himself puts it (personal communication): *"Higher level experts are intended to be explicitly ignorant of the details of the state of the agent at any resolution more detailed than their action choice. Therefore, the problem is really a POMDP from their perspective. It's easy to design unfriendly state decompositions that make this disastrous. The key point is that it is highly desirable to deny them information – the chief executive of [a major bank] doesn't really want to know how many paper clips his most junior bank clerk has – but arranging for this to be benign in general is difficult."*

In the DS framework, however, hierarchical credit assignment via frequently used, automatically generated subprograms becomes trivial in principle. For instance, suppose policies are programs built from a general programming language that permits parameterized conditional jumps to arbitrary code addresses (Dickmanns, Schmidhuber, & Winklhofer, 1987; Ray, 1992; Wiering & Schmidhuber, 1996; Schmidhuber et al., 1997b; Schmidhuber, Zhao, & Schraudolph, 1997a). DS will simply keep successful hierarchical policies that partially reuse code (subprograms) via appropriate jumps. Again, partial observability is not an issue.

2.4   DS Advantage 4: Non-Hierarchical Abstract Credit Assignment

Hierarchical learning of macros and reusable subprograms is of interest but limited. Often there are *non*-hierarchical (nevertheless exploitable) regularities in solution space. For instance, suppose we can obtain solution B by replacing every action *"turn(right)"* in solution A by *"turn(left)."* B will then be regular in the sense that it conveys little additional conditional algorithmic information, given A (Solomonoff, 1964; Kolmogorov, 1965; Chaitin, 1969; Li & Vitányi, 1993), that is, there is a short algorithm computing B from A. Hence B should not be hard to learn by a smart RL system that already found A. While DPRL cannot exploit such regularities in any obvious manner, DS in general algorithm spaces does not encounter any fundamental problems in this context. For instance, all that is necessary to find B may be a modification of the parameter *"right"* of a single instruction *"turn(right)"* in a repetitive loop computing A (Schmidhuber et al., 1997b).

2.5   DS Advantage 5: Metalearning Potential

In a given environment, which is the best way of collecting reward? Hierarchical RL? Some sort of POMDP-RL, or perhaps analogy-based RL? Combinations thereof? Or other nameless approaches to exploiting algorithmic regularities in solution space? A smart learner should find out by itself, using experience to improve its own credit assignment strategy (metalearning or "learning to learn") (Lenat, 1983; Schmidhuber, 1987). In principle, such a learner should be able to run *arbitrary* credit assignment strategies, and discover and use "good" ones, without wasting too much of its limited life-time (Schmidhuber et al., 1997a). It seems obvious that DPRL does not provide a useful basis for achieving this goal, while DS seems more promising as it does allow for searching spaces populated with arbitrary algorithms, including metalearning algorithms. I will come back to this issue later.

Disclaimer: of course, solutions to almost all possible problems are irregular and do not share mutual algorithmic information (Kolmogorov, 1965; Solomonoff, 1964; Chaitin, 1969; Li & Vitányi, 1993). In general, learning and generalization are therefore impossible for any algorithm. But it's the comparatively few, exceptional, low-complexity problems that receive almost all attention of computer scientists.

2.6   Advantage 6: Exploring Limited Spatio-Temporal Predictability

Knowledge of the world may boost performance. That's why exploration is a major RL research issue. How should a learner explore a spatio-temporal domain? By predicting and learning from success/failure what's predictable and what's not.

Most previous work on exploring unknown data sets has focused on selecting single training exemplars maximizing traditional information gain (Fedorov, 1972; Hwang, Choi, Oh, & II, 1991; MacKay, 1992; Plutowski, Cottrell, & White, 1994; Cohn, 1994). Here typically the concept of a surprise is defined in Shannon's sense (Shannon, 1948): some event's surprise value or information content is the negative logarithm of its probability. This inspired simple reinforcement learning approaches to pure exploration (Schmidhuber, 1991a; Storck, Hochreiter, & Schmidhuber, 1995; Thrun & Möller, 1992) that use adaptive predictors to predict the entire next input, given current input and action. The basic idea is that the action-generating module gets rewarded in case of predictor failures. Hence it is motivated to generate action sequences leading to yet unpredictable states that are "informative" in the classic sense. Some of these explorers actually like white noise simply because it is so unpredictable, thus conveying a lot of Shannon information. Compare alternative, hardwired exploration strategies (Sutton & Pinette, 1985; Kaelbling, 1993; Dayan & Sejnowski, 1996; Koenig & Simmons, 1996).

Most existing systems either always predict all details of the next input or are limited to picking out simple statistic regularities such as "performing action A in discrete, fully observable environmental state B will lead to state C with probability 0.8." They are not able to limit their predictions solely to certain computable aspects of inputs (Schmidhuber & Prelinger, 1993) or input sequences, while ignoring random and irregular aspects. For instance, they cannot even express (and therefore cannot find) complex, abstract, predictable regularities such as *"executing a particular sequence of eye movements, given a history of incomplete environmental inputs partially caused by a falling glass of red wine, will result in the view of a red stain on the carpet within the next 3 seconds, where details of the shape of the stain are expected to be unpredictable and left unspecified."*

General spatio-temporal abstractions and limited predictions of this kind apparently can be made only by systems that can run fairly general algorithms mapping input/action sequences to compact internal representations conveying only certain relevant information embedded in the original inputs. For instance, there are many different, realistic, plausible red stains — all may be mapped onto the same compact internal representation predictable from all sequences compatible with the abstraction "falling glass." If the final input sequence caused by eye movements scanning the carpet does not map onto the concept "red stain" (because the glass somehow decelerated in time and for some strange reason never touched the ground), there will be a surprise. There won't be a surprise, however, if the stain exhibits a particular, unexpected, irregular shape, because there was no explicit confident expectation of a particular shape in the first place.

The central questions are: In a given environment, in absence of a state model, how to extract the predictable concepts corresponding to algorithmic regularities that are not already known? How to discover novel spatio-temporal regularities automatically among the many random or unpredictable things that should be ignored? Which novel input sequence-transforming algorithms do indeed compute reduced reduced internal representations permitting reliable predictions?

Usually we cannot rely on a teacher telling the system which concepts are interesting, such as in the EURISKO system (Lenat, 1983). The DPRL framework is out of the question due to issues of partial observability. Lookup-table approaches like those used in more limited scenarios are infeasible due to the huge number of potentially interesting sequence-processing, event-memorizing algorithms. On the other hand, it is possible to use DS-like methods for building a "curious" embedded agent that differs from previous explorers in the sense that it can limit its predictions to fairly arbitrary, computable aspects of event sequences and thus can explicitly ignore almost arbitrary unpredictable, random aspects (Schmidhuber, 1999). It constructs initially random algorithms mapping event sequences to abstract internal representations (IRs). It also constructs algorithms predicting IRs from IRs computed earlier. Its goal is to learn novel algorithms creating IRs useful for correct IR predictions, without wasting time on those learned before. This can be achieved by a co-evolutionary scheme involving two competing modules collectively designing single algorithms to be executed. The modules have actions for betting on the outcome of IR predictions computed by the algorithms they have agreed upon. If their opinions differ then the system checks who's right, punishes the loser (the surprised one), and rewards the winner. A DS-like RL algorithm forces each module to increase its reward. This motivates each to lure the other into agreeing upon algorithms involving predictions that surprise it. Since each module essentially can put in its veto against algorithms it does not consider profitable, the system is motivated to focus on those computable aspects of the environment where both modules still have confident but different opinions. Once both share the same opinion on a particular issue (via the loser's DS-based learning process, e.g., the winner is simply copied onto the loser), the winner loses a source of reward — an incentive to shift the focus of interest onto novel, yet unknown algorithms. There are simulations where surprise-generation of this kind can actually help to speed up external reward (Schmidhuber, 1999).

2.7   Summary

Given the potential DS advantages listed above (most of them related to partial observability), it may seem that the more ambitious the goals of some RL researcher, the more he/she will get drawn towards methods for DS in spaces of fairly general algorithms, as opposed to the more limited DPRL-based approaches.

Standard DS does suffer from major disadvantages, though, as I will point out later for the case of realistic, stochastic worlds.

3   Typical Applications

Both DPRL and DS boast impressive practical successes. For instance, there is the world-class DPRL-based backgammon player (Tesauro, 1994), although it's not quite clear yet (beyond mere intuition) why exactly it works so well. And DS has proven superior to alternative traditional methods in engineering domains such as wing design, combustion chamber design, turbulence control (the historical origins of "evolutionary computation"). There are overviews (Schwefel, 1995; Koumoutsakos P. & D., 1998) with numerous references to earlier work.

Will DS' successes in such domains eventually carry over to learning sequential behavior in domains traditionally approached by variants of DPRL? At the moment little work has been done on DS in search spaces whose elements are sequential behaviors (Schmidhuber et al., 1997b), but this may change soon. Of course, the most obvious temporal tasks to be attacked by DS are not board games but tasks that violate DPRL's Markovian assumptions. It does not make sense to apply low-bias methods like DS to domains that satisfy the preconditions of more appropriately biased DPRL approaches.

Parity. I will use the parity problem to illustrate this. The task requires to separate bitstrings of length $n > 0$ (n integer) with an odd number of zeros from others. n-bit parity in principle is solvable by a 3-layer feedforward neural net with n input units. But learning the task from training exemplars by, say, backpropagation, is hard for $n > 20$, due to such a net's numerous free parameters. On the other hand, a very simple finite state automaton with just one bit of internal state can correctly classify arbitrary bitstrings by sequentially processing them one bit at a time, and switching the internal state bit on or off depending on whether the current input is 1 or 0.

A policy implementing such a sequential solution, however, cannot efficiently be learned by DPRL. The problem is that the task violates DPRL's essential Markovian precondition: the current input bit in a training sequence does not provide the relevant information about the previous history necessary for correct classification.

Next we will see, however, that parity can be quickly learned by the most trivial DS method, namely, random search (RS). RS works as follows: *REPEAT randomly initialize the policy and test the resulting net on a training set UNTIL solution found.*

Experiment. Our policy is the weight matrix of a standard recurrent neural network. We use two architectures (A1, A2). A1(k) is a fully connected net with 1 input, 1 output, and k hidden units, each non-input unit receiving the traditional bias connection from a unit with constant activation 1.0. A2 is like A1(10), but less densely connected: each hidden unit receives connections from the input unit, the output unit, and itself; the output unit sees all other units. All activation functions are standard: $f(x) = (1 + e^{-x})^{-1} \in [0.0, 1.0]$. Binary inputs are -1.0 (for 0) and 1.0 (for 1). Sequence lengths n are randomly chosen between 500 and 600. All variable activations are set to 0 at each sequence begin. Target information is provided only at sequence ends (hence the relevant time delays comprise at least 500 steps; there are no intermediate rewards). Our training set consists of 100 sequences, 50 from class 1 (even; target 0.0) and 50 from class 2 (odd; target 1.0). Correct sequence classification is defined as "absolute error at sequence end below 0.1". We stop RS once a random weight matrix (weights randomly initialized in [-100.0,100.0]) correctly classifies all training sequences. Then we test on the test set (100 sequences).

In all simulations, RS eventually finds a solution that classifies all test set sequences correctly; average final absolute test set errors are always below 0.001 — in most cases below 0.0001. In particular, RS with A1 ($k = 1$) solves the problem within only 2906 trials (average of 10 trials). RS with A2 solves it within 2797 trials on average. RS for architecture A2, but without self-connections for hidden units, solves the problem within 250 trials on average. See a previous paper (Hochreiter & Schmidhuber, 1997) for additional results in this vein.

RS is a dumb DS algorithm, of course. It won't work within acceptable time except for the most trivial problems. But this is besides the point of this section, whose purpose is to demonstrate that even primitive DS may yield results beyond DPRL's abilities. Later, however, I will discuss smarter DS methods.

What about GP? Given the RS results above, how can it be that parity is considered a difficult problem by many authors publishing in the DS-based field of "Genetic Programming" (GP), as can be seen by browsing through the proceedings of recent GP conferences? The reason is: most existing GP systems are extremely limited because they search in spaces of programs that do not even allow for loops or recursion — to the best of my knowledge, the first exception was (Dickmanns et al., 1987). Hence most GP approaches ignore a major motivation for search in program space, namely, the repetitive reuse of code in solutions with low algorithmic complexity (Kolmogorov, 1965; Solomonoff, 1964; Chaitin, 1969; Li & Vitányi, 1993).

Of course, all we need to make parity easy is a search space of programs that process inputs sequentially and allow for internal memory and loops or conditional jumps. A few thousand trials will suffice to generalize perfectly to n-bit parity for *arbitrary* n, not just for special values like those used in the numerous GP papers on this topic (where typically $n << 30$).

4   DS Theory

The arguments above emphasize DS' ability to deal with general algorithm spaces as opposed to DPRL's limited spaces of reactive mappings. Which theoretical results apply to this case?

Non-incremental & Deterministic. We know that Levin Search (LS) (Levin, 1973, 1984; Li & Vitányi, 1993) is optimal in deterministic and *non*incremental settings, that is, in cases where during the search process there are no intermediate reinforcement signals indicating the quality of suboptimal solutions. LS generates and tests computable solution candidates s in order of their Levin complexities

$$Kt(s) = \min_{q}\{-logD_P(q) + log \ t(q,s)\},$$

where program q computes s in $t(q, s)$ time steps, and $D_P(q)$ is q's Solomonoff-Levin probability (Levin, 1973, 1984; Li & Vitányi, 1993). Now suppose some algorithm A is designed to find the x solving $\phi(x) = y$, where ϕ is a computable function mapping bitstrings to bitstrings. For instance, x may represent a solution to a maze task implemented by $\phi(x) = 1$ iff x leads to the goal. Let n be a measure of problem size (such as the number of fields in the maze), and suppose A needs at most $O(f(n))$ steps (f computable) to solve problems of size n. Then LS also will need at most $O(f(n))$ steps (Levin, 1973, 1984; Li & Vitányi, 1993). Unlike GP etc., LS has a principled way of dealing with unknown program runtimes — time is allocated in an optimal fashion. There are systems that use a probabilistic LS variant to discover neural nets that perfectly generalize from extremely few training examples (Schmidhuber, 1995, 1997), and LS implementations that learn to use memory for solving maze tasks unsolvable by DPRL due to highly ambiguous inputs (Schmidhuber et al., 1997b).

Almost all work in traditional RL, however, focuses on *incremental* settings where continual policy improvement can bring more and more reward per time, and where experience with suboptimal solution candidates helps to find better ones. Adaptive Levin Search (ALS) (Schmidhuber et al., 1997b; Wiering & Schmidhuber, 1996) extends LS in this way: whenever a new candidate is more successful than the best previous one, the underlying probability distribution is modified to make the new candidate more likely, and a new LS cycle begins. This guarantees that the search time spent on each incremental step (given a particular probability distribution embodying the current bias) is optimal in Levin's sense.

It does not guarantee, though, that the total search time is spent optimally, because the probability adjustments themselves may have been suboptimal. ALS cannot exploit *arbitrary* regularities in solution space, because the probability modification algorithm itself is fixed. A machine learning researcher's dream would be an incremental RL algorithm that spends overall search time optimally in a way comparable to non-incremental LS's.

Incremental & Deterministic. Which theoretical results exist for incremental DS in general program spaces? Few, except for the following basic, almost trivial one. Suppose the environment allows for separating the search phase into repeatable, deterministic trials such that each trial with a given policy yields the same reward. Now consider stochastic hill-climbing (SHC), one of the simplest DS methods:

1. Initialize vector-valued policy p, set variables $BestPolicy := p$, $BestResult := -\infty$. **2.** Measure reward R obtained during a trial with actions executed according to p. **3.** If $BestResult > R$ then $p := BestPolicy$, else $BestPolicy := p$ and $BestResult := R$. **4.** Modify p by random mutation. Go to **2**.

If (1) both environment and p are deterministic, and if (2) the environment and all other variables modified by p (such as internal memory cells whose contents may have changed due to actions executed according to p) are reset after each trial, then the procedure above will at least guarantee that performance cannot get worse over time. If step **4** allows for arbitrary random mutations and the number of possible policies is finite then we can even guarantee convergence on an optimal policy with probability 1, given infinite time. Of course, if the random mutations of step **4** are replaced by a systematic enumeration of all possible mutations, then we also will be able to guarantee finite (though exponential in problem size) time[1]. Similar statements can be made about alternative DS methods such as GP or evolutionary programming.

Of course, in real-world settings *no* general method can be expected to obtain optimal policies within reasonable time. Typical DS practitioners are usually content with suboptimal policies though. The next section, however, will address even more fundamental problems of DS.

5   DS: Problems with Unknown Delays and Stochasticity

Overview. As mentioned above, DS in policy space does not require certain assumptions about the environment necessary for traditional RL. For instance, while the latter is essentially limited to memory-free, reactive mappings from inputs to actions, DS can be used to search among fairly arbitrary, complex, event-memorizing programs (using memory to deal with partial observability), at least in simulated, deterministic worlds. In realistic settings, however, reliable policy evaluations are complicated by (a) unknown delays between action sequences and observable effects, and (b) stochasticity in policy and environment. Given a limited life-time, how much time should a direct policy searcher spend on policy evaluations to obtain reliable statistics? Despite the fundamental nature of this question it has not received much attention yet. Here I evaluate an efficient approach based on the *success-story algorithm* (SSA). It provides a radical answer prepared for the worst case: it *never* stops evaluating any previous policy modification except those it undoes for lack of empirical evidence that they have contributed to lifelong reward accelerations. I identify SSA's fundamental advantages over traditional DS on problems involving unknown delays and stochasticity.

The problem. In realistic situations DS exhibits several fundamental drawbacks: (**1**) Often there are unknown temporal delays between causes and effects. In general we cannot be sure that a given trial was long enough to observe all long-term rewards/punishments caused by actions executed during the trial. We do not know in advance how long a trial should take. (**2**) The policy may be stochastic, i.e., the learner's actions are selected nondeterministically according to probability distributions conditioned on the policy. Stochastic policies are widely used to prevent learners from getting stuck. Results of policy evaluations, however, will then *vary from trial to trial*. (**3**) Environment and reward may be stochastic, too. And even if the environment is deterministic it may appear stochastic from an individual learner's perspective, due to partial observability.

Time is a scarce resource. Hence all direct methods face a central question: to determine whether some policy is really useful in the long run or just appears to

---

[1] Note that even for the more limited DPRL algorithms until very recently there have not been any theorems guaranteeing finite convergence time (Kearns & Singh, 1999).

be (e.g., because the current trial was too short to encounter a punishing state, or because it was a lucky trial), how much time should the learner spend on its evaluation? In particular, how much time should a single trial with a given policy take, and how many trials are necessary to obtain statistically significant results without wasting too much time? Despite the fundamental nature of these questions not much work has been done to address them.

Basic idea. There is a radical answer to such questions: Evaluate a previous policy change at any stage of the search process by looking at the entire time interval that has gone by since the change occurred — at any given time aim to use *all* the available empirical data concerning long-term policy-dependent rewards! A change is considered "good" as long as the average reward per time since its creation exceeds the corresponding ratios for previous "good" changes. Changes that eventually turn out to be "bad" get undone by an efficient backtracking scheme called the *success-story algorithm* (SSA). SSA always takes into account the latest information available about long-term effects of changes that have appeared "good" so far ("bad" changes, however, are not considered again). Effectively SSA adjusts trial lengths retrospectively: at any given time, trial starts are determined by the occurrences of the remaining "good" changes representing a success story. The longer the time interval that went by since some "good" change, the more reliable the evaluation of its true long-term benefits. No trial of a "good" change ever ends unless it turns out to be "bad" at some point. Thus SSA is prepared for the worst case. For instance, no matter what's the maximal time lag between actions and consequences in a given domain, eventually SSA's effective trials will encompass it.

What's next. The next section will explain SSA in detail, and show how most traditional direct methods can be augmented by SSA. Then we will experimentally verify SSA's advantages over traditional direct methods in case of noisy performance evaluations and unknown delays.

6 Success-Story Algorithm (SSA)

Here we will briefly review basic principles (Schmidhuber et al., 1997a). An agent lives in environment E from time 0 to unknown time T. Life is one-way: even if it is decomposable into numerous consecutive "trials", time will never be reset. The agent has a policy POL (a set of modifiable parameters) and possibly an internal state S (e.g., for short-term memory that can be modified by actions). Both S and POL are variable dynamic data structures influencing probabilities of actions to be executed by the agent. Between time 0 and T, the agent repeats the following cycle over and over again ($\mathcal{A}$ denotes a set of possible actions):

REPEAT:
select and execute some $a \in \mathcal{A}$ with conditional probability $P(a \mid POL, S, E)$.[2]

Action a will consume time and may change E, S, and POL.

---

[2] Instead of using the expression *policy* for the conditional probability distribution P itself we reserve it for the agent's modifiable data structure POL.

Learning algorithms (LAs). $LA \subset A$ is the set of actions that can modify POL. LA's members are called *learning algorithms* (LAs). Previous work on metalearning (Schmidhuber et al., 1997a, 1997b) left it to the system itself to compute execution probabilities of LAs by constructing and executing POL-modifying algorithms. In this paper we will focus on a simpler case where all LAs are externally triggered procedures. Formally this means that $P(a \in LA \mid POL, S, E) = 1$ if E is in a given "policy modification state" determined by the user, and $P(a \in LA \mid POL, S, E) = 0$ otherwise. For instance, in some of the illustrative experiments to be presented later, SHC's mutation process will be the only LA. Alternatively we may use LAs that are in fact GP-like crossover strategies, or a wide variety of other policy-modifying algorithms employed in traditional DS methods.

Checkpoints. The entire lifetime of the agent can be partitioned into time intervals separated by special times called *checkpoints*. In general, checkpoints are computed dynamically during the agent's life by certain actions in A executed according to POL itself (Schmidhuber et al., 1997a). In this paper, however, for simplicity all checkpoints will be set in advance. The agent's k-th checkpoint is denoted c_k. Checkpoints obey the following rules: (1) $\forall k \ \ 0 < c_k < T$. (2) $\forall j < k \ \ c_j < c_k$. (3) Except for the first, checkpoints may not occur before at least one POL-modification has been computed by some LA since the previous checkpoint.

Sequences of POL-modifications (SPMs). SPM_k denotes the sequence of POL-modifications computed by LAs in between c_k and c_{k+1}. Since LA execution probabilities may depend on POL, POL may in principle influence the way it modifies itself, which is interesting for things such as metalearning. In this paper's experiments, however, we will focus on the case where exactly one LA (a simple mutation process like the one used in stochastic hill-climbing) is invoked in between two subsequent checkpoints.

Reward and goal. Occasionally E provides real-valued reward. The cumulative reward obtained by the agent between time 0 and time $t > 0$ is denoted $R(t)$, where $R(0) = 0$. Typically, in large (partially observable) environments, maximizing cumulative expected reinforcement within a limited life-time would be too ambitious a goal for any method. Instead designers of direct policy search methods are content with methods that can be expected to find better and better policies. But what exactly does "better" mean in our context? Our agent's obvious goal at checkpoint t is to generate POL-modifications accelerating reward intake: it wants to let $\frac{R(T) - R(t)}{T - t}$ exceed the current average speed of reward intake. But to determine this speed it needs a previous point $t' < t$ to compute $\frac{R(t) - R(t')}{t - t'}$. How can t' be specified in a general yet reasonable way? Or, to rephrase the central question of this paper: if life involves unknown temporal delays between action sequences and their observable effects and/or consists of many successive "trials" with nondeterministic, uncertain outcomes, how long should a trial last, and how many trials should the agent look back into time to evaluate its current performance?

The *success-story algorithm* (to be introduced next) addresses this question in a way that is prepared for the worst case: once a trial of a new policy change has begun it will *never* end unless the policy change itself gets undone (by a simple backtracking mechanism which ensures that trial starts mark long-term reward accelerations).

Enforcing success stories. Let V denote the agent's time-varying set of past checkpoints that have been followed by long-term reward accelerations. Initially V is empty. v_k denotes the k-th element of V in ascending order. The *success-story criterion* (SSC) is satisfied at time t if either V is empty (trivial case) or if

$$\frac{R(t) - R(0)}{t - 0} < \frac{R(t) - R(v_1)}{t - v_1} < \frac{R(t) - R(v_2)}{t - v_2} < \ldots < \frac{R(t) - R(v_{|V|})}{t - v_{|V|}}.$$

SSC demands that each checkpoint in V marks the beginning of a long-term reward acceleration measured up to the current time t. SSC is achieved by the *success-story algorithm* (SSA) which is invoked at every checkpoint:

1. WHILE SSC is not satisfied: Undo all POL modifications made since the most recent checkpoint in V, and remove that checkpoint from V.

2. Add the current checkpoint to V.

"Undoing" a modification means restoring the preceding POL — this requires storing past values of POL components on a stack prior to modification. Thus each POL modification that survived SSA is part of a bias shift generated after a checkpoint marking a lifelong reward speed-up: the remaining checkpoints in V and the remaining policy modifications represent a "success story."

Trials and "effective" trials. All checkpoints in V represent starts of yet unfinished "effective" trials (as opposed to externally defined trials with prewired starts and ends). No effective trial ever ends unless SSA restores the policy to its state before the trial started. The older some surviving SPM, the more time will have passed to collect statistics concerning its long-term consequences, and the more stable it will be if it is indeed useful and not just there by chance.

Since trials of still valid policy modifications never end, they embody a principled way of dealing with unknown reward delays. No matter what's the maximal causal delay in a given environment, eventually the system's effective trials will encompass it.

Metalearning? An interesting example of long delays between actions and effects is provided by metalearning (learning a learning algorithm or credit assignment algorithm) (Lenat, 1983; Schmidhuber, 1987; Schmidhuber et al., 1997a). For instance, suppose some "metalearning action sequence" changes a learner's credit assignment strategy. To evaluate whether the change is good or bad, apparently we need something like a "meta-trial" subsuming several lower-level "normal" trials in which instances of additional policy changes produced by the modified learning strategy somehow get evaluated, to collect evidence concerning the quality of the modified learning strategy itself. Due to their very nature such meta-trials will typically consume a lot of time. SSA, however, addresses this issue in a natural and straight-forward way. There is no explicit difference between trials and meta-trials. But new effective trials do get opened within previously started, yet unfinished effective trials. What does this mean? It means that earlier SPMs automatically get evaluated as to whether they set the stage for later "good" SPMs. For instance, SSA will eventually discard an early SPM that changed the policy in a way that increased the probability of certain later SPMs causing a waste of time on evaluations of useless additional policy changes. That is, SSA automatically measures (in terms of reward/time ratios affected by learning and testing processes) the impact of early learning on later learning: SSA prefers SPMs making "good" future SPMs more likely. Given action sets that allow for composition of general credit assignment strategies from simple LAs, SSA will prefer probabilistic learning algorithms leading to better probabilistic learning algorithms. And it will end meta-trials as soon as they violate the constraints imposed by the success-story criterion, just like it does with "normal" trials.

Implementing SSA. SSA guarantees that SSC will be satisfied after each checkpoint, even in partially observable, stochastic environments with unknown delays. (Of course, later SSA invocations using additional, previously unavailable, delayed information may undo policy changes that survived the current checkpoint.) Although inequality (1) contains $|V|$ fractions, SSA can be implemented efficiently: only the two most recent still valid sequences of modifications (those "on top of the stack") need to be considered at a given time in an SSA invocation. A *single* SSA invocation, however, may invalidate *many* SPMs if necessary.

7   Illustration: How SSA Augments DS

Methods for direct search in policy space, such as stochastic hill-climbing (SHC) and genetic algorithms (GAs), test policy candidates during time-limited trials, then build new policy candidates from some of the policies with highest evaluations observed so far. As mentioned above, the advantage of this general approach over traditional RL algorithms is that few restrictions need to be imposed on the nature of the agent's interaction with the environment. In particular, if the policy allows for actions that manipulate the content of some sort of short-term memory then the environment does not need to be fully observable — in principle, direct methods such as Genetic Programming (Cramer, 1985; Banzhaf et al., 1998), adaptive Levin Search (Schmidhuber et al., 1997b), or Probabilistic Incremental Program Evolution (Sałustowicz & Schmidhuber, 1997), can be used for searching spaces of complex, event-memorizing programs or algorithms as opposed to simple, memory-free, reactive mappings from inputs to actions.

As pointed out above, a disadvantage of traditional direct methods is that they lack a principled way of dealing with unknown delays and stochastic policy evaluations. In contrast to typical trials executed by direct methods, however, an SSA trial of any previous policy modification *never* ends unless its reward/time ratio drops below that of the most recent previously started (still unfinished) effective trial. Here we will go beyond previous work (Schmidhuber et al., 1997a, 1997b) by clearly demonstrating how a direct method can benefit from augmentation by SSA in presence of unknown temporal delays and stochastic performance evaluations.

Task (Schmidhuber & Zhao, 1999). We tried to come up with the simplest task sufficient to illustrate the drawbacks of standard DS algorithms and the way SSA overcomes them. Hence, instead of studying tasks that require to learn complex programs setting and resetting memory contents (as mentioned above, such complex tasks provide a main motivation for using DS), we use a comparatively simple two-armed bandit problem.

There are two arms A and B. Pulling arm A will yield reward 1000 with probability 0.01 and reward -1 with probability 0.99. Pulling arm B will yield reward 1 with probability 0.99 and reward -1000 with probability 0.01. *All rewards are delayed by 5 pulls.* There is an agent that knows neither the reward distributions nor the delays. Since this section's goal is to study policy search under uncertainty we equip the agent with the simplest possible stochastic policy consisting of a single variable p $(0 \leq p \leq 1)$: at a given time arm A is chosen with probability p, otherwise B is chosen. *Modifying the policy in a very limited, SHC-like way (see below) and observing the long-term effects is the only way the agent may collect information that might be useful for improving the policy.* Its goal is to maximize the entire reward obtained during its life-time which is limited to 30,000 pulls. The maximal cumulative reward is 270300 (always choose arm A), the minimum is -270300 (always choose arm B). Random arm selection yields expected reward 0. [3]

Obviously the task is non-trivial, because the long-term effects of a small change in p will be hard to detect, and will require significant statistical sampling.

It is besides the point of this paper that our prior knowledge of the problem suggests a more informed alternative approach such as "pull arm A for N trials, then arm B for N trials, then commit to the best." Even cleverer optimizers would try various assumptions about the delay lengths and pull arms in turn until one was statistically significantly better than the other, given a particular delay assumption. We do not allow this, however: we make the task hard by requiring the agent to learn solely from observations of outcomes of limited, SHC-like policy mutations (details below). After all, in partially observable environments that are much more complex and realistic (but less analyzable) than ours this often is the only reasonable thing to do.

---

[3] The problem resembles another two-armed bandit problem for which there is an optimal method due to Gittins (Gittins, 1989). Our unknown reward delays, however, prevent this method from being applicable — it cannot discover that the current reward does not depend on the current input but on an event in the past. In addition, Gittins' method needs to discount future rewards relative to immediate rewards. Anyway, this footnote is besides the point of this paper whose focus is on direct policy search — Gittins' method is not a direct one.

Stochastic Hill-Climbing (SHC). SHC may be the simplest incremental algorithm using direct search in policy space. It should be mentioned, however, that despite its simplicity SHC often outperforms more complex direct methods such as GAs (Juels & Wattenberg, 1996). Anyway, SHC and more complex population-based direct algorithms such as GAs, GP, and evolution strategies are equally affected by the central questions of this paper: how many trials should be spent on the evaluation of a given policy? How long should a trial take?[4]

We implement SHC as follows: **1.** Initialize policy p to 0.5, and real-valued variables *BestPolicy* and *BestResult* to p and 0, respectively. **2.** If there have been more than $30000 - TrialLength$ pulls then exit (*TrialLength* is an integer constant). Otherwise evaluate p by measuring the average reward R obtained during the next *TrialLength* consecutive pulls. **3.** If *BestResult* $> R$ then $p := BestPolicy$, else *BestPolicy* $:= p$ and *BestResult* $:= R$. **4.** Randomly perturb p by adding either -0.1 or +0.1 except when this would lead outside the interval $[0,1]$. Go to **2.**

Problem. Like any direct search algorithm SHC faces the fundamental question raised in section 2: how long to evaluate the current policy to obtain statistically significant results without wasting too much time? To examine this issue we vary *TrialLength*. Our prior knowledge of the problem tells us that *TrialLength* should exceed 5 to handle the 5-step reward delays. But due to the stochasticity of the rewards, much larger *TrialLengths* are required for reliable evaluations of some policy's "true" performance. Of course, the disadvantage of long trials is the resulting small number of possible training exemplars and policy changes (learning steps) to be executed during the limited life which lasts just 30,000 steps.

Comparison 1. We compare SHC to a combination of SSA and SHC, which we implement just like SHC except that we replace step **3** by a checkpoint (SSA-invocation — see section 6).

Comparison 2. To illustrate potential benefits of policies that influence the way they learn we also compare to SSA applied to a primitive "self-modifying policy" (SMP) with *two* modifiable parameters: p (with same meaning as above) and "learning rate" δ (initially 0). After each checkpoint, p is replaced by $p + \delta$, then δ is replaced by $2 * \delta$. In this sense SMP itself influences the way it changes, albeit in a way that is much more limited than the one in previous papers (Schmidhuber et al., 1997a; Schmidhuber, 1999). If $\delta = 0$ then it will be randomly set to either 0.1 or -0.1. If $\delta > 0.5$ ($\delta < -0.5$) then it will be replaced by 0.5 (-0.5). If $p > 1$ ($p < 0$) then it will be set to 1 (0).

One apparent danger with this approach is that accelerating the learning rate may result in unstable behavior. We will see, however, that SSA precisely prevents this from happening by eventually undoing those learning rate modifications that are not followed by reliable long-term performance improvement.

---

[4] In fact, population-based approaches will suffer even more than simple SHC from unknown delays and stochasticity, simply because they need to test many policies, not just one.

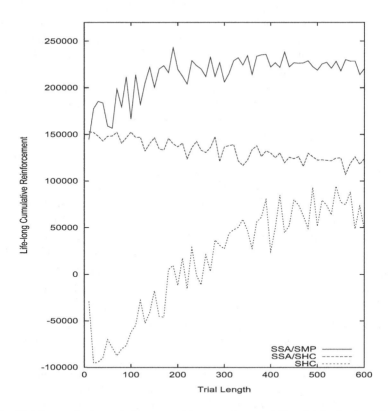

Fig. 1. *Total cumulative reinforcement (averaged over 100 trials) obtained by SHC (bottom), SSA/SHC (middle), SSA/SMP (top) for varying trial lengths. The picture does not change much for even longer trial lengths.*

Results. For all three methods Figure 1 plots lifelong cumulative reward (mean of 100 independent runs) against *TrialLength* varying from 10 to 600 pulls with a step size of 10 pulls. For most values of *TrialLength*, SHC fails to realize the long-term benefits of choosing arm A. SSA/SHC, however, always yields satisfactory results because it does not care whether *TrialLength* is much too short to obtain statistically significant policy evaluations. Instead it retrospectively readjusts the "effective" trial starts: at any given checkpoint, each previous checkpoint in V marks the begin of a new trial lasting up to the current checkpoint. Each such trial start corresponds to a lifelong reward-acceleration. The corresponding policy modifications gain more and more empirical justification as they keep surviving successive SSA calls, thus becoming more and more stable.

Still, SSA/SHC's performance slowly declines with increasing *TrialLength* since this implies less possible policy changes and less effective trials due to limited life-time. SSA/SMP (comparison **2**), however, does not much suffer from this problem since it boldly increases the learning rate as long as this is empirically observed to accelerate long-term reward intake. As soon as this is not the case any longer, however, SSA prevents further learning rate accelerations, thus avoiding unstable behavior. This primitive type of learning algorithm self-modification outperforms SSA/SHC. In fact, some of the surviving effective trials may be viewed as "metalearning trials": SSA essentially observes the long term effects of certain learning rates whose values are influenced by the policy itself, and undoes those that tend to cause "bad" additional policy modifications setting the stage for worse performance in subsequent trials.

Trials Shorter Than Delays. We also tested the particularly interesting case $TrialLength < 5$. Here SHC and other direct methods fail completely because the policy tested during the current trial has nothing to do with the test outcome (due to the delays). The SSA/SHC combination, however, still manages to collect cumulative performance of around 150,000. Unlike with SHC (and other direct methods) there is no need for *a priori* knowledge about "good" trial lengths, exactly because SSA retrospectively adjusts the *effective* trial sizes.

Comparable results were obtained with much longer delays. In particular, see a recent article (Schmidhuber, 1999) for experiments with much longer life-times and unknown delays of the order of $10^6 - 10^7$ time steps.

A Complex Partially Observable Environment. This section's focus is on clarifying SSA's advantages over traditional DS in the simplest possible setting. It should be mentioned, however, that there have been much more challenging SSA applications in partially observable environments, which represent a major motivation of direct methods because most traditional RL methods are not applicable here. For instance, a previous paper (Schmidhuber et al., 1997a) describes two agents A and B living in a partially observable 600×500 pixel environment with obstacles. They learn to solve a complex task that could not be solved by various TD(λ) Q-learning variants (Lin, 1993). The task requires (1) agent A to find and take a key "key A"; (2) agent A go to a door "door A" and open it for agent B; (3) agent B to enter through "door A", find and take another key "key B"; (4) agent B to go to another door "door B" to open it (to free the way to the goal); (5) one of the agents to reach the goal. Both agents share the same design. Each is equipped with limited "active" sight: by executing certain instructions, it can sense obstacles, its own key, the corresponding door, or the goal, within up to 50 pixels in front of it. The agent can also move forward, turn around, turn relative to its key or its door or the goal. It can use short-term memory to disambiguate inputs — unlike Jaakkola et al.'s method (1995), ours is not limited to finding suboptimal stochastic policies for POEs with an optimal solution. Each agent can explicitly modify its own policy via special actions that can address and modify the probability distributions according to which action sequences (or "subprograms") are selected (this also contributes to making the set-up highly non-Markovian). Reward is provided only if one of the agents touches the goal. This agent's reward is 5.0; the other's is 3.0 (for its cooperation — note that asymmetric reward also introduces competition). Due to the complexity of the task, in the beginning the goal is found only every 300,000 actions on average (including actions that are primitive LAs and modify the policy). No prior information about good initial trial lengths is given to the system. Through self-modifications and SSA, however, within 130,000 goal hits (10^9 actions) the average trial length decreases by a factor of 60 (mean of 4 simulations). Both agents learn to cooperate to accelerate reward intake, by retrospectively adjusting their effective trial lengths using SSA.

While this previous experimental research has already demonstrated SSA's applicability to large-scale partially observable environments, a study of why it performs well has been lacking. In particular, unlike the present work, previous work (Schmidhuber et al., 1997a) did not clearly identify SSA's fundamental advantages over alternative DS methods.

8   Relation to Market Models

There is an interesting alternative class of RL systems that also combines aspects of DS and traditional RL. It exploits ideas from the field of economy that seem naturally applicable in the context of multiagent RL, and (unlike Q-learning etc.) are not necessarily limited to learning reactive behavior. In what follows I will ignore the extensive original financial literature and briefly review solely some work on RL economies instead. Then I will relate this work to SSA.

Classifier Systems and Bucket Brigade. The first RL economy was Holland's meanwhile well-known bucket brigade algorithm for classifier systems (Holland, 1985). Messages in form of bitstrings of size n can be placed on a global message list either by the environment or by entities called classifiers. Each classifier consists of a condition part and an action part defining a message it might send to the message list. Both parts are strings out of $\{0, 1, \_\}^n$ where the '$\_$' serves as a 'don't care' if it appears in the condition part. A non-negative real number is associated with each classifier indicating its 'strength'. During one cycle all messages on the message list are compared with the condition parts of all classifiers of the system. Each matching classifier computes a 'bid' based on its strength. The highest bidding classifiers may place their message on the message list of the next cycle, but they have to pay with their bid which is distributed among the classifiers active during the last time step which set up the triggering conditions (this explains the name bucket brigade). Certain messages result in an action within the environment (like moving a robot one step). Because some of these actions may be regarded as 'useful' by an external critic who can give payoff by increasing the strengths of the currently active classifiers, learning may take place. The central idea is that classifiers which are not active when the environment gives payoff but which had an important role for setting the stage for directly rewarded classifiers can earn credit by participating in 'bucket brigade chains'. The success of some active classifier recursively depends on the success of classifiers that are active at the following time ticks. Unsuccessful classifiers are replaced by new ones generated with the help of GAs.

Holland's original scheme is similar to DPRL algorithms such as Q-learning in the sense that the bids of the agents correspond to predictions of future reward. On the other hand, the scheme does not necessarily require full environmental observability. Instead it partly depends on DS-like evolutionary pressure absent in traditional RL. E.g., bankrupt agents who spent all their money are removed from the system.

Holland's approach, however, leaves several loopholes that allow agents to make money without contributing to the success of the entire system. This led to a lot of follow-up research on more stable RL classifier economies (Wilson, 1994, 1995; Weiss, 1994; Weiss & Sen, 1996) and other related types of RL ecomomies (see below). This work has closed some but possibly not all of the original loopholes.

Prototypical Self-referential Associating Learning Mechanisms. Pages 23-51 of earlier work (Schmidhuber, 1987) are devoted to systems called PSALM1 - PSALM3. Like in Holland's scheme, competing/cooperating RL agents bid for executing actions. Winners may receive external reward for achieving goals. Unlike in Holland's scheme, agents are supposed to learn the credit assignment process itself (metalearning). For this purpose they can execute actions for collectively constructing / connecting / modifying agents, for assigning credit (reward) to agents, and for transferring credit from one agent to another. To the best of my knowledge, PSALMs are the first machine learning systems that enforce the important constraint of total credit conservation (except for consumption and external reward): no agent can generate money from nothing. This constraint is not enforced in the original bucket brigade economy, where new agents enter with freshly created money (this may cause inflation and other problems). Reference (Schmidhuber, 1987) also inspired the *neural* bucket brigade (NBB), a slightly more recent but less general approach enforcing money conservation, where money is "weight substance" of a reinforcement learning neural net (Schmidhuber, 1989).

Hayek Machine (Baum & Durdanovic, 1998). PSALM3 does not strictly enforce individual property rights. For instance, agents may steal money from other agents and temporally use it in a way that does not contribute to the system's overall progress. Hayek machines are constitutional economies that apparently do not suffer from such "parasite problems" (although there is no proof yet at the moment). Hayek2 (Baum & Durdanovic, 1998) — the most recent Hayek variant — is somewhat reminiscent of PSALM3 (agents may construct new agents, and there is money conservation), but avoids several loopholes in the credit assignment process that may allow some agent to profit from actions that are not beneficial for the system as a whole. Property rights of agents are strictly enforced. Agents can create children agents and invest part of their money into them, and profit from their success. Hayek2 learned to solve rather complex blocks world problems (Baum & Durdanovic, 1998). The authors admit, however, that possibly not all potential loopholes rewarding undesired behavior have been closed by Hayek2.

COINs/Wonderful Life Utility (Wolpert, Tumer, & Frank, 1999). Perhaps the only current RL economy with a sound theoretical foundation is the COllective INtelligence (COIN) by Wolpert, Tumer & Frank (1999). A COIN partitions its set of agents into "subworlds." Each agent of a given subworld shares the same local utility function. Global utility is optimized by provably making sure that no agent in some subworld can profit if the system as a whole does not profit. COINs were successfully used in an impressive routing application.

SSA and Market Models. One way of viewing SSA in an economy-inspired framework is this: the current "credit" of a policy change equals the reward since its creation divided by the time since its creation. A policy change gets undone as soon as its credit falls below the credit of the most recent change that has not been undone yet. After any given SSA invocation the yet undone changes reflect a success-story of long-term credit increases.

To use the parent/child analogy (Baum & Durdanovic, 1998): at a given time, any still valid policy change may be viewed as a (grand-)parent of later policy changes for which it set the stage. Children that are more profitable than their ancestors protect the latter from being undone. In this way the ancestors profit from making successful children. Ancestors who increase the probability of non-profitable offspring, however, will eventually risk oblivion.

9   Conclusion

Direct search (DS) in policy space offers several advantages over traditional reinforcement learning (RL). For instance, DS does not need *a priori* information about world states and the topology of their interactions. It does not care whether the environment is fully observable. It makes hierarchical credit assignment conceptually trivial, and also allows for many alternative, non-hierarchical types of abstract credit assignment.

Existing DS methods, however, do suffer from fundamental problems in presence of environmental stochasticity and/or unknown temporal delays between actions and observable effects. In particular, they do not have a principled way of deciding when to stop policy evaluations.

Stochastic policy evaluation by the success-story algorithm (SSA) differs from traditional DS. SSA never quits evaluating any previous policy change that has not yet been undone for lack of empirical evidence that it has contributed to a lifelong reward acceleration. Each invocation of SSA retrospectively establishes a success history of surviving self-modifications: only policy changes that have empirically proven their long-term usefulness so far get another chance to justify themselves. This stabilizes the "truly useful" policy changes in the long run.

Unlike many traditional value function-based RL methods, SSA is not limited to fully observable worlds, and does not require discounting of future rewards. It shares these advantages with traditional DS algorithms. Unlike stochastic hill-climbing and other DS methods such as genetic algorithms, however, SSA does not heavily depend on *a priori* knowledge about reasonable trial lengths necessary to collect sufficient statistics for estimating long-term consequences and true values of tested policies.

On the other hand, many DS methods can be augmented by SSA in a straightforward way: just measure the time used up by all actions, policy modifications, and policy tests, and occasionally insert checkpoints that invoke SSA. In this sense SSA's basic concepts are not algorithm-specific — instead they reflect a novel, general way of thinking about how "true" performance should be measured in RL systems using DS in policy space.

Since SSA automatically collects statistics about long-term effects of earlier policy changes on later ones, it is of interest for improving the credit assignment method itself (Schmidhuber et al., 1997a).

Although the present paper's illustrative SSA application is much less complex than our previous ones, it is the first to provide insight into SSA's fundamental advantages over traditional DS methods in case of stochastic policy evaluations and unknown temporal delays between causes and effects.

Market models are similar to traditional DPRL in the sense that the bids of their agents correspond to predictions of future reward used in DPRL algorithms such as Q-learning. On the other hand, they are similar to DS in the sense that they incorporate evolutionary pressure and do not obviously require full environmental observability and Markovian conditions but can be applied to agents whose policies are drawn from general program spaces. For example, bankrupt agents who spent all their money are usually replaced by mutations of more successful agents. This introduces Darwinian selection absent in traditional DPRL.

SSA shares certain aspects of market models. In particular, at a given time any existing policy modification's reward/time ratio measured by SSA may be viewed as an investment into the future. The policy modification will fail to survive once it fails to generate enough return (including the reward obtained by its own "children") to exceed the corresponding investment of its "parent", namely, the most recent *previous*, still existing policy modification.

Future research will hopefully show when to prefer pure market models over SSA and vice versa. For instance, it will be interesting to study whether the former can efficiently deal with long, unknown causal delays and highly stochastic policies and environments.

Acknowledgments. Thanks to Sepp Hochreiter, Jieyu Zhao, Nic Schraudolph, Fred Cummins, Luca Gambardella for valuable comments. This work was supported in part by SNF grant 21-43'417.95 "Incremental Self-Improvement" and SNF grant 2100-49'144.96 "Long Short-Term Memory".

References

Andre, D. (1998). Learning hierarchical behaviors. In *NIPS'98 Workshop on Abstraction and Hierarchy in Reinforcement Learning*.

Banzhaf, W., Nordin, P., Keller, R. E., & Francone, F. D. (1998). *Genetic Programming – An Introduction*. Morgan Kaufmann Publishers, San Francisco, CA, USA.

Barto, A. G., Sutton, R. S., & Anderson, C. W. (1983). Neuronlike adaptive elements that can solve difficult learning control problems. *IEEE Transactions on Systems, Man, and Cybernetics, SMC-13*, 834–846.

Baum, E. B., & Durdanovic, I. (1998). Toward code evolution by artificial economies. Tech. rep., NEC Research Institute, Princeton, NJ. Extension of a paper in Proc. 13th ICML'1996, Morgan Kaufmann, CA.

Bellman, R. (1961). *Adaptive Control Processes.* Princeton University Press.

Bertsekas, D. P., & Tsitsiklis, J. N. (1996). *Neuro-dynamic Programming.* Athena Scientific, Belmont, MA.

Bowling, M., & Veloso, M. (1998). Bounding the suboptimality of reusing sub-problems. In *NIPS'98 Workshop on Abstraction and Hierarchy in Reinforcement Learning.*

Chaitin, G. (1969). On the length of programs for computing finite binary sequences: statistical considerations. *Journal of the ACM, 16,* 145–159.

Coelho, J., & Grupen, R. A. (1998). Control abstractions as state representation. In *NIPS'98 Workshop on Abstraction and Hierarchy in Reinforcement Learning.*

Cohn, D. A. (1994). Neural network exploration using optimal experiment design. In Cowan, J., Tesauro, G., & Alspector, J. (Eds.), *Advances in Neural Information Processing Systems 6,* pp. 679–686. San Mateo, CA: Morgan Kaufmann.

Cramer, N. L. (1985). A representation for the adaptive generation of simple sequential programs. In Grefenstette, J. (Ed.), *Proceedings of an International Conference on Genetic Algorithms and Their Applications* Hillsdale NJ. Lawrence Erlbaum Associates.

Dayan, P., & Hinton, G. (1993). Feudal reinforcement learning. In Lippman, D. S., Moody, J. E., & Touretzky, D. S. (Eds.), *Advances in Neural Information Processing Systems 5,* pp. 271–278. San Mateo, CA: Morgan Kaufmann.

Dayan, P., & Sejnowski, T. J. (1996). Exloration bonuses and dual control. *Machine Learning, 25,* 5–22.

Dickmanns, D., Schmidhuber, J., & Winklhofer, A. (1987). Der genetische Algorithmus: Eine Implementierung in Prolog. Fortgeschrittenenpraktikum, Institut für Informatik, Lehrstuhl Prof. Radig, Technische Universität München..

Digney, B. (1996). Emergent hierarchical control structures: Learning reactive/hierarchical relationships in reinforcement environments. In Maes, P., Mataric, M., Meyer, J.-A., Pollack, J., & Wilson, S. W. (Eds.), *From Animals to Animats 4: Proceedings of the Fourth International Conference on Simulation of Adaptive Behavior, Cambridge, MA,* pp. 363–372. MIT Press, Bradford Books.

Eldracher, M., & Baginski, B. (1993). Neural subgoal generation using backpropagation. In Lendaris, G. G., Grossberg, S., & Kosko, B. (Eds.), *World Congress on Neural Networks,* pp. III–145–III–148. Lawrence Erlbaum Associates, Inc., Publishers, Hillsdale.

Fedorov, V. V. (1972). *Theory of optimal experiments.* Academic Press.

Gittins, J. C. (1989). *Multi-armed Bandit Allocation Indices.* Wiley-Interscience series in systems and optimization. Wiley, Chichester, NY.

Harada, D., & Russell, S. (1998). Meta-level reinforcement learning. In *NIPS'98 Workshop on Abstraction and Hierarchy in Reinforcement Learning.*

Hochreiter, S., & Schmidhuber, J. (1997). LSTM can solve hard long time lag problems. In Mozer, M. C., Jordan, M. I., & Petsche, T. (Eds.), *Advances in Neural Information Processing Systems 9*, pp. 473–479. MIT Press, Cambridge MA.

Holland, J. H. (1975). *Adaptation in Natural and Artificial Systems.* University of Michigan Press, Ann Arbor.

Holland, J. H. (1985). Properties of the bucket brigade. In *Proceedings of an International Conference on Genetic Algorithms.* Hillsdale, NJ.

Huber, M., & Grupen, R. A. (1998). Learning robot control using control policies as abstract actions. In *NIPS'98 Workshop on Abstraction and Hierarchy in Reinforcement Learning.*

Humphrys, M. (1996). Action selection methods using reinforcement learning. In Maes, P., Mataric, M., Meyer, J.-A., Pollack, J., & Wilson, S. W. (Eds.), *From Animals to Animats 4: Proceedings of the Fourth International Conference on Simulation of Adaptive Behavior, Cambridge, MA*, pp. 135–144. MIT Press, Bradford Books.

Hwang, J., Choi, J., Oh, S., & II, R. J. M. (1991). Query-based learning applied to partially trained multilayer perceptrons. *IEEE Transactions on Neural Networks, 2*(1), 131–136.

Jaakkola, T., Singh, S. P., & Jordan, M. I. (1995). Reinforcement learning algorithm for partially observable Markov decision problems. In Tesauro, G., Touretzky, D. S., & Leen, T. K. (Eds.), *Advances in Neural Information Processing Systems 7*, pp. 345–352. MIT Press, Cambridge MA.

Juels, A., & Wattenberg, M. (1996). Stochastic hillclimbing as a baseline method for evaluating genetic algorithms. In Touretzky, D. S., Mozer, M. C., & Hasselmo, M. E. (Eds.), *Advances in Neural Information Processing Systems*, Vol. 8, pp. 430–436. The MIT Press, Cambridge, MA.

Kaelbling, L. (1993). *Learning in Embedded Systems.* MIT Press.

Kaelbling, L., Littman, M., & Cassandra, A. (1995). Planning and acting in partially observable stochastic domains. Tech. rep., Brown University, Providence RI.

Kearns, M., & Singh, S. (1999). Finite-sample convergence rates for Q-learning and indirect algorithms. In Kearns, M., Solla, S. A., & Cohn, D. (Eds.), *Advances in Neural Information Processing Systems 12.* MIT Press, Cambridge MA.

Kirchner, F. (1998). Q-learning of complex behaviors on a six-legged walking machine. In *NIPS'98 Workshop on Abstraction and Hierarchy in Reinforcement Learning.*

Koenig, S., & Simmons, R. G. (1996). The effect of representation and knowedge on goal-directed exploration with reinforcement learnign algorithm. *Machine Learning, 22*, 228–250.

Kolmogorov, A. (1965). Three approaches to the quantitative definition of information. *Problems of Information Transmission, 1*, 1–11.

Koumoutsakos P., F. J., & D., P. (1998). Evolution strategies for parameter optimization in jet flow control. *Center for Turbulence Research – Proceedings of the Summer program 1998, 10*, 121–132.

Lenat, D. (1983). Theory formation by heuristic search. *Machine Learning, 21.*

Levin, L. A. (1973). Universal sequential search problems. *Problems of Information Transmission, 9*(3), 265–266.

Levin, L. A. (1984). Randomness conservation inequalities: Information and independence in mathematical theories. *Information and Control, 61*, 15–37.

Li, M., & Vitányi, P. M. B. (1993). *An Introduction to Kolmogorov Complexity and its Applications.* Springer.

Lin, L. (1993). *Reinforcement Learning for Robots Using Neural Networks.* Ph.D. thesis, Carnegie Mellon University, Pittsburgh.

Littman, M. (1996). *Algorithms for Sequential Decision Making.* Ph.D. thesis, Brown University.

Littman, M., Cassandra, A., & Kaelbling, L. (1995). Learning policies for partially observable environments: Scaling up. In Prieditis, A., & Russell, S. (Eds.), *Machine Learning: Proceedings of the Twelfth International Conference*, pp. 362–370. Morgan Kaufmann Publishers, San Francisco, CA.

MacKay, D. J. C. (1992). Information-based objective functions for active data selection. *Neural Computation, 4*(2), 550–604.

McCallum, R. A. (1996). Learning to use selective attention and short-term memory in sequential tasks. In Maes, P., Mataric, M., Meyer, J.-A., Pollack, J., & Wilson, S. W. (Eds.), *From Animals to Animats 4: Proceedings of the Fourth International Conference on Simulation of Adaptive Behavior, Cambridge, MA*, pp. 315–324. MIT Press, Bradford Books.

McGovern, A. (1998). acquire-macros: An algorithm for automatically learning macro-action. In *NIPS'98 Workshop on Abstraction and Hierarchy in Reinforcement Learning.*

Moore, A., & Atkeson, C. G. (1993). Prioritized sweeping: Reinforcement learning with less data and less time. *Machine Learning, 13*, 103–130.

Moore, A. W., Baird, L., & Kaelbling, L. P. (1998). Multi-value-functions: Efficient automatic action hierarchies for multiple goal mdps. In *NIPS'98 Workshop on Abstraction and Hierarchy in Reinforcement Learning.*

Plutowski, M., Cottrell, G., & White, H. (1994). Learning Mackey-Glass from 25 examples, plus or minus 2. In Cowan, J., Tesauro, G., & Alspector, J. (Eds.), *Advances in Neural Information Processing Systems 6*, pp. 1135–1142. San Mateo, CA: Morgan Kaufmann.

Ray, T. S. (1992). An approach to the synthesis of life. In Langton, C., Taylor, C., Farmer, J. D., & Rasmussen, S. (Eds.), *Artificial Life II*, pp. 371–408. Addison Wesley Publishing Company.

Rechenberg, I. (1971). Evolutionsstrategie - Optimierung technischer Systeme nach Prinzipien der biologischen Evolution. Dissertation.. Published 1973 by Fromman-Holzboog.

Ring, M. B. (1991). Incremental development of complex behaviors through automatic construction of sensory-motor hierarchies. In Birnbaum, L., & Collins, G. (Eds.), *Machine Learning: Proceedings of the Eighth International Workshop*, pp. 343–347. Morgan Kaufmann.

Ring, M. B. (1993). Learning sequential tasks by incrementally adding higher orders. In S. J. Hanson, J. D. C., & Giles, C. L. (Eds.), *Advances in Neural Information Processing Systems 5*, pp. 115–122. Morgan Kaufmann.

Ring, M. B. (1994). *Continual Learning in Reinforcement Environments*. Ph.D. thesis, University of Texas at Austin, Austin, Texas 78712.

Sałustowicz, R. P., & Schmidhuber, J. (1997). Probabilistic incremental program evolution. *Evolutionary Computation*, 5(2), 123–141.

Samuel, A. L. (1959). Some studies in machine learning using the game of checkers. *IBM Journal on Research and Development*, 3, 210–229.

Schmidhuber, J. (1987). Evolutionary principles in self-referential learning, or on learning how to learn: the meta-meta-... hook. Institut für Informatik, Technische Universität München..

Schmidhuber, J. (1989). A local learning algorithm for dynamic feedforward and recurrent networks. *Connection Science*, 1(4), 403–412.

Schmidhuber, J. (1991a). Curious model-building control systems. In *Proc. International Joint Conference on Neural Networks, Singapore*, Vol. 2, pp. 1458–1463. IEEE.

Schmidhuber, J. (1991b). Learning to generate sub-goals for action sequences. In Kohonen, T., Mäkisara, K., Simula, O., & Kangas, J. (Eds.), *Artificial Neural Networks*, pp. 967–972. Elsevier Science Publishers B.V., North-Holland.

Schmidhuber, J. (1991c). Reinforcement learning in Markovian and non-Markovian environments. In Lippman, D. S., Moody, J. E., & Touretzky, D. S. (Eds.), *Advances in Neural Information Processing Systems 3*, pp. 500–506. San Mateo, CA: Morgan Kaufmann.

Schmidhuber, J. (1995). Discovering solutions with low Kolmogorov complexity and high generalization capability. In Prieditis, A., & Russell, S. (Eds.), *Machine Learning: Proceedings of the Twelfth International Conference*, pp. 488–496. Morgan Kaufmann Publishers, San Francisco, CA.

Schmidhuber, J. (1997). Discovering neural nets with low Kolmogorov complexity and high generalization capability. *Neural Networks*, 10(5), 857–873.

Schmidhuber, J. (1999). Artificial curiosity based on discovering novel algorithmic predictability through coevolution. In Angeline, P., Michalewicz, Z., Schoenauer, M., Yao, X., & Zalzala, Z. (Eds.), *Congress on Evolutionary Computation*, pp. 1612–1618. IEEE Press, Piscataway, NJ.

Schmidhuber, J., & Prelinger, D. (1993). Discovering predictable classifications. *Neural Computation*, 5(4), 625–635.

Schmidhuber, J., & Zhao, J. (1999). Direct policy search and uncertain policy evaluation. In *AAAI Spring Symposium on Search under Uncertain and Incomplete Information, Stanford Univ.*, pp. 119–124. American Association for Artificial Intelligence, Menlo Park, Calif.

Schmidhuber, J., Zhao, J., & Schraudolph, N. (1997a). Reinforcement learning with self-modifying policies. In Thrun, S., & Pratt, L. (Eds.), *Learning to learn*, pp. 293–309. Kluwer.

Schmidhuber, J., Zhao, J., & Wiering, M. (1997b). Shifting inductive bias with success-story algorithm, adaptive Levin search, and incremental self-improvement. *Machine Learning*, *28*, 105–130.

Schwefel, H. P. (1974). Numerische Optimierung von Computer-Modellen. Dissertation.. Published 1977 by Birkhäuser, Basel.

Schwefel, H. P. (1995). *Evolution and Optimum Seeking*. Wiley Interscience.

Shannon, C. E. (1948). A mathematical theory of communication (parts I and II). *Bell System Technical Journal, XXVII*, 379–423.

Singh, S. (1992). The efficient learning of multiple task sequences. In Moody, J., Hanson, S., & Lippman, R. (Eds.), *Advances in Neural Information Processing Systems 4*, pp. 251–258 San Mateo, CA. Morgan Kaufmann.

Solomonoff, R. (1964). A formal theory of inductive inference. Part I. *Information and Control, 7*, 1–22.

Solomonoff, R. (1986). An application of algorithmic probability to problems in artificial intelligence. In Kanal, L. N., & Lemmer, J. F. (Eds.), *Uncertainty in Artificial Intelligence*, pp. 473–491. Elsevier Science Publishers.

Storck, J., Hochreiter, S., & Schmidhuber, J. (1995). Reinforcement driven information acquisition in non-deterministic environments. In *Proceedings of the International Conference on Artificial Neural Networks, Paris*, Vol. 2, pp. 159–164. EC2 & Cie, Paris.

Sun, R., & Sessions, C. (2000). Self-segmentation of sequences: automatic formation of hierarchies of sequential behaviors. *IEEE Transactions on Systems, Man, and Cybernetics: Part B Cybernetics, 30*(3).

Sutton, R. S. (1988). Learning to predict by the methods of temporal differences. *Machine Learning, 3*, 9–44.

Sutton, R. S. (1995). TD models: Modeling the world at a mixture of time scales. In Prieditis, A., & Russell, S. (Eds.), *Machine Learning: Proceedings of the Twelfth International Conference*, pp. 531–539. Morgan Kaufmann Publishers, San Francisco, CA.

Sutton, R. S., & Pinette, B. (1985). The learning of world models by connectionist networks. *Proceedings of the 7th Annual Conference of the Cognitive Science Society*, 54–64.

Sutton, R. S., Singh, S., Precup, D., & Ravindran, B. (1999). Improved switching among temporally abstract actions. In *Advances in Neural Information Processing Systems 11*. MIT Press. To appear.

Teller, A. (1994). The evolution of mental models. In Kenneth E. Kinnear, J. (Ed.), *Advances in Genetic Programming*, pp. 199–219. MIT Press.

Tesauro, G. (1994). TD-gammon, a self-teaching backgammon program, achieves master-level play. *Neural Computation, 6*(2), 215–219.

Tham, C. (1995). Reinforcement learning of multiple tasks using a hierarchical CMAC architecture. *Robotics and Autonomous Systems, 15*(4), 247–274.

Thrun, S., & Möller, K. (1992). Active exploration in dynamic environments. In Lippman, D. S., Moody, J. E., & Touretzky, D. S. (Eds.), *Advances in Neural Information Processing Systems 4*, pp. 531–538. San Mateo, CA: Morgan Kaufmann.

Wang, G., & Mahadevan, S. (1998). A greedy divide-and-conquer approach to optimizing large manufacturing systems using reinforcement learning. In *NIPS'98 Workshop on Abstraction and Hierarchy in Reinforcement Learning*.

Watkins, C. J. C. H., & Dayan, P. (1992). Q-learning. *Machine Learning, 8*, 279–292.

Watkins, C. (1989). *Learning from Delayed Rewards*. Ph.D. thesis, King's College, Oxford.

Weiss, G. (1994). Hierarchical chunking in classifier systems. In *Proceedings of the 12th National Conference on Artificial Intelligence*, Vol. 2, pp. 1335–1340. AAAI Press/The MIT Press.

Weiss, G., & Sen, S. (Eds.). (1996). *Adaption and Learning in Multi-Agent Systems*. LNAI 1042, Springer.

Wiering, M., & Schmidhuber, J. (1998). HQ-learning. *Adaptive Behavior, 6*(2), 219–246.

Wiering, M., & Schmidhuber, J. (1996). Solving POMDPs with Levin search and EIRA. In Saitta, L. (Ed.), *Machine Learning: Proceedings of the Thirteenth International Conference*, pp. 534–542. Morgan Kaufmann Publishers, San Francisco, CA.

Williams, R. J. (1992). Simple statistical gradient-following algorithms for connectionist reinforcement learning. *Machine Learning, 8*, 229–256.

Wilson, S. (1994). ZCS: A zeroth level classifier system. *Evolutionary Computation, 2*, 1–18.

Wilson, S. (1995). Classifier fitness based on accuracy. *Evolutionary Computation, 3(2)*, 149–175.

Wolpert, D. H., Tumer, K., & Frank, J. (1999). Using collective intelligence to route internet traffic. In Kearns, M., Solla, S. A., & Cohn, D. (Eds.), *Advances in Neural Information Processing Systems 12*. MIT Press, Cambridge MA.

Automatic Segmentation of Sequences through Hierarchical Reinforcement Learning

R. Sun and C. Sessions

[1] CECS Dept, University of Missouri, Columbia, MO 65211, USA
[2] University of Alabama, Tuscaloosa, AL 35487, USA

1 Introduction

Sequential behaviors (sequential decision processes) are fundamental to cognitive agents. The use of reinforcement learning (RL) for acquiring sequential behaviors is appropriate, and even necessary, when there is no domain-specific a priori knowledge available to agents (Sutton 1995, Barto et al 1995, Kaelbling et al 1996, Bertsekas and Tsitsiklis 1996, Watkins 1989). Given the complexity and differing scales of events in the world, there is a need for hierarchical RL that can produce action sequences and subsequences that correspond with domain structures. This has been demonstrated time and again, in terms of facilitating learning and/or dealing with non-Markovian dependencies, e.g., by Dayan and Hinton (1993), Kaelbling (1993), Lin (1993), Wiering and Schmidhuber (1998), Tadepalli and Dietterich (1997), Parr and Russell (1997), Dietterich (1997), and many others. Different levels of action subsequencing correspond to different levels of abstraction. Thus, subsequencing facilitates hierarchical planning as studied in traditional AI as well (Sacerdoti 1974, Knoblock, Tenenberg, and Yang 1994, Sun and Sessions 1998).

However, we noticed the shortcomings of structurally pre-determined hierarchies in RL (whereby structures are derived from a priori domain knowledge and thus fixed). The problems of such hierarchies include cost (because it is costly to obtain a priori domain knowledge to form hierarchies), inflexibility (because the characteristics of the domain for which fixed hierarchies are built can change over time), and lack of generality (because domain-specific hierarchies most likely vary from domain to domain). Even when limited learning is used to fine tune structurally pre-determined hierarchies (Parr and Russell 1997, Dietterich 1997), some of these problems persist.

A more general approach would be to automatically develop hierarchies (of actions), from scratch, based only on some generic structures (such as a fixed number of levels) and to automatically tailor details of structures and their parameters with reinforcement learning. What this process amounts to is automatically *segmenting* action sequences (self-segmentation) and creating a hierarchical organization of action subsequences (which can be viewed as "macro-actions" or "subroutines"). Subsequences resulting from self-segmentation may be reused

R. Sun and C.L. Giles (Eds.): Sequence Learning, LNAI 1828, pp. 241–263, 2000.
© Springer-Verlag Berlin Heidelberg 2000

throughout a sequence or by different sequences (i.e, shared among different tasks). [1] In the end we have a hierarchical organization of sequential behaviors.

Although segmentation is evidently important, some existing hierarchical RL models either do not involve segmentation (i.e., using pre-determined hierarchies or segmentations) or involve only domain-specific segmentation processes. In contrast, we will address the issue of learning segmentation without (or with little) domain-specific knowledge or procedures (Ring 1991, Schmidhuber 1992, Weiss 1995, Thrun and Schwartz 1995).

A difficult issue that we face in RL is how to deal with (non-Markovian) temporal dependencies (that is, situations in which state transition probabilities are determined not only by the current state and action but also by previous ones, due to partial observability; Lin 1993, McCallum 1996, Kaelbling et al 1996). [2] Such dependencies can create problems in reinforcement learning. Through the use of reinforcement learning at different levels, we may seek out proper configurations of non-Markovian temporal dependencies, with the goal of reducing dependencies through segmenting at proper places at different levels so as to facilitate the learning of the overall task.

Therefore, we need to deal with the following issues: (1) automatic (self) segmentation of sequences, with each segment to be handled differently by a different module, to reduce or remove non-Markovian temporal dependencies; (2) automatic development of common subsequences (that is, subroutines or subtasks) that can be used in various places of a sequence and/or in different sequences, to simplify non-Markovian dependencies and to form compact representations; (3) moreover, segmentation without (or with little) a priori domain-specific knowledge as embodied in domain-specific structures, domain-specific ways of creating such structures, and so on (because relying on a priori knowledge leads to a lack of generality).

2   Review of RL

Reinforcement learning (RL) has received a great deal of attention recently. RL can be viewed as an on-line variation of value-iteration dynamic programming (DP). DP in general can be defined as follows: there is a 5-tuple: (S, U, T, P, g), in which S is the set of state, U is the set of actions, and T is the probabilistic state transition function that maps the current state and the current action to a new state in the next time step. P is the (reactive) stationary *policy* that determines the action at the current time step given the current state: $P(s_t) = u_t$. g is the

---

[1]   When adaptive formation of hierarchies is carried out in a multiple-task context, the learning of different sequences can influence each other, and common subsequences may emerge. As a result, different tasks may share some subsequences (subroutines; Thrun and Schwartz 1995).

[2]   In such situations, optimal actions at one point may be dependent on not only the current state but also states and actions occurring some time ago. See Sondik (1978), Monahan (1982), and Puterman (1994) for treatments of POMDPs (partially observable Markovian decision processes.

cost (or reward) function that maps certain states and/or actions to real values. That is, in DP, there is a discrete-time system, the state transitions of which depend on actions performed by an agent. In probabilistic terms, a Markovian process is in the working in determining a new state (from state transition) after an action is performed: $prob(s_{t+1}|s_t, u_t, s_{t-1}, u_{t-1}, ...) = prob(s_{t+1}|s_t, u_t) = p_{s_t, s_{t+1}}(u_t)$, where u_t is determined based on the policy P (assuming $u_t = P(s_t)$). In this process, costs (or rewards) can occur for certain states and/or actions. Normally the costs/rewards accumulate additively, with or without a discount factor.

The cumulative cost/reward estimate (which we will denote as J) that results from following an optimal policy of actions satisfies the Bellman optimality equation:

$$J(s_t) = \max_u \sum_{s_{t+1} \in S} p_{s_t, s_{t+1}}(u)(g(s_t) + \gamma J(s_{t+1}))$$

where g denotes cost/reward (which is assumed to be a function of states), s_t is any state and s_{t+1} is the new state resulting from action u. Or, using the notation $Q(s_t, u_t)$ (where $\max_u Q(s, u) = J(s)$), we have

$$Q(s_t, u_t) = \sum_{s_{t+1} \in S} p_{s_t, s_{t+1}}(g(s_t) + \gamma \max_u Q(s_{t+1}, u))$$

Based on the Bellman optimality equation, there are a number of on-line (RL) algorithms for learning Q or J functions. One is the Q-learning algorithm of Watkins (1989). The updating is done completely on-line, without explicitly using probability estimates:

$$Q(s_t, u_t) := (1 - \alpha)Q(s_t, u_t) + \alpha(g(s_t) + \gamma \max_{u_{t+1}}(Q(s_{t+1}, u_{t+1})))$$

$$= Q(s_t, u_t) + \alpha(g(s_t) + \gamma \max_{u_{t+1}}(Q(s_{t+1}, u_{t+1})) - Q(s_t, u_t))$$

where u_t is determined by an action policy that allows sufficient exploration (Bertsekas and Tsitsiklis 1996). For example, it can be based on the Boltzmann distribution:

$$prob(s_t, u_t) = \frac{e^{Q(s_t, u_t)/\tau}}{\sum_u e^{Q(s_t, u)/\tau}}$$

where τ is the temperature that determines the degree of randomness in action selection (other policies are also possible; Bertsekas and Tsitsiklis 1996). The updating is done based on actual state transition instead of transition probabilities; that is, on-line "simulation" is performed. With enough sampling, the transition frequency from s_t and u_t to s_{t+1} should approach $p_{s_t, s_{t+1}}(u_t)$, and thus provides an estimation. Therefore, the result will be the same values as in the earlier specification of Q values. Such learning allows completely autonomous learning from scratch, without a priori domain knowledge.

3   The SSS Algorithm

Below we will present an approach for automatically developing hierarchical reinforcement learning systems, the SSS algorithm, which stands for *Self Segmentation of Sequences*. Different from usually Markovian domains for Q-learning, we will deal with non-Markovian domains (partially observable Markovian decision processes), where an agent observes local information that constitutes an observational state (or an observation; Bertsekas and Tsitsiklis 1996) but not a true state. The true state may be determined from the history of observational states. We create a hierachical structure that involves multiple modules (each with either little or no memory) for dealing with such domains, without a priori domain knowledge. (In the following discussion, the term "state" in general refers to observational states.)

3.1   The General Idea

The general idea is as follows: There are a number of individual action modules (referred to as Q modules below). Each of them selects actions to be performed at each step. However, for each Q module, there is also a corresponding controller CQ, which determines at each step whether the Q module should continue or relinquish control. When a Q module currently in control relinquishes its control, a higher-level controller, AQ, will decide which Q module should take over next from the current point on. So, in any given state, a pair of Q and CQ should be in control. When the CQ selects *continue*, the Q will select an action with regard to the current state that will affect the environment and thus generate reinforcement from the environment. When the CQ selects *end*, the control is returned to AQ, which will then proceed immediately to select (with regard to the current state) another CQ (and its corresponding Q) to take over. This cycle then repeats itself (cf. the idea of "options"; Precup et al 1998).

Each component in this system is learned from scratch (in contrast to e.g. Precup et al 1998, Dieterich 1997). Let us look into how each component learns:

- Each Q module tries to receive as much reinforcement as possible before it is forced to give up. i.e., performs optimization within a local segment (a set of adjacent states). However, local segments change over time and thus the world is not static for a Q module. That is, the learning of self-segmentation (determined jointly by CQ and AQ) is concurrent with the local learning of Q modules. The non-static situation adds to the complexity of learning.
- Each CQ tries to determine at the current point whether it is more advantageous to terminate the corresponding Q module or to let it continue, in terms of maximizing the overall reinforcement. [3] A CQ considers whether or not

---

[3]   If the Q module is continued, the overall reinforcement is the (discounted) sum of all the reinforcements that will be received by the Q module plus the (discounted) sum of reinforcement that will be received by subsequent Q's (since the active Q module will be terminated eventually). If the Q module is terminated, the overall reinforcement is the (discounted) sum of all the reinforcement that will be received by subsequent Q's.

to give up based on which way will lead to more overall reinforcement. This is partially determined by the performance of all Q's executed subsequently and by the selection made by AQ. So, the CQ has to deal with the problem of dynamic interaction.

- AQ tries to learn the selection of Q modules at various points (by an abstract control action), by evaluating which selection will lead to more overall reinforcement. Again this is not a static situation: which states becomes decision points for AQ is partially determined by CQ's (which determines when to give control back to AQ, which is in turn determined by Q's, which select actions that generate reinforcement). As each Q and CQ pair learns, the selection by AQ may have to change also.

This two-level structure can be extended to more than two levels.

3.2   The Algorithm

The Overall Specification Let s denote the observational state of an agent at a particular moment (not necessarily a complete description). Assume reinforcements are associated with the current observational state: $g(s)$. We will focus on Q-learning to illustrate our idea (although other RL algorithms are also applicable). Let us look into a minimal structure: a two level hierarchy, in which there are three types of learning modules:

- Individual action module Q: Each performs actions and learns through Q-learning.
- Individual controller CQ: Each CQ learns when a Q module (corresponding to the CQ) should continue its control and when it should give up the control. The learning is accomplished through (separate) Q-learning.
- Abstract controller AQ: It performs and learns abstract control actions, that is, which Q module to select under what circumstances. The learning is accomplished through (separate) Q-learning.

The overall algorithm is as follows:

- 1. Observe the current state s.
- 2. The currently active Q/CQ pair takes control. If there is no active one (when the system first starts), go to step 5.
- 3. The active CQ selects and performs a control action based on $CQ(s, ca)$ for different ca. If the action chosen by CQ is *end*, go to step 5. Otherwise, the active Q selects and performs an action based on $Q(s, a)$ for different a.
- 4. The active Q and CQ performs learning. Go to step 1.
- 5. AQ selects and performs an abstract control action based on $AQ(s, aa)$ for different aa, to select a Q/CQ pair to become active.
- 6. AQ performs learning. Go to step 1.

Learning The learning rules, along with explanations of their purposes, are detailed as follows.

– Individual action modules. For the active Q_k, when neither the current action nor the next action by the corresponding CQ_k is *end*, [4] we use the usual Q-learning rule:

$$\Delta Q_k(s,a) = \alpha(g(s) + \gamma \max_{a'} Q_k(s',a') - Q_k(s,a))$$

where s' is the new state resulting from action a in state s.

Explanation: When CQ_k decides to continue, Q_k learns to estimate reinforcement generated (1) by its current action and (2) by its subsequent actions (assuming a greedy policy: taking the action that has the highest value in a state), (3) plus the reinforcement generated later by other modules after Q_k/CQ_k relinquishes control (see the next learning rule). The value of Q_k is the sum of the estimates of these three parts.

When the current action of CQ_k (in s) is *continue* and the next action of CQ_k (in s') is *end*, the Q_k module receives as reward the maximum value of AQ:

$$\Delta Q_k(s,a) = \alpha(g(s) + \gamma \max_{aa'} AQ(s',aa') - Q_k(s,a))$$

where s' is the new state (resulting from action a in state s) in which control is returned to AQ by CQ_k, and aa is any abstract action of AQ.

Explanation: As the corresponding CQ terminates the control of the current Q module, AQ has to take an abstract action in state s', the value of which is the (discounted) total reinforcement that will be received from that point on (by the whole system), if that action is taken and if thereafter the greedy policy (taking the action that has the highest value in the current state) is followed by AQ and the current (stochastic) policies are followed in all the other modules. So, at termination, the Q module learns the total (discounted) reinforcement that will be received by the whole system thereon (if the greedy policy is followed by AQ and the current stochastic policies are followed by the other modules). Combining the explanations of the above two rules, we see that a Q module decides its action based on which action will lead to higher overall reinforcement from the current state on (both by itself and by subsequent modules). [5]

Remarks: If reinforcement is given only at the end when the goal is reached, the above learning rules amount to assigning a reward to a module based on the number of steps to the goal from the state in which it was terminated. Instead of counting the number of steps to the goal, we simply use discounting of reinforcement to achieve the same effect (because the total amount of discounting is determined by the number of steps to the goal). Thus, when Q is terminated, it estimates in

---

[4] Note that there is a one-step delay in the application of the learning rule.

[5] Note that we are being optimistic about the selections to be made by AQ. An alternative (the SARSA learning rule) is to use $AQ(aa,s)$ in the above formula, where aa is the actual abstract action taken by AQ. But that change will not produce an estimated average of reinforcement unless the learning rules for AQ are changed accordingly.

this way how close it has gotten to the goal at that point. In this way, we do not need to use separate rewards for individual modules (which require a priori domain knowledge to set up). The same can be said about CQ below.

- Individual controllers. For the corresponding CQ_k, there are also two separate learning rules, for the two different actions. When the current action by CQ_k is *continue*, the learning rule is the usual Q-learning:

$$\Delta CQ_k(s, continue) = \alpha(g(s) + \gamma \max_{ca'} CQ_k(s', ca') - CQ_k(s, continue))$$

where s' is the new state resulting from action *continue* in state s and ca' is any control action by CQ_k.

Explanation: When CQ_k decides to continue, it learns to estimate reinforcement generated by the actions of the corresponding Q_k, assuming that CQ_k gives up control whenever *end* has a higher value, plus the reinforcement generated after Q_k/CQ_k relinquishes control (see the next learning rule). That is , CQ_k learns the value of *continue* as the sum of the expected reinforcement generated by Q_k until $CQ_k(end) > CQ_k(continue)$ and the expected reinforcement generated by subsequent modules thereafter.

When the current action by CQ_k is *end*, the learning rule is

$$\Delta CQ_k(s, end) = \alpha(\max_{aa} AQ(s, aa) - CQ_k(s, end))$$

where aa is any abstract control action by AQ.

Explanation: That is, when a CQ ends, it learns the value of the best abstract action to be performed by AQ, which is equal to the (discounted) total reinforcement that will be accumulated by the whole system from the current state on (if the greedy policy is followed by AQ and the current stochastic policies are followed by the other modules). Combining the above two learning rules, in effect, the CQ module learns to make its decisions by comparing whether giving up or continuing control will lead to more overall reinforcement from the current state on.

- Abstract controllers. For AQ, we have the following learning rule:

$$\Delta AQ(s, aa) = \alpha(ag(s) + \gamma^m \max_{aa'} AQ(s', aa') - AQ(s, aa))$$

where aa is the abstract control action that selects a Q module to take control, s' is the new state (after s) in which AQ is required to make a decision, m is the number of time steps taken to go from s to s' (used in determining the amount of discounting γ^m), and ag is the (discounted) cumulative reinforcement received after the abstract control action for state s and before the next abstract control action for state s' (that is, $ag(s) = \sum_{k=0,1,\ldots,m-1} g(s_k)\gamma^k$, where $s_0 = s$ and $s_m = s'$).

Explanation: AQ learns the value of an abstract control action that it selects, which is the (discounted) cumulative reinforcement that the chosen Q module will accrue before AQ has to make another abstract action decision, plus the accumulation of reinforcement from the next abstract action on, assuming the greedy policy will be followed by AQ and the current (stochastic) policies will be followed by the other modules. In other words, AQ estimates the total reinforcement to be accrued (if it is greedy and all the other modules follow their current policies). So in effect AQ learns to select lower-level modules by comparing what selections lead to more overall reinforcement from the current point on.

Technically, we only need either CQ's or AQ, but not both, since their values are closely related (if an identical input representation is given to them). However, as we will discuss later, we have to keep them separate when we have more than two levels. Furthermore, if we introduce different input representations for different levels, we must keep them separate (even in the case of two levels). Finally, if we want these modules to be independent, autonomous entities (agents), then the separation of CQs and AQ is justified on the basis of separate learning by separate entities.

Temporal Representation in Modules In SSS, we may need to construct temporal representations, in order to avoid excessive segmentation when there is too much temporal dependency. One possibility is recurrent neural networks (e.g., Elman 1990). RNNs have been used to represent temporal dependencies of various forms in much previous work, such as Elman (1990), Lin (1993), Whitehead and Lin (1995), and Giles et al (1995). RNNs have shortcomings, such as long learning time, possible inaccuracy, possibly improper generalizations, and so on. Theoretically, a RNN can memorize arbitrarily long sequences, but practically, due to limitations on precision, the length of a sequence that can be memorized is quite limited (Lin 1993).

As a more viable alternative to RNNs, we may use decision trees in RL, along the line of McCallum (1996), which splits a state if a statistical test shows that there are significant differences among the cases covered by that state (that is, if the state can be divided into two states by adding features from preceding steps and provide more accurate assessment of the (discounted) cumulative reinforcement that will be received). Compared with a priori specifications of non-Markovian temporal dependencies (i.e., specifying exactly which preceding step is relevant ahead of the time), this method is more widely applicable, because a priori knowledge may not be available. Compared with RNNs, this method can be more robust, because, due to limited precision, temporal representation in RNNs can fade away quickly over a few steps and thus RNNs may have trouble dealing with long-range dependencies. Compared with using a full-scale temporal representation such as the n-fold state space method (in which an n-fold state space is made up of states and their corresponding $n - 1$ preceding states), the advantage of this method is that it may (ideally) seek out those and only those relevant preceding steps that are involved in temporal dependencies and thus reduces the complexity of representation. The shortcoming of the method is that, if unconstrained, the search for relevant historic features can be exhaustive and thus costly.

3.3 Extensions to More Levels

The above specification is with respect to a two-level hierarchy, the component of which can be denoted as $AQ_0(= Q)$, $CQ_0(= CQ)$, and $AQ_1(= AQ)$. We call it the zeroth-order system. We can easily extend it to more levels. That is, on top of AQ_0's, CQ_0's, and AQ_1's, we have AQ_2 for selecting among AQ_1's as well as CQ_1 that determines when the corresponding AQ_1 should give up. We obtain a first-order system this way. Then, on top of AQ_2's, we can have AQ_3 for selecting among AQ_2's and CQ_2's for determining termination. That is, we use a number of first-order systems to develop a second-order system. This process can be repeated for any number of times.

At any step, there should always be an active AQ_i/CQ_i pair at each level i (where $i = 0, 1, ..., M$). We use k (or j) to denote the pair of controllers that is active. Here is the algorithm:

/* using a bottom-level module */
- 1. Observe the current state s.
- 2. The currently active bottom-level pair, AQ_0^k/CQ_0^k, takes control. If there is no active one, set i to M, activate the controller AQ_M/CQ_M, and go to step 5.
- 3. The active CQ_0^k selects an action based on $CQ_0^k(s, ca)$ for different ca. If the action chosen by CQ_0^k is end, set i to 1 and go to step 5. Otherwise, the corresponding AQ_0^k selects and performs an action based on $AQ_0^k(s, a)$ for different a.
- 4. The active AQ_0^k and CQ_0^k perform learning in their respective ways. Go to step 1.
/* moving up or down the hierarchy */
- 5. The currently active controller at level i, CQ_i^k/AQ_i^k, takes control. CQ_i^k selects an action based on $CQ_i^k(s, ca)$ for different ca. (CQ_M always selects $continue$.)
- 6. If the CQ_i^k decision is to continue, an CQ_{i-1}^j/AQ_{i-1}^j pair is selected by AQ_i^k and activated ($i > 0$).
- 6.1. CQ_i^k and AQ_i^k perform learning respectively.
- 6.2. If $i-1 > 0$, set i to $i-1$ and go to step 5 (moving down the hierarchy). Otherwise, go to step 3 (reaching the bottom of the hierarchy).
- 7. If the CQ_i^k decision is to end, find the currently active controller at the higher level $i + 1$, CQ_{i+1}^j/AQ_{i+1}^j ($i < M$).
- 7.1. CQ_i^k and AQ_i^k perform learning respectively.
- 7.2. Set i to $i+1$ and go to step 5 (moving up the hierarchy) ($i < M$).

The new learning rules are as follows (where p is a penalty term, which is set to 0 in our experiments).

- For the active AQ_0^k, when neither the current action nor the next action (at the next time step) by CQ_0^k is end:

$$\Delta AQ_0^k(s, a) = \alpha(g(s) + \gamma \max_{a'} AQ_0^k(s', a') - AQ_0^k(s, a))$$

where s' is the new state resulting from an action a in state s. When the current action by CQ_0^k is *continue* but the next action by CQ_0^k is *end*,

$$\Delta AQ_0^k(s,a) = \alpha(g(s) + \gamma \max_{aa'} AQ_1^j(s',aa') - p - AQ_0^k(s,a))$$

where p is a penalty for moving up the hierarchy and s' is the new state resulting from action a in state s. AQ_1^j is the active module at the higher level at the next time step (s').

- For the active CQ_0^k, there are two separate learning rules for two different actions:

$$\Delta CQ_0^k(s, continue) = \alpha(g(s) + \gamma \max_{ca'} CQ_0^k(s',ca') - CQ_0^k(s,continue))$$

$$\Delta CQ_0^k(s, end) = \alpha(\max_{aa} AQ_1^j(s,aa) - p - CQ_0^k(s,end))$$

where s' is the new state resulting from an action by AQ_0^k in state s and p is a penalty for moving up the hierarchy. AQ_1^j is the active module at the higher level at the current time step.

- For the active AQ_i^k, where $i = 1, 2, ..., M$, we have the following learning rule, when both the current action and the next action by the corresponding CQ_i^k is *continue*:

$$\Delta AQ_i^k(s,aa) = \alpha(ag(s) + \gamma^m \max_{aa'} AQ_i^k(s',aa') - AQ_i^k(s,aa))$$

where aa is the abstract control action that selects a lower-level module, s' is the new state encountered (after aa is completed), m is the number of time steps taken to go from s to s' (used for determining the amount of discounting γ^m), and $ag(s)$ is the (discounted) cumulative reinforcement received after the current abstract control action for state s and before the next abstract control action for state s' (that is, $ag(s) = \sum_{k=0,1,...,m-1} g(s_k)\gamma^k$, where $s_0 = s$ and $s_m = s'$). When the current action by the corresponding CQ_i^k is *continue* but the next action by the CQ_i^k is *end*,

$$\Delta AQ_i^k(s,aa) = \alpha(ag(s) + \gamma^m \max_{aa'} AQ_{i+1}^j(s',aa') - p - AQ_i^k(s,aa))$$

where aa is the abstract control action that selects a lower-level module, s' is the new state encountered (after aa is completed). AQ_{i+1}^j is the active module at the higher level when s' is encountered.

- For the active CQ_i^k, where $i = 1, 2, ..., M$, we have the following learning rule for *end*:

$$\Delta CQ_i^k(s, end) = \alpha(\max_{aa} AQ_{i+1}^j(s,aa) - p - CQ_i^k(s,end))$$

where p is a penalty for moving up a hierarchy and AQ_{i+1}^j is the active module at the higher level at the current time step. We have the following learning rule for *continue*:

$$\Delta CQ_i^k(s, continue) = \alpha(ag(s) + \gamma^m \max_{ca'} CQ_i^k(s',ca') - CQ_i^k(s,continue))$$

where s' is the next state in which CQ_i^k is to make a decision, and m is the number of time steps taken to go from s to s'.

Note that, at different levels, we can set different learning rates and temperatures (for CQ_is and AQ_is). Note also that, although a two-level hierarchy can be easily simplified (if the same representation is used throughout) by examining the values of all the CQ's without using AQ at all in the selection of lower-level modules, a hierarchy of more than two levels cannot be easily collapsed into one level in this way. Hierarchical decision making has its advantages.

4   Analysis

4.1   Analysis of Non-markovian Dependencies

Let us examine several special cases of non-Markovian dependencies that are particularly suitable for SSS. For simplicity, we will assume that a two-level hierarchy is used. We use "non-Markovian tasks" to refer to tasks in which non-Markovian dependencies (as defined in section 1) exist, and "Markovian tasks" to refer to tasks in which no such dependencies exist.

1. Using Markovian subsequencing to turn non-Markovian tasks into Markovian ones. This is the simplest case of dealing with non-Markovian dependencies, which was addressed by a similar but more limited model proposed by Wiering and Schmidhuber (1998). An example used in Wiering and Schmidhuber (1998) is as follows: An agent is supposed to turn left at the first intersection, and then turn right at the second. Thus it is a non-Markovian sequence, as the second turn is dependent on the first turn (assuming that states are composed of visual indicators for intersections and other features). However, if we make a switch to a different (sub)sequence after the first turn, we then have a chain of two Markovian subsequences, instead of one non-Markovian sequence. Through the use of subsequencing, a non-Markovian sequence may become multiple Markovian sequences in a chain, as higher-level chaining provides the necessary context for local Markovian decision making. The action modules (for handling respective subsequences) have different policies, in accordance with the global context, i.e., their respective positions in a chain. [6]
   Segmentation that turns a non-Markovian sequence into multiple Markovian sequences in a chain can be accomplished by SSS through (implicitly) comparing overall reinforcement received through segmentation at different points. Both the higher-level and lower-level modules use atemporal representation in this case (i.e., without memory of any sort). Because a better way of segmentation will lead to a higher amount of overall reinforcement, eventually better ways of segmentation will likely dominate. [7] This is an

---

[6] Clearly, not all non-Markovian sequences with long-range dependencies can be handled this way. The scenario represents a small portion of non-Markovian situations.

[7] We cannot guarantee that though, because it is possible to be trapped in a "local minimum". The same caveat applies below.

extension of the approach of Wiering and Schmidhuber (1998). In Wiering and Schmidhuber's (1998) model, an a priori determined chain of modules is used, and each module has to select a subgoal and keep running until the goal is achieved (and cannot be flexibly switched off).

2. Using non-Markovian subsequencing to turn non-Markovian tasks into Markovian ones. When non-Markovian dependencies are dense but limited within small temporal segments (subsequences), if we can isolate and deal with separately these small segments, the overall task can be treated as Markovian. The difficulty lies in how we determine these local segments. Using a two-level structure in which the lower level uses temporal representation and the higher level uses atemporal representation, SSS can determine relevant subsequences through (implicitly) comparing overall reinforcement received through segmentation at different points. Segmentation at the proper points that separate local segments will result in the largest overall reinforcement (because such segmentation leads to capturing all the dependencies), and therefore those points will likely be adopted. The algorithm typically adjusts the lengths of subsequences in different modules to accommodate the different lengths of the non-Markovian dependencies in different local segments. [8]

   We refer to such a process as "automatic temporal localization of non-Markovianness". We refer to sequences in which non-Markovian dependencies can be localized as having the "temporal locality property" (as opposed to the "spatial locality property" assumed in Dayan and Hinton 1993 for deriving their spatially hierarchical model). Although local non-Markovian dependencies can be handled by further segmentation without the use of temporal representation, it is unwieldy to do so, because too many segments may be generated and thus too many modules may be needed.

3. Using Markovian subsequencing and non-Markovian meta-sequencing for handling long-range (but sporadic) non-Markovian dependencies. Using a two-level structure in which the lower level uses atemporal representation and the higher level uses temporal representation, SSS can seek out and handle long-range dependencies. Under the assumption that long-range dependencies are sporadic, the higher-level process will determine those points in a sequence that are involved in a non-Markovian dependency, while the lower-level processes will handle Markovian processes in between. Ideally, the segmentation of subsequences occurs at those points that are involved in long-range dependencies. The SSS algorithm is capable of such segmentation, because it can (implicitly) compare overall reinforcement received through segmentation at different points and tend to find the best way(s) of segmentation that results in the largest reinforcement. Given the higher-level temporal representation and the lower-level atemporal representation, segmentation at those points that are involved in long-range dependencies

---

[8] In addition, local non-Markovian processes can be different from each other, and thus the very segmentation into these local subsequences captures certain global non-Markovian dependencies (as in the first case).

will result in the largest overall reinforcement (because such segmentation leads to capturing all the dependencies without involving other states unnecessarily), and therefore those points will likely be adopted.

4. Separating the handling of coexisting short-range and long-range non-Markovian dependencies. Our approach can also be suitable for dealing with a mixture of long-range and short-range (global and local) non-Markovian dependencies. In the presence of both types of dependencies, SSS typically finds a way of separating different (global or local) dependencies and treat them separately. Using temporal representation at both the higher and lower level, the separation of the two types of dependencies is accomplished by comparing overall reinforcement received through segmentation at different points. The better ways of segmentation that treat global and local non-Markovian dependencies separately and correctly should result in more overall reinforcement eventually. This separation may have various advantages. For example, it may simplify the overall complexity of temporal representation. It may also facilitate the convergence of learning. [9]

In all, SSS learns to use both global and local contexts through seeking out proper configurations of temporal structures (global and local dependencies).

We can characterize different dimensions of non-Markovian temporal dependencies as follows:

— Degree of dependency: the maximum number of previous states that the current step is dependent on. In one extreme, the degree can be unlimited or infinite. In the other extreme, the degree can be zero, in which case there is no temporal dependency.
— Distance of dependency: the maximum number of steps between the current step and the furthest previous state that the current step is dependent on (given all the intermediate steps). In one extreme, the distance can be unlimited or infinite. In the other extreme, the distance can be zero.
— Density of dependency: the ratio between the degree of dependency and the distance of dependency.

According to these dimensions, (1) sporadic long-range dependencies involve long *distance* but low *density* temporal dependencies. Thus they can be handled by Markovian subsequencing and non-Markovian meta-sequencing, because such dependencies can be captured as segmentation points and handled by temporal representation at the higher level, which makes the lower level Markovian (because non-Markovian dependencies are of long distance and low density, they need not show up in lower-level processes). (Note that it is also possible

---

[9] Local non-Markovian processes can be different from each other, and thus the segmentation per se captures certain (global) non-Markovian dependencies. So it is also possible to use atemporal representation at the higher level if such representation is sufficient to handle existent global non-Markovian dependencies (as in the first case).

that Markovian subsequencing and non-Markovian meta-sequencing can handle
a non-Markovian task with long *distance*, high *density*, and high *degree* temporal
dependencies, if subsequencing can insulate lower-level processes from such dependencies, as in the case of e.g. the parity problem when presented sequentially.)
(2) Using Markovian subsequencing (without non-Markovian meta-sequencing)
to turn a non-Markovian task into a Markovian task is a special case in which
low-*density* (long- or short-*distance*) dependencies disappear when the task is
properly segmented, due to, on the one hand, the localization of the lower-level
processes and, on the other hand, the insulation of most of the states from the
higher-level process. These processes likely become Markovian because the low-
density temporal dependencies are likely absorbed by the chain of Markovian
processes. (3) Using non-Markovian subsequencing to turn non-Markovian tasks
into Markovian ones typically involves temporal dependencies that are of short
distance (but maybe of high *density* and of high *degree*) and can be localized
within the lower-level processes. (4) Separating the handling of coexisting global
and local non-Markovian dependencies typically involves cases in which temporal
dependencies are of varied *distances* that are preferably bifurcated (i.e., naturally separated into two categories: long-*distance* and short-*distance*), so that
each type can be handled by a corresponding level.

4.2   Analysis of Difficulties

The major difficulties SSS faces are the following:

- Large search space. The simultaneous learning of multiple levels (involving
  abstract control, control, and individual action modules) results in a much
  larger search space in which the system has to find an optimal (or near optimal) configuration. In comparison, structurally pre-determined hierarchical
  RL has much smaller spaces to deal with.
- Cross-level interactions. Between any two adjacent levels, the higher-level
  control interacts with the lower-level control. In other words, the learning
  of the lower-level control is based on the higher-level control, but in turn
  the higher-level control need also to adapt based on the learning and performance of the lower-level control. Thus, there are complex dynamic interactions (section 3.1). Structurally pre-determined hierarchies do not deal with
  such problems
- Within-level interactions. Interactions can occur among different modules
  at the same level too. Due to learning, the performance of one module can
  change and therefore affect other modules. While these other modules adapt
  to the change through learning, their outcomes in turn affect the original
  module. Again, there are complex, dynamic interactions.

There are in general three possible training regimes (all of which can be used
in our model), from the computationally simplest, which reduces most the interactions between different components of a hierarchical system, to the most
complex, as follows:

- Incremental elemental-to-composite learning (Lin 1993, Singh 1994): first train the system using only "elemental" tasks (with each elemental task being mapped to a particular module) and then, after the completion of the training on elemental tasks, train the system using composite tasks (which are composed of elemental tasks). There is in effect no autonomous self-segmentation in this case. Segmentation is pre-determined. This is therefore the easiest setting.
- Simultaneous elemental-and-composite learning (Singh 1994, Tham 1994): train the whole system using both elemental and composite tasks (each associated with a task label) simultaneously. In this case, the elemental tasks, learned along with composite tasks, provide the clues for segmenting the composite tasks. So the segmentation in this case is not autonomous either.
- Simultaneous composite learning: train all the components of the system simultaneously using the same composite tasks with the same reinforcement information from the environment; in other words, the system learns to decompose the task autonomously by itself. This is the most difficult setting and the focus of this work.

Thus, although SSS can accommodate any of these methods, it does not require separate training for different modules, incremental training that goes from elemental to composite tasks, or simultaneous training of composite and elemental tasks (pre-segmentation). SSS instead relies on reinforcement for completely autonomous self-segmentation: It compares different amounts of reinforcement resulting from different ways of segmentation and tends to choose the best way(s) on that basis.

5   Experiments

We will discuss two examples below. The first domain is taken from McCallum (1996 b). It is chosen because it is simple but involves multiple possible segments, which is useful in illustrating our approach. The second domain is taken from Tadepalli and Dietterich (1997), which demonstrates the reuse of segments. In each domain, we will show that proper configurations of modules can be learned. For simplicity, we will use a two-level hierarchy.

Maze 1 In this maze, there are two possible starting locations and one goal location. The agent occupies one cell at a time and at each step obtains local information (observation) concerning the four adjacent cells (the left, right, above, and below cell) regarding whether each is an opening or a wall. It can make a move to any adjacent cell at each step (either go left, go right, go up, or go down). But if the adjacent cell is a wall, the agent will remain in the original cell at the end of the step. See Figure 1, where "1" indicates the starting cells. Each number indicates an observational state (i.e., an observation, not a true state) as perceived by the agent. In this domain, the minimum path length (i.e., the number of steps of the optimal path from either starting cell to the goal cell) is

6. When not all the paths are optimal, the average path length is a measure of the overall quality of a set of paths. The reinforcement structure (for applying Q-learning) is simple: The reward for reaching the goal location is 1, and no other reward (or punishment) is given.

The parameter settings for Q-learning modules are as follows: the Q value discount rate is 0.95, the initial learning rates for all modules $(\alpha_Q^0, \alpha_{AQ}^0, \alpha_{CQ}^0)$ are uniformly 0.9, the learning rates change according to $\alpha^t = \alpha^{t-1}/t^{1/5}$ (where t is the number of episodes completed), the initial temperatures are $\tau_Q^0 = 0.5$ and $\tau_{AQ}^0 = \tau_{CQ}^0 = 0.9$, and the temperatures change according to $\tau^t = \tau^{t-1}/t^{1/2}$ (where t is the number of episodes completed). The total number of training episodes is 5,000. The number of steps allowed in each episode during learning is 100 (an episode ends when the limit is reached, or as soon as the goal is reached)

As shown in Figure 1, the three cells marked as "5" are perceived to be the same by the agent. However, different actions are required in these cells in order to obtain the shortest paths to the goal. Likewise, the two cells marked as "10" are perceived to be the same but require different actions. In order to remove non-Markovian dependencies in each module, we can divide up each possible sequence (from one of the starting cells to the goal) into a number of segments so that, when different modules are used for these segments, a consistent policy can be adopted in each module.

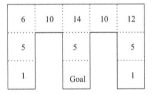

Fig. 1. A maze requiring segmentation. Each number (randomly chosen) indicates an unique observational state as perceived by the agent.

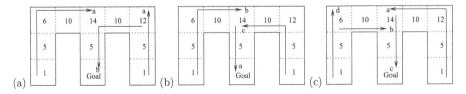

Fig. 2. Different segmentations: (a) using two modules, (b) using three modules, (c) using four modules. Each arrowed line indicates an action (sub)sequence produced by a module, learned by SSS.

As confirmed by the results of our experiments, a single agent (with atemporal representation) could not learn the task at all (the learning curve was flat), due to oscillations (and averaging) of Q values. Adding temporal representation (i.e., memory) may partially remedy the problem, but this approach has difficulty dealing with long-range dependencies (see earlier discussions) and, moreover, it is not comparable with SSS using atemporal representation. Thus it was not used here. On the other hand, as confirmed by the experiments, SSS can segment sequences to remove non-Markovian dependencies. In this domain, it can be easily verified that a minimum of two Q/CQ pairs (modules) are needed in order to remove non-Markovian dependencies in each module. See Figure 2. However, finding the optimal paths using only two modules is proven difficult, because the agent has to be able to find switching points (between the two modules) that are exactly right for a sequence. In general, in this domain, the more modules there are, the easier the segmentation can be done (that is, the faster the learning is). This is because the more modules there are, the more possibilities (alternatives) there are for a proper segmentation that removes non-Markovian dependencies. [10] An ANOVA analysis (number of modules x block of training) shows that there is a significant main effect of number of modules ($p < 0.05$) and a significant interaction between number of modules and block of training ($p < 0.05$), which indicates that the number of modules has significant impact on the learning performance. The performance of the resulting systems is shown in Figure 3, under two conditions: using the completely deterministic policy in each module, or using a stochastic policy (with the Boltzmann distribution action selection with $\tau = 0.006$). In either case, as indicated by Figures 3, there are significant performance improvements in terms of percentages of the optimal path traversed and in terms of the average path length, when we go incrementally from 2 modules to 14 modules. Pairwise t tests on successive average path lengths confirmed this conclusion ($p < 0.05$). See Figure 3 for the test results.

As a variation, to reduce the complexity of this domain and thus to facilitate learning, we limit the starting location to one of the two cells. This setting is easier because there is no need to be concerned with the other half of the maze (see Figure 4). The learning performance is indeed enhanced by this change. We found that this change leads to better learning performance using either two, three, or four modules. Another possibilities for reducing the complexity is to always start with one module. Again, the learning performance is enhanced by this change. Therefore, the segmentation performance is determined to a large extent by the inherent difficulty of the domain that we deal with. The performance changes gradually in relation to the change in the complexity of the domain.

In all, the above experiments demonstrated that proper segmentation was indeed possible using SSS. Through learning a set of Markovian processes (with atemporal representations at both the higher and lower level), SSS removed non-

---

[10] When there are more modules available, there are more possibilities of segmentation. For example, some of the possible ways of segmentation, using three and four modules, are shown in Figure 2.

# of modules	Perc Optimal Path $\tau = 0$	Perc Optimal Path $\tau = 0.006$	Avg Path Length $\tau = 0.006$	Pairwise t test $T(> 2.33)$
2	32%	30%	17.32	
3	46%	44%	10.54	5.387
4	66%	59%	9.50	4.959
6	83%	70%	9.33	3.649
10	90%	76%	8.88	2.617
14	92%	81%	8.10	2.184
18	93%	84%	7.50	1.207
22	96%	87%	7.53	0.175

Fig. 3. The effect of number of modules on the performance (after learning), in terms of the percentage of optimal paths and the average path length (with the maximum length of 24 imposed on each path).

Markovian dependencies and handled the sequences using a (learned) chain of Markovian processes. It was also clear from the experiments that it was not guaranteed that the segmentation (learning) process would succeed. The convergence to optimal solutions was probabilistic (as illustrated by Figure 3).

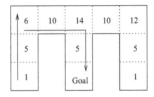

Fig. 4. A possible segmentation using two modules, when only one starting location is allowed.

Maze 2 In this maze, there is one starting location at one end (marked as "2") and one goal location at the other. However, before reaching the goal location, the agent has to reach the top of each of the three arms. At each step, the agent obtains local observation concerning the four adjacent cells regarding whether each is an opening or a wall. See Figure 5, where each number indicates an observational state (an observation) as perceived by the agent. The agent can make a move to any adjacent cell at each step (either go left, go right, go up, or go down). But if the adjacent cell is a wall, the agent will remain in the original cell at the end of the step. The reward for reaching the goal location (after visiting the tops of all the three arms) is 1.

The parameter settings for the modules are as follows: the Q value discount rate is 0.97, the initial learning rates for all the modules $(\alpha_Q^0, \alpha_{AQ}^0, \alpha_{CQ}^0)$ are uniformly 0.9, the learning rates change according to $\alpha^t = \alpha^{t-1}/t^{1/5}$ (where t is the number of episodes completed), the initial temperatures are $\tau_Q^0 = 0.6$ and

$\tau_{AQ}^0 = \tau_{CQ}^0 = 0.8$, and the temperatures change according to $\tau^t = \tau^{t-1}/t^{1/2}$. The total number of training episodes is 10,000. The number of steps allowed in each episode during learning is 200 (an episode ends when the limit is reached, or as soon as the goal is reached after having reached the tops of all the three arms).

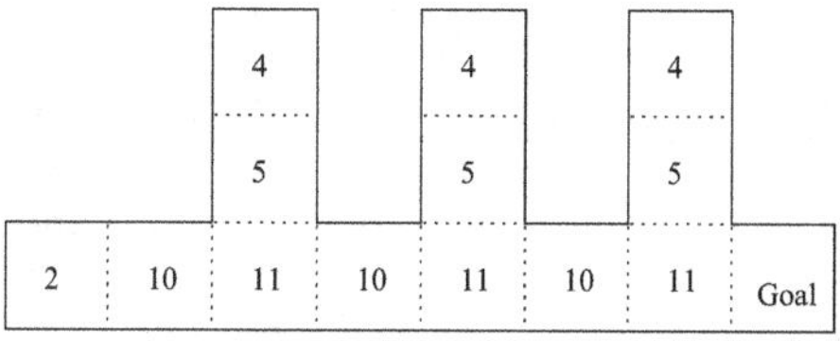

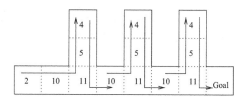

Fig. 5. Maze 2: A maze requiring segmentation and reuse of modules. Each number (randomly chosen) indicates an observational state as perceived by the agent.

Fig. 6. A segmentation using only two modules. Each arrowed line indicates an action sequence produced by a module, learned by SSS. The two modules alternate.

In this domain, the shortest path consists of 19 steps. A minimum of two modules (two Q/CQ pairs) are needed (using atemporal input representation), in order to remove non-Markovian dependencies through segmentation and thus to obtain the shortest path. (As confirmed by the results of our experiments, a single agent with atemporal representation cannot learn the task at all.) With two modules, there is exactly one way of segmenting the sequence (considering only the shortest path to the goal): switching to a different module at the top cell of each arm (marked as "4") and switching again at the middle cell between any two arms (marked as "10"). See Figure 6. As confirmed by our experiments, this segmentation allows repeated use of the same modules along the way to the goal. Reuse of modules lead to the *compression* of sequences. When more modules are added, reuse of modules might be reduced: a third module, for example, can be used in place of the second use of module 1 (Figure 6).

As shown by the experiments, in this domain, unfortunately, learning does not become easier when we add more modules. This is because, in this domain, there is only exactly one way of segmentation (that is, switching at the top cell of each arm and at the cell between any two arms) that may lead to an optimal path, and thus there is no advantage in using more modules. Instead, we observed in the experiments a slight (but statistically significant) decrease of performance when more modules are added, in terms of both the learning process and the learned product. In general, the more modules we have, the slower the learning is. An ANOVA analysis (number of modules x block of training) shows that there is a significant main effect of number of modules ($p < 0.05$) and a significant interaction between number of modules and block of training ($p < 0.05$), which indicates that the number of modules has significant negative (detrimental) impact on learning. After learning, in terms of the performance of the resulting systems, we looked into both percentages of the optimal path (under both the deterministic and stochastic condition) and average path lengths (under both conditions). See Figures 7. The t test shows that the increases in average path lengths (i.e., the degradation of performance), corresponding to the increases from 2 to 3 modules and from 3 to 4 modules, are statistically significant.

# of modules	Perc Optimal Path $\tau = 0$	Perc Optimal Path $\tau = 0.001$	Avg Path Length $\tau = 0.001$	Pairwise t test $T(> 2.33)$
2	60%	52%	22.51	
3	43%	38%	23.85	8.600
4	27%	20%	24.85	4.010
5	27%	22%	25.42	1.281

Fig. 7. The effect of number of modules on the performance (after learning), in terms of the percentage of optimal paths and the average path length (with a maximum length of 39).

In all, the experiments in this domain further demonstrated the point made earlier regarding the feasibility of self-segmentation. Non-Markovian dependencies were removed through a set of Markovian processes (with atemporal representations). Furthermore, the experiments demonstrated the reuse of a module (in several different places) in a sequence or, in other words, the possibility of subroutines that could be called into use any number of times.

Reuse of modules has significant advantages. It leads to the compression of descriptions of sequences. Moreover, it allows the handling of sequences that cannot be (efficiently) handled otherwise. For example, the above domain could not be handled by simpler models in which segmentation was limited to a linear chaining (of a small number of modules) without any way for reusing modules (such as Wiering and Schmidhuber 1998). However, a simpler model might handle the domain by using six or more modules so that a chain of six modules could be formed. This approach resulted in inefficiency. While a minimum of two modules was required for SSS in this domain, Wiering and Schmidhuber's model required at least 6 modules in order to obtain the optimal path. If we increased the number of arms to, say, 10, then at least 20 modules would be required by Wiering and Schmidhuber's model, while two modules would still suffice with SSS.

Note that we did not experimentally compare SSS with e.g. Precup et al (1998), Dietterich (1997), and Parr and Russell (1997), because these algorithms require a substantial amount of a priori domain knowledge and thus are not comparable to SSS. On the other hand, although Parr and Russell (1995) and McCallum (1996b) deal with partial observability without requiring a priori knowledge, they do not segment sequences and develop hierarchies of subsequences, and thus are not comparable to SSS in that sense.

6   Summary

The advantages of the algorithm can be summarized as follows:

- In SSS, there are no pre-determined hierarchies, no a priori domain-specific structures to help with the formation of hierarchies, no domain-specific built-in ways for creating hierarchies, and so on. In sum, there is no use of a priori domain-specific knowledge in forming hierarchies.
- SSS uses only one single learning principle (that is, the maximization of expected reinforcement).
- SSS seeks out somewhat proper (and sometimes optimal) configurations of hierarchical structures, in correspondence with temporal dependency structures of a domain (extending Wiering and Schmidhuber 1998).
- SSS is able to develop subroutines, which can potentially be reused at different points of a sequence (unlike Wiering and Schmidhuber 1998), or shared by multiple (different) sequences (as in Thrun and Schwartz 1995).
- In terms of classical planning, with hierarchical structuring, SSS can be viewed as performing planning at different levels of abstraction (Knoblock et al 1994), with lower-level modules being macro-actions.

There is much further work that can be done along the line outlined here. For example, we need to scale the algorithm up to deal with much larger state spaces, in which function approximation or other schemes must be used to handle the complexity of Q values, and the speed of convergence must also be expressly dealt with. We need to look into domains with probabilistic state transitions and/or noisy observations. We may also want to adaptively determine the number of levels in such systems through learning, in the same way as the adaptive determination of segmentation points within each level.

Acknowledgements: This work is supported in part by Office of Naval Research grant N00014-95-1-0440.

References

F. Bacchus and Q. Yang, (1994). Downward refinement and the efficiency of hierarchical problem solving. *Artificial Intelligence.* 71, 1, 43-100.

D. Bertsekas and J. Tsitsiklis, (1996). *Neuro-Dynamic Programming.* Athena Scientific, Belmont, MA.

A. Cassandra, L. Kaelbling, and M. Littman, (1994). Acting optimally in partially observable stochastic domains. *Proc. of 12th National Conference on Artificial Intelligence.* Morgan Kaufmann, San Mateo, CA.

L. Chrisman, (1993). Reinforcement learning with perceptual aliasing: the perceptual distinction approach. *Proc. of AAAI.* 183-188. Morgan Kaufmann, San Mateo, CA.

P. Dayan and G. Hinton, (1993). Feudal reinforcement learning. *Advances in Neural Information Processing Systems.* MIT Press, Cambridge, MA.

T. Dietterich, (1997). Hierarchical reinforcement learning with MAXQ value function decomposition. $http://www.engr.orst.edu/ \sim tgd/cv/pubs.html$.

J. Elman, (1990). Finding structure in time. *Cognitive Science.* 14, 179-212.

P. Frasconi, M. Gori, and G. Soda, (1995). Recurrent neural networks and prior knowledge for sequence processing. *Knowledge Based Systems.* 8, 6, 313-332.

C.L. Giles, B.G. Horne, and T. Lin, (1995). Learning a class of large finite state machines with a recurrent neural network. *Neural Networks*, 8 (9), 1359-1365.

L. Kaelbling, (1993). Hierarchical learning in stochastic domains: preliminary results. *Proc. of ICML*, 167-173. Morgan Kaufmann, San Francisco, CA.

L. Kaelbling, M. Littman, and A. Moore, (1996). Reinforcement learning: A survey. *Journal of Artificial Intelligence Research*, 4, 237-285.

C. Knoblock, J. Tenenberg, and Q. Yang, (1994). Characterizing abstraction hierarchies for planning. *Proc of AAAI'94.* 692-697. Morgan Kaufmann, San Mateo, CA.

L. Lin, (1993). *Reinforcement Learning for Robots Using Neural Networks.* Ph.D. Thesis, Carnegie Mellon University, Pittsburgh.

A. McCallum, (1996). Learning to use selective attention and short-term memory in sequential tasks. *Proc. Conference on Simulation of Adaptive Behavior.* 315-324. MIT Press, Cambridge, MA.

A. McCallum, (1996 b). *Reinforcement Learning with Selective Perception and Hidden State.* Ph.D Thesis, Department of Computer Science, University of Rochester, Rochester, NY.

G. Monohan, (1982). A survey of partially observable Markov decision processes: theory, models, and algorithms. *Management Science*, 28 (1), 1-16.

R. Parr and S. Russell, (1995). Approximating optimal policies for partially observable stochastic domains. *Proc. of IJCAI'95.* 1088-1094. Morgan Kaufmann, San Mateo, CA.

R. Parr and S. Russell, (1997). Reinforcement learning with hierarchies of machines. *Advances in Neural Information Processing Systems 9*. MIT Press, Cambridge, MA.

D. Precup, R. Sutton, and S. Singh, (1998). Multi-time models for temporary abstract planning. *Advances in Neural Information Processing Systems 10*. MIT Press, Cambridge, MA.

M. Puterman, (1994). *Markov Decision Processes*. Wiley-Inter-science. New York.

M. Ring, (1991). Incremental development of complex behaviors through automatic construction of sensory-motor hierarchies. *Proc. of ICML*. 343-347. Morgan Kaufmann, San Francisco, CA.

E. Sacerdoti, (1974). Planning in a hierarchy of abstraction spaces. *Artificial Intelligence*. 5, 115-135.

J. Schmidhuber, (1992). Learning complex, extended sequences using the principle of history compression. *Neural Computation*, 4 (2), 234-242.

J. Schmidhuber, (1993). Learning unambiguous reduced sequence descriptions. *Advances in Neural Information Processing Systems*, 291-298.

S. Singh, (1994). *Learning to Solve Markovian Decision Processes*. Ph.D Thesis, University of Massachusetts, Amherst, MA.

E. Sondik, (1978). The optimal control of partially observable Markov processes over the infinite horizon: discounted costs. *Operations research*, 26 (2).

R. Sun and T. Peterson, (1999). Multi-agent reinforcement learning: weighting and partitioning. *Neural Networks*, Vol.12 No.4-5. pp.127-153.

R. Sun and C. Sessions, (1998). Learning plans without a priori knowledge. *Adaptive Behavior*, in press. A shortened version appeared in *Proceedings of WCCI-IJCNN'98*, vol.1, 1-6. IEEE Press, Piscateway, NJ.

R. Sutton, (1995). TD models: modeling the world at a mixture of time scales. *Proc. of ICML*. Morgan Kaufmann, San Francisco, CA.

P. Tadepalli and T. Dietterich, (1997). Hierarchical explanation-based reinforcement learning. *Proc. International Conference on Machine Learning*. 358-366. Morgan Kaufmann, San Francisco, CA.

C. Tham, (1995). Reinforcement learning of multiple tasks using a hierarchical CMAC architecture. *Robotics and Autonomous Systems*. 15, 247-274.

S. Thrun and A. Schwartz, (1995). Finding structure in reinforcement learning. *Neural Information Processing Systems*. MIT Press, Cambridge, MA.

C. Watkins, (1989). *Learning with Delayed Rewards*. Ph.D Thesis, Cambridge University, Cambridge, UK.

S. Whitehead and L. Lin, (1995). Reinforcement learning of non-Markov decision processes. *Artificial Intelligence*. 73 (1-2). 271-306.

M. Wiering and J. Schmidhuber, (1998). HQ-learning. *Adaptive Behavior*, 6 (2), 219-246.

Hidden-Mode Markov Decision Processes for Nonstationary Sequential Decision Making

Samuel P.M. Choi, Dit-Yan Yeung, and Nevin L. Zhang

Department of Computer Science,
Hong Kong University of Science and Technology
Clear Water Bay, Kowloon, Hong Kong
{pmchoi,dyyeung,lzhang}@cs.ust.hk

1   Introduction

Problem formulation is often an important first step for solving a problem effectively. In sequential decision problems, Markov decision process (MDP) (Bellman [2]; Puterman [22]) is a model formulation that has been commonly used, due to its generality, flexibility, and applicability to a wide range of problems. Despite these advantages, there are three necessary conditions that must be satisfied before the MDP model can be applied; that is,

1. The environment model is given in advance (a completely-known environment).
2. The environment states are completely observable (fully-observable states, implying a Markovian environment).
3. The environment parameters do not change over time (a stationary environment).

These prerequisites, however, limit the usefulness of MDPs. In the past, research efforts have been made towards relaxing the first two conditions, leading to different classes of problems as illustrated in Figure 1.

Model of Environment

		Known	Unknown
		Completely Observable	
States of Environment	Completely Observable	MDP	Traditional RL
	Partially Observable	Partially Observable MDP	Hidden-state RL

Fig. 1. Categorization into four related problems with different conditions. Note that the degree of difficulty increases from left to right and from upper to lower.

R. Sun and C.L. Giles (Eds.): Sequence Learning, LNAI 1828, pp. 264–287, 2000.

This paper mainly addresses the first and third conditions, whereas the second condition is only briefly discussed. In particular, we are interested in a special type of nonstationary environments that repeat their dynamics in a certain manner. We propose a formal model for such environments. We also develop algorithms for learning the model parameters and for computing optimal policies.

Before we proceed, let us briefly review the four categories of problems shown in Figure 1 and define the terminology that will be used in this paper.

1.1   Four Problem Types

Markov Decision Process

MDP is the central framework for all the problems we discuss in this section. An MDP formulates the interaction between an agent and its environment. The environment consists of a state space, an action space, a probabilistic state transition function, and a probabilistic reward function. The goal of the agent is to find, according to its optimality criterion, a mapping from states to actions (i.e. policy) that maximizes the long-term accumulated rewards. This policy is called an *optimal policy*. In the past, several methods for solving Markov decision problems have been developed, such as value iteration and policy iteration (Bellman 1).

Reinforcement Learning

Reinforcement learning (RL) (Kaelbling *et al.* 12; Sutton and Barto 28) is originally concerned with learning to perform a sequential decision task based only on scalar feedbacks, without any knowledge about what the correct actions should be. Around a decade ago researchers realized that RL problems could naturally be formulated into incompletely known MDPs. This realization is important because it enables one to apply existing MDP algorithms to RL problems. This has led to research on *model-based* RL. The model-based RL approach first reconstructs the environment model by collecting experience from its interaction with the world, and then applies conventional MDP methods to find a solution. On the contrary, *model-free* RL learns an optimal policy directly from the experience. It is this second approach that accounts for the major difference between RL and MDP algorithms. Since less information is available, RL problems are in general more difficult than the MDP ones.

Partially Observable Markov Decision Process

The assumption of having fully-observable states is sometimes impractical in the real world. Inaccurate sensory devices, for example, could make this condition difficult to hold true. This concern leads to studies on extending MDP to partially-observable MDP (POMDP) (Monahan 20; Lovejoy 17; White III 29). A POMDP basically introduces two additional components to the original

MDP, i.e. an observation space and an observation probability function. Observations are generated based on the current state and the previous action, and are governed by the observation function. The agent is only able to perceive observations, but not states themselves. As a result, past observations become relevant to the agent's choice of actions. Hence, POMDPs are sometimes referred to as non-Markovian MDPs. Traditional approaches to POMDPs (Sondik 26; Cheng 5; Littman *et al.* 15; Cassandra *et al.* 4; Zhang *et al.* 31) maintain a probability distribution over the states, called *belief state*. It essentially transforms the problem into an MDP one with an augmented (and continuous) state space. Unfortunately, solving POMDP problems exactly is known to be intractable in general (Papadimitriou and Tsitsiklis 21; Littman *et al.* 14).

Hidden-State Reinforcement Learning

Recently, research has been conducted on the case where the environment is both incompletely known and partially observable. This type of problems is sometimes referred to as hidden-state reinforcement learning, incomplete perception, perception aliasing, or non-Markovian reinforcement learning. Hidden-state RL algorithms can also be classified into model-based and model-free approaches. For the former, a variant of the Baum-Welch algorithm (Chrisman 8) is typically used for model reconstruction, and hence turns the problem into a conventional POMDP. Optimal policies can then be computed by using existing POMDP algorithms. For the latter, research efforts are diverse, ranging from state-free stochastic policy (Jaakkola *et al.* 11), to recurrent Q-learning (Schmidhuber 24; Lin and Mitchell 13), to finite-history-window approach (McCallum 19; Lin and Mitchell 13). Nevertheless, most of the model-free POMDP algorithms yield only sub-optimal solutions. Among the four classes of problems aforementioned, hidden-state RL problems are expected to be the most difficult.

1.2   Nonstationary Environments

Traditional MDP problems typically assume that environment dynamics (i.e., MDP parameters) are always fixed (i.e., *stationary*). This assumption, however, is not realistic in many real-world applications. In elevator control (Crites and Barto 9), for example, the passenger arrival and departure rates can vary significantly over one day, and should not be modeled by a fixed MDP.

Previous studies on nonstationary MDPs (Puterman 22) presume that changes of the MDP parameters are exactly known in every time step. Given this assumption, solving nonstationary MDP problems is trivial, as the problem can be recast into a stationary one (with a much larger state space) by performing state augmentation. Nevertheless, extending the idea to incompletely-known environmental changes (i.e., to the reinforcement learning framework) is far more difficult.

In fact, RL (Kaelbling *et al.* 12; Sutton and Barto 28) in nonstationary environments is an impossible task if there exists no regularity in the way environment dynamics change. Hence, some degree of regularity must be assumed.

Typically, nonstationary environments are presumed to change slowly enough such that on-line RL algorithms can be employed to keep track of the changes. The online approach is memoryless in the sense that even if the environment ever reverts to the previously learned dynamics, learning must still start all over again. There are a few heuristic approaches along this line (Littman and Ackley 16; Sutton 27; Sutton and Barto 28).

1.3   The Properties of Our Proposed Model

Herein we propose a formal environment model (Choi *et al.* 7) for the nonstationary environments that repeat their dynamics over time. Our model is inspired by observations from an interesting class of nonstationary RL tasks. Throughout this section we illustrate the properties of such nonstationary environments by using the elevator control problem as an example.

Property 1: A Finite Number of Environment Modes

The first property we observed is that environmental changes are confined to a finite number of *environment modes*. Modes are stationary environments that possess distinct environment dynamics and require different control policies. At any time instant, the environment is assumed to be in exactly one of these modes. This concept of modes seems to be applicable to many, though not all, real-world tasks. In the elevator control problem, a system might operate in a morning-rush-hour mode, an evening-rush-hour mode and a non-rush-hour mode. One can also imagine similar modes for other real-world control tasks, such as traffic control, dynamic channel allocation (Singh and Bertsekas 25), and network routing (Boyan and Littman 3).

Property 2: Partially Observable Modes

Unlike states, environment modes cannot be directly observed. Instead, the current mode can only be estimated according to the past state transitions. It is analogous to the elevator control example in that the passenger arrival rate and pattern can only be partially observed through the occurrence of pick-up and drop-off requests.

Property 3: Modes Evolving as a Markov Process

Normally, mode transitions are stochastic events and are independent of the control system's response. In the elevator control problem, the events that change the current mode of the environment could be an emergency meeting in the administrative office, or a tea break for the staff on the 10th floor. Obviously, the elevator's response has no control over the occurrence of these events.

Property 4: Infrequent Mode Transitions

Mode transitions are relatively infrequent. In other words, a mode is more likely to retain for some time before switching to another one. Take the emergency meeting as an example, employees on different floors take time to arrive at the administrative office, and thus would generate a similar traffic pattern (drop-off requests on the same floor) for some period of time.

Property 5: Small Number of Modes

It is common that, in many real-world applications, the number of modes is much fewer than the number of states. In the elevator control example, the state space comprises of all possible combinations of elevator positions, pick-up and drop-off requests, and certainly would be huge. On the other hand, the mode space could be small. For instance, an elevator control system can simply have the three modes as described above to approximate the reality.

Based on these properties, an environment model is now proposed. The whole idea is to introduce a mode variable to capture environmental changes. Each mode specifies an MDP and hence completely determines the current state transition function and reward function (property 1). A mode, however, is not directly observable (property 2), and evolves with time according to a Markov process (property 3). The model is therefore called *hidden-mode model*.

Note that the hidden-mode model does not impose any constraint to satisfy properties 4 and 5. In other words, the model is flexible enough to work for environments where these two properties do not hold. Nevertheless, as will be shown later, these properties can be utilized to help the learning in practice.

The hidden-mode model also has its limitations. For instance, one may argue that the mode of an environment should preferably be continuous. While this is true, for tractability, we assume the mode is discrete. This implies that our model, as for any other model, is only an abstraction of the real world. Moreover, we assume that the number of modes is known in advance. We will seek to relax these assumptions in future research.

1.4   Related Work

Our hidden-mode model is closely related to the nonstationary environment model proposed by Dayan and Sejnowski (10). Although our model is more restrictive in terms of representational power, it involves much fewer parameters and is thus easier to learn. Besides, other than the number of possible modes that should be known in advance, we do not assume any other knowledge about the way environment dynamics change[1]. Dayan and Sejnowski, on the other hand, assume that one knows precisely how the environment dynamics change.

---

[1] That is, the transition probabilities of the Markov process governing mode changes, though fixed, are unknown in advance.

The hidden-mode model can also be viewed as a special case of the hidden-state model, or *partially observable Markov decision process* (POMDP). As will be shown later, a hidden-mode model can always be represented by a hidden-state model through state augmentation. Nevertheless, modeling a hidden-mode environment via a hidden-state model will unnecessarily increase the problem complexity. We discuss the conversion from the former to the latter in Section 2.2.

1.5   Our Focus

In order for RL to take place, one may choose between the model-based and model-free approaches. This paper is primarily concerned with the model-based approach, and concentrates on how a hidden-mode model can be learned based on the Baum-Welch algorithm. The issue of finding the optimal policy will only be addressed briefly.

1.6   Organization

The rest of this paper is organized as follows. In the next section, we describe the hidden-mode model by defining the hidden-mode Markov decision process (HM-MDP) and illustrate how it can be reformulated into a POMDP. Section 3 will subsequently discuss how a hidden-mode model can be learned in two different representations — a POMDP or an HM-MDP. A variant of the Baum-Welch algorithm for learning HM-MDP is proposed. These two approaches are then compared empirically in Section 4. In Section 5, we will briefly discuss how hidden-mode problems can be solved. Then we highlight the assumptions of our model and discuss its applicability in Section 6. Finally, Section 7 pinpoints some directions for future research and Section 8 summarizes our research work.

2   Hidden-Mode Markov Decision Processes

This section presents our hidden-mode model. Basically, a hidden-mode model is defined as a finite set of MDPs that share the same state space and action space, with possibly different transition functions and reward functions. The MDPs correspond to different modes in which a system operates. States are completely observable and their transitions are governed by an MDP. In contrast, modes are not directly observable and their transitions are controlled by a Markov chain. We refer to such a process as a *hidden-mode Markov decision process* (HM-MDP). Figure 2 gives an example of HM-MDP.

2.1   Formulation

Formally, an HM-MDP is defined as an 8-tuple $(Q, S, A, X, Y, R, \Pi, \Psi)$, where Q, S and A represent the sets of modes, states and actions respectively; the mode transition function X maps mode m to n with a fixed probability of x_{mn}; the state transition function Y defines transition probability, $y_m(s, a, s')$, from state

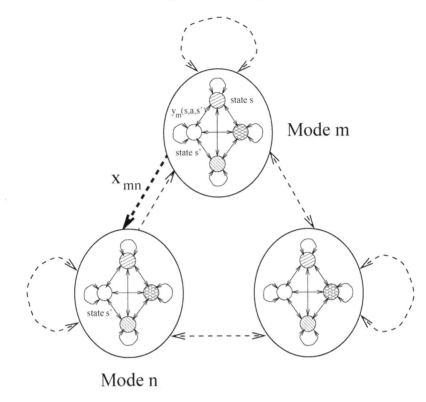

Fig. 2. A 3-mode, 4-state, 1-action HM-MDP. The values x_{mn} and $y_m(s, a, s')$ are the mode and state transition probabilities respectively.

s to s' given mode m and action a; the stochastic reward function R returns rewards with the mean value $r_m(s, a)$; Π and Ψ denote the prior probabilities of the modes and of the states respectively. The evolution of modes and states is depicted in Figure 3.

2.2   Reformulating HM-MDP as POMDP

HM-MDP is a subclass of POMDP. In other words, it is always possible to reformulate the former as a special case of the latter. In particular, one may take an ordered pair of any mode and observable state in the HM-MDP as a hidden state in a POMDP, and any observable state of the former as an observation of the latter. Suppose the observable states s and s' are in modes m and n respectively. These two HM-MDP states together with their corresponding modes form two hidden states $\langle m, s \rangle$ and $\langle n, s' \rangle$ for its POMDP counterpart. The transition probability from $\langle m, s \rangle$ to $\langle n, s' \rangle$ is then simply the mode transition probability x_{mn} multiplied by the state transition probability $y_m(s, a, s')$. For an M-mode, N-state, K-action HM-MDP, the equivalent POMDP thus has N observations and MN hidden states. A formal reformulation is detailed in Figure 4.

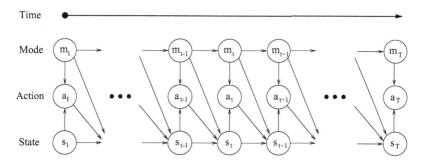

Fig. 3. The evolution of an HM-MDP. Each node represents a mode, action or state variable. The arcs indicate dependencies between the variables.

$$POMDP = (S', A', T', R', Z', Q', \Pi')$$

$$S' = Q \times S, \ Z' = S, \ A' = A$$

$$T' : \{p_{ij}(a) = x_{mn} \cdot y_m(s, a, s') \mid i = \langle m, s \rangle \ \in S', \ j = \langle n, s' \rangle \ \in S'\}$$

$$Q' : \{q_i(a, s') = \begin{cases} 1 & : \quad \text{if } s = s' \\ 0 & : \quad \text{if } s \neq s' \end{cases} \mid i = \langle m, s \rangle \ \in S', \ s' \in Z'\}$$

$$R' : \{r_i(a) = r_m(s, a) \mid i = \langle m, s \rangle \ \in S'\}$$

$$\Pi' = \{\pi'_i = \pi_m \cdot \psi_s \mid i = \langle m, s \rangle \ \in S'\}$$

Fig. 4. Reformulating HM-MDP into POMDP

Note that $S', A', T', R', O', Q', \Pi'$ are the state space, action space, state transition function, reward function, observation space, observation function, and prior state probabilities of the resulting POMDP respectively. The following lemmas prove that HM-MDPs are indeed a subclass of POMDPs.

Lemma 1. *The HM-MDP to POMDP transformation satisfies the state transition function requirement, namely* $\sum_j p_{ij}(a) = 1$.

Proof: From the transformation, we know that

$$\sum_j p_{ij}(a) = \sum_{\langle n, s' \rangle \in Q' \times S'} p_{\langle m, s \rangle, \langle n, s' \rangle}(a)$$

$$= \sum_{n \in Q'} \sum_{s' \in S'} x_{mn} \cdot y_m(s, a, s')$$

$$= \sum_{n \in Q'} x_{mn} \cdot \sum_{s' \in S'} y_m(s, a, s')$$

$$= \sum_{n \in Q'} x_{mn} \cdot 1$$

$$= 1 \hspace{4cm} \square$$

Lemma 2. *HM-MDPs form a subclass of POMDPs.*

Proof: Given an HM-MDP and its corresponding POMDP, there is a 1-1 mapping from the mode-state pairs of the HM-MDP into the states of the POMDP. This implies that for every two different pairs of mode and state $\langle m, s \rangle$ and $\langle m', s' \rangle$, there are corresponding distinct states in the POMDP. The transformation ensures that the two states are the same if and only if $m = m'$ and $s = s'$. It also imposes the same transition probability and average reward between two mode-state pairs and for the corresponding states in the POMDP. It implies that the transformed model is equivalent to the original one. Therefore HM-MDPs are a subclass of POMDPs. $\hspace{2cm} \square$

Figure 5 demonstrates the reformulation for a 3-mode, 4-state, 1-action HM-MDP and compares the model complexity with its equivalent POMDP. Note that most state transition probabilities (dashed lines) in the POMDP are collapsed into mode transition probabilities in the HM-MDP through parameter sharing. This saving is significant. In the example, the HM-MDP model has a total of 57 transition probabilities, while its POMDP counterpart has 144. In general, an HM-MDP contains much fewer parameters ($N^2MK + M^2$) than its corresponding POMDP (M^2N^2K).

3   Learning a Hidden-Mode Model

Now it becomes clear that there are two ways to learn a hidden-mode model: either learning an HM-MDP directly, or learning an equivalent POMDP. In this section, we first briefly discuss how the latter can be achieved by a variant of the Baum-Welch algorithm, and then develop a similar algorithm for HM-MDP.

3.1   Learning a POMDP Model

Traditional research in POMDP (Monahan 20; Lovejoy 17) assumes a known environment model and is concerned with finding an optimal policy. Chrisman (8) was the first to study the learning of POMDP models from experience.

Chrisman's work is based on the Baum-Welch algorithm, which was originally proposed for learning hidden Markov models (HMMs) (Rabiner 23). Based on the fact that a POMDP can be viewed as a collection of HMMs, Chrisman proposed a variant of the Baum-Welch algorithm for POMDP. This POMDP Baum-Welch algorithm requires $\Theta(M^2N^2T)$ time and $\Theta(M^2N^2K)$ storage for

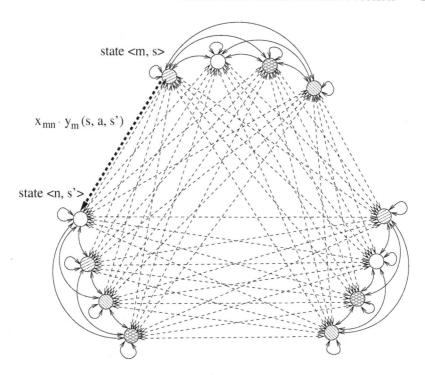

state <m, s>

$x_{mn} \cdot y_m(s, a, s')$

state <n, s'>

Fig. 5. Reformulating a 3-mode, 4-state, 1-action HM-MDP described in Figure 2 as an equivalent POMDP. For brevity, exact transition probability values are not shown. State s of mode m in Figure 2 is relabeled as $<m, s>$. Note that HM-MDP has much fewer model parameters than its POMDP counterpart.

learning an M-mode, N-state, K-action HM-MDP, given T data items. However, Chrisman's algorithm does not learn the reward function. One possible extension is to estimate the reward function by averaging the obtained rewards, weighted by the estimated state certainty. The effectiveness of the algorithm will be examined in the next section.

3.2 HM-MDP Baum-Welch Algorithm

We now extend the Baum-Welch algorithm to the learning of an HM-MDP model. The outline of the algorithm, called HM-MDP Baum-Welch, is shown in Figure 6. This new algorithm is similar to the POMDP version, except that the auxiliary variables are redefined.

The intuition behind both algorithms remains the same; i.e., estimating the parameters of the hidden variables by counting their expected number of transitions. This counting, however, can only be inferred from the observations by maintaining a set of auxiliary variables. Suppose that the number of transitions from the hidden variable i to j is known, the transition probability from i to j

Given a collection of data and an initial model parameter vector $\bar{\theta}$.
repeat
  $\theta = \bar{\theta}$
  Compute forward variables α_t. (Figure 7)
  Compute backward variables β_t. (Figure 8)
  Compute auxiliary variables ξ_t and γ_t. (Figure 9)
  Compute the new model parameter $\bar{\theta}$. (Figure 10)
until $\max\limits_i |\bar{\theta}_i - \theta_i| < \epsilon$

Fig. 6. The skeleton of HM-MDP Baum-Welch algorithm

can then be computed by the following equation:

$$\Pr(j|i) = \frac{\text{the number of transitions from } i \text{ to } j}{\text{the number of visits to } i}$$

where the denominator is simply the numerator summing over all j.

The central problem now becomes how to count the transitions of the hidden variables. While its exact value is unknown, it is possible to estimate the expected value through inferences on the observation sequence. We define $\xi_t(i,j)$ as the expected number of state transitions from i to j at time step t. Given a sequence of T observations, i.e., $T-1$ transitions, the total number of transitions from state i to j becomes $\sum\limits_{t=1}^{T} \xi_t(i,j)$, and the total number of visits to i is $\sum\limits_{j} \sum\limits_{t=1}^{T} \xi_t(i,j)$.

Thus far, our algorithm is not different from the standard Baum-Welch algorithm. The key difference between the two algorithms comes from the inference part (i.e., maintaining the auxiliary variables). As the observed state sequence is shifted one step forward in our model, additional attention is needed for handling the boundary cases. In the subsequent sections, the intuitive meanings and definitions of the auxiliary variables will be given.

Computing Forward Variables

Let the collection of data D be denoted as (S, A, R), where S is the observation sequence $s_1 s_2 \cdots s_T$, A the random[2] action sequence $a_1 a_2 \cdots a_T$, and R the reward sequence $r_1 r_2 \cdots r_T$. We define forward variables $\alpha_t(i)$ as $\Pr(s_1, s_2, ..., s_t, m_{t-1} = i | \theta, A)$, i.e. the joint probability of observing the partial state sequence from s_1 up to s_t and the mode at time $t-1$ being in i, given the model θ and the random action sequence A. To compute the forward variables efficiently, a dynamic programming approach is depicted in Figure 7.

---

[2] It is worth mentioning that although the optimal action is a function of modes and states, the choice of action should be at random in the model-learning phase, or called exploration phase.

Computing Forward Variables:

for all $i \in Q$,
$$\alpha_1(i) = \psi_{s_1}$$

for all $i \in Q$,
$$\alpha_2(i) = \pi_i \, \psi_{s_1} \, y_i(s_1, a_1, s_2)$$

for all $j \in Q$,
$$\alpha_{t+1}(j) = \sum_{i \in Q} \alpha_t(i) \, x_{ij} \, y_j(s_t, a_t, s_{t+1})$$

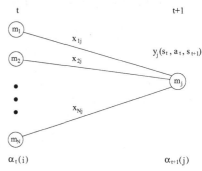

Fig. 7. Computing forward variables

Computing Backward Variables

Backward variable $\beta_t(i)$ denotes the probability $\Pr(s_{t+1}, s_{t+2}, \cdots, s_T | s_t, m_{t-1} = i, \theta, \mathsf{A})$, which represents the probability of obtaining the partial state sequence s_{t+1}, s_{t+2} up to s_T, given the state s_t, the mode being i at time $t - 1$, the model θ, and the random action sequence A. Unlike forward variables, backward variables are computed backward from β_T. The computational steps required for the backward variables are illustrated in Figure 8.

Computing Backward Variables:

for all $i \in Q$,
$$\beta_T(i) = 1$$

for all $i \in Q$,
$$\beta_t(i) = \sum_{j \in Q} x_{ij} \, y_j(s_t, a_t, s_{t+1}) \, \beta_{t+1}(j)$$

for all $i \in Q$,
$$\beta_1(i) = \sum_{j \in Q} \pi_j \, y_j(s_1, a_1, s_2) \, \beta_2(j)$$

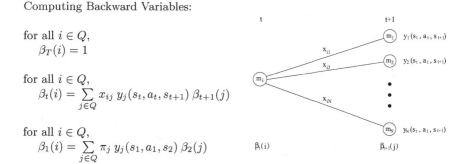

Fig. 8. Computing backward variables

Computing Auxiliary Variables

With the forward and backward variables, two additional auxiliary variables $\xi_t(i,j)$ and $\gamma_t(i)$ can now be defined. Formally, $\xi_t(i,j)$ is defined as $\Pr(m_{t-1} = i, m_t = j | \mathsf{S}, \mathsf{A}, \theta)$, i.e. the probability of being in mode i at time $t-1$ and in mode j at time t, given the state and action sequences, and the model θ. Figure 9 depicts how the forward and backward variables can be combined to compute $\xi_t(i,j)$.

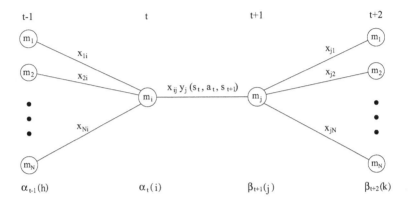

Computing Auxiliary Variables:
For all $i, j \in Q$,
$$\xi_t(i,j) = \frac{\alpha_t(i) \, x_{ij} \, y_j(s_t, a_t, s_{t+1}) \, \beta_{t+1}(j)}{\sum\limits_{k \in Q} \alpha_T(k)}$$

For all $i \in Q$,
$$\gamma_t(i) = \sum_{j \in Q} \xi_{t+1}(i,j)$$

Fig. 9. Computing auxiliary variables

Auxiliary variable $\gamma_t(i)$ is defined as $\Pr(m_t = i | \mathsf{S}, \mathsf{A}, \theta)$, i.e. the probability of being in mode i at time t, given the state and action sequences, and the model θ. Then $\gamma_t(i)$ is simply the sum of $\xi_{t+1}(i,j)$ over all possible resultant modes j; that is,

$$\gamma_t(i) = \sum_{j=1}^{N} \xi_{t+1}(i,j)$$

Parameter Reestimation

With these auxiliary variables, the model parameters can be updated. In particular, the prior mode distribution π_i, i.e. the probability of being in mode i at time $t = 1$, is simply the auxiliary variable $\gamma_1(i)$.

The mode transition probability x_{ij} is the number of mode transitions from i to j divided by the number of visits to mode i. Although these two values cannot be known exactly, they can be estimated by summing up the variables ξ and γ respectively:

$$\bar{x}_{ij} = \frac{\text{expected number of mode transitions from } i \text{ to } j}{\text{expected number of visits to mode } i}$$

$$= \frac{\displaystyle\sum_{t=2}^{T} \xi_t(i,j)}{\displaystyle\sum_{t=1}^{T-1} \gamma_t(i)}$$

Similarly, the state transition probabilities and reward function can be reestimated by the following:

$$\bar{y}_i(j,k,l) = \frac{\text{expected number of visits to mode } i \text{ state } j, \text{ with action } k \text{ and resulting in } l}{\text{expected number of visits to mode } i \text{ state } j, \text{ with action } k}$$

$$= \frac{\displaystyle\sum_{t=1}^{T-1} \gamma_t(i)\, \delta(s_t, j)\, \delta(a_t, k)\, \delta(s_{t+1}, l)}{\displaystyle\sum_{h \in S} \sum_{t=1}^{T-1} \gamma_t(i)\, \delta(s_t, j)\, \delta(a_t, k)\, \delta(s_{t+1}, h)}$$

$$\bar{r}_i(j,k) = \frac{\text{expected reward received by taking action } k \text{ at mode } i \text{ state } j}{\text{expected number of visits to mode } i \text{ state } j \text{ with action } a}$$

$$= \frac{\displaystyle\sum_{t=1}^{T-1} \gamma_t(i)\, \delta(a_t, k)\, \delta(s_t, j)\, r_t}{\displaystyle\sum_{t=1}^{T-1} \gamma_t(i)\, \delta(a_t, k)\, \delta(s_t, j)}$$

The function $\delta(a, b)$ is defined as 1 if $a = b$, or 0 otherwise. It is used for selecting the particular state and action. For a small data set, it is possible that some states or actions do not occur at all. In that case, the denominators of the formulae are equal to zero, and the parameters should remain unchanged. Figure 10 summarizes the parameter reestimation procedure.

$$\bar{x}_{ij} = \begin{cases} \dfrac{\sum\limits_{t=2}^{T} \xi_t(i,j)}{\sum\limits_{t=1}^{T} \gamma_t(i)} & : \quad \text{if denominator} \neq 0 \\[2em] x_{ij} & : \quad \text{otherwise} \end{cases}$$

$$\bar{y}_i(j,k,l) = \begin{cases} \dfrac{\sum\limits_{t=1}^{T-1} \gamma_t(i)\,\delta(s_t,j)\,\delta(s_{t+1},l)\,\delta(a_t,k)}{\sum\limits_{l \in S} \sum\limits_{t=1}^{T-1} \gamma_t(i)\,\delta(s_t,j)\,\delta(s_{t+1},l)\,\delta(a_t,k)} & : \quad \text{if denominator} \neq 0 \\[2em] y_i(j,k,l) & : \quad \text{otherwise} \end{cases}$$

$$\bar{r}_i(j,k) = \begin{cases} \dfrac{\sum\limits_{t=1}^{T-1} \gamma_t(i)\,\delta(a_t,k)\,\delta(s_t,j)\,r_t}{\sum\limits_{t=1}^{T-1} \gamma_t(i)\,\delta(a_t,k)\,\delta(s_t,j)} & : \quad \text{if denominator} \neq 0 \\[2em] r_i(j,k) & : \quad \text{otherwise} \end{cases}$$

$$\bar{\pi}_i = \gamma_1(i)$$

Fig. 10. Parameter reestimation for HM-MDP Baum-Welch algorithm

It is not difficult to see that the HM-MDP Baum-Welch algorithm requires only $\Theta(M^2T)$ time and $\Theta(MN^2K + M^2)$ storage, which gives a significant reduction when compared with $\Theta(M^2N^2T)$ time and $\Theta(M^2N^2K)$ storage in the POMDP approach.

4   Empirical Studies

This section empirically examines the POMDP Baum-Welch[3] and HM-MDP Baum-Welch algorithms in terms of the required data size and time. Experiments on various model sizes and settings were conducted. The results are quite consistent. In the following, some details of a typical run are presented for illustration.

4.1   Experimental Setting

The experimental model is a randomly generated HM-MDP with 3 modes, 10 states and 5 actions. Note that this HM-MDP is equivalent to a fairly large

---

[3] Chrisman's algorithm also attempts to learn a minimal possible number of states. Here we are concerned only with learning of the model parameters.

POMDP, with 30 hidden states, 10 observations and 5 actions. In order to simulate the infrequent mode changes, each mode is set to have a minimum probability of 0.9 in looping back to itself. In addition, each state of the HM-MDP has 3 to 8 non-zero transition probabilities, and rewards are uniformly distributed between $r_m(s, a) \pm 0.1$. This reward distribution, however, is not disclosed to the learning agents.

The experiments were run with data of various sizes, using the same initial model. The model was also randomly generated in the form of HM-MDP. To ensure fairness, the equivalent POMDP model was used for POMDP Baum-Welch learning. For each data set, the initial model was first loaded, and the selected algorithm iterated until the maximum change of the model parameters was less than a threshold of 0.0001. After the algorithm terminated, the model learning time was recorded, and the model estimation errors were computed. The experiment was then repeated for 11 times with different random seeds in order to compute the median.

4.2   Performance Measure

The HM-MDP and POMDP Baum-Welch algorithms learn a hidden-mode model in different representations. To facilitate comparison, all models were first converted into POMDP form. Model estimation errors can then be measured in terms of the minimum difference between the learned model and the actual model. As the state indices for the learned model might be different from the actual one, a renumbering of the state indices is needed. In our experiment, an indexing scheme that minimizes the sum of the squares of differences on the state transition probabilities between the learned and the actual models was used (provided the constraints on the observation probabilities are preserved). Figure 11 (a) and (b) report respectively the sum of the squares of differences on the transition function and on the reward function using this indexing scheme.

Regarding the computational requirement of the algorithms, the total CPU running time was measured on a SUN Ultra I workstation. Table 1 reports the model learning time in seconds.

Table 1. CPU time in seconds

Approach	Data Set Size				
	1000	2000	3000	4000	5000
HM-MDP	4.60	18.72	15.14	9.48	10.07
POMDP	189.40	946.78	2164.20	3233.56	4317.19

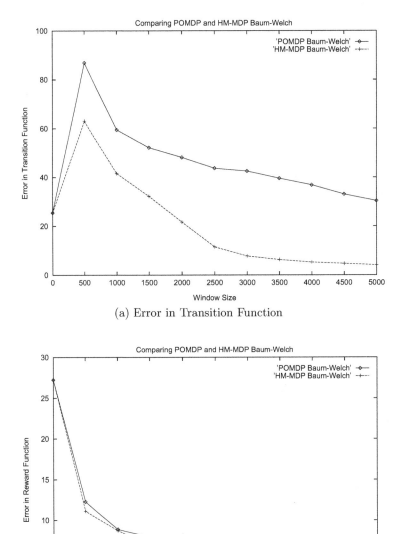

(a) Error in Transition Function

(b) Error in Reward Function

Fig. 11. Model learning errors in terms of the transition probabilities and rewards. All environment models are in their POMDP form for comparison. The errors are measured by summing the squares of differences on the state transition probabilities and on the reward function respectively.

4.3   Empirical Results

Conclusion can now be drawn. Generally speaking, both algorithms can learn a more accurate environment model as the data size increases (Figure 11). This result is not surprising since both algorithms are statistically based, and hence their performances rely largely on the amount of data provided. When the training data size is too small (less than 1000 in this case), both algorithms perform about equally poorly. However, as the data size increases, HM-MDP Baum-Welch improves substantially faster than POMDP Baum-Welch.

Our experiment reveals that HM-MDP Baum-Welch was able to learn a fairly accurate environment model with a data size of 2500. POMDP Baum-Welch, on the contrary, needs a data size of 20000 (not shown) in order to achieve a comparable accuracy. In fact, in all the experiments we conducted, HM-MDP Baum-Welch always required a much smaller data set than the POMDP Baum-Welch. We believe that this result holds in general because in most cases, an HM-MDP consists of fewer free parameters than its POMDP counterpart.

In terms of computational requirement, HM-MDP Baum-Welch is much faster than POMDP Baum-Welch (Table 1). We believe this is also true in general for the same reason described above. In addition, computational time is not necessarily monotonically increasing with the data size. It is because the total computational requirements depend not only on the data size, but also on the number of iterations being executed. From our experiments, we notice that the number of iterations tends to decrease as the data size increases.

5   Solving Hidden-Mode Problems

In this section we describe briefly how hidden-mode problems can be solved. Since HM-MDPs are a special class of POMDPs, a straightforward approach is first to convert a hidden-mode problem into a POMDP one and subsequently to apply POMDP algorithms. Nevertheless, POMDP algorithms do not exploit the special structures of HM-MDPs. Herein, we develop a value iteration approach for HM-MDPs[4]. The main idea of the algorithm is to exploit the HM-MDP structure by decomposing the value function based on the state space. This algorithm is akin to the POMDP value iteration conceptually but is much more efficient.

5.1   Value Iteration for HM-MDPs

Many POMDP algorithms maintain a probability distribution over the state space known as *belief state*. As a result, a policy is a mapping from belief states to actions. In HM-MDPs, a probability distribution over the mode space is maintained. We name it *belief mode*. Unlike the POMDP approach, the belief mode divides the belief states into an observable part (i.e. the observable states) and an unobservable part (i.e. the hidden modes). This representation minimizes

---

[4]   A more detailed description of the algorithm can be found in (Choi 6).

the number of hidden variables. For every observed state and action, the belief mode b is updated as follows.

$$b_{s'}^a(m') = \frac{\sum_{m \in Q} \Pr(m'|m) \cdot \Pr(s'|m, s, a) \cdot b(m)}{\sum_{m' \in Q} \sum_{m \in Q} \Pr(m'|m) \cdot \Pr(s'|m, s, a) \cdot b(m)}$$

$$= \frac{\sum_{m \in Q} x_{m'm} \cdot y_m(s, a, s') \cdot b(m)}{\sum_{m' \in Q} \sum_{m \in Q} x_{m'm} \cdot y_m(s, a, s') \cdot b(m)}$$

where $b_{s'}^a(m')$ is the probability of being in mode m', given the action a and the state s'. The numerator computes the likelihood of the next mode and the denominator is the normalization factor.

An HM-MDP policy now becomes a mapping from belief modes and states to actions. Specifically, an optimal action for a belief mode b and the current state s maximizes the following value function:

$$V(b, s) = \max_{a \in A} \left(\sum_{m \in Q} r_m(s, a) \cdot b(m) + \gamma \sum_{s' \in S} \Pr(s'|b, s, a) V(b_{s'}^a, s') \right) \qquad (1)$$

where $r_m(s, a)$ is the reward function and γ is the discount factor. Since s is a discrete variable, one can view the value function V as $|S|$ value functions. Note that these decomposed value functions are still piecewise linear and convex. One can therefore use Equation (1) for the value iteration to compute the optimal value function for each state in S.

5.2   Empirical Results

We implement Equation (1) by using a variant of incremental pruning (Zhang and Liu 31; Cassandra *et al.* 4) and run the program on a SPARC Ultra 2 machine. A number of experiments were conducted based on some simplified real-world problems. The descriptions of the problems can be found in (Choi 6). Table 2 gives a summary of the tasks. In these experiments, a discount factor of 0.95 and a solution tolerance of 0.1 were used. Table 3 reports the CPU time in seconds, the number of vectors in the resulting value functions, and the number of required epochs. While incremental pruning is considered as one of the most efficient POMDP algorithms, our experiment showed that it is unable to solve any of these problems within the specified time limit.

There are two main reasons why the HM-MDP approach is more efficient than the POMDP one. First, the dimension of the vector is significantly reduced from $|Q| \cdot |S|$ to $|Q|$. Second, the most time-consuming part of the algorithm, namely the cross sum operation, no longer needs to be performed on the whole value function due to decomposition of the value function.

Table 2. HM-MDP problems

Problem	Modes	States	Actions
Traffic Light	2	8	2
Sailboat	4	16	2
Elevator	3	32	3

Table 3. Solving HM-MDP problems by using incremental pruning

Problem	POMDP Approach			HM-MDP Approach		
	Time	Vectors	Epochs	Time	Vectors	Epochs
Traffic Light	>259200	-	-	4380	404	114
Sailboat	>259200	-	-	170637	1371	112
Elevator	>259200	-	-	186905	3979	161

6 Discussions

The usefulness of a model depends on the validity of the assumptions made. In this section, we revisit the assumptions of HM-MDP, discuss the issues involved, and shed some light on its applicability to real-world nonstationary tasks. Some possible extensions are also discussed.

A Finite Number of Environment Modes

MDP is a flexible framework that has been widely adopted in various applications. Among these there exist many tasks that are nonstationary in nature and are more suitable to be characterized by several, rather than a single, MDPs. The introduction of distinct MDPs for modeling different modes of the environment is a natural extension to those tasks.

One advantage of having distinct MDPs is that the learned model is more comprehensible: each MDP naturally describes a mode of the environment. In addition, this formulation facilitates the incorporation of prior knowledge into the model initialization step.

Partially Observable Modes

While modes are not directly observable, they may be estimated by observing the past state transitions. It is a crucial, and fortunately still reasonable, assumption that one needs to make.

Although states are assumed to be observable, it is possible to extend the model to allow partially observable states, i.e., to relax the second condition mentioned in Section 1. In this case, the extended model would be equivalent in representational power to a POMDP. This could be proved by showing the reformulation of the two models in both directions.

Modes Evolving as a Markov Process

This property may not always hold for all real-world tasks. In some applications, such as learning in a multi-agent environment or performing tasks in an adversary environment, the agent's actions might affect the state as well as the environment mode. In that case, an MDP instead of a Markov chain should be used to govern the mode transition process. Obviously, the use of a Markov chain involves fewer parameters and is thus preferable whenever possible.

Infrequent Mode Transitions

This is a property that generally holds in many applications. In order to characterize this property, a large transition probability for a mode looping back to itself can be used. Note that this is introduced primarily from a practical point of view, but is not a necessary condition for our model. In fact, we have tried to apply our model-learning algorithms to problems in which this property does not hold. We find that our model still outperforms POMDP, although the required data size is typically increased for both cases.

Using high self-transition probabilities to model rare mode changes may not always be the best option. In some cases mode transitions are also correlated with the time of a day (e.g. busy traffic in lunch hours). In this case, time (or the mode sequence) should be taken into account for identifying the current mode. One simple way to model this property is to strengthen left-to-right transitions between modes, as in the left-to-right HMMs.

Small Number of Modes

This nice property significantly reduces the number of parameters in HM-MDP compared to that in POMDP, and makes the former more applicable to real-world nonstationary tasks.

The number of states can be determined by the learning agent. States can be distinguished by, for instance, transition probabilities, mean rewards, or utilities. McCallum (19) has detailed discussions on this issue.

Likewise, the number of modes can be defined in various ways. After all, modes are used to discern changes of environment dynamics from noise. In practice, introducing a few modes is sufficient for boosting the system performance. More modes might help further, but not necessarily significantly. A trade-off between performance and response time must thus be decided. In fact, determining the optimal number of modes is an important topic that deserves further studies.

7   Future Work

There are a number of issues that need to be addressed in order to broaden the applicability of HM-MDPs. First, the number of modes is currently assumed to be known. In some situations, choosing the right number of modes can be difficult. Hence, we are now investigating the possibility of using Chrisman's or McCallum's hidden-state-splitting techniques (Chrisman 8; McCallum 18) to remove this limitation. Next, the problem-solving algorithm we presented here is preliminary. Further improvement, such as incorporating the point-based improvement technique (Zhang *et al.* 30), can be achieved. We are also investigating an algorithm that further exploits the characteristics of the HM-MDP. We will present this algorithm in a separate paper. Finally, the exploration-exploitation issue is currently ignored. In our future work, we will address this important issue and apply our model to real-world nonstationary tasks.

8   Summary

Making sequential decisions in nonstationary environments is common in real-world problems. In this paper we presented a formal model, called hidden-mode Markov decision process, for a broad class of nonstationary sequential decision tasks. The proposed model is based on five properties observed in a special type of nonstationary environments, and is applicable to many traffic control type problems. Basically, the hidden-mode model is defined as a fixed number of partially observable modes, each of which specifies an MDP. While state and action spaces are fixed across modes, the transition and reward functions may differ according to the mode. In addition, the mode evolves according to a Markov chain.

HM-MDP is a generalization of MDP. In addition to the basic MDP characteristics, HM-MDP also allows the model parameters to change probabilistically. This feature is important because many real-world tasks are nonstationary in nature and cannot be represented accurately by a fixed model. Nevertheless, the hidden-mode model also adds uncertainty to the model parameters and makes the problem, in general, more difficult than the MDPs.

HM-MDP is a specialization of POMDP; it can always be transformed into a POMDP with an augmented state space. While POMDPs are superior in terms of representational power, HM-MDPs require fewer parameters, and therefore can provide a more natural formulation for certain type of nonstationary problems. Our experiments also show that this simplification significantly speeds up both the model-learning and the problem-solving procedures of HM-MDPs.

9   Acknowledgment

This research work is supported by Hong Kong Research Grants Council Grant: HKUST6152/98E.

References

R. E. Bellman, (1957). *Dynamic Programming*. Princeton University Press, Princeton, NJ.

R. E. Bellman, (1957). A Markovian decision process. *Journal of Mathematics and Mechanics*, 6:679–684.

J. A. Boyan and M. L. Littman, (1994). Packet routing in dynamically changing networks: a reinforcement learning approach. In *Advances in Neural Information Processing Systems 6*, pages 671–678, San Mateo, California. Morgan Kaugmann.

A. R. Cassandra, M. L. Littman, and N. Zhang, (1997) Incremental pruning: A simple, fast, exact algorithm for partially observable Markov decision processes. In *Uncertainty in Artificial Intelligence*, Providence, RI.

H.-T. Cheng, (1988). *Algorithms for Partially Observable Markov Decision Processes*. PhD thesis, University of British Columbia, British Columbia, Canada.

S. P. M. Choi, (2000). *Reinforcement Learning in Nonstationary Environments*. PhD thesis, Hong Kong University of Science and Technology, Department of Computer Science, HKUST, Clear Water Bay, Hong Kong, China, Jan.

S. P. M. Choi, D. Y. Yeung, and N. L. Zhang, (1999). An environment model for nonstationary reinforcement learning. In *Advances in Neural Information Processing Systems 12*. To appear.

L. Chrisman, (1992). Reinforcement learning with perceptual aliasing: The perceptual distinctions approach. In *AAAI-92*.

R. H. Crites and A. G. Barto, (1996). Improving elevator performance using reinforcement learning. In D. Touretzky, M. Mozer, and M. Hasselmo, editors, *Advances in Neural Information Processing Systems 8*.

P. Dayan and T. J. Sejnowski, (1996). Exploration bonuses and dual control. *Machine Learning*, 25(1):5–22, Oct.

T. Jaakkola, S. P. Singh, and M. I. Jordan, (1995). Monte-Carlo reinforcement learning in non-Markovian decision problems. In G. Tesauro, D. S. Touretzky, and T. K. Leen, editors, *Advances in Neural Information Processing Systems 7*, MA. The MIT Press.

L. P. Kaelbling, M. L. Littman, and A. W. Moore, (1996). Reinforcement learning: A survey. *Journal of Artificial Intelligence Research*, 4:237–285, May.

L. J. Lin and T. M. Mitchell, (1992). Memory approaches to reinforcement learning in non-Markovian domains. Technical Report CMU-CS-92-138, Carnegie Mellon University, School of Computer Science.

M. L. Littman, A. R. Cassandra, and L. P. Kaelbling, (1995a). Learning policies for partially observable environments: Scaling up. In A. Prieditis and S. Russell, editors, *Proceedings of the Twelfth International Conference on Machine Learning*, pages 362–370, San Francisco, CA. Morgan Kaufmann.

M. L. Littman, A. R. Cassandra, and L. P. Kaelbling, (1995b). Efficient dynamic-programming updates in partially observable Markov decision processes. Technical Report TR CS-95-19, Department of Computer Science, Brown University, Providence, Rhode Island 02912, USA.

M. L. Littman and D. H. Ackley, (1991). Adaptation in constant utility non-stationary environments. In R. K. Belew and L. Booker, editors, *Proceedings of the Fourth International Conference on Genetic Algorithms*, pages 136–142, San Mateo, CA, Dec. Morgan Kaufmann.

W. S. Lovejoy, (1991). A survey of algorithmic methods for partially observed Markov decision processes. *Annals of Operations Research*, 28:47–66.

A. McCallum, (1993). Overcoming incomplete perception with utile distinction memory. In *Tenth International Machine Learning Conference*, Amherst, MA.

A. McCallum, (1995). *Reinforcement Learning with Selective Perception and Hidden State*. PhD thesis, University of Rochester, Dec.

G. E. Monahan, (1982). A survey of partially observable Markov decision processes: Theory, models and algorithms. *Management Science*, 28:1–16.

C. H. Papadimitriou and J. N. Tsitsiklis (1987). The complexity of Markov decision processes. *Mathematics of Operations Research*, 12(3):441–450.

M. L. Puterman (1994). *Markov Decision Processes: Discrete Stochastic Dynamic Programming*. John Wiley and Sons.

L. R. Rabiner, (1989). A tutorial on hidden Markov models and selected applications in speech recognition. *Proceedings of the IEEE*, 77(2), Feb.

J. H. Schmidhuber (1990). Reinforcement learning in Markovian and non-Markovian environments. In D. S. Lippman, J. E. Moody, and D. S. Touretzky, editors, *Advances in Neural Information Processing Systems*, volume 3, pages 500–506, San Mateo, CA. Morgan Kaufmann.

S. Singh and D. P. Bertsekas, (1997). Reinforcement learning for dynamic channel allocation in cellular telephone systems. In *Advances in Neural Information Processing Systems 9*, 1997.

E. J. Sondik, (1971). *The Optimal Control of Partially Observable Markov Processes*. PhD thesis, Stanford University, Stanford, California, USA.

R. S. Sutton, (1990). Integrated architectures for learning, planning, and reacting based on approximating dynamic programming. In *Proceedings of the Seventh International Conference on Machine Learning*, pages 216–224. Morgan Kaufmann.

R. S. Sutton and A. G. Barto, (1998). *Reinforcement Learning: An Introduction*. The MIT Press.

C. C. White III, (1991). Partially observed markov decision processes: A survey. *Annals of Operations Research*, 32.

N. L. Zhang, S. S. Lee, and W. Zhang, (1999). A method for speeding up value iteration in partially observable markov decision processes. In *Proceeding of 15th Conference on Uncertainties in Artificial Intelligence*.

N. L. Zhang and W. Liu, (1997). A model approximation scheme for planning in partially observable stochastic domains. *Journal of Artificial Intelligence Research*, 7:199 – 230.

Pricing in Agent Economies Using Neural Networks and Multi-agent Q-Learning

Gerald Tesauro

IBM T. J. Watson Research Center

1 Introduction

Reinforcement Learning (RL) procedures have been established as powerful and practical methods for solving Markov Decision Problems. One of the most significant and actively investigated RL algorithms is Q-learning (Watkins, 1989). Q-learning is an algorithm for learning to estimate the long-term expected reward for a given state-action pair. It has the nice property that it does not need a model of the environment, and it can be used for on-line learning. A number of powerful convergence proofs have been given showing that Q-learning is guaranteed to converge, in cases where the state space is small enough so that lookup table representations can be used (Watkins and Dayan, 1992). Furthermore, in large state spaces where lookup table representations are infeasible, RL methods can be combined with function approximators to give good practical performance despite the lack of theoretical guarantees of convergence to optimal policies.

Most real-world problems are not fully Markov in nature – they are often non-stationary, history-dependent and/or not fully observable. In order for RL methods to be more generally useful in solving such problems, they need to be extended to handle these non-Markovian properties. One important application domain where the non-Markovian aspects are paramount is the area of multi-agent systems. This area is expected to be increasingly important in the future, due to the potential rapid emergence of "agent economies" consisting of large populations of interacting software agents engaged in various forms of economic activity. The problem of multiple agents simultaneously adapting is in general non-Markov, because each agent provides an effectively non-stationary environment for the other agents. Hence the existing convergence guarantees do not hold, and in general, it is not known whether any global convergence will be obtained, and if so, whether such solutions are optimal.

Some progress has been made in analyzing certain special case multi-agent problems. For example, the problem of "teams," where all agents share a common utility function, has been studied by Crites and Barto (1996), and by Stone and Veloso (1999). Likewise, the purely competitive case of zero-sum utility functions has been studied in Littman (1994), where an algorithm called "minimax-Q" was proposed for two-player zero-sum games, and shown to converge to the optimal value function and policies for both players. Sandholm and Crites studied simultaneous Q-learning by two players in the Iterated Prisoner's Dilemma game

R. Sun and C.L. Giles (Eds.): Sequence Learning, LNAI 1828, pp. 288–307, 2000.

(Sandholm and Crites, 1995), and found that the learning procedure generally converged to stationary solutions. However, the extent to which those soluti- ons were "optimal" was unclear. Recently, Hu and Wellman (1998) proposed an algorithm for multi-agent Q-learning in two-player general-sum games. This algorithm is an important first step, but does not yet appear to be useable for practical problems, because it assumes that policies followed by both players will be Nash equilibrium policies. This requires unbounded rationality of all agents, as well as full knowledge of the state transitions and of the utility functions of all players. Furthermore, the potential problem of choosing from amongst multiple Nash equilibria is not addressed. This could be a serious problem, since Nash equilibria tend to proliferate when there is sufficiently high emphasis on future rewards, i.e., a large value of the discount parameter γ (Kreps, 1990).

The present work examines simultaneous Q-learning in an economically mo- tivated two-player game. The players are assumed to be two sellers of similar or identical products, who compete against each other on the basis of price. At each time step, the sellers alternately take turns setting prices, taking into account the other seller's current price. After the price has been set, the consumers then respond instantaneously and deterministically, choosing either seller 1's product or seller 2's product (or no product) based on the current price pair (p_1, p_2), leading to an instantaneous reward or profit (U_1, U_2) given to sellers 1 and 2 respectively. Although not required by Q-learning, it is assumed for purposes of comparing with game-theoretic solutions that both sellers have full knowledge of the expected consumer response for any given price pair, and in fact have full knowledge of both profit functions.

This work builds on prior research reported in Tesauro and Kephart (2000), which examined the effect of including foresight, i.e. an ability to anticipate longer-term consequences of an agent's current action. Two different algorithms for agent foresight were presented: (i) a generalization of the minimax search procedure in two-player zero-sum games; (ii) a generalization of the Policy Ite- ration method from dynamic programming, in which both players' policies are simultaneously improved, until self-consistent policy pairs are obtained that op- timize expected reward over two time steps. It was found that including foresight in the agents' pricing algorithms generally improved overall agent profitability, and usually damped out or eliminated the pathological behavior of unending cyclic "price wars," in which long episodes of repeated undercutting amongst the sellers alternate with large jumps in price. Such price wars were found to be rampant in prior studies of agent economy models (Kephart, Hanson and Sai- ramesh, 1998; Sairamesh and Kephart, 1998) when the agents use "myopically optimal" or "myoptimal" pricing algorithms that optimize immediate reward, but do not anticipate the longer-term consequences of an agent's current price setting.

There are three primary motivations for studying simultaneous Q-learning. First, if Q-functions can be learned simultaneously and self-consistently for both players, the policies implied by those Q-functions should be self-consistently op- timal. (The meaning of "optimal" here and throughout this chapter is that the

Q-function accurately represents discounted long-term reward obtained by following the Q-derived policy, and that no other policy can obtain superior long-term discounted reward.) In other words, an agent will be able to correctly anticipate the longer-term consequences of its own actions, the other agents' actions, and will correctly model the other agents as having an equivalent capability. Hence the classic problem of infinite recursion of opponent models will be avoided. In contrast, in other approaches to adaptive multi-agent systems, these issues are more problematic. For example, Hu and Wellman (1996) study the situation of a single "strategic" agent, which is able to anticipate the market impact of its pricing actions, in a population of "reactive" agents, which have no such anticipatory capability. Likewise, Vidal and Durfee (1998) propose a recursive opponent modeling scheme, in which level-0 agents do no opponent modeling, level-1 agents model the opponents as being level-0, level-2 agents model the opponents as being level-1, etc.. In both of these approaches, there is no effective way for an agent to model other agents as being at an equivalent level of depth or complexity.

The second advantage of Q-learning is that the solutions should correspond to deep lookahead: in principle, the Q-function represents the expected reward looking infinitely far ahead in time, exponentially weighted by a discount parameter $0 < \gamma < 1$. In contrast, the prior work of Tesauro and Kephart (2000) was based on shallow finite lookahead. Finally, in comparison to directly modeling agent policies, the Q-function approach seems more extensible to the situation of very large economies with many competing sellers. Approximating Q-functions with nonlinear function approximators such as neural networks seems intuitively more feasible than approximating the corresponding policies. Furthermore, in the Q-function approach, each agent only needs to maintain a single Q-function for itself, whereas in the policy modeling approach, each agent needs to maintain a policy model for every other agent; the latter seems infeasible when the number of sellers is large.

The remainder of this chapter is organized as follows. Section 2 describes the structure and dynamics of the model two-seller economy, and presents three economically-based models of seller profit (Price-Quality, Information-Filtering, and Shopbot) which are known to be prone to price wars when agents myopically optimize their short-term payoffs. System parameters are chosen to place each of these systems in a price-war regime. Section 3 describes implementation details of Q-learning in these model economies. As a first step, the simple case of ordinary Q-learning is considered, where one of the two sellers uses Q-learning and the other seller uses a fixed pricing policy (the myopically optimal, or "myoptimal" policy). Section 4 examines the more interesting and novel situation of simultaneous Q-learning by both sellers. Section 5 studies single-agent Q-learning in these models using neural networks, and compares the results to those of section 3 using lookup tables. Finally, section 6 summarizes the main conclusions and discusses promising directions and challenges for future work.

2   Model Agent Economies

Real agent economies are likely to contain large numbers of agents, with complex details of how the agents behave and interact with each other on multiple time scales. In order to make initial progress, a number of simplifying assumptions are made. The economy is restricted to two competing sellers, offering similar or identical products to a large population of consumer agents. The sellers compete on the basis of price, and it is assumed that prices are discretized and can lie between a minimum and maximum price, such that the number of possible prices is at most a few hundred. This renders the state space small enough that it is feasible to use lookup tables to represent the agents' pricing policies and expected utilities. Time in the simulation is also discretized; at each time step, the consumers compare the current prices of the two sellers, and instantaneously and deterministically choose to purchase from at most one seller. Hence at each time step, for each possible pair of seller prices, there is a deterministic reward or profit given to each seller. The simulation can iterate forever, and there may or may not be a discounting factor for the present value of future rewards.

It is worth noting that the consumers are not regarded as "players" in the model. The consumers have no strategic role: they behave according to an extremely simple, fixed, short-term greedy rule (buy the lowest priced product at each time step), and are regarded as merely providing a stationary environment in which the two sellers can compete in a two-player game. This is clearly a simplifying first step in the study of multi-agent phenomena, and in future work, the models will be extended to include strategic and adaptive behavior on the part of the consumers as well. This will change the notion of "desirable" system behavior. In the present model, desirable behavior would resemble "collusion" between the two sellers in charging very high prices, so that both could obtain high profits. Obviously this is not desirable from the consumers' viewpoint.

Regarding the dynamics of seller price adjustments, it is assumed that the sellers alternately take turns adjusting their prices, rather than simultaneously setting prices (i.e. the game is extensive form rather than normal form). The choice of alternating-turn dynamics is motivated by two considerations: (a) As the number of sellers becomes large and the model becomes more realistic, it seems more reasonable to assume that the sellers will adjust their prices at different times rather than at the same time, although they probably will not take turns in a well-defined order. (b) With alternating-turn dynamics, one can stay within the normal Q-learning framework where the Q-function implies a deterministic optimal policy: it is known that in two-player alternating turn games, there always exists a deterministic policy that is as good as any non-deterministic policy (Littman, 1994). In contrast, in games with simultaneous moves (for example, rock-paper-scissors), it is possible that no deterministic policy is optimal, and that the existing Q-learning formalism for MDPs would have to be modified and extended so that it could yield non-deterministic optimal policies.

Q-learning is studied in three different economic models that have been described in detail elsewhere Sairamesh and Kephart, 1998; Kephart, Hanson and

Sairamesh, 1998; Greenwald and Kephart, 1999). The first model, called the "Price-Quality" model (Sairamesh and Kephart, 1998), models the sellers' products as being distinguished by different values of a scalar "quality" parameter, with higher-quality products being perceived as more valuable by the consumers. The consumers are modeled as trying to obtain the lowest-priced product at each time step, subject to threshold-type constraints on both quality and price, i.e., each consumer has a maximum allowable price and a minimum allowable quality. The similarity and substitutability of seller products leads to a potential for direct price competition; however, the "vertical" differentiation due to differening quality values leads to an asymmetry in the sellers' profit functions. It is believed that this asymmetry is responsible for the unending cyclic price wars that emerge when the sellers employ myoptimal pricing strategies.

The second model is an "Information-Filtering" model described in detail in Kephart, Hanson and Sairamesh (1998). In this model there are two competing sellers of news articles in somewhat overlapping categories. In contrast to the vertical differentiation of the Price-Quality model, this model contains a horizontal differentiation in the differing article categories. To the extent that the categories overlap, there can be direct price competition, and to the extent that they differ, there are asymmetries introduced that again lead to the potential for cyclic price wars.

The third model is the so-called "Shopbot" model described in Greenwald and Kephart (1999), which is intended to model the situation on the Internet in which some consumers may use a Shopbot to compare prices of all sellers offering a given product, and select the seller with the lowest price. In this model, the sellers' products are exactly identical and the profit functions are symmetric. Myoptimal pricing leads the sellers to undercut each other until the minimum price point is reached. At that point, a new price war cycle can be launched, due to buyer asymmetries rather than seller asymmetries. The fact that not all buyers use the Shopbot, and some buyers instead choose a seller at random, means that it can be profitable for a seller to abandon the low-price competition for the bargain hunters, and instead maximally exploit the random buyers by charging the maximum possible price.

An example economic profit function, taken from the Price-Quality model, is as follows: Let p_1 and p_2 represent the prices charged by seller 1 and seller 2 respectively. Let q_1 and q_2 represent their respective quality parameters, with $q_1 > q_2$. Let $c(q)$ represent the cost to a seller of producing an item of quality q. Then the profits per item sold by sellers 1 and 2 are given by $p_1 - c(q_1)$ and $p_2 - c(q_2)$ respectively. Now, according to the model of consumer behavior described in Sairamesh and Kephart (1998), each consumer has a minimum quality threshold and a maximum price threshold, and these threshold values are uniformly distributed between 0 and 1 throughout the consumer population. This implies that in the absence of competition, the market share obtained by seller i will be given by $(q_i - p_i)$; this represents the elimination of consumers with quality thresholds greater than q_i and price thresholds less than p_i. Combining the market share calculation with the profit per item calculation, one can show analytically that in the limit of infinitely many consumers, the instantaneous utilities (profits per consumer) U_1 and U_2 obtained by seller 1 and seller 2 respectively are given by:

$$U_1 = \begin{cases} (q_1 - p_1)(p_1 - c(q_1)) & \text{if } 0 \leq p_1 \leq p_2 \text{ or } p_1 > q_2 \\ (q_1 - q_2)(p_1 - c(q_1)) & \text{if } p_2 < p_1 < q_2 \end{cases} \tag{1}$$

$$U_2 = \begin{cases} (q_2 - p_2)(p_2 - c(q_2)) & \text{if } 0 \leq p_2 < p_1 \\ 0 & \text{if } p_2 \geq p_1 \end{cases} \tag{2}$$

A plot of the profit landscape for seller 1 as a function of prices p_1 and p_2 is given in figure 1, for the following parameter settings: $q_1 = 1.0$, $q_2 = 0.9$, and $c(q) = 0.1(1 + q)$. (These specific parameter settings were chosen because they are known to generate harmful price wars when the agents use myoptimal policies.) In this figure, the myopic optimal price for seller 1 as a function of seller 2's price, $p_1^*(p_2)$, is obtained for each value of p_2 by sweeping across all values of p_1 and choosing the value that gives the highest profit. For small values of p_2, the peak profit is obtained at $p_1 = 0.9$, whereas for larger values of p_2, there is eventually a discontinuous shift to the other peak, which follows along the parabolic-shaped ridge in the landscape. An analytic expression for the myopic optimal price for seller 1 as a function of p_2 is as follows (defining $x_1 = q_1 + c(q_1)$ and $x_2 = q_2 + c(q_2)$):

$$p_1^*(p_2) = \begin{cases} q_2 & \text{if } 0 \leq p_2 < x_1 - q_2 \\ p_2 & \text{if } x_1 - q_2 \leq p_2 \leq \frac{1}{2}x_1 \\ \frac{1}{2}x_1 & \text{if } p_2 > \frac{1}{2}x_1 \end{cases} \tag{3}$$

Similarly, the myopic optimal price for seller 2 as a function of the price set by seller 1, $p_2^*(p_1)$, is given by the following formula (assuming that prices are discrete and that ϵ is the price discretization interval):

$$p_2^*(p_1) = \begin{cases} c(q_2) & 0 \leq p_1 \leq c(q_2) \\ p_1 - \epsilon & \text{if } c(q_2) \leq p_1 \leq \frac{1}{2}x_2 \\ \frac{1}{2}x_2 & \text{if } p_1 > \frac{1}{2}x_2 \end{cases} \tag{4}$$

There are also similar profit landscapes for each seller in the Information-Filtering model and in the Shopbot model. In all three models, it is the existence of multiple, disconnected peaks in the landscapes, with relative heights that can change depending on the other seller's price, that leads to price wars when the sellers behave myopically.

In these models it is assumed for simplicity that the players have essentially perfect information. They can model the consumer behavior perfectly, and they also have perfect knowledge of each other's costs and profit functions. Hence the model is in essence a two-player perfect-information deterministic game, similar to games like chess. The main differences are that the utilities are not strictly zero-sum, there are no terminating or absorbing nodes in the state space, and payoffs are given to the players at every time step, rather than at terminating nodes.

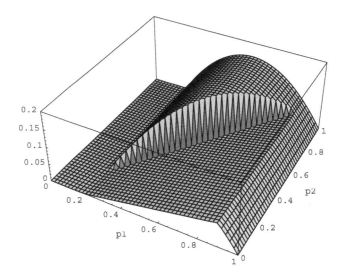

Fig. 1. Sample profit landscape for seller 1 in Price-Quality model, as a function of seller 1 price p_1 and seller 2 price p_2.

As mentioned previously, the possible seller prices are constrained to lie in a range from some minimum to maximum allowable price. The prices are discretized, so that one can create lookup tables for the seller profit functions $U(p_1, p_2)$. Furthermore, the optimal pricing policies for each seller as a function of the other seller's price, $p_1^*(p_2)$ and $p_2^*(p_1)$, can also be represented in the form of table lookups.

3   Single-Agent Q-Learning

Let us first consider ordinary single-agent Q-learning vs. a fixed myoptimal opponent pricing strategy in the above two-seller economic models. The procedure for Q-learning is as follows. Let $Q(s, a)$ represent the discounted long-term expected reward to an agent for taking action a in state s. The discounting of future rewards is accomplished by a discount parameter γ such that the value of a reward expected at n time steps in the future is discounted by γ^n. Assume that the $Q(s, a)$ function is represented by a lookup table containing a value for every possible state-action pair, and assume that the table entries are initialized to arbitrary values. Then the procedure for solving for $Q(s, a)$ is to infinitely repeat the following two-step loop:

1. Select a particular state s and a particular action a, observe the immediate reward r for this state-action pair, and observe the resulting state s'.

2. Adjust $Q(s, a)$ according to the following equation:

$$\Delta Q(s, a) = \alpha[r + \gamma \max_b Q(s', b) - Q(s, a)] \tag{5}$$

where α is the learning rate parameter, and the max operation represents choosing the optimal action b among all possible actions that can be taken in the successor state s' leading to the greatest Q-value. A wide variety of methods may be used to select state-action pairs in step 1, provided that every state-action pair is visited infinitely often. For any stationary Markov Decision Problem, the Q-learning procedure is guaranteed to converge to the correct values, provided that α is decreased over time with an appropriate schedule.

In this pricing application, the distinction between states and actions is somewhat blurred. It is assumed here that the "state" for each seller is sufficiently described by the other seller's last price, and that the "action" is the current price decision. This should be a sufficient state description because no other history is needed either for the determination of immediate reward, or for the calculation of the myoptimal price by the fixed-strategy player. The definitions of immediate reward r and next-state s' have also been modified for the two-agent case. The next state s' is defined as the state that is obtained, starting from s, of one action by the Q-learner and a response action by the fixed-strategy opponent. Likewise, the immediate reward is defined as the sum of the two rewards obtained after those two actions. These modifications were introduced so that the state s' would have the same player to move as state s. (A possible alternative to this, which was not investigated, is to include the side-to-move as additional information in the state-space description.)

In the simulations reported below, the sequence of state-action pairs selected for the Q-table updates were generated by uniform random selection from amongst all possible table entries. The initial values of the Q-tables were generally set to the immediate reward values. (Consequently the initial Q-derived policies corresponded to myoptimal policies.) The learning rate was varied with time according to:

$$\alpha(t) = \alpha(0)/(1 + \beta t) \tag{6}$$

where the initial learning rate $\alpha(0)$ was usually set to 0.1, and the constant $\beta \sim 0.01$ when the simulation time t was measured in units of N^2, the size of the Q-table. (N is the number of possible prices that could be selected by either player.) A number of different values of the discount parameter γ were studied, ranging from $\gamma = 0$ to $\gamma = 0.9$.

Results for single-agent Q-learning in all three models indicated that Q-learning worked well (as expected) in each case. In each model, for each value of the discount parameter, exact convergence of the Q-table to a stationary optimal solution was found. The convergence times ranged from a few hundred sweeps through each table element, for smaller values of γ, to at most a few thousand updates for the largest values of γ. In addition, the profitability of the converged Q-function's policy was measured by running the Q-policy against the other player's myopic policy from 100 random starting states, each for 200 time steps, and averaging the resulting cumulative profit for each player. It was found that, in each case, the seller achieved greater profit against a myopic opponent by using a Q-derived policy than by using a myopic policy. (This was true even for $\gamma = 0$, because, due to the redefinition of Q updates summing over two time steps, the case $\gamma = 0$ effectively corresponds to a two-step optimization, rather than the one-step optimization of the myopic policies.) Furthermore, the cumulative profit obtained with the Q-derived policy monotonically increased with the increasing γ (as expected).

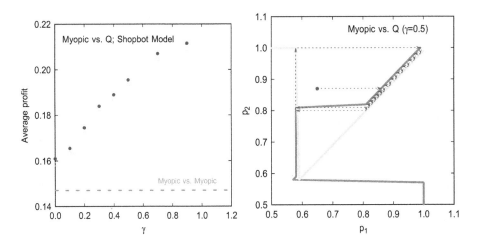

Fig. 2. Results of single-agent Q-learning in the Shopbot model. (a) Average profit per time step for Q-learner (seller 1, filled circles) and myopic seller (seller 2, open circles) vs. discount parameter γ. Dashed line indicates baseline expected profit when both sellers are myopic. (b) Cross-plot of Q-derived price curve (seller 1) vs. myopic price curve (seller 2) at $\gamma = 0.5$. Dashed line and arrows indicate a temporal price-pair trajectory using these policies, starting from filled circle.

It was also interesting to note that in many cases, the expected profit of the myopic opponent also increased when playing against the Q-learner, and also improved monotonically with increasing γ. The explanation is that, rather than better exploiting the myopic opponent, as would be expected in a zero-sum game, the Q-learner instead reduced the region over which it would participate in a mutually undercutting price war. Typically one finds in these models that with myopic vs. myopic play, large-amplitude price wars are generated that start at very high prices and persist all the way down to very low prices. When a Q-learner competes against a myopic opponent, there are still price wars starting at high prices, however, the Q-learner abandons the price war more quickly as the prices decrease. The effect is that the price-war regime is smaller and confined to higher average prices, leading to a closer approximation to cooperative or collusive behavior, with greater expected utilites for both players.

An illustrative example of the results of single-agent Q-learning is shown in figure 2. Figure 2(a) plots the average profit for both sellers in the Shopbot model, when one of the sellers is myopic and the other is a Q-learner. (As the model is symmetric, it doesn't matter which seller is the Q-learner.) Figure 2(b) plots the myopic price curve of seller 2 against the Q-derived price curve (at $\gamma = 0.5$) of seller 1. One can see that both curves have a maximum price of 1 and a minimum price of approximately 0.58. The portion of both curves lying along the diagonal indicates undercutting behavior, in which case the seller will respond to the opponent's price by undercutting by ϵ, the price discretization interval.

Given any initial state (p_1, p_2), the system dynamics in figure 2(b) can be obtained by alternately applying the two pricing policies. This can be done by a simple iterative graphical construction, in which one first holds p_2 constant and moves horizontally to the $p_1(p_2)$ curve, and then one holds p_1 constant and moves vertically to the $p_2(p_1)$ curve. We see in this figure that the iterative graphical construction leads to an unending cyclic price war, whose trajectory is indicated by the dashed line. Note that the price-war behavior begins at the price pair $(1, 1)$, and persists until a price of approximately 0.83. At this point, seller 1 abandons the price war, and resets its price to 1, leading once again to another round of undercutting.

The amplitude of this price war is diminished compared to the situation in which both players use a myopic policy. In that case, seller 1's curve would be a mirror image of seller 2's curve, and the price war would persist all the way to the minimum price point, leading to a lower expected profit for both sellers.

4   Multi-agent Q-Learning

Let us now examine the more interesting and challenging case of simultaneous training of Q-functions and policies for both sellers. The approach is to use the same formalism presented in the previous section, and to alternately adjust a random entry in seller 1's Q-function, followed by a random entry in seller 2's Q-function. As each seller's Q-function evolves, the seller's pricing policy is correspondingly updated so that it optimizes the agent's current Q-function. In modeling the two-step payoff r to a seller in equation 5, the opponent's current policy is used, as implied by its current Q-function. The parameters in the experiments below were generally set to the same values as in the previous section. In most of the experiments, the Q-functions were initialized to the immediate-reward values (so that the policies corresponded to myopic policies), although other initial conditions were explored in a few experiments.

For simultaneous Q-learning in the Price-Quality model, robust convergence to a unique pair of pricing policies is obtained, independent of the value of γ, as illustrated in figure 3(b). This solution also corresponds to the solution found by generalized minimax and by generalized DP in Tesauro and Kephart (2000). Note that repeated application of this pair of price curves leads to a dynamical trajectory that eventually converges to a fixed-point located at $(p_1 = 0.9, p_2 = 0.4)$. A detailed analysis of these pricing policies and the fixed-point solution is presented in Tesauro and Kephart (2000). In brief, for sufficiently low prices of seller 2, it pays seller 1 to abandon the price war and to charge a very high price, $p_1 = 0.9$. The value of $p_2 = 0.4$ then corresponds to the highest price that seller

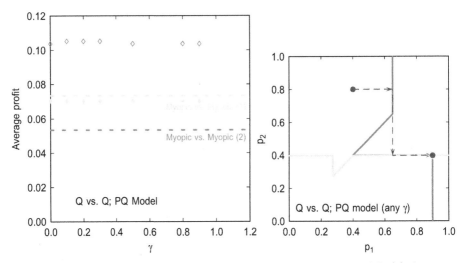

Fig. 3. Results of simultaneous Q-learning in the Price-Quality model. (a) Average profit per time step for seller 1 (solid diamonds) and seller 2 (open diamonds) vs. discount parameter γ. Dashed line indicates baseline myopic vs. myopic expected profit. Note that seller 2's profit is higher than seller 1's, even though seller 2 has a lower quality parameter. (b) Cross-plot of Q-derived price curves (at any γ). Dashed line and arrows indicate a sample price dynamics trajectory, starting from the filled circle. The price war is eliminated and the dynamics evolves to a fixed point indicated by an open circle.

2 can charge without provoking an undercut by seller 1, based on a two-step lookahead calculation (seller 1 undercuts, and then seller 2 replies with a further undercut). Note that this fixed point does not correspond to a (one-shot) Nash equilibrium, since both players have an incentive to deviate, based on a one-step lookahead calculation.

The cumulative profits obtained by the pair of pricing policies are plotted in figure 3(a). It is interesting that seller 2, the lower-quality seller, actually obtains a significantly higher profit than seller 1, the higher-quality seller. In contrast, with myopic vs. myopic pricing, seller 2 does worse than seller 1.

In the Shopbot model, exact convergence of the Q-functions was not found for all values of γ. However, in those cases where exact convergence was not found, there is very good approximate convergence, in which the Q-functions and policies converged to stationary solutions to within small random fluctuations. Different solutions were obtained at each value of γ. Symmetric solutions, in which the shapes of $p_1(p_2)$ and $p_2(p_1)$ are identical, are generally obtained obtained at small γ, whereas a broken symmetry solution, similar to the Price-Quality solution, is obtained at large γ. There is also a range of γ values, between 0.1 and 0.2, where either a symmetric or asymmetric solution could be obtained, depending on initial conditions. The asymmetric solution is counter-intuitive, because one would expect that the symmetry of the two sellers' profit functions would lead to a symmetric solution. In hindsight, one can apply the same type

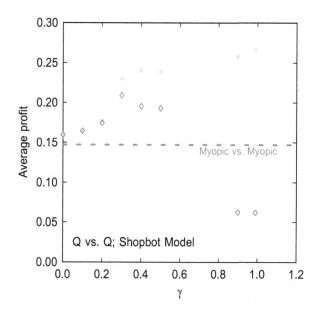

Fig. 4. Average profit per time step obtained by simultaneous Q-learners seller 1 (solid diamonds) and seller 2 (open diamonds) in the Shopbot model, as a function of discount parameter γ. Dashed line indicates baseline myopic vs. myopic expected profit.

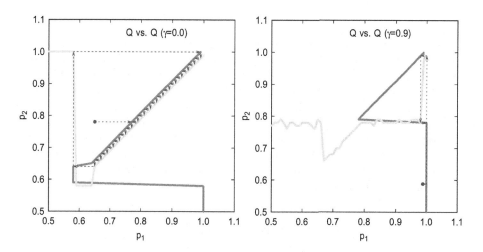

Fig. 5. Cross-plots of Q-derived pricing policies obtained by simultaneous Q-learning in the Shopbot model. (a) Q-derived price curves at $\gamma = 0$; the solution is symmetric. Dashed line and arrows indicate a sample price dynamics trajectory. (b) Q-derived price curves at $\gamma = 0.9$; the solution is asymmetric.

of reasoning as in the Price-Quality model to explain the asymmetric solution. A plot of the expected profit for both sellers as a function of γ is shown in figure 4. Plots of the symmetric and asymmetric solution, obtained at $\gamma = 0$ and $\gamma = 0.9$ respectively, are shown in figure 5.

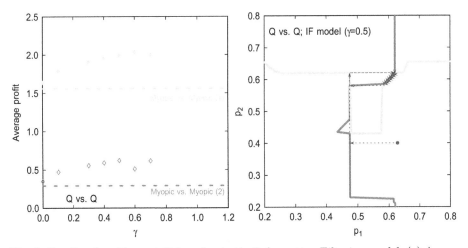

Fig. 6. Results of multi-agent Q-learning in the Information-Filtering model. (a) Average profit per time step for seller 1 (solid diamonds) and seller 2 (open diamonds) vs. discount parameter γ. (The data points at $\gamma = 0.6, 0.7$ represent unconverged Q-functions and policies.) Dashed lines indicates baseline expected profit when both sellers are myopic. (b) Cross-plot of Q-derived price curves at $\gamma = 0.5$.

Finally, in the Information-Filtering model, simultaneous Q-learning produced exact or good approximate convergence only for small values of γ ($0 \leq \gamma \leq 0.5$). For large values of γ, no convergence was obtained. The simultaneous Q-learning solutions yielded reduced-amplitude price wars, and montonically increasing profitability for both sellers as a function of γ, at least up to $\gamma = 0.5$. A few data points were examined at $\gamma > 0.5$, and even though there was no convergence, the Q-policies still yielded greater profit for both sellers than in the myopic vs. myopic case. A plot of the Q-derived policies and system dynamics for $\gamma = 0.5$ is shown in figure 6(b). The expected profits for both players as a function of γ is plotted in figure 6(a).

5   Q-Learning with Neural Networks

Using lookup tables to represent Q-functions as described in the previous two sections can only be feasible for small-scale problems. It is likely that the situations that will be faced by software agents in the real world will be too large-scale and complex to tackle via lookup tables, and that some sort of function approximation scheme will be necessary. This section examines the use of multi-layer neural networks to represent the Q-functions in the same economic models studied previously. Some initial results are presented for the case of a single adaptive QNN (Q-learning neural network) agent, training vs. a fixed-strategy myopic agent, as was described previously in section 3.

The neural networks studied here are multi-layer perceptrons (MLPs) as used in back-propagation. The same Q-learning equation 5 is used as previously, however, the quantity $\Delta Q(s, a)$ is interpreted as the output error signal used in a backprop-style gradient calculation of weight changes. As in the previous sections, the state-action pairs (s, a) are chosen by uniform random exploration, although there is some preliminary evidence that somewhat better policies can be obtained by training on actual trajectories. Also in the experiments below, a fixed learning-rate constant $\alpha = 0.1$ was used, rather than the time-varying schedule $\alpha(t)$ described previously. This appears to give a significant speed increase at the cost of only a slight degradation in final network performance.

One of the most important issues in using neural networks is the design of the input state representation scheme. Schemes that incorporate specialized knowledge of the domain can often do better than naive representation schemes. The only knowledge included here is that it is important for a seller to know whether its price is greater than, less than, or equal to the other seller's price. This suggests a coding scheme using five input units. The first two units represent the two seller prices (p_1, p_2) as real numbers, and the remaining three units are binary units representing the three logical conditions $[p_1 < p_2]$, $[p_1 = p_2]$, and $[p_1 > p_2]$.

In the experiments below, the networks contained a single linear output unit, and a single hidden layer of 10 hidden units, fully connected to the input layer. For the Shopbot model, the network appeared to reach peak profitability within a few hundred sweeps. However, its ability to approximate the correct Q-function after this amount of training was generally poor, with the worst accuracy obtained at large values of γ. Furthermore, the improvement in approximation error with training was extremely slow, and continued to decrease at an extremely slow rate for as long as the training was continued. Typical training runs lasted for several tens of thousands of sweeps through all possible price pairs. In the case of $\gamma = 0$ an extremely long training run of several million sweeps was performed, after which the approximation accuracy was quite good, but the error was still decreasing at a very slow rate.

The difficulty in obtaining accurate function approximation could have resulted from inaccurate targets $\Delta Q(s, a)$ used in training, or it could be due to intrinsic limitations in the function approximator itself. In a separate series of experiments, neural nets were trained with exact targets provided by the lookup tables, and this yielded no measurable advantage in approximation accuracy, suggesting that the problem is not due to inaccurate heuristic teacher signals in equation 5.

During the neural net training runs, the expected performance of the neural net policy was periodically measured vs. the myopic opponent. While the absolute error in the Q-function improved monotonically, the policy's expected profit was found to reach a peak relatively quickly (usually withing 100-200 sweeps, but longer for large γ) and then either level off or decrease slightly. A plot of the peak expected profit for each training run as a function of γ is shown in figure 8. For comparison, the expected profit of the exact optimal policy, obtained by lookup table Q-learning, is also plotted. It is encouraging to note that, although the absolute accuracy of the neural net Q-function is poor and improves extremely slowly, the resulting policies nevertheless give reasonably decent performance and can be trained relatively quickly. This once again re-emphasizes a point found in other successful applications of neural nets and reinforcement learning: the neural net approach can often give a surprisingly strong policy, even though the absolute accuracy of the value function is poor.

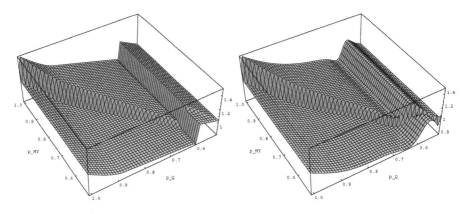

Fig. 7. Plot of the Q-function for single-agent Q-learning vs. a myopic opponent in the Shopbot model at $\gamma = 0.7$. p_Q is the Q-learner's price and p_MY is the myopic player's price. (a) Exact optimal Q-function obtained by lookup table Q-learning. (b) Neural network approximation to the Q-function.

An illustration of the quality of neural net function approximation compared to an exact lookup table solution is shown in figure 7. (This network was trained for 50,000 sweeps through all possible price pairs, and displays significantly better function approximation than at the point where peak profitability is first reached.) We can see that the neural net approximates the flat and smoothly curving portions of the landscape quite well. It also correctly fits the diagonal discontinuity along the undercutting line $p_Q < p_{MY}$, primarily due to knowledge engineering of an additional input feature to represent this discontinuity. However, the neural net fits poorly the second discontinuity in the low p_Q regime; this results in a suboptimal policy.

Results of simultaneous Q-learning in the Shopbot model are plotted in figure 9. These runs appear to reach peak performance after a few thousand sweeps. With further training, the approximation error continues to decrease slowly, but no improvement in policy strength is observable. Note that the average profit in figure 9 compares quite favorably with figure 4. The Q-derived policies for

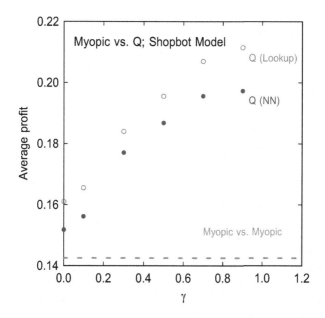

Fig. 8. Plot of expected profit for a single Q-learning agent, training against a fixed myopic opponent, in the Shopbot model, as a function of γ. Filled circles represent a neural network Q-learner, while open circles represent a lookup table Q-learner. Each data point represents the best policy obtained during a training run. By comparison, the baseline myopic vs. myopic expected profit is indicated by the dashed line.

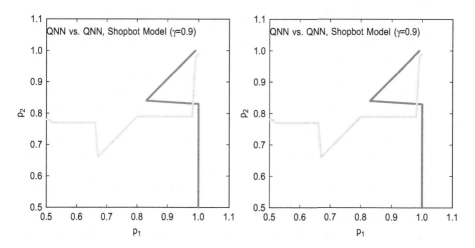

Fig. 9. Results of simultaneous neural network Q-learning in the Shopbot model. (a) Average profit per time step for seller 1 (solid diamonds) and seller 2 (open diamonds) vs. discount parameter γ. Dashed line indicates baseline myopic vs. myopic expected profit. (b) Cross-plot of Q-derived price curves at $\gamma = 0.9$.

$\gamma = 0.9$ in figure 9 have roughly the same qualitative shape as the curves in figure 5 based on lookup tables. Preliminary results for the Information-Filtering also demonstrate the same qualitative relationship between neural net policies and lookup table policies. (These networks only had 5 hidden units; it seems likely that significant improvements could be obtained by increasing the number of hidden units.)

6 Summary

This chapter has examined single-agent and multi-agent Q-learning in three models of a two-seller economy in which the sellers alternately take turns setting prices, and then instantaneous utilities are given to both sellers based on the current price pair. Such models fall into the category of two-player, alternating-turn, arbitrary-sum Markov games, in which both the rewards and the state-space transitions are deterministic. The game is Markov because the state space is fully observable and the rewards are not history dependent.

In all three models (Price-Quality, Information-Filtering, and Shopbot), large-amplitude cyclic price wars are obtained when the sellers myopically optimize their instantaneous utilities without regard to longer-term impact of their pricing policies. It is found that, in all three models, the use of Q-learning by one of the sellers against a myopic opponent invariably results in exact convergence to the optimal Q-function and optimal policy against that opponent, for all allowed values of the discount parameter γ. The use of the Q-derived policy yields greater expected profit for the Q-learner, with monotonically increasing profit as γ increases. In many cases, it has a side benefit of enhancing social welfare by also giving greater expected profit for the myopic opponent. This comes about by reducing the amplitude of the undercutting price-war regime, or in some cases, eliminating it completely.

The more interesting and challenging situation of simultaneously training Q-functions for both sellers has also been studied. This is more difficult because as each seller's Q-function and policy change, it provides a non-stationary environment for adaptation of the other seller. No convergence proofs exist for such simultaneous Q-learning by multiple agents. Nevertheless, despite the absence of theoretical guarantees, generally good behavior of the algorithm was found. In two of the models (Shopbot and Price-Quality), exact or very good approximate convergence was obtained to simultaneously self-consistent Q-functions and optimal policies for any value of γ, whereas in the Information-Filtering model, simultaneous convergence was found for $\gamma \leq 0.5$. In the Information-Filtering and Shopbot models, monotonically increasing expected utilities for both sellers were also found for small values of γ. In the Price-Quality model, simultaneous Q-learning yields an asymmetric solution, corresponding to the solution found in Tesauro and Kephart (2000), that is highly advantageous to the lesser-quality seller, but slightly disadvantageous to the higher-quality seller, when compared to myopic vs. myopic pricing. A similar asymmetric solution is also found in the

Shopbot model for large γ, even though the profit functions for both players are symmetric.

For each model, there exists a range of discount parameter values where the solutions obtained by simultaneous Q-learning are self-consistently optimal, and outperform the solutions obtained in Tesauro and Kephart (2000). This is presumably because the previously published methods were based on limited lookahead, whereas the Q-functions in principle look ahead infinitely far, with appropriate discounting.

It is intruiging that simultaneous Q-learning works well in these models, despite the lack of theoretical convergence proofs. Sandholm and Crites also found that simultaneous Q-learning generally converged in the Iterated Prisoner's Dilemma game. These empirical findings suggest that a deeper theoretical analysis of simultaneous Q-learning may be worth investigating. There may be some underlying theoretical principles that can explain why simultaneous Q-learning works, for at least certain classes of arbitrary-sum utility functions.

Some initial steps have also been taken in combining nonlinear function approximation, using neural nets, with the Q-learning approach. It was found that a single neural net Q-learner facing a myopic opponent can exhibit reasonably good pricing policies, despite difficulties in obtaining an accurate approximation to the Q-function. Two neural networks performing simultaneous Q-learning were also able to obtain pricing policies that match the qualitative characteristics of lookup table policies, and with profitabilities close to the lookup table results.

In addition to replacing lookup tables with function approximators, several other important challenges will also be faced in extending this approach to larger-scale, more realistic simulations. First, the three economic models used here quite deliberately ignored frictional effects such as agent search costs. Such effects can damp out price wars, and can lead to different system behaviors such as partial equilibria that support stable price differentiation. Eventually such frictional effects will have to be considered, although it has been argued in prior studies of these models (Sairamesh and Kephart, 1998; Kephart, Hanson and Sairamesh, 1998; Greenwald and Kephart, 1999) that frictional effects in Web-based agent economies will be considerably smaller than in traditional human economies. Also, with many sellers, the concept of sellers taking turns adjusting their prices in a well-defined order becomes problematic. This could lead to an additional combinatorial explosion, if the mechanism for calculating expected reward has to anticipate all possible orderings of opponent responses.

Furthermore, while these economic models have a moderate degree of realism in their profit functions, they are unrealistic in the assumptions of knowledge and dynamics. In the work reported here, the state space was fully observable infinitely frequently at zero cost and with zero propagation delays. The expected consumer response to a given price pair was instantaneous, deterministic and fully known to both players. Indeed, the players' exact profit functions were fully known to both players. It was also assumed that the players would alternately take turns equally often in a well-defined order in adjusting their prices.

Under such assumptions of knowledge and dynamics, one could hope to develop an algorithm that could calculate in advance something like a game-theoretic optimal pricing algorithm for each agent.

However, in realistic agent economies, it is likely that agents will have much less than full knowledge of the state of the economy. Agents may not know the details of other agents' profit functions, and indeed an agent may not know its own profit function, to the extent that buyer behavior is unpredictable. The dynamics of buyers and sellers may also be more complex, random and unpredictable than what assumed here. There may also be information delays for both buyers and sellers, and part of the economic game may involve paying a cost in order to obtain information about the state of the economy faster and more frequently, and in greater detail. Finally, one may expect that buyer behavior will be non-stationary, so that there will be a more complex co-evolution of buyer and seller strategies.

While such real-world complexities are daunting, there are reasons to believe that learning approaches such as Q-learning may play a role in practical solutions. The advantage of Q-learning is that one does not need a model of either the instantaneous payoffs or of the state-space transitions in the environment. One can simply observe actual rewards and transitions and base learning on that. While the theory of Q-learning requires exhaustive exploration of the state space to guarantee convergence, this may not be necessary when function approximators are used. In that case, after training a function approximator on a relatively small number of observed states, it may then generalize well enough on the unobserved states to give decent practical performance. Several recent empirical studies have provided evidence of this (Tesauro, 1995; Crites and Barto, 1996; Zhang and Dietterich, 1996).

Acknowledgements. The author thanks Jeff Kephart and Amy Greenwald for helpful discussions.

References

R. H. Crites and A. G. Barto, (1996). "Improving elevator performance using reinforcement learning." In: D. Touretzky et al., eds., Advances in Neural Information Processing Systems 8, 1017-1023, MIT Press.

A. Greenwald and J. O. Kephart, (1999). "Shopbots and pricebots." Proceedings of IJCAI-99, 506-511.

J. Hu and M. P. Wellman, (1996). "Self-fulfilling bias in multiagent learning." Proceedings of ICMAS-96, AAAI Press.

J. Hu and M. P. Wellman, (1998). "Multiagent reinforcement learning: theoretical framework and an algorithm." Proceedings of ICML-98, Morgan Kaufmann.

J. O. Kephart, J. E. Hanson and J. Sairamesh, (1998). "Price-war dynamics in a free-market economy of software agents." In: Proceedings of ALIFE-VI, Los Angeles.

D. Kreps, (1990). *A Course in Microeconomic Theory*. Princeton NJ: Princeton University Press.

M. L. Littman, (1994). "Markov games as a framework for multi-agent reinforcement learning," Proceedings of the Eleventh International Conference on Machine Learning, 157–163, Morgan Kaufmann.

J. Sairamesh and J. O. Kephart, (1998). "Dynamics of price and quality differentiation in information and computational markets." Proceedings of the First International Conference on Information and Computation Economics (ICE-98), 28–36, ACM Press.

T. W. Sandholm and R. H. Crites, (1995). "On multiagent Q-Learning in a semi-competitive domain." 14th International Joint Conference on Artificial Intelligence (IJCAI-95), Workshop on Adaptation and Learning in Multiagent Systems, Montreal, Canada, 71–77.

P. Stone and M. Veloso, (1999). "Team-partitioned, opaque-transition reinforcement learning." *Proceedings of the Third International Conference on Autonomous Agents*, 206–212. New York: ACM Press.

G. Tesauro, (1995). "Temporal difference learning and TD-Gammon." *Comm. of the ACM*, **38:3**, 58–67.

G. J. Tesauro and J. O. Kephart, (2000). "Foresight-based pricing algorithms in agent economies." *Decision Support Sciences*, to appear.

J. M. Vidal and E. H. Durfee, (1998). "Learning nested agent models in an information economy," *J. of Experimental and Theoretical AI*, **10(3)**, 291-308.

C. J. C. H. Watkins, (1989). "Learning from delayed rewards." Doctoral dissertation, Cambridge University.

C. J. C. H. Watkins and P. Dayan, (1992). "Q-learning." *Machine Learning* **8**, 279–292.

W. Zhang and T. G. Dietterich, (1996). "High-performance job-shop scheduling with a time-delay TD(λ) network." In: D. Touretzky et al., eds., Advances in Neural Information Processing Systems 8, 1024-1030, MIT Press.

Multiple Forward Model Architecture for Sequence Processing

Raju S. Bapi[1,3] and Kenji Doya[2,3]

[1] Dept. of Computer & Information Sciences, University of Hyderabad
[2] CREST, Japan Science and Technology Corporation
[3] Kawato Dynamic Brain Project, ERATO, JST

1   Introduction

Serial order is an important aspect of human and animal behavior and continues to receive attention. In spite of research over many years, it is not yet completely understood how the brain solves the serial order of motor behavior problem (Rosenbaum 10). However, in recent years there has been rapid progress in the domain of sequence processsing both in the neuroscience literature (electrophysiology on animals and imaging studies on humans) and in computational learning literature.

In the sequence learning literature, various researchers used neural networks (for example, Bapi & Doya 1, Dominey 2, Elman 3, etc.) to learn multiple sequences. Problems with such approaches are long training times and catastrophic forgetting. Recently, Wolpert and Kawato (16) proposed multiple paired forward-inverse models architecture for human motor learning and successfully applied it to the problem of manipulation of multiple objects (Haruno et al. 4). They argued that such paired models enable learning and retrieval of the appropriate models based on environmental context and facilitate smooth interpolation for generalization. These models also avoid the catastrophic forgetting problem since simulations demonstrate that the model switching is robust (Haruno *et al.* 4). In the current work we extend this approach to sequence learning. We propose a multiple forward model (MFM) architecture for sequence processing. The key idea is that sequence learning and switching is based on prediction errors. After introducing the details of the proposed architecture, we will review the experimental findings of Tanji and Shima (15) on monkeys. The aim of the current work is to take these experimental results as an example case and test the proposed MFM architecture.

2   MFM Architecture

A forward model is defined as one that predicts the response output $y(t+1)$, given the inputs $x(t)$ to the system. In the sequence processing context, a forward model predicts the next action $y(t+1)$, given the previous response $y(t)$. Figure 1 shows the MFM architecture.

R. Sun and C.L. Giles (Eds.): Sequence Learning, LNAI 1828, pp. 308–320, 2000.

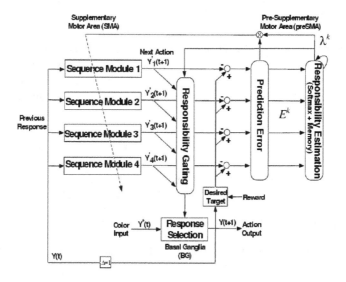

Fig. 1. Neural Network Architecture

In the following we describe the processing steps in order. Firstly, the network is presented with the the previous response $y(t)$. Each of the *Sequence Modules* predicts the next action $y^k(t + 1)$ based on the previous response. These predictions are gated by the responsibility factors λ^k in the *Responsibility Gating* module to generate a predicted response. The *Response Selection* module combines the predicted response with the input to generate the actual action output $y(t + 1)$. Errors resulting from the comparison of the desired target to the predicted response of each module are sent to the *Prediction Error* module. *ResponsibilityEstimation* module transforms the prediction errors into responsibility factors λ^k. λ^k signify the relative appropriateness of modules in the current context and drive hebbian learning in the sequence modules. The above processing steps are repeated till the sequence switching becomes stable. We now present the detailed equations.

2.1 Sequence Module Output

Each sequence module k predicts the next action $\hat{y}^k(t+1)$ based on the previous response $y(t)$.

$$\hat{y}_j^k(t + 1) = f \left(\sum_i w_{ji}^k(t) y_i(t) \right) \tag{1}$$

2.2   Response Selection

The predicted response is used in two ways. Firstly, it is used to generate the actual action output $y_j(t+1)$. Predicted response from each sequence module $\hat{y}^k(t)$ is gated by the corresponding responsibility factor $\lambda^k(t)$ and the final output is chosen by $g(\cdot)$, either the maximum function or a suitable stochastic function.

$$y_j(t+1) = g\left(\sum_{k=1} \lambda^k(t)\hat{y}_j^k(t)\right) \tag{2}$$

2.3   Responsibility Estimation

The second use of the predicted responses is to calculate the responsibility factors.

Prediction Error The prediction error $E^k(t)$ of each module is calculated based on the predicted response $\hat{y}_j^k(t)$ and the desired target $y_j^{\star\star}(t)$.

$$error_j^k(t) = (y_j^{\star\star}(t) - \hat{y}_j^k(t)) \tag{3}$$

$$E^k(t) = \frac{1}{2}\sum_j \left(error_j^k(t)\right)^2 \tag{4}$$

Responsibility We assume that the probability $p^k(t)$ of the kth module being the appropriate predictor is proportional to the exponential of the error $E^k(t)$ with a scaling factor $\sigma(t)$.

$$p^k(t) = \epsilon e^{\frac{-E^k(t)}{\sigma(t)^2}} \tag{5}$$

The responsibility estimation module keeps a memory of the previous $p^k(t-\delta)$ values, where $\delta = 0,...,\Delta$. Responsibility factor $\lambda^k(t)$ is then calculated by normalizing the product of all the probabilities.

$$\lambda^k(t) = \frac{\prod_{\delta=0}^{\Delta} p^k(t-\delta)}{\sum_i \prod_{\delta=0}^{\Delta} p^i(t-\delta)} \tag{6}$$

The combination of using the exponential function and normalization amounts to using a softmax operation in the responsibility estimation. The use of past probability values ensures that modules are not switched around wildly.

2.4   Learning in the Sequence Modules

Hebbian learning in the sequence modules is gated by the responsibility factor. Thus at any time, the module that predicts the best learns the most. Although in the current formulation the forward models work as one-step-ahead predictors, they can be designed as more general predictors with longer sequential context.

$$w_{ji}^k(t+1) = w_{ji}^k(t) + \eta \lambda^k error_j^k(t) \cdot$$
$$\hat{y}_j^k(t)(1 - \hat{y}_j^k(t))y_i(t-1) \tag{7}$$

In the next section we present the details of the experiments of Tanji and Shima on monkeys. The specific equations used to reproduce the results of Tanji and Shima are given in the Appendix. The subsequent section presents the simulation results.

3   Studies on Monkeys

Tanji and colleagues devised a sequence learning paradigm and made single cell electrode recordings in behaving monkeys while they performed sequential arm movements. The recordings have been made in various areas in the anteriror part of the neocortex, including the supplementary motor area (SMA), the pre-supplementary motor area (preSMA), the premotor cortex (PM), and the motor cortex (MI). All these areas are hypothesized to be participating in the learning and/or execution of the external-input-driven and/or internally-generated sequential motor acts (Tanji 14). After describing the experimental setup, a summary of results from various experiments will be given below.

3.1   Experimental Details

Monkeys were initially trained to respond with a push, pull or turn movement on a handle when presented with a red, yellow, or green color light, respectively, on a display panel. After establishing the color-to-action mapping, they were required to sequence these elementary actions by observing a succession of color lights and recalling the appropriate movement at every step. In this manuscript we will refer to the four sequences as I:123, II:132, III:321, and IV:312. The trials when color lights preceded movements were called, 'Visual Trials (VT)' and the other trials when there were no colored lights were called 'Memory Trials (MT)'. In a block of trials, monkeys experienced 5 VT followed by 6 MT. They were taught four such sequences till they achieved 95% success rate on each sequence. After this stage, single cell recordings were made while monkeys performed several blocks of trials. Each block used a different sequence and the order of appearance of different sequences varied semi-randomly. The end of a block is signaled by random flashing of lights which also indicated a change in the sequence.

3.2   Experimental Results

In the present study, we focus on the results of single unit recordings in SMA and PreSMA. SMA recordings (Tanji & Shima 15) revealed a significant activation exhibiting two main properties: i) *sequence-specific activity*: activity of some cells preceded specifically before the performance of a particular sequence (say, Turn-Pull-Push) and ii) *transition-specific activity*: some cells were tonically active after performing a specific movement and before initiating a particular next movement (say, Push followed by Pull). In contrast, the activity of majority of cells in the MI was selective to single movements but not sequence-specific. While SMA cells were mainly active in the MT phase, cells in PM were active only during the VT phase and cells in MI were active during all phases of the task. Some cells in preSMA were active only during the very first VT, possibly signifying the start of a new sequence and thus specifying the need for a change in motor plan (Shima *et al.* 11). In this article learning of sequence and transition specificity is demonstrated using MFM architecture.

4   Simulation Results

Detailed equations used in the simulations are shown in the Appendix. Each sequence is presented to the network successively for 5 blocks. All the four sequences are shown to the network, the order of presentation being randomized. Each block consists of 5 VT followed by 6 MT as in the monkey experiments. During the VT, the network has access to the desired target and hence the learning progresses in a supervised fashion. In the current simulations, during the VT period we assume that the appropriate (colored) light-to-movement mapping has already been established and thus the network performs at 100% accuracy. However, during the MT the desired output is not available and is calculated based on the reward. For example, if the predicted response is incorrect, then the desired target is set as the opposite of the actual response (for example, 110 for 001). Thus the learning during the MT progresses in a semi-supervised fashion.

4.1   Long Term Behavior of the Network

Simulation results for 132 blocks are shown in Figure 2. The top row shows the randomized presentation of all the four sequences during the simulations. The second and third rows show how the responsibility factor λ varies as sequences are learnt during the last visual and memory trials, denoted as λ-VT5 and λ-MT6 respectively. The bottom row shows the number of steps performed correctly (performance accuracy) in the last memory trail (MT6) as simulations progressed. It can be observed that as the switching became stable, the performance accuracy also improved. For example, although Module 3 initially captured both Sequence I (123) and Sequence II (132), specialization for Sequence II (132) developed by 20th block and stayed stable since then. More details are shown in later figures below.

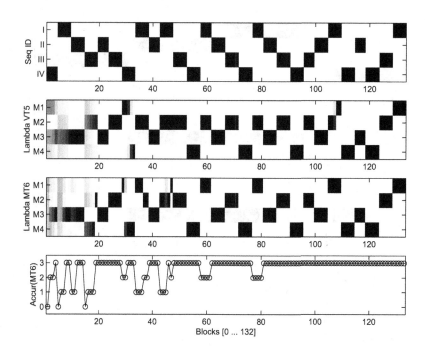

Fig. 2. Results for all the blocks are shown. Legend: Modules – M1 : Module 1; M2 : Module 2; M3 : Module 3; M4 : Module 4; Sequence IDs – I : 123, II : 132, III : 321, IV : 312

For clarity, various snapshots during the intermediate blocks are shown in Figures 3, 4 and 5. Figure 3 shows that the performance in the early blocks is erratic and that Module 3 is active during the presentation of Sequences IV, I, and II in the 6th memory trial (see the graph on the third row – λ-MT6).

By the 30th block in Figure 4, we see that Sequences II and III are represented by Modules 3 and 2, respectively and that for Sequences IV and I switching is not yet stable. However, by the end of the simulation the switching became stable and specialized (SeqI:M1, SeqII:M3, SeqIII:M2, SeqIV:M4) as shown in Figure 5.

4.2   Short Term Behavior of the Network

Short term behavior of the network during single blocks (Block 38 and 132) is shown in Figures 6 and 7. Sequence I is presented to the network during both these blocks. During the early stages the network did not arrive at a stable switching solution for Sequence I. As shown in Figure 6, the network locked into an incorrect module (Module number 3 which represents Sequence II) by the end of the 5th VT and as a consequence there are significant number of errors of recall during the subsequent 6 MTs. In comparison, after extensive training

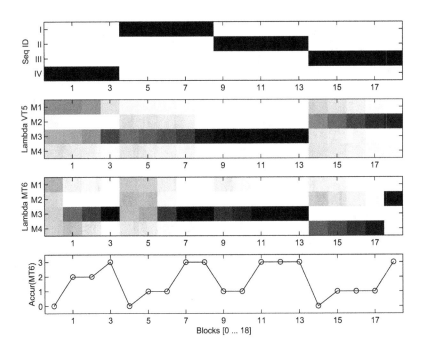

Fig. 3. Results from blocks 0-18 are shown. Legends as in Figure 2.

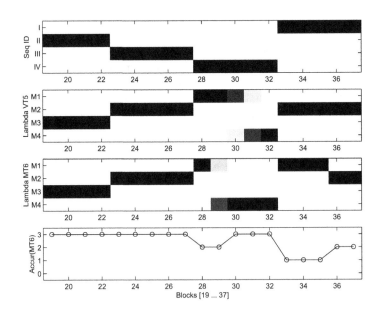

Fig. 4. Results of Blocks 19-37 are shown. Legends as in Figure 2.

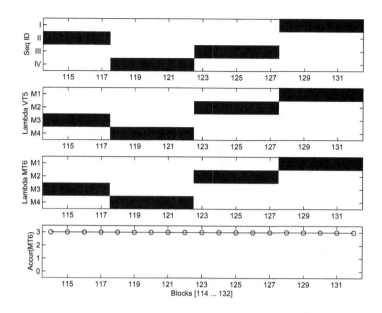

Fig. 5. Results of Blocks 114-132 are shown. Legends as in Figure 2.

(by block 132 as shown in Figure 7), Module 1 specialized in Sequence I and the recall was accurate during all of the MTs.

4.3   Discussion of Results

Thus the learning of sequence specificity and stable switching among learned sequences is achieved by this architecture. Each module learns the sequence transitions appropriate to the sequence that the module specializes in. For example, Module 1 learns the transitions 1-to-2 and 2-to-3. In the current formulation, sequence specificity in the modules arises as a result of learning the appropriate transitions.

Although sequence and transition specificity are demonstrated, detailed comparison between the results of monkey experiments and the simulations is left as future work.

5   Summary

Here we put forward some preliminary hypotheses about the brain areas whose functionality is captured in the MFM architecture (also indicated in Figure 1): *SequenceModules* mimic the function of the SMA, the *Responsibility Estimation* may take place in the preSMA. One of the roles attributed to the basal ganglia is context dependent response selection (Houk et al. 5) and this aspect is attributed to the *ResponseSelection* module in the proposed architecture.

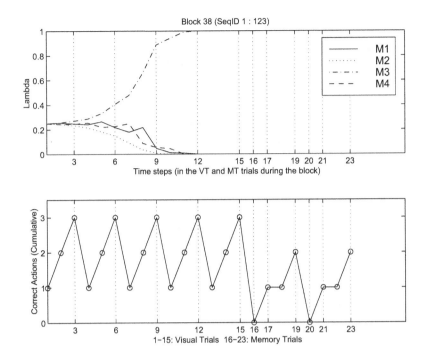

Fig. 6. Detailed Results of 38th block are shown.

In the current simulations, complex sequence learning, where the individual elements of a sequence may be repeating, is not demonstrated. A more general approach would be to use recurrent networks for sequence modules in place of purely feed-forward networks. Simulations of the general version are in progress.

The notion of modularity and its usefulness in solving complex problems by decomposing them into sub problems has been addressed in several previous studies (for example, Jacobs et al. 6; Sun & Peterson 12). Hierarchical organization of the modules is also studied (for example, Jordan & Jacobs 7; Parr & Russell 8; Precup & Sutton 9; Tani & Nolfi 13). The architecture studied here also falls in the general framework of the previous studies. However we pursue the idea of hierarchical mixture of experts with a goal to studying them as functional models of sequential planning in biological systems. Although the current architecture consists only of one level, the concept can be extended to multiple levels of hierarchy. In such a hierarchical system, module switching at any level will be affected not only by the the responsibility esitmations at the current level but also by the values at the other levels. In one such formulation, a network can be set up such that the sequential context encoded at each level increases as one moves up the hierarchy. Hierarchical networks are of immense use in the domains of natural language processing and sequential planning.

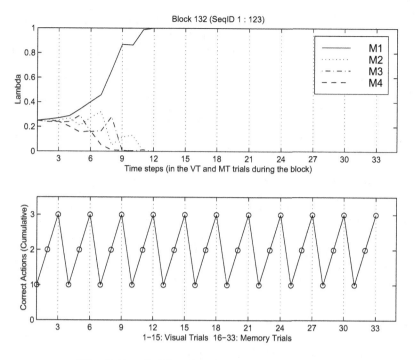

Fig. 7. Detailed Results of 132nd block are shown.

References

R. S. Bapi and K. Doya, (1998). A sequence learning architecture based on cortico-basal ganglionic loops and reinforcement learning. In *Proceedings of the 5th International Conference on Neural Information Processing*, 1, 260–263.

P. F. Dominey, (1995). Complex sensory-motor sequence learning based on recurrent state representation and reinforcement learning. *Biological Cybernetics*, 73, 265–274.

J. Elman, (1990). Finding structure in time. *Cognitive Science*, 14, 179–211.

M. Haruno, D. M. Wolpert, and M. Kawato, (1999). Multiple paired forward-inverse models for human motor learning and control. In M. J. Kearns, S. A. Solla, and D. A. Cohen (Eds.), *Advances in Neural Information Processing Systems*, 11, MIT Press, Cambridge, MA, USA, pp. 31–37.

J. C. Houk, J. L. Davis, and D. G. Beiser, editors, (1995). *Models of information processing in the basal ganglia*. MIT Press, Cambridge, MA, USA.

R. A. Jacobs, M. I. Jordan, S. J. Nowlan, and G. E. Hinton, (1991). Adaptive mixtures of local experts. *Neural Computation*, 3, 79–87.

M. I. Jordan and R. A. Jacobs (1994). Hierarchiacal mixtures of experts and the EM algorithm. *Neural Computation*, 6, 181–214.

R. Parr and S. Russell, (1998). Reinforcement learning with hierarchies of machines. In M. I. Jordan, M. J. Kearns and S. A. Solla (Eds.), *Advances in Neural Information Processing Systems*, 10, MIT Press, Cambridge, MA, USA, pp. 1043–1049.

D. Precup and R. S. Sutton, (1998). Multi-time models for temporally abstract planning. In M. I. Jordan, M. J. Kearns and S. A. Solla (Eds.), *Advances in Neural Information Processing Systems*, 10, MIT Press, Cambridge, MA, USA, pp. 1050–1056.

D. A. Rosenbaum, (1991). *Human Motor Control*. Academic Press, San Diego, CA, USA.

K. Shima, H. Mushiake, N. Saito, and J. Tanji, (1996). Role for cells in the presupplementary motor area in updating motor plans. *Proceedings of the National Academy of Science USA*, 93, 8694–8698.

R. Sun and T. Peterson, (1999). Multi-agent reinforcement learning: weighting and partitioning. *Neural Networks*, 12, 727–753.

J. Tani and S. Nolfi, (1999). Learning to perceive the world as articulated: an approach for hierarchical learning of sensory-motor systems . *Neural Networks*, 12, 1131–1141.

J. Tanji, (1994). The supplementary motor area in the cerebral cortex. *Neuroscience Research*, 19, 251–268.

J. Tanji and K. Shima, (1994). Role for supplementary motor area cells in planning several movements ahead. *Nature*, 371, 29, 413–416.

D. M. Wolpert and M. Kawato, (1998). Multiple paired forward and inverse models for motor control. *Neural Networks*, 11, 1317–1329.

Appendix A – Equations

A.1 k^{th} Forward Sequence Model Output

$$\hat{y}_j^k(t+1) = f\left(\sum_{i=0}^{4} w_{ji}^k(t)y_i(t)\right);$$

$$\text{where, } j = 1, 2, 3 \text{ (Action Ouputs)}$$
$$k = 1, 2, 3, 4 \text{ (Modules / Sequences)}$$
$$i = 0, 1, 2, 3, 4 \text{ (Inputs)}$$

$$y_i(0) = \begin{cases} 1 \ i = 0 \text{ (Bias node)} \\ 0 \ i = 1, 2, 3 \\ 1 \ i = 4 \text{ (Ready node)} \end{cases}$$

$$y_i(t) = \begin{cases} 1 & i = 0 \\ \{0, 1\} \ i = 1, 2, 3 \text{ (Previous Response)} \\ 0 & i = 4 \end{cases}$$

$$\hat{y}_j^k(t+1) \in (0, 1); \text{ (Module Output)}$$

$$f(x) = \frac{1}{1 + e^{-4x}}; \text{ (Sigmoid Function)}$$

A.2 Response Selection

$$y_j(t+1) = \begin{cases} 1 \; j = m \\ 0 \; j \neq m \end{cases}$$

where,

$$m = max_j \left(y_j^\star(t) + \sum_{k=1}^{4} \lambda^k(t) \hat{y}_j^k(t) \right);$$

$$y_j^\star(t) = \begin{cases} \text{Desired Target} & \text{in VT} \\ 0 & \text{in MT} \end{cases}$$

$$j = 1, 2, 3$$

A.3 Responsibility Estimation

A.3.1 Prediction Error

$$error_j^k(t) = (y_j^{\star\star}(t) - \hat{y}_j^k(t))$$

$$y_j^{\star\star}(t) = \begin{cases} y_j(t) & \text{if Correct Trial} \\ 1 - y_j(t) & \text{if Error Trial} \end{cases}$$

$$E^k(t) = \frac{1}{2} \sum_j \left(error_j^k(t) \right)^2$$

A.3.2 Responsibility

$$p^k(t) = e^{\frac{-E^k(t)}{\sigma(t)^2}}$$

$$\lambda^k(t) = \frac{\prod_{\delta=0}^{3} p^k(t - \delta)}{\sum_{i=1}^{4} \prod_{\delta=0}^{3} p^i(t - \delta)}$$

$$\sigma(t+1) = \alpha\sigma(t) + (1 - \alpha)\frac{1}{\Delta} \sum_{\delta=0}^{\Delta} min \left[E^k(\delta) \right]$$

$$\text{where, } p^k(t) = \frac{1}{4}; t \leq 0, k = 1, 2, 3, 4$$

$$\sigma(0) = 3$$

Note 1: The scaling factor keeps a running average of the best prediction error and thus ensures that the responsibility is not locked onto one module prematurely.

Note 2: p and σ values are reset at the beginning of every block of 11 trials (6 visual and 5 memory). Whereas, all other variables are reset at the beginning of every trial.

A.4 Weight Update in the kth Forward Sequence Model

$$w_{ji}^k(t+1) = w_{ji}^k(t) + \eta\lambda^k error_j^k(t)\hat{y}_j^k(t)(1 - \hat{y}_j^k(t))y_i(t-1)$$

$$w_{ji}^k(0) \in (0,1)(\text{Uniformly distributed random values})$$

Integration of Biologically Inspired Temporal Mechanisms into a Cortical Framework for Sequence Processing

Hervé Frezza-Buet[1], Nicolas Rougier[2], and Frédéric Alexandre[2]

[1] Supélec,
France
[2] Loria,
France

1 Introduction

Time is an important dimension in many real-world problems. This is particularly true for behavioral tasks where the temporal factor is critical. Consider for example the analysis of a perceptual scene or the organization of behavior in a planning task. Temporal problems are often solved using temporal techniques like Markovian Models or Dynamic Time Warping. Classical connectionist models are powerful for pattern matching tasks but exhibit some weaknesses in dealing with dynamic tasks involving the temporal dimension. Thus, they are efficient for off-line statistical data processing, but must be adapted for situated tasks which are intrinsically temporal.

This adaptation can correspond to the coupling of connectionist models with classical temporal techniques, thus yielding hybrid models (Sun and Alexandre 1997). It can also correspond to the design of new connectionist architectures with specific abilities for temporal processing. We have proposed in the past a classification for temporal connectionist architectures (Durand and Alexandre 1996). Following this classification, these networks can be described according to the way time is represented within the architecture.

Architectures with an *external* representation of time correspond to classical neural networks like multilayer perceptrons in which only the input space is modified to include the temporal dimension and some specific mechanisms are added. The Time Delay Neural Network (TDNN) is a typical example of this kind of system. This model was introduced by (Waibel et al. 1989) to learn and recognize phonemes in automatic speech recognition tasks. The input space is a window on a spectral representation of speech with frequency and time axes, and a mechanism of weight sharing ensures invariance of position in time. Apart from that, the general architecture of a TDNN is a classical multilayer perceptron learning with a backpropagation algorithm. Models with such an external representation suffer from serious limitations because time is considered as a dimension similar to other spatial or physical dimensions.

Architectures with an *internal* representation of time are specific architectures designed for the purpose of dynamic information processing and are thus not

R. Sun and C.L. Giles (Eds.): Sequence Learning, LNAI 1828, pp. 321–348, 2000.

classical architectures with an adapted input space. The internal representation of time in these architectures can be built either in an implicit or an explicit way.

Concerning the *implicit* method, typical architectures are recurrent neural networks (Pearlmutter 1990), that manage time via the succession of their internal steady states. In this case, the current output is obtained as a function of the current input state and of the context, obtained from a copy of the previous internal state of the network (Elman 1990). This representation is called implicit because the succession of events only appears implicitly, through the context layer.

On the contrary, the *explicit* method for the internal representation of time clearly implements time through sequences of events that can be detected directly inside the network. Close to Markovian principles, these architectures include units that represent events, and links that represent transition probabilities between these events, thus yielding explicit sequence representations within the network. Models using this strategy of representation are often (but not always (Béroule 1990)) inspired by cortical functioning, either for memory mechanisms (Ans et al 1994) or for more general sensorimotor tasks (Alexandre 1996). Here the main problem is to design learning rules for establishing these temporal links and to integrate the latter with other classical spatial links.

The biological validity of these various strategies for time representation inside neural networks has been discussed elsewhere (Durand and Alexandre 1996). We just mention here that the external strategy could correspond to the processing of temporal sensory input like auditory input (Suga 1990), the internal implicit strategy could correspond to the highest levels of time integration (Dominey et al. 1995), (Elman 1990) and the internal explicit strategy could correspond to some biological models of cortical functioning (Burnod 1989). Many neurobiologically plausible mechanisms of time processing have been proposed in the past. They are generally using an internal representation of time. Some of the most typical will be reviewed in section 2.

Beyond this local view on specific temporal mechanisms, the goal of this chapter is to emphasize the idea of integrating these mechanisms into a more general framework, allowing a better exploitation and articulation between them. As will be discussed in section 3, the cerebral cortex may be seen as a set of functionally and architecturally different modules, each devoted to specific aspects of time processing. Building modular architectures gathering and coupling these abilities can undoubtedly offer new temporal properties, particularly if integrated behavioral tasks are investigated, as reported in section 4.

2   Temporal Mechanisms in Biological Modeling

Even if the whole neural network domain often draws (more or less tightly) on biological inspiration, mechanisms like activation functions or learning rules are often designed with no reference to time, whereas a real neuron is a dynamic system that evolves over time. In this section, some biologically inspired temporal models of neurons available in the literature will be presented. All of them have been designed in order to model experimental data from conditioning paradigms involving stimulus associations, sequence management, or the ability to keep cues in memory during a delay period. Underlying temporal mechanisms will be described here and related to the functioning and to the learning of neurons. The experimental framework and the fitting of the models to the data will not be mentioned and the reader might refer to cited papers for further information concerning those points.

2.1   Functioning Mechanisms

In simple terms, neuronal functioning can be explained as follows. Dendrites receive signals from other neurons and transmit them to the soma and the axon. Then, a non-linear functioning causes an output signal to be propagated on the axon toward other connected neurons. This signal constitutes a spike train. Only the quantity and the timing of spikes code the information. In classical neuronal models, a continuous value, the activation, stands for the mean frequency of the firing rate and thus hides individual neuronal temporal behavior. On the contrary, it is exploited by some more biologically inspired models.

Spiking neurons One of the lowest levels of description of neuronal temporal behavior is the spike itself (Gerstner 1998). In the so-called spiking neuron approach, neuronal activity is fully reported with, for each neuron i, the set of its firing times.

$$F_i = \{t_i^{(1)}, \cdots, t_i^{(n)}\} \tag{1}$$

Based on these elementary data, various neuronal operations can be implemented (Gerstner 1998). They can investigate rate coding (with an average over time, over several cycles or over a population of neurons) or pulse coding (strategies of coding based on synchronicity of spike timing).

Several models of neurons, from the simplest to the most complex (e.g. compartmental), have also been designed within this formalism (Maass and Bishop 1998). For example, the Spike Response Model describes the neuronal state $u_i(t)$ at time t (which can be interpreted as the cell membrane potential) as the sum of the neuronal response to its own spikes (refractory period with negative kernel $\eta_i(s)$) and the response to presynaptic spikes (excitatory (resp. inhibitory) postsynaptic potential given by a positive (resp. negative) kernel $\epsilon_{ij}(s)$), as written in equation 2.

$$u_i(t) = \sum_{t_i^{(f)} \in F_i} \eta_i(t - t_i^{(f)}) + \sum_{j \in \Gamma_i} \sum_{t_j^{(f)} \in F_j} w_{ij} \epsilon_{ij}(t - t_j^{(f)}) \tag{2}$$

where Γ_i is the set of neurons connected to neuron i and w_{ij} corresponds to the synaptic strength of the connection between the neurons i and j.

This formalism has the advantage of being established at a very low (and thus precise) level of time. It has also given rise to a variety of theoretical as well as applied studies (Maass and Bishop 1998) which now establish spiking neurons as a full domain of research. However, the corresponding drawback of this formalism is that its low level of granularity implies a large amount of computation even for a simple network of neurons. Another drawback is related to the lack of well established learning rules at this level of description. That is one reason why it is important to keep in mind other formalisms describing these (and other related) temporal mechanisms.

The leaky integrator At a higher level of description than the spike, explicit temporal functions can also be used to obtain a neuronal temporal behavior. In the simple leaky integrator model (SLI), the input to a neuron at time t, denoted by $I(t)$, can take a continuous value between zero and one (Reiss and Taylor 1991). Then, the membrane potential $A(t)$ is written as:

$$A(t+1) = f(I).I(t) + (1 - f(I)).A(t) \qquad (3)$$

where the function $f(I)$ is defined, with constants a and d:

$$f(I) = d(1 - I) + aI. \qquad (4)$$

Finally, the output of the neuron is computed via the Heaviside function H as:

$$Out(t+1) = H(A(t) - 0.5) \qquad (5)$$

As illustrated in figure 1, functions A and f are such that they provide to the neuronal internal state a wave input attack in the time $1/ln(a)$ and a wave input decay in the time $1/ln(d)$. It is thus possible to determine the shape of the activity with the choice of constants a and d. Of course, these phenomena can also be obtained within the spiking neuron formalism (Gerstner 1998), but at a much higher computational cost.

This *trace* mechanism, describing neurons as leaky integrators, makes the neuronal activity last longer than its input. We will explain below how this mechanism is important for a network to properly learn and recall sequences.

The gated dipole Synaptic functioning has also been studied, with differential equations over time describing at each time the variation of some state variables, as in the SLI model. This approach has led to many models, sharing common features. These features are described below, on the basis of the gated dipole model introduced by Grossberg (Grossberg 1984). The model is a good illustration of the kind of complex temporal behavior that can arise from straightforward equations.

The gated dipole is grounded on the modeling of synaptic dynamics. The role of the synapse is to transfer a signal from presynaptic to postsynaptic nervous fibers. Let t be the (continuous) time parameter, $S(t)$ the value of the presynaptic activity, $T(t)$ the value of the postsynaptic activity and $z(t)$ the conductance of

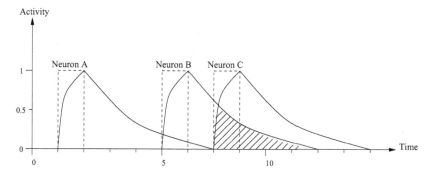

Fig. 1. This figure represents the typical shape of activity obtained with a trace mechanism. It also illustrates how this mechanism enables two events occurring at distinct instants to have lasting activities, to meet and to interact via learning

the synapse provided by chemical neurotransmitters. Equation 6 describes the way S is transmitted through the synapse over time, figure 2 illustrates it.

$$T(t) = S(t).z(t) \tag{6}$$

A perfect conduction would correspond to a constant conductance $z(t)$ over time. When $S(t)$ occurs (becomes non null), some previously stored neurotransmitters are emitted to provide conductance (this is considered as instantaneous in the model). The synapse continuously produces neurotransmitters to "refill" the stock until saturation. The production and consumption of neurotransmitters can then be described with equation 7.

$$\frac{d}{dt}z(t) = A.(B - z(t)) - S(t).z(t) \tag{7}$$

The first term of equation 7 represents the production of neurotransmitters, with a speed A, until the level B. The second term is the consumption of neurotransmitters by the signal $S(t)$. If signal $S(t)$ is kept constant, production and consummation of neurotransmitters complement each other and the output signal $T(t)$ reaches an equilibrium value such that:

$$\frac{d}{dt}z(t) = 0 = A.(B - z(t)) - S(t).z(t)$$
$$\Rightarrow z(t) = \frac{AB}{A + S(t)} \quad \Rightarrow \quad T(t) = \frac{AB.S(t)}{A + S(t)} \tag{8}$$

The function $T = f(S)$ at the equilibrium state is non-linear, monotonic increasing and saturates with the value AB. Such a function is similar to the sigmoidal transfer function used with the classical formal neuron. Outside the equilibrium case, the dynamics of the synapse, shown in figure 2, have interesting temporal properties. For example, overshoots and undershoots can trigger events when

$S(t)$ respectively sets and resets. Moreover, the decay from overshoot to habituation can be considered as a progressively decaying *trace* of the burst of S. The concept of trace is useful to correlate time separated events, as will be discussed later.

This model is suitable for detecting transitions of signals and illustrates well the kind of temporal properties easily obtained by using appropriate intrinsically temporal models.

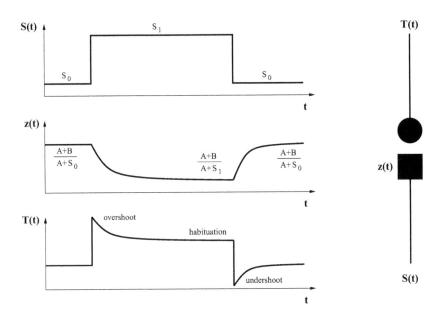

Fig. 2. The gated dipole, from (Grossberg 1984).

2.2   Learning Mechanisms

Classical static learning mechanisms are often based on Hebbian rules, which compute weight variations from the correlation between presynaptic and postsynaptic activities, according to the rule:

$$\Delta W_{ij} = \alpha S_i . T_j \tag{9}$$

This static view is obviously an approximation since it is clear that, as a consequence of presynaptic activity, postsynaptic activity is not simultaneous but consecutive to presynaptic activity. Several temporal learning mechanisms have been proposed and take this constraint into account.

The common feature that underlies these mechanisms is the use of traces, so that instantaneous correlations between traces of signals signify temporal correlations of those signals (cf. figure 1). The shapes of the traces, and the properties of the learning rules, endow the models with their own specific properties.

Learning the earliest predictor Adaptive behavior has been widely studied throughout classical (Pavlov 1927) and instrumental (Skinner 1938) conditioning. The classical conditioning experiment is described in the following terms in (Sutton and Barto 1981):

> ..., the subject is repeatedly presented with a neutral conditioned stimulus, that is, a stimulus that does not cause a response other than orienting responses, followed by an unconditioned stimulus (UCS), which reflexively causes an unconditioned response (UCR). After a number of such pairings of the CS and the UCS-UCR, the CS comes to elicit a response of its own, the conditioned response (CR), which closely resembles the UCR or some part of it.

There exist several variations of this simple experiment. For example, one can try to condition the subject with the help of several CS_i. The point is that the delay separating CS_i from UCS (inter-stimulus interval or ISI) plays a crucial role in the success or failure of the conditioning. Neural modeling takes this point into account. Furthermore, a large amount of experimental paradigms (overshadowing, blocking, etc.) give serious clues concerning the temporal mechanisms underlying conditioning.

Sutton and Barto (Sutton and Barto 1981) propose a model based on activity traces which is able to take these kinds of data into account. The model is grounded in a formal neuron (cf. figure 3) where input x_0 is the value of the UCS, other inputs x_i are respective values of the CS_i and y is indifferently the CR or the UCR.

The model is driven by the following equations, where f is a sigmoid function, α and β are positive constants with $0 \leq \alpha, \beta < 1$ and c is a positive constant determining the learning rate:

$$\overline{x}_i(t+1) = \alpha \overline{x}_i(t) + x_i(t) \tag{10}$$

$$\overline{y}(t+1) = \beta \overline{y}(t) + (1 - \beta)y(t) \tag{11}$$

$$y(t) = f[\sum_{j=1}^{n} w_j(t)x_j(t)] \tag{12}$$

$$\forall i \in [1..n], w_i(t+1) = w_i(t) + c[y(t) - \overline{y}(t)]\overline{x}_i(t) \tag{13}$$

Each input x_i and y has a trace activity, respectively $\overline{x}_i$ and $\overline{y}$. At the beginning of conditioning, in the case of a single CS (corresponding to a single input x), the output y is activated at the same time as UCS (or x_0) because of the fixed weight w_0. Meanwhile, if $\overline{x}$ is active, it will increase its weight w since this

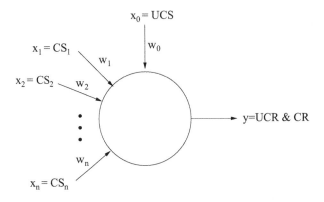

Fig. 3. The adaptive element of (Sutton and Barto 1981).

latter is proportional to $(y(t) - \overline{y}(t))$ and $\overline{x}$. It will then soon be able to trigger the output on its own. The adaptive element has learned to trigger a response whenever CS is present just before UCS. As in the classical conditioning paradigm, the delay separating the onset of CS and UCS plays a crucial role since learning only occurs in case of temporal overlap between a positive trace of x and a "burst" of $(y(t) - \overline{y}(t))$.

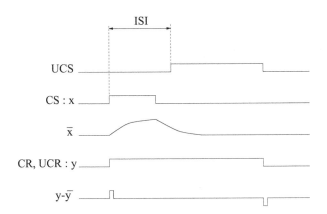

Fig. 4. Time courses of element variables after conditioning. CS elicits a response of its own.

Another aspect of classical conditioning is the context factor, which may be determinant during the learning phase. For example, when a first association

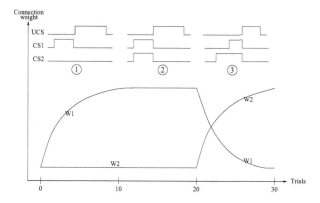

Fig. 5. The blocking paradigm. As long as CS_2 is not the earliest predictor (step 1 and 2), w_2 remains unchanged. As soon as CS_2 becomes the earliest predictor (step 3), w_1 decreases to zero while w_2 reaches its asymptotic value.

$CS_1 \rightarrow CR$ has been learned, the addition of a new CS_2 contingent to CS_1 generally implies a very weak $CS_2 \rightarrow CR$ association or no association at all. This phenomenon is called "blocking" and is modeled by the Rescorla-Wagner theory (Rescorla and Wagner 1972) which states that *organisms only learn when events violate their expectations*. Figure 5 shows the evolution of weights for such a blocking paradigm, where three phases can be distinguished:

1. This is a classical conditioning experiment with only one CS_1. Weight w_1 is then increased up to its asymptotic value.
2. A second CS_2 contingent to CS_1 is added, but, since learning has occurred at a previous phase, output (triggered by CS_1) onset is now overlapping with CS_1 onset. CS_2 is then unable to learn anything since its trace activity $\overline{x}_2$ is not positive during the output onset. Weights w_1 and w_2 remain the same.
3. CS_2 onset is now earlier than CS_1, trace activity $\overline{x}_2$ is now positive during the output onset (triggered by CS_1), weight w_2 is then increased. The consequence is that output will be triggered sooner and sooner by CS_2 up to the point where $\overline{x}_1$ will be positive during the output offset. Then w_1 will be decreased to zero. CS_2 has become a better predictor of UCS than CS_1.

Learning the date of the predictor Learning the earliest predictor is useful for anticipating the consequence of an event. However, if the time interval that separates the event and its consequence is nearly constant, it may be useful to be ready only when the consequence occurs. A mechanism allowing the memorization of this time interval has been proposed in (Grossberg and Schmajuk 1987), (Grossberg and Schmajuk 1989). This mechanism is grounded on a trace that arises after the burst of a signal and then shuts down. This defines a time interval, after the burst of the signal, and correlation can be computed during this interval. The idea is then to provide many synapses with different time constants, and thus to allow an overlap during complementary intervals. The model is called the Spectral Timing Model.

Let us first describe the functioning of one synapse, and then the use of a range of such synapses for anticipation. Let I_{CS} be a conditioned signal (a step function), and I_{UCS} be the unconditioned signal. When learning has occurred, I_{UCS} has to be anticipated when it should occur, according to I_{CS}. Synapse i is described by three variables, according to the following equations, where f is a sigmoidal function.

$$\frac{d}{dt}x_i = \alpha_i[-Ax_i + (1 - Bx_i)I_{CS}] \tag{14}$$

$$\frac{d}{dt}y_i = C(1 - y_i) - Df(x_i) \tag{15}$$

$$\frac{d}{dt}z_i = Ef(x_i)y_i[-z_i + I_{UCS}] \tag{16}$$

Equation 14 allows x_i to transmit I_{CS} with a delay, depending on parameters. Equation 15 describes spontaneous production of neurotransmitter y_i and consumption of this neurotransmitter when the synapse transmits x_i. This equation is similar to equation 7. As a delayed signal x_i is transmitted through the synapse, using neurotransmitter y_i, the transmitted value of x_i, i.e the product $f(x_i)y_i$, is a trace of the occurrence of I_{CS}. Then, equation 16 describing the strength of association z_i performs the evolution of z_i toward I_{UCS}, but only when the trace of I_{CS} is strong enough. The shape of the traces for a high α_i (in plain line) and for low α_i (in dashed line) is illustrated in figure 6.

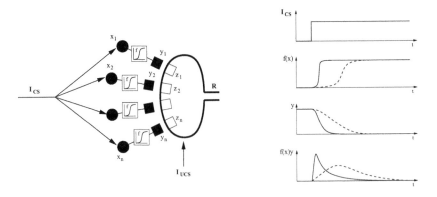

Fig. 6. Spectral Timing Model, from (Grossberg and Schmajuk 1987).

Spectral timing consists then in endowing a neuron with a battery of synapses, having different values α_i, for correlations with a given I_{CS} (cf. figure 6).

The response of the neuron is then given by equation 17.

$$R = \left[\sum_i f(x_i) y_i . z_i - F \right]^+ \quad \text{with} \quad \begin{cases} x^+ = x \ \text{ if } x \geq 0 \\ x^+ = 0 \ \text{ otherwise} \end{cases} \tag{17}$$

The behavior of the neuron then consists in responding to an I_{CS} by summing traces that have been associated with I_{UCS} (they have a high z_i value). The response then occurs at the moment when I_{UCS} should occur.

Finally, let us mention that the spectral timing paradigm has also been successfully implemented with a range of leaky integrators as a model of frontal cortex (Dominey et al. 1995).

Context-dependent learning The models previously discussed were grounded on classical conditioning experiments, and deal with the association of two signals. Some other models describe a synapse concerned with a third signal, modulating the associative role of the synapse. This defines the concept of the synaptic triad.

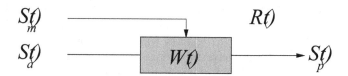

Fig. 7. The synaptic triad, from (Dehaene and Changeux 1989).

The synaptic triad model of Dehaene and Changeux (Dehaene and Changeux 1989), illustrated in figure 7, involves a presynaptic activity $S_a(t)$, a postsynaptic activity $S_p(t)$, and a modulation signal $S_m(t)$ that acts on the synaptic weight $W(t)$. The weight $W(t)$ is a trace of the modulation activity.

$$W(t+1) = \begin{cases} \alpha_p W(t) + (1 - \alpha_p) W^m(t) \ \text{ if } S_m(t) > 0.5 \\ \alpha_d W(t) \hspace{4.2cm} \text{ if } S_m(t) < 0.5 \end{cases} \tag{18}$$

The α_p and α_d parameters are in the range $[0, 1]$. The weight $W(t)$ is a trace that increases toward the current maximal authorized weight $W^m(t)$ when the modulation signal $S_m(t)$ is high, and decreases otherwise. The contribution of all the synapses i to the output signal $S_p(t)$ is given by:

$$S_p(t+1) = \sum_i W^i(t) S_a^i(t) \tag{19}$$

The temporal learning rule for the triad actually computes the value W^m of the synapse. The learning rule is given by:

$$\delta W^m(t) = \beta R(t) \frac{W(t)}{W^m(t)} S_a(t) (2 S_p(t) - 1) \tag{20}$$

The function $R(t)$ is a reinforcement signal, related to the experimental frame-work of the model (Dehaene and Changeux 1989). It will be considered as a positive constant and will not be discussed here. The maximal weight W^m in-creases according to the cooccurence of presynaptic signal S_a and postsynaptic signal S_p, as for Hebbian learning rules, but this occurs only when the trace W of S_m is close to its maximum value. The signal S_m can be viewed as a *context* value, and the synapse will conduct signals only when the context is active (cf. equation 19).

More complex contextual rules have been developed since the initial model by Dehaene and Changeux, dealing with non-simultaneity of presynaptic and postsynaptic signals, i.e one has to come before the other when context is active in order to increase the weight of the synapse (see (Guigon 1993) for example).

2.3   Biological Temporal Mechanisms

This overview of some functioning and neuronal learning mechanisms illustrates the variety of temporal neuronal properties that can be exploited in artificial neural networks (and that are absent in classical static models). As mentioned above, these mechanisms are generally used to model experimental data and often stick to the experimental framework. They have to be integrated in a more complete architecture in order to address wider range of real-world problems. For example, this has been successfully done for radar imaging by Grossberg and colleagues (Gove et al. 1995), (Grossberg et al. 1995).

Engineering-like applications, like autonomous robot control, are often tack-led by Markov Decision Processes such as Q-Learning (Watkins 1989) (see (Litt-man 1996) for a good overview of these techniques). In the latter case, time is considered as a discrete parameter, ordering a series of synchronous interactions between the agent and the external world. However, this kind of approach seems to be seldom applied to real asynchronous problems.

Biological models may be an efficient way to overcome this difficulty, due to the robustness of temporal mechanisms like the trace concept. Our claim is that the integration within a cortical framework of such elementary biologically-inspired mechanisms can lead to efficient systems for real-world applications.

3   Cortical Modeling

The goal of establishing a framework for cortical modeling is to bridge the gap between the isolated temporal mechanisms and the distributed and polymodal nature of the cerebral cortex itself. This makes it possible to efficiently express complex behaviors, including several temporal resolutions. Before proposing (in the next section) our computational models for this framework, we report the outline of the biological model that underlies it. The reader can refer to the original description of the model (Burnod 1989) for more details about the un-derlying biological data. These data yield two levels of description. First, at the global level, architectural and functioning data give hints about different kinds of processing regions in the cortex, and information pathways between them. Second, at a more local level, neuronal circuitry is described together with the corresponding functioning and learning rules.

3.1   The Global Level: A Network of Areas

The global description of the four major lobes (frontal, parietal, temporal and occipital) with the functional description of the cortex proposed by Brodmann as early as 1909 (Brodmann 1909), gives precious hints for a functional approach. It makes the distinction of four major types of areas, as illustrated in figure 8 and described below (using the formalism of this figure).

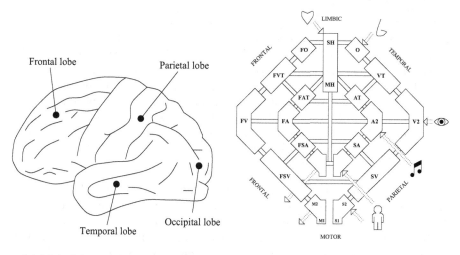

(a) Main lobes of the cerebral cortex

(b) Model of the connectivity between cortical areas (adapted from (Burnod 1989))

Fig. 8. Anatomical and functional view of the cerebral cortex

Sensory areas These mono-modal areas map the sensory information coming from the different body receptors which can be divided into five main sensory poles (auditory (A), visual (V), somesthesic (S), olfactory (O) and internal molecular (SH)). Moreover, the information flow is structured in such a way that topology is conserved from peripheral receptors to cortical sensory areas. A fixed mono-modal perceptive sequence can be encoded at this level.

Motor areas (M) These mono-modal areas allow the performing of actions upon the internal world (e.g. hormonal secretion) or the external world (e.g hand movement). Actions can be executed simultaneously but also coordinated in a complex sequence of movements (but fixed at this level).

Posterior associative areas These polymodal areas, including temporal and parietal areas, are crucial to cortical organization since they allow the linking of at least two areas, one with the other. They will for instance allow direct sensorimotor coordination encoding in the case of a link between a sensory and a motor area (e.g. hand-eye coordination). Moreover, these associative areas may also link two sensory areas or two other associative areas, allowing in this way the construction of a more structured and integrated representation of information. Stereotypical sensorimotor sequences (e.g. reaching one's mouth with one's hand) can be learned in these areas.

Prefrontal associative areas From a functional point of view, prefrontal associative areas have to be distinguished from their posterior counterparts. The former are generally action-oriented and play a major role in temporal organization of behavior. Furthermore, the privileged relations with the posterior cortex (cf. fig.8(b)) and the presence of specific temporal mechanisms within prefrontal units (bistable) make prefrontal areas able to construct and coordinate dynamic temporal sequences grounded on posterior ones (e.g. guidance of the hand toward a goal in the focus of attention).

Information pathways To throw light on the nature of cortical organization, cortical modeling defines a framework for a distributed polymodal representation of information. The integration of numerical data into more structured and "sub-symbolic" reference frames is possible throughout a hierarchy of polymodal areas. We are thus offered a way of keeping to some extent the robustness of numerical data while manipulating this data at a higher level. These cortical mechanisms involve (mainly in the posterior cortex) statistical and slow learning, and perform a kind of extraction of the world regularities through the construction of stereotyped temporal sequences. The ability to model complex and more dynamic behaviors requires additional mechanisms that can be provided by frontal areas or even by extra-cortical structures. The cortical network is not fully interconnected but defines via associative areas *three privileged pathways between the motor system, the internal state and the perception of the outside world* in the following way:

 - parietal areas relate the outside world with the motor system
 - temporal areas relate the outside world with the internal state
 - frontal areas relate the internal state with the motor system

Moreover, as shown in figure 8(b), there are privileged connections between frontal areas and posterior cortex: each posterior area is mirrored within the frontal lobes. This anatomical design suggests an interlaced cooperation between perceptive posterior representation and frontal motor ones, for the temporal organization of behaviour. Indeed, frontal areas are believed to play a central role in most complex temporal behaviors such as anticipation, planning, working memory or any other dynamic temporal sequencing behavior.

3.2   The Local Level: Neuronal Assemblies

A more detailed analysis of the inner organization of the cortical sheet may also describe this as a large set of elementary circuits: the cortical minicolumns. Each of those minicolumns receives a subset of the intra or extra-cortical information and because of the topological property of the cortical areas, neighboring minicolums will tend to receive the same subset of information. These groups of minicolumns are called maxicolumns: they share the same information subset but are able to apply different filters on it. The model of the cortical column reported in (Burnod 1989) describes the functioning and learning properties of such maxicolumns, which are different from those of the formal neuron.

Architecture The cortical minicolumn (also called cortical column) is a group of a maybe a hundred interconnected neurons where activity is essentially related to the pyramidal neurons while the other neurons, excitatory or inhibitory interneurons, mainly participate in the inner mechanism of the column. Moreover, the cortical column is a six layered structure (cf. figure 9) where layers I to III allow communication with other cortical columns while layers IV to VI allow communication with extra-cortical structures. Depending on the area the column belongs to, the size of each layer may vary greatly.

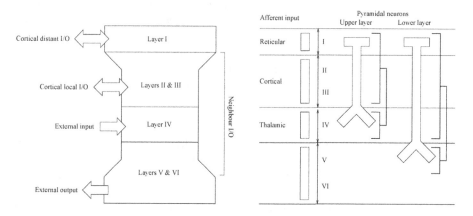

Fig. 9. The six layered structure of the cortical column and the corresponding input/output data channels

Basic operations The inner mechanisms of the column result in three possible distinct levels of activity for the pyramidal neurons:

- Inhibited level E0 represents very weak activity
- Low level E1 represents small variations of relatively low frequencies (5Hz to 10Hz). We will refer to this priming state as the *call state*
- High level E2 represents a much higher frequency (50Hz to 100Hz). We will refer to this state as the *satisfaction state*

Spatial filters As said before, a maxicolumn is a set of several neighboring cortical columns sharing the same subset of information and constitutes a functional module. As long as there is no specialization of these columns, they will often be activated in a moderate way for any pattern of information. Learning is then the ability for a minicolumn to become specialized on a precise pattern of information while others in the same maxicolumn are inhibited (coupling/uncoupling). This task corresponds to filtering or feature extraction.

Spatio-temporal filters Cortical columns are able to activate themselves at three distinct levels. Activation of a column at level E2 requires the simultaneous activation of both cortical and thalamic inputs. Consequently, when a column A receives a cortical input alone or a thalamic input alone, it will not reach level E2 but rather level E1. This activity E1 is nonetheless propagated to all neighboring columns. If among them, one (C) is excited via its thalamic input, it will reach level E2 and will produce an extra-cortical action (whatever the target). This action will then modify the thalamic context, which may now be propitious for the activation of column A to level E2. Column A will then learn to preferentially call column C since this latter is favorable to the excitation of the former (cf. figure 10). This mechanism may be seen to some extent as a goal directed search: the level E1 is a *desired* or *calling* state, while level E2 is the *satisfaction* state.

The temporal mechanism of spreading intra-cortical activation indeed allows the search for sequences that are able to satisfy the calling column. Learning will then consist in slowly orienting the call activity toward columns that help to reach the satisfaction state.

Bistable units All the prefrontal area units share a common mechanism: the bistable mechanism. Bistable units possess two stable states: *a resting state* and *a sustaining state*. Both ON (at rest to sustained activity) and OFF (sustained activity to rest) transitions require an external activity (e.g. external stimuli A and B) to be performed (cf. figure 11). Thus, while cortical posterior columns are only able to organize sequences at one level (e.g. A-B-C), frontal ones are able to organize hierarchical sequences (e.g. (A-(B-C))).

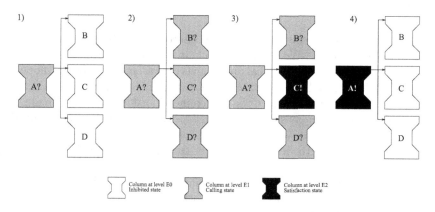

Fig. 10. 1) Column A receives cortical input and activates itself to level "E1" **2)** Activity is spread to neighbouring columns **3)** Thalamic context allows the activation of column C to level "E2", an action is performed that modifies the thalamic context **4)** Thalamic context modification allows column A to reach activation level "E2". Learning will occur and column A will learn to preferentially call column C.

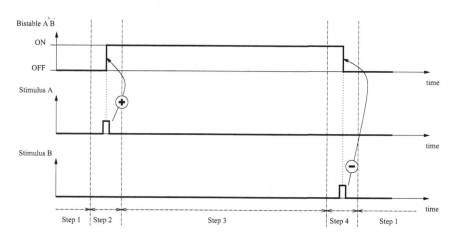

Fig. 11. 1) Bistable A^+B^- is at rest **2)** Detection of stimulus A produces the ON transition on the bistable A^+B^- **3)** The bistable activity is sustained **4)** Detection of stimulus B produces the OFF transition on the bistable A^+B^-

4   Cortical Temporal Mechanisms for Computer Science Purposes

As computer scientists, we are specifically interested in efficient software design for real-world problems. We think that such an engineering oriented purpose can benefit from the study of biological data. Nevertheless, most biological models are not suitable for immediate software integration, but have rather been designed to explain experimental data. Classical connectionist models, like multi-layer perceptrons or Kohonen's Self Organizing Maps can be viewed as the adaptations of biological models to software engineering constraints, adding mechanisms such as backpropagation with derivable transfer functions, or explicit winner-takes-all.

Concerning computation of temporal information, which is crucial when addressing real problems, a biological framework also appears to be helpful (cf. section 3). As is shown by the attempts we have mentioned, adaptation of biological temporal models to information processing is not obvious, and mechanisms that arise from such attempts appear to be heterogeneous (cf. section 1). We propose that one way to design reusable algorithms is to refer as precisely as possible to a cortical framework, allowing us to deal with highly integrated architectures. Integrated temporal processing implies different levels of time computation that have to be consistent one with each other. Within the same cortical paradigm, presented in section 3, we first describe low level (small time constant) mechanisms that are applied to temporal pattern recognition. We then consider causality detection, applied to the learning of higher level reactive abilities of an autonomous robot. Finally, we look at temporal mechanisms involved in neural planning with bistable units.

4.1   Monomodal Sequences within a Map

The Temporal Organization Map (TOM) architecture (Durand and Alexandre 1996) has been proposed as a model of the auditory cortex and applied to speech processing. At the lowest level, a simple cochlea model (Hartwich and Alexandre 1997) performs a spectral transformation of the speech signal. The processing level is a map of super-units, each super-unit standing for a maxicolumn, as described in section 3.2. As a first temporal mechanism, each super-unit has a spatio-temporal receptive field. The spatial field corresponds to the integration of a set of contiguous fibers from the cochlea model. The temporal field corresponds to a leaky integration, controlled by a decay parameter. This short term memory allows the integration of activation within an interval of time.

The second temporal mechanism is performed within the processing map. It corresponds to intra-map temporal links between super-units which can build explicit sequences of activation within the map. Robustness to sequence distortion (insertion or deletion) is obtained through the interaction of both temporal mechanisms. A division mechanism was also implemented and leads to specializations within super-units in order to differentiate sequences passing through the same units.

This model was applied to spoken digit recognition using some classical benchmarks in speech processing (Durand and Alexandre 1996). It has obtained performances similar to the best stochastic models, with a better performance given the temporal and spatial complexity of the algorithm.

4.2 Multimodal Causality Sequences for Reactive Integrated Behaviour

The mechanism described here is related to internal computation within an artificial cortical map. The maxicolumns (see section 3.2) of the map are involved in the learning of temporal regularities, and are the basic units of the model. As such, a unit represents a population of synchronous cortical columns that receive the same information. Three kinds of activation have been defined, as described for a single cortical column (Burnod 1989).

First, unit i stores an *excitation* activity E_i^{exci} as soon as the perceptive events e_i it is associated with occur. Another associated recency signal E_i^{rec} is used as a trace of the occurrence of the event. It is initialized to 1 and linearly decays over time. When it reaches 0, the stored intensity E_i^{exci} is reset to 0. The use of two variables E_i^{exci} and E_i^{rec} prevents the confusion of strong old events with weak recent ones.

Second, a *call* activity of unit i means that event e_i is useful, and has to occur. For simplification here, this activity will be considered as a boolean value (1 or 0), whereas it is, in the model, a continuous value, representing the strength of the request for e_i.

Third, when a specific event that was requested through the call activity has occured (excitation of a called unit), the unit is said to be *satisfied*.

Learning by specialization When learning occurs at the level of a cortical maxicolumn, columns inside the maxicolumn, that were synchronously firing, separate into two asynchronous parts. Each part can split again, further refining learning (see (Burnod 1989) for details). As units of the model represent synchronous columns, the effect of learning at the level of a unit is the creation of a new unit, both units representing the new synchronous sets of columns.

Temporal learning rule The aim of the learning rule presented here is to build sequences of units, based upon perception. Let us suppose that a given unit i is called, and that the associated event e_i always occurs after another event e_j, i.e. after E_j^{exci} of unit j is set. It is then possible to conclude that getting e_j is a means to get the requested e_i, i.e. call activity has to spread from unit i to unit j. If we consider unit i as the goal "getting occurrence of e_i" when it is called, unit j can be viewed as a subgoal to be called. The learning rule described in equation 21 allows the detection of the goal/sub-goal relationships between units, by increasing weights between units. When a subgoal is detected, it splits, and the split unit is devoted to receiving a call activity from the goal. As it is called after the call activity at the level of the goal, the subgoal can play the role of a goal for other units in the map, in order to extend the causal sequence.

Let i be the unit whose subgoals are detected by using the mechanism, and j one of the other units in the map. The weight w_{ij}, initially null, represents the causal relationship between i and j, and the splitting of j occurs when it reaches 1. A flag δ_{ij} is associated with each w_{ij}. Weights are updated according to the procedure 21.

$$
\begin{aligned}
&\text{if } E_j^{\text{rec}} = 1,\ \delta_{ij} \leftarrow 1. \\
&\text{if } E_i^{\text{rec}} = 1 \text{ and } E_i^{\text{call}} = 1,\ (\text{satisfaction of } i) \\
&\quad \text{case } E_j^{\text{rec}} = M^i \text{ and } M^i > 0 : w_{ij} \leftarrow w_{ij} + \tau . E_j^{\text{rec}} . E_j^{\text{exci}} \\
&\quad \text{case } 0 < E_j^{\text{rec}} < M^i \qquad : w_{ij} \leftarrow w_{ij} + \tau . (E_j^{\text{rec}} - M^i) . E_j^{\text{exci}} \\
&\quad \text{case } E_j^{\text{rec}} = 0 \qquad\qquad\ : w_{ij} \leftarrow w_{ij} - \theta \\
&\quad \text{in all cases} \qquad\qquad\quad : \delta_{ij} \leftarrow 0 \\
&\text{else if } E_i^{\text{call}} = 1 \text{ and } E_j^{\text{rec}} \text{ reaches } 0, \\
&\qquad\qquad\qquad\qquad\qquad w_{ij} \leftarrow w_{ij} - \tau' . E_j^{\text{exci}} . \delta_{ij} \\
&\quad \text{else nothing to compute.}
\end{aligned}
\qquad (21)
$$

Parameters τ and τ' are fixed learning rates, the symbol $\leftarrow$ stands for variable setting and $M^i = \max_j E_j^{\text{rec}}$. Learning w_{ij} occurs only when unit i is a goal ($E_i^{\text{call}} = 1$). When an event e_j occurs ($E_j^{\text{rec}} = 1$), the flags δ_{kj} for all k are raised. If the goal i is satisfied ($E_i^{\text{rec}} = 1$ and $E_i^{\text{call}} = 1$), the weight w_{iJ} to unit E_J that has been excited the most recently ($E_J^{\text{rec}} = M^i$) increases, proportional to both the recency and the stored intensity E_j^{exci} of the event e_J. For the other j units that are "quite recent" ($E_j^{\text{rec}} > 0$), the weights w_{ij} are decreased, proportionally to the relative age $E_j^{\text{rec}} - M^i$ of e_j occurrence, and also according to E_j^{exci}, consistent with the rule for unit J. The mechanism for the most recent unit J and the other recent j is a competition for recency, detecting the last predictor of the goal satisfaction. Events that have not occurred before the satisfaction of the goal i ($E_j^{\text{rec}} = 0$) are decreased with a decay value. Note that satisfaction of the goal j resets the flags δ_{ij} of related weights w_{ij}. If an event e_j occurs, without being followed by the satisfaction of the goal, i.e the trace E_j^{rec} reaches 0, if the goal is still being called ($E_i^{\text{call}} = 1$) and if it has not been satisfied since the occurrence of e_j (the flag δ_{ij} is still raised), then the weight w_{ij} is decreased.

This mechanism has been shown to be robust to different kinds of temporal noise, mainly distortion of sequences, insertion of events, permutation of items in the sequence (Frezza-Buet and Alexandre 1999). It is suitable for detecting sequences of causality between perceptive events that are intrinsically asynchronous, which is the case for real perception. Finally, the mechanism allows the detection of the last predictor, as opposed to Sutton and Barto rules (see section 2.2) that detect the earliest. This is important since spreading calls from a goal to its successive subgoals requires the learning of all intermediate events of a perceptive sequence, and not only the first, even if it is actually predictive of the last.

Application This mechanism has been used inside each map of a multi-map architecture for robot control (Frezza-Buet and Alexandre 1998b). This architecture contains many maps for detecting multi-modal events that are linked with the mechanism presented here. The multimodal sequences that are learned are the basis for a competition within units in the model. This competition allows the robot to trigger the appropriate action at each time, according to the needs that initiate call activities, according to the perception that initiates excitation activities, and to the knowledge concerning the world stored in the w_{ij}. The cortical framework, that drives the design of the map architecture, coupled with the local temporal mechanism described in this section, has led here to an efficient control architecture endowing the robot with the ability to learn elaborated reactive behavior from its experience in the environment.

4.3   Context Detection for Bistable Transitions

The previously described model deals with one level sequences (no sub-sequences), providing procedural abilities for reactive behavior. This model refers to posterior cortex functionalities. As we are interested in more complex behaviors, involving planning on the basis of connectionist computation, we are currently studying prefrontal functions. Some early modeling results will be presented here briefly, in order to introduce the use of the context manipulation mechanism detailed here, allowing temporal scheduling of actions.

Prefrontal modeling framework for neural planning As mentioned in section 3, prefrontal functionality is grounded on cortical columns having a bistable activity pattern. The model described now is an attempt to use this ability for planning the behaviour of the robot. Compared with a biological description of the cortex, and more precisely of the prefrontal lobe, our functional approach is of course very rough, but it has to be seen in the context of the design of efficient and highly integrated control architectures. In this modeling framework, prefrontal cortex is a set of units connected to posterior cortex units with one-to-one connections (cf. figure 12). The posterior cortex part of the model is similar to the one mentioned in section 4.2. It is a module allowing complex servo-control oriented computation, i.e. a call activity at the level of a posterior unit (the P_is in figure 12) triggers an elaborated action of the robot, as "facing the current target" for example. Then, the role of the prefrontal cortex part of the model (the F_is in figure 12) is to schedule posterior calls, in order to plan the behaviour of the robot towards finding rewarding situations.

This scheduling, described in (Burnod 1989) and in a more computer science oriented way in (Frezza-Buet and Alexandre 1998a), is illustrated by the following example. Let us suppose that a sequence of events $a - b - c$ has to be performed for getting a reward. That means that posterior units P_a, P_b and P_c have to be excited in that order, after successive calls in these three units. The role of associated frontal units F_a, F_b and F_c (cf. figure 12) is then the following. First F_a triggers a call on posterior unit P_a. As a consequence of this call, let us suppose that event e_a occurs, meaning that P_a is excited. Then, F_a sends call activity to F_b, that calls P_b to get e_b in the same way. When e_b occurs, F_b transmits the call to F_c that enables the occurrence of the rewarded event e_c. The significance of this sequence, compared with the posterior model of section 4.2, is the way failures of calls are managed. Let us suppose that the call in P_a triggered by F_a in the previous example is not followed by the event e_a that makes P_a excited. That means that the current context does not allow the getting of this event, and that something else has to be done before getting e_a is possible. What has to be done before is the activation of another sequence of events (they may involve motor events as a consequence of calls), noted $aa - ab$ in figure 12. The failure of the call in F_a makes F_a have a sustained specific activity (transition ON of the bistable) that *stacks* the purpose of calling P_a without calling it anymore. Then, a call is transmitted to F_{aa}. When sequence $aa - ab$ has been performed, the perceptive world is supposed to be in a context that allows e_a to occur subsequently to a call in P_a. The detection of this context, which is the temporal mechanism described in this section, triggers the OFF transition of bistable activity in F_a. The effect of this latter transition is first to stop storing the call that previously failed, and second to retry it, by calling P_a again (the call is popped out from the stack). Due to the use of $aa - ab$, this call now allows e_a to occur, and F_a transmits a call to F_b as in the non failing case presented first.

Context detection, which is crucial for the neuronal stacking allowed by the frontal cortex model, has to be robust to the intrinsic asynchronousness of perceptions. This context detection, which is the learning rule for frontal sequences in the model, is presented now and details concerning the use of this mechanism for robot control can be found in (Frezza-Buet and Alexandre 1998a).

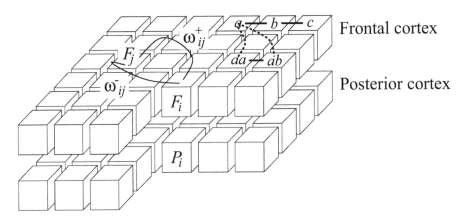

Fig. 12. Prefrontal modeling framework.

Asynchronous context detection The purpose of the mechanism is to enable a bistable frontal unit F_i (cf. figure 12) to learn perceptive context. This context must ensure that a call on the corresponding P_i will succeed in getting the associated event e_i. At the level of F_i, let us consider two events e_i^+ and e_i^-, respectively representing the success of call in A_i and its failure (F_i gives up calling A_i). Learning occurs during both e_i^+ and e_i^-, as detailed below.

For any frontal connection between F_i and F_j, a couple of weights (w_{ij}^+, w_{ij}^-) are used. Weights w_{ij}^+ and w_{ij}^- store correlations between excitation in P_j and respective events e_i^+ and e_i^-. Using these weights, two kinds of contextual activities $\tilde{c}_i$ and $\hat{c}_i$ are computed, according to equations 22 where operator $[x]^+$ returns x if $x > 0$ and 0 otherwise.

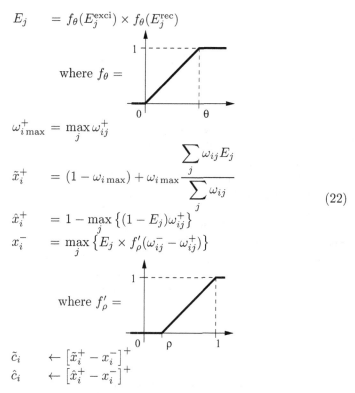

$$E_j = f_\theta(E_j^{\text{exci}}) \times f_\theta(E_j^{\text{rec}})$$

where $f_\theta =$

$$w_{i\,\text{max}}^+ = \max_j w_{ij}^+$$

$$\tilde{x}_i^+ = (1 - w_{i\,\text{max}}) + w_{i\,\text{max}} \frac{\sum_j w_{ij} E_j}{\sum_j w_{ij}}$$

$$\hat{x}_i^+ = 1 - \max_j \left\{ (1 - E_j) w_{ij}^+ \right\}$$

$$x_i^- = \max_j \left\{ E_j \times f_\rho'(w_{ij}^- - w_{ij}^+) \right\}$$

where $f_\rho' =$

$$\tilde{c}_i \leftarrow \left[\tilde{x}_i^+ - x_i^- \right]^+$$

$$\hat{c}_i \leftarrow \left[\hat{x}_i^+ - x_i^- \right]^+$$

(22)

The value E_j is the trace of excitation activity of P_j (intensity of e_j modulated by its recency). The value $\tilde{x}_i^+$ is the fitting of the E_j distribution to the stored w_{ij}^+ weights. If no strong correlation has been detected between any E_j and e_i^+ ($w_{i\,\text{max}}^+$ is weak), the w_{ij}^+ are not significant, the context $\tilde{x}_i^+$ is then good by default (close to 1). The context value $\tilde{x}_i^+$ is sensitive to changes in the E_j distribution, allowing the detection that the current distribution is going closer to the ideal one (defined by the w_{ij}^+). As this context is too permissive for reliable context detection, another context value $\hat{x}_i^+$ is defined, which is high when the E_j distribution matches exactly the w_{ij}^+. Finally, if one of the current E_j has been detected as being correlated to e_i^- without being correlated to e_i^+ ($\omega_{ij}^- - \omega_{ij}^+$ is high), this E_j is predictive of the failure of the call, and the x_i^- context value is high. Using the contexts $\tilde{x}_i^+$, $\hat{x}_i^+$ and x_i^-, two respectively permissive and not permissive contexts $\tilde{c}_i$ and $\hat{c}_i$ are defined.

As $\hat{c}_i$ is reliable, it is used to trigger the OFF transition of F_i. On the other hand $\tilde{c}_i$, being sensitive to the improvement of the distribution of perception, is used to sustain bistable activity of F_i until $\hat{c}_i$ allows the OFF transition.

The learning rule for the wij^+ is straightforward, once the previous values are computed (cf. equation 23). Note that the ω_{ij}^- are computed only when the call fails but it was supposed to succeed ($\hat{c}_i > 0$).

$$
\begin{aligned}
&\text{For all } j, \\
&\quad \text{When } e_i^+ \text{ occurs} \\
&\qquad \tau^+ = \tau \\
&\qquad \omega_{ij}^+ \leftarrow (1 - \tau^+)\omega_{ij}^+ + \tau^+ E_j \\
&\quad \text{When } e_i^- \text{ occurs} \\
&\qquad \tau^- = \tau \times \hat{c}_i \\
&\qquad \omega_{ij}^- \leftarrow (1 - \tau^-)\omega_{ij}^- + \tau^- E_j
\end{aligned}
\tag{23}
$$

Interest of the context learning mechanism The context detection is robust (Frezza-Buet 1999) to asynchronous perception, due to correlation with traces. It also enables one to separate events E_j that are often occurring whenever a call in P_i succeeds (e_i^+) or not (e_i^-) from the events E_j that are responsible for the failure. This mechanism, coupled with stacking properties of bistable activation, is involved in the scheduling of action schemes, synchronizing calls towards the posterior cortex model by defining when a sub-sequence has succeeded. Learned contexts are also used to determine which sub-sequence to call when a call fails. Finally, the same context mechanism has been reused, detecting distribution of call activities among the frontal units, to learn which schemes are not compatible with the execution of others.

4.4   Discussion

The design of mechanisms presented in this section is driven by engineering constraints (robustness, integration into an efficient architecture), that lead us not just to stick to the biological background. Using biological inspiration for such purposes is constrained by a trade off between biological validity and computational efficiency. Nevertheless, cortical modeling offers us a framework to develop highly integrated applications. These open architectures can then be refined and extended consistently.

5   Conclusion

The main goal of this chapter was to present a cortical framework in which isolated neurobiologically inspired mechanisms can be integrated. It was shown in particular that these mechanisms can act at different levels of time, for different kinds of elementary functions. Data from cortical organization and functioning offer a framework for embedding these mechanisms in a way that yields neuro-biological plausibility at the neuronal as well as the behavioral level.

As a conclusion, in a schematic way, we can now consider in turn the mechanisms and their time scale, with the corresponding neuronal and behavioral description.

1. The time scale of one millisecond corresponds, at the neuronal level, to the duration of a spike and to the duration of synaptic transmission from one neuron to its closest neighbors. It thus corresponds to the minimal time scale for a bit of information. At the behavioral level, coincidence detectors, in peripheral neural structures, can work at this time scale.

2. The time scale of ten milliseconds corresponds, at the neuronal level in the central structures, to the coding level of spike intervals, since the maximal frequency cannot exceed 100 Hz in these structures. This thus corresponds to the minimal timing from one area to the next. At the behavioral level, it corresponds to the focus of attention or to the timing of feedback information flow from an higher level to a lower level map.

3. The time scale of one hundred milliseconds corresponds, at the neuronal level, to the activation dynamics of a population of neurons, which are locally synchronized at this time scale. It is the basic timing of activities in the cortex which are linked with simple sensory and motor events. At the behavioral level, it corresponds to the minimal reaction times from the first processing layer (stimulus) to the last (recognition or action). It is thus the minimal time for the simplest sensorimotor loops.

4. The time scale of one second corresponds, at the neuronal level, to the time scale of the basic processes which can result in learning. Neurons in the higher levels of associative cortex can stay active on this time scale, even if the stimulus is no longer present. At the behavioral level, it corresponds to the time scale of correspondences between sensory and motor events on different modalities which can produce reinforcement. It also corresponds to a level of information processing which has strong intrinsic regulations within modalities (for example, the exploration of an object).

5. The time scale of ten seconds corresponds, at the neuronal level, to the typical time scale of working memory in the frontal regions of the cortex. The learning mechanism is performed by the control of bistable states of frontal neurons in order to build stacks. At the behavioral level, this time scale corresponds to the processes in the frontal cortex allowing the organization of temporal aspects of behavior like the exploration of a scene.

6. The time scale of one hundred seconds and more corresponds, at the neuronal level, to the very long time constants of some neuronal intrinsic metabolic and genetic processes. Rhythms with long periods can be produced by such structures as the reticular formation and the hypothalamic nuclei. Such internal clocks can influence cortical activity by modulators which can switch the intrinsic temporal programs of large populations of cortical neurons. At

the behavioral level, these biological rhythms can have large contextual influence (like emotion) and can produce global regulation of the behavioral programs within the whole network.

On the one hand, each basic temporal mechanism that we have presented above can be related to one (or two consecutive) of these temporal resolutions and to the corresponding neuronal and behavioral mechanisms. On the other hand it is clear that a fully plausible behavioral model should include all of the six levels of time. In any case, it should not be restricted to one or two levels. We believe that the cortical framework that we have presented here allows one to work at the same time at these different temporal levels, with the corresponding behavioral abilities.

References

Alexandre, F. (1996). Connectionist cognitive processing for invariant pattern recognition. In *Proceedings International Conference on Pattern Recognition*.

Ans, B., Coiton, Y., Gilhodes, J., and Velay, J. (1994). A neural network model for temporal sequence learning and motor programming. *Neural Networks*.

Béroule, D. (1990). Guided propagation : current state of theory and application. In Soulié, F. F. and Hérault, J., editors, *Neurocomputing. NATO ASI Serie*. Springer Verlag Berlin Heidelberg.

Brodmann, K. (1909). *Vergleichende Lokalisationslehre der grobhirnrinde*. J.A. Barth, Leipzig.

Burnod, Y. (1989). *An adaptive neural network the cerebral cortex*. Masson.

Dehaene, S. and Changeux, J.-P. (1989). A simple model of prefrontal cortex function in delayed-response task. *Journal of Cognitive Neuroscience*, 1(3):244–261.

Dominey, P., Arbib, M., and Joseph, J.-P. (1995). A model of corticostriatal plasticity for learning oculomotor associations and sequences. *Journal of Cognitive Neuroscience*, 7(3):311–336.

Durand, S. and Alexandre, F. (1996). TOM, a new temporal neural network architecture for speech signal processing. In *Proceedings IEEE International Conference on Acoustics, Speech and Signal Processing*, Atlanta.

Elman, J. L. (1990). Finding structure in time. *Cognitive Science*, 14:179–211.

Frezza-Buet, H. (1999). *Un modèle de cortex pour le comportement motivé d'un agent neuromimétique autonome*. PhD thesis, Université Henri Poincaré Nancy I. In french.

Frezza-Buet, H. and Alexandre, F. (1998a). Multimodal sequence learning with a cortically-inspired model. In *JCIS98, Association for Intelligent Machinery*, volume 2, pages 24–27.

Frezza-Buet, H. and Alexandre, F. (1998b). Selection of action with a cortically-inspired model. In *Seventh European Workshop on Learning Robots*, pages 13–21.

Frezza-Buet, H. and Alexandre, F. (1999). Specialization within cortical models: An application to causality learning. In *Proceedings of the 7th European Symposium on Artificial Neural Networks*.

Gerstner, W. (1998). Spiking neurons. In Maass, W. and Bishop, C., editors, *Pulsed Neural Networks*. Bradford Book, MIT Press.

Gove, A., Grossberg, S., and Mingolla, E. (1995). Brightness perception, illusory contours, and corticogeniculate feedback. *Visual Neuroscience*, 12:1027–1052.

Grossberg, S. (1984). Some normal and abnormal behavioral syndromes due to transmitter gating of opponent processes. *Biological Psychiatry*, 19(7):1075–1117.

Grossberg, S., Mingolla, E., and Williamson, J. (1995). Synthetic aperture radar processing by a multiple scale neural system for boundary and surface representation. *Neural Network*, 8:1005–1028.

Grossberg, S. and Schmajuk, N. A. (1987). Neural dynamics of attentionally modulated pavlovian conditioning : Conditioned reinforcement, inhibition, and opponent processing. *Psychobiology*, 15(3):195–240.

Grossberg, S. and Schmajuk, N. A. (1989). Neural dynamics of adaptive timing and temporal discrimination during associative learning. *Neural Network*, 2:79–102.

Guigon, E. (1993). *Modelisation des proprietes du cortex cerebral : Comparaison entre aires visuelles, motrices et préfrontales*. PhD thesis, École centrale de Paris. in English.

Hartwich, E. and Alexandre, F. (1997). A Speech Recognition System using an Auditory Model and TOM Neural Network. In Pearson, O.-W., Steele, N.-C., and Albrecht, R.-F., editors, *Proceedings International Conference of Artificial Neural Nets and Genetic Algorithms*, Norwich. Springer Verlag.

Littman, M. L. (1996). *Algorithms for Sequential Decision Making*. PhD thesis, Department of Computer Science at Brown University.

Maass, W. and Bishop, C., editors (1998). *Pulsed Neural Networks*. MIT Press.

Pavlov, I. P. (1927). *Conditioned Reflexes (V.Anrep, trans.)*. London: Oxford University Press".

Pearlmutter, B. A. (1990). Dynamic recurrent neural networks. Technical Report CMU-CS-90-196, Carnegie Mellon University.

Reiss, M. and Taylor, J. (1991). Storing temporal sequences. *Neural Networks*, 4:773–787.

Rescorla, W. A. and Wagner, A. R. (1972). *Classical conditioning II: Current research and theory*, chapter A theory of Pavlovian conditioning: Variations in the effectiveness of reinforcement and non-reinforcement. Black, A.H. and Prokasy, W. F., appleton-century-crofts edition.

Skinner, B. (1938). *The Behavior of Organisms.*

Suga, N. (1990). Cortical computational maps for auditory imaging. *Neural Networks*, 3:3–21.

Sun, R. and Alexandre, F., editors (1997). *Connectionist - Symbolic Interpretation; from Unified to Hybrid Approaches.* Lawrence Erlbaum Associates.

Sutton, R. S. and Barto, A. G. (1981). Toward a modern theory of adaptative network : Expectation and prediction. *Psychological Review*, 88(2):135–170.

Waibel, A., Hanazawa, T., Hinton, G., Shikano, K., and Lang, K. (1989). Phoneme recognition using time delay neural networks. In *IEEE Transactions on Acoustics Speech and Signal Processing*, volume 37.

Watkins, C. J. (1989). *Learning from delayed rewards.* PhD thesis, University of Cambridge.

Attentive Learning of Sequential Handwriting Movements: A Neural Network Model

Stephen Grossberg[1] and Rainer W. Paine[2]

Department of Cognitive and Neural Systems[3]
Center for Adaptive Systems, Boston University
677 Beacon Street, Boston, MA 02215 U.S.A.
http:www.cns.bu.edu/Profiles/Grossberg
E-mail: steve@bu.edu

1. Introduction

Much sensory-motor behavior develops through imitation, as during the learning of handwriting by children (Burns, 1962; Freeman, 1914; Iacoboni et al., 1999). Such complex sequential acts are broken down into distinct motor control synergies, or muscle groups, whose activities overlap in time to generate continuous, curved movements that obey an inverse relation between curvature and speed. How are such complex movements learned through attentive imitation? Novel movements may be made as a series of distinct segments that may be quite irregular both in space and time, but a practiced movement can be made smoothly, with a continuous, often bell-shaped, velocity profile. How does learning of sequential movements transform reactive imitation into predictive, automatic performance?

A neural model is summarized here which suggests how parietal, frontal, and motor cortical mechanisms, such as difference vector encoding, interact with adaptively-timed, predictive cerebellar learning during movement imitation and predictive performance (Grossberg & Paine, 2000). To initiate movement, visual attention shifts along the shape to be imitated and generates vector movement using motor cortical cells. During such an imitative movement, cerebellar Purkinje cells with a spectrum of delayed response profiles sample and learn the changing directional information and, in turn, send that learned information back to the cortex and eventually to the muscle

---

[1] Supported in part by the Defense Advanced Research Projects Agency and the Office of Naval Research (DARPA/ONR N00014-95-1-0409), and by the National Science Foundation (NSF IRI-97-20333).

[2] Supported in part by the Defense Advanced Research Projects Agency and the Office of Naval Research (DARPA/ONR N00014-95-1-0409, ONR N00014-92-J-1309), and by the National Institutes of Health (NIH 1-R29-DC02952-01).

[3] Acknowledgments: The authors wish to thank Robin Amos and Diana Meyers for their valuable assistance in the preparation of the manuscript and graphics.

R. Sun and C.L. Giles (Eds.): Sequence Learning, LNAI 1828, pp. 349-387, 2000.

synergies involved. If the imitative movement deviates from an attentional focus around a shape to be imitated, the visual system shifts attention, and may make an eye movement back to the shape, thereby providing corrective directional information to the arm movement system.

This imitative movement cycle repeats until the corticocerebellar system can accurately drive the movement based on memory alone. A cortical working memory buffer transiently stores the cerebellar output and releases it at a variable rate, allowing speed scaling of learned movements which is limited by the rate of cerebellar memory read-out. Movements can be learned at variable speeds if the density of the spectrum of delayed cellular responses in the cerebellum varies with speed. Learning at slower speeds facilitates learning at faster speeds. Size can be varied after learning while keeping the movement duration constant (isochrony). Context-effects arise from the overlap of cerebellar memory outputs. The model is used to simulate key psychophysical and neural data about learning to make curved movements, including a decrease in writing time as learning progresses; generation of unimodal, bell-shaped velocity profiles for each movement synergy; size and speed scaling with preservation of the letter shape and the shapes of the velocity profiles; an inverse relation between curvature and tangential velocity; and a Two-Thirds Power Law relation between angular velocity and curvature.

2. Model Precursors

The new model, called Adaptive VITEWRITE (AVITEWRITE), builds on two previous movement models. The first is the Vector Integration to Endpoint (VITE) model (Bullock & Grossberg, 1988a, 1988b, 1991) (Figure 1). The VITE model successfully explained psychophysical and neurobiological data about how synchronous multi-joint reaching trajectories could be generated at variable speeds. VITE was later expanded (Bullock, Cisek, & Grossberg, 1998) to explain how arm movements are influenced by proprioceptive feedback and external forces, among other related factors. The firing patterns of six distinct cell types in cortical areas 4 and 5 were also simulated during various movement tasks (Kalaska et al., 1990). In order to allow a greater focus on issues related to the learning of curved movements, the AVITEWRITE model avoids explicit descriptions of muscle dynamics, and therefore uses components of the earlier VITE models of Bullock and Grossberg (1988a, 1988b, 1991).

A second basis for the AVITEWRITE model is the VITEWRITE model of Bullock, Grossberg, and Mannes (1993), (Figure 2). The curved trajectories of handwriting require more than simple point-to-point movements. Curved handwriting trajectories appear to be generated by sequences of movement synergies (Bernstein, 1967; Kelso, 1982), or groups of muscles working together to drive the limb in prescribed directions, whose activities overlap in time (Morasso et al., 1983; Soechting & Terzuolo, 1987; Stelmach et al., 1984). VITEWRITE uses such a synergy-overlap strategy to generate curved movements from individual, target-driven strokes. A key issue faced by all models which seek to generate curves by overlapping strokes is how to appropriately time the strokes to generate a particular curve. VITEWRITE avoids an explicit representation of time in the control of synergy activation by using features of the movement itself; namely, times of zero or of maximum velocity, to trigger activation of a subsequent synergy. However, movement in VITEWRITE is controlled by a predefined sequence of "planning vectors" which cause unimodal velocity profiles for the synergies that control each directional component of a curve. VITEWRITE does not address how these planning vectors may be discovered, learned, and stored in a self-organizing process which can generate unimodal velocity profiles for each directional component of a curved movement. This challenge is met by the *adaptive* VITEWRITE model.

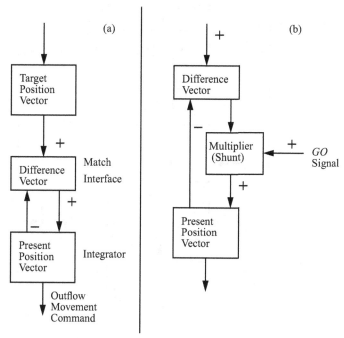

Fig. 1. (a) A match interface within the VITE model continuously computes a difference vector (*DV*) between the target position vector (*TPV*) and a present position vector (*PPV*), and adds the difference vector to the present position vector. (b) A *GO* signal gates execution of a primed movement vector and regulates the rate at which the movement vector updates the present position command. (Adapted with permission from Bullock and Grossberg, 1988a.)

AVITEWRITE describes how the complex sequences of movements involved in handwriting can be learned through the imitation of previously drawn curves. Although the system described herein could be modified to learn from the actual movements of a teacher, the present model learns by imitating the product of that teacher's movements, the static image of a written letter. AVITEWRITE shows how initially segmented movements with multimodal velocity profiles during the early stages of learning can become the smooth, continuous movements with the unimodal, bell-shaped velocity profiles observed in adult humans Abend et al., 1982; Edelman & Flash, 1987; Morasso, 1981; Morasso et al., 1983) after multiple learning trials. Early, error-prone handwriting movements with many visually reactive, correctional components gradually improve over time and many learning trials, to become automatic, error-free movements which can even be performed without visual feedback. A key factor in this transition is the use of synergy-based learning (see below), which retains some degree of stability across otherwise highly variable practice trials.

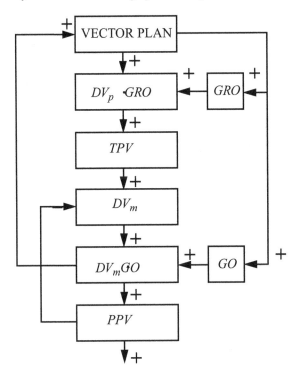

Fig. 2. The VITEWRITE model of Bullock et al. (1993). A Vector Plan functions as a motor program that stores discrete planning vectors DV_p in a working memory. A GRO signal determines the size of script and a GO signal its speed of execution. After the vector plan and these will-to-act signals are activated, the circuit generates script automatically. Size-scaled planning vectors DV_pGRO are read into a target position vector (TPV). An outflow representation of present position, the present position vector (PPV), is subtracted from the TPV to define a movement difference vector (DV_m). The DV_m is multiplied by the GO signal. The net signal DV_mGO is integrated by the PPV until it equals the TPV. The signal DV_mGO is thus an outflow representation of movement speed. Maxima or zero values of its cell activations may automatically trigger read-out of the next planning vector DV_p.. (Reproduced with permission from Bullock et al., 1993.)

The AVITEWRITE model architecture is briefly outlined below (Figure 3) and described later in detail in the Model Description (Figure 9). At the start of movement, visual attention (1) focuses on the current hand position and moves to select a target position (2) on the curve being traced. A Difference Vector representation (3) of the distance and direction to the target is formed between the current hand position (*PPV*) and the new target position (*TPV*). This Difference Vector activates the appropriate muscle synergy (4) to drive a reactive movement to that target. At the same time, a cerebellar adaptive timing system (5) (Fiala et al., 1996) learns the activation pattern of the muscle synergy involved in the movement and begins to cooperate or compete (6) with reactive visual attention for control of the motor cortical trajectory generator (7). A working memory (8) transiently stores learned motor commands to allow them to be executed at decreased speeds as the speed and size of trajectory generation are volitionally controlled through the basal ganglia (9). Reactive visual control takes over when memory causes mistakes. Both the movement trajectory and the memory are then corrected, allowing memory to take over control again. As successive, visually reactive movements are made to a series of attentionally chosen targets on the curve, a memory is formed of the muscle synergy activations needed to draw that curve. After tracing the curve multiple times, memory alone can yield error-free movements.

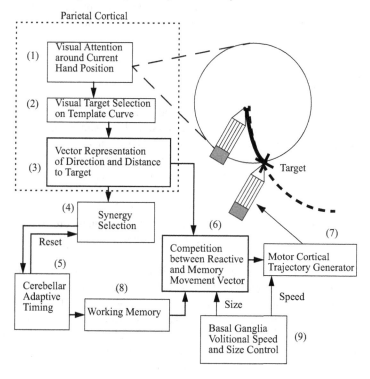

Fig. 3. Conceptual diagram of the AVITEWRITE architecture. Numbers in parentheses indicate the order of discussion in the text.

Several properties of human handwriting movements emerge when AVITEWRITE learns to write a letter. Size and speed can be volitionally varied (Figure 3, (9)) after learning while preserving letter shape and the shapes of the velocity profiles (Plamondon & Alimi, 1997; Schillings et al., 1996; van Galen & Weber, 1998; Wann & Nimmo-Smith, 1990; Wright, 1993). Isochrony, the tendency for humans to write letters of different sizes in the same amount of time, is also demonstrated (Thomassen & Teulings, 1985; Wright, 1993). Speed can be varied during learning, and learning at slower speeds facilitates future learning at faster speeds (Alston & Taylor, 1987, p. 115; Burns, 1962, pp. 4 45-46; Freeman, 1914, pp. 83-84). Unimodal, bell-shaped velocity profiles for each movement synergy emerge as a letter is learned, and they closely resemble the velocity profiles of adult humans writing those letters (Abend et al., 1982; Edelman & Flash, 1987; Morasso, 1981; Morasso et al., 1983). An inverse relation between curvature and tangential velocity is observed in the model's performance (Lacquaniti et al., 1983). It also yields a Two-Thirds Power Law relation between angular velocity and curvature, as seen in human writing under certain conditions (Lacquaniti et al., 1983; Thomassen & Teulings, 1985; Wann et al., 1988). Finally, context effects become apparent when AVITEWRITE generates multiple connected letters, reminiscent of carryover coarticulation in speech (Hertrich & Ackermann, 1995; Ostry et al., 1996), and similar to handwriting context effects reported by Greer and Green (1983), and Thomassen and Schomaker (1986).

3. Movement Synergies

Movement synergies are groups of muscles that work together in a common task. The brain seems to control complex movement tasks, such as walking or handwriting, by issuing commands to a few muscle synergies, as opposed to specifying the movement parameters for scores of individual muscles separately (Bizzi et al., 1998; Buchanan et al., 1986; Kelso, 1982; Turvey, 1990). Using muscle synergies greatly simplifies the control and planning of movement by lessening the number of degrees of freedom requiring executive control (Bernstein, 1967; Turvey, 1990). Only at lower levels of the central nervous system, such as in the brainstem and spinal cord, would the motor synergy commands branch out to individual muscles. A key question is how these movement synergies are controlled.

Human movements can be broken down into individual movement segments, or strokes. Each stroke corresponds to the activities of particular muscle synergies. When the muscle synergies controlling a limb are activated synchronously (Figure 4b), there is a tendency to make simple, straight movements (Hollerbach & Flash, 1982; Morasso, 1986) with bell-shaped velocity profiles (Abend et al., 1982; Morasso, 1981; Morasso et al., 1983), (Figure 4b). Curved movements may be generated by a linear superposition of straight strokes due to asynchronous synergies (Figure 4a and 4c) (Morasso et al., 1983; Soechting & Terzuolo, 1987; Stelmach et al., 1984). Thus, a key issue is how the timing of strokes is determined. In curved movements, each synergy generates its own bell-shaped velocity profile. A simple example is a "U" curve (Figure 5), drawn as a combination of three strokes: one for a synergy in the negative, vertical direction; a second in the positive, horizontal direction; and a final stroke in the positive, vertical direction (Figures 5b and 5c). The observation that the curved movements of handwriting obey an inverse relation between curvature and velocity (Lacquaniti et al., 1983) can be attributed to the direction reversal and synergy switching which occurs at points of high curvature, as at the bottom of a "U" curve (Figure 5d and 5e).

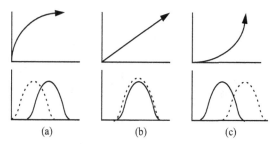

Fig. 4. Varying the relative timing of synergy activation can yield different curved movements. Synchronous synergy activation yields straight movements (b) while asynchronous synergy activation can yields curved movements in (a) and (c). The dotted and solid curves represent synergies that control movements in the positive y and x directions, respectively.

4. The VITE Model of Reaching

How is movement direction represented in the brain? Much research (e.g., Andersen et al., 1995; Georgopoulos et al., 1982, 1989, 1993; Mussa-Ivaldi, 1988) suggests that motor and parietal cortex compute a vectorial representation of movement direction in motor and/or spatial coordinates. The VITE model (Bullock & Grossberg, 1988a, 1988b, 1991) showed how a vectorial representation of movement direction and length could generate straight reaching movements with bell-shaped velocity profiles (Figure 1). Such a Difference Vector (DV) is computed as the difference from an outflow representation of the current hand position, or Present Position Vector (PPV), to a target, or Target Position Vector (TPV) (Figure 6). The DV is multiplied by a gradually increasing GO signal, that is under volitional control, whose growth rate can be changed to alter movement speed while preserving movement direction and length (Figure 1). The "GO" signal seems to be generated with in the basal ganglia (Hallett & Khoshbin, 1980; Georgopoulos et al., 1983; Horak & Anderson, 1984a, 1984b; Berardelli et al., 1996; Turner & Anderson, 1997; Turner et al., 1998). The DV times the GO signal is an outflow representation of movement velocity that is integrated at the PPV until the present position of the hand reaches the target.

The VITE model explains behavioral and neural data about how a motor synergy can be commanded to generate a synchronous, multi-joint reaching trajectory at variable speeds. VITE describes how synchronous movements may be generated across synergistic muscles with automatic compensation for the different total contractions undergone by each muscle group. Many properties of human reaching movements emerge from VITE's performance, including the equifinality of movement synergies, a rate-dependence of velocity profile asymmetries, and variations in the ratio of maximum to average movement velocities (Bullock & Grossberg, 1988a, 1988b, 1991).

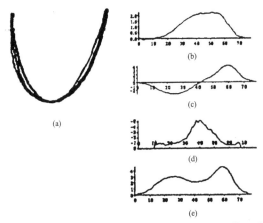

(a)

(b)

(c)

(d)

(e)

Fig. 5. (a) A "U" curve written by a human; (b) and (c): x and y direction velocity profiles, respectively; (d) movement curvature; (e) tangential velocity. (Reproduced with permission from Edelman and Flash, 1987.)

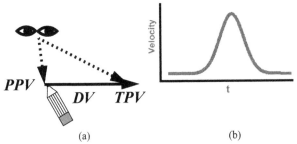

(a)   (b)

Fig. 6. (a) Illustration of a Difference Vector (DV) formed from the current hand location, given by a Present Position Vector (PPV), to a Target Position Vector (TPV). The DV is integrated in a VITE circuit to generate a straight movement with a bell-shaped velocity profile (b).

The expanded VITE model of Bullock, Cisek, and Grossberg (1998) assigned functional roles to six cell types in movement-related, primate cortical areas 4 and 5, and integrated them into a system which is capable of "continuous trajectory formation; priming, gating, and scaling of movement commands; static and inertial load compensation; and proprioception" (Bullock et al., 1998, p. 48). In this more detailed model, Difference Vector cells resemble the activity of posterior parietal area 5 phasic cells, while Present Position Vector cells behave like anterior area 5 tonic cells.

The VITEWRITE model of Bullock, Grossberg, and Mannes (1993) (Figure 2) extended the VITE reaching model to explain handwriting data. In VITEWRITE, curved movements are generated using a velocity-dependent stroke-launching rule that allows *asynchronous* superposition of sequential muscle synergy activations with unimodal, bell-shaped velocity profiles for each synergy. Scaling the size of *DV*s by multiplication with a volitional *GRO* signal allows size scaling without significantly altering the trajectory shape or the shape of the velocity profile. Similarly, altering the size of the volitional *GO* signal alters trajectory speed without changing trajectory shape. The movements generated by VITEWRITE yield the inverse relation between curvature and tangential velocity observed in human performance, as well as the Two-Thirds Power law relation between angular velocity and curvature observed in humans under some writing conditions (Lacquaniti et al., 1983; Thomassen & Teulings, 1985; Wann et al., 1988). VITEWRITE also shows how size scaling of individual synergies via separate *GRO* signals can change the style of writing without altering velocity profile shape. Such independent scaling of muscle synergy commands is supported by the study of Wann and Nimmo-Smith (1990), which yielded data that "do not support common scaling for x and y dimensions" (p. 111).

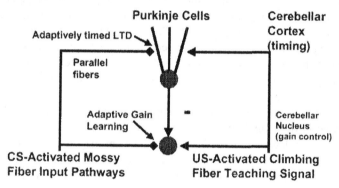

Fig. 7. Cerebellar spectral timing circuit: Long Term Depression (LTD) occurs over at the parallel fiber-Purkinje cell synapse when an unconditioned stimulus (US) is paired with a conditioned stimulus (CS) over multiple presentations. (Adapted with permission from Grossberg and Merrill, 1996). See text for details.

The Adaptive VITEWRITE model yields performance which is equally consistent with available handwriting data. In addition, AVITEWRITE addresses the main limitation of VITEWRITE, which is its inability to learn and remember the motor plan that, once learned, yields such good performance. The original VITEWRITE model does not address "the self-organizing process that discovers, learns, and stores representations of movement commands" (Bullock et al., 1993, p. 22). The pattern of "planning vectors" which formed VITEWRITE's motor program, or plan, needed to be predefined in order for the system to generate a movement or write a particular letter.

In contrast, AVITEWRITE learns how to generate letters by itself, and then remembers how to write them. The cost in so doing is a considerably larger learned memory. It remains to be seen whether and how the very parsimonious synergy-launching rule that was used in VITEWRITE can be assimilated into this learning scheme.

6. Adaptive Timing in the Cerebellum

Given that curved movements may be generated by asynchronous activation of multiple muscle synergies, we need to understand how the time-varying activation of asynchronous muscle synergies, or strokes, is learned. Several mechanisms have been proposed to learn how to adaptively time responses to stimuli. Possible timing mechani<sms include delay lines (Moore et al., 1989; Zipser, 1986), a spectrum of slow responses with different reaction rates in a population of neurons (Bartha et al., 1991; Bullock et al., 1994; Grossberg & Merrill, 1992, 1996; Grossberg & Schmajuk, 1989; Jaffe, 1992), and temporal evolution of the network activity pattern (Buonomano & Mauk, 1994; Chapeau-Blondeau & Chauvet, 1991). Given the need to learn time delays of up to four seconds in eye blink conditioning, delay lines of sufficient length do not appear to be present in the cerebellar cortex (Fiala et al., 1996; Freeman, 1969). Network noise over a four second interval seems to preclude temporal network evolution mechanisms (Buonomano & Mauk, 1994; Fiala et al., 1996).

Accumulating evidence suggests that adaptively timed learning of strokes may be achieved by *spectraltiming* in the cerebellum. Fiala et al. (1996) and others (Ito, 1984; Perrett et al., 1993) have suggested that the cerebellum may be involved in the opening of a timed gate to express a learned motor gain, as when a rabbit learns to blink after hearing a tone previously associated with an air puff. In this conception (Figure 7), a signal associated with a Conditioned Stimulus (CS) arrives via the cerebellar (mossy fiber)-to-(parallel fiber) pathway at a population of Purkinje cells and triggers a series of phase-delayed activation profiles, or depolarizations, of the Purkinje cells, called a Purkinje cell "spectrum" (Figure 8b). When a signal associated with a subsequent Unconditioned Stimulus (US) arrives via climbing fibers at some fixed Interstimulus Interval (ISI) after the CS, then Long Term Depression (LTD) of active Purkinje cells may occur at that time (Figure 8a), leading to disinhibition of the cerebellar nuclei at that time (Figure 7); hence the term "adaptive timing" (Fiala et al., 1996; Grossberg & Merrill, 1992, 1996; Grossberg & Schmajuk, 1989). The staggered temporal pattern of Purkinje cell depolarizations following the initial CS ensures that some Purkinje cells will be active, and subject to Long Term Depression, at the time that the US arrives via the climbing fibers (Figure 8a).

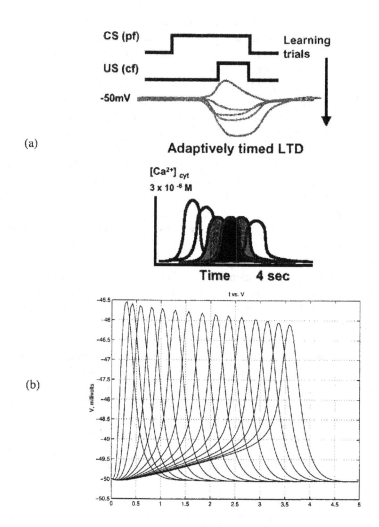

Fig. 8. (a) Purkinje cell spectrum (bottom) and adaptively timed Long Term Depression (LTD) over multiple CS-US pairings. As the unconditioned stimulus (US) arrives over multiple learning trials at a fixed interstimulus interval after the conditioned stimulus (CS), LTD occurs at those Purkinje cells which are active when the US arrives (shaded response curves). (b) Purkinje cell depolarization spectrum from Fiala et al. (1996) equations. Continuous glutamate input = 10 microM. (Adapted with permission from Fiala et al., 1996.)

Fiala et al. (1996) utilized biochemical mechanisms of the metabotropic glutamate receptor (mGluR) system to simulate how learning of adaptively timed Long Term Depression, or LTD, of Purkinje cells occurs and causes disinhibition of cerebellar nuclei during classical conditioning. Fiala et al. (1996) showed that a Purkinje cell spectrum could learn to respond to two conditioned stimuli with different interstimulus intervals (p. 3770). AVITEWRITE takes this approach one step further. Instead of learning one or two responses at discrete points in time, as in the conditioning task, it is hypothesized that the cerebellar adaptive timing mechanism can also learn a continuous response over time in sequential tasks like handwriting.

For a continuous handwriting task, different Purkinje cell spectra are activated by the commands corresponding to different muscle synergies. The climbing fiber unconditioned stimuli act as error-based signals that train the Purkinje cells to become hyperpolarized in specific temporal patterns that lead to correctly shaped writing movements. The level of depression of a given Purkinje cell determines the extent of cerebellar nucleus disinhibition during that Purkinje cell's activation and thus the learned gains for controlling a particular muscle synergy during a brief time window of movement. When these brief, individual movement commands are summed over the entire Purkinje cell population with staggered, overlapping cell activations, a continuously changing pattern of muscle synergy activations may be generated which can yield curved planned movements. In the AVITEWRITE model, this cerebellar adaptive timing module forms part of an integrated sequential learning and generation system (Figures 3 and 9) that also uses elements of VITE cortical and basal ganglia trajectory formation for visually reactive movements to targets and synergy-based spectral activation, as well as ideas from VITEWRITE about how working memories can build curved movements from overlapping synergies in a way that preserves shape-invariant volitional speed and size scaling.

This view of a cerebellar role in handwriting is consistent with data showing that there is cerebellar activity during drawing, and that the cerebellum is more active when lines are retraced than in new line generation because error detection (deviation from the lines) occurs during retracing but not new line generation (Jueptner & Weiller, 1998). Since the cerebellum is more active during error corrections, it is likely that climbing fibers (Figure 7) are signaling movement error, leading to Long-Term Depression or LTD of Purkinje cell-parallel fiber synapses (Gellman et al., 1985; Ito, 1991; Ito & Karachot, 1992; Oscarsson, 1969; Simpson et al., 1996). In a similar vein, the cerebellum may also be involved in a variety of complex sequential tasks. It is known that there is a cerebellar role in procedural memory. In a sequential button press task, lesions to the dentate nucleus cause deficits in learning and memory (Lu et al., 1998). Further, Doyon et al. (1998) demonstrated through studies using a sequential finger movement task that the cerebellum and striatum are involved in the automatization and long-term retention of motor sequence behavior.

In addition to showing how the cerebellum may be involved in learning a sequential handwriting task, the AVITEWRITE model also shows how the cerebellum may encode movement velocity. It is known that Purkinje cell simple spike discharge is direction- and speed-dependent (Coltz et al., 199a; Ebner, 1998). Simple spikes result from summation of excitatory postsynaptic potentials at parallel fiber-Purkinje cell synapses, across multiple Purkinje cell dendrites (Ghez, 1991, p. 631). AVITEWRITE assumes that movement context information, such as the movement direction and speed, is carried via the parallel fibers to the Purkinje cell populations controlling particular muscle synergies. Further, complex spike discharge of Purkinje cells is "spatially tuned and strongly related to movement kinematics" (Fu et al., 1997). A complex spike results when a single action potential is carried to a Purkinje cell via a climbing fiber, triggering a large Purkinje cell action potential followed by a high-frequency burst of smaller action potentials (Ghez, 1991, p. 631). In AVITEWRITE, the climbing fiber inputs act as error-correcting signals which train Purkinje cells that control particular muscle synergies to become hyperpolarized at the appropriate times during movement. AVITEWRITE therefore assumes that the climbing fiber signal is dependent on the direction and amplitude of a required corrective movement. The required corrective movement is different from, and possibly in the opposite direction to, the actual movement of that particular muscle synergy, which is reflected in simple spike activity. In fact, Coltz et al. (1999b) have found that complex spike discharge is direction- and speed-dependent, and that it is related to directions opposite those of the corresponding simple spikes, and to speeds different from those of the simple spikes. This appears to be further evidence that climbing fibers transmit a movement error signal. The model suggests how, using a spectrum of phase-delayed Purkinje cell activations based on adaptive timing mechanisms, learned cerebellar outputs may code movement gain and velocity.

7. AVITEWRITE Model

AVITEWRITE uses visual spatial attention to determine where the hand will move to imitate a curve. Attention is modeled algorithmically since it is not the main focus of the present study. The model assumes that attention may be focused within a circular region around the present fixation point. Attention is initially focused around the current hand position on a template curve (Figure 9). Attention then shifts along the curve to another target (*TPV*: Target Position Vector) on the shape that lies within an attentional radius of the current hand position (*PPV*: Present Position Vector). How this is modeled will be more explicitly stated below.

In support of the model's use of spatial attention, experimental data suggest that superior frontal, inferior parietal, and superior temporal cortex are part of a network for voluntary attentional control (Hopfinger et al., 2000) which is critical for directing "unpracticed movements in man" (Richer et al., 1999, p. 1427). Jueptner et al. (1997a, 1997b) reported that the prefrontal cortex was activated in a finger movement-sequence learning task during new learning but not during automatic performance after learning. Further, the left dorsal prefrontal cortex was reactivated "when subjects paid attention to the performance of the prelearned sequence" (Jueptner et al., 1997b, p. 1313). Evidence for an interaction between parietal and frontal lobe activity and cerebellar activity was found by Arroyo-Anllo and Botez-Marquard (1998). The authors found that humans with olivopontocerebellar atrophy suffered deficits in copying a simple figure and in immediate visual spatial memory, "consistent with the hypothesis that the cerebellum is involved in visual spatial working memory... and that it modulates parietal lobe- and frontal lobe-mediated functions" (p. 52).

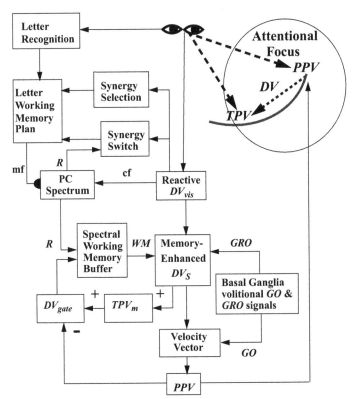

Fig. 9. AVITEWRITE architecture: cf = climbing fiber; DV_{gate} = Gating Difference Vector; DV_s = Size-scaled, memory-enhanced Difference Vector; DV_{vis} = Visual Difference Vector; GO = Volitional speed control signal; GRO = Volitional size control signal; mf = mossy fiber; PC = Purkinje cell; PPV = Present Position Vector; R = Adaptively timed cerebellar output; TPV = Target Position Vector; TPV_m = Memory-modulated Target Position Vector; WM = Spectral Working Memory Buffer output.

AVITEWRITE uses spatial attention to constrain the choice of the target positions that drive imitative tracing of a curve. The model assumes that these targets are selected within an attentional "tube" that is swept out by shifts in attention around the curve (Figure 10). If there is no memory, or if movement deviates from the attentional radius around the curve being traced due to memory inaccuracy, then a new target is chosen on the curve. Each choice of a new TPV from the current PPV defines a visual Difference Vector, or DV_{vis}, that is constrained to point forward along the template curve and remain within an attentional radius (r_a) of it, or else return the hand to within a distance r_a of the curve if it has exceeded it. More details about the target selection algorithm are described below. The TPVs are used to form difference vectors, DV_{vis}, that both drive the movement and act as teaching signals to train a cerebellar spectral memory via climbing fiber inputs.

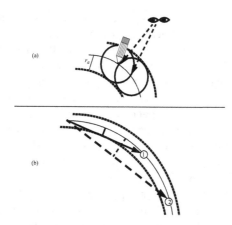

Fig. 10. Illustration of target selection: (a) Targets are chosen so as to keep the movement within an attentional radius, depicted as a circle around the current hand/pencil tip position, of the curve being traced. Superposition of these circular foci of attention as attention shifts across space generates an attentional "tube" around the template curve, shown as dotted lines. (b) Target 1 is possible because movement to it would not exceed the attentional radius, r_a, from the curve being traced, whereas Target 2 is invalid because r_a would be exceeded.

Once a target is chosen, vision provides direction and amplitude information, in the form of the difference vector, DV_{vis}, to a trajectory generator which can combine temporally overlapping muscle synergy activations to generate curved movements whose speed and size are volitionally controlled. Evidence for the use of visual difference vectors has been reported by several investigators. For example, in a study of human visuomanual pointing to a visual target on a horizontal plane, Vindras and Viviani (1998) found that final hand position appeared to be "coded as a vector represented in an extrinsic frame of reference centered on the hand" (p. 569). Similarly, in the Schwartz and Moran (1999) study of cell population vectors in motor and premotor cortex during drawing movements, "population vectors predicted direction (vector angle) and speed (vector length) throughout the drawing task" and that the "2/3 power law described for human drawing was also evident in the neural correlate of the monkey hand trajectory" (p. 2705).

Forming a visual difference vector to a target on the template curve includes activation of the appropriate muscle synergy to generate movement to that target. The trajectory generator then starts to integrate the memory-enhanced difference vector, DV_s, generating a velocity vector that drives movement to the target (Figure 9). At the beginning of learning, when there is not yet a memory contribution to movement control, DV_s equals DV_{vis} multiplied by a volitional size-scaling *GRO* factor. While movement towards the visual target is occurring, adaptively timed learning of the muscle synergy activations required to reach that target occurs. The cerebellum is activated by active muscle synergies. The model assumes that different synergies activate different spectral memories to learn and store corrective movement commands.

In the simulations (Figures 13), four separate spectral memories are formed for positive and negative, horizontal and vertical movement synergies, respectively. The use of separate synergy-activated spectral memories allows the model to learn a consistent movement despite the existence of variable errors on learning trials. It also allows muscle synergy-switching with independent control of each synergy.

A new synergy is activated at the start of movement and whenever there is a reversal in movement direction, requiring activation of a different synergistic set of muscles. Prior to learning, the synergies needed to begin a movement are determined by the value of DV_{vis}. For example, when starting the letter "U" when there is no prior memory of this letter, a DV_{vis} is formed which initially points in the negative y and positive x-directions. Purkinje cell spectra corresponding to the negative y and positive x-direction synergies therefore begin sampling the climbing fiber error/teaching signal. As memory starts to form, the model assumes that a visual representation of the letter is categorized by inferotemporal and prefrontal mechanisms in the "what" cortical processing stream, and that a visual cue is used to sample the appropriate synergies used to perform a given letter from memory (Figure 11). Although not modeled explicitly, AVITEWRITE assumes that a working memory, possibly in prefrontal cortex, forms a category representation of each letter which controls adaptive pathways to all the synergies. The letter category determines which cerebellar spectra, corresponding to the particular synergies needed to write that letter, are activated via mossy fiber inputs. Only those adaptive pathways that were modified due to prior learning will read-out nonzero values of the cerebellar spectral memory output, R. In order to initiate writing of a learned letter, the letter category triggers the initial spectra that control the synergies needed to start the movement. When writing the letter "U" for example, the letter category memory activates spectra corresponding to the negative y and positive x-direction synergies at the beginning of movement. The letter category representation also stores the identities of the other (the positive y) spectra involved in generating that particular letter. Their order of activation is determined automatically by the synergy switching rule described below.

Synergy switching is accomplished as follows in the model. If the total movement direction, determined by the sum of the reactive visual Difference Vector (DV_{vis}) and the cerebellar spectral memory (R) in Figure 9, changes sign, then a new synergy and Purkinje cell spectrum are activated. No new spectral components are activated in the spectrum from the prior synergy, although those components which are active at the time of the synergy switch continue to respond until they decay spontaneously. Such spectral behavior is supported by the responses of the biochemically-detailed Fiala et al. (1996) model to the sudden cessation of glutamate input to the Purkinje cells from the parallel fibers. In the Fiala et al. (1996) simulations, spectral components which are active at the time of input cessation remain active for a time while decaying spontaneously, whereas no new spectral components respond once the glutamate input has been shut off. The term spectral activity is here used to indicate the time-varying change in Ca^{2+} concentration and potential of a Purkinje cell following parallel fiber inputs. When writing a letter "U", a negative y-direction muscle synergy starts the movement. One Purkinje cell spectrum would learn to correct all the negative y-synergy movement errors. At the bottom of the "U", the y-synergy would reverse, triggering activation of a new spectrum to learn to correct the positive y-synergy errors. At this point, input to the negative y-synergy spectrum would be stopped; e.g., by shutting off the glutamate input released from parallel fibers in the Fiala et al. (1996) model equations, and the spectra active at the time of the direction reversal would decay.

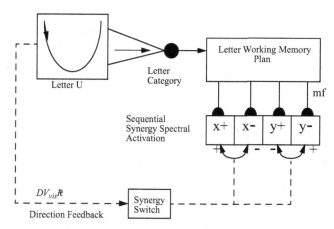

Fig. 11. Working Memory (*WM*) representation of a letter category that determines the sequential order of readout of synergy specific spectra for the positive and negative, *x* and *y* synergies, x+, x-, y+, and y-. Synergy switching is triggered by a change in sign of the total movement direction, $DV_{vis} + R$. mf = mossy fiber.

Error-driven movement learning is mediated by climbing fiber error signals, based on the Difference Vector *TPV–PPV* between the target position and the present hand position. The climbing fiber signal modifies the parallel fiber/Purkinje cell synaptic efficacy by triggering patterns of Long Term Depression across the Purkinje cell populations that control the respective muscle synergies. As the Purkinje cells' activity becomes more depressed, their target cerebellar nucleus becomes disinhibited (Figure 7), thereby enhancing muscle synergy activation over time according to the temporal pattern of Purkinje cell population activity.

The AVITEWRITE model incorporates competition between reactive movement and memory-based movement control systems. The model hypothesizes that the cerebellar motor memory competes for control of movement with cortical areas that guide reactive movements based on visual input (Caminiti et al., 1999; Dagher et al., 1999; Jueptner et al., 1997a, 1997b; Jueptner & Weiller, 1998; Kawashima et al., 2000; Sadato et al., 1996). In the model, the reactive visual difference vector (DV_{vis}) and the learned output from cerebellar memory (*R*), transiently stored in a working memory buffer (*WM*) described below, are combined to form the Memory-Enhanced Difference Vector, DV_S. The DV_S is, in turn, multiplied by a volitional size-scaling *GRO* signal to yield the size-scaled, memory-enhanced Difference Vector, DV_s. When the memory contribution to DV_s is strong enough, then the cerebellar memory determines

DV_s and DV_{vis} decays to zero. A visual difference vector (DV_{vis}) will be formed to a target if either of two conditions is met:

First, if the memory is too small (below some threshold value), then the system waits for a brief period of time in case another memory is becoming active. If no memory grows beyond the threshold by the end of this time period, then a reactive visual DV_{vis} is formed in the manner described above. This DV_{vis} drives the reactive movement toward a target. Second, if an error is made due to a movement deviating from the attentional radius around the template curve, then a corrective visual DV_{vis} is formed which determines DV_s and drives a corrective movement. The difference between the target and present positions $(TPV–PPV)$ generates a cerebellar teaching signal that updates the memory. Memory again takes over control once the trajectory reenters the attentional focus around the template curve, at which time DV_{vis} decays to zero. Thus, on-line error correction occurs which automatically shuts off as the system successfully learns to generate the desired curve. As learning proceeds, error-prone movements become successively more accurate until no errors are made and memory alone controls the movement. Once memory can control the movement without errors, the learned movement can be correctly executed without visual feedback.

As in the original VITEWRITE model Bullock et al. (1993), a volitional *GO* signal scales movement speed in AVITEWRITE by altering the trajectory generator's rate of difference vector (DV_s) integration. However, the rate of predefined memory "planning vector" readout in VITEWRITE was a function of the movement's velocity. It is still unclear how such a rule can hold across learning trials during which initial variability in strokes and speeds eventually converges to a unimodal velocity profile.

When one turns to spectral learning to overcome this difficulty, one needs to face a different problem; namely, the rate with which cerebellar Purkinje cells can read out the synaptic weights that form their motor memory is limited. In other words, attempting to alter movement speed by changing the *GO* signal by a factor of 2.8 to match the range of human speeds (Wright, 1993) would not necessarily alter the rate at which the cerebellum reads out its stored motor commands by a comparable factor. AVITEWRITE hypothesizes that the rate at which the motor commands are retrieved from cerebellar long term memory defines the maximum possible rate at which error-free, memory-driven sequential handwriting movements can be made.

How can learned movements be made across a wide range of speeds while keeping trajectory shape and velocity profiles relatively constant if the variability of the long term motor memory readout rate is limited? Van Galen (1991) suggested that working memory buffers between handwriting "processing modules" may "accommodate for time frictions between information processing activities in different modules" (p. 182). AVITEWRITE hypothesizes that a working memory system helps to write at a wide range of speeds even if the read-out rate of cerebellar spectra does not change. This working memory system, with movement speed-dependent motor command readout, is not to be confused with the prefrontal working memory assumed to store letter category representations discussed earlier but not explicitly modeled in AVITEWRITE. Experimental data support the idea that working memory function may influence movement speed. For example, several authors have found that lesions causing spatial working memory deficits also cause increased movement speed. Ventral hippocampal lesions (Bannerman et al., 1999), cholinergic basal forebrain lesions (Waite et al., 1995), and NMDA receptor antagonism (Kretschmer & Fink, 1999) impair both spatial working memory and cause an increase in movement speed. Pleskacheva et al. (2000) found that voles with smaller hippocampal mossy fiber projections exhibited poorer spatial working memory and increased movement speed. Zhou et al. (1999) found that some neurons in the medial and lateral areas of the septal complex, which has close reciprocal connections with the hippocampus, display movement speed-related activity. Chieffi & Allport (1997) found support for the hypothesis that "short-term memory for a visually-presented location within reaching space" is represented in a "motoric code" (p. 244).

The AVITEWRITE model hypothesizes that the learned cerebellar movement commands are transiently stored in a working memory buffer (WM in Figure 9) which can read out those commands at a variable rate which is less than or equal to the rate at which motor commands are retrieved from the cerebellar spectral memory. The motor commands stored in the working memory are combined with the reactive visual difference vector (DV_{vis}) and scaled by the volitional, size-controlling GRO signal to form the memory-enhanced, size-scaled difference vector (DV_s) discussed above. A *memorymodulated* movement target (TPV_m) is generated from the memory-enhanced difference vector by adding DV_s to the current value of TPV_m. At the beginning of movement, TPV_m is initialized to the starting position of the hand; that is, to the initial value of the Present Position Vector (PPV).

When an animal is making sequential movements to a series of targets, it must read out the next target from working memory as it reaches the current target in order to continue the sequence. In AVITEWRITE, a subsequent motor command is loaded from working memory and executed only when the previous memory-modulated target (TPV_m) is reached. A memory-derived target has been reached when the present hand position (PPV) equals the position of TPV_m. The difference vector from PPV to TPV_m is defined as DV_{gate} (Figure 9). Thus, when DV_{gate} reaches zero or becomes negative, TPV_m has been reached and the next command is loaded from the working memory buffer (WM). (Alternatively, one could use a small, non-zero threshold value of DV_{gate} to trigger WM readout.) The working memory of AVITEWRITE allows the volitionally controlled GO signal to alter movement speeds of both reactive and learned movements, while preserving trajectory shape and the shapes of the velocity profiles, by altering the rate of memory readout relative to the speed of the movement. The maximum speed at which a learned movement can be executed without error is determined by the rate of long term memory readout from the cerebellar spectral memory. In the model, removal of the cortical working memory buffer impairs the system's ability to decrease the speed of learned movements while preserving their kinematic features, such as shape and velocity profile invariance. The model hereby offers one possible explanation for the experimentally observed movement speed increases following spatial working memory impairment.

(a)

(b)

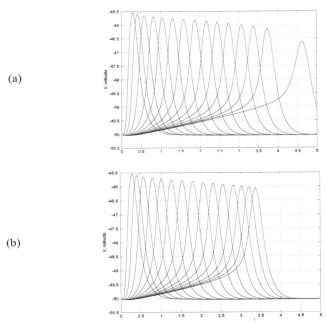

Fig. 12. (a) Purkinje cell depolarization spectrum from the Fiala et al. (1996) equations. Continuous glutamate input = 5 microM. (b) Continuous glutamate input = 25 microM. Note that the spectrum is more dense and spans a shorter time than in (a).

One consequence of decreasing movement speed and the rate of motor command readout from the working memory buffer is that visual error feedback will be delayed. If the Purkinje cells responsible for triggering the erroneous movement have returned to their baseline activity by the time that the error feedback arrives via climbing fibers, then the parallel fiber/Purkinje cell synaptic weights will not be modified and the error will be repeated on the next learning trial. Such late error feedback may "correct" the wrong synaptic weights if other Purkinje cells in the population are active at the time that the climbing fiber signal arrives. A corrective movement could still be learned by modifying the weights of the Purkinje cells which are active when the error signal arrives, but it could be too late for it to significantly improve the movement trajectory. Further, it might even worsen performance if the curvature of the template curve near the current position of the moving hand has changed since the time the error occurred and the corrective movement points away from the curve at the time it is made. AVITEWRITE proposes the following solution to the problem of delayed error feedback to the cerebellar Purkinje cell spectrum. This solution is consistent with the fact that increasing the conditioned stimulus intensity can "speed up the clock" in the rabbit nictitating membrane paradigm which earlier versions of spectral learning were used to model (Grossberg & Schmajuk, 1989, p. 93). In the model, the density of the Purkinje cell responses over time varies during learning as a function of the volitionally controlled *GO* signal that controls movement speed. For learning at slow movement speeds, the density of Purkinje cell responses over time is decreased. This decreased density allows the activities of the Purkinje cells responsible for a given component of a movement synergy command to span a greater period of time so that more of them may be active at the time that the error feedback arrives. As speed increases, error feedback arrives sooner and Purkinje cell spectral density increases so that more cells are active sooner to sample the earlier error feedback. Simulations of the biochemically-predictive spectral timing model of Fiala et al. (1996) demonstrated that the rate of Purkinje cell response – that is, the spectral density – can be decreased by decreasing the amount of glutamate released at the parallel fiber/Purkinje cell synapse (Figure 12). By varying spectral density with speed in AVITEWRITE, successful learning may occur over a wider range of speeds. The mathematical equations and parameters that define the model are given in Grossberg and Paine (2000).

8. Model Simulations

Computer simulations illustrate the following model prooperties: (1) the model's ability to learn to generate cursive letters with realistic velocity profiles; (2) generation of an inverse relation between curvature and tangential velocity; (3) generation of a Two-Thirds Power Law relation between curvature and velocity; (4) the ability to vary the movement speed during learning, with a gradual increase in speed as learning proceeds; (5) variable speed performance of learned movements with preservation of the movement shape and the shape of the velocity profile; (6) the ability to vary the size of movements while maintaining isochrony as well as the shape of the velocity profiles; and (7) the ability to yield coarticulatory context effects, such as variation of letter size and downstroke duration due to adjacent letters.

Learning a Letter. Figures 13 and 14 illustrate the learning process as AVITEWRITE learns to write the cursive letter l by tracing a template curve for thirty-seven trials. On early trials, mistakes are made as the newly forming memory competes for control of the movement with visually reactive movements to targets on the curve. Memory control is initially poor and requires corrective reactive movements which yield a segmented trajectory and a velocity profile that consists of several discrete peaks. As learning proceeds over multiple trials, performance gradually improves and the writing time decreases until, on trial thirty-seven in this case, the memory representation of the synergy activations is able to drive an accurate, fast writing movement which does not deviate from the attentional radius around the template curve.

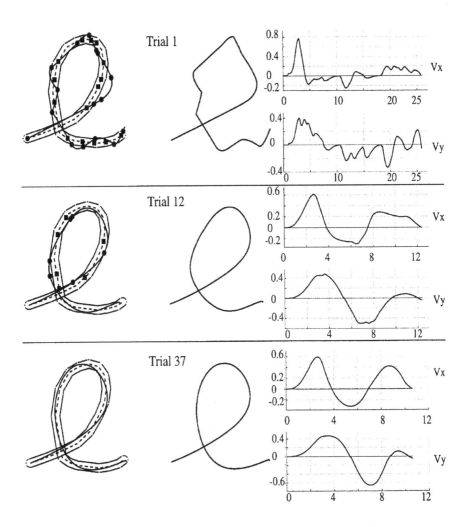

Fig. 13. Learning the letter *l*. *Left*: The attentional focus is illustrated by the tube around the dashed template curve. Circles indicate the *PPV* when a new target, marked by a square, is chosen, either because memory is too small or because the *PPV* has exceeded the distance, r_a, from the template curve. *Middle*: AVITEWRITE's *l* viewed in isolation. *Right*: x (top) and y (bottom) velocity profiles, Vx, Vy. (a) Learning trial 1; (b) Learning trial 12; (c) Final learning trial 37. The letter is now drawn without deviating from the attentional radius around the template curve. Note also that the writing time has decreased from over 25 to under 11 time units.

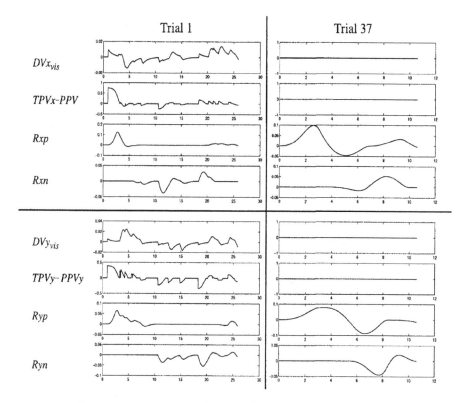

Fig. 14. Model components during learning of the letter *l* of Figure 3.12. *Left*: trial 1; *Right*: trial 37; *Top*: Positive and negative *x* synergies; *Bottom*: Positive and negative *y* synergies;

Figure 14 shows the dynamics of several model components during the learning process. The visual difference vector (DV_{vis}) from the present position (PPV) to a target (TPV) is integrated through time as it competes with memory, R, to control the movement. If R is less than a threshold value of ε or if movement exceeds a distance r_a from the template curve, then a target, TPV, is chosen and DV_{vis} grows toward the value of $TPV - PPV$. If $R > \varepsilon$ and the PPV is within a distance r_a of the template curve, then DV_{vis} decays toward zero. The Purkinje cell population response, R, which forms the cerebellar memory output, is shaped by learning as the parallel fiber/Purkinje cell synaptic weights are modified based on the error signal $TPV - PPV$. Note that on trial 37 (right side of figure), memory alone controls movement and keeps it within the attentional radius r_a of the template curve. No errors are made and DV_{vis} and $TPV - PPV$ equal zero throughout the learned movement. Figure 15 shows the corresponding spectral activations during trial 37. Figure 16 shows a sample of how the model can learn all the letters of the alphabet.

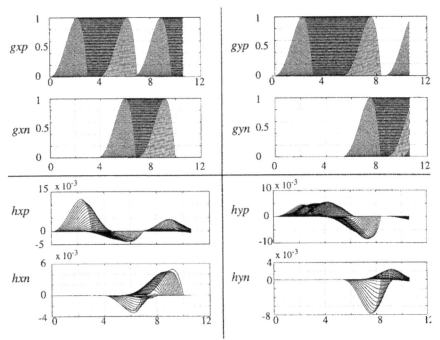

Fig. 15. Purkinje cell spectra during trial 37 of learning the letter *l*: *Top*: Spectrum of Purkinje cell responses (*g*) generated using Equation (2). Input to the spectrum of one synergy is shut off when the net movement direction, given by $DV_{vis} + R$, changes sign. A new synergy and Purkinje cell spectrum are then activated. Such synergy switching occurs at approximately times $t = 4$ and 7 in the positive and negative *x* synergies (left: *gxp*, *gxn*) and $t = 6$ and 9 in the positive and negative *y* synergies (right: *gyp*, *gyn*). *Bottom*: The pattern of learned Purkinje cell activations (*h*) formed when *g* is gated by the parallel fiber/Purkinje cell synaptic weights (*z* in Equation 3) formed during learning.

Inverse Relation between Curvature and Velocity. Figure 17 compares three letters learned by AVITEWRITE with similar letters written by adult human subjects (Edelman & Flash, 1987). Unimodal x and y velocity profiles are generated for each synergy by both humans and AVITEWRITE, as is the inverse relation between tangential velocity and curvature. The peaks in curvature near the ends of the simulated trajectories are the result of the x and y velocities (Vx, Vy) getting very small, with Vx and Vy << 1. The curvature:

$$C = \frac{(Vx \cdot Ay) - (Vy \cdot Ax)}{(Vx^2 + Vy^2)^{1.5}} \tag{1}$$

approaches infinity as the sum of Vx^2 and Vy^2 approaches zero. This effect is not seen in the human data shown in Figure 17 because the curvature has been truncated prior to the end of the velocity profile where velocity reaches zero. Terms $\ddot{x}$ and $\ddot{y}$ are the x and y acceleration, respectively.

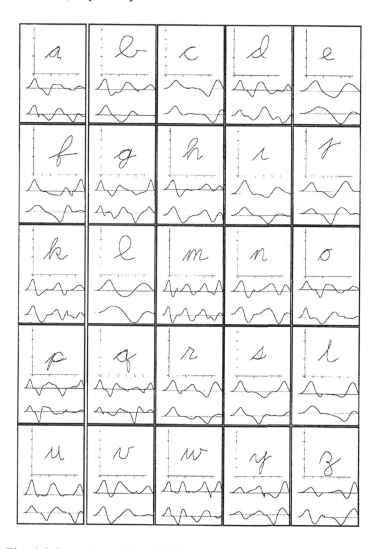

Fig. 16. The alphabet as learned by AVITEWRITE; Each panel contains a letter at the top with the x velocity profile in the middle and the y velocity profile at the bottom. All letters were learned at the relative scale shown here. The cross in the t, the letter x, and the dots on the i and j were omitted because they involved discontinuities in the movement, with lifting of the pen from the page and hand repositioning.

The Two-Thirds Power Law. As curvature increases, the angular velocity required to move through the curve in a given amount of time also increases. Thus, angular velocity is a function of the curvature. This relation is quantified by the Two-Thirds

Power Law, which states that the angular velocity is proportional to the curvature raised to the two-thirds power (Lacquaniti et al., 1983):

$$A = kC^{\frac{2}{3}},\tag{2}$$

where A = angular velocity, C = curvature, and k is a proportionality constant. Equivalently,

$$V_{\text{tan}} = kr^{\frac{1}{3}},\tag{3}$$

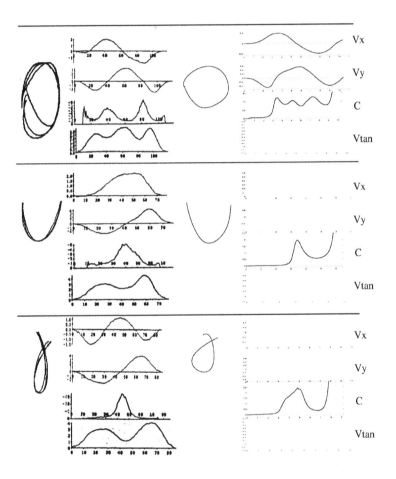

Fig. 17. *Left*: Human writing with x and y velocity profiles (Vx,Vy), movement curvature (C), and tangential velocity (Vtan) (Reproduced with permission from Edelman & Flash, 1987). *Right*: Similar shapes learned by AVITEWRITE.

where V_{tan} = tangential velocity, r = radius of curvature ($1/C$), and k is a proportionality constant. The law was originally reported to hold mainly for elliptical movements (Lacquaniti et al., 1983). Since then, others (Wann et al., 1988, p. 635) have reported that the law holds for handwriting movements at fast speeds. The law is violated when "size differences and translation are combined in a word" (Thomassen & Teulings, 1985, p. 260). Nevertheless, the law holds under many conditions in human handwriting movements. The Two-Thirds Power Law relation emerges from the learning process described in the current model (Figure 18). The Two-Thirds Power Law prediction of tangential velocity becomes unrealistically large as the curvature of the movement becomes very small ($C \ll 1$), as may occur near the beginning and end of a movement (Figure 17), causing the large spikes in the power law predictions in Figure 18. Smoothing the acceleration, as would be done by the motor plant, reduces the number of these spikes.

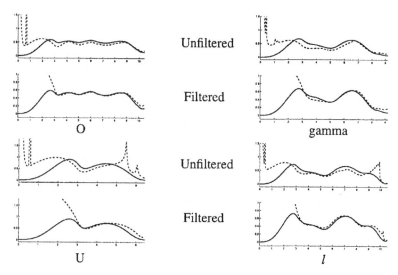

Fig. 18. Two-Thirds Power Law predictions (dotted lines) of tangential velocity compared to the actual tangential velocity (solid lines) of AVITEWRITE for the letters O, U, gamma, and *l*. For each letter, the top panel shows the power law prediction calculated using the unfiltered model acceleration profile, and the bottom panel with filtered outputs.

Variable Speeds During Learning. A task must usually be performed more slowly during the early stages of learning than at later stages. Increasing the speed of performance before the motor system has adequately learned the task results in more errors. Such a gradual speed increase occurs while learning to play musical instruments or a new language. A similar phenomenon occurs during the learning of handwriting movements (Alston & Taylor, 1987, p. 115; Burns, 1962, pp. 45-46; Freeman, 1914, pp. 83-84).

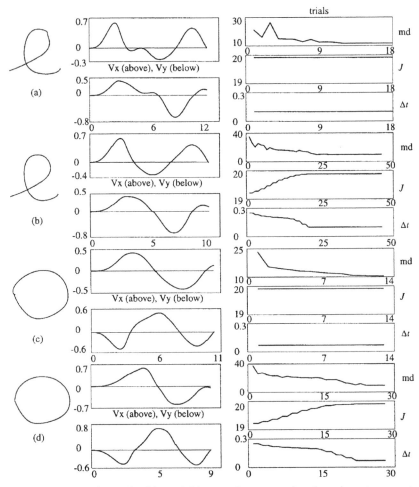

Fig. 19. Letters learned with variable speed compared to learning at a constant, fast speed. In (a) and (c), the *GO* signal (*J*) and spectral density (calibrated by •*t*) were held constant (*J* = 20, •*t* = 0.1). In (b) and (d), the *GO* signal and spectral density were incrementally increased every two trials (starting at *J* = 19.25, •*t* = 0.25; ending at *J* = 20, •*t* = 0.1). The result was an increase in the range of movement durations. (a) through (d): *Left*: Letter learned by AVITEWRITE; *Middle*: *x* and *y* velocity profiles, Vx, Vy; *Right*: (top) trials versus movement duration (md); (middle) *J* over the course of learning; (bottom) •*t* over the course of learning.

Figure 19 shows that this gradual decrease of movement duration over multiple learning trials is a feature of AVITEWRITE's learning as well. The decrease in movement duration over the course of learning in AVITEWRITE may occur for two reasons: (1) In the early trials, the memory is not yet fully developed. As a result, the movement repeatedly deviates from the attentional radius around the template curve being traced, and the total distance moved may exceed the length of the template curve (Figure 13a). As learning progresses, the movement remains within the attentional radius more and more, so the total movement distance may decrease (Figures 13b, and 13c). (2) Since fewer DV_{vis}'s contribute to forming the memory at earlier trials (the memory forms a cumulative representation of all the DV_{vis}'s over all past learning trials), the size of the memory signal R may be smaller at a given time for earlier trials as compared to later trials. Movement velocity scales with the size of the cerebellar memory output, R. This increase in the size of the memory signal over the course of learning can also lead to a speed increase and a decrease in movement duration as learning progresses.

In addition to a decrease of movement duration resulting from the learning mechanism described above, a person may also voluntarily alter the speed of a movement. The model allows for such speed scaling during learning by varying the volitional GO signal along with the density of the cerebellar spectra which are sampling the movement error signals. Altering spectral density can also alter the size of the memory signal, R, generated at a given time. Since the movement velocity is proportional to the size of R, the speed is altered both by changes in the GO signal and by changes in the spectral density. If the execution rate of movement commands stored in the working memory is reduced by decreasing movement speed via the GO signal, error feedback to the cerebellum is delayed.

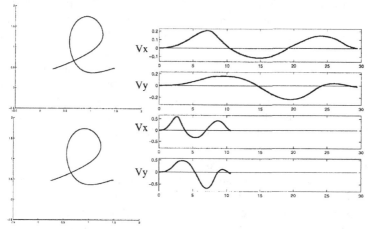

Fig 20. Speed scaling of the letter l with preservation of the letter shape and the shape of the x and y velocity profiles, Vx, Vy. *Top*: Letter l with the GO signal input $J = 7$. *Bottom*: Letter l with the GO signal input $J = 20$.

Speed-Scaling of a Learned Movement. Previously learned movements can be written at a wide range of speeds with relatively little distortion of the shape of the movement or the velocity profiles. Wright (1993) has shown that the speed of handwriting movements can be varied by a factor of about 2.8 (a range of 0.6 to 1.66 times the baseline speed) without significantly altering the letter shape. Presumably, no new learning takes place during such speed-scaling since the letters have been written by the subjects for years.

The model yields speed-scaling by a comparable factor without shape or velocity profile distortion, as shown in Figure 20. These results are obtained through the use of a working memory buffer which transiently stores the outputs of the cerebellar long term memory and sends them on to the motor apparatus at a rate which can be decreased relative to the rate of cerebellar readout (Figure 9). Speed is altered by varying the size of the *GO* signal.

If learning has been completed at some final spectral density, altering spectral density thereafter can result in distortions of the movement and its velocity profile. Thus, attempting to control the speed of learned movements by altering spectral density alone may trigger new movement errors. Instead, AVITEWRITE uses the volitional *GO* signal in conjunction with the working memory system to yield speed scaling with shape invariance. Since no new learning is required, and hence no delayed error feedback, the spectral density is kept constant at the value reached on the last learning trial at which error-free movement was achieved. The model assumes that an attentional gate couples the *GO* signal and spectral density during attentive imitation, but that they are decoupled during automatic performance of a previously learned letter.

Size Scaling and Isochrony. Size can be scaled in the model by varying the volitional *GRO* signal in Figure 9. Using the same *GRO* value for both horizontal and vertical directions will uniformly alter the size of a letter without altering the ratio of height to width (Figure 21). However, Wann and Nimmo-Smith (1990) have shown that humans do alter this ratio when scaling letter sizes; that is, vertical and horizontal sizes can be scaled independently. In their experiment of size scaling, subjects were found to increase the horizontal (x) component of movement by 46% and the vertical (y) component by 78% (p. 111). Figure 22 shows the result of a simulation in which different *GRO* values are used for the horizontal and vertical directions, with the x synergies' *GRO* signal Sx increased 46% and Sy by 78%, relative to the value used during learning.

Human handwriting exhibits isochrony; namely, the tendency for shapes of different sizes to be drawn in the same amount of time. Isochrony is also a feature of the model's performance, as seen in Figures 21 and 22. Isochrony in humans is observed at small sizes, but it fails at large sizes; that is, the isochrony principle is valid within the "neighborhood of normal letter heights (approx. 0.5 cm) [but the] writing time will increase at some point where force demands become too high" (Thomassen & Teulings, 1985, p. 255). "Writing time is not invariant across changes in writing size, but increases by a small amount" (Wright, 1993, p. 49). These limits of isochrony may be due to the physical limitations of the hand/arm system and/or limits of the central force-control mechanisms of the brain, as exemplified in the extreme case of Parkinson's disease patients who appear to have a "reduced capability to maintain a given force level for the [prolonged] stroke time periods" required when letter size is greatly increased (Van Gemmert et al., 1999, p. 685).

Coarticulatory Context Effects in Handwriting. How a cursive letter is written may be affected by adjacent, connected letters. Thomassen and Schomaker (1986) demonstrated context effects which they assume are due to coarticulation; that is, "anticipatory and overlapping instructions to the motor system" (p. 257). Different sets of muscles with separate goals can be working simultaneously, or the same set of muscles can be receiving motor commands to carry out separate goals. In the latter case, the muscles' movements may be a summation or averaging of the commands they receive. If conflicting commands are received, some muscles in a group which usually work together toward a common goal may carry out one command while other muscles in the group carry out other commands (Ohman, 1965, pp. 166, 168; Fowler et al., 1993, p. 179).

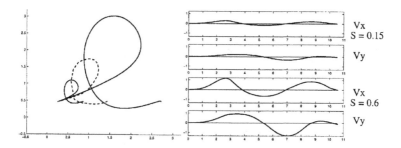

Fig. 21. Size scaling with isochrony. The dashed letter *l* is the template curve traced during learning with a baseline, size-scaling *GRO* signal S = 0.3. S = 0.15 for the smaller, solid *l* written by AVITEWRITE, and S = 0.6 for the larger, solid *l*. Both the large and the small *l* are written in the same amount of time, as seen in the *x* and *y* velocity profiles, Vx, Vy.

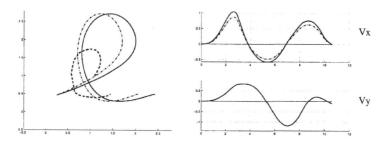

Fig. 22. Independent scaling of horizontal and vertical components of size. The small, dashed letter *l* is the template curve traced during learning with a baseline, size-scaling *GRO* signal parameters $S_x = S_y = 0.3$. The two larger *l*'s both have a *y GRO* signal parameter $S_y = 0.53$. The large, dash-dotted *l* has an *x GRO* signal of $S_x = 0.44$ corresponding to the dotted *x* velocity profile, Vx, while the large, solid *l* has $S_x = 0.53$ with a solid *x* velocity profile.

Thomassen and Schomaker (1986) found that "more rapid writers... display stronger context effects than slower writers" (p. 257). This finding is consistent with the observed increase in speech *carryover coarticulation* with increases in speaking rate. "Carryover" ("perseverative", "left to right") coarticulation occurs when new motor commands are given before the previous commands have been fully executed. Muscles then begin contracting in a new pattern before the previous pattern of muscle contractions has been completed (Ostry et al., 1996).

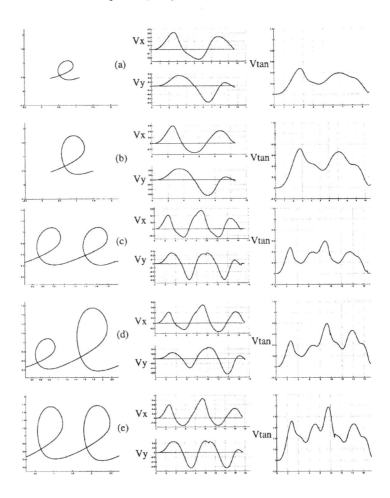

Fig. 23. Simulated combinations of the letters *e* and *l*. *Left*: The letters; *Middle*: x and y velocity profiles, Vx, Vy; *Right*: Tangential velocity, Vtan.

The idea that some of the observed context effects in handwriting are due to carryover coarticulation was tested as follows. Connected letters were simulated with varying degrees of overlap of the corresponding spectral memories. In other words, the degree of superposition between adjacent letters was varied. The letters *e* and *l* were learned by the modeled system (Figures 23). The learned memory traces were then read out successively with varying degrees of overlap. Some of the downstroke duration and size effects observed by Thomassen and Schomaker (1986) were replicated by varying the degree of superposition between adjacent letters. In the simulation of the word *eele*, shown in Figure 24, the relative timing of the loading of the previously learned letter memories was varied and the sizes of the letters were compared. The second *e* becomes smaller than the other *e*'s when its superposition increases with the large vertical upstroke of the following *l*, thereby canceling a large part of the *e* downstroke (Figures 24b and 24c). Increasing the time separation between letters can eliminate the coarticulatory size effects in the model, as seen in Figure 24a.

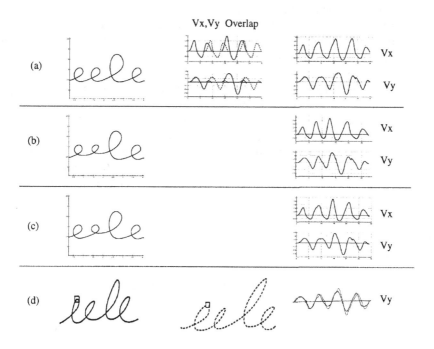

Fig. 24. Simulations of coarticulation: (a) through (c): Simulated *eele* with varying degrees of overlap between the letters. Timing relations are as follows. (a) 6.6, 6.6, 7 (The second letter begins 6.6 time units after the first; the third starts 6.6 after the second, and the fourth starts 7 time units after the third, corresponding to the second V*x* zero crossings shown in V*x* Overlap.) V*x*,V*y* Overlap show the overlapping velocity profiles of the individual letters. (b) 5, 5, 7; (c) 6.6, 5, 7; (d) Human writing of *eele* by two subjects (Figure (d) reproduced with permission from Thomassen & Schomaker, 1986). The dotted *y* velocity profile, V*y*, corresponds to the dotted *eele*.

9. Conclusion

The AVITEWRITE model clarifies aspects of how a person learns to make curved handwriting movements. This model incorporates elements of two previous groups of models: spectral timing models that analyze cerebellar learning (Fiala, Grossberg, & Bullock, 1996; Grossberg & Merrill, 1992; Grossberg & Schmajuk, 1989) and the VITE and VITEWRITE models of how the cerebral cortex and basal ganglia work together to control the read-out of trajectory commands (Bullock & Grossberg, 1988a, 1988b, 1991; Bullock, Grossberg & Mannes, 1993). The AVITEWRITE model hereby seeks to clarify how the cerebral cortex, cerebellum, and basal ganglia may interact during complex learned movements. There is both cooperation and competition between reactive vision-based imitation and planned memory readout. The cooperation includes interactions between cortical difference vectors and cerebellar learning. The competition arises between cerebellar control of learned movements and error-driven, cortical control of reactive movements to attentionally chosen visual targets. The model suggests that there is an automatic shift in the balance of movement control between these cortical and cerebellar processes during the course of learning. Reactive movements are made to attentionally chosen targets on a curve at the same time as movement error signals are generated which allow the cortico-cerebellar system to learn how to draw the curve. Memory-based movements gradually supersede visually-driven movements as learning progresses. Finally, the model shows how challenging psychophysical properties of planar hand movements may emerge from this cortico-cerebellar-basal ganglia interaction.

References

Abend, W., Bizzi, E., Morasso, P. (1982). Human arm trajectory formation. *Brain.* 105, 331-348.

Alston, J., Taylor, J. (1987). Handwriting: Theory, research, and practice. New York: Nichols.

Andersen, R., Essick, G., Siegel, R. (1985). Encoding of spatial location by posterior parietal neurons. *Science.* 230, 456-458.

Andersen, R. (1995). Encoding of intention and spatial location in the posterior parietal cortex. *CerebralCortex* . 5, 457-469.

Arroyo-Anllo, E.M., Botez-Marquard, T. (1998). Neurobehavioral dimensions of olivoponto-cerebellar atrophy. *JournalofClinicalandExperimentalNeuropsychology* . 20, 52-59.

Bannerman, D.M., Yee, B.K., Good, M.A., Heupel, M.J., Iversen, S.D., Rawlins, J.N. (1999). Double dissociation of function within the hippocampus: a comparison of dorsal, ventral, and complete hippocampal cytotoxic lesions. *BehavioralNeuroscience* . 113, 1170-1188.

Bartha, G.T., Thompson, R.F., Gluck, M.A. (1991). Sensorimotor learning and the cerebellum. In M. Arbib, J. Ewert (Eds.). Visual structures and integrated functions. Berlin: Springer.

Berardelli, A., Hallet, M., Rothwell, J.C., Agostino, R., Manfredi, M., Thompson, M., Thompson, P.D., Marsden, C.D. (1996). Single-joint rapid arm movements in normal subjects and in patients with motor disorders. *Brain.* 119, 661-674.

Bernstein, N. (1967). The coordination and regulation of movements. London: Pergamon Press.

Bizzi, E., Saltiel, P., Tresch, M. (1998). Modular organization of motor behavior. *Zeitschriftfur Naturforschung* [C]. 53, 510-7.

Buchanan, T.S., Almdale, D.P.J., Lewis, J.L., Rymer, W.Z. (1986). Characteristics of synergic relations during isometric contractions of human elbow muscles. *JournalofNeurophysiology*. 56, 1225-1241.

Bullock, D., Cisek, P., Grossberg, S. (1998). Cortical networks for control of voluntary arm movements under variable force conditions. *CerebralCortex* . 8, 48-62.

Bullock, D., Fiala, J.C., Grossberg, S. (1994). A neural model of timed response learning in the cerebellum. *NeuralNetworks* . 7, 1101-1114.

Bullock, D., Grossberg, S. (1988a). The VITE model: A neural command circuit for generating arm and articulator trajectories. In J. Kelso, A. Mandell, M. Shlesinger (Eds.). Dynamic patterns in complex systems. Singapore: World Scientific.

Bullock, D., Grossberg, S. (1988b). Neural dynamics of planned arm movements: Emergent invariants and speed-accuracy properties during trajectory formation. *Psychological Review*. 95, 49-90.

Bullock, D., Grossberg, S. (1991). Adaptive neural networks for control of movement trajectories invariant under speed and force rescaling. *HumanMovementScience* . 10, 3-53.

Bullock, D., Grossberg, S., Mannes, C. (1993). A neural network model for cursive script production. *BiologicalCybernetics* . 70, 15-28.

Buonomano, D.V., Mauk, M.D. (1994). Neural network model of the cerebellum: Temporal discrimination and the timing of motor responses. *NeuralComputation* . 6, 38-55.

Burns, P.C. (1962). Improving handwriting instruction in elementary schools. Minneapolis (pp. 45-46). Minneapolis, MN: Burgess Publishing Co.

Caminiti, R., Genovesio, A., Marconi, B., Mayer, A.B., Onorati, P., Ferraina, S., Mitsuda, T., Giannetti, S., Squatrito, S., Maioli, M.G., Molinari, M. (1999). Early coding of reaching: Frontal and parietal association connections of parieto-occipital cortex. *EuropeanJournal of Neuroscience*. 11, 3339-3345.

Chapeau-Blondeau, F., Chauvet, G. (1991). A neural network model of the cerebellar cortex performing dynamic associations. *BiologicalCybernetics* . 65, 267-279.

Chieffi, S., Allport, D.A. (1997). Independent coding of target distance and direction in visuo-spatial working memory. *PsychologicalResearch* . 60, 244-250.

Coltz, J.D., Johnson, M.T.V., Ebner, T.J. (1999a). Cerebellar Purkinje cell simple spike discharge encodes movement velocity in primates during visuomotor arm tracking. *TheJournalofNeuroscience* . 19, 1782-1803.

Coltz, J.D., Johnson, M.T.V., Ebner, T.J. (1999b). Cerebellar Purkinje cell complex spike discharge during visuomotor arm tracking in primates: Relationships to movement parameters and comparisons to simple spike discharge. *SocietyforNeuroscienceAbstracts* . 25, 372.

Dagher, A., Owen, A.M., Boecker, H., Brooks, D.J. (1999). Mapping the network for planning: a correlational PET activation study with the Tower of London task. *Brain*. 122, 1973-1987.

Doyon, J., LaForce Jr., R., Bouchard, G., Gaudreau, D., Roy, J., Poirier, M., Bedard, P., Bedard, F., Bouchard, J. (1998). Role of the striatum, cerebellum and frontal lobes in the automatization of a repeated visuomotor sequence of movements. *Neuropsychologia*. 36, 625-641.

Ebner, T.J. (1998). A role for the cerebellum in the control of limb movement velocity. *Current OpinioninNeurobiology* . 8, 762-769.

Edelman, S., Flash, T. (1987). A model of handwriting. *BiologicalCybernetics* . 57, 25-36.

Fiala, J., Grossberg, S., Bullock, D. (1996). Metabotropic glutamate receptor activation in cerebellar Purkinje cells as substrate for adaptive timing of the classically conditioned eyeblink response. *TheJournalofNeuroscience* . 16, 3760-3774.

Fowler, C., Saltzman, E. (1993). Coordination and coarticulation in speech production. *LanguageandSpeech* . 36, 171-195.

Freeman, F.N. (1914). The teaching of handwriting (pp. 83-84). Boston, MA: Houghton-Mifflin, The Riverside Press Cambridge.

Freeman, J.A. (1969). The cerebellum as a timing device: an experimental study in the frog. In R. Llinas (Ed.). Neurobiology of cerebellar evolution and development, pp. 397-420. Chicago: American Medical Association.

Fu, Q.G., Mason, C.R., Flament, D., Coltz, J.D., Ebner, T.J. (1997). Movement kinematics encoded in complex spike discharge of primate cerebellar Purkinje cells. *Neuroreport*. 8, 523-529.

Gellman, R., Gibson, A.R., Houk, J.C. (1985). Inferior olivary neurons in the awake cat: Detection of contact and passive body displacement. *JournalofNeurophysiology* . 54, 40-60.

Georgopoulos, A.P., DeLong, M.R., Crutcher, M.D. (1983). Relations between parameters of step-tracking movements and single cell discharge in the globus pallidus and subthalamic nucleus of the behaving monkey. *TheJournalofNeuroscience* . 3, 1586-1598.

Georgopoulos, A.P., Kalaska, J.F., Caminiti, R., Massey, J.T. (1982). On the relations between the direction of two-dimensional arm movements and cell discharge in primate motor cortex. *TheJournalofNeuroscience* . 2, 1527-1537.

Georgopoulos, A.P., Lurito, J.T., Petrides, M., Schwartz, A.B., Massey, J.T. (1989). Mental rotation of the neuronal population vector. *Science*. 243, 234-236.

Georgopoulos, A.P., Taira, M., Lukashin, A. (1993). Cognitive neurophysiology of the motor cortex. *Science*. 260, 47-52.

Ghez, C. (1991). The Cerebellum. In E.R. Kandel, J.H. Schwartz, T.M. Jessel (Eds.). Principles of neural science, pp. 626-646. New York: Elsevier Science Publishers.

Greer, K., Green, D. (1983). Context and motor control in handwriting. *ataPsychologica* . 54, 205-215.

Grossberg, S., Merrill, J. (1992). A neural network model of adaptively timed reinforcement learning and hippocampal dynamics. *CognitiveBrainResearch* . 1, 3-38.

Grossberg, S., Merrill, J. (1996). The hippocampus and cerebellum in adaptively timed learning, recognition, and movement. *JournalofCognitiveNeuroscience* . 8, 257-277.

Grossberg, S., Paine, R. (2000) A neural model of corticocerebellar interactions during attentive imitation and predictive learning of sequential handwriting movements. *NeuralNetworks* . in press.

Grossberg, S., Schmajuk, N. (1989). Neural dynamics of adaptive timing and temporal discrimination during associative learning. *NeuralNetworks* . 2, 79-102.

Hallett, M., Khoshbin, S. (1980). A physiological mechanism of bradykinesia. *Brain*. 103, 301-314.

Hertrich, I., Ackermann, H. (1995). Coarticulation in slow speech: Durational and spectral analysis. *LanguageandSpeech* . 38, 159-187.

Hollerbach, J.M., Flash, T. (1982). Dynamic interactions between limb segments during planar arm movement. *BiologicalCybernetics* . 44, 67-77.

Hopfinger, J.B., Buonocore, M.H., Mangun, G.R. (2000). The neural mechanisms of top-down attentional control. *NatureNeuroscience* . 3, 284-291.

Horak, F.B., Anderson, M.E. (1984a). Influence of globus pallidus on arm movements in monkeys, I. Effects of kainic acid-induced lesions. *JournalofNeurophysiology* . 52, 290-304.

Horak, F.B., Anderson, M.E. (1984b). Influence of globus pallidus on arm movements in monkeys, II. Effects of stimulation. *JournalofNeurophysiology* . 52, 305-322.

Iacoboni, M., Woods, R.P., Brass, M., Bekkering, H., Mazziotta, J.C., Rizzolatti, G. (1999). Cortical mechanisms of human imitation. *Science.* 286, 2526-2528.

Ito, M. (1984). The cerebellum and neural control (pp. 325-349). New York: Raven.

Ito, M. (1991). The cellular basis of cerebellar plasticity. *CurrentOpinioninNeurobiology* . 1, 616-620.

Ito, M., Karachot, L. (1992). Protein kinases and phosphatase inhibitors mediating long-term desensitization of glutamate receptors in cerebellar Purkinje cells. *Neurosciences Research.* 14, 27-38.

Jaffe, S. (1992). A neuronal model for variable latency response. In F.H. Eeckman (Ed.). Analysis and modeling of neural systems. Boston: Kluwer Academic Publishers.

Jueptner, M., Frith, C.D., Brooks, D.J., Frackowiak, R.S., Passingham, R.E. (1997a). Anatomy of motor learning. II. Subcortical structures and learning by trial and error. *JournalofNeurophysiology.* 77, 1325-1337.

Jueptner, M., Stephan, K.M., Frith, C.D., Brooks, D.J., Frackowiak, R.S., Passingham, R.E. (1997b). Anatomy of motor learning. I. Frontal cortex and attention to action. *Journalof Neurophysiology.* 77, 1313-1324.

Jueptner, M., Weiller, C. (1998). A review of differences between basal ganglia and cerebellar control of movements as revealed by functional imaging studies. *Brain.* 121, 1437-1449.

Kalaska, J.F., Cohen, D.A.D., Prud'homme, M.J., Hyde, M.L. (1990). Parietal area 5 neuronal activity encodes movement kinematics, not movement dynamics. *ExperimentalBrainResearch.* 80, 351-364.

Kawashima, R., Okuda, J., Umetsu, A., Sugiura, M., Inoue, K., Suzuki, K., Tabuchi, M, Tsukiura, T., Narayan, S.L., Nagasaka, T., Yanagawa, I., Fujii, T., Takahashi, S., Fukuda, H., Yamadori, A. (2000). Human cerebellum plays an important role in memory-timed finger movement: an fMRI study. *JournalofNeurophysiology* . 83, 1079-1087.

Kelso, J.A.S. (Ed.) (1982). Human motor behavior. Hillsdale, NJ: Lawrence Erlbaum.

Kretschmer, B.D., Fink, S. (1999). Spatial learning deficit after NMDA receptor blockade and state-dependency. *BehaviouralPharmacology* . 10, 423-428.

Lacquaniti, F., Terzuolo, C., Viviani, P. (1983). The law relating the kinematic and figural aspects of drawing movements. *ActaPsychologica* . 54, 115-130.

Lu, X., Hikosaka, O., Miyachi, S. (1998). Role of monkey cerebellar nuclei in skill for sequential movement. *JournalofNeurophysiology* . 79, 2245-2254.

Moore, J.W., Desmond, J.E., Berthier, N.E. (1989). Adaptively timed conditioned responses and the cerebellum: A neural network approach. *BiologicalCybernetics* . 62, 17-28.

Morasso, P. (1981). Spatial control of arm movements. *ExperimentalBrainResearch* . 42, 223-227.

Morasso, P. (1986). Understanding Cursive Script as a Trajectory Formation Paradigm. In H. Kao, G. van Galen, R. Hoosain (Eds.). Graphonomics: Contemporary research in handwriting, pp. 137-167. New York: Elsevier Science Publishers.

Morasso, P., Mussa Ivaldi, F.A., Ruggiero, C. (1983). How a discontinuous mechanism can produce continuous patterns in trajectory formation and handwriting. *ActaPsychologica* . 54, 83-98.

Mussa-Ivaldi, F. (1988). Do neurons in the motor cortex encode movement direction? An alternative hypothesis. *NeuroscienceLetters* . 91, 106-111.

Ohman, S. (1965). Coarticulation in VCV utterances: spectrographic measurements. *Journalof theAcousticalSocietyofAmerica* . 39, 151-168.

Oscarsson, O. (1969). Termination and functional organization of the dorsal spino-olivocerebellar path. *TheJournalofPhysiologyLondon)*   200, 129-149.

Ostry, D., Gribble, P., Gracco, V. (1996). Coarticulation of jaw movements in speech production: is context sensitivity in speech kinematics centrally planned? *TheJournalofNeuroscience.* 16, 1570-1579.

Perrett, S.P., Ruiz, B.P., Mauk, M.D. (1993). Cerebellar cortex lesions disrupt learning-dependent timing of conditioned eyelid responses. *TheJournalofNeuroscience* . 13, 1708-1718.

Plamondon, R., Alimi, A. (1997). Speed/accuracy trade-offs in target-directed movements. *BehavioralandBrainSciences* . 20, 279-349.

Pleskacheva, M.G., Wolfer, D.P., Kupriyanova, I.F., Nikolenko, D.L., Scheffrahn, H., Dell'Omo, G., Lipp, H.P. (2000). Hippocampal mossy fibers and swimming navigation learning in two vole species occupying different habitats. *Hippocampus.* 10, 17-30.

Richer, F., Chouinard, M.J., Rouleau, I. (1999). Frontal lesions impair the attentional control of movements during motor learning. *Neuropsychologia.* 37, 1427-1435.

Sadato, N., Ibanez, V., Deiber, M.P., Campbell, G., Leonardo, M., Hallett, M. (1996). Frequency-dependent changes of regional cerebral blood flow during finger movements. *JournalofCerebralBloodFlowandMetabolism* . 16, 23-33.

Schillings, J., Meulenbroek, R., Thomassen, A. (1996). Limb segment recruitment as a function of movement direction, amplitude, and speed. *JournalofMotorBehavior* . 28, 241-254.

Schwartz, A.B., Moran, D.W. (1999). Motor cortical activity during drawing movements: Population representation during lemniscate tracing. *Journal of Neurophysiology* . 82, 2705-2718.

Simpson, J.I., Wylie, D.R., De Zeeuw, C.I. (1996). On climbing fiber signals and their consequence(s). *BehavioralandBrainSciences* . 19, 384-398.

Soechting, J., Terzuolo, C. (1987). Organization of arm movements. Motion is segmented. *Neuroscience.* 23, 39-51.

Stelmach, G., Mullins, P., Teulings, H. (1984). Motor programming and temporal patterns in handwriting. In J. Gibbon, L. Allan (Eds.). *Timing and Time Perception,Anals of the NewYorkAademyofSciences* . 423, 144-157.

Thomassen, A., Schomaker, L. (1986). Between-letter context effects in handwriting trajectories. In H. Kao, G. van Galen, R. Hoosain (Eds.). Graphonomics: Contemporary research in handwriting, pp. 253-272. New York: North-Holland: Elsevier Science Publishers.

Thomassen, A., Teulings, H. (1985). Time, size and shape in handwriting: Exploring spatio-temporal relationships at different levels. In J. Michon, J. Jackson, (Eds.). Time, mind, and behavior, pp. 253-263. Berlin: Springer-Verlag.

Turner, R.S., Anderson, M.E. (1997). Pallidal discharge related to the kinematics of reaching movements in two dimensions. *JournalofNeurophysiology* . 77, 1051-1074.

Turner, R.S., Grafton, S.T., Votaw, J.R., Delong, M.R., Hoffman, J.M. (1998). Motor subcircuits mediating the control of movement velocity: A PET study. *JournalofNeurophysiology.* 80, 2162-2176.

Turvey, M.T. (1990). Coordination. *AmericanPsychologist* . 45, 938-953.

van Galen, G.P. (1991). Handwriting: Issues for a psychomotor theory. *HumanMovementScience.* 10, 165-191.

van Galen, G.P., Weber, J. (1998). On-line size control in handwriting demonstrates the continuous nature of motor programs. *ActaPsychologica* . 100, 195-216.

van Gemmert, A.W., Teulings, H.L., Contreras-Vidal, J.L., Stelmach, G.E. (1999). Parkinson's disease and the control of size and speed in handwriting. *Neuropsychologia.* 37, 685-694.

Vindras, P., Viviani, P. (1998). Frames of reference and control parameters in visuomanual pointing. *Journal of Experimental Psychology Human Perception and Performance*   . 24, 569-591.

Waite, J.J., Chen, A.D., Wardlow, M.L., Wiley, R.G., Lappi, D.A., Thal, L.J. (1995). 192 immunoglobulin G-saporin produces graded behavioral and biochemical changes accompanying the loss of cholinergic neurons of the basal forebrain and cerebellar Purkinje cells. *Neuroscience*. 65, 463-476.

Wann, J., Nimmo-Smith, I., Wing, A. (1988). Relation between velocity and curvature in movement: equivalence and divergence between a power law and a minimum-jerk model. *Journal of Experimental Psychology Human Perception and Performance*   . 14, 622-637.

Wann, J.P., Nimmo-Smith, I. (1990). Evidence against the relative invariance of timing in handwriting. *The Quarterly Journal of Experimental Psychology*   . 42A, 105-119.

Wright, C.E. (1993). Evaluating the special role of time in the control of handwriting. *Acta Psychologica*. 82, 5-52.

Zhou, T.L., Tamura, R., Kuriwaki, J., Ono, T. (1999). Comparison of medial and lateral septal neuron activity during performance of spatial tasks in rats. *Hippocampus*. 9, 220-234.

Zipser, D. (1986). A model of hippocampal learning during classical conditioning. *Behavioral Neuroscience*. 100, 764-776.

About Editors

Ron Sun: Dr. Ron Sun is an Associate Professor at University of Missouri-Columbia. He received his Ph.D in 1991 from Brandeis University in computer science. Dr. Ron Sun's research interests center around the study of intellegence and cognition, especially in the areas of commonsense reasoning, human and machine learning, multi-agent systems, and hybrid connectionist models. He is the author of over 100 papers, and has written, edited or contributed to 15 books, including the book *Integrating Rules and Connectionism for Robust Commonsense Reasoning*, published by John Wiley and Sons. For his paper on integerating rule-based reasoning and connectionist models, he received the 1991 David Marr Award from Cognitive Science Society. He organized and chaired many conferences and workshops in his areas of interest. He has also been on the program committees of the National Conference on Artificial Intelligence (AAAI-93, AAAI-97, AAAI-99), International Joint Conference on Neural Networks (IJCNN-99, IJCNN-00), and many other conferences, and has been an invited/plenary speaker for some of them. Dr. Sun is the co-editor-in-chief of the journal Cognitive Systems Research (Elsevier). He also serves on the editorial boards of Connection Science, Applied Intelligence, and Neural Computing Surveys. He is a member of AAAI, INNS, and Cognitive Science Society, and a senior member of IEEE.

C. Lee Giles: Dr. C. Lee Giles is a Senior Research Scientist at NEC Research Institute. He is adjunct faculty at the Institute for Advanced Computer Studies of University of Maryland, Computer and Information Science Department at University of Pennsylvania, Department of Computer Science of Columbia University, and a member of DIMACS. His current research interests are in basic and applied research in intelligent information processing systems. He has published over 150 journal and conference papers, book chapters, edited books and proceedings in these areas. He recently coedited with R. Sun and J. Zurada a special issue of IEEE Transactions on Neural Networks on "Neural Networks and Hybrid Intelligent Models" and with M. Gori a book on Adaptive Processing of Sequences and Data Structures. Several of his papers have won or been nominated for best paper awards. He serves on many conference program committees and has helped organize many meetings and workshops. He has served on the editorial boards of IEEE Intelligent Systems, IEEE Transactions on Knowledge and Data Engineering, IEEE Transactions on Neural Networks, Journal of Computational Intelligence in Finance, Journal of Parallel and Distributed Computing, Neural Networks, Neural Computation, Optical Computing and Processing, and Applied Optics. He is a Fellow of the IEEE, a member of AAAI, ACM, INNS, AAAS, the Internet Society, and OSA.

Author Index

Lecture Notes in Artificial Intelligence (LNAI)

Lecture Notes in Computer Science